Lecture Notes in Computer Science   9753

Commenced Publication in 1973
Founding and Former Series Editors:
Gerhard Goos, Juris Hartmanis, and Jan van Leeuwen

More information about this series at http://www.springer.com/series/7409

Panayiotis Zaphiris · Andri Ioannou (Eds.)

Learning and Collaboration Technologies

Third International Conference, LCT 2016
Held as Part of HCI International 2016
Toronto, ON, Canada, July 17–22, 2016
Proceedings

 Springer

Editors
Panayiotis Zaphiris
Cyprus University of Technology
Lemesos
Cyprus

Andri Ioannou
Cyprus University of Technology
Lemesos
Cyprus

ISSN 0302-9743   ISSN 1611-3349 (electronic)
Lecture Notes in Computer Science
ISBN 978-3-319-39482-4   ISBN 978-3-319-39483-1 (eBook)
DOI 10.1007/978-3-319-39483-1

Library of Congress Control Number: 2016940324

LNCS Sublibrary: SL3 – Information Systems and Applications, incl. Internet/Web, and HCI

Printed on acid-free paper

This Springer imprint is published by Springer Nature
The registered company is Springer International Publishing AG Switzerland

Foreword

The 18th International Conference on Human-Computer Interaction, HCI International 2016, was held in Toronto, Canada, during July 17–22, 2016. The event incorporated the 15 conferences/thematic areas listed on the following page.

A total of 4,354 individuals from academia, research institutes, industry, and governmental agencies from 74 countries submitted contributions, and 1,287 papers and 186 posters have been included in the proceedings. These papers address the latest research and development efforts and highlight the human aspects of the design and use of computing systems. The papers thoroughly cover the entire field of human-computer interaction, addressing major advances in knowledge and effective use of computers in a variety of application areas. The volumes constituting the full 27-volume set of the conference proceedings are listed on pages IX and X.

I would like to thank the program board chairs and the members of the program boards of all thematic areas and affiliated conferences for their contribution to the highest scientific quality and the overall success of the HCI International 2016 conference.

This conference would not have been possible without the continuous and unwavering support and advice of the founder, Conference General Chair Emeritus and Conference Scientific Advisor Prof. Gavriel Salvendy. For his outstanding efforts, I would like to express my appreciation to the communications chair and editor of *HCI International News*, Dr. Abbas Moallem.

April 2016   Constantine Stephanidis

HCI International 2016 Thematic Areas and Affiliated Conferences

Thematic areas:

- Human-Computer Interaction (HCI 2016)
- Human Interface and the Management of Information (HIMI 2016)

Affiliated conferences:

- 13th International Conference on Engineering Psychology and Cognitive Ergonomics (EPCE 2016)
- 10th International Conference on Universal Access in Human-Computer Interaction (UAHCI 2016)
- 8th International Conference on Virtual, Augmented and Mixed Reality (VAMR 2016)
- 8th International Conference on Cross-Cultural Design (CCD 2016)
- 8th International Conference on Social Computing and Social Media (SCSM 2016)
- 10th International Conference on Augmented Cognition (AC 2016)
- 7th International Conference on Digital Human Modeling and Applications in Health, Safety, Ergonomics and Risk Management (DHM 2016)
- 5th International Conference on Design, User Experience and Usability (DUXU 2016)
- 4th International Conference on Distributed, Ambient and Pervasive Interactions (DAPI 2016)
- 4th International Conference on Human Aspects of Information Security, Privacy and Trust (HAS 2016)
- Third International Conference on HCI in Business, Government, and Organizations (HCIBGO 2016)
- Third International Conference on Learning and Collaboration Technologies (LCT 2016)
- Second International Conference on Human Aspects of IT for the Aged Population (ITAP 2016)

Conference Proceedings Volumes Full List

Learning and Collaboration Technologies

Program Board Chairs: **Panayiotis Zaphiris, Cyprus, and Andri Ioannou, Cyprus**

- Ruthi Aladjem, Israel
- Anastasios A. Economides, Greece
- Maka Eradze, Estonia
- Mikhail Fominykh, Norway
- David Fonseca, Spain
- Francisco José García Peñalvo, Spain
- Béatrice Hasler, Switzerland
- Mustafa Murat Inceoglu, Turkey
- Tomaž Klobučar, Slovenia
- Birgy Lorenz, Estonia
- Ana Loureiro, Portugal
- Maria Mama-Timotheou, Cyprus
- Efi Nisiforou, Cyprus
- Antigoni Parmaxi, Cyprus
- Maria Perifanou, Greece
- Nicos Souleles, Cyprus
- Aimilia Tzanavari, USA
- Telmo Zarraonandia, Spain
- Maria Zenios, Cyprus

The full list with the program board chairs and the members of the program boards of all thematic areas and affiliated conferences is available online at:

http://www.hci.international/2016/

HCI International 2017

The 19th International Conference on Human-Computer Interaction, HCI International 2017, will be held jointly with the affiliated conferences in Vancouver, Canada, at the Vancouver Convention Centre, July 9–14, 2017. It will cover a broad spectrum of themes related to human-computer interaction, including theoretical issues, methods, tools, processes, and case studies in HCI design, as well as novel interaction techniques, interfaces, and applications. The proceedings will be published by Springer. More information will be available on the conference website: http://2017.hci.international/.

General Chair
Prof. Constantine Stephanidis
University of Crete and ICS-FORTH
Heraklion, Crete, Greece
E-mail: general_chair@hcii2017.org

http://2017.hci.international/

Contents

Instructional Design

Interaction Techniques and Platforms for Learning

Learning Performance

Web-based, Mobile and Ubiquitous Learning

Collaboration Technologies

Cultural and Social Aspects of Learning and Collaboration Technologies

Instructional Design

Learning4Work. Designing a New Evaluation System Based on Scenario Centered Curriculum Methodology: The Pre-test

David Fonseca[✉], August Climent, Lluís Vicent,
and Xavier Canaleta

GRETEL- Grup de Recerca en Technology Enhanced Learning,
La Salle Universitat Ramon Llull, Barcelona, Spain
{fonsi,augc,vicent,xavic}@salle.url.edu

Abstract. This paper aims to provide the theoretical framework and methodology for the definition of data collection tools designed to assess the effectiveness and impact of training envisaged by the LEARNING4WORK project. This project is based on the development of learning strategies within the framework of Vocation Training, in order to improve learning processes and make them more applicable in the real working world while minimizing the number of student drop-outs. Learning methods are re-conceptualized through the use of immersive worlds and role and project-orientated-learning. Scenario Centered Curriculum (SCC) was applied to promote the acquisition and development of international cooperation skills through the use of Information Communication Technologies (ICT) tools and systems. The paper focuses on the design process of the evaluation initial questionnaires (or Pre-test), starting from the theoretical framework established in the field of learning in formal, informal and non-formal educational contexts, applied to an innovative vision of education and training, centered on the learner's future professional role.

Keywords: Enhanced learning · Collaboration technologies · Lifelong learning · User centered evaluation · Usability · Satisfaction · User profile

1 Introduction

1.1 The Partners and Main Objectives of the Project

Ten partners make up the Consortium of the Project. La Salle Campus Barcelona (FUNITEC-Ramon Llull University, Spain), has the role of coordinating partner and there are three other main partners: FIDAE (Federazione istituti di attività educative) and ISP (Intesa SanPaolo Fromazione Scpa) in Italy, and ASSEDIL (Association Europeenne des Directeurs d'Institutions Lasalliennes) in France, plus the six other associate partners that are the vocational training centers in which the Project will be developed: 2 in Spain (La Salle Palma School, and Salesians de Sarrià), 2 in Italy (Instituto Cavanis and Suore Salesiane dei Sacri Couri) and 2 in France (Ensemble Solaire Jeanne d'Arc and Groupe Scolaire Saint Joseph La Salle).

© Springer International Publishing Switzerland 2016
P. Zaphiris and A. Ioannou (Eds.): LCT 2016, LNCS 9753, pp. 3–13, 2016.
DOI: 10.1007/978-3-319-39483-1_1

The fundamental objectives of the Project are to:

- Extend the use of practical, motivating, effective and international learning methodologies in the vocational training sectors in Spain, France and Italy,
- Increase the success rate of the students through providing experiences which they find highly-motivating and which also require a certain degree of individual commitment,
- Create a bank of educational program based in immersive worlds, projects and roles,
- Foment international co-operation through joint projects carried out by heterogeneous work groups made up of members from different social and cultural backgrounds,
- Pinpoint the degree to which different learning innovations can be applied to a group of students (role, online, international, etc.),
- Verify whether these new methodologies manage to meet the objectives set out and compare these results with those of traditional learning techniques used in Vocational Training centers.

These objectives are set out in the framework of the European Union (EU) strategic priorities 2014–2020 in reference to: "The development of basic and transversal skills, the development of adapted evaluation systems, an increased and more intensive use of ICTs, more cohesion between the different evaluation systems and the promotion of the transfer of learning strategies and methodologies among the countries of the EU".

1.2   Project Phases

The Project is divided into five stages which are in turn organized into activities:

- Preparation: The activity program is reviewed by the main partners.
- Content Generation: The main partners have the responsibility to design the teaching materials for the courses, a guide to the SCC teaching methodology and a guide on the evaluation methods used in the learning and professional insertion process.
- Implantation: The teachers of the schools are trained in the method to implement both traditional and SCC methodologies in two courses: A pilot program with the Search Engine Optimization (SEO) course is carried out to compare traditional methodologies with the SCC; and the results of the learning are analyzed and the second year students are taught the Mobile Commerce (MOBCOM) course using SCC methodology in all the centers.
- Tracking: Collection of data from students' performance and employability.
- Results analysis and breakdown at the end of each of these courses.

The methodology for the development of the project is based on a two-phase spiral model. Initially the learning methodologies are implemented in the traditional form in a school in each of the three countries and then the same training is implemented in a different school using the SCC methodology. It is hoped that the impact and results of the project will strengthen pedagogical capabilities in the vocational training sector in the following ways:

- Reduction in school absence and increase motivation and commitment from the student,
- Increased satisfaction level of the students,
- Creation of the need to learn, from their roles with the immersive world proposed,
- Creation of a certain degree of rivalry in the completion of ubiquitous tasks thanks to the use of various ICT systems,
- Boost knowledge of students' mother tongue and the establishment of a lingua franca to carry out international tasks,
- Train the students and those already working and ensure that they are fully prepared to carry out the work expected of an officially qualified technician.

1.3 SCC Assessment

The experimental model suggested by the L4W project is based on a new SCC approach and on the training programs development methods. SCC is a methodology inherently based on objectives. Its objectives are the same ones as those pursued by students when undertaking an education or training course and actively attending a particular training program. Its objectives should coincide with those same objectives set by students when thinking about their job and career aspirations. SCC is built on activities: i.e. activities concerning the adoption of the SCC methodology must be related to the long-term goals set by students in view of their specific roles to be played in real life. A SCC should starts with the definition of what the scenario is or will be. Subsequently, within the given scenario, the training provider shall decide, on the basic elements to be developed, the specific conditions and "parallel" or "side" elements to be implemented to enhance students' ability to play their role in their future professional career. SCC works in any complex learning environment, as long as mentors are available and willing to coach students in their learning process and future realistic roles to play. A meaningful experimental environment of such a scenario must therefore be put in place. This environment can be built on the web or at school. In both cases, teamwork and mentoring, as well as the subsequent evaluation of products resulting from these specific activities, are the key pivot around which the teaching methodology revolves. It is therefore fundamental to start from the teachers' training, in the first place, and only later provide training to students themselves.

In order to fulfill our objectives, we need to develop a new approach that, on the one hand, takes into account the evaluation questions related to the project success, effectiveness and impact generated by the latter on the target audience; and on the other hand, it addresses the issue of evaluation of learning and tools useful for the transparency and validation of skills acquired by students through an innovative methodology aiming at developing not only vertical professional skills but also transversal soft skills and key skills.

2 Related Work

The SCC approach directly recalls the acquisition and validation dynamics of skills (such as life skills, key skills, and citizenship skills), which become a central element in the evaluation processes [1]. The issue of skills has progressively come to the limelight on the international scene, calling the attention of vocational training and education scholars, production organizations and policy makers [2]. As repeatedly stressed, being skilled implies in itself a social dimension, since someone can be recognized as competent, without necessarily acquiring skills though academic qualifications. At the same time, it implies an effective action dimension focusing on the flexibility and adaptability of competences as such on different levels, across the board.

At school, competences have been at the center of the debate for years; yet, the issue of how to assess them is underestimated, since the complexity of all the underlying issues is not directly taken into account, also considering the fact that some of these skills are prescriptive. Nowadays, we can find different references into the literature developing the "edumetrics" concept [3, 4], which has deepened the theme of competence assessment, by highlighting its specificity and discussing the translatability of psychometric criteria generally used in testing in the domain of education.

It is necessary to strengthen curricular (school) programming based on core competences, in order to facilitate the early acquisition of active citizenship competences at school. This would be desirable also in view of a wider dissemination of inquiry learning methodologies addressed to the most disadvantaged recipients who need to reposition of their skills in evidence based perception and self-assessment processes and more "manageable" cognitive processes. In this sense, intensifying the use of systems promoting the mutual recognition of European qualifications for employment, improving matching between job descriptions and skill profiles of diplomas and qualifications (European Skills/Competences, Qualifications and Occupations), can and must be regarded as a process involving all the training processes that are expressed in terms of learning outcomes. In addition, a lively debate has emerged on the link between instrument referencing systems, such as EQF (European Qualification Framework), with the national qualifications frameworks, NQF (National Qualification Framework), starting from the enhancement of already existing transparency and traceability tools, in particular, ECVET (European Credit system for Vocational Education and Training).

2.1 What to Assess and Why

Assessing training is always a difficult task, since it is closely connected to the context where (formal, non-formal and informal) training to be assessed has taken place and to the type of assessment approach that has been used. Generally, in the literature on training evaluation, two major theoretical approaches can be found: evaluation training and effectiveness training. The former is based on the evaluation of learning outcomes achieved at the end of training, in other words is based on the effectiveness of training that was provided. In the former approach, objectives, content and design of training become the object of evaluation; in the latter approach, however, the training process is examined in all its stages (pre, ongoing and post) considering the variables that might have influenced the effectiveness of training activities. Assessment supports and fosters the quality development of an education and training system because it:

- Identifies the strengths and weaknesses of an education and training system and action,
- Observes and analyses how resources are used,
- Involves and empowers the stakeholders engaged in the training system and actions,
- Ensures that a change has indeed occurred with effects on the institutional and social context,
- Allows to identify critical issues in a primary phase using Pre and Profile tests, and using mixed methods (combining quantitative and qualitative approaches) for a better interpretation of the results [5].

When we try to incorporate new educational methods using different technologies, we need to incorporate them into teaching in a controlled manner; there are some risks that need to be controlled before one can improve not only the curriculum but also student skills and knowledge. With technology, the professor must be trained and capable of providing full-time support to students: he or she must be capable of offering a good and precise explanation of the practice and methodology, must correctly select the applications, and must provide clear final objectives. Previous studies describe "critical mistakes" in the implementation of educational technology - mistakes that can generate negative perceptions among the students and which need to be avoided [6–10]. The need of and justification for incorporating IT into the educational process are particularly relevant, and they are described in the main roles of the European Higher Education Area (EHEA), which runs the university studies of member countries, including Spain, where this project was undertaken [11].

2.2 Mixed-Methods Assessment for Pedagogical Purposes

Quantitative and qualitative approaches have historically been the main methods of scientific research. Currently, a hybrid approach to experimental methodology has emerged that takes a more holistic view of methodological problems: the mixed-methods research approach. This model is based on a pragmatic paradigm that contemplates the possibility of combining quantitative and qualitative methods to achieve complementary results.

The value of research lays not so much in the epistemology of the method but in its effectiveness [12]. On the one hand, quantitative research focuses on analyzing the degree of association between quantified variables, as promulgated by logical positivism; therefore, this method requires induction to understand the results of the investigation. Because this paradigm considers that phenomena can be reduced to empirical indicators that represent reality, quantitative methods are considered objective [13, 14]. On the other hand, qualitative research focuses on detecting and processing intentions. Unlike quantitative methods, qualitative methods require deduction to interpret results. The qualitative approach is subjective, as it is assumed that reality is multifaceted and not reducible to a universal indicator [15].

The current methods in UX do not necessarily include the end user to participate in the creative process of the product. Most of them are guides of imagination exercises to be more emphatic with the user in concrete scenarios as cognitive walkthroughs [16], or user persons [17]. On the other hand, there are also qualitative methods far from usability standards which allow obtaining subjective information from users themselves, such as contextual design [18], or diary methods [19].

To provide a quality management, which is likely to attain objectives and to meet users' needs, it is necessary to rely on timely information on the efficiency and effectiveness of the training schedule. The main need that arises from a training project is to:

- Check the internal consistency of the programming procedures that are implemented and to describe the gap between expectations, processes and outcomes, resulting from the procedures in use,
- Describe the effectiveness of innovation processes that are implemented in terms of: enhancement of knowledge, expertise, skills, activities of each individual, change in attitudes and behaviors of individuals and organizations, impact of innovation on the professional, social and institutional context, and identify the transferability elements emerging from the innovation process, in order to translate them into educational policy choices.

3 Pre-test in SCC Applied to SEO and MOBCOM Courses

The SCC approach introduces an innovation element in the educational process, where it supposes an adjustment of content and models of learning units to the expected use of these tools by students in the workplace and in professional contexts. The implementation of the evaluation model is subdivided into three phases:

- First phase: research activities aimed at identifying the SCC approach centered variables. This phase aims to define the assumptions and provides for the definition and analysis of the critical variables measured; the identification and determination of strategic processes on which the assessment process is to be based; and the data collection tool development.
- In the second phase, tools will be administered and data will be collected within the sample made up of the teachers and learners community and in the control group (population not covered by the action).
- In the third phase, the processing of results will take place to answer the evaluative questions posed during the model development, by means of a comparison between the built model (initial research hypothesis) and the results obtained in terms of effectiveness and impact. The final phase is intended to predict any changes in the model, compared to the preliminary setup of the training model.

The methodological approach that has been adopted aims to give an account, on the one hand, of the complexity of the research field, in terms of enlargement of training systems (formal, non-formal, informal); SCC approach consideration; key process analysis in terms of skills development and performance of the extreme variability of training behaviors by organizations. In the process of design the test, we need to identify and choice the indicators to be obtained in order to validate our methodology. The indicators can be metaphorically understood as signals, "arrows" that specify, clarify and describe the characteristics or properties of training to differentiate, to take evolution under control, to observe the direct and indirect effects caused by the project on individuals and their related institutions.

To formulate effectiveness and impact indicators and to identify areas subject to assessment it is necessary to remind, explicitly, and to explore the main features that characterize the SCC method and its building procedures, such as the development of learning units. For example, some aspects to be reviewed are:

- The meaning of training unit of learning,
- The reasons why the SCC approach is chosen,
- The implications on teachers' work,
- The SCC/modulation relationship for students' learning, etc.

3.1   Courses Assessment

The following Table 1 shows the basic scheme of the courses assessment:

Table 1. Course assessment. (1) For traditional and SCC groups. (2) Only to evaluate in the SCC group. (3) For local classes and international groups: one school of each country will develop the MOBCOM course in an international model, in collaboration with the selected schools of the other countries.

Course	Type	Assessment task	When?	Assessment components
SEO	Both (1)	1.- Technological profile	Before start	Quantitative survey using Likert scale
		2.- Motivation (2)		
	Both (1)	3.- General skills	At the end of the course	Mixed method: quantitative test with Likert scale and qualitative evaluation in focus group according to Bipolar Laddering (BLA) technique [20]
		4.- Specific skills		
		5.- Usability of the method		
		6.- Student satisfaction		
MOBCOM	SCC (3)	1.- Technological profile	Before start	Quantitative survey using Likert scale
		2.- Motivation		
	SCC (3)	3.- General skills	At the end of the course	Mixed method: quantitative test with Likert scale and qualitative evaluation in focus group according to BLA
		4.- Specific skills		
		5.- Usability of the method		
		6.- Student satisfaction		
		7.- International impact		
		8.- Efficiency of SCC		

Table 2. Pre-test 1: Technological Student Profile. Questions 1 and 2: 5-Daily, 4-Occasionally, 3-Only at school, 2-Rarely, 1-Never. Questions 4,5,7 and 8: A-Very much, B-Somewhat, C-Slight, D-Note at all.

Name:_____Email:_____ Fem/Male	Age:_____			
1.- How often do you use your computer?	5	4	3	2	1
2.- How often do you use services of Internet?	5	4	3	2	1
3.- Which devices do you usually use to access Internet (select): PC / Computer at school / Smartphone / Tablet / I don't use Internet/ Other (specify):				
4.- Identify level of knowledge of the following programs				
Word Processing	A	B	C	D
Multimedia presentations	A	B	C	D
Hypertext	A	B	C	D
Spreadsheets	A	B	C	D
Image processing	A	B	C	D
Audio/video production	A	B	C	D
Concept maps	A	B	C	D
Publication of audio/video	A	B	C	D
Social media tools	A	B	C	D
5.- What is your degree of competence in each following systems?				
Blog	A	B	C	D
Forum	A	B	C	D
Wiki	A	B	C	D
Text chat	A	B	C	D
Audio/Video conference	A	B	C	D
Electronic mail	A	B	C	D
Social networks	A	B	C	D
e-Learning platforms	A	B	C	D
6.- Have you participated in ICT training courses? YES, recently / Yes, but not recently / NO				
If Yes, please specify: forums / sharing materials / synchr. meetings / (audio / video) Conference / meetings in person / blended / e-learning / other (specify):				
7.- If you have answer YES to question 6, express an evaluation of the following indicators:				
ICT training path corresponds to initial expectations	A	B	C	D
ICT training path corresponds to professional interests	A	B	C	D
Positive effects on didactic practice	A	B	C	D
Quality teaching materials	A	B	C	D
8.- In your school experience using ICT	A	B	C	D
9.- Using ICT, which of the following tools hay you used/ use? Computer laboratory / IWB - Interactive Whiteboard / Personal devices (tablet-smartphone) / Other:				
10.- Select the ICT systems that you have used: Moodle / Edmodo / Google Apps / Youtube / Other:				
11.- Have you ever used digital educational content to promote your idea or product? YES/NO				
If Yes, please specify: Content created with word processing soft / with presentation soft / with the Whiteboard soft / with educational soft / e-book / other:				

Preliminary information on the students profile and their initial motivation are basic information in order to develop the methodology proposed. With the information extracted from these surveys we can detect differences across countries and educational institutions and the motivation of the students of the schools involved in the project.

3.2   Designing the Pre-test

With all the data collected we can adapt the method in function of the characteristics of the students, their needs, or for example technology difficulties of the students. The pre-test was designed to ask students about the technologies they are familiar with, possess or use (Table 2), and their motivation in front of the use of SCC methodology (Table 3). This information provides us with the level of advanced preparation using interconnected systems through different devices such as computers, mobile phones, tablets, etc. A classical mistake is assuming the presence of knowledge, use or possession of technologies required to complete a project; when this assumption is later proved wrong, the experiment fails due to the design errors in the implementation and development processes.

Table 3. Pre-test 2: Student Motivation using SCC Methodology. Questions 1 and 2: 5-Daily, 4-Occasionally, 3-Only at school, 2-Rarely, 1-Never. Questions 4,5,7 and 8: A-Very much, B-Somewhat, C-Slight, D-Note at all.

Name:_____ Email:_____ Fem/Male / Age: _____
1) What do you expect form the course SCC?
2) Have you ever heard of SCC before? YES/NO, If yes, in which regard?
3) Do you like the idea of engaging in a learning which simulated a real work situation, in which you assume an important role in order to solve problems and / or achieve goals? YES / NO
If so, what do you consider your personal motivations for participation
If not, what do you consider your personal reasons for not participating
4) You think you can be a good work team member on a specific project?
5) Among the various moments of which will consist of the learning experience SCC, which you think are the most interesting for you and why? (More choices are possible)
5.1.- To simulate a real work commitment.   YES/NO – Why?: 5.2.- Working in a team.   YES/NO – Why?: 5.3.- To use new technologies.   YES/NO – Why?: 5.4.- Doing less theory and more practice.   YES/NO – Why?: 5.5.- To practice one or more foreign languages. YES/NO – Why?:
6) What are your personal experiences of participation in structured situations of group and/or business (eg. Sports, associations, small jobs, work in the family business, etc); concisely express your feelings about it; Describe the abilities that followed?
7) What benefits you expect to gain from a training course focused on the SCC?

4   Conclusions

The paper presents the design of a specific pre-test for testing the student profile and motivation in a course where we adapt the SCC methodology. Scenario Centered Curriculum is being applied to promote the acquisition and development of international cooperation skills through the use of Information Communication Technologies (ICT) tools and systems. The L4W project is based on the development of learning strategies within the framework of Vocation Training, in order to improve learning processes and make them more applicable in the real working world while minimizing the number of student drop-outs. Learning methods are re-conceptualized through the use of immersive worlds and role and project-orientated-learning. As we have demonstrated the process of designing the assessment surveys it is critical in order to obtain the complete feedback of the student. The collected information allows us to evaluate the impact of the new educational methods proposed and the need of change any educational exercise or strategy, something that it is very easy to find according with the fact of work in three different educational sectors as are the Spanish, French and Italian schools. At the moment of the publication of this paper (2016, February), we are collecting the data and beginning the analysis of the Pre-Test data, following the schedule of the project.

Acknowledgments. The *Learning4work* project is supported by the European Union with its program Erasmus+ ES01-KA202-004845. The present work only expresses the opinion and points of view of its authors and both the National Agency and the European Commission are not responsible for any direct or derivate use that can be done form the contents presented in the same one.

Funded by
the European Union

References

1. Turnbull, A.P.: Exceptional Lives: Special Education in Today's Schools. Merrill/Prentice Hall, Order Department, Old Tappan (1995)
2. Mertens, D.M.: Research and Evaluation in Education and Psychology: Integrating Diversity with Quantitative, Qualitative, and Mixed Methods. Sage Publications, Thousand Oaks (2014)
3. Dierick, S., Dochy, F.: New lines in edumetrics: new forms of assessment lead to new assessment criteria. Stud. Educ. Eval. **27**(4), 307–329 (2001)
4. Baartman, L.K., Prins, F.J., Kirschner, P.A., Van Der Vleuten, C.P.: Determining the quality of competence assessment programs: a self-evaluation procedure. Stud. Educ. Eval. **33**(3), 258–281 (2007)
5. Fonseca, D., Redondo, E., Villagrasa, S.: Mixed-methods research: a new approach to evaluating the motivation and satisfaction of university students using advanced visual technologies. Univ. Access Inf. Soc. **14**(3), 1–22 (2004)

6. Redondo, E., Giménez, L., Valls, F., Navarro, I., Fonseca, D., Villagrasa, S.: High vs. low intensity courses: student technological behavior. In: Proceedings of the 3rd International Conference on Technological Ecosystems for Enhancing Multiculturality, pp. 77–82. ACM, October 2015
7. Daccord, T.: 5 Critical mistakes schools make with iPads (and how to correct them) (2012). http://www.edudemic.com. Accessed 29 Aug 2013
8. Shareski, D.: The ten worst practices in educational technology (2010). http://kibrown. wordpress.com. Accessed 29 Aug 2013
9. Muir, M.: The two mistakes teachers make when teaching with technology (2012). http:// multiplepathways.wordpress.com/. Accessed 29 Aug 2013
10. Cuban, L.: The technology mistake: confusing access to information with becoming educated (2012). http://www.washingtonpost.com/blogs. Accessed 29 Aug 2013
11. Martín-Calero, C.G.: Innovación docente: Docencia y TICS. Universidad de Valladolid, Valladolid (2008)
12. Tashakkori, A., Teddlie, C.: Foundations of Mixed Methods Research: Integrating Quantitative and Qualitative Approaches in the Social and Behavioral Science. Sage Publications Inc., Thousand Oaks (2004)
13. Sale, J.E.M., Lohfeld, L.H., Brazil, K.: Revisiting the quantitative-qualitative debate: implications for mixed methods research. Qual. Quant. **36**(1), 43–53 (2002)
14. Vigo, M., Aizpurua, A., Arrue, M., Abascal, J.: Quantitative assessment of mobile web guidelines conformance. Univ. Access Inf. Soc. **10**(1), 33–49 (2011)
15. Pfeil, U., Zaphiris, P.: Applying qualitative content analysis to study online support communities. Univ. Access Inf. Soc. **8**(1), 1–16 (2010)
16. Wharton, C., Rieman, J., Lewis, C., Polson, P.: The cognitive walkthrough method: a practitioner's guide. In: Nielsen, J., Mack, R.L. (eds.) Usability Inspection Methods, pp. 105–141. Wiley, New York (1994)
17. Cooper, A.: The Inmates are Running the Asylum: Why High-Tech Products Drive us Crazy and How to Restore the Sanity, p. 199. Macmillan Publishing Co., Inc., Indianapolis (1999)
18. Beyer, H., Holtzblatt, K.: Contextual Design: Defining Customer-Centered Systems. Morgan Kaufmann Publishers Inc., San Francisco (1998)
19. Bolger, N., Davis, A., Rafaeli, E.: Diary methods: capturing life as it is lived. Ann. Rev. Psychol. **54**, 579–616 (2003)
20. Pifarré, M., Tomico, O.: Bipolar laddering (BLA): a participatory subjective exploration method on user experience. In: Proceedings of the 2007 Conference on Designing for User Experiences, p. 2. ACM, November 2007

Cooperative Micro Flip Teaching

Francisco J. García-Peñalvo[1(✉)], Ángel Fidalgo-Blanco[2],
María Luisa Sein-Echaluce[3], and Miguel Ángel Conde[4]

[1] GRIAL Research Group, University of Salamanca, Salamanca, Spain
fgarcia@usal.es
[2] Technical University of Madrid, Madrid, Spain
angel.fidalgo@upm.es
[3] University of Zaragoza, Zaragoza, Spain
mlsein@unizar.es
[4] GRIAL Research Group, University of León, León, Spain
miguel.conde@unileon.es

Abstract. This work integrates two aspects whose positive impact on learning has been tested flip teaching and cooperation among students. In this proposal the faculty/students of a subject use, throughout the flip teaching technique, the resources created by students of a different degree. The theme of the resources is about teamwork competence, topic in which students create and later use the resources. The paper describes how to use and organize the generated and shared resources by the students, using the proposed teaching/learning methodology that is so called Micro Flip Teaching. Also, the results of the students' usefulness perception are presented.

Keywords: Flip Teaching · Cooperation · Knowledge management system · Educational innovation

1 Introduction

Flip Teaching methodology is based on two key actions: move at home the activities that are usually done in the classroom (such as master lectures); and move into the classroom those that are usually done at home (like homework). Traditional education is based on lectures where the teacher acts as the emitting source of knowledge and students as passive recipients. Moreover, in carrying out academic works, students have an active role, whether they are individual or collective works. According to this, Flip Teaching implies, on one hand, taking advantages from the presence of faculty and students in a common location (e.g. the classroom) to achieve an active participation, because of an authentic interaction in the classroom is the basic element for active learning The ideal environment for active learning should motivate students to interact, perform activities, and reflect on their learning [1]. On the other hand, Flip Teaching looks for that students at home emulate the behavior they usually have in the classroom.

The first proposals being made to bring the lessons home and work in the classroom, emerged in 2000. Lage et al. [2] call this technique "Inverting the classroom",

P. Zaphiris and A. Ioannou (Eds.): LCT 2016, LNCS 9753, pp. 14–24, 2016.
DOI: 10.1007/978-3-319-39483-1_2

while Baker [3] names it "Classroom Flip". Ever since there have been new names like "Flip Teaching", "Flipped Classroom" or "Flipped Learning".

Although there is no common model for application of this technique [4], there exist lots of works that use the video as a substitute for the master lecture. However, there is no uniformity in the activities undertaken in class. It can be said that this "inversion" of times can help to optimize spaces for discussions, debates, laboratories, projects, practical activities in class, and the fostering of collaboration. The four pillars that make Flip teaching possible are flexible environments, learning culture, intentional content, and professional teachers [5]. The Observatory of Education Innovation of the *Tecnológico de Monterrey* [6] has also detected a tendency to integrate inverted learning with other approaches, for example, combining peer instruction [7], self-paced learning according to objectives, adaptive learning [8–10], and the use of leisure to learn.

Thus, Flip Teaching model is based on the idea of increasing interaction among students and their responsibility for their own learning [11], using virtual learning environments as supported tool [12–14]. These virtual environments allow students the access to the learning resources and the possibility to make questions and interchange materials throughout the forums, because it is mandatory that the students have availability of help at home [15].

With this regard, students often share learning resources with their peers through social networks [16]. Teachers can take advantage from this situation organizing these shared resources and stimulating their production. Some research works have shown that resources production means a stimulus for students, as a way to explain their experience relating to a specific subject or the context where learning occurs [17]. Also, the use of contents created by students stimulates the creation of new resources by themselves. Thus a spiral is established where contents are produced, classified, organized and used [18].

Most of the Flipped Teaching experiences reviewed by the authors showed that the typical out of the classroom activities are based on videos, most of them created by the faculty. It is less common, but some teachers also use external videos to the academic scope.

The approach of this work is based on the use, under the model of "Flip Teaching", of students' produced resources in order to analyze the students' perception on the usefulness of these resources.

This way, the main novelty of this work is that out the classroom activity is based on videos provided by both faculty and student (to substitute the master lectures) and online resources (generated by the students as supplementary learning material). All this by establishing criteria for integrating the resources, generated by students, with those generated by teachers.

The research done with this experience contributes with:

- A study of the resources that students create for each of the situation, which generates a continuous knowledge. It includes its format, scope and usefulness.
- Identification, study and analysis of the learning activities where the created resources may be involved. Besides, there are activities that integrate both faculty's resources and students' resources.

- A qualitative study of the students' perception about the learning improvement throughout the use of the generated resources.
- A qualitative study of the willingness to share their learning resources with others peers.

The rest of the paper is organized as follow. Section 2 presents the proposed Flip Teaching model. Section 3 explains the research context. Section 4 discusses the results. Finally, Sect. 5 closes the paper with its conclusions.

2 Flip Teaching Proposed Model

In this paper a Flip teaching method has been defined and it is so called Micro-Flip Teaching (MFT). The feature of this model is that it is not necessary to apply it to the whole subject. Its application is simple with easy to follow notes. It uses free cloud-computing accessible technologies, such as Screencast, Dropbox or Drive. The model has been tested with a positive impact in the learning improvement [19].

MFT model has three stages, as it is shown in Fig. 1: (1) Outside the classroom activity; (2) Binding activity; and (3) Inside the classroom activity.

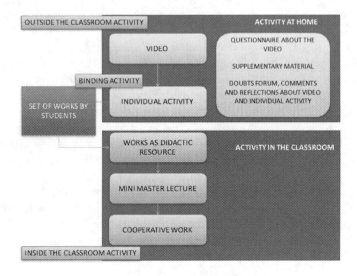

Fig. 1. Micro Flip Teaching (MFT) model

2.1 Activity at Home

It really is an activity that takes place outside the classroom, although termed "at home". The aim is not to transfer the full master lecture, but the most significant of the same through a video lasting no longer than ten minutes. The reason is that there are cognitive studies demonstrating the novelty of any stimulus tends to disappear after ten minutes [20]. Moreover, each video has an associated questionnaire to verify that students have seen the video; a forum for questions, comments and reflections (simulates the doubts that may arise during a class) and supplementary material.

2.2   Binding Activity

It is a key activity to establish a connection between the activities inside and outside the classroom [21]. This activity consists of making an individual work where students apply the explained concepts in the outside the classroom activity. Works are sent to the faculty for correction or they are published in a shared forum with all the students. This activity's duration is thirty minutes.

2.3   Activity in the Classroom

Faculty knows the doubts previously (through the forum available on the activity at home) and the degree of learning of such terms (through the work done in binding activity). From that prior knowledge the activity in the classroom is structured in a series of steps:

- Step 1. The results of the work of the binding activity are used as a teaching resource (both those that are well designed as the rest). Students present the work, after that a discussion begins about the reasons why it is right or wrong. Running time twenty minutes.
- Step 2. The faculty gives a mini master lecture for ten minutes.
- Step 3. Cooperative work where the learning resources generated until that moment are used. The duration is thirty minutes.

This model takes into account the knowledge that is used during the activity at home and that was generated previously by other students; specifically, as "master lecture" and "supplementary material".

The method can be used with the support of any Learning Management System because it is used as a driver of the process (resource management, forums, etc.).

3   Research Context

This research has been done during 2015–2016 academic year in the Programming Fundamentals subject of the first year of the Biotechnology degree in the Technical University of Madrid. This subject is taught in the first semester and was followed by sixty students.

The resources used for this case were created by students of the subject of Informatics and Programming for the previous academic year 2014–2015. This subject was taught in the first year and belongs to the degree of Engineer of Energy of the Technical University of Madrid.

The MFT method was applied for the development of teamwork competence (TWC) of the students in the 2015–2016 academic year. Thus, TWC was the theme of the created resources by the students the academic year before, also regarding the development of the TWC.

Figure 2 shows how the generated resources are integrated in the activity in the classroom by both faculty and a selection of students and, as supplementary material, students may access to the stored resources in a knowledge management system called

BRACO (*Buscador de Recursos de Aprendizaje Cooperativo*) [16, 22]. It is a system that allows storing, identifying, organizing and searching knowledge using ontologies. It is characterized by its capacity of converting individual or grouping knowledge into organizational knowledge [23].

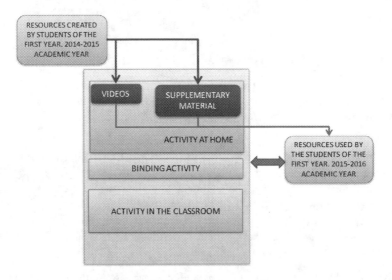

Fig. 2. Model applied on experience

Students make the binding activity organized in teams and each activity corresponds with several stages of the TWC development. People that compose the team interact among them through forums, wikis and online storage systems. This way, faculty may have evidences enough to follow the advances and to finally evaluate the TWC. This method is called Comprehensive Training Model of the Teamwork Competence (CTMTC) and has the main property of allowing faculty teach and evaluate the TWC both individually and by-group [24, 25].

The activity in the classroom is based on the use of the outcomes of the teamwork (TW) as didactical resource. Student teams expose the way they have done a specific TW stage and its outcomes. Faculty and the rest of the students make questions, reflect or contrast the presented outcomes with their own outcomes.

Teacher's role is based on how to use the students' expositions as didactical resource; for example, teacher may explain the reasons of the mistakes and may correct them in a public way. The others student teams use the exposed works to modify their own works. After that, a mini master lecture about the next TW stage is done. The process continues during four more sessions till the end of the TWC development.

The results presented in the next section correspond to two different studies. The first was made with students that created and shares the resources during 2014–2015 academic year and the second was made with the students that used those resources during 2015–2016 academic year.

4   Results

4.1   Resources Generated by Students in 2014–2015 Academic Year

Sixty students participated in this experience. They were organized in ten work teams with six people by team. Six teams generated useful resources and the others did not generated resources or the resources generated were not valid due to low quality issues (considered by the faculty evaluation of the work done).

The six teams have created thirty-nine resources whose typology is presented in Table 1. All these resources have been used in the activity at home in the following way:

- Nine resources have been integrated, alongside the teachers' ones, in the Learning Management System used in the subject (Moodle platform).
- Thirty-nine resources are accessible for the students, as supplementary material, in BRACO knowledge management system.

Table 1. Generated and shared contents in 2014–2015 academic course

Number and type of generated and shared by the students	
Videos (explanations of TW development and of the TW itself)	12
Web site (final result of TW)	6
Files (results of the intermediate stages of TW)	21

4.2   Students' Perception of the Use of the Resources in 2015–2016 Academic Year

In the academic course 2015–2016, once completed the training process and before the teachers carry out the evaluation, a survey among the participating students was conducted. The survey was voluntary and from a population of sixty students answered it fifty-five.

The survey has twenty-seven questions about the development of TWC and the students' profile, organized in the following way: four questions about Learning-Enthusiasm-Organization; eight questions about the Contents; two questions about Evaluation-Workload; five questions about their general opinion of the subject development; and eight questions about participant's characteristics. Some questions use a Likert scale 1–5, (1- Completely disagree; 2- Somewhat agree; 3- Neither agree nor disagree; 4- Sufficient agree; and 4- Strongly agree).

Table 2 shows the ration of the received answers regarding the questions about how the students used, in the activity at home, the created resources that were available in a web site, alongside with other teachers' materials. Tables 3 and 4 present the questions related to BRACO system (where the supplementary material was organized). It is attempted to measure the ease of access to supplementary material and its usefulness when performing the different stages of TWC development. Finally, it is asked for the intention of students to share the resources that they have created with others, see Table 5.

Table 2. Using videos of teachers and students in 2015–2016 academic year

Q5. Indicate the degree of agreement with the following statements (%):

	1	2	3	4	5
I have seen works in the recommended web site before I started TW	0	2	4	55	40
I think the works in the recommended web site have been useful to decide the TW theme	2	7	24	40	27

Table 3. BRACO resources used in 2015–2016 academic year

Q7. Indicate the number of resources that have seen among those found through BRACO:

	%
None	4
Between 2 and 4	31
Between 5 and 7	45
More than 7	20

Table 4. Ease and usefulness of BRACO in 2015–2016 academic year

Q10. Express your level of agreement with the following statements about the impact of the contents of BRACO in the development of teamwork (%)

	1	2	3	4	5
BU1. I have found easy to access BRACO resources	2	4	20	**55**	16
BU2. I have found BRACO useful for the phase "Mission and objectives"	2	5	13	**55**	25
BU3. I have found BRACO useful for the phase "Normative"	4	2	15	**53**	27
BU4. I have found BRACO useful for the phase "Responsibilities map"	4	4	22	**49**	22
BU5. I have found BRACO useful for the phase "Timetable"	4	4	27	**45**	20
BU6. I have found BRACO useful for the phase "Implementation phase"	4	5	24	**49**	18
BU7. I have found BRACO useful for the phase "Storage"	5	16	**40**	35	4
BU8. I have found BRACO useful for the phase "Final result"	7	7	16	**40**	29

Table 5. Resource sharing

Q12. With whom would you share in the future the resources you have created during the development of TW?	
	%
With my friends	5
With other teams of my teaching group	18
With other teams of my degree	24
With other teams of other degrees	3
With who ask me resources	50

5 Discussion

As in other previous research works, it has been demonstrated the usefulness of students create, share and use resources that have been previously created by other students (peer content creation) [17]. This case about knowledge creation demonstrates that students is able to create useful resources in different formats (video, web pages and files), which improves their learning. Moreover, students have willingness to share resources (50 % share with anyone and 24 % with the same degree). Both creation and sharing of resources brings benefits to student learning [26]. Sharples et al. [27] mention to Sidney Pressey (author of "Psychology and the New Education", 1933) that affirms that "Pupils are saved, in the words of Pressey, from educational drudgery and incompetence by joining online communities, asking questions, seeking answers, creating and sharing resources". Therefore, it must be strengthened by faculty the creation, organization and use of these resources.

Students were asked with which groups they would shared the resources they have created. They were allowed only one choice in order to know their preferences. 50 % of students would share their resources with anyone who asked them and 3 % would share it with other degrees, compared with 24 % who would share with their same degree partners. This situation is shocking because these students have used resources created by students from another degree. For this reason, it is key that the generated knowledge will be managed through a knowledge management system that all students in the same organization can access, to prevent the sharing of resources depends on "if they ask me a resource or not". This is possible in the presented proposal and a BRACO ontology has been defined depending on the degrees where the knowledge is created.

With regard to the use of the recommended web site outside the classroom, where the resources of both faculty and students are integrated, the 94 % of students recognizes that used it. The impact of this resource usage has been significant, for example, the 67 % of the students has been conditioned to choose the type of work to be done.

In relation to the rest of the resources used by students, and accessible as supplementary material through BRACO, it is shown that they have used it. Only 4 % of students did not use any resources, however 96 % have used some of these resources and 65 % used five or more resources. Therefore, it demonstrates that students use the resources generated by students of other degrees.

Regarding the use of resources on a particular stage of teamwork, in all phases except one, between 65 % and 80 % of the students recognized that the students' generated resources stored in BRACO have been useful or very useful for them.

For the "Storage" phase, only 39 % of students have seemed useful these resources; it will be necessary to consider whether the provided materials do not help in that task or whether the students already have sufficient knowledge and they do not need additional support. Therefore, teachers must analyze these resources and find out the reason of this. This leads to the conclusion that a measuring tool of the usefulness should be used in order to promote and review the resource creation in those parts of the subject where exist the perception that they have not been helpful.

6 Conclusions

It has shown the organization of resources created by students in order to used them for students of other degrees throughout the Micro Flip Teaching method, including both individuals and grouping activities in which ones the resources are useful and suitable. Also, the students' positive perception regarding the effect of the use of these resources in their learning has been studied. Moreover, other important contribution of the research done is the students' good willingness to share the created resources, but still it is necessary to work to improve it.

This method is easily transferable to any subject regardless of the discipline taught. In addition, it can be used in a timely manner in those parts of the subject where students have poorer academic results or there will be more complex topics.

Acknowledgements. We would like to thank the Government of Aragón, the European Social Fund and the Ministry of Education of the Region of Castilla-León for their support. Finally, the authors would like to express their gratitude to the research groups (LITI, http://www.liti.es; GIDTIC, http://gidtic.com and GRIAL, http://grial.usal.es).

References

1. Felder, R.M., Brent, R.: Active learning: an introduction. ASQ High. Educ. Br. **2**, 1–5 (2009)
2. Lage, M.J., Platt, G.J., Treglia, M.: Inverting the classroom: a gateway to creating an inclusive learning environment. J. Econ. Educ. **31**(1), 30–43 (2000)
3. Baker, J.W.: The 'classroom flip': using web course management tools to become the guide by the side. In: Chambers, J.A. (ed.) Selected Papers from the 11th International Conference on College Teaching and Learning, pp. 9–17. Florida Community College at Jacksonville, Jacksonville (2000)
4. CCL GUIDE: Learning story. Flipped classroom. What is the flipped classroom model, and how to use it? University of Minho, Portugal (2013). http://creative.eun.org/c/document_library/get_file?uuid=b0845def-9c31-476d-a3be-52a04c1e23a0&groupId=96459. Accessed 18 Feb 2016

 5. Ramírez-Monoya, M.S., Ramírez-Hernández, D.C.: Inverted learning environments with technology, innovation and flexibility: student experiences and meanings. J. Inf. Technol. Res. **9**, 18–33 (2016)
 6. Observatory of Educational Innovation of the Tecnológico de Monterrey: Flipped Learning. Tecnológico de Monterrey (2014). http://observatorio.itesm.mx/edutrendsaprendizajeinvertido. Accessed 25 Feb 2016
 7. Fulton, K.P.: Time for Learning: Top 10 Reasons Why Flipping the Classroom can Change Education. Corwin Press, California (2014)
 8. Lerís López, D., Vea Muniesa, F., Velamazán Gimeno, Á.: Aprendizaje adaptativo en Moodle: Tres casos prácticos. Educ. Knowl. Soc. **16**, 138–157 (2015)
 9. Berlanga, A., García-Peñalvo, F.J.: Learning technology specifications: semantic objects for adaptive learning environments. Int. J. Learn. Technol. **1**, 458–472 (2005)
10. Berlanga, A.J., García-Peñalvo, F.J.: Learning design in adaptive educational hypermedia systems. J. Univ. Comput. Sci. **14**, 3627–3647 (2008)
11. Bergmann, J., Sams, A.: Flip Your Classroom: Reach Every Student in Every Class Every Day. International Society for Technology in Education, New York (2012)
12. García-Peñalvo, F.J., García Carrasco, J.: Los espacios virtuales educativos en el ámbito de Internet: Un refuerzo a la formación tradicional. Educ. Knowl. Soc. **3** (2002)
13. García-Peñalvo, F.J.: Advances in E-Learning: Experiences and Methodologies. Information Science Reference (formerly Idea Group Reference), Hershey (2008)
14. García-Peñalvo, F.J., Seoane-Pardo, A.M.: Una revisión actualizada del concepto de eLearning. Décimo Aniversario. Educ. Knowl. Soc. **16**, 119–144 (2015)
15. Yoshida, H.: Perceived usefulness of "flipped learning" on instructional design for elementary and secondary education: with focus on pre-service teacher education. Int. J. Inf. Educ. Technol. **6**(6), 430–434 (2016)
16. Fidalgo Blanco, A., Sein-Echaluce Lacleta, M.L., García-Peñalvo, F.J., Pinilla-Martínez, J.: BRACO: Buscador de Recursos Académicos Colaborativos. En: La Sociedad del Aprendizaje. Actas del III Congreso Internacional sobre Aprendizaje, Innovación y Competitividad. CINAIC 2015 (14–16 de Octubre de 2015, Madrid, España), pp. 469–474 (2015)
17. Sein-Echaluce, M.L., Fidalgo-Blanco, A., García-Peñalvo, F.J.: Students' knowledge sharing to improve learning in engineering academic courses. Int. J. Eng. Educ. (IJEE) **32** (2), 1024–1035 (2016)
18. Séin-Echaluce, M.L., Fidalgo Blanco, Á., García-Peñalvo, F.J., Conde, M.Á.: A knowledge management system to classify social educational resources within a subject using teamwork techniques. In: Zaphiris, P., Ioannou, A. (eds.) LCT 2015. LNCS, vol. 9192, pp. 510–519. Springer, Heidelberg (2015)
19. Sein-Echaluce, M.L., Fidalgo-Blanco, A., García-Peñalvo, F.J.: Metodología de enseñanza inversa apoyada en b-learning y gestión del conocimiento. La Sociedad del Aprendizaje. Actas del III Congreso Internacional sobre Aprendizaje, Innovación y Competitividad. CINAIC 2015 (14–16 de Octubre de 2015, Madrid, España), pp. 464–468 (2015)
20. Medina, J.: Brain Rules: 12 Principles for Surviving and Thriving at Work, Home, and School. Pear Press, Edmonds, WA (2008)
21. Strayer, F.J.: How learning in an inverted classroom influences cooperation, innovation and task orientation. Learn. Environ. Res. **15**, 171–193 (2012)
22. García-Peñalvo, F.J., Sein-Echaluce Lacleta, M.L., Fidalgo-Blanco, Á.: Educational innovation management. A case study at the University of Salamanca. In: Alves, G.R., Felgueiras, M.C. (eds.) Proceedings of the Third International Conference on Technological Ecosystems for Enhancing Multiculturality (TEEM 2015), pp. 151–158. ACM, New York (2015)

23. Fidalgo-Blanco, A., Sein-Echaluce, M.L., García-Peñalvo, F.: Epistemological and ontological spirals: from individual experience in educational innovation to the organisational knowledge in the university sector. Progr. Electron. Libr. Inf. Syst. **49**(3), 266–288 (2015)
24. Lerís, D., Fidalgo, A., Sein-Echaluce, M.L.: A comprehensive training model of the teamwork competence. Int. J. Learn. Intellect. Cap. **11**(1), 1–19 (2014)
25. Fidalgo-Blanco, Á., Sein-Echaluce, M.L., García-Peñalvo, F.J., Conde, M.Á.: Using learning analytics to improve teamwork assessment. Comput. Hum. Behav. **47**, 149–156 (2015)
26. Sein-Echaluce, M.L., Fidalgo-Blanco, A., García-Peñalvo, F.J.: A repository of students' resources to improve the teamwork competence acquisition. In: ACM (eds.) TEEM 2015, Porto, Portugal, 07–09 October 2015, pp. 173–180. ACM, New York (2015). doi:http://dx. doi.org/10.1145/2808580.2808607
27. Sharples, M., Adams, A., Ferguson, R., Gaved, M., McAndrew, P., Rienties, B., Weller, M., Whitelock, D.: Innovating Pedagogy 2014: Open University Innovation Report 3. The Open University, Milton Keynes (2014). http://www.openuniversity.edu/sites/www. openuniversity.edu/files/The_Open_University_Innovating_Pedagogy_2014_0.pdf. Accessed 18 Feb 2016

Microinteractions and a Gamification Framework as a Mechanism for Capturing 21st Century Skills

Evangelos Kapros$^{(\boxtimes)}$ and Kathy Kipp

Learnovate Centre, Trinity College Dublin
Unit 28, Trinity Technology & Enterprise Campus, Pearse Street,
Dublin 2, Ireland
{evangelos.kapros,kkipp}@scss.tcd.ie
http://www.learnovatecentre.org/

Abstract. This paper describes a pedagogical design to capture 21st Century Skills. The pedagogical design includes three key components: a pedagogical frame, a gamification framework, and microinteraction-based interaction design. The focus was on secondary education (K-12), but the pedagogical design is generic and flexible enough to be appropriated for other purposes. Moreover, the paper describes how the three components of the pedagogical design can be implemented into a software tool for authentic classroom environments and informal settings. The tool would allow the capturing of 21st Ce. Skills, their formative assessment, and the metacognitive awareness of skill development. The contribution of this project is twofold: firstly, the production of a concrete set of pedagogical design guidelines and, secondly, design guidelines towards the implementation of a proof-of-concept prototype for use in classroom environments.

Keywords: Pedagogical design · Microinteractions · Gamification

1 Introduction

This paper describes a pedagogical design to capture 21st Century Skills. Already in 1999, there was a realisation that the workforce and the workplace landscape was changing rapidly, and training would need to reflect these changes, in what was called "21st Century Skills for 21st Century Jobs" [14]. Despite the initial focus on the workplace, and the recognition that competency-based-education is not a new concept[1] [13], opportunities to re-surface much desirable student-centred pedagogies were also recognised [11].

With regard to scaling such approaches, one well-known approach in K-12 is the Programme for International Student Assessment (PISA), developed by

---

[1] Papers from the 70 s go so far as mapping U.S. efforts to capture competencies during the 20 s and 30 s back to the operationalisation of WWI [2,5,9].

© Springer International Publishing Switzerland 2016
P. Zaphiris and A. Ioannou (Eds.): LCT 2016, LNCS 9753, pp. 25–35, 2016.
DOI: 10.1007/978-3-319-39483-1_3

the Organisation for Economic Co-operation and Development (OECD)[2]. Other attempts include the Assessment and Teaching of 21st Century Skills (ATC21S) project[3] and the Collaborative Assessment Alliance[4].

These attempts have been criticised with a number of arguments [7]; however, one aspect that was of special interest to us was that current approaches seem to be tightly-coupled with specific tasks. Thus, it can be the case that the obtained results are a matter of the students' skills as much as they are the result of task design.

In contrast, we set out to develop a task-independent approach so that it would scale and maintain its flexibility at the same time. Our intention is to develop a pedagogical design which will be developed as a software tool to be deployed at institutions of primarily K-12, but also Higher Education. While this is our initial focus, our design has no component that explicitly excludes informal education settings. Our approach is described below.

2   Pedagogical Design

2.1   Research Direction

Our Pedagogical Design is rooted in the Core Questions of this Research Project:

1. What are 21st Century Skills?
2. What learning innovations are being used to promote them?
3. What techniques/methodologies are being employed to assess them?
4. What technologies are being used to promote 21st Century Skills and their assessment?

And are given shape by the project objectives:

- To create a common framework for how 21st Century Skills can be assessed;
- To be able to assess informal learning and social activity from learners; in particular, to research new methods of assessment which can interpret, visualise and comparatively assess learning activity implicitly and continuously;
- To create a software tools in which multiple methods and approaches to assessment can take place.

2.2   Design Recommendations

With these questions and objectives focusing the initial research, a literature review was done around these areas to identify current trends in 21st Ce. skills, 21st Ce. skills assessment, and the state of art pedagogical design surrounding both of these areas.

From this research, the following pedagogical recommendations were made in regards to where gaps in innovation currently exist within this space:

---

[2] http://www.oecd.org/pisa/.
[3] http://www.atc21s.org/.
[4] http://caa21.org/.

Vertical and horizontal mobility: Anything designed should be able to cross grade level and content area as opposed to being grade or subject specific.

Not activity specific: Anything designed should be more than a once-off activity and have longevity and breadth to it, as opposed to being a singular activity that a student/teacher only interacts with once.

Authentic classroom dynamic: Anything designed should fit within the authentic classroom dynamic and become an extension of regular classroom practice as opposed to being something that interferes, prohibits, or breaks up the standard rhythm of instruction.

Additionally, recommendations were made that whatever demonstrator was built should:

Activate student skill literacy: Student understanding of the skills is not being addressed global focus seems to have jumped straight to the assessment of the skill without focusing on the teaching of the skill.

Be based in experiential learning: As opposed to forcing a context for the skill if possible the pedagogy should be rooted in a naturally occurring learning experience (a pseudo experiential learning situation).

Offer formative assessment for learning: Typical assessment activities in this area are either summative or disjointed formative and there should be a more streamlined and continuous formative assessment that promotes true and deep learning.

And lastly, the recommendations were made that:

The design be flexible: As it is clear that this is not a defined space the demonstrator should be flexible and dynamic offering many options for future design and extension of the original frame.

Data be viewed as baseline: That the data generated from the experience be something that is not limiting and can be used to establish a baseline for future development.

With this in mind, it was established that the best direction for development was in the self-assessment space as self-assessment allows for the flexibility established within the recommendations and is not a path being pursued by most developers at the moment and has the potential for more innovation. Additionally, self-assessment:

- Activates student understanding of 21st Ce. skills, providing knowledge base and direct instruction for what is implicit (literacy of 21st Ce. skills and assessment)
- Is personalised and allows for goal setting, continuous feedback, strength and deficit identification and formative assessment
- Allows for metacognitive awareness to increase student responsibility for skill development
- Informs classroom choices in all three realms of the educative relationship (student-teacher-knowledge) and is universally applicable

The decision was then made to create a 21st Ce. century skills self-assessment app. With the knowledge that this app would be trialled in Ireland, the frame that was chosen for the 21st Ce. skills was that used by the National Council for Curriculum and Assessment (NCCA) [8]. The NCCA refer to these skills as the Key Skills and have created 'rubrics' for them at both the Junior Cycle (K-8) and Senior Cycle Level (K-12). For the purposes of the demonstrator, the Junior Cycle Key Skills frame has been selected. However, the pedagogical frame described below, the gamification framework, and the microinteraction design of the next sections are not limited to this setting and have been designed to be as generic and flexible as possible.

2.3   Pedagogical Frame

The pedagogical frame in this use case is based on assessment strategies for self-directed learning and utilizes the conceptual design of manage, monitor and modify in regards to student behaviour around 21st Ce. skills. Specifically, the model of reference is model [3] of self-directed learning and their process-design model for feedback and continuous learning.

Generally, the frame consists of a phase which:

1. Starts with an identification of an experiential learning instances (a tagging of one of the identified 21st Ce. skills on the home page)
2. Continues with benchmarked experiences (an answering of either a quick answer multiple choice or free text question to activate student literacy and learning within the tagged skill)
3. Ends with the selection of an exemplar (student uploading of personal evidence of work in the skill) and a self-assessment (self-rating based on reflection)

To support this, a frame was selected with the steps of each design phase being built using a blend of feedback spirals and metacognitively scaffolded benchmark prompts that are designed to activate experiential learning (using Bloom's revised taxonomy [1], Wiggins & McTighe's Six Facets of Understanding [16], and Zimmerman's Phases and Subprocess of Self-Regulation [17]).

In regards to the specific self-assessment activities, benchmark activities within each phase are based on Rolheiser's growth scheme for teacher implementation of stages of student self-assessment [10], and student self-rating is done using a modified version of Marzano's 4-Point Self-Assessment Scale [6].

In regards to the specific creation and scaffolding of content within the onboarding, benchmarked experiences and exemplar questions and tasks, Bloom's revised taxonomy was used to formulate questions and tasks as was the concept of knowledge acquisition needing to occur prior to knowledge application.

3   Gamification Framework

This section describes and explains a gamified system for the aforementioned pedagogical design, mainly focusing on a proof-of-concept tablet app. The system consists of a tablet app, and a group of players who are students. The way the system will be designed and deployed is explained below, using the 6D Gamification Design Framework [15].

3.1 Description of the Gamified System

The system consists of a tablet app, a website, and players who meet in real life to participate in class activities. The players with the role of a student will be using the tablet app. The setting is a physical and synchronous classroom environment for the majority of the game tasks, and other environments for a few tasks. No asynchronous teaching or learning is assumed, but is not prohibited either.

The students will use the tablet app to identify *each moment in class when they are active in one of the 21st Ce. skills* defined by the NCCA (Collaboration, Communication, Creativity, Self-management, Information management) [8]. The home screen provides the students with a selection of the skills and they have to tap the appropriate choice each time they have used a skill in the classroom (e.g., Alice taps "Creativity" after solving a new problem in Mathematics). To validate this input without interrupting the class, the app will occasionally ask the student to perform short *benchmark tasks* after they have tapped a skill. However, these validation benchmarks will not appear each and every time the student has selected a skill. These self-assessment activities are organised in *levels* (phases) of increasing difficulty and are rewarded as described in the following sections. A preliminary on-boarding phase has been designed in a way that it can be delivered by the teacher in class without consuming too much time off a class session. Moreover, to clear a phase the student will have to upload an *exemplar* of an achievement of theirs that reflects each skill.

This gamified self-assessment process is suitable for both the Junior and the Senior Cycle and is not affected by pedagogical decisions with regard to the language of the assessment. Thus, it can facilitate multiple models of 21st Ce. Skills, multiple education systems, curricula, age groups, taught modules, or languages. Many of these benefits derive from the curriculum-independent nature of the self-assessment pedagogy itself, and not specifically from the gamification process.

The role of other stakeholders such as the teachers and parents is beyond the scope of this paper.

3.2 Define Business Objectives

One main reason why a design decision was made to gamify the process is that the self-assessment process is a continuous one. Indeed, the pedagogy is based on the continuous feedback spiral described in [3].

Since self-assessment is an iterative process, it is only safe to assume that initial iterations will produce poorer results than subsequent ones. Competence in self-assessment depends greatly on familiarisation with the assessment language. Thus, it is important to keep motivation among students high until they reach a stage where they will produce rich self-assessment material.

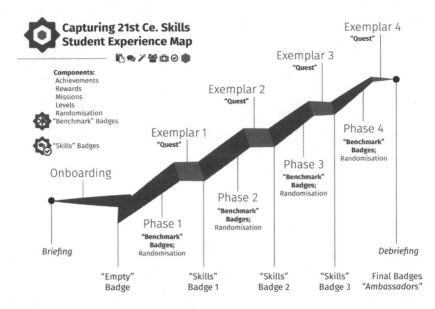

Fig. 1. The student user-experience map for the capturing of the 21st Ce. skills. A "Hero Journey" experience is designed by phases of increasing difficulty, microcredentials as rewards, and personalised solutions (exemplars) to "quests".

Gamification can facilitate getting the best out of students' self-assessments by keeping them in a mental state of flow [4]. A state of flow is one where the students immerse into their tasks and thus they are more likely to respond in a qualitatively appropriate way.

3.3   Delineate Target Behaviours

The target behaviours are the following. Firstly, tagging. That is, a player is expected to use the system to *digitally tag a physical activity*. That is, a key performance indicator (KPI) of the system will be the amount of user activity related with identifying that they have used a 21st Ce. skill in the classroom.

Secondly, a target behaviour is the player to explain their involvement with the skills. That is, a KPI of the system is the amount and the quality of user activity around the benchmark tasks during the phases, and the uploaded exemplars at the end of each phase (see Fig. 1).

3.4   Describe Your Players

The players are young, and relatively tech savvy (as we assume that their schools has provided them with tablet devices). While the pedagogical design and the overall gamification framework (phases, exemplars, etc.) have nothing that absolutely prescribes a tablet app and could be used with paper-based forms, the age of the players favours a digital solution.

The players, depending on their exact age, could have a varying level of workload and this could affect the use of the system. New students could use the system more due to excitement about its novelty, while near-graduation students could be affected by the current system's high appreciation of examination results and focus on those rather than on 21st Ce. skills.

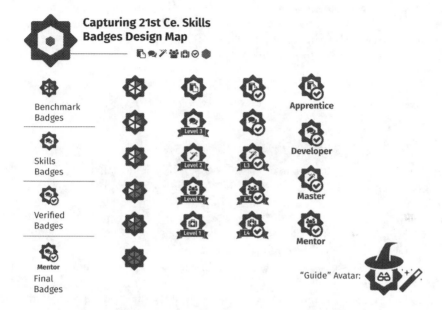

Fig. 2. Various designs for badges for the system. Benchmark badges also function as a progress indicator within a phase, while skills badges can indicate both progress across all phases and Marzano scale. Badges can be verified—but not evaluated—by teachers. A "guide" avatar is designed to provide guidance to the students.

3.5   Devise Activity Loops

The main activity loop will be to tag classroom activities in the system/app. Moreover, if the user has tagged a skill a set number of times they will be asked to complete a short benchmark task. Finally, the users get to upload an exemplar work of theirs for each skill that represents their best example of what each skill looks like in practice. For the main activity, the feedback is a simple notification that they have performed the tagging (see about microinteractions at the section below). For the benchmark and the exemplar tasks, the users will receive digital badges within the system (see Fig. 2). These badges would be designed so as to assign a status to users depending on their self-assessment and could include some teacher validation (not evaluation, rather validation in the sense of avoiding plagiarism etc.).

3.6   Dont Forget the Fun!

All the points said above, it is expected that satisfaction, within-school civic-duty-like fun, not necessarily playful fun is going to be the key motivator for players to participate in the system. Fun is seeked by expanding intrinsic motivation, it is not the goal that the aforementioned badges will be a major motivation force. Rather, extrinsic motivations will provide moments of instant gratification for sticking with the system, while, using again the examples of Alice tagging "Creativity" in a Mathematics activity, the Mathematics activity itself is supposed to be the playful fun of the system[5]. This can be conveyed to the users via the app visual design and text. However, various benchmark tasks can be designed so as to have playful elements. A "guide" avatar, designed to provide guidance to the students, can also consist an element of playful behaviour.

3.7   Deploy the Appropriate Tools

The appropriate tool here is a tablet app. The tablet app is intended to capture skills on the spot. Moreover, one can see their badges and previous exemplars.

A tablet is preferred since it is a mobile device which is less cumbersome for text input than a mobile phone. It allows on-the-spot capturing of skills and also to complete benchmark tasks that would require text input (e.g., "What does it mean to be excellent at Collaboration?"). Larger screen real-estate at tablets also means that browsing history or an overview of exemplars is better than using a mobile device.

As the players are young and tech savvy, they shouldn't have any difficulty in using this technology.

Overall, our gamification framework suggests the design of a finite game, where (i) mastery, ownership, and identity are the chief motivators, (ii) there are clear checkpoints as victory conditions, (iii) levels of difficulty, levels, rewards (badges), reinforcement through teacher validation of the badges, and quests (exemplars) are the game mechanics, (iv) and status, achievement, and feedback by the teacher are the social interactions.

4   Microinteraction Design

The pedagogical design and the gamification framework described above can result in many different implementations, but they all require a single interaction: *to digitally tag the physical activity of the skill* by tapping the appropriate choice each time they have used a skill in the classroom (e.g., Alice taps "Creativity" after solving a new problem in Mathematics). This interaction is a microinteraction: microinteractions are "contained product moments that revolve around a single use case—they have one main task" [12] and they consist of four parts:

---

[5] There is lack of evidence to suggest that it is even feasible to substitute most fun in-class activities with a piece of software.

www.learnovatecentre.org

Fig. 3. The microinteraction for the capturing of the 21st Ce. skills. A user performs some activity in the classroom and then in the app they tag it by tapping the respective option. The system gives them feedback about the success of the microinteraction. Two possible designs for different tablet platforms are presented.

Triggers: The trigger (see Fig. 3) that initiates the microinteraction is the user. The user performs some activity in the classroom and then in the app they tag it by tapping the respective option.

Rules: The rules for tagging are explained during an on-boarding phase to the students, and also by the teachers. It is anticipated that teachers would adapt the use of the tool to their teaching style. From the system's point of view, the rule is that the microinteraction needs to be triggered and then it will give feedback to the user or will initiate a loop (see the fourth part of microinteractions below).

Feedback: Feedback needs to be kept to a minimum in order to avoid interruptions of teaching in the classroom. A "thumbs up" icon with an informative text about which skill has been tagged should appear (see Fig. 3).

Modes and loops: Two extension loops of the tagging microinteraction for the capturing of the 21st Ce. skills are based on user behaviour as described below:

— After a user taps a skill for a certain number of times (as in Fig. 3) they are prompted to perform a benchmark task (see Fig. 4 left).
— After they have performed all the benchmark tasks for a phase, they are asked to upload an exemplar of the skill to move to the next phase (see Fig. 4 right).
— After the user has completed either a benchmark task or an exemplar, they receive their respective badge (see Fig. 2).

Overall, the aforementioned microinteraction design has a twofold intention. Its simplicity aims to enhance the usability and the user experience of the system. Moreover, the interaction design needs to facilitate the use in an authentic classroom environment and not interrupt teaching.

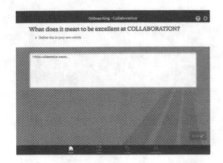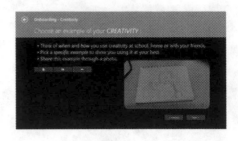

www.learnovatecentre.org

Fig. 4. Extension loops of the tagging microinteraction for the capturing of the 21st Ce. skills. After a user taps a skill for a certain number of times (as in Fig. 3) they are prompted to perform a benchmark task (left). After they have performed all the benchmark tasks of a phase they are asked to upload an exemplar of the skill to move to the next phase (right).

5 Preliminary Findings

We have sense-checked the pedagogical framework and the microinteractions-based and gamified design with a small sample of teachers and students. The response was positive and our design has been described by these few teachers as "filling the gap" in the area of skills assessment. The students perceived that they would benefit in raising their awareness around the skills. The response was from a small sample and to present conclusive findings a trial should be conducted with a prototype software application.

To this end, to day we have started developing a software tablet application which incorporates the ideas of this paper. Trials with the demonstrator have been scheduled with both the K-12 and the Higher Education sector and we anticipate that the data collected from these will yield interesting results.

6 Conclusions

In conclusion, the original project objectives of creating a framework for the assessment 21st Ce. Skills that would be independent of (formal or informal) a singular activity and which could be implemented in a software application were met successfully.

Moreover, we have designed a microinteraction-based gamified framework that accompanies the pedagogical design, which has the potential to enhance the user experience and the usability of skills assessment without interrupting the in-classroom activities.

A forthcoming trial with a software tool that incorporates the aforementioned principles is going to validate this approach, its flexibility, and its scalability.

Acknowledgments. This research is supported by the Learnovate Centre at Trinity College, the University of Dublin. The Learnovate Centre is funded under the Technology Centre Programme through the Government of Ireland's state agencies Enterprise Ireland and IDA Ireland.

References

1. Anderson, L.W., Krathwohl, D.R. (eds.): A Taxonomy for Learning, Teaching, and Assessing: A Revision of Bloom's Taxonomy of Educational Objectives. Allyn and Bacon, Boston (2001)
2. Callaghan, R.E.: Education and the Cult of Efficiency. Chicago University, Chicago (1962)
3. Costa, A.L., Kallick, B.: Learning and Leading with Habits of Mind: 16 Essential Characteristics for Success. Association for Supervision and Curriculum Development, Alexandria (2008)
4. Csíkszentmihályi, M.: Flow: The Psychology of Optimal Experience. Harper & Row, New York (1990)
5. Davies, I.: Objectives in Curriculum Design. McGraw Hill, New York (1976)
6. Marzano, R.J.: Classroom Assessment and Grading that Work. Association for Supervision and Curriculum Development, Alexandria (2006)
7. Murphy, S.: The pull of PISA: uncertainty, influence, and ignorance. Inter-Am. J. Educ. Democracy **3**(1), 27–44 (2010)
8. National Council for Curriculum, Assessment: Key Skills framework. NCCA (2009)
9. Neumann, W.: Educational responses to the concern of proficiency'. In: Grant, G. (ed.) On Competence: A Critical Analysis of Competence Based Reform in Higher Education. Jossey Bass, San Francisco (1979)
10. Rolheiser, C.: Self-evaluation.. Helping Students Get Better at It! A Teachers Resource Book. Cooperative Learning Evaluation Assessment Research Group, Toronto (1996)
11. Rotherham, A.J., Willingham, D.: 21st century skills the challenges ahead. Educ. Leadersh. **67**(1), 16–21 (2009). ASCD
12. Saffer, D.: Microinteractions. O'Reilly Media, San Francisco (2014)
13. Spady, W.G.: Competency based education: a bandwagon in search of a definition. Educ. Researcher **6**(1), 9–14 (1977)
14. Stuart, L.: 21st Century Skills for 21st Century Jobs. A Report of the U.S. Department of Commerce, U.S. Department of Education, U.S. Department of Labor, National Institute for Literacy and Small Business Administration. U.S. Government Printing Office (1999)
15. Werbach, K., Hunter, D.: For the Win: How Game Thinking Can Revolutionize Your Business. Wharton Digital Press, Philadelphia (2012)
16. Wiggins, G., McTighe, J.: Understanding by Design, 2nd edn. ASCD, Alexandria (2005)
17. Zimmerman, B.J.: From cognitive modeling to self-regulation: a social cognitive career path. Educ. Psychol. **48**(3), 135–147 (2013)

Creating Instructor Dashboards to Foster Collaborative Learning in On-Line Medical Problem-Based Learning Situations

Maedeh Assadat Kazemitabar[1]([⊠]), Stephen Bodnar[1],
Peter Hogaboam[2], Yuxin Chen[2], Juan Pablo Sarmiento[3],
Susanne P. Lajoie[1], Cindy Hmelo-Silver[2], Ricki Goldman[3],
Jeffrey Wiseman[4], and Lapki Chan[5]

[1] Department of Educational and Counselling Psychology,
McGill University, Montreal, Canada
maedeh.kazemi@mail.mcgill.ca,
{stephen.bodnar2,susanne.lajoie}@mcgill.ca
[2] School of Education, Indiana University Bloomington, Bloomington, IN, USA
phogaboa@umail.iu.edu, yc58@iu.edu,
chmelosi@indiana.edu
[3] Department of Administration Leadership and Technology,
New York University, New York, USA
{jps651,rgl07}@nyu.edu
[4] Center for Medical Education, McGill University, Montreal, Canada
jeffrey.wiseman@mcgill.ca
[5] School of Biomedical Sciences, The University of Hong Kong,
Hong Kong, China
lapki@hkucc.hku.hk

Abstract. Problem-based learning (PBL) refers to a student-centered pedagogy in which students collaborate with each other to solve complex problems. There are many benefits to this approach, such as improving student problem-solving skills, developing group-work skills and motivation. However, it is built upon low student-teacher ratios, which places increased demands on instructors, making traditional forms of PBL costly to implement in large-enrolment courses). This suggests that it is important to find ways to extend expert facilitation to multiple groups. Based on this approach, we have implemented an online, asynchronous learning environment entitled HOWARD (Helping Others With Argumentation and Reasoning Dashboard) which aims to foster multiple small PBLs and boost their instructional capacity. Beyond supporting instructors to handle multiple groups at the same time, our computer-supported PBL environment can allow learners to connect across cultures and disciplines, enabling them to interact beyond boundaries of location, time and space.

Keywords: Problem-based learning · Computer-supported collaborative learning · Multi-cultures · Visualization tools · Online dashboard · Patient/physician communication

© Springer International Publishing Switzerland 2016
P. Zaphiris and A. Ioannou (Eds.): LCT 2016, LNCS 9753, pp. 36–47, 2016.
DOI: 10.1007/978-3-319-39483-1_4

1 Introduction

1.1 Problem-Based Learning (PBL)

Problem based learning (PBL) is a student-centered pedagogy in which students collaborate with each other to solve complex and ill-structured problems (Hmelo-Silver and Barrows 2006). In this pedagogy, the objective of the instruction is to help students learn knowledge and reasoning skills as they learn in context. In it, the teacher's role switches from providing content knowledge to facilitating and guiding the students' interactions towards their learning goals (Hung et al. 2008). There are many benefits to this student-centered pedagogical approach, such as improving students' problem-solving and group-work skills, enriching their higher order thinking, motivation and deep internalization of students' knowledge. By solving complex real-world problems in a PBL setting, such important skills can be developed to enhance students' academic and professional competencies.

1.2 What is Involved in Providing PBL?

Context. Ill-structured real-world problems (often interdisciplinary) provide the context of the PBL environment. Although PBL has been traditionally used in the medical domain, it has been extended to other domains; e.g. mathematics, psychology, business education.

Collaboration spaces. A Learning Space is a distinguished social feature in PBL (Roscelle and Teasley 1995). It serves as a platform to afford learning materials and tools for learners to discuss key concepts and critical knowledge (Hmelo-Silver 2013). By participating in collaborative activities, learners share thoughts, discuss rationale, negotiate conflicts, and generate recommendations to solve complex problems. According to Hmelo-Silver (2013), a learning space could be divided into: (a) a problem space to discuss general content related with a problem case; and (b) a related conceptual space to discuss specific problems and related concepts at hand.

Scaffolding learners. Teachers need to take roles as facilitator whose main tasks should be modeling, coaching and fading (Hmelo-Silver and Barrows 2006). Scaffolding is support provided to students based on their personal needs, learning processes and levels of understanding. As students take more responsibilities for their own learning and become experienced and advanced in PBL, instructors fade their support progressively to motivate students to take more control of their learning.

Scaffolding facilitators. In complex PBL situations (e.g., multiple PBL groups or novel technology-supported PBL environments), facilitators themselves may require additional support. Using a "Wizard of Oz" approach a wizard teacher can support the other facilitators (Lajoie et al. 2014). In particular, wizards support the facilitators by observing the teaching process and noticing issues with the instructional content and student interactions that the facilitator might have overlooked. On such occasions, wizards may provide support by discussing and reminding facilitators to organize their instruction to correspond with students' dynamic learning processes and the development of learning activities.

1.3   Challenges of PBL

Various limitations of PBL have been discussed for some time. Two much-discussed limitations are: (a) the difficulty of scaling up small-group (b) challenges in assessing individual learning outcomes, etc. (Martinez-Maldonado et al. 2012). One main challenge of traditional PBL is the low student-teacher ratio. Students tackle questions that are significantly more open-ended and ill-structured than those in traditional instruction, and hence success often hinges on facilitation, monitoring and guidance from the instructor. The increased demand on instructing the team has made traditional forms of PBL difficult and costly to implement in large-enrolment courses.

Efforts to scale-up while maintaining the pedagogical approach have included peer tutoring, and facilitators that periodically visit multiple groups (Hmelo-Silver 2013). Other efforts have modified the pedagogical model to reduce the need for a facilitator (Abdelkhalek et al. 2010). However, research to date shows that when fostering multiple small-group PBLs simultaneously, facilitators' awareness of individual small-group PBL interactions is limited and requires considerable additional support (Martinez Maldonado et al. 2012). Our design aims to structure pedagogy and technology to provide this additional support to PBL facilitators working with multiple collaborative groups.

1.4   Technology-Enhanced PBL

Breakthroughs in technology may empower facilitators and boost their instructional capacity, allowing larger numbers of learners to participate and interact within a scaled-up PBL setting. Many researchers are interested in using technology with opportunities for supporting and scaffolding learners in a PBL context (e.g., Lajoie et al. 2014). Computer-supported PBL broadens the range of application of PBL across cultures and disciplines, and enables learners to interact and connect beyond boundaries of location, time and space. Technology may also support scaling-up PBL by allowing instructors to facilitate multiple groups at the same time. Recent PBL environments are structured and designed in technology-rich contexts (e.g., computer-supported learning environments). New technologies and cognitive tools have been exploited to enhance and empower the development of PBL. The features of technology-rich PBL environments may include: (1) shared collaborative learning spaces, (2) a collection of computer-mediated cognitive tools, and (3) use of visualizations. PBL has also been widely used in online learning environments via different models and media. Online PBL can be delivered in asynchronous or synchronous communications, or a mixture of the two. It has gained great popularity in recent years for its many instructional capabilities and its adaptability to a variety of contexts.

The components of online PBL contribute in different ways: whiteboards can be designed to foster students' brainstorming activities; chat spaces can promote students' flow of thought; threaded discussion forums encourage the exchange and discussion of ideas; other interactive and collaborative learning spaces may increase learners' engagement, creativity, reflection and productivity (Jonassen 1995).

2 Value of the Present Research

This research aims to investigate ways to support PBL facilitators working with multiple small PBL groups. To do so, we designed online tools to boost instructional capacity. These tools were brought together in an online learning environment entitled HOWARD (Helping Others With Argumentation and Reasoning Dashboard). It is expected that the PBL methodology in tandem with the technological competences of the designed learning environment will aid in making PBL-type teaching methods viable option for large courses. The platform may also allow for the implementation of courses across countries and cultures, aiding students to tackle problems of intercultural communication and awareness of context.

3 The Study

This research is situated in the context of an important but minimally attended medical domain: that of effectively breaking bad news to patients (Baile et al. 2000). In the realm of medical instruction and practice, emphasis has been placed in recent years to the relevance of communicational skills in the context of health services, and the impact that these soft skills have in proficient medical practice. One of these is the communication of problematic news. The manner in which this is done can alter a patient's course of decisions and actions, potentially impacting on his/her relations with the health system and treatment, emotional and mental health and, importantly, his/her immediate social context (family, workplace, friends). The way in which, for example, a person is informed about a venereal disease and whether or not this information should be shared with a spouse or partner has immediate consequences in the health of a whole family group.

The PBL course developed in the context of this research aims to help medical students learn from the critical assessment and group discussion of contrasting video-case based scenarios to foster their clinical decision making, and also enrich their communication skills in challenging situations about emotionally sensitive issues. Third and fourth year medical students will be recruited and take an online multiday workshop, with synchronous and asynchronous capabilities, and with the assessment and facilitation of a group of instructors. Students are organized in groups, which may belong to the same medical school or multi-cultural groups from different parts of the globe. The groups have deadlines and the course is taken in a given time frame (synchronous), but the individual activities each group member performs can be executed asynchronously. All of the relevant activities are conducted online through HOWARD.

4   HOWARD Interface

As described above, The HOWARD system is a web application designed to support asynchronous PBL workshops. This workshop involves three types of users: students, instructors and instructor-facilitators (who aid the instructors). Each user type participates in the workshop differently. Figure 1 provides an overview of the different user types and their interactions.

The overall layout for the site is similar for the different user types. A video column on the left side of the site provides access to video materials. A navigation bar at the bottom allows learners to access the site's different features, which are loaded dynamically into the main working space in the center of the screen. Hereafter we describe how this structure is used to implement user interfaces for the three user types in our workshops, beginning with students.

4.1   Student Interface

Students who log in for a workshop for the first time are directed to the guide page. The guide provides background information on the aims of the workshop (i.e., giving bad news) and the instruction method (i.e., PBL). Brief introductions to the website include frequently-asked-questions and a video guide providing an overview of the system.

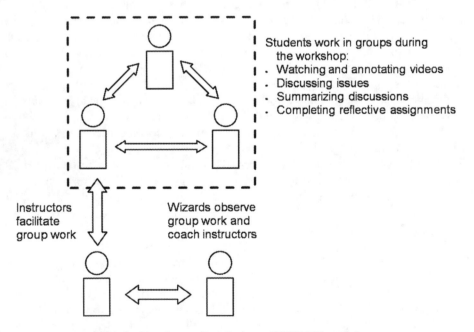

Fig. 1. User interactions during a HOWARD workshop

After reading through the guide, learners are expected to visit the "Today's Tasks" page. This page presents learners with a list of tasks to complete each day of the workshop and serves as pedagogical scaffolding to help students stay engaged, while providing them with a sense of progress. The task list is updated daily by an instructor. The general work-flow would involve students visiting the task list, and then visiting other parts of the site to complete those tasks. At present, the learner is responsible for tracking their progress through the workshop using the list. As they complete tasks, they return back to the task page to mark items complete. To help avoid having learners forget to update the status of their tasks, a reminder prompt is shown when learners log out from the system.

In order to replicate the advantages of traditional PBL in new technological PBL environments face-to-face PBL in HOWARD, we have attempted to provide an environment which adapts this learning approach to an asynchronous on-line environment. Our approach is to combine a discussion space, implemented as a threaded chat, with a collaborative text editor that can be used as a whiteboard.

Figure 2 shows the interface we have developed for group collaboration. Learners access the space using the 'Home' item on the navigation bar. The middle area of the screen is the discussion area. This collaborative writing space enables the traditional affordances of group work and discussion, such as sharing thoughts, discussing perspectives, negotiating conflict and designing and generating recommendations, while at the same time allowing the students insights to be available not only for further revision, but for the assessment by the instructing team. Special steps have been taken to facilitate asynchronous communication (to support learners from different time zones). First, learners are notified of new messages or whiteboard edits by means of a small badge-style notification indicator that appears on the navigation bar. Second,

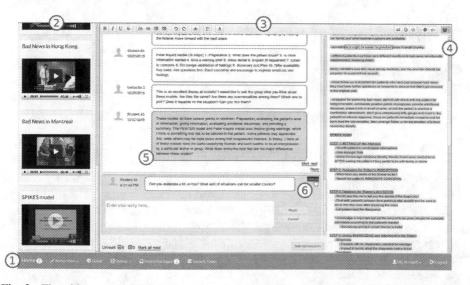

Fig. 2. The video annotation interface. Annotations students create are visible to other group members to promote discussion.

color is used to distinguish between old posts that the user has seen (colored white) with new posts that the user has not yet read (colored blue). After a user has read a post, they mark it as 'read' by clicking on the provided 'Read' link which changes the color to white. Because new posts can appear for both the most recent and older conversations, indicators visible on the bottom left of the discussion area are provided. These show learners how many unread posts exist and where these posts are located relative to the currently visible area (either above or below).

A collaborative whiteboard is located to the right of the discussion area. The whiteboard is built on the open-source text-editing platform Etherpad that allows learners to collaboratively write in real-time. Typically, this space is used as a real whiteboard would be, to summarize and record important points from the discussions that take place. Background color is used to attribute regions of text to their authors, with each learner having a unique color within a group.

To approximate the ability in face-to-face PBL to point to things on a real whiteboard, we have developed a group workspace feature that allows learners to link their posts in the discussion area with text located on the whiteboard. This is accomplished by selecting a region of text, typing a message in the discussion area and then posting. For other students who are reading these linked posts, locating the target text is accomplished by clicking a look-up button on the top-right corner of the post. Look-ups can also be performed from the whiteboard. In both cases, the relevant text is highlighted and automatically scrolled into view.

The video materials visible in the video column to the left of the group work space are a second important workshop resource. Videos are the medium used to present students with cases, i.e. examples of doctors providing patients with bad news. In the present course design, we provide two cases situated in different socio-cultural contexts, Montreal and Hong Kong. As a way of increasing engagement, we have leveraged code from the Open Video Annotation Project to implement an interface for annotating the videos. Learners first select a video to annotate from the video column, after which the video annotation tool loads in the main working space (see Fig. 3).

The video annotation tool allows learners to select regions of the video and attach a comment or observation. These annotations foster a dialogue among the students across time zones (specifically in cases of international collaboration), encouraging peer-based and intercultural learning, with the students feeding from the reflections and interactions with other members of the group.

A third and final key component of the online workshop is related to assessment. To evaluate progress made during the workshop, learners complete two reflective writing activities on private "Reflection" whiteboards shared only with their instructor. The interface provided by a private whiteboard is identical to a group whiteboard made full-screen without a discussion space, similar to a typical word processing environment. These private whiteboards contain questions for the student to reflect on and answer, and a submission button to notify an instructor when an assignment is ready for review. The system notifies a learner when their assignment has been reviewed using the same badge-style notification employed for group discussion changes. Feedback on the assignments, as well as other general messages from instructors, can be accessed via the 'Instructor Input' menu item which launches an email-style inbox.

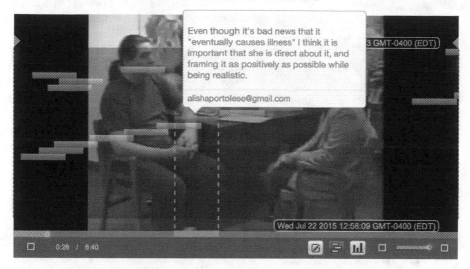

Fig. 3. The student user interface, consisting of navigation bar (1), video column (2) discussion space (3) and collaborative whiteboard (4). New chat messages appear blue (5). Chat messages allow students to link to whiteboard text (6) (Color figure online).

Before describing the instructor view of the platform, we first briefly mention that the actions that learners perform while using the system are logged. The purpose of this logging is two-fold: first, it allows a learner analytics module to process the log data and generate visualizations and other summaries to provide instructors with information on the activities of the group that help to gauge their progress and participation and flag groups or individuals in need of attention. Second, the log data provides researchers with a description of the learning process and an opportunity to associate behavior patterns during the activities with learning outcomes. This can also be used to investigate whether a design feature has the intended effect. We now present the instructor view of the system.

4.2   Instructor Interface

The instructor interface provides access to information on the participation and progress of the groups and a means to provide feedback on the group discussions and activities. For brevity, we focus on one aspect of the interface: the dashboard which is designed to facilitate the monitoring of group activities. Each group is represented on the dashboard page with four visualizations arranged in a row (see Fig. 4). We describe each of the visualizations below.

The left-most area of the dashboard shows information reflecting individual and group 'health'. A pie chart breaks down the participation levels of each student by analyzing the number of words they type in their group discussions and on the whiteboard. Below the pie chart, progress bars display various group-level information. The first progress bar shows group participation relative to other groups. If groups participate approximately the same amount, then all group bars appear green. However, for groups that deviate from each other, the bars for low-ranking groups are flagged with yellow or red to attract the instructor's attention. The second progress bar shows the overall progress for the group, measured as the mean level of tasks completed. A more detailed view of individual students' progress status is available by clicking on the label. The bottom-most progress bars show two related measures of student-instructor interaction. The student-instructor act ratio shows amount of attention the group has received, while instructor focus shows the amount of attention received relative to the other groups.

To the right, we see the 'Latest Activities' news feed which lists the various activities of group members in reverse chronological order. To avoid a cluttered display, the details of the acts are hidden until the instructor hovers over an event with the mouse. In some cases, the notification is provided as a hyperlink to provide convenient access to the particular discussion post, video annotation or other written content produced by the learners. An 'instructor only' filter can be applied to the notification feed to make it easier for instructors to review the activities they have completed. The visualization located at the top-right of the dashboard is a social network analysis diagram representing the interactions of the group members in the discussion space. Student users are represented by nodes. Larger nodes indicate more output and color indicating their location. Arcs joining the nodes show which given learner has replied to whom in the discussion space, with thicker arcs indicating more words exchanged.

Fig. 4. The instructor dashboard provides information on student participation and progress (1), recent activities (2), interaction trends between group members (3) and commonly discussed terms (4) (Color figure online).

Finally, a word cloud shows the frequency of different words being used in the discussions and the whiteboard, with more frequent words appearing larger. Common stop words are excluded.

Besides the dashboard, there are a number of other menu items on the instructor navigation bar. We briefly describe those:

1. *Student whiteboards*: This menu item provides links to discussion spaces for each group the instructor is managing. A discussion space loads as it would appear to the students, and the instructor can observe what is happening more closely, or contribute to discussions within the chat space or the whiteboard.
2. *Send Input*: This feature is for sending notifications to a group or to all groups.
3. *Assignments*: Allows instructors to see which students have submitted what assignments at a glance. When a student submits an assignment, an indicator appears which also links directly to the assignment. When instructors have reviewed the assignment and left feedback, they can click on a button to notify the student.
4. *Wizard chat*: This item provides access to a private space where instructors and wizards can discuss any concerns that come up during the course of a workshop. The space is identical to a student group's work space, but access is limited to the instructor and the wizard.
5. *Materials*: Clicking on the item loads a tabbed page where instructors can perform administrative functions typical of a learning system, such as creating users, managing groups and creating or distributing learning materials.

4.3   The Instructor-Facilitator Interface

In addition to students and instructors that take part in a workshop, there are also 'wizards'; these are PBL facilitators who monitor the interactions of the instructors and their groups but do not interact directly with the students. Instead, they function as a coach who provides tips and guidance to the instructors during a workshop. This is specifically in order to support facilitators in managing the cognitive load of their multiple group PBL instruction.

Their web interface is much the same as the instructors, i.e. they have access to the dashboard visualizations and the group discussions as well as the other menu items. Two aspects of the wizard interface are different from the other groups:

1. *'Mark Flag' notifications*: Wizards have the ability to send messages to instructors, via the 'Mark Flag' item, to direct their attention to different areas of the site. Creating a 'Mark Flag' message is similar to creating a typical email message, with the exception that these messages record page location information (the page the wizard is viewing while typing the message). When an instructor receives a 'Mark Flag' message in their notification feed, they can click on it to access it.
2. *Instructor Chats*: A final menu item specific to the wizard interface is the 'Instructor Chats' item, which provides links to the Wizard-Instructor private chat areas for each of the instructors.

5   Value and Future Directions

We conducted a pilot test of the platform in a week-long workshop for medical students, focused on breaking bad news. Instructors used HOWARD to monitor PBL groups and provide support to students as they reasoned through a bad news delivery case. As our aim is to increase the instructional capacity of PBL instructors, our preliminary analysis is focused on their instructors' felt needs and goals.

Facilitation is a primary concern for instructors. During post-interviews, instructors focused on three values: (1) gaining a sense of students' understanding to encourage participation and emotional engagement, and (2) managing the multiple interfaces and pathways to respond to students and the instructor-facilitator. (3) the value of and need for finding ways to conduct PBL online.

The asynchronous aspect of the design creates a challenge for instructors in terms of having a sense of what students' instructional needs. As one instructor noted:

> When I am teaching a student live, just by looking at their body language I can tell. Are they in distress, or are they liking this? In the online system, you can't tell….I lose the insight that I can get from having a human conversation to know, is this teaching on task, on target, or not? In a live setting, I would be able to pick that up in body language very quickly, as a tutor. In a pure online asynchronous setting, I'm completely blind to that…Students are trained to do their medical writing in as dispassionate, and in an unemotional, like, this is science, this is what I observed… So students are writing as if they would be writing medical records, they would deliberately hide any emotions, or deliberately remove any emotions from what it is that they would be writing down.

This finding suggests that future interventions should take a broader consideration of organization-specific cultures when designing for online environments and modes of communication. Beyond national cultures, organizational cultures may impact students' participation and emotional engagement.

The value of PBL in medical education has been strongly voiced by the medical community for many years. The primary benefit is that students encounter a problem as they would in actual practice: as ill-structured, complex, and often lacking a correct answer. As one of our workshop instructors noted:

> "I guess that, part of it is that, medical students so often feel, "I am not good enough, I'm never going to be as good as Dr. Y." I spend a lot of time as an educator, helping them realize that their opinion counts so much, that sometimes it is more important than what is in the literature. It is important because later on, when you go into practice as a physician, there are many questions in medicine that cannot be answered by the literature. And so then you are still faced with having to come to, what seems to be a reasonable decision with your patient. And people call that non-evidence based. But that's 99 % of medicine. So that what they are doing in these small groups, is that in a way, they are doing in my opinion, a very authentic medical thinking activity, where their own opinion and their own conceptions and misconceptions form a very important part of what it is they are thinking about and what they are doing."

HOWARD is designed to help both the student and the teacher by providing asynchronous tools for supporting individual and group interactions to foster PBL discussions about patient cases. The HOWARD tools support instructors through learning analytic metrics about the group process as well as through a 'Wizard of Oz' technique to support teacher attention to the instructional context.

The value of our design is in finding ways to make PBL more accessible by working to extend the instructional capacity of a PBL instructor. However, we are finding that an iterative design process is necessary, as each new technological capability brings with it new challenges to address. Focused on preserving the core value of authentic and ill-structured problems, and the challenges of facilitating, our future directions include (1) testing the design in a multi-group PBL instructional session, (2) Reduction of features and pathways, and (3) refining dashboard visualizations to focus on learning-relevant details (rather than activity-relevant details).

References

Abdelkhalek, N., Hussein, A., Gibbs, T., Hamdy, H.: Using team-based learning to prepare medical students for future problem-based learning. Med. Teach. **32**(2), 123–129 (2010)

Baile, W.F., Buckman, R., Lenzi, R., Glober, G., Beale, E.A., Kudelka, A.P.: SPIKES—a six-step protocol for delivering bad news: application to the patient with cancer. Oncologist **5**(4), 302–311 (2000)

Hmelo-Silver, C.E.: The International Handbook of Collaborative Learning. Routledge, Abingdon (2013)

Hmelo-Silver, C.E., Barrows, H.S.: Goals and strategies of a problem-based learning facilitator. Interdisc. J. Prob.-Based Learn. **1**(1), 4 (2006)

Hung, W., Jonassen, D.H., Liu, R.: Problem-based learning. Handb. Res. Educ. Commun. Technol. **3**, 485–506 (2008)

Jonassen, D.H.: Supporting communities of learners with technology: a vision for integrating technology with learning in schools. Educ. Technol. **35**(4), 60–63 (1995)

Lajoie, S.P., Hmelo-Silver, C.E., Wiseman, J.G., Chan, L.K., Lu, J., Khurana, C., Kazemitabar, M.: Using online digital tools and video to support international problem-based learning. Interdisc. J. Prob.-Based Learn. **8**(2), 6 (2014)

Martinez Maldonado, R., Kay, J., Yacef, K., Schwendimann, B.: An interactive teacher's dashboard for monitoring groups in a multi-tabletop learning environment. In: Cerri, S.A., Clancey, W.J., Papadourakis, G., Panourgia, K. (eds.) ITS 2012. LNCS, vol. 7315, pp. 482–492. Springer, Heidelberg (2012)

Roschelle, J., Teasley, S.D.: The construction of shared knowledge in collaborative problem solving. In: O'Malley, C. (ed.) Computer Supported Collaborative Learning, pp. 69–97. Springer, Heidelberg (1995)

Increasing the Quality of Use Case Definition Through a Design Thinking Collaborative Method and an Alternative Hybrid Documentation Style

Alexandra Matz[✉] and Panagiotis Germanakos

User Experience, Products & Innovation ICD, SAP SE,
Dietmar-Hopp-Allee 16, 69190 Walldorf, Germany
{alexandra.matz, panagiotis.germanakos}@sap.com

Abstract. Use cases are a critical milestone in the User Centered Design process referring to a list of action steps that define an interaction between two entities sharing a common goal. They express a structural representation of a usage scenario aiming to generate highly usable prototypes and user interfaces of a system or application. However, today, use cases are often not sufficiently created and documented, or they are not in the expected quality. The lack of a step-by-step collaborative approach towards the composition of more inclusive and readable use cases create unnecessary iterations increasing the cost, time, and resources utilization in an organization. Hence, in this paper we propose a Design Thinking collaborative method based on an alternative hybrid use case documentation style that enhances active participation and learning across team members. We emphasize on the methodology and tool and we present the benefits as those extracted from real-life business scenarios.

Keywords: User centered design · User experience · Collaborative learning · Use cases · Design thinking · User interfaces · User research

1 Introduction

Use cases are considered one of the most important tools of user research and user experience design since they encapsulate a crucial activity step in the User Centered Design (UCD) process, which guides the main philosophy and strategy of most companies today during the development of their business applications and systems. Use cases, in more practical terms, show the aim and the subsequent objectives of a system and the assigned user roles (also called actors), by expressing a list of steps and interactions among them towards a common goal. They could be written in a textual form or represented with the use of flow charts, sequence charts, Petri nets, or programming languages [1, 2]. In order for use cases to be effective and consequently convey the expected outcomes during the design and development of software solutions, they should be readable and understandable by all project stakeholders, sponsors and the end-users. Usually, their development is taking place after the creation of storyboards and before the actual design of the mock-ups and/or prototypes. It is the

© Springer International Publishing Switzerland 2016
P. Zaphiris and A. Ioannou (Eds.): LCT 2016, LNCS 9753, pp. 48–59, 2016.
DOI: 10.1007/978-3-319-39483-1_5

step that more abstract and fuzzy descriptions of the activities and tasks are transformed into tangible interactions between the involved entities (user roles and system). The more precise and inclusive a use case is the higher the probability to develop more qualitative user interfaces and system designs that will increase the user experience of the end-users.

However, one of the biggest problems nowadays in large organizations is that often project teams, that usually consist of different roles with diverse backgrounds and perspectives, miss to define use cases correctly (if not omit them) given the tight time delivery schedules and the lack of: (a) a consistent collaborative methodology that could put the various suggested use case styles into practice, enabling continuous learning and generating cumulative knowledge of real-life situations, and (b) a use case documentation tool that could ensure the same level of understanding and acceptability by all. Empirical research has shown that working and learning in highly synergetic collaborative environments [3] increase engagement, active participation, creativity, responsibility and awareness across project team members leading to deeper learning and more sophisticated and innovative solutions to real-world problems.

Thus, in this paper we outline a use case framework namely *Usee*, emphasizing on the methodology for creating use cases applying Design Thinking (DT – [4]) and facilitating collaboration, empathy, and integrative thinking and learning among project team members in large organizations during the software development process; and an alternative definition of a hybrid (diagrammatic and textual) use cases documentation style that bridges possible knowledge gaps and enhances understanding of their added value and use.

2   Related Work and Challenges in Large Organizations

The construction and documentation of use cases as an approach for identifying and capturing more inclusively the functional and behavioral requirements for the development of software systems is not new. It is also referred to as use case driven development (that could also be suitably aligned with the agile development methodology [5]), and has been gradually widely adopted, with the necessary modifications and alignments, to the business and process models of many large organizations. Jacobson et al. [6] was the first back in 1986 that created a number of techniques (textual, structural and visual modeling) for specifying and analyzing use cases, in an attempt to more comprehensively capture software requirements of large-scaled systems. Since then, many researchers, mostly from the area of software and systems engineering, approached adequately the topic suggesting different methods for developing and documenting use cases. Even though minor or significant variations in their viewpoints can be identified with respect to the style of presentation or the formulation of the content, most of them agree that, broadly speaking, there is not a standard way to create a use case, as there are no universally defined components or structures that could satisfy all the needs through a unique representation of the various parts it consists of (apart from some distinct items used across the various recommendations such as the actors, purpose or goals, preconditions and interactions). Yet, the length, complexity and the detail that a use case could be described in is guided predominantly from the case or the situation under investigation, the specific characteristics or its surrounding contextual factors. Fowler and Scott presented in [7] various use cases, class diagrams and inter-action models using the UML language distinguishing between the title, main success scenario and extensions (an outcome condition of the various interactions derived from the main success scenario) as the body of a use case. Cockburn, in one of his highly used textbooks [2], maintained a more flexible open approach (one column of text) in the writing of use cases and separated those that need to be described at higher level (casual) from those that need to be detailed more extensively (fully dressed). For Cockburn sometimes even a more simple structure of a use case composed only from the primary actor, scope, level and the story (in a narrative format describing the situation) might be sufficient for the needs of a project. He suggested a number of symbols to graphically indicate the subsequent levels of a use case ranging from the very high summary, summary, user goal (preferred level aka "goal level" or "sea level"), to sub-function and the too low level. A variation of this style could be considered the one-column table or the two-column table, which, even though extensively used today in the business sector, someone could argue that the within lines might hinder the flow of the actual writing [2]. In general, the purely textual layouts have the disadvantage that they maintain a serial or column approach with no clear (visual) distinction of the actors or the flow of infor-mation. This could be proved overwhelming especially in big and complex scenarios (though a useful rule of thumb is that a use case should not be in total more than nine action steps). Other use case styles are the Rational Unified Process (RUP – [8]), IF-Statement style, Occam style, and the Diagram style as nicely outlined by Cockburn in his book [2]. Finally, Constantine and Lockwood introduced the essential use case (aka business use case), where they used a structured narrative (conversation format), for capturing the user interface requirements and the purpose or the intentions that influence an interaction [9]. Therefore, there are various ways for creating use cases like in a diagrammatic format (using e.g. the UML language), in textual format (e.g. in a table), or using index cards (as introduced by Beck and Cunningham [10] in [11]).

However, most of these approaches refer to specific roles, as software engineers or developers, who have more technical skills, knowledge and training and embrace a particular way of thinking driven by their expertise. Nowadays, large-scaled software development project teams consist of heterogeneous roles (such as product owners and managers, architects, developers, user researchers, interaction and visual designers, etc.), tackling the real-life problems with innovative solutions usually found in the boundaries of their expertise. Hence, in order to achieve a successful and effective development of use cases, we must first face an existing challenge, especially in large organizations, of how to develop a method that will be able to bridge the knowledge gaps, experiences, educational backgrounds, and business roles of the various stake-holders. For such a method to be successful, it should share attributes, notations and semantics that will enable an active participation and learning through their continuous interaction, while participants are located in the same physical space or collaborate through virtual environments. Main concern is to maintain a common level of under-standing and breadth and depth of analysis to the benefit of all. This way teams will be able to take advantage of the diversified capabilities and expertise of its members towards their common goal that is the creation of seamless, functional and highly usable user interfaces and systems. More specifically, we have currently identified, to the best of our knowledge, a number of problems, among others, that hinder the smooth development and understanding of use cases, and which can be broadly distinguished as the:

- *Lack of a consistent collaborative methodology for creating use cases.* Even though there are noteworthy guidelines in the literature, as briefly discussed above, describing the various parts and components of use cases, there is not a consistent methodology showing how these could be applied by a project's team members in a consistent and collaborative manner. Inevitably, this creates different perspectives, lack of common understanding and acceptability of their potential benefit. Furthermore, ad-hoc or different approaches are utilized across teams resulting to not having a highly synergetic development process and a homogeneous outcome that could be cross-validated. Consequently, in many cases the same use cases (often belonging to different user roles) are re-defined driven by the different scope and viewpoints of various project teams, and leading to redundancies and/or incomparable results.

  In addition, the existence of such a collaborative methodology could increase the monitoring and support during the development process ensuring the expected qualitative definition of use cases. In particular, the lack of a subsequent step-by-step approach towards turning/interpreting more abstract statements (i.e. found in the previous process step, namely "Storyboards") to more deterministic/specific ones that serve as the basis of interaction design and functionality create unnecessary repetitions increasing the cost and time consumption. For example, many times we observed team members to use statements as, a user 'thinks', 'considers', 'evaluates', etc., instead of 'reports', 'chooses', 'deletes', etc., that could move the interaction process forward and could clearly indicate "who has the ball" each time in an interaction.

- *Lack of a hybrid (diagrammatic and textual) documentation style.* Currently, apart from the more "technical" UML based graphical styles, most project team members use pure textual or tabular style formats for the creation/documentation of their use cases. Inevitably, this creates confusion to those that follow the UCD approach, since it presupposes a totally different way of thinking than the one they used to have until this point in the process. The transition from a graphical high-level description method (as is Storyboards) to a pure text-based specific statements write-up creates inconsistencies and mental gaps to the participants and difficulties of adopting their way of thinking to this style. Also, this tabular format does not facilitate ease of use interaction and quick cross check validation among use cases since they are composed of pure text that masks the relevant information overwhelming the team members during the analysis (or consolidation) phase. For example, it is not easy to compare their length or their level of detail. Furthermore, there is no distinction between the user role and the system (they both belong under one column), and also there is no provision for marking possible repetitions among two activities or interaction points between two entities, that could be measurable and give added-value to one interaction step (i.e. the relationship of the two entities at a particular stage of the process). Finally, there are no interaction lines indicating the flow of information as traditionally most of data modelling tools use for the representation of information.

3   The *Usee* Collaborative Framework

In response to the above challenges and concerns, we outline in this section a use cases framework namely *Usee*, that aims to provide the basis for an end-to-end process of developing, validating and sharing qualitative use cases among projects' stakeholders. It provides components and tools that facilitate an effective collaboration, proactive support, knowledge sharing and learnability to the various transdisciplinary teams that participate in large-scaled projects and have the same objective; to increase the usability and user experience of user interfaces, applications and systems to the benefit of the end-users. The framework comprises of three main entities:

(a) *The User Interface*. It enables users to: (i) manage use cases (create new, review and modify existing), (ii) manage personas, (iii) maintain rules and messages which will facilitate the syntactical and semantical validations of use case data, and (iv) research, analyze and compare existing use cases through statistical methods and tools for their level of similarity, complexity, semantic quality, etc.

(b) *The Cloud Application Server*. It consists of four plus one components: (i) the use case maintenance, where the creation (providing two alternative ways: step-by-step and/or Graphical (WYSIWYG)), maintenance and storage of use cases data are handled; (ii) the use case administration, where the semantical and syntactical algorithms as well as the validation rules and messages are handled; (iii) the use cases and personas analysis and research, where various statistical models and comparison algorithms are executed, (iv) the persona maintenance, where the viewing and creation of personas' data are facilitated; and also (v) the cloud system administration, accommodating system and user administration.

(c) *The Cloud Usee Collaboration Network*. It is composed of three elements: (i) and (ii) refer to the use case and persona collaboration and discussion forum, where project teams can publish/share their use cases and personas and discuss related questions and issues, and (iii) the open source use case rule framework, where use case rules and algorithms can be shared, extended and modified by the network community, and which can be downloaded to the *Usee* application server.

Furthermore, the framework it will provide the possibility to upload use cases and personas to the SAP User Experience Communities (https://experience.sap.com and https://www.experiencesplash.com), in order to run usability validation tests with customers and end-users. Finally, there will be the provision of inviting customers for these usability validation sessions through the SAP Customer Engagement (CEI) initiative.

A fundamental prerequisite for the generation of qualitative use cases using the *Usee* framework is their comprehensive composition in a highly synergetic collaborative manner and their inclusive documentation in a style that will be understandable and purposeful for all the participating members of a project team. Accordingly, for the purpose of this paper, at first, we suggest a Design Thinking-based methodological approach liable to increase teams' learnability and efficiency towards the development of their use cases while at the same time reducing unnecessary time consuming and costly iterations. At a second level, we describe the main parts, structure and attributes of a new re-designed alternative hybrid (diagrammatic and textual) form for documenting use cases (as this will be extracted by the *Usee*), that increases customization, readability, comparability and enhances flexibility of use.

3.1   A Use Case Collaborative Methodology Using an Alternative Hybrid Style

As stated above the suggested collaborative methodology for the composition of use cases is based on the Design Thinking approach which is widely used in large organizations. DT originates as far back as the late 1980s and early 1990s when the need for a different, creative as well as innovative resolution of challenges emerged in the fields of engineering and architecture [12]. In DT, the approaches and problem solving methods of designers are merged with the viewpoints and practices of technology and business. As a result, it has evolved into a discipline that helps to strategically design and create products that satisfy the needs of users while at the same time opening up new business opportunities for companies [13]. DT advocates an open mindset and constant learning by observing and thoroughly understanding a problem space. Using the different skills and backgrounds of a multi-functional Design Thinking team, this approach helps to uncover new ideas through sharing of insights and by building on the ideas of others. During the entire process, keeping the open mindset remains important. If an idea or a method does not suffice, teams are prepared to not stick to one path, but re-iterate and even throw away ideas and start-over. To fail early in the process, and to fail often is encouraged as it allows constant learning through iterating on ideas as well as prototypes and helps to create innovative and at the same time solid and validated solutions.

Hence, this collaboration method apart from increasing the engagement, intrinsic motivation, empathy, learnability, and bridging diverse perspectives and backgrounds as those dictated by the various business roles, adheres to a number of teamwork dynamics as is: the facilitation of active and meaningful participation towards achieving the shared goals defined by the case at hand; the team-oriented approach to creativity, problem-solving and decision making; recognition of variable communication patterns; optimization of interpersonal trust and information processing; experiential skills development to effectively engage the main challenges teams usually face, like conflict resolution; etc. [14]. The biggest asset though derived from this constructive collaboration is the cumulative knowledge for a specific business situation that can be reproducible and retrofitted back to the business case at hand or to other teams dealing with similar cases saving effort, possible redundancies and resources. This is achieved through the creation of open ended opportunities (e.g. extensive engagement in open ended tasks) for the participants who have to construct their own learning objects and flexible knowledge through active experimentation, observation, reflection and conceptualization of their experience (two well-known approaches that support this method are Kolb's Experiential Learning Model [15] and the Problem-Based Learning [16]).

However, a necessary condition for a use case to be successful while teams are working in a DT collaborative mode is to perform continuous iterations and validation based on the situation-specific objectives and the main success scenario that they have decided upon at the very beginning of the process. The material and information that should be available at this stage combine the analysis and outcomes from the end-user research, conducted earlier through interviews, observations, field studies, etc., during the requirements collection phase. Typically, these deliverables include the personas, user story maps, activity flows, task analysis, storyboards, etc., that will determine the content and will guide the information flow and action steps of a use case. Once those are sufficiently documented then the team can proceed to the creation of the first use case which will in turn sketch the grounds, in the next step, for the interaction and visual design of the user interface, before the actual system integration and development starts (see Fig. 1).

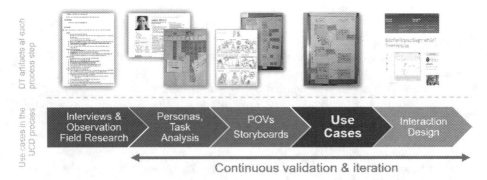

Fig. 1 The use cases in the UCD process and related DT artifacts

We hereafter describe the suggested components of the alternative hybrid style that teams could employ for creating their use cases (see Fig. 2b). For a better understanding of its realization in a real business situation we give next to each attribute an example based on a hypothetical scenario related to the 'Resolve Leave Request Conflicts' case. Structure-wise the proposed layout is composed of two main parts:

(a) The more *static part* which contains the following data:
   i. **Use Case ID** – used for cross reference and linking with the corresponding persona (*e.g. UC0001*);
   ii. **Use Case Name** – short use case name (*e.g. Resolve Leave Requests Conflicts*);
   iii. **Primary Role** – the user role who uses the system to fulfill a specific goal (*e.g. Manager – Linda*);
   iv. **Secondary Role** (optional) – the user role who receives information from the system, but is not the primary user (*e.g. Employee*);
   v. **Use Case Goal** (or Point of View (POV) – it describes the user's goal; what does (s)he wants to achieve; User + Need + Insight (*e.g. Linda needs a way to review the leave requests of her team in order to ensure no absence conflicts*);
   vi. **Background** – includes short description in free format about the scenario and any necessary assumptions (*e.g. Linda has a large team and often she*

receives many leave requests. Due to the nature of the work many times she comes across with leave request conflicts. Therefore, prior to the approval of a leave request she needs to see whether any leaves overlap exist);

vii. **Pre-conditions** – it describes the prerequisites which should be true before the use case can start (*e.g. Access to the system and authorization to view and approve her team's requests*); and

viii. **Trigger** – it identifies the action or event(s) that gets the use case started (*e.g. Linda received a leave request from an employee and opened the notification*).

(b) The more *dynamic part* which contains entity boxes (representing the user and the system), interaction lines, alternative paths, failure cases, and repetition notations. More specifically:

i. An **entity box** is broken down into three sections: (a) the first (left) section indicates the **number of the activity** (*e.g. 3*), (b) the second (middle) section describes the **action steps** that needs to be undertaken by the user to achieve a goal using the main path (*e.g. The system provides details about the conflicting leaves and graphically indicates the overlapping days*), and (c) the third (right) section describes the **user interaction data** and data sources (internal or external) needed to complete the action steps (*e.g. Employee names, leave dates, date timeline, conflict indicator, etc.*);

ii. The interaction lines describe the **interaction points** (numbered as Ia (Interaction a), Ib, Ic, etc.), expressing the relationships among the user and the system. They are the interception points among two actions and show how the interactions are situated in contexts of use. Each interaction point shows the reaction of the system on a required action from the user and vice-versa. Interaction points can be used for various reasons such as further analysis of signifying the path and the length of a use case, comparison among the same or similar use cases belonging to different applications and/or roles, point of reference on complex and iterative (i.e. loops) use cases, isolation and in depth analysis of a particular relationship (for example teams can use statistical models and methods to apply a more detailed quantitative and/or qualitative analysis with respect to i.e. effectiveness, efficiency, of an interaction among two actors), etc.;

iii. The **alternative paths** are ways in which the main success case can succeed, and they are placed under the entity box they are referring to, denoted by the number of activity, followed by the number of the alternative path, followed by a small description (in our case, *e.g. 3a. The system proposes how to resolve this conflict, i.e. it considers the employee's tasks, remaining days, etc. and suggests an optimized leave period*);

iv. The **failure cases** describe possible ways in which the main success case can fail and they are denoted by the letter *F*, followed by the number of activity, followed by the number of the failure case, followed by a small description (*e.g. F3a. The suggested days are outside the period the Employee wants to go on vacation*); and

v. Lastly, a dotted line connecting two or more entity boxes describes possible **repetition(s)** of specific action steps (*e.g. Action steps 2 to 4 might need to be iterated*).

At the very end of the suggested style there is another more static part, called **Annotations**, where teams can take note of clarifications, references, information that are noteworthy, need to be re-visited or to be considered in the future pertinent to the specific use case or activity steps (e.g. in action step 3 Linda has to decide whether she will accept the suggestion by the system or she will try manually to find a solution to the problem.)

3.2   Use Cases Documentation, Generation and Storage

The *Usee* application, implemented in both mobile and desktop technological environments, will provide a unique tool to compose and document use cases (see Fig. 2a) generated in the hybrid use cases style described above. The documentation will follow a fully controlled cloud-based creation process providing the necessary step-by-step guidance, support and storage. More specifically, this application will add value to project team members in various ways, such as: (a) initially, while users entering the data of a use case (already worked out in the DT collaborative mode) through the smart user interface, dedicated validation mechanisms will check for similarities e.g. of roles entered or goals. In case of potential similarity, the user will be prompted and enabled to review the existing use cases and the related information. This way we will increase transparency across development units and will avoid producing duplicate or similar use cases for a similar or the same role or user activity; (b) it will increase learnability by providing immediate feedback through suggestions and validations of the inserted text based on rules which will ensure the quality of the content, e.g. instead of phrases like, a user 'thinks' or 'considers', the application will propose 'reports' or 'chooses'; and (c) it will inform users in real-time about the strength and the quality of their use case, based on the interaction steps and flow, etc. Currently, the *Usee* application is in the development phase. However, apart from the DT collaborative methodology, a

Fig. 2 (a) The *Usee* wireframes and (b) the generated alternative hybrid use cases style

visually enriched Microsoft Excel-based template consisting of the components detailed earlier is available and used by project teams with encouraging results and feedback as we discuss below.

4 Benefits Derived from Usability Tests in Real-Life Scenarios

During the last two years the proposed use cases methodology and style have been extensively validated in numerous workshops internally in SAP with product development teams and externally with various co-innovation customers, accommodating positive feedback and acceptability. More specifically, the meta-analysis of the observations, interviews and focus groups yielded a number of benefits for the teams and the quality of their products' design and development. The added value of the suggested approach can be summarized as follows:

(a) *Enhanced flexibility and adaptability.* It is based upon the well-established DT method, where most project teams are familiar with and trained. A team's members need to continue to work together in a flexible and iterative manner, following the described use cases guidelines for their development. In this context, they can (re)define entities, shuffle the action steps and the interaction flow until they reach to an acceptable qualitative version. Furthermore, they can all actively participate and brainstorm, embracing the same understanding irrespective of their different knowledge backgrounds.

(b) *Speed up processing.* It maintains the same level of approach to the benefit of a project's team members. This means, there is no need to switch their working context i.e. jumping from a more visual thinking (e.g. storyboards), to pure tabular and textual format.

(c) *Ease of use.* It is more concentrated and presents a balanced visual and textual representation of data, showing clearly the flow of all the pertinent information with respect to one activity (as most data flow diagrams), leveraging the cognitive overload of team members.

(d) *Increased clarity.* There is a clear visual distinction between the user and the system, and their respective activities.

(e) *Ease of customization.* It provides an easy of use and quick comparison among two or more use cases, allowing quick adjustments irrespective of the various contexts of use. It also enables the rapid association with the elements of a persona (where a user role is detailed, i.e. tasks, needs, requirements), and of transparent identification of overlaps (i.e. same use case different roles or applications, or same role/use case but different applications).

(f) *New functionality.* Except of the repetition dotted line which indicates a possible loop among two activities, the suggested interaction points are revealed from the interaction/activity of two entities. A team's members can further compare or analyze (i.e. by isolating and applying an in depth analysis of a particular/key relationship of two entities) or can use them as point of reference on complex and iterative use cases.

5 Conclusions

Nowadays, use cases are increasingly used by organizations to document their business processes, to detect behavioral system requirements and identify how it reacts in different conditions. A use case primarily shows the interaction between a user and a system when (s)he tries to accomplish a goal given a specific business scenario. Even though use cases refer to a critical step of the UCD process ensuring the usability and acceptability of user interfaces and interaction designs of a system, quite often teams do not compose them sufficiently or even miss to address them. This happens on hand due to the tight schedule delivery constraints or limitation of resources and on the other hand due to the lack of a guided collaborative approach that will increase engagement, active involvement, learnability, or simply will motivate them to pursue them. In addition, it seems that the divergent business roles, backgrounds, experiences and skills of individuals that usually participate in the UCD product development process in large organizations cannot fully take advantage of the existing use cases documentation styles and tools since they fail to facilitate the same level of understanding; creating many times confusion, disorientation or overwhelming the team members.

In light of the abovementioned challenges, in this paper we have proposed a DT collaborative method for creating use cases as well as a new alternative hybrid use case style for their documentation in the context of the *Usee* framework. The main aim is to facilitate the inclusive and qualitative generation of comparable use cases through continuous learning and active participation of all stakeholders that share the same goals. From the usability tests and validations we conducted so far, in various business scenarios and with different size and kinds of business roles and teams, we could conclude that there is a positive tendency, acceptability, and satisfaction towards the utilization of the suggested method and tool. This is really encouraging for the future of this work since it could increase the business value of companies by facilitating a more sound communication among the various stakeholders and enhance clarity and understanding of their business cases. Future work includes the release of the *Usee* application as a final product and the further validation of the proposed solution in different business settings and more complex business scenarios in an attempt to further enhance and optimize its use.

Acknowledgements. We would like to thank our colleagues Mandana Samii and Timo Bess for the visual enhancements of the proposed use case definition style, our managers Matthias Berger and Joerg Roesbach for their support and allocation of resources as well as all the product organizations, teams (especially the Suite Engineering UX team), customers and individuals in SAP, who have participated in the usability tests and provided their constructive comments and valuable suggestions.

References

1. Wiegers, K.: Software Requirements, 2nd edn. Microsoft Press, Redmond (2003). ISBN 10:0735618798
2. Cockburn, A.: Writing Effective Use Cases. Addison-Wesley, Boston (2001). ISBN 0-201-70225-8

3. Barkley, E.F., Cross, K.P., Major, C.H.: Collaborative Learning Techniques, A Handbook for College Faculty. Wiley, Hoboken (2014)
4. Plattner, H., Meinel, C., Leifer, L. (eds.): Design Thinking: Understand – Improve – Apply. Springer Science & Business Media, Berlin (2011). ISBN 10:364226638X
5. Cohn, M.: Succeeding with Agile: Software Development Using Scrum. Addison-Wesley Professional, Boston (2009). ISBN 10:0321579364
6. Jacobson, I., Christerson, M., Jonsson, P., Overgaard, G.: Object-Oriented Software Engineering – A Use Case Driven Approach, 1st edn. Addison-Wesley Professional, Boston (1992). ISBN 978-0-201-54435-0
7. Fowler, M., Scott, K.: UML Distilled – A Brief Guide to the Standard Object Modeling Language, 2nd edn. Addison Wesley, Boston (1999). ISBN 0-201-65783-X
8. Kruchten, P.: The Rational Unified Process: An Introduction. Addison-Wesley Professional, Boston (2004). ISBN 0-321-19770-4
9. Constantine, L.L., Lockwood, A.D.L.: Software for Use: A Practical Guide to the Models and Methods of Usage-Centered Design. ACM Press/Addison-Wesley, New York (1999). ISBN 0-201-92478-1
10. Beck, K., Cunningham, W.: A laboratory for teaching object oriented thinking. ACM Sigplan Not. **24**(10), 1–6 (1989)
11. Ambler, S.W.: The Object Primer: Agile Model-Driven Development with UML 2.0. Cambridge University Press, Cambridge (2004)
12. Rowe, G.P.: Design Thinking. The MIT Press, Cambridge (1987). ISBN 978-0-262-68067-7
13. Brown, T.: Harvard Business Review, pp. 84–92, June 2008
14. Levi, D.: Group Dynamics for Teams. Sage Publications, Thousand Oaks (2013). ISBN 10:1412999537
15. Kolb, D.: Experiential Learning as the Science of Learning and Development. Prentice Hall, Englewood Cliffs (1984)
16. Hmelo-Silver, C.E.: Problem-based learning: what and how do students learn? Educ. Psychol. Rev. **16**(3), 235–266 (2004)

Reflections on eLearning Storyboard for Interaction Design

Nor'ain Mohd Yusoff[1]([✉]) and Siti Salwah Salim[2]

[1] Faculty of Computing and Informatics,
Multimedia University, 63100 Cyberjaya, Selangor, Malaysia
norain.yusoff@mmu.edu.my
[2] Faculty of Computer Science and Information Technology,
University of Malaya, 50603 Kuala Lumpur, Malaysia
salwa@um.edu.my

Abstract. The purpose of this paper is to highlight several fundamental questions surrounding eLearning storyboards: (1) What exactly is a storyboard? (2) What significance does a storyboard can bring in different industries? (3) How does the design process take place in eLearning storyboard? Finally, (4) What is the role that eLearning storyboard plays for its user(s)? Issues pertaining to the community of practice i.e. social and collaborative task support and agility of the design process that can facilitate task performance and effective communication between designers are discussed and recommended for future works.

Keywords: eLearning storyboard · Multimedia design tool

1 Introduction

In Human-Computer Interaction (HCI), designer draws or sketches a storyboard to see what the interface does and how it is used to accomplish the tasks in real usage scenarios. It is also regarded as low fidelity prototyping in designing system interfaces, that looks like, or very close to the actual product or design solution. This is because it uses materials that are different from the intended final version such as papers and cardboard. Nevertheless, the use and application of storyboard has been extended to other industries including in the design and development for eLearning courseware, hence the name eLearning storyboard. Users of eLearning storyboard have been diversified from a storyboard designer to the eLearning manager, information manager, and head department of eLearning unit and subject-matter experts in different fields. In delivering high quality user experience (UX) to these users, eLearning storyboard communities would depend on how well does the interaction designers understand the intended product that need to be designed and developed. As we look across a number of theoretical and empirical studies, it had been identified that the essential ideas about what an eLearning storyboard has not been addressed and discussed in a manner that can be used by the interface designers, UX practitioners, information architects, software engineers, human factors experts, information systems analysts and/or social scientists to introduce or improve the existing system designs.

© Springer International Publishing Switzerland 2016
P. Zaphiris and A. Ioannou (Eds.): LCT 2016, LNCS 9753, pp. 60–69, 2016.
DOI: 10.1007/978-3-319-39483-1_6

The goal of this paper is to highlight several essential ideas regarding eLearning storyboard. This paper begins with defining storyboard in general. It continues by providing some significance use of storyboard in different industries. The design process and roles that an eLearning storyboard plays will be discussed. Finally, a discussion about designing interactions and human factors for eLearning storyboard will be presented along with some recommendations for future research.

2 Defining Storyboard

In general, a storyboard can be defined in many ways, such as:

- "A series of sketches that are used as a planning tool to visually show how the action of a story unfolds" [22, p. 11]
- "An illustrated view, like a comic book, of how the producer or director envisions the final version of a production will look" [20]
- "An outline or a draft line of a production made up of consequential pictures" [5]
- "Script is a verbal plan for a story, while storyboard is a plan for visualisation of that story" [8]
- "Storyboards are series of sketches that indicate how sequences of events should take place. They are similar to cartoon panels because they have pictures with captions explaining the scenes and any possible dialogue" [19, p. 3]

In summary, a storyboard is explained as a technique for illustrating and outlining an interaction between a person (people) and a product(s) in narrative format, which includes a series of drawings, sketches, or pictures and words that tell a story. Another name for storyboard is "narration". Narration board is described as a "valuable design tool to the design team as it provides a common visual-based medium to share the common understanding of future design developments" [24, p. 276]. The visual-based elements are important to the designers because it assists them in visualising and developing ideations for future design solutions.

3 Significant of Storyboard in Different Industries

Storyboards are used in a range of industries. Some significant uses of storyboards across different industries include [22, p. 13]:

- Advertising campaigns: storyboards are used to sell campaign strategies to clients or for use in focus group. These storyboards reflect campaign ideas that are highly detailed and include only key frames.
- Video games: storyboards are used to create each scene of the game, including cinematic and full-motion video sequences that introduce a story and act as the user's reward for excelling in game play.
- Multimedia: storyboards are used to sketch each of the screens along with notes about the content of particular images, the functions of specific button and how the video and sound is to be presented. These storyboards assist in developing CD-ROMs for education or training.

- Web design: storyboards are used for the web design development in defining and grouping elements such as graphics, animations, videos and illustrations. These storyboards assist the web development team to understand the structure of a site and how that information is presented.
- Industrial and governmental videos: storyboards are used to present ideas to clients when creating industrial and/or governmental videos. These storyboards promote effective decision making, help to set strategies and solve problems.

4 Design Process in eLearning Storyboard

To date, there are few researches on storyboarding design process have been found specifically for eLearning storyboard. While most researches in storyboard have been focusing on the design process for designing products [23] and system interface designs [21], this section reviews such works that are related, including Marie and Klein's and Donahue's reports on eLearning storyboard. Van der Lelie described the five phases of the product design process of a storyboard. Each design process is accompanied with its own design activities, purpose, visualisation style and the forms it will produce [23]. Van der Lelie's product design process of storyboard focuses on different visualisation style for each design cycle. As shown in Fig. 1, Van der Lelie's storyboarding design process practices agility in the five phases of storyboarding, which are analysis, synthesis, simulation, evaluation and decision. Throughout the design process, design teams interactions are reported in the synthesis and simulation phases (refer Fig. 1).

Ideas and concepts are generated from the design team to evoke comments, judgment or acceptance in the processing phase. Interestingly, Van der Lelie's storyboarding design process was influenced by the visualisation style used in relation to the design phase and the intended goal. Truong et al. provided five significant attributes of storyboards for demonstrating system interfaces in HCI [21]. These attributes can be significant in designing interfaces within the processing of an eLearning storyboard. The attributes are as follows [21, p. 15]:

- Level of detail: This refers to how many objects and actors might be presented in a particular frame, level of photorealism and display of the entire scene or only details of the interface.
- Inclusion of text: It refers to the texts, either through the tagline narrations for each pane or within individual frames as speech, thought bubbles, or labels and signs which represents in the real life environment. The designers can also choose to depict the story entirely using visual elements without text.
- Inclusion of people and emotions: This refers to the renditions of human characters to build empathy for potential users, display motivation, or convey other intangible elements.
- Number of frames: It refers to the number of panels presented in a single storyboard, which can consist between 1 and more than 20 frames. Truong et al. said 3 and 6 frames are regarded as minimum size to show single activity. However, multiple features and activities are usually shown in multiple storyboards.

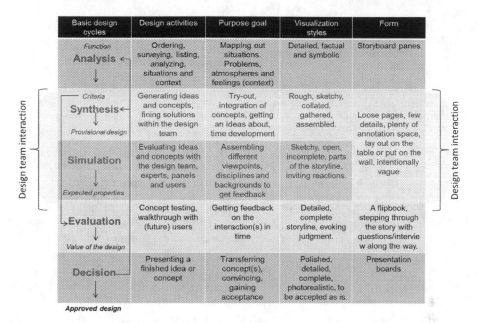

Basic design cycles	Design activities	Purpose goal	Visualization styles	Form
Function **Analysis** ← ↓	Ordering, surveying, listing, analyzing, situations and context	Mapping out situations. Problems, atmospheres and feelings (context)	Detailed, factual and symbolic	Storyboard panes
Criteria **Synthesis** ← ↓ *Provisional design*	Generating ideas and concepts, fining solutions within the design team	Try-out, integration of concepts, getting an ideas about, time development	Rough, sketchy, collated, gathered, assembled.	Loose pages, few details, plenty of annotation space, lay out on the table or put on the wall, intentionally vague
Simulation ↓ *Expected properties*	Evaluating ideas and concepts with the design team, experts, panels and users	Assembling different viewpoints, disciplines and backgrounds to get feedback	Sketchy, open, incomplete, parts of the storyline, inviting reactions.	
↳ **Evaluation** ↓ *Value of the design*	Concept testing, walkthrough with (future) users	Getting feedback on the interaction(s) in time	Detailed, complete storyline, evoking judgment.	A flipbook, stepping through the story with questions/interview along the way.
Decision ⌐ ↓	Presenting a finished idea or concept	Transferring concept(s), convincing, gaining acceptance	Polished, detailed, complete, photorealistic, to be accepted as is.	Presentation boards

Design team interaction (left margin)
Design team interaction (right margin)

Approved design

Fig. 1. Five phases of design process in storyboard for product design (Source: Van der Lelie [23])

– Portrayal of time: It refers to the explicit time indication passing within a storyboard or use transitions that convey changes over time.

Marie and Klein reported a detailed design guideline for developing storyboards that can lead to faster client approval and fewer editing during the design and development process [13]. The detailed design was categorised into three design processing activities. First the design activity that refers to the analysis of five requirements of eLearning development, which are content gathering and analysis, high level design, detailed design, storyboarding and web-based training modules i.e. alpha, beta and final phases. Second is the design activity that refers to the detailed design development which includes the following steps: identifying learners, gathering and analysing contents, developing instructional objectives, identifying instructional strategies and identifying the flow of the content. This document on detailed design needs to be approved before continuing to the next step. Apparently, this document had become a guideline for the storyboarding process. Finally, the design activity that refers to the storyboard template which are reviewed and compared in terms of its alignment with the detailed design in storyboard development. Hence, Marie and Klein's guidelines can be significant for structuring design process activities in the development of an eLearning storyboard framework. Since design documents are the core and most extensive activity in developing eLearning storyboards, six strategies to assist the designer's task are offered, as follows [6, p. 4]:

– Graphic themes must be consistent and clear with the interface before the early phase in design process.

- Combination of instructional methods can be used to provide information in the eLearning course, such audio, graphical illustrations and case studies
- Interactivity for course development should be agreed.
- Testing or evaluations of the course should be included
- Constraints in course development such as scaling or deemphasising of extraneous or non-critical information from subject-matter experts need to be emphasised.
- A preliminary course plan to structure the format, sequence and presentation of a specific content need to be developed. This high-level outline may include the breakdown of the course's objectives and content into modules, recommended interactivity to support the contents and length estimation for each module, as well as a flow chart to visualise the complex interaction or branching.

From the review of these literatures, four important findings had been identified. Firstly, Van der Lelie has shown agility practices and visualisation strategies in the storyboarding design process as well as the element of design team interaction in the synthesis and simulation phases of the storyboarding design process. Secondly, Truong et al. provided three attributes which can be significant for designing interfaces within the processing of eLearning storyboard. Thirdly, Marie and Klein's reported on the detailed design guidelines for developing storyboards that can be used to structure design process activities in the development of an eLearning storyboard framework. Finally, Donahue's strategies for design document activities can be used to assist design team in documenting contents for the eLearning storyboard.

5 Roles of eLearning Storyboard

A storyboard in the context of eLearning course development is used to document the eLearning design. It provides the content in a visual format which will be customized based on the needs of the eLearning team members, similar to the practise in the instructional design field, for example; the instructional designers needs to provide the detail in the storyboard that is needed by the subject-matter experts in order to produce an effective eLearning [18]. Hence, in this section, there are two roles of eLearning storyboard identified in the literature. Firstly it acts as an instructional design tool and secondly, as a communication tool.

5.1 An Instructional Design Tool

A storyboard can assist in the instructional design process. This is because the storyboard that is used for developing eLearning courseware contains scenarios and their processes, which describe elements, purposes about the assignment, in addition to its components. These components can be animations, sounds, pictures, texts, graphics and interactive interaction. Each component describes the kind of interaction it should behave like during the actual implementation, as well as where the amount and positions of these components are being planned in storyboarding. When the scenarios and descriptive components have been completed, the storyboard will be passed to the multimedia developers to translate the requirements into a form of multimedia courseware [18]. Brandon provides several steps that lead to the creation of eLearning storyboard. As shown in Fig. 2, the production storyboard is created in the instructional design process before it ends and being handover to the multimedia development team. Each of these steps is meant to reduce the possibility of mistakes and to preserve the integrity and value in the eLearning design process. Briefly, the steps are described as follows [1]:

- The priority of business needs is identified.
- The job objectives (in terms of outcomes and accomplishments) are outlined to fulfil the needs.
- The tasks of a learner are being analysed to accomplish each outcome.
- Available methods and tools to accomplish each outcome are listed out.
- The approximations are identified to help the learners develop the needed skills in a learning setting.
- Formal learning objectives can be defined
- Formal learning objectives are organised into learning progressions
- A flowchart is created to set up the sequence of learning activities
- Draft storyboards are created to provide a basis for reviewing the course plan with subject-matter experts.
- Draft storyboards are transformed into production storyboards that will guide the developers. These production storyboards can also serve as a checklist for the final summative evaluation before its release.

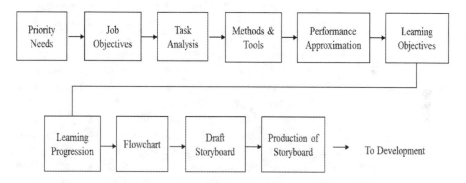

Fig. 2. Steps in eLearning storyboard creation (Source: Brandon [1])

5.2 A Communication Tool

In general, the eLearning storyboard is used to communicate eLearning design which "provides the details from the designers that are needed by the developers in order to produce an eLearning application on time and within budget" [1]. Brandon stated that the eLearning storyboard provides a communication channel between at least three disciplines contributing to the final product; instructional design, graphic design and technology. There are three significances of a storyboard in producing effective eLearning through the support of communication [1]:

- Storyboard completely documents eLearning design
- The brainstorming which accompanies work on the storyboard may assist the creative process and result in a better design
- Storyboard provides an important basis for project management, control and communication.

In achieving communication using storyboards, some works have been demonstrated by Haesen et al. and Malizia et al. Haesen et al. demonstrated principles and techniques which were derived from comics that can facilitate and support communication in the process of storyboarding [9]. The approach is called 'Collaborative Multidisciplinary user-centred Software engineering (COMuICSer). This approach formalises the way storyboards are created and at the same time preserving the creative aspects of storyboarding to provide greater involvement for all team members and end-users in an engineering processes. Malizia et al. demonstrated the principle of back-channel communications in emergency management in their emergency storyboard system (eStoryS) where it provides combinations of tools including storyboards in mash up application [12].

6 Discussion and Recommendations

Based on the information to the fundamental questions raised about eLearning storyboard, we identified two important supports in eLearning storyboard. Firstly, social support is needed to shift the paradigm of storyboarding away from the individual user practices to social practices. Better tools should be designed to encourage participatory and collaborative modes of designing among designers [10]. Secondly, agility support is needed to move away from linear process. It is suggested that computer-based instructional design tools such as the eLearning storyboard should move towards an agile design process in order to be more effective in adapting to the designers' activities [7]. Current practices in instructional design were interpreted by Häkkinen as nonlinear, cyclical and iterative process‖ [10, p. 466], therefore, the need for agility is important as it enables the change in requirements and allows flexibility in reaching common understanding among the design team. In order to meet this need, one of the techniques that can be used to reach common understand among the designers is to apply the shared visualisation in eLearning storyboard design [15]. Among the techniques includes collaborative concept mapping, collaborative discussion board and collaborative annotation where shared visualisation can help eLearning storyboard designers to pre-plan the eLearning structure or discuss virtually in an e-discussion room. Besides, shared visualisation that works for distributed eLearning team should allow participatory design in both web-based and mobile-based applications.

In addition, the design process in eLearning storyboard should be more adaptive and agile, where instructional design team can carry out their work in a flexible and interactive manner [10]. Software designers should find initiatives and effort to design and develop eLearning storyboard applications that can provide agility, tightly linked design-analysis-redesign cycles, and able to move toward artefacts improvement [2, 11]. Interestingly, Douglas said that any instructional system can be more effective if its components have well defined functions to perform under adaptive or people-oriented, rather than predictive and process-oriented. It explains how such feature that allows the adaptive design and agility is needed in eLearning storyboard.

Apart from these two roles, there is another important role in the component of an eLearning storyboard that worth investigating is the shared cognitive aspects that are needed to support interactions between eLearning storyboard designers. This is because the cognitive task activities are commonly shared between the designers. Designers share cognitive tasks activities which includes; deciding on the storyboard content, organising the structure for storyboard design, recalling the analysis requirements before storyboarding, and evaluating the storyboard design production.

According to Cannon-Bowers and Salas [3], as these cognitive activities were being shared, designers will develop shared mental model, resulting in better task performance and more effective communication. This notion had been discussed by Nor'ain and Salim [14, p. 281] in the team's cognitive research in human–computer interaction. In their work, they presented a schematic model of social-based vs. shared situation awareness-based approaches. The two perspectives on the shared cognition shown in the model can be used by HCI researchers who aim to solve a particular problem in team cognition by selecting the appropriate shared cognitive models for specific types of systems and applications. For example, if the researcher is investigating shared situation awareness in an emergency response system, he/she can use distributed the situation awareness model to analyse the process of decision making of that system. Similarly, the collaborative design in eLearning storyboard can be investigated using the shared mental model theory to analyse the practise of agility process.

In addition, more attempts to understand storyboard in terms of the tools, concepts and frameworks, similar to one written by Nor'ain and Salim [17] are needed. In this paper, the storyboard has been reviewed and analysed with regard to the three aspects of eLearning design requirements; collaborative design environment, iterative process methodology and designer-centeredness support. In understanding the problem in eLearning storyboard, another work has been done by Nor'ain and Salim to investigate problem aspects of the cognitive task and the storyboarding skills required of subject-matter experts using the cognitive task analysis technique in HCI [16].

With respect to our discussion earlier, we can see the important issues here is to warrant the needs that support the interaction design for eLearning storyboard, which include collaborative work, agile storyboarding design process methodology and achieving shared mental model. As suggested by Häkkinen [10], Douglas [7], Jonassen [11] and Bratt [2], future needs of softwares that applied the agile design process to assist designers' roles is essential and recommended. In all, in addition to the social and agility elements, this study sheds light on the importance of shared mental model, which is needed to support eLearning storyboard users' interactions. It suggests how these insights can contribute to improving humanness for the community of practices of eLearning storyboards, which can be offered by interface designers, UX practitioners, information architects, software engineers, human factors experts, information systems analysts and social scientists.

7   Conclusion

This paper discusses the fundamental questions with regards to the meaning, significance, design process and the roles of storyboards. From the discussion, some information that has been synthesised and concluded, are as follow:

- E-Learning storyboarding design process consists of three main design activities:
  analysis, design document and design template. It is found that design document is
  the core and most extensive design activity that requires strategies to assist the task
  of design team.
- E-Learning storyboard performs roles in assisting instructional design process and
  communication among team designers.
- Storyboard tools, concepts and framework use different approaches and need different kinds of support.
- Storyboard system that can assist collaborative tasks for the design team should be
  able to function as a communication tool as well as performing the design
  instructions. However, what is more needed in supporting designers' interaction is
  the functionality to adapt changes in the design process. Therefore, interface
  designers or software engineers can look forward a new paradigm of agile storyboarding process.
- E-Learning storyboard needs social and agility support for designers' interaction. In
  addition to these needs, the notion of shared mental model is important to support
  the shared cognitive aspects between them.

Acknowledgments. We would like to thank the Ministry of Higher Education Malaysia -
Exploratory Research Funding Scheme (project ID: EP20120612006) and Multimedia University
(project IDs: IP20110707004 and IP20120511020) for funding this research study.

References

1. Brandon, B.: Storyboards tailored to you: do-it-yourself magic arrows. Learn. Solut. Mag.
   (2004).   http://www.learningsolutionsmag.com/articles/304/storyboards-tailored-to-you-do-
   it-yourself-magic-arrows. Accessed 12 Dec 2009
2. Bratt, S.: A framework for agile instructional development. In: World Conference on
   E-Learning in Corporate, Government, Healthcare, and Higher Education 2011, Honolulu,
   Hawaii, USA (2011). http://www.editlib.org/p/38993
3. Cannon-Bowers, J.A., Salas, E.: Reflections on shared cognition. J. Organ. Behav. **22**(2),
   195–202 (2001)
4. Chapman, B.L.: Tools for design and development of online instruction. In: Spector, J.M.,
   Merrill, M.D., van Merrienboer, J., Driscoll, M.P. (eds.) Handbook of Research on
   Educational Communications and Technology, pp. 671–684. Lawrence Erlbaum, New York
   (2008)
5. Cristiano, G.: Analyzing Storyboard, 2nd edn. Iradidio Books, Los Angeles (2005)
6. Donahue, M.: The design document: your blueprint for e-Learning standards and
   consistency. Learn. Solut. e-Mag.™ 1–9 (2005)

7. Douglas, I.: Issues in software engineering of relevance to instructional design. TechTrends **50**(5), 28–35 (2006). doi:10.1007/s11528-006-0035-z

8. Glebas, F.: Directing the Story: Professional Storytelling and Storyboarding Techniques. Elsevier Inc. Oxford (2009)

9. Haesen, M., Meskens, J., Luyten, K., Coninx, K.: Draw me a storyboard: incorporating principles & techniques of comics. In: Proceedings of the 24th BCS Interaction Specialist Group Conference, Dundee, United Kingdom (2010)

10. Häkkinen, P.: Challenges for design of computer-based learning environments. Br. J. Educ. Technol. **33**(4), 461–469 (2002). doi:10.1111/1467-8535.00282

11. Jonassen, D.H.: Instructional design as design problem solving: An iterative process. Educ. Technol. **48**(3), 21 (2008)

12. Malizia, A., Bellucci, A., Diaz, P., Aedo, I., Levialdi, S.: eStorys: a visual storyboard system supporting back-channel communication for emergencies. J. Vis. Lang. Comput. **22**(2), 150–169 (2011). doi:10.1016/j.jvlc.2010.12.003

13. Marie, G., Klein, J.: Developing effective detailed design documents and WBT/CBT storyboards. In: World Conference on E-Learning in Corporate, Government, Healthcare, and Higher Education 2008, Las Vegas, Nevada, USA (2008)

14. Nor'ain, M.Y., Salim, S.S.: Social-based versus shared situation awareness-based approaches to the understanding of team cognitive research in HCI. In: (i-USEr 2014) 3rd International Conference on User Science and Engineering, Shah Alam, Malaysia, 2nd–5th September 2014

15. Nor'ain, M.Y., Salim, S.S.: A systematic review of shared visualisation to achieve common ground. J. Vis. Lang. Comput. **28**, 83–99 (2015). doi:10.1016/j.jvlc.2014.12.003. Open Access. Elsevier Science

16. Nor'ain, M.Y., Salim, S.S.: Investigating cognitive task difficulties and expert skills in e-Learning storyboards using a cognitive task analysis technique. Comput. Educ. **58**(1), 652–665 (2012). doi:10.1016/j.compedu.2011.09.009

17. Mohd Yusoff, N., Salim, S.S.: A review of storyboard tools, concepts and frameworks. In: Zaphiris, P., Ioannou, A. (eds.) LCT 2014, Part I. LNCS, vol. 8523, pp. 73–82. Springer, Heidelberg (2014)

18. Okur, M.R., Gümüs, S.: Storyboarding issues in online course production process. Procedia – Soc. Behav. Sci. **2**(2), 4712–4716 (2010). doi:10.1016/j.sbspro.2010.03.755

19. Pardew, L.: Beginning Illustration and Storyboarding for Games. Course Technology, Boston (2004)

20. Simon, M.: Storyboard: Motion in Art, 3rd edn. Elsevier Inc. Oxford (2007)

21. Truong, K.N., Hayes, G.R., Abowd, G.D.: Storyboarding: an empirical determination of best practices and effective guidelines. In: Proceedings of the 6th Conference on Designing Interactive Systems, University Park, PA, USA (2006)

22. Tumminello, W.: Exploring Storyboarding, 1st edn. Thomson-Delmar Learning, Canada (2005)

23. Van der Lelie, C.: The value of storyboards in the product design process. Pers. Ubiquit. Comput. **10**(2–3), 159–162 (2006). doi:10.1007/s00779-005-0026-7

24. Wong, C.Y., Khong, C.W.: Quantifying the narration board for visualising final design concepts by interface designers. In: Jacko, J.A. (ed.) HCI 2007. LNCS, vol. 4550, pp. 273–282. Springer, Heidelberg (2007)

Constructive Learning Using Flip-Flop Methodology: Learning by Making Quizzes Synchronized with Video Recording of Lectures

Umida Stelovska[1], Jan Stelovsky[2(✉)], and John Wu[1]

[1] parWinr Inc., 415 Oakmead Parkway, Sunnyvale, CA 94085, USA
{umida,johnwu}@parwinr.com
[2] Department of Information and Computer Sciences,
University of Hawaii at Manoa, 1680 East-West Road,
Honolulu, HI 96822, USA
janst@hawaii.edu

Abstract. This article introduces the concept of Constructive Learning where students' comprehension is augmented by active creation of teaching materials. It highlights the potential of the Flip-Flop instructional methodology that involves students in creating quizzes synchronized with video recordings of lectures. The premise is that as students create questions, correct and incorrect answers, hints and hint links that lead to relevant resources, they get in depth understanding of the content presented in the video. Peer evaluation is also an integral part of the methodology. The collected data can be used for grading and as a resource pool for future quizzes. We describe the online tools that support the students and instructors. While this method was primarily developed for the use in flipped/inverted classroom settings, it can be applied do any MOOCs or other lecture screencasts or training that employs videos.

Keywords: Instructional methods · Constructive learning · Constructivist learning · Training videos · MOOC · Flipped classroom · Inverted classroom · Course design · Educational technology

1 Introduction

The maxim that 'Learning by teaching' is one of the best - if not the best - method of learning has been around for centuries. Search for his topics on Google Scholar shows 1,570 entries. Among these, numerous books and articles (e.g., [1–4], and Wikipedia summary and references [5]) are devoted to listing the advantages of various approaches to accomplish this maxim and present entire curricula development techniques based on the notion that students learn more and more profoundly if they need to present material to other students and challenge their understanding of the content.

Moreover, 'Active Learning' (see references in Wikipedia [6] and research survey in [7]) and 'Constructivist Learning' concepts – based on Piaget's theory and popularized by Vygotskii [8], also see Wikipedia [9] – have been widely accepted and

© Springer International Publishing Switzerland 2016
P. Zaphiris and A. Ioannou (Eds.): LCT 2016, LNCS 9753, pp. 70–81, 2016.
DOI: 10.1007/978-3-319-39483-1_7

integrated into the typical curricula. One of the tenets of these educational categories is that students should be involved in discovering and creating knowledge rather than simply absorbing lectures.

Search for the term 'flipped classroom' on Internet returns over 5 million entries. Search for 'MOOC' returns 8.5 million page finds. Undoubtedly these fairly recently introduced educational concepts and technologies are popular and gaining ground.

According to the top searches on Internet: 'The flipped classroom is a pedagogical model in which the typical lecture and homework elements of a course are reversed. Short video lectures are viewed by students at home before the class session, while in-class time is devoted to exercises, projects, or discussions.' For overview of flipped classroom approaches and how they fit in the landscape of educational categories see for instance [7, 10].

Typically, the flipped methodology relies on lectures that were recorded on as video. In particular, MOOC (massive open online course, see [11, 12] and Wikipedia [13] for discussion of proliferation and pros and cons of MOOCs) use video recordings of lectures to reach audiences often dispersed around the world. When flipped methodology is employed, the students view the video ahead of the class time and the instruction is devoted to exercises that practice the topics covered in the video lecture. While numerous educational institutions reported marked improvement of student outcomes on high school as well as on university level when flipped classroom is based on video recordings, there is a significant research literature as well as numerous popular journal articles that question their effectiveness (e.g., [14, 15]).

Our experience confirms the criticism, as we found that the most significant disadvantage of the flipped methodology is that here is no guarantee that the students have paid enough attention and understood the lecture while watching the video recording. Using the traditional instructional approach, learners digest a lecture in a controlled environment, mostly void of noise, artificial interruptions and other distractions. Since the flip classroom mandates that students view the lecture at home or in another environment of their choice, they may choose to do so in a noisy coffee shop or in a room shared with siblings who demand their attention. While cell phones are typically banned in a classroom setting, it is quite unlikely that a student will switch off his smart phone and not pick up he call when his girlfriend calls. In particular, it is very unlikely that the students will choose to view a video lecture or even its more difficult segments more than one time, even if they were insecure whether they understood enough of its topics. As a consequence, a substantial percentage of our students often come unprepared so that some of the class time needs to be devoted to reviewing the lecture material rather than to practice and exercises.

To alleviate in particular these disadvantages of flipped classroom and MOOC-based learning, we have developed a 'Flip-flop' method supported by extensive online technology means that involves students in 'constructive' learning by creating teaching materials tightly connected with lecture recordings.

2   Flip-Flop Basics

We propose to augment the inverted 'flip' methodology by an additional 'flop' element that ensures that the students not only review the video lecture, but - which is more important – makes it very likely that they get deeply involved with the topics presented in the screencast and attempt to understand the covered topics well at home before they come to the classroom.

The method is simple: the students construct quizzes that are synchronized with the video recording of a lecture. Moreover, they take quizzes that fellow students created. When they are then exposed to additional practical exercises in the classroom setting, we can expect that they digested the topics they viewed at home well enough that the instructor does not need to spend extra time explaining the subject in detail again and the classroom session can be devoted to the actual practical exercises.

While quiz-making as an educational technology is not new concept and even several commercial companies offer quiz making facilities based on video lectures – e.g., [16, 17], our methodology augments this concept in several important areas: Our quizzes feature feedbacks, hints and hint links and allow the author to choose from a variety of ways to synchronize tasks with the video – paused tasks stop the video while 'segment' tasks are displayed during the length of the corresponding video segment. Moreover, the author of a quiz can choose whether to show which answer is the correct one even when an incorrect answer was selected. Besides multiple-choice type of questions, we support poll tasks – which are important for peer evaluations – as well as 'pinboard tasks' where the author just pins text or an image without requiring the quiz-taker to respond. There is also a gamification element: Correctly answered questions increase the student's score for this quiz. It is up to the author of the quiz to determine the maximum points per task and whether the number of possible points decreases with time.

Since this tightly structured and systematic approach does not explicitly fit the well-documented and researched educational methodologies, we propose the term 'constructive education' for approaches and technologies that require the students to construct teaching materials based on and synchronized with recordings of educational lessons.

2.1   Quiz-Taking and Quiz-Making Technology

The quiz-taking tool plays the lecture screencast in the left pane while the right pane shows the corresponding task: In Fig. 1 the student has answered the question correctly and is rewarded by a smiley face and received 14 points. Notice that the feedback offers an additional information that explains why the chosen answer is indeed correct.

If the student selects the wrong answer, she receives no points and the feedback might indicate why the chosen answer is incorrect, preferably pointing out the likely misconception. This is depicted in Fig. 2.

Note that there is a "Hint" button in the top right corner. When clicked, dialog shows short text paragraph that may lead the student on the right path towards

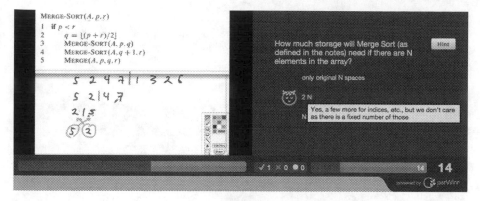

Fig. 1. Taking a quiz: selecting a correct choice displays a feedback that offers additional information.

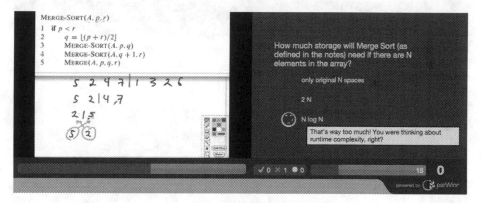

Fig. 2. Taking a quiz: selecting an incorrect choice displays a feedback that points out a possible misconception.

answering the question. As shown in Fig. 3, underneath the hint text is "Analysis of Merge Sort" button that when clicked opens an external webpage within another tab of the browser.

The most important aspect of the Flip-Flop method consists, however, in creating quizzes, not just taking them. Using our simple-to-use authoring tool, students split portions of the lecture video recording that has been posted on a common video platform (such as YouTube) into - typically three to five minutes long - consecutive segments, and add a task to each of the segments. While multiple-choice are the most commonly used tasks, we don't discourage students from using poll or pinboard tasks.

The screenshot in Fig. 4 shows the Flip-Flop authoring tool. The left side of the screen is devoted to the video and its segments. The current third segment is highlighted in green and the handles allow the author to determine the beginning and the end of the sentiment. The larger handles define the beginning and the end of the quiz.

Notice that this entire quiz covers approximately one fourth of the entire video. The right pane defines the task associated with the current segment. Here, the author has typed in the question, the hint, the answers and the feedbacks that where shown to the quiz-taker in Figs. 1, 2, and 3.

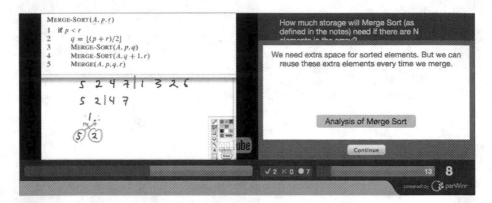

Fig. 3. Taking a quiz: hint with a link to a related resource page

To make the authoring tool initially easier to use for a beginner, the user can choose to display labels rather than icons for the buttons. Moreover, each button has a tooltip that is displayed when the cursor hovers over it for a while.

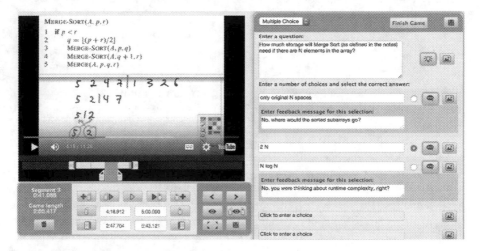

Fig. 4. Creating a quiz: multiple-choice task synchronized with a segment of video and entries for hint text, hint link label, hint link URL, and for choice feedback.

Once the quiz has been created, the author is provided with a simple embed string that when pasted into a page lets the peer students take the quiz. In the modern browsers, no additional web page elements (i.e. HTML code) are necessary.

2.2   Quiz-Making as Learning by Teaching

The Flip-Flop methodology has several advantages: In order to construct a meaningful quiz, the students need to understand the lecture and are likely to review the video recording one or more times until they do so.

In order to add a task, the students have to come up with a question that relates to the topic discussed in the specific lecture segment, with the correct answer, as well as with a few incorrect answers. They may well find that coming up with a relevant question is not always easy.

Moreover, while the correct answer is often quite obvious once the question is decided upon, formulating several incorrect, but not completely irrelevant choices is not a trivial matter: An incorrect answer cannot be partially correct and should not be obvious or easy to guess. And even when it is quite easy to formulate the first wrong answer, additional non-trivial incorrect answers are typically more and more difficult to come up with.

We encourage the students to accompany each of the answers with the feedback that will be displayed once an answer has been selected and emphasize that they should not just use the simple "Yes", "You got it!", "Wrong", or "Really?" feedbacks, but come up with more meaningful reasoning why the answer is good or not. In particular, a good strategy is to point out the misconception that is likely to be the reason behind choosing the incorrect answer.

Adding a hint requires additional skills: Since the length of the hint text is severely limited, students need to summarize their knowledge of the topic. They also need to formulate the hint so that it does not reveal the correct answer and only points towards the right direction.

When creating a hint button that leads to another web page, students practice another set of skills that are and will be increasingly in demand: searching for resources. In order to add a link button, the student has to look for web pages that relate to the question and decide which one of the found pages is the most appropriate, e.g., which explains the topic in more detail – or even better – then mentioned in the video lecture itself. Needless to say, the students are likely to deepen their understanding of the topic at hand from each of the resources they considered. Also, they need to judge the quality of these resources and their appropriateness for the level of course.

Last but not least, having to formulate all the components of a task is an exercise that may improve the students' writing skills.

Peer evaluation is another important component of the inverted classroom that is integrated in Flip-Flop methodology and supported by its tools. The student author has to add several predefined poll questions at the end of each quiz that allow the peers who take her quiz to judge the quality of all the quiz components: the questions, the correct answers, the incorrect answers, the feedbacks, the hint, and the hint links. Figure 5 shows one such poll task being entered within the authoring tool. Obviously, defining

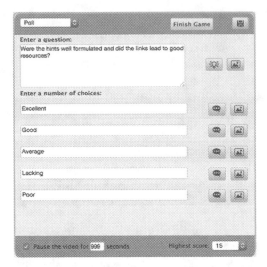

Fig. 5. Defining a peer evaluation task

all these default poll questions is a chore that cannot be automated and we will describe the tools that simplify these and other chores in the next section.

3   Flip-Flop Techniques and Technology

To support pilot experiment that is a currently underway we have expanded the system tools to make Flip-Flop more structured and easier to deploy. The students in a 300-level computer science course that has been previously inverted have been sub-divided into randomly selected groups of four students. Each student had to construct a quiz and then also take the quizzes constructed by the other three students in the group. Thus the students are not only the authors of one quiz, but are confronted with several other quizzes related to the same lecture and necessarily have to compare their quiz with the work of their colleagues. Every quiz has to include a question that identifies the student taking the quiz followed by the aforementioned peer evaluation poll. Naturally, the instructor is encouraged to take the students' quizzes and submit her own evaluations.

The course encompasses more than 70 screencasts that are typically up to 20 min long. Each screencast has been subdivided into four approximately five minutes long. These subsections are assigned to every group member so that each student in the group creates a quiz from a different part of the screencast. Therefore every student either creates a quiz or takes a quiz from all the parts of the lecture video.

To facilitate the chores of assigning students to groups whose composition changes every week, subdividing the videos into quizzes, and creating segments and the cor-responding tasks within each of the quizzes, we have developed an online scheduling tool depicted in Fig. 6. This tool lists all the screencasts, subdivides them row-wise into subsections. Every group occupies a column where the blue name identifies the student who is in charge of creating the corresponding quiz.

The screencast titles, thumbnails and ids are links to the videos posted on YouTube. Notice that underneath each of these links is another link to the webpage that contains the topic notes. This feature makes it convenient for the students to consult the corresponding notes while watching a video. We even encourage the students to use the notes while constructing a quiz since even if they copy and paste text from the notes into a question and an answer, they will have to reformulate the text in most cases and they will rarely find there the alternative incorrect answers.

Hovering the cursor over the name of an author brings up the menu displayed in Fig. 7. As the tooltip indicates, the "Take Quiz" item serves two purposes: Since it is a link the quiz page, the group members can use it to take the quiz. For the author of the quiz it serves as check that her web page is functional, i.e., whether the corresponding file on the server is in the correct folder, and has the correct name and permissions.

The "Save Template" item greatly simplifies the author's menial and otherwise considerably time-consuming chores in defining the quiz segments, multiple-choice tasks and peer evaluation polls. After the author uploads such a template within the authoring tool, she is presented with a default quiz that has already all these components. For instance, the start and end points of the quiz and of each its segments shown in Fig. 4 have been created with such a template. Note that since the peer evaluation poll questions are the same for all quizzes, the template completely eliminates any effort in defining them.

But the template is not only a time-saving device – it allows the student author to fully concentrate on the creative aspect of constructing a quiz rather than being distracted by chores that do not foster her learning experience.

The template has another subliminal side-effect: Under the guise of providing all the features a task may incorporate, it equips every multiple-choice question with one correct and two incorrect answers, every answer with a default feedback, and every task with a hint and a hint link. Therefore the student needs to delete some of these components if she does not want to provide them. Not only is this an extra step, but we suspect that students will hesitate to delete proposed elements and step up to the challenge of creating the corresponding content even though we expressly mention that they will not be penalized for simplifying the default quiz.

The last two menu items further simplify the author's chores – they notifying the other members of her group via email that the quiz is ready.

To help the students to get familiar and confident in using the tools we have developed extensive tutorials that describe the individual tool features as well as strategies that may improve the quality of their quizzes.

Our Flip-Flop technology offers another tool that supports the instructor. The online Quiz Evaluation tool shown in Fig. 8 presents the students and their quizzes in a hierarchical fashion that allows the instructor to drill down the work of every student to the level of individual quiz components. She can not only view all the questions, answers and their correctness (according to the author), feedbacks and hints, she can also access the documents referenced by the hint links because each of these links this represented by buttons that leads to the corresponding web page. The number of questions answered correctly when a student took quizzes is currently only displayed in

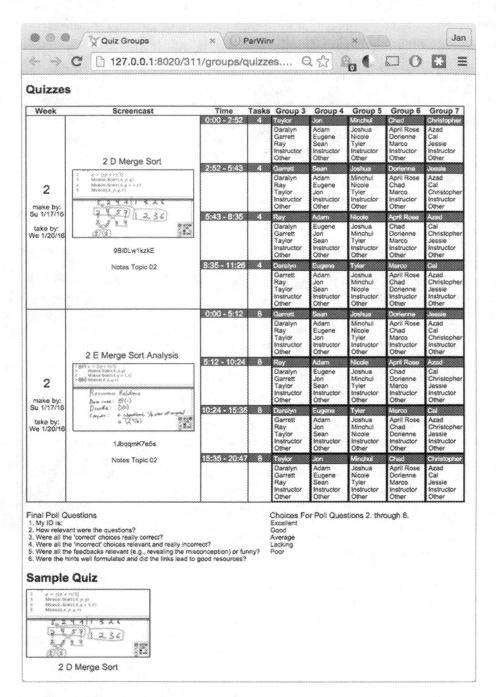

Fig. 6. Scheduling tool: subdivision into groups, screencast segments. Note links to screencasts on YouTube, web pages with topics notes, and splits of time segments for a quiz.

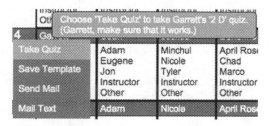

Fig. 7. Scheduling tool facilities: note tooltips and Save Template item that greatly simplifies quiz making chores.

summarily fashion, as the correctness would have to be first approved by an expert to be used as a reliable measure.

Notice that the peer evaluation scores are also displayed in brackets after the quiz titles. We intend to improve the visualization this peer evaluation, for instance in the form of the customary partially filled stars.

Another feature which is still under construction, is the instructor' evaluation of the students work. While currently the instructor can already provide the same scores as the student within the red pop-up dialogue, we intend to develop scoring for each of the individual test components as well as an easy way to correct and improve them. Moreover, we plan to incorporate additional grading facilities within our tools.

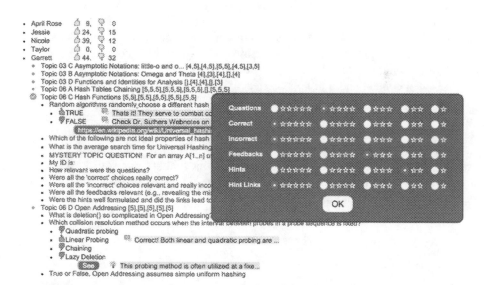

Fig. 8. Instructor's tool: drilling-down students' quizzes: note results achieved in all quizzes (thumbs-up and -down next to students' names), feedbacks in gray, buttons for hint links. Clicking the green check icon next to the quiz title displays a dialog where instructor can enter her own evaluation of the quiz.

4 Conclusions

The Flip-Flop methodology makes the concept of "learning by teaching" a well-defined and structured method supported by concrete technology. As students create and take each other's quizzes they practice skills that are essential to comprehension: asking questions, judging the correctness of answers, summarizing information and searching for resources.

The Flip-Flop tools support not only students while they create and take quizzes based on lecture screencasts, they facilitate peer evaluations, and provide the instructor with a wealth of data. This data can, for instance, make the task that most instructors like the least - the grading - less time consuming. Moreover, instructors can be reuse past quizzes in their future courses.

5 Future Plans

The Flip-Flop methodology will be investigated in detail during the Fall 2016 semester using surveys, data analysis as well as neuro-physiological methods [18].

The underlying technology can be further developed to simplify creating quizzes: For instance, video transcript and analysis of the audio track can help determine good beginning and end of segments within the video.

As the students develop expertise in creating quizzes and experience what makes a good quiz while taking the quizzes by their peers we expect that strategies emerge that can be reused in future courses. For instance, students are likely develop preference for paused questions as opposed to questions that appear while a segment plays or intersperse relaxing 'pinboards' and opinion polls in between difficult tasks.

Artificial intelligence will benefit the quiz authors as it can suggest questions based on the video content and transcript, correct answers, as well as documents to be used hint links. For instance, we are discussing with IBM whether IBM Watson [19] can be integrated into the Flip-Flop tools. On the other hand, artificial intelligence frameworks can benefit from the experts' knowledge while as they construct Flip-Flop quizzes. To use IBM Watson, a client must first 'ingest' documents and then 'train' Watson with questions and correct answers and that is exactly what hint links and quiz tasks provide.

Further interesting and enhancements would become possible once the database of tasks reaches substantial volume. For instance, it will become feasible to choose tasks randomly for a particular screencast or give precedence to tasks with higher evaluation scores.

References

1. Duran, D.: Learning-by-teaching. Evidence and implications as a pedagogical mechanism. In: Innovations in Education and Teaching International, pp. 1–9 (2016)
2. Hanke, U.: Learning by teaching. In: Seel, N.M. (ed.) Encyclopedia of the Sciences of Learning, pp. 1830–1832. Springer, Heidelberg (2012)

3. Goodlad, S., Hirst, B.: Peer Tutoring: A Guide to Learning by Teaching. Nichols Publishing, New York (1989)
4. Biswas, G., Segedy, J.R., Bunchongchit, K.: From design to implementation to practice a learning by teaching system: Betty's Brain. Int. J. Artif. Intell. Edu. pp. 1–5 (2015)
5. Wikipedia. https://en.wikipedia.org/wiki/Learning_by_teaching
6. Wikipedia. https://en.wikipedia.org/wiki/Active_learning
7. Bishop, J.L., Verleger, M.A.: The flipped classroom: a survey of the research. In: ASEE National Conference Proceedings, Atlanta, GA (2013)
8. Vygotskii, L.S.: Mind in Society: The Development of Higher Psychological Processes. Harvard University Press, Cambridge (1978)
9. Wikipedia. https://en.wikipedia.org/wiki/Constructivism_(philosophy_of_education)
10. Wikipedia. https://en.wikipedia.org/wiki/Flipped_classroom
11. Baggaley, J.: MOOC rampant. Distance Educ. **34**(3), 368–378 (2013)
12. Christensen, G., Steinmetz, A., Alcorn, B., Bennett, A., Woods, D., Emanuel, E.J.: The MOOC phenomenon: who takes massive open online courses and why? Available at SSRN 2350964. November 2013
13. Wikipedia. https://en.wikipedia.org/wiki/Massive_open_online_course
14. Vardi, M.Y.: Will MOOCs destroy academia? Commun. ACM **55**(11), 5–10 (2012)
15. San Jose State to Michael Sandel: Keep your MOOC off our campus. Boston Globe. 3 May 2013
16. Kahoot! https://getkahoot.com/ways-to-play
17. Zaption. https://www.zaption.com
18. Stelovsky, J., Minas, R.K., Stelovska, U., Wu, J.: Applying Augmented Cognition to Flip-Flop Methodology. Proceedings of HCII 2016 Conference. Springer, Toronto (2016)
19. Meet Watson. http://www.ibm.com/smarterplanet/us/en/ibmwatson/

PLMan: Towards a Gamified Learning System

Carlos Villagrá-Arnedo, Francisco J. Gallego-Durán,
Rafael Molina-Carmona$^{(\boxtimes)}$, and Faraón Llorens-Largo

Cátedra Santander-UA de Transformación Digital,
Universidad de Alicante, Alicante, Spain
{villagra,fgallego,rmolina,faraon}@dccia.ua.es

Abstract. Gamification is set to be a disruptive innovation in the field
of education in the next years, as a way to encourage learning, since
when the fun impregnates the learning process, motivation increases and
stress is reduced. However, most experiences in learning gamification just
remain on the surface, just offering a layer of standardized game elements
such as badges, leader boards and medals. Instead, a deeper transformation of the learning process is needed, making up a true process reengineering. As a practical example, PLMan learning system is presented,
an attempt to redefine the learning process in the context of a particular
subject. It is based on a unique and simple type of problem: solving mazes
of the PLMan game, an adaptation of the famous *Pac-Man* game. The
maze, as the building block of our learning strategy, has a set of properties that allows us to introduce all the features of games in the learning
process. From this experience some important lessons about the gamification of the teaching-learning process can be obtained: the importance
of fun as a consequence of learning, the need of having an immediate
feedback of our actions, the trial and error possibility as a major source
of learning and progress, the relevance of experimentation and creativity
as a means to develop the learners skills and the importance of autonomy
to give the learners the control of their learning process. All these features are propellants for learning and a way to improve the motivation
of learners.

Keywords: Gamification · Learning · Game learning

1 Introduction

Playing is learning. From our earliest childhood, we experience our environment
to learn. As a result of this learning, we have fun and therefore, we call it
playing. As we grow, the words *game* or *playing* seem unserious and we use
learning instead, but playing and learning are the same thing. All this has not
gone unnoticed by researchers in the field of learning and, as a result, research on
the use of games in education is experiencing a particular boom. No researcher
questions today about the ability of games to teach. The controversy focuses on
what skills, contents or capabilities can be taught through games.

© Springer International Publishing Switzerland 2016
P. Zaphiris and A. Ioannou (Eds.): LCT 2016, LNCS 9753, pp. 82–93, 2016.
DOI: 10.1007/978-3-319-39483-1_8

In such a technological world like today's, the paradigm of massive games are video games. Numerous studies have demonstrated the ability of video games to teach, identifying what features make these games so educational as fun. Going one step beyond, can we use these features in other processes that are not games themselves? We call this gamification.

Gamification is defined as applying the principles of video games design, the use of the mechanics and the elements of a game in any process, beyond the specific context of video games. Many gamification proposals remain on the surface: they just provide a veneer to the process, adorning it with elements that give the aspect of the game: an attractive interface, badges, ratings, leader boards, medals... However, the process itself is unchanged. This supposed gamification actually does not include the key features that a game should have: fun, autonomy, tolerance to error, experimentation, progressivity, and so on.

From our point of view, the gamification must penetrate that surface and imbue the whole process. True gamification is a process rethinking to incorporate all the features of games to the core of the learning process. This is not a simple task that, like any other process reengineering, requires a thorough study of the process to be gamified. The aim of this paper is determining the key elements, strategies and features that make gamification a true process reengineering. To exemplify the results, a practical case is proposed: PLMan.

Section 2 presents the concepts and previous works about games and gamification. Our proposal about the features of a gamified system is presented in Sect. 3. Section 4 is devoted to explain the design and construction of a particular gamified experience. Finally, the conclusions and future work are presented in Sect. 5.

2 Background

2.1 Games and Gamification

The continued development and strong penetration in society of video games is unquestionable. Video games have changed the way our youth (and adults) conceive reality and interact with each other [12,20]. According to Prensky [16] computer games attract players for several reasons: they encourage participation, motivate users to gradually achieve small goals, offer immediate rewards or punishments, and allow the difficulty of each level to be adapted according to players abilities, age or knowledge of the game. The reflection that this reality provokes is straighforward: can video games be used in other contexts than entertainment to motivate people to do any activity? And if so, how can it be done?

Gamification comes out from this question. It is defined as applying the principles of video games design, the use of the mechanics, dynamics and the elements of a game in any process, beyond the specific context of video games [23]. Gamification was included in Gartner hype cycle about Emerging Technologies 2011. In 2012, it was included in the peak of inflated expectations, expecting to get the plateau of productivity in a period between five and ten years. In 2013, gamification was considered in the peak of expectations but falling in 2014 in trough of disillusionment, and even disappearing in 2015. This was already foreseen in the Gartner consultants report *Gamification 2020: What Is the Future of Gamification?* [1], which considered that gamification was going to get to trough of disillusionment in 2013 and 2014, mainly because it is difficult to understand the design of video games and the strategies that motivate players, resulting in fake applications of gamification due to superficial applications of the concept. They even forecasted for 2014 that 80 % of applications based on this philosophy would fail to satisfy business needs due to a bad design. However, the correct application of the video games principles will have a strong impact in many fields, becoming a transforming force together with other emergent technologies.

Games and gamification can be very powerful tools for improving different processes, particularly learning process. Numerous studies indicate that games encourage learning, since when the fun impregnates the learning process, motivation increases and stress is reduced. As Koster [10] says, immediate feedback reinforces by endorphins and dopamine neurons and links involved in the accurate prediction, which gives the player the feeling commonly known as fun. Particularly the use of video games increases satisfaction while learning and memorization are also improved [14]. This is because a complete immersion of the players on the task being done occurs [3], allowing them to decide what to do at all times. It is important to add that during the game, immediately after each action, the player receives response information, enabling learning by trial and error.

Gamification is to take advantage of both the psychological predisposition of people to participate in games like the benefits of the own game to motivate and improve the performance of the participants. This approach applied to the educational world has a promising way to go [17].

2.2   Gamified Learning

Education is one of the fields where gamification will become a disruptive innovation, mainly in tech-based learning (eLearning) and lifelong learning. According to NMC Horizon Report 2013 [7], gamification was one of the two technologies experiencing growing interest in education in a mid-term (two to three years). The report states that using gamification and games in a wide way are two sides of the same coin. Recent reports, such as the one of 2016 [8], state that this stage is already overtaken and new terms, such as *Measuring Learning*, *Personalized Learning* and *Adaptive Learning*, appear. Those terms go deeper in the concept of gamification as a process redesign to adapt to learners' rythm.

Therefore, as international referenced reports say, we can conclude that the following years are crucial worldwide to determine if gamification, particularly its correct application to different experiences, will be able to consolidate the great expectations on it, in general, but also in education in particular, where it is expected that these years are the key point. That is why high doses of both research and clear justification of using gamification techniques are necessary, based on quality indicators. A lot of analysed experiences, reports and aspects reflect the interest in gamification, but the evidence and, perfectly clear for experts, is that we are in front of the first steps, just isolated items that overlap, but, in the end, not facing the core of gamification: gamifying all the learning process. Reengineering the whole process is needed, taking into account since the beginning the principles of gamification in order to design a successful gamified experience. Nowadays, according to Kapp [9], there are two types of gamification: structural gamification and content gamification. Structural gamification is the application of game-elements to propel a learner through content with no alteration or changes to the content itself. The content does not become game-like, only the structure around the content [15]. Content gamification is the application of game elements and game thinking to alter content to make it more game-like.

For a discipline to be mature, the design methodology must be clearly defined and accepted. In gamification, nevertheless, many experiences fail because the solutions are just a mix of pieces from game components with no formal design process. There has been some effort to define design frameworks for gamification, and a complete review can be found in [13]. Some interesting experiences are the one of González et al. [5] that present a conceptual architecture for an Intelligent Tutorial System that includes gamification elements as key components, or the work of Domínguez et al. [2] that describes a gamification plugin for an e-learning platform, collecting quantitative and qualitative data in the process.

3 Gamification Proposal

3.1 The Essence of Games

There are several works that explore the essence of games, as a first step to transplant their lessons to gamification. Among them, one of the most frequently mentioned studies is the one by Werbach (Pyramid of the elements [22]), which is based in the article by Hunike et al. [6]. This analysis shows the game elements in a pyramid (Fig. 1) where the lower elements are the basis on which the higher ones are built.

This model states that the most important aspect in a game is at the top of the pyramid, the so-called *dynamics*. To be able to create these *dynamics*, elements of the lower step are needed, that is, the *mechanics* that, in turn, require the elements in the pyramid base, the *components*. Therefore, to produce *emotions* in the players (a *dynamic*), a game could use the *chance*, *rewards* and *challenges*, or any combination elements in the *mechanics* level. In turn, *challenges* could be made up of *achievements* and *points* to win a *combat*, for instance.

Obviously, all these elements are part of the essence of a lot of video games. However, not all elements are present in all games. For example, some classic games such as "The Secret of Monkey Island" [4] or "Alone in the Dark" [11], classified as adventure games, have no rankings, virtual goods or even points. Furthermore, the mere addition of game elements is not enough to have a funny motivating gaming experience, since there are games that include most of these elements but are not funny at all. So, are there other aspects to consider?

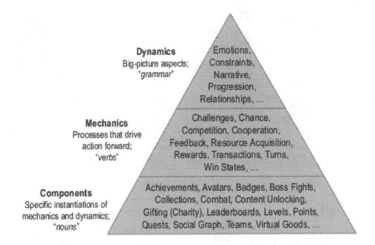

Fig. 1. Pyramid of the elements of Werbach

3.2   Motivation as a Principle

Motivation plays a central role in every gamification process, as one of the main propellants for human activity. Motivation can be informally defined as the set of reasons for a person to act in a certain way. There are two types of motivation: extrinsic and intrinsic motivation, and both should strongly influence the design of a gamified system. For good results, the elements must be designed in search of intrinsic motivation, always with an appropriate balance of extrinsic motivation (without overdoing it). All this is situated within a psychological theory known as the Self-Determination Theory [18]. This theory tries to explain the factors that influence the motivation, stating that there is a continuum from amotivation to intrinsic motivation, which passes through several intermediate levels of extrinsic motivation.

Making a summary of this theory, it can be said that there are three key factors for people to be in a state of intrinsic motivation to perform a task:

- *Autonomy:* they must perceive that they make the task willingly, not being forced, and always in position to control the process with their own decision criterion.
- *Competence:* it is imperative to feel that the task is feasible or practicable. Someone feeling incapable of performing a task cannot be intrinsically motivated to do it.
- *Meaning:* the task should mean something to the doer. If the task has no value or meaning for the person, it can be perceived as useless and it cannot generate intrinsic motivation.

As a conclusion, a necessary condition to obtain a successful gamified process is incorporating some of the main game elements (dynamics, mechanics and components) but a deeper redesign of the process is needed to produce intrinsic motivation by offering autonomy and meaning, and considering the proficiency level of the players.

3.3 Gamification of the Learning Process

A process is a set of interrelated activities that interact to achieve a result. In the context of education, the learning process is the set of activities that produce learning as a result. Reengineering a process is rethinking and redesigning its activities to better achieve the objectives of the process, usually with a lower cost. When dealing with the learning process, reengineering it implies that the rethinking and redesign are done to get better results in the learning outcomes as well as increasing the efficiency and effectiveness, in a broad sense.

To define the learning process it is necessary to determine the activities and the way they are related. In the following sections a study about the learning activities and their relations is presented, together with the main features that, from our point of view, are needed for a effective reengineering so that a deep gamification is achieved.

Learning Activities. Learning activities are the building blocks to construct a learning process. As a result of performing the learning activities, the student should have developed the expected capabilities and skills. For the learning activities to take part in an effective gamified learning experience, they should have the following features:

- *Meaning:* the activity must be linked to the subject to be taught, that is, the contents of the subject must be needed to correctly perform the activities. For instance, the activity "calculating the derivative of x^2" has a meaning in the context of learning derivatives, but it has no meaning for a History course.
- *Score:* there must be any way to assess how good is the activity result, that is, there must be a score or measurement of the degree of correctness of the result. For instance, the activity "solve a crossword puzzle" can be scored by indicating the percentage of correct words in the puzzle solution.
- *Automatic assessment:* this feature is related to the previous one. The possibility of automatically assess the results of the activity is crucial to obtain an immediate feedback from the system with no human intervention.
- *Progressiveness:* it should be possible to progressively increase the difficulty of the activity, so that there is the possibility of designing simple activities to train basic competences and complex activities to train advances competences. For example, the "crossword puzzle" activity can be designed to increase its difficulty by incorporating more complex words progressively.
- *Experimentation and creativity:* usually, learning activities are designed to have only one possible solution (the case of "multiple choice tests" is paradigmatic). However, the reality is not closed and usually has infinite possible interpretations. Providing activities with multiple solutions and paths to explore, allows experimentation, creativity and decision making.
- *Game "flavour":* if possible, it is interesting to give some aspect of game to the activity. A "crossword puzzle" is preferable to a "word definition" activity, for instance.

Learning Path. Isolated activities do not make up a course. A motivating learning experience is achieved when the activities are linked with the others to built a learning path. Instead of sequential series of activities, a network of activities is proposed, so that every student can make up their own learning path performing the different activities (the nodes of the network) following the links between the activities. The combination of the activities in different ways allow the development of the following features:

- *Autonomy:* the students are owners of their own learning process. So, there should be some mechanism that allows them to make their own decisions to choose their own learning pace.
- *Challenge:* there must be an adequate level of challenge in the proposed activities, so that learners enter a state of *flow* [19], that is, they have a feeling of complete and energized focus in the activity, with a high level of enjoyment and fulfillment.
- *Rewards:* performing an activity should always have a reward. Usually, the reward is the resulting mark once the activity is assessed or, in other cases, some other rewards like additional benefits or social recognition.
- *Levels:* to maintain the sense of progression and challenge, there should be some levels of achievement and a system of blockage. This way, once a level is achieved, the rewards are obtained and the following levels are unblocked.
- *Trial and error:* people learn from their own mistakes, so error should not be penalized. Trial and error is a very natural and effective learning strategy that must be allowed and even promoted.

To illustrate the construction of a gamified learning system based on these principles, an example is set out in the next section. The use of a practical case can help to identify the key aspects and facilitate the understanding.

4   PLMan Learning System

The PLMan Learning System is a custom-made gamified, automated learning system that gives support to a first-year subject whose aim is to introduce students into Computational Logic. It will be used as an example to illustrate the design and construction of a gamified learning system.

The platform is structured around a gamified Website that manages all the information and elements of the system and allows the interaction of the actors (students and teachers). This is the entrance point for the students, who can download the learning activities, upload their solutions, obtain their marks and receive some predictions of the system about their learning progress. The teachers, on their behalf, enter the system to manage the students activity, introduce new activities, assign the initial stage and difficulty level of the activities and monitor the students progress. The gamified Website is the place that lodges the most superficial game elements, so that the students can have a game-like picture of their progress. To do so, elements like badges, leaderboards, and progression bars, among others, are introduced.

Nevertheless, the most interesting contribution is the internal redefinition of the learning process to achieve the desired deep gamification. The elements of the PLMan Learning System and how they are structured to make up the gamified experience are presented in the following sections. For each element, the strategies to fulfill the desired features are explained.

4.1   Learning Activities: PLMan Game

As it was stated before, learning activities are the blocks to build a gamified learning experience. PLMan game was designed to be used as the learning activity, bearing in mind that the objective of the course is learning Computational Logic. PLMan [21] is a game that challenges students to solve some *Pac-Man*-like mazes by means of logic programming in Prolog language. The fact of using a game as learning activity predispose students to accept it as a funny task. It has, definitely, an evident *game flavour*.

In PLMan students create automated controllers for Mr. PLMan, the main character. The goal is making these automated controllers able to eat all the dots of a given maze, dodging the perils. Automated controllers are developed in Prolog programming language, constructing sets of rules to reason about the maze and decide actions, so performing this activity will lead students to improve their level of logic thinking and develop their Prolog skills. Therefore, the activity has a *meaning* for the subject to be learned. An example maze along with an automated controller written in Prolog is shown in Fig. 2.

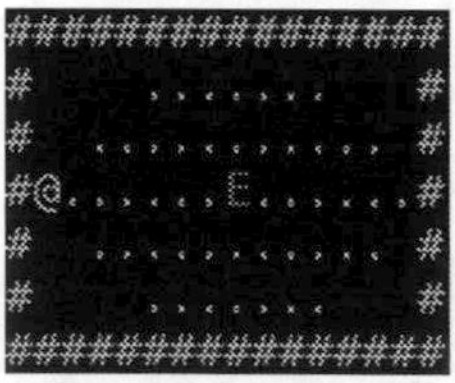

```
:- use_module('pl-man-game/main').
plman :- see(normal, up,         '.'), doAction(move(up)).
plman :- see(normal, down,       '.'), doAction(move(down)).
plman :- see(normal, left,       '.'), doAction(move(left)).
plman :- see(normal, right,      '.'), doAction(move(right)).
plman :- see(normal, down-left,  'E'), doAction(move(left)).
plman :- see(normal, down-left,  '.'), doAction(move(down)).
plman :- doAction(move(right)).
```

Fig. 2. Example maze along with the Prolog knowledge base that controls Mr. PLMan (@) to eat all the dots dodging the enemy (E)

PLMan is a turn-based game. Each turn, Mr. PLMan can perform one of these four generic actions in one of 4 orthogonal direction (`up`, `down`, `left`, `right`):

- `move(Direction)`: move one cell towards the direction.
- `get(Direction)`: get the object placed at the contiguous cell.
- `drop(Direction)`: drop the current object (reverse of `get`).
- `use(Direction)`: use the object towards one the direction.

The game ends when Mr. PLMan succeeds (all the dots in the maze are eaten) or fails (it comes across an enemy or bomb, the limit of turns is reached or there is a time-out during execution).

The combined effect of the sequence of actions will lead to a possible solution. It is important to highlight that the solution is not, in general, unique. Therefore, the student can obtain their own solution, introducing their own strategies. This way, along with the open possibilities offered by the game, the *experimentation* is encouraged and the *creativity* is favored.

An important feature for an activity is scoring its results. In this case, the *score* is the percentage of dots eaten, so there is a way of measuring the degree of correctness of the solution. Additionally, some punishments are also added to the score to enforce testing, code revision and detailed behaviour design. Punishments are applied in case of collision with a wall, invalid or erroneous action with the objects, or rule failure if no clause is successful in a given turn.

Each time students develop any new controller for a given maze, they are *automatically assessed*. The fact of using a programming language like Prolog makes available some automatic tools that can be incorporated to the system. This way the score is obtained immediately, as soon as the solution is uploaded to the system.

Mazes are designed to have an increasing difficulty, requiring progressively more programming abilities. In the first mazes, simple rules in the form "If you see an enemy to your left, move right" are enough to construct successful controllers. As the game progresses, more difficult mazes are delivered, requiring more complex controllers to succeed. This leads students to learn Prolog programming, as well as logic thinking and small bits of Artificial Intelligence. These features allows the introduction of the *progressiveness* in the activity, so that it allows training from very simple to quite complex contents and skills.

4.2   Learning Path

Once the activities are defined, a second important question is the way they are combined so that the reengineered learning process is complete. The learning experience is conceived as a network, so that the activities are considered as nodes of the network, and the links between the activities represent the conditions to pass from one activity to the other. The objective of this scheme is allowing the generation of different adapted learning paths and the implementation of the desired features described in Sect. 3.3.

The feature of progressiveness given to the activities, explained in the previous section, allows the definition of different *levels* of difficulty. More than 400 different mazes have been made for PLMan, with different layouts, objects to get and use, enemies and obstacles to avoid and even problems to solve. These mazes are organized into 4 main stages and up to 5 levels of difficulty per stage.

The stages are sorted by increasing difficulty, so that as one moves from one stage to the next one, new knowledge about the programming language is required to overcome it. Thus, for stage 1 it is only required the use of simple rules and the maze is deterministic (the maze remains unchanged between executions). Stage 2 maintains deterministic mazes but incorporates the use of multiple conditions in the rules. In stage 3 some indeterminacy is added and in stage 4 indeterminism and possible situations to control increase. To progress from one stage to another, a minimum score is needed, so a block/unblock strategy can be implemented.

At each stage, students have to solve 1 to 5 different mazes. Although the required knowledge and skills to solve every maze in a stage are the same, there are different levels of difficulty for the different possible mazes. In fact, to get each new maze for solving, students start by pick up their desired difficulty level among valid levels for the stage in which they are. The greater the difficulty level, the more the contribution to the final grade. Then, the system presents them with a random maze from their selected level of difficulty.

The students can solve offline as many mazes as they want in every stage, so that they can decide upload the solution to advance to a new stage (if unblocked) when they feel confortable with their developed knowledge and skills. As a consequence, students have a feeling of progress and *challenge* that stimulates them and maintain them in the state of flow. Moreover, the fact of selecting their desired difficulty levels gives the student some control to their learning path, promoting their *autonomy* and decision making.

Students use PLMan software to develop and test their solutions to each maze they get assigned. Every time they have developed a solution they consider to be working, they submit the solution through the PLMan Website. The automated system runs the solution and evaluates their score and marks. The accumulated marks make up the system *rewards*. The system shows detailed evaluation to the students and, if they complete more than 75 % of the maze, they unlock the next maze and can continue. If not, they have to improve their solution and send it again until they achieve 75 % or more.

The system is designed in the aim of formative assessment, considering that students need to learn from their own mistakes without being penalized for it. Because of this, students do not have a limit of submissions for a given maze. The system always consider the best solution they have submitted to give them marks. Partially solved mazes also contribute to their final grade proportionally to the percentage solved of the maze. This is the way to perform a *trial and error* strategy.

5   Conclusions and Further Work

In this paper we have presented our experience designing and developing a gamified learning experience. Few years ago, reports foresaw that gamification was set to be a disruptive innovation in the field of education. Now, is the time for the gamification to take off. However, experiences in learning gamification are, by now, quite limited and usually stay on the surface, just offering a layer of standardized elements such as badges, leader boards and medals. A fun and efficient gamified learning experience is much more than a mix of game mechanics, dynamics and components. Mature gamification experiences must go further in their proposals. In this context, we propose a deeper transformation of the learning process, making up a true process reengineering.

Our proposal claims an active learning, promoting the intrinsic motivation of the students, who learn for their own satisfaction. Students have different abilities and learn at different rates. A gamified strategy for learning must be closer to students interests and provide them with some autonomy getting their best. The key is moving towards an adaptive gamified student-centered learning model.

From our experience we have learned some important lessons about the gamification of the learning process: the importance of fun as a consequence of learning, the need of having an immediate feedback of our actions, the trial and error possibility as a major source of learning and progress, the relevance of experimentation and creativity as a means to develop the learners skills and the importance of autonomy to give the learners the control of their learning process, among others. All these features are propellants for learning and a way to improve the motivation of learners.

These lessons have guided the design of a gamified learning system to help students to develop their knowledge and skills in the context of a computational logic subject. The result is an operative platform that provides a gamified learning experience that fulfills the desired features.

Certainly there are aspects that are subject to discussion but we consider them as a starting point for teachers who want to approach the world of gamification. In the future, we plan to improve the system and enrich the experience with the students' feedback.

References

1. Burke, B.: Gamification 2020: What is the future of gamification? Technical report, Gartner, November 2012
2. Domínguez, A., Saenz-de Navarrete, J., de Marcos, L., Fernández-Sanz, L., Pagés, C., Martínez-Herráiz, J.J.: Gamifying learning experiences: practical implications and outcomes. Comput. Educ. **63**, 380–392 (2013)
3. Freitas, S.D., Neumann, T.: The use of exploratory learning for supportingimmersive learning in virtual environments. Comput. Educ. **52**(2), 343–352 (2009)
4. Gilbert, R.: The secret of monkey island (1990)
5. González, C., Mora, A., Toledo, P.: Gamification in intelligent tutoring systems, pp. 221–225. ACM Press (2014)
6. Hunicke, R., Leblanc, M., Zubek, R.: MDA: a formal approach to game design and game research. In: Proceedings of the Challenges in Games AI Workshop, Nineteenth National Conference of Artificial Intelligence, pp. 1–5 (2004)
7. Johnson, L., Adams, S., Cummins, M., Estrada, V., Freeman, A., Ludgate, H.: The NMC horizon report: 2013 higher education edition. Technical report, New Media Consortium (2013)
8. Johnson, L., Adams Becker, S., Cummins, M., Estrada, V., Freeman, A., Hall, C.: NMC Horizon Report: 2016 Higher Education Edition. New Media Consortium; EDUCAUSE Learning Initiative, Austin Texas [S.l.] (2016)
9. Kapp, K.: The Gamification of Learning and Instruction: Game-based Methods and Strategies for Training and Education. Wiley, New York (2012)
10. Koster, R., Wright, W.: A Theory of Fun for Game Design. Paraglyph Press, Pittsburgh (2004)

11. Loguidice, B., Barton, M.: Vintage Games: An Insider Look at the History of Grand Theft Auto, Super Mario, and the Most Influential Games of All Time. Focal Press/Elsevier, Boston (2009)
12. McGonigal, J.: Reality Is Broken: Why Games Make Us Better and How They Can Change the World. Penguin Group, New York (2011)
13. Mora, A., Riera, D., González, C., Arnedo-Moreno, J.: A Literature Review of Gamification Design Frameworks, pp. 1–8. IEEE, September 2015
14. Moreno-Ger, P., Burgos, D., Torrente, J.: Digital games in eLearning environments: current uses and emerging trends. Simul. Gaming 40(5), 669–687 (2009)
15. Pastor, H., Satorre, R., Molina, R., Gallego, F., Llorens, F.: Can moodle be used for structural gamification? In: INTED 2015 Proceedings of the 9th International Technology, Education and Development Conference, IATED, 2–3 March 2015, pp. 1014–1021 (2015)
16. Prensky, M.: Digital Game-Based Learning. McGraw-Hill, New York (2001)
17. Prensky, M.: Don'T Bother Me Mom-I'M Learning!. Paragon House Publishers, New York (2006)
18. Ryan, R.M., Deci, E.L.: Self-determination theory and the facilitation of intrinsic motivation, social development, and well-being. Am. Psychol. 55(1), 68–78 (2000)
19. Schell, J.: The Art of Game Design: A Book of Lenses. Morgan Kaufmann Publishers Inc., San Francisco (2008)
20. Turkle, S.: Alone Together: Why We Expect More from Technology and Less from Each Other. Basic Books, New York (2011)
21. Villagrá-Arnedo, C., Castel De Haro, M., Gallego-Durán, F.J., Pomares Puig, C., Suau Pérez, P., Cortés Vaíllo, S.: Real-time evaluation. In: Proceedings of the 1st International Conference on Education and New Learning Technologies, IATED, EDULEARN 2009, Barcelona, Spain, pp. 3361–3369, July 2009
22. Werbach, K., Hunter, D.: For the Win: How Game Thinking Can Revolutionize Your Business. Wharton Digital Press, Philadelphia (2012)
23. Werbach, K., Hunter, D.: For The Win: How Game Thinking Can Revolutionize Your Business. Wharton Digital Press, Philadelphia (2012)

An Analysis of Applying the Short Bridge Method to Digital Education

Renata Zilse[(⊠)], Tiago Primo, Fernando Koch, and Andrew Koster

SAMSUNG Research Institute, São Paulo, Brazil
{renata.borges,tiago.t,fernando.koch,andrew.k}@samsung.com

Abstract. This work seeks to build a new kind of classroom experience by rethinking how educational content is currently transmitted and consumed at schools. This work presents the results of applying the Short Bridge Method in the education context. We evaluate how this approach contributes to the class composition process by providing tools that support educators and school administrators to plan courses aligned with students' necessities and learning pace. We present our methodology to identify the work flows and artifacts that impact the class composition activities to support educators and school administrators for personalized learning environments. The results allowed us to understand and map the teacher's behavior during class preparation and define a set of practices to be incorporate in class composition software.

1 Introduction

A real improvement in worldwide levels of schooling can be perceived in the expected decrease of the number of people without formal education: 12 % in 2010 to 3 % in 2050. Together with this, we can observe the fast spread of broadband mobile internet and the improvement of information access for all citizens, regardless their origin [4].

In addition, the constant behavior changes between generations are transforming the main kind of knowledge acquisition and also opening space for novel education methodologies that became more individualized, customized and interactive. This new approach increases the teachers work, and even causes uncomfortable situations related to a misconception that technologies will replace traditional teachers.

Teachers are under information overload whilst selecting learning objects from the growing source of Open Educational Resources like YouTube for schools, Khan Academy and MIT OpenCourseWare. These professionals face the challenge of selecting the objects that are both aligned with their preferences and they believe will help improving learning performance and student engagement.

Dealing with educational issues teachers need to follow growing content demand, deal with the school and students technological choices, and understand the dynamics and pedagogical aspects of digital educational resources.

Faced with those endeavors, some research questions arose: are the present class composing and performance processes the same since new medias emerged?

© Springer International Publishing Switzerland 2016
P. Zaphiris and A. Ioannou (Eds.): LCT 2016, LNCS 9753, pp. 94–102, 2016.
DOI: 10.1007/978-3-319-39483-1_9

How is the Teacher class composition process facing information overload? Can smart technological educational tools help Teachers in this aspect?

An alternative to cope with those research questions would be the use of the Bridge Method. Initially developed in 1998 by Dayton et al. [1] and further quoted by many GUI researches, the Bridge method aims to bring knowledge about how to go from User Requirements to User Interface in a interactive system — how to bridge the gap. Translating the subjects mental models in a flowchart, the method also brings a consensual interaction map considering all stakeholders and important touch points. The Authors recommendation about the activity duration however was too long which frustrated their wider use. In 2004 Zilse and Moraes [6] suggested that a shorter version of the original method could be applied to any interactive systems and also any project where specific user interactions (virtual or physical) should be mapped in blueprints, The Short Bridge Method. Focusing on simple, viable, and feasible interactions between participants during a period together the method helps to identify user flows, bottlenecks and features.

Since then the method has been applied routinely to map the user desired actions in User Experience Design processes. For instance, the process would allow to identify the Teachers journey map, from the class composition to the class review, highlighting important issues. To validate the Short Bridges findings we analyze a case study, part of a Digital Teaching Platform (DTP), a Brazilian Samsung Research Institute ongoing project [3].

As a result, we modeled the Teachers work with consequent optimization of operational costs and betterment of education process. We believe that the application of the proposed method will improve the user experience by translating the teacher mental models in applied educational solutions. Also, we contributed with to help teachers to rethink the classroom as whole. Focusing not just in the content but how it is transmitted and consumed by the students, leading to pedagogical practices that contributes with class composition and stimulate students knowledge sharing. This paper is organized as following: (1) the Short Bridge method application to the understanding and mapping of the teachers mental model related to class composition processes within the information overload context; (2) the methods outputs analysis; (3) evaluation and validation of these outputs in the real case study and; (4) the Results and outcomes for further studies propositions.

2   Short Bridge Method

2.1   Preliminaries

Based on The Bridge method, the Short Bridge version is also an user centered method, focused in potential users (including his particulars, tasks and environment), who's the job must be supported by an application [1]. The main attribute of this method is to clarify the user interface by the user requirements detailed by the main users, bridging the gap between both. In this shorter approach we established application like any product or solution interacted by users, and the interface like any touch point between the user and referred application. Ultimately, the method is a collaborative one that purposes to specify the user experience itself in a top-down point of view (user experience and interaction) [5].

2.2   Application

The short version of The Bridge Method workshop, originally played from 3 to 7 workshops days, is organized to range from 2 to 6 h, according to the complexity of the theme, in a sharper point of view. The necessary materials are A4 sheets, pencils, a large board or big sheets (where the user flow will be drawn), colorful Post-its and boards pens. About the subjects, the creators of The Bridge method recommend five participants collaborating with their expertise in a rich discussion, bringing solutions to challenges presented. The subjects were chosen by the following criteria:

- two different skilled users in distinct subject relevant axis of experience: two teachers were invited, one specialist in Learning and planning Methods and a post-graduation teacher;
- one UX Designer or HCI Usability professional: we chose the first;
- one Developer or Computer Scientist: chosen an expert;
- one System Engineering or Technical Documenter: chosen first.

The Short Bridge Method should follow the 4 steps in the workshop plus one to Report (see Fig. 1), where: Step 1, Actions (16 % of workshop time) is a warming moment and when each participant list his personal relevant and desired actions for the theme and begins to understand the user's actions at all from the other participants point of view; Step 2, Tasks (34 % of workshop time) is when users helped by others participants express the actions in tasks flows; Step 3, Features (34 % of workshop time) is when some solutions for the found problems means features (task objects); Step 4, Validation (16 % of workshop time), a kind of usability test; and finally the Short Bridge method additional Step +1, Report with the detailed outputs.

Fig. 1. The 4+1 steps of the workshop for applying the Short Bridge method

2.3   Outputs

With the application of the Short Bridge method we could map the teachers mental model for class composition activities and build a flow chart encompassing the process. By its application results, we could confirm the interconnection between the class composition and class execution activities, so both were detailed in this study. Organizing and stimulating a guided discussion between the participants, it was possible to identify the main actors of each phase of the process and map the related and desired stages. Also we were able to specify some features and roles for each actor. Such outputs can be used for any system development that intends to build solutions for this domain. To present the results, as recommended by the shorter version presented, we used the flow chart based on the Garrett visual vocabulary [2]. It shows a process summary, focusing to the actions-key, simplifying the final result.

As presented in the user flow chart of Fig. 2, the Class Building Process consists basically in two phases and 6 key actions (hexagonal shapes):

- Class Composition Phase 1 composed by (A) Class Script Build, (B) Class Planning and Execution of Lessons and (C) Emulate and Test Class;
- Class Execution Phase 2 composed by (D) Provide Class; 5, Share Class; and (E) Class Evaluation by Feedbacks.

The main actors are: Teacher, Academic Coordinator and Academic Platform.

The first phase, Class Composition, is when Teacher prepares his classes or the whole class period. His/Her work starts with the Classes Script build or review (A). Class Planning and Execution of Lessons (B) is a dynamic action composed by the search and compilation of physical or digital contents and resources, typically the educational objects, tailored to recovered, copied or new lessons and activities. This is the heaviest phase, when the teacher searches for examples, activities and media elements like videos, digital exercises or graphics to enhance the class content. After finishes a class composition, frequently the Teacher emulates and tests his class (C) to verify the consistency, deepness, and time, to evaluate if it is appropriated for the students profile. It is very common Teacher tests the learning object he/she is adding doing essays to verify the validity of it. The evaluation of those results leads to the review of lessons, educational contents, new assessments and even, a re-planning of the class. Within the participants discussions we identified five features often used by Teacher when playing the Class Planning and Execution of Lessons action (B): (1) Adds/Review content items; (2) Records Audio/Video by him/herself, something or event; (3) Adds Links to complementary contents in books, handouts, internet or applications; (4) Integrate Medias like videos, games, labs or activities; and (5) Combine skills and abilities that will rank the class at all over an Academic Platform. All of those features were recommendations based on the Teachers point of view based on their current experience with unintegrated software solutions to do so. Today this Teacher deals with many sources and kinds of information causing an overload to manage. The (B) action Class Composition and Execution of Lessons is the hardiest of all the building class process.

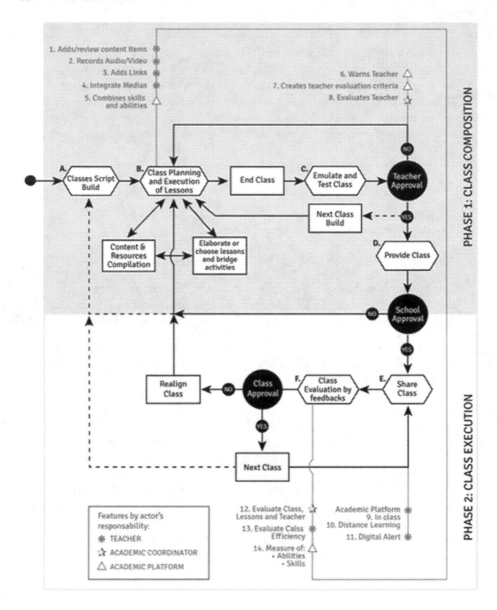

Fig. 2. Process flow chart of the full process for classroom education

After the class or all periods classes were done Teacher shares it with school (D, Provide Class) to a board approval. At this step it was identified new features: (6) Warms Teacher about approval or not; (7) Creates Teacher evaluation criteria; and (8) Evaluates Teacher. All of them addressed to School management and its mapped actors (Academic Coordinator and Platform) allowing evaluation just in time.

Once approved by the School, Teacher goes to the Class Execution second phase. He/She teaches In Class or Distance Learning (E, Share Class). Sometimes he/she anticipates digital alert with classs topics to students by intranet, e-mail, Facebook or Whatsapp (features 9, 10 and 11 also mapped and highlighted in the Flowchart). The Teacher always gets feedback from students by comments, behaviors, assessments or questions during the class time and from others schools educators (F, Class Evaluation by feedbacks). The related features of this action are: (12) Evaluate Class, Lessons and Teacher, assigned to the Academic Coordinator; (13) Evaluate Class Efficiency, assigned to the Teacher; and (14) Measure of acquired abilities and skills, assigned to the Academic Platform. This information will form the basis of his/her knowledge about the class students and will be useful for future classes reviews or even for new ones. By this reason the features mapped on this action (F) are linked to the features mapped on the action (B). Without a consistent Class Evaluation by feedbacks the Class Composition and Execution of Lessons (action B) quality is compromised.

3   Evaluation

We evaluated the flow chart of Fig. 2 in two phases, corresponding to the two phases of digital education: class preparation and class execution. The evaluation of phase 1 was performed during a set of field trials, with the support of a prototype DTP specifically designed to support the highlighted activities. Our results were obtained due to a collaboration with two teachers at public high schools in Manaus, Brazil, to create digital classroom content that were complementary to their regular mathematics classes.

3.1   Case Study

Because the user interface of the DTP Composer element was still in development, the first phase was not executed directly on the platform, but rather the Teachers indicated what content they wanted to use, and we manually composed the classroom material for use on the platform. In this manner, the Teachers created their class plan and content, and used us as an interface with the software platform. In particular, the Teachers searched for online videos, and used these, in combination with educative slides to compose most of their material. They further used exercises based on the book material their school uses, and indicated interactive content that the book publisher makes available to the schools. We composed an electronic book integrating all these materials, or if unavailable, substituting them with equivalent content. This, in turn, was validated by the Teachers, who suggested further changes. This corresponds with the cycles we see in phase 1 of the flow chart of Fig. 2, where we expected various back-and-forth discussions between class planning, content compilation and Teacher/school approval. However, the main focus of our evaluation was on the class execution process, which we could evaluate more rigorously due to the prototype software being ready for use in the classroom.

The class execution phase was evaluated in five classes in two public high schools in Manaus, with in total 180 students participating in the classes. In the classes, both the teacher and all the students used the tablet with the DTP Content Player prototype that we developed in accordance with the output from the Short Bridge method. We evaluated student and teacher satisfaction with the prototype using a satisfaction survey during the class, and interviews after the classes.

3.2   Results

The case study reinforces that the application of methods that brings people to a co-creation processes is the better way to achieve natural and easy solutions. These kinds of process should be the basis of any digital and interactive application that intends to help people. And the Short Bridge Method applies well as a way to understand the mental model of the target system users.

The field trials, allowed us to identify that educational applications must focus on the "chain of teaching"; considering the administrative staff (pedagogical designers and directors), the school pedagogical plan, the class itself and the post-class evaluation. The sequence and correlation between the actions and system's functionalities should be oriented to meet these stakeholders.

The Class Planning and Execution of Lessons could be confirmed as the harder action of the Class Building Process. Empowering the teacher during their class composition activities is crucial, specially when considering this bottleneck. Many teachers spend too much time searching and tailoring educational contents. One teacher remarked that "if there are 10 ways to resolve a question, I will teach all of them. I think that each person has his way to learn and will choose the best manner to do that." Their time is limited, and it would be interesting for them to focus on pedagogical alternatives that could improve the content assimilation by the students.

The Short Bridge method as a tool to identify the user experience involved in schools allowed us to get insights regarding the design and development of seamless educational solutions for school environments.

4   Conclusion

The Short Bridge collaborative method, with two different skilled Teachers participation and engagement, brings knowledge about the user journey and experience very relevant for the Digital Platform development. Even considering the results related and dependent of them domain, it was possible to confirm the Teacher information overload perception highlighting the harder action in the Class Building Process: the Teacher Class Planning and Execution of Lessons. Motivated to help teachers to rethink the classroom as whole, the focus on this action allow us to propose a virtual environment where the mapped features could be easily controlled (Fig. 3). We hope so to support Teachers to plan courses aligned with students' necessities and learning pace minimizing his/her overload while the activities could be easily performed.

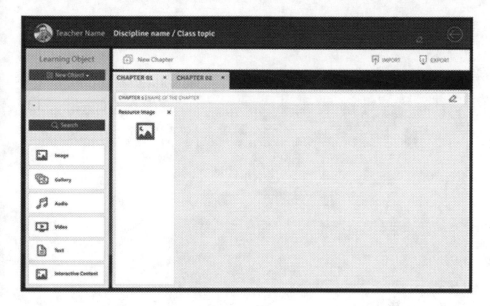

Fig. 3. Wireframe of the Composition tool for completing the action Class Planning and Execution of Lessons (B)

The User Flow Chart represent the actions of the Teacher taking into account other stakeholders (called actors) pointed by the main participants. They are essential for the perfect execution of the Building Classes Process. The features pointed are also relevant but should be tested in a more accurate and focused research.

Although the Teacher Planning Class Process use case was a specific topic, we can verify that the Short Bridge Method application works to any interactive processes. The focus is the user action and his necessities for the studied system. The attributes and features are not protagonists. The purpose of the method is to provide a better experience for the user to achieve a goal. Further studies should be done for better validation of the Class Composition first phase (actions A to D) with new experiments in a real case field trial.

References

1. Dayton, T., McFarland, A., Kramer, J.: Bridging user needs to object oriented GUI prototype via task object design. In: User interface design, pp. 15–56 (1998)
2. Garrett, J.J.: A visual vocabulary for describing information architecture and interaction design (2002). http://www.jjg.net/ia/visvocab/. Accessed 10 Feb 2016
3. Koster, A., Primo, T., Koch, F., Oliveira, A., Chung, H.: Towards an educator-centred digital teaching platform: the ground conditions for a data-driven approach. In: Proceedings of the 15th IEEE Conference on Advanced Learning Technologies (ICALT), Hualien, Taiwan, pp. 74–75. IEEE (2015)

4. Malik, K.: Human Development Report 2013 – The Rise of the South: Human Progress in a Diverse World. Human Development Reports, United Nations Development Programme (2013)
5. Reichenauer, A., Komischke, T.: A comprehensive process model for usable information architecture systems: integrating top-down and bottom-up information architecture. Hum. Comput. Interact. Int. Proc. 1, 223–227 (2003)
6. Zilse, R., Moraes, A.: Utilização do método the bridge para o processo de arquitetura de informação em website universitário. In: 3o Congresso Internacional de Ergonomia e Usabilidade, Design de Interfaces e Interação Homem-Computador, Rio de Janeiro, Brazil, pp. 48–55. PUC-Rio (2004)

Interaction Techniques and Platforms for Learning

Enhancing Collaboration and Facilitating Children's Learning Using TUIs: A Human-Centered Design Approach

Wafa Almukadi[1,2(✉)] and Guy A. Boy[1]

[1] School of Human-Centered Design, Innovation and Art,
Florida Institute of Technology, 150 West University Boulevard,
Melbourne, FL 32901, USA
Walmukadi2013@my.fit.edu, gboy@fit.edu
[2] Computing and Information Technology College,
Information System Department,
King Abdulaziz University, Jeddah, Saudi Arabia

Abstract. Human-Computer Interaction (HCI) literature already suggests that Tangible User Interfaces (TUIs) can support children learning. This paper presents a human-centered design approach of TUIs applied for reading tasks in the classroom for children aged 5 to 8 years. This approach is also supported by agile software and hardware development. We focused on language learning by building 3-letter words. We also discover the remarkable advantage of TUIs to support collaboration with teachers and the others children in the achievement of such tasks. We discuss related human-system integration issues, and more specifically tangibility and emerging collaboration factors elicited from formative evaluation results.

Keywords: Author keywords tangible user interface · Learning · Children · Engagement · Collaboration · Fun · Human-centered design

1 Introduction

The Human-Computer Interaction (HCI) community works on TUIs for around two decades [20]. More recently, TUI in children learning's environments started to have an impact showing interesting possibilities from various viewpoints such as usability, learning, collaboration, and fun [10, 20]. Several research efforts have been carried out and provided empirical evidence and theoretical validations of the benefits of TUIs on learning outcomes [10, 19]. Many applications [15–18] developed for children in a large variety of domains and tasks. However, results show potential influence processes related to learning, while still no conclusive evidence of measuring learning outcomes [20]. This paper will discuss how TUIs can enhance children's learning environment that facilitates learning overall. It presents an interactive tangible learning system for children age 5 to 8, designed to facilitate language learning with 3-letter words. An empirical experiment was performed with 9 children to evaluate the affect of TUIs in children's learning environment.

© Springer International Publishing Switzerland 2016
P. Zaphiris and A. Ioannou (Eds.): LCT 2016, LNCS 9753, pp. 105–114, 2016.
DOI: 10.1007/978-3-319-39483-1_10

1.1 What Do Children Like and Do Not Like in the Classroom?

A discussion session involving 17 children aged 5 to 8 (11 girls and 6 boys) and 4 teachers were conducted in a local school to explore what children like in their classroom and what they don't like. Findings are summarized as follows:

- Children don't like sitting at a desk, they prefer booths or round tables that can fit groups of children and provide more freedom to move;
- Children don't like to be tested;
- Children like to be rewarded;
- Children like to use interactive tool to learn, such as tablet and iPad;
- Children like to have fun while learning supported by games and stories;
- Children like working together.

In addition, teachers involved endorsed the benefit of serious games designed for learning and problem-solving purposes, which can replace traditional exercises and entertain children. Children like to play, and playing facilitates learning. Based on these findings we claimed that using TUIs in children classroom could enhance children's learning by supporting interactivity, collaboration, embodiment, and pleasure [20]. At the same time, TUIs support what children and teachers prefer.

2 Why Tangible User Interface?

Human-Centered Design (HCD) [4] promotes involving potential future users into the design process. It typically consists in iterative loops that include ideation, prototype development, formative evaluation and validation. At a higher level of abstraction, HCD dictates looking for emerging properties of technology being developed, as well as organizational and human factors [4, 12]. Children are involved in affective exploration by creating imaginary and rich artificial life through play. TUIs in the classroom provide children with useful support for such exploration and knowledge acquisition. This tangible reading and writing environment enables children to acquire knowledge by acting (i.e., moving letter cubes among each other to form words).

TUIs provide a playful environment that facilitates children's overall development and learning [9, 10]. Providing such playful environments in classrooms increases children's engagement [16], offers freedom, motivation, and also learning through natural activities that fit into children's everyday contexts [5, 19]. Moreover, TUIs support collaboration of several users interacting with their environment as well as among each other [10, 16, 19]. Collaborative learning increases productivity levels [5], boosting confidence and self-esteem of children. Furthermore, TUIs require little cognitive effort to learn how to use systems, enabling students to focus exclusively on objects and tasks [19].

We claim that use of TUIs in the classroom, more specifically for language-learning purposes, improves learning outcomes. Demonstration of this claim led us to develop a TUI prototype that supports language learning by "building" and spelling 3-letters words, for children age 4 to 8. We tested the prototype in local school, involving 9 children (4 girls and 5 boys).

3 The Proposed TUI System

The proposed prototype designed as a portable lightweight and low-cost TUI based on open source framework reacTIVision[1]. The system's design support children's familiarity with letter-cubes manipulation. This result is corroborated by [19] results telling that children better grasp an abstract concept when its concrete representation can be grasped physically [18]. We considered Antle's five TUIs properties for children's [3]. The components of our prototype are (Fig. 1):

Fig. 1. The proposed TUI system components with a running example of 3-letter words "HEN"

A medium-size transparent box, which has a useful table-top surface that enables children to manipulate letter-cubes on it. A black foam board has been added around the playing surface to define the playing area.

- Three blocks represent the system objects; we call them blocks. Blocks are input objects. They afford gesture-based interaction, flexibility, reliability [16] and children familiarity acquisition. Four sides of each block have fiducial markers (Fig. 2) providing each of them with a unique ID representing a letter (note that two sides are left for future work). The resulting 3-block system enables the manipulation of 12 letters. Letters C, F, H, and B belong to Block1. Letters A, U, O, and E belong to Block2. Letters T, G, N, and X belong to Block3. The system enables 23 different

---

[1] http://reactivision.sourceforge.net/.

meaningful 3-letter words: cat, fat, hat, bat, act, hug, hut, hot, cut, tab, fun, hen, fan, can, tub, bag, bug, hog, bog, cot, fox, fog, and box. These words were recommended by teachers that we interviewed as the most common learning words for children 5–8 years old.

- A web-camera (Logitech HD webcam C615) enabling optical marker recognition is placed at the bottom of the box.
- A laptop is used to run the system framework, application, and display output. The application is coded by Processing[2].

3.1   How Does the System Work?

We chose an easy topic of 3-letter words that is familiar with our audience age because we wanted to focus on activity (i.e., what children effectively do) and not only the task (i.e., what children are requested to do), as well as TUI impact in the classroom. Children have the task to discover meaningful words. Children have to manipulate blocks on all four sides, which have optical markers, to "build" a meaningful word. Letters are not attached to the blocks. The idea behind that is to boost children curiosity and challenge them by providing game atmosphere. Whenever children obtain a meaningful 3-letter word, such as "HEN", an image corresponding to the word is immediately displayed together with the text message, "You got the word HEN", as well as clapping sounds is played. Conversely, if children build a non-meaningful word (e.g., "BFG"), nothing happens, (i.e. no negative feedback is provided). The overall principle is to encourage children to explore at their own pace further possibilities and thus motivate them to improve their vocabulary and spelling.

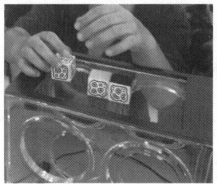 

Fig. 2. On the left, three tangible objects with fiducial makers. On the right, close look to the fiducial markers that are attached to objects

---

[2] https://processing.org/.

4 Evaluation Study

A pilot study conducted at a local school. A group of 9 children aged 5 to 8 (4 girls and 5 boys) participated in the study. The experiment took place in a classroom after school day. We observed children's interactions with the system (i.e., activity), and learning outcomes.

4.1 Methods

We adapted Hanna's guidelines for usability testing with children [7]. Furthermore, we choose the co-discovery evaluation approach for the observation of children's activities. This approach consists in letting children collaborate with each other to learn how to interact with the proposed system [11]. We also used the Peer Tutoring method [8] where children who used the system can teach their friends what to do. After completing requested tasks, children were requested to complete a questionnaire using smiley ometer [13].

4.2 The Study Scenario

Children were brought into the classroom and asked to individually write 3-letter words that they know (Fig. 3). They had 20 min to complete the task. Our main goal was to observe children's behavior and interactivity, and build a basis for comparison with equivalent behavior using the TUI system. Another goal of this first task was to know children's knowledge level. After that, they asked to play together using the TUI system for 20 min (Fig. 4). Following the session, they were asked to fill in an evaluation sheet consisting of questionnaire with a smiley ometer for 10 min.

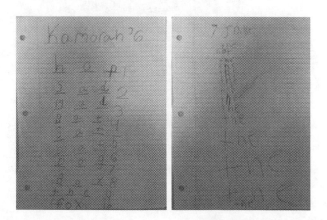

Fig. 3. An example of children hand writing, on the left six years old got 10 words, on the right 7 years old got 2words.

Fig. 4. Children play with the TUI system in classroom

Children were introduced to the system as a new game consisting in learning 3-letter words. They had to explore various ways of combining blocks. In practice, children stood around the TUI system and tried to play with it. A six years old child began to align the blocks and turned them on different sides until he achieved a meaningful word. With no request, this child, who tried the system first, started to guide other children and taught them how to build successful words, using a Peer Tutoring approach implicitly. After a while, three children were leading the group and showed them how to use the TUI system. They expressed their thoughts loudly and discussed about various possibilities of building words. After the session, children sat at a table to complete a paper evaluation sheet (Fig. 5).

Fig. 5. Children completing evaluation sheet

5   Results and Discussion

The researcher who conducted the study mainly focused on observing children's activities, taking notes, taking pictures, and video recording the "playground". A volunteer teacher provided help with children interaction and organizing the sessions.

During the first session, children were first very quiet, staring at each other and at the ceiling. Some children put their heads on the table pretending they were tired and needed to sleep. Others complained that they didn't know any words. Then the volunteer teacher provided some examples orally. Consequently, children started to fill in their sheets. A few children tried to talk with others silently, asking about some words. Two children exchange their sheets to help each other.

When children started using the TUI system, they were very active and curious about how the system worked and how could these objects represent letters. They started by grasping the blocks and examined them by looking at and touching them. Children interacted with the system smoothly by discovering how to use it without asking for help. Children collaborated very well while they thought aloud about 3-letter words, continuously spelling. They explained meaning of some words to their peers such as "cot and bog" pointed to the pictures displayed on the screen. The room was full of children giggling and laughing, which proved their happiness and fun. After completing the evaluation form, children asked us when they could use the system again. They also asked if it was possible to leave the system and suggested visiting them in their classroom at least once a week.

Regarding performance results, since we could not guaranty task completeness, we counted the number of words that children were able to "build" in 20 min. During the first session, children were able to successfully build 14 words. During the second session, they were able to build, 20 words. In addition, during the first session none of them learned new vocabulary, while during the second session 3 children, ages 5, 6, and 7, learned two new words "cot" and "bog". Learning happened when other children built these words, so they started asking about their meaning and pointed to the image displayed in the screen to show the meaning (i.e., using a connotation cognitive process). Some children used the words "cot" and "bog" in a sentence to explain their meaning.

Since this paper focuses on children activity and collaboration, we need to evaluate children engagement as an important factor of children's playful learning experiences. Engagement defined as a kind of mindfulness and awareness requiring cognitive effort and deep processing of new information [1]. Some researches evaluate engagement by the amount of time spent on and off a particular task [1]. In our case it was difficult to count the time spent for building words. However, it was suggested that observing children behaviors such as smiles, laughing, frowns, and yawns are more reliable indicators of engagement or lack of engagement [6, 14]. Based on previous suggested principles on measuring engagement [6, 14], we deduced that children in the first session showed lack of engagement clearly appearing in their behaviors, such as staring at the ceiling, putting their heads down on the desks, verbalizing negative expressions, such as, "I feel tired, I want to sleep, I don't know any 3-letter words". In the second session, we observed that children were very much engaged, based on their face expressions, laughs and giggling sounds, letters and words screaming, and positive expressions such as "yes, yeah, easy, cool, and nice". Children like feedback whether audio, text, or image, which keeps them more engaged representing their success.

An important factor that emerged during the experiment is collaboration. Not only the TUI system supports collaboration among children, but it also affords collaboration (i.e., it naturally suggests collaboration). Children collaborated also by giving turns to

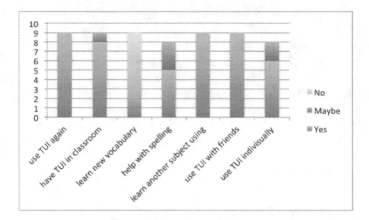

Fig. 6. Results of evaluation sheet

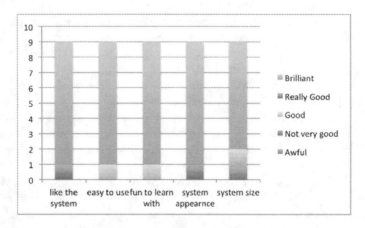

Fig. 7. Results of smiley ometer

their peers and taught each other how to use the system. Observational analysis revealed that children were much more active in terms of moving their bodies, guessing and expressing themselves. Figures 6 and 7 show the results of children questionnaire.

6 Summary

Human-centered design of using a TUI system in the classroom greatly contributes to facilitate children's learning and enhance collaboration. Our language-learning experimental results show that a TUI system used in a classroom with children 5–8 years old supports exploratory learning, collaboration, engagement, and enjoyment. Tangibility is crucial for the manipulation of abstract concepts and learning through the manipulation of equivalent physical objects. TUIs enable children to express themselves through natural body movements, interactivity, collaboration and having fun. Consequently, providing behaviors of exploration, social interaction, manipulation of objects, movement, and enjoyment while learning.

7 Future Work

Regarding the small sample size (9 children); we could not perform a significant quantitative analysis. Planned studies are in progress that involves more children. We already started to extend the approach to numbers and basic math [2]. Future work includes comparison experiments between abstract objects that are presented in this paper (objects with no letters) and objects with letters to explore the effect of physical correspondence on learning and engagement.

Acknowledgements. We thank all the teachers, children, and participants. Thanks to the University Park elementary school and district of Brevard public school. Special thanks to Sally Sabawi, Jeri Moore, Karen Strauss, and Theresa Nicolette. Thanks to Dr. Kolski, Dr. Stephane, and Dr. Read for their feedback and comments.

References

1. Africano, D., Berg, S., Lindbergh, K., Lundholm, P., Nilbrink, F., Persson, A.: Designing tangible interfaces for children's collaboration. In: CHI 2004 Extended Abstracts on Human Factors in Computing Systems, ACM Press, pp. 853–868 (2004)
2. Almukadi, W., Stephane, A.L.: BlackBlocks: tangible interactive system for children to learn 3-letter words and basic math. In: Proceedings of the 2015 ACM International Conference on Interactive Tabletops & Surfaces, pp. 421–424 (2015)
3. Antle, A.: Tangibles: five properties to consider for children. In: CHI 2007 Workshop on Tangibles, pp. 1–10 (2007)
4. Boy, G.A. (ed.): The Handbook of Human-Machine Interaction: A Human-Centered Design Approach. Ashgate Publishing Ltd., Farnham (2012)
5. Fails, J.A., Druin, A., Guha, M.L., Chipman, G., Simms, S., Churaman, W.: Child's play: a comparison of desktop and physical interactive environments. In: ACM Proceedings of the 2005 Conference on IDC, pp. 48–55 (2005)
6. Hanna, L., Neapolitan, D., Risden, K.: Evaluating computer game concepts with children. In: Proceeding of the 2004 Conference on IDC: Building A Community, pp. 49–56. ACM Press IDC (2004)
7. Hanna, L., Risden, K., Alexander, K.: Guidelines for usability testing with children. Interactions **4**(5), 9–14 (1997)
8. Hoysniemi, J., Hamalainen, P., Turkki, L.: Using peer tutoring in evaluating the usability of a physically interactive computer game with children. Interact. Comput. **15**(2), 203–225 (2003)
9. Inhelder, B., Piaget, J., Iverson, J.M., Goldin-Meadow, S.: The Early Growth of Logic in the Child; Gesture Paves the Way for Language Development. Norton, New York (1964)
10. Marshall, P.: Do tangible interfaces enhance learning? In: ACM Proceedings of the 1st International Conference on TEI, pp. 163–170 (2007)

11. Mazzone, E., Xu, D., Read, J.C.: Design in evaluation: reflections on designing for children's technology. In: Proceedings 21st British HCI Group Annual Conference on People and Computers: HCI But Not as We Know It, vol. 2, pp. 153–156. BCS (2007)
12. Norman, D.A.: Things That Make Us Smart: Defending Human Attributes in the Age of the Machine. Basic Books, New York (1993)
13. Read, J.C.: Validating the Fun Toolkit: an instrument for measuring children's opinions of technology. Cogn. Technol. Work **10**(2), 119–128 (2008)
14. Read, J.C., MacFarlane, S.J., Casey, C.: Endurability, engagement and expectations: measuring children's fun. In: Proceedings of the IDC, pp. 189–198. Shaker Publishing, Germany (2002)
15. Ryokai, K., Marti, S., Ishii, H.: I/O brush: drawing with everyday objects as ink. In: Proceedings of CHI 2004, pp. 303–310 (2004)
16. Sheridan, J.G., Short, B.W., Van Laerhoven, K., Villar, N., Kortuem, G.: Exploring cube affordance: towards a classification of non-verbal dynamics of physical interfaces for wearable computing. In: IET Eurowearable, 2003, pp. 113–118. IEEE (2003)
17. Sylla, C.: Designing a tangible interface for collaborative storytelling to access' embodiment and meaning making. In: Proceedings of the 12th ACM International Conference on IDC, pp. 651–654 (2013)
18. Wang, D., et al.: E-Block: a tangible programming tool for children. In: Adjunct Proceedings of the 25th Annual ACM Symposium on User Interface Software and Technology (2012)
19. Xu, D.: Design and evaluation of tangible interfaces for primary school children. In: Proceedings of the 6th ACM International Conference on IDC, pp. 209–212 (2007)
20. Zaman, B., Vanden Abeele, V., Markopoulos, P., Marshall, P.: Editorial: the evolving field of tangible interaction for children: the challenge of empirical validation. Pers. Ubiquit. Comput. **16**(4), 367–378 (2012)

Interactive Augmented Reality: A New Approach for Collaborative Learning

Poonpong Boonbrahm[✉], Charlee Kaewrat, and Salin Boonbrahm

School of Informatics, Walailak University,
Tha Sala, Nakhon Si Thammarat 80160, Thailand
poonpong@gmail.com, Charlee.qq@gmail.com,
salil.boonbrahm@gmail.com

Abstract. This study aims at using new technology, interactive augmented reality (AR), to establish collaborative learning. Interactive augmented reality means that virtual objects can be interacted and displayed in real world which made them easy to understand or easy to work with. In this paper, we have developed a system to support collaborative work in which users can be in different locations and use interactive augmented reality technology to help them doing collaborative work which in this case is completing a 3D jigsaw puzzle. For the interactive AR system, Unity 3D game engine was used on a Vuforia platform. Apples' iPads were chosen as the device to perform the task due to ease of use, good camera quality and good display for AR applications. The results show that the two users can collaborate by helping each other to get the job done in AR environment.

Keywords: Collaboration learning · Augmented reality · Interactive

1 Introduction

Collaborative learning is, by definition, a situation in which two or more people learn or work on something together [1]. Collaborative learning has a benefit in which people can share their expertise to make something faster or help others learn new things or understand more clearly about a problem or create new knowledge from sharing of their expertise. Examples of collaborative learning are group projects, joint problem solving and other activities [2]. With today technology, collaborative learning can expand beyond collaboration in classrooms to global collaboration in which two or more people can interact to make effective learning. Augmented reality technology is one of the new technologies that have been adopted for this purpose. Unlike its counterpart, virtual reality, in which students are immersed into virtual world, augmented reality generates 3D virtual objects which students can interact as in the real world, making them more interesting to learn. In collaborative augmented reality systems, users can collaborate by face-to-face, remote or a combination of both. Researches on augmented reality and their applications in the field of education have been investigated by many researchers but for collaborative learning, it is just the beginning. To make collaborative learning more interesting and useful, participants in the group should be able to interact on the same topics, or the same object. Interaction

© Springer International Publishing Switzerland 2016
P. Zaphiris and A. Ioannou (Eds.): LCT 2016, LNCS 9753, pp. 115–124, 2016.
DOI: 10.1007/978-3-319-39483-1_11

with the virtual object in augmented reality technology means people can interact, rotate or even grab the object while others can observe how that reaction affects the virtual object.

In this research, we have set up an experiment for two peoples working at different locations but in the same network to perform an AR collaborative learning. These two persons will attempt to help each other to finish the same puzzle board using their real hands in an AR environment.

2   Related Work

Research on computer supported collaborative work has been done for many years. At first, past research emphasized on communications, meeting support, and coordination and procedures [3]. Recently, due to advance in technology, especially in computer graphics, it has been possible for virtual reality (VR) and augmented reality (AR) applications to emerge and be applied to computer supported collaborative work [4]. Collaborative augmented reality can be applied in many areas ranging from education, manufacturing, health sciences, entertainment and others. Research on developing prototype of virtual and augmented reality applications in remote collaboration for process modeling has been done by Poppe et al. [5] with the aim to help increasing sense of immersion in an intuitive shared work and task space. Interaction amongst users is also a point of interest both in the situation of face-to-face and remote interaction. Billinghurst and Kato [6] have shown that using the characteristics of augmented reality such as seamless interaction between real and virtual environment, the ability to enhance reality, the presence of spatial cues for face-to-face and remote collaboration, different interfaces for face-to-face and remote collaboration were developed. In their demonstration, users could share physical workspace, create an interface for three dimensional Computer Supported Cooperative Work (CSCW). Testing for remote collaboration, AR conferencing interface were developed for this purpose. Another interesting experiment on interaction between two persons in augmented reality environment was developed by Yan et al. [7]. In this experiment, two users who were in different places played ping-pong against each other by using real paddles over the network. Studies on multiple users interacted with two and three dimensional data in augmented environment using tangible user interfaces have also been investigated [8]. Some researchers preferred to work on mobile collaborative augmented reality. For example, Reitmayr and Schmalsteig [9] built a mobile collaborative augmented reality system that supported true stereoscopic 3D graphics with user interface and direct interaction with virtual objects. Wichert [10] developed a mobile augmented reality 3D Tetris game for multiple users as an example of a collaborative augmented reality system. The game shows how to distribute the functionality in collaboration.

For specific areas of collaborative augmented reality applications, education or learning seemed to be the most popular. Kaufmann [11] gave a brief insight into the potential and challenges of using Augmented Reality in education with an example of experience gained from development of collaborative AR applications specifically designed for mathematics and geometry. Gonzales et al. [12] showed how to use mobile technology and augmented reality to enhance collaborative learning on cultural and natural heritage. The project involved forty students and four faculty members. The evaluation results have shown a high rate of success in both pedagogic and technical aspects.

Research on the interaction of users and virtual objects in augment reality environment are also important to collaborative training. There are many concept of interaction that can be used in collaborative training but the most effective one is real hand interaction. There are many techniques for tracking hands and virtual objects such as using the execution of grasp and release gestures [13]. The grasp and release gestures are recognized by estimating the positions of the user's thumb and forefinger visually. If there is a virtual object within the region between these fingers, and the surface is touching both fingers, then the object is grabbed. If the distance is far apart, the object is released. There is another method proposed by Boonbrahm et al. [14]. They used virtual fingers to grab the virtual object. In this case, distance between virtual finger and virtual objects must be calculated carefully. With this technique, grabbing the virtual object will be done naturally and can be used in collaborative work as well especially for the work that required moving virtual object from one place to another.

3 Methodology

In terms of collaborative learning, people usually prefer face-to-face interaction using conversation, gesture, gaze and non-verbal cues to communicate. However, there are many cases within real environment face-to-face interaction is not possible due to either geographical location or other factors. In this paper, we aim to prove the concept that interactive augmented reality can be used as a new way for collaborative learning. The concept is that more than two people can collaborate by interacting with the same object as long as they are in the same network, even though they are in different locations or using different tools. In our set-up experiment, there are two or more users locating at different area but in the same WiFi network, using their hands to interact with the environment in order to help each other to accomplish a common job, which in this case is completing a puzzle. In fact, the collaboration can be anything ranging from building a small toy to making a virtual house. But for demonstration purpose, we used jigsaw puzzle to prove the concept. In this setup, Unity 3D game engine was used on the Vuforia platform. Interaction with the virtual objects by hand includes touching, lifting and grabbing. Friction was applied to the surface of both virtual fingers and objects. For the devices to perform in this experiment, Apples' iPads was chosen due to its ease of use and its good camera and display quality for AR applications. There are three components that have to be accomplished in order to facilitate the experiment which include communication framework, virtual interaction and network requirement.

3.1   Framework

In this experimental set up, there are two users at different locations, connected to the same WiFi network, trying to help each other to complete the puzzle with their own hands. The proposed framework is shown in Fig. 1.

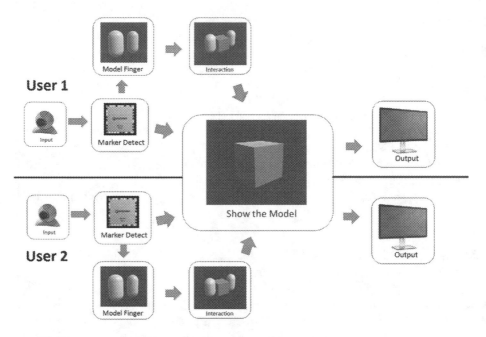

Fig. 1. Proposed framework for interactive collaborative augmented reality system

As shown in Fig. 1, there are two users collaborating to interact with the model which in this case is the puzzle. Each user has one set of markers to transform their fingers to become the virtual fingers so that they can interact with the piece of puzzle. The piece of puzzle is also a virtual object and it interacts with virtual fingers. The shared model as shown at the center of Fig. 1 represents the puzzle that is one of the four puzzle pieces as shown in Fig. 2.

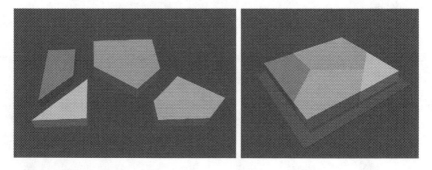

Fig. 2. Puzzle before and after completion through collaboration

Since the pieces of puzzle are shared at the center for both users to interact with, there must be some signs to tell whether that piece of the puzzle is being used by other user or not. To solve this problem, we have assigned them to change color when one user touching them or picking them up. Figure 3 demonstrates this change.

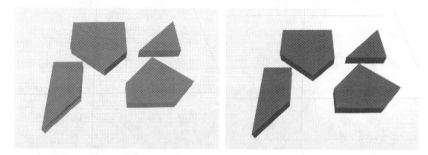

Fig. 3. Color of the puzzle changed from blue to green or red when users touch or grab the puzzle respectively (Color figure online).

Another part that needs attention is the output. In this case, output is the display that shows what happened when the interaction occurred. In order to interact from one side, users at both sides need to know what happened to the system. When one user grabs or touches the puzzle on his or her side, the user can see his or her virtual fingers touching or grabbing the puzzle as shown in Fig. 4 but the user at the other side can only see the movement of the puzzle and the change in color. This condition will make collaboration more effective because users realized what is happening.

Fig. 4. User1 can see his or her virtual fingers in the left picture while user2 knows from the change of color indicating that user1 is now touching the piece that have turned green as shown in the right picture (Color figure online).

3.2 Interaction Between Fingers and Objects

Since interaction can occur only between virtual objects, if we want to use our fingers to pick up things or grabbing something, we have to change them into virtual fingers.

In order to do that, we stick AR markers to them and change them into virtual objects. In our case, we choose cylindrical markers for this purpose. Since cylindrical marker can fit onto the fingers, so touching or picking objects up will make the participants feel like using their own fingers. Figure 5 shows the cylindrical markers and their virtual models which they appear just like real fingers.

Fig. 5. Cylindrical markers and virtual models

To make virtual fingers to be able to grab the virtual object, some physical properties such as surface, volume, density, friction and collision detection properties for rigid body have to be applied to them. With this setup, the virtual finger will have better grab due to the properties of the surface.

3.3 Network

As mentioned before, interactive augmented reality for collaborative system will work best if they are in the same network. This network can be either WiFi or Bluetooth. If the location of each user is not far apart, Bluetooth will work fine but if it is not, we need to use WiFi network. For this experiment, the regular household Wi-Fi with a bandwidth of 8 Mbps was used. We can setup the network in two ways depends on resources and stability of the system. The first setup used only mobile devices as a host and client. Figure 6 shows how the network operates. If one device is assigned as a host, it will create a virtual object to be used in operation which in this study, is the puzzle. In the case that another user joins the network as client, the host will clone its virtual object to be used by the client device. This cloning object will behave just like the parent object, except that it will only be seen by the client.

In case that the system needs to be more stable, the second way to setup is to use a powerful desktop computer attached to the LAN implemented as a host and the joining mobiles using WiFi as clients. Figure 7 shows how to setup such network. In this case, the virtual object which is the puzzle system will be created only once and both users can share this object.

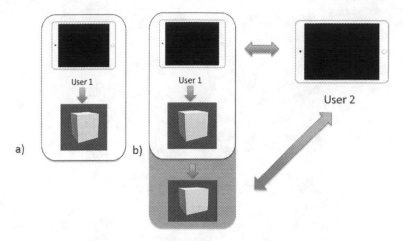

Fig. 6. Network setup for mobile-mobile collaboration

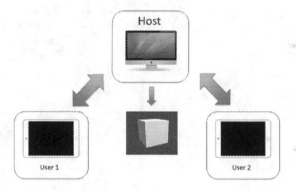

Fig. 7. Network setup using desktop computer as a host for mobile-mobile collaboration

4 Experimental Setup

After setting up all the requirements for testing the concept of using interactive augmented reality in collaborative learning, we have started the experiment by having two users using iPads (as host and client) with augmented reality software installed. The users were asked to help each other to put the puzzle pieces together by using their hands under augmented reality environment. Since we have applied all the physical properties to both fingers and objects, all the parts behave like the real puzzle, so when it touches each other, it slipped. To avoid that, we have to add one piece of virtual model performed as a frame to keep the puzzle within the range as shown in Fig. 8.

Figures 9, 10 and 11 show how the two users performed and what they saw on their display screens.

Fig. 8. Puzzle sheet with frame

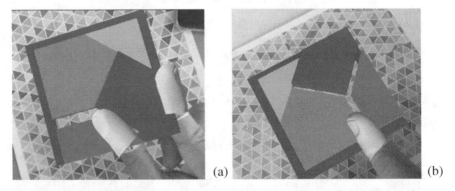

(a)   (b)

Fig. 9. Activity of user1 (a) grabbing a piece of puzzle and user2 (b) touching one puzzle piece (Color figure online)

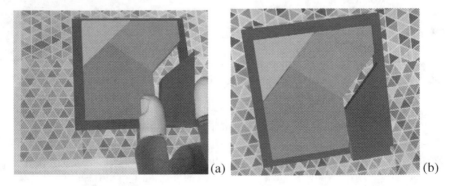

(a)   (b)

Fig. 10. Activity performed by user1 (a) and user2 (b)

When user1 grabs one piece of the puzzle, that piece changes color from blue to red as shown in Fig. 9(a) while user2 touches the other piece and that piece becomes green see Fig. 9(b). Since user on one side cannot see the finger of user on the other side, color will be used to tell whether it was grabbed or touched by the other user. Figure 10 shows the activity that happened by two users, but this time the second user did not interact with the puzzle.

After collaborate in finishing the puzzle, both display will be the same but may be in different viewpoint as seen in Fig. 11.

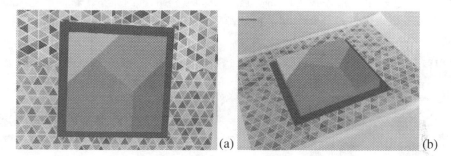
(a)   (b)

Fig. 11. Finishing job as seen by user1 (a) and user2 (b)

5 Results and Discussion

From the experiment, we can see that two users can collaborate in helping each other to complete a job without interacting on the same virtual object at the same time. The only thing that we found which have caused some issues is the stability of the network and the compatible of the devices. In case that one device is more powerful than the other, the movement of the 3D objects on the powerful one will be faster making real time collaboration not possible. The bandwidth of the WiFi is another issue. From our experiment, the suitable bandwidth should be at least 8 Mbps. This concept can be applied to other kind of teaching and learning such as in project based learning, active learning and etc. Besides that, since augmented reality is the technology that deals with virtual object, so all topics related to some kinds of interaction between objects can be simulated for easy understanding. For example, it can be applied in chemistry, physics and biology. With new way of learning like flipped class room in which collaboration amongst students and students with teacher is necessary, collaborative augmented reality seems to fit in nicely as well. Beside teaching and training, some kinds of work that need collaboration such as manufacturing, architecture and business could exploit this opportunity.

6 Conclusions

With the advance in technology like augmented reality in which virtual objects can be visualize in real world along with new user interface and ability of the users to interact with the virtual objects, it is possible to create a new way of learning. This new way of learning not only saves time and budgets for learning new things or to understand difficult topics, but it also creates a sense of working as a team. Groups of student or workers can share their expertise and to create new knowledge with this new way of learning.

Acknowledgements. This research is partially supported by the grant from Institute of Research and Development (under the contract WU57606), Walailak University, Thailand.

References

1. https://en.wikipedia.org/wiki/Collaborative_learning
2. Cerbin, B.: Collaborative Learning Techniques Workshop, Center for Advancing Teaching and Learning, UW-La Crosse (2010)
3. Eseryel, D., Ganesan, R., Edmons, G.S.: Review of computer-supported collaborative work systems. Educ. Technol. Soc. **5**(2), 130–136 (2001)
4. Billinghurst, M., Weghorst, S., Furness III, T.: Shared space: an augmented reality approach for computer supported collaborative work. Virtual Reality **3**, 25–36 (1998)
5. Poppe, E., Brown, R., Johnson, D., Recker, J.: A prototype augmented reality collaborative process modelling tool. In: 9th International Conference on Business Process Management, Clemont-Ferrand, France, pp. 1–5 (2011)
6. Billinghurst, M., Kato, H.: Collaborative augmented reality. CACM-CollabAR **45**(7), 64–70 (2002). ACM Digital Library
7. Yan, Y., Chen, X., Li, X.: Collaborative augmented reality ping-pong via markerless real rackets. In: 2011 International Conference on Virtual Reality and Visualization, pp. 136–143 (2011)
8. Regenbrecht, H.T., Wagner, M.T.: Interaction in a collaborative augmented reality environment. In: CHI 2002: Changing the World, Changing Ourselves, pp. 504–505 (2002)
9. Reitmayr, M., Schmalsteig, D.: Mobile collaborative augmented reality. In: ISAR 2001, NewYork, USA (2001)
10. Wichert, R.: Collaborative gaming in a mobile augmented reality environment. In: The Ibero-American Symposium in Computer Graphics 2002, pp. 31–37 (2002)
11. Kaufmann, H.: Collaborative augmented reality in education. In: Imagina Conference 2003, Monaco-Mediax, Monaco (2003)
12. Gonzales, F., Villareejo, L., Miralbell, O., Gomis, J.M.: How to use mobile technology and augmented reality to enhance collaborative learning on cultural and natural heritage? An e-learning experience. Mediterr. J. Educ. Res. **14a**, 497–502 (2013)
13. Figueiredo, L., Anjos, R.D., Lindoso, J., Neto, E., Roberto, R., Silva, M., Teichrieb, V.: Bare hand natural interaction with augmented objects. In: Extended Abstracts of the IEEE International Symposium on Mixed and Augmented Reality 2013, Adelaide, SA, Australia (2013)
14. Boonbrahm, P., Kaewrat, C.: Assembly of the virtual model with real hands using augmented reality technology. In: Shumaker, R., Lackey, S. (eds.) VAMR 2014, Part I. LNCS, vol. 8525, pp. 329–338. Springer, Heidelberg (2014)

Software Architectures Supporting Human-Computer Interaction Analysis: A Literature Review

Juan Cruz-Benito[(⊠)], Roberto Therón,
and Francisco J. García-Peñalvo

Department of Computers and Automatics, GRIAL Research Group,
University of Salamanca, Salamanca, Spain
{juancb, theron, fgarcia}@usal.es

Abstract. This paper presents a Literature Review on software architectures that support Human-Computer Interaction analysis processes. Despite of software architectures and Human-Computer interaction are not new research fields; there are not much scientific papers that cover the relation of both (at least in the Web of Science and Scopus databases used). The Literature Review presented covers the relationship between both fields, conducting the research using 3 questions proposed by the authors in order to discover the current state of art of this software architectures that supports HCI, to research about the different trends in the field of software engineering that help in the design, definition and exploitation of them and to find out if there is in the literature an application to the field of eLearning of these software complex systems that deal with HCI analysis. Regarding the results of the Literature Review, authors pre-sent a classification of the papers reviewed by 24 common features discovered, helping the readers and others researchers to know how these software architectures work with different kind of HCI analysis approaches, how are designed, what are the goals of applying this kind of system for the analysis, or what are the application contexts.

Keywords: Human-computer interaction · HCI · Software architectures · Analysis · Literature review · eLearning

1 Introduction

The systems that retrieve and analyze information from the users' interaction with software systems are currently a trend topic. Human-Computer Interaction is a research area in continuous development [1], and increasingly important in the current times regarding the arising of topics like Big Data, User Experience (UX), etc. and the strong scope that puts the Business world in the monetization of online systems through improving the HCI related areas and by the creation of a data-driven culture [2, 3] that enables decision-making processes were the users' interaction is the key point and the users are the main actor [4].

Within the development of the HCI there are many areas involved where researchers could collaborate. Besides those mentioned previously (Big Data, UX, etc.) many

© Springer International Publishing Switzerland 2016
P. Zaphiris and A. Ioannou (Eds.): LCT 2016, LNCS 9753, pp. 125–136, 2016.
DOI: 10.1007/978-3-319-39483-1_12

authors have proposed complex software systems and software architectures that feature the work with data related to users' interaction [5–8]. The application of these works on complex systems and software architectures enables the current advances on different areas like, for example, measuring UX metrics [9], performing data analytics (distributing computation, creating complex data pipelines between different systems, etc.), enabling decision making supported by data visualizations and visual analytics [10, 11], Internet of Things (IoT) processes where users are involved directly [7], Learning and Learning Analytics [12–17], sales revenue measuring across different platforms, data-driven marketing using several third-party applications [18], etc. Some of these solutions are intended to interconnect in a better way different existing services and systems in order to enable new ways of collaboration between platforms and software systems [19], empowering sets of applications with a common goal or developing smooth processes in work related with data.

The aim of this paper is to present a Literature Review (LR) on software architectures that support the Human-Computer Interaction (HCI) analysis, emphasizing on discovering how these software architectures work with different kind of HCI analysis approaches (devices and environments where the interaction analysis is performed, etc.), how are designed (using software engineering) and to find out if there is a niche in the reviewed literature related to the application of software architectures that support HCI analysis regarding to eLearning environments.

The following sections Theoretical Background, Literature Review and Conclusions present different relevant aspects about the fundamental theoretical background needed to understand the key points of the software architectures and Human-Computer Interaction fields used in this paper, present the literature review performed (methodology, results, etc.) and some conclusions about the knowledge retrieved from this LR.

2   Theoretical Background

The Software Architectures are not a new thing in Computer Sciences. From the 90's the work and research about this topic has been a constant, due the need of adapting the concepts, design and foundations to the new challenges that appear continuously with the new trends in Computer Sciences, the new frameworks, the new needs, etc. But, even assuming that the concept is not new, what is a Software Architecture? How can be defined a Software Architecture?

Regarding the literature, there are many authors that have defined and worked about this concept, but can be remarked the definitions provided by Kruchten [20] and by Bass et al. [21]: according to Kruchten, a Software Architecture is "[…] the set of significant decisions about the organization of a software system, the selection of the structural elements and their interfaces by which the system is composed, together with their behavior as specified in the collaborations among those elements, the composition of these structural and behavioral elements into progressively larger subsystems, and the architectural style that guides this organization -these elements and their interfaces, their collaborations, and their composition" [20]. On the other hand, Bass et al. provide another simpler definition, where they compress the concept to: "The Software Architecture of a system is the set of structures needed to reason about the system, which comprise the software elements, relations among them, and properties of both" [21].

On the other hand, the Human-Computer Interaction is a process of information transfer between both entities, or in other way, and according to Dix [22] "the Human-Computer Interaction is the study of the way in which computer technology influences human work and activities". The analysis of how occurs this interaction, give actionable insights to designers and creators of technology about how people utilize and understand the technology, and obviously, give them keys on how improve this relation. According to Dix [22], the foundations of the HCI field are the *Usability, Observation and Empirical Data, Design and Methodology, Representation and Analysis* and *Implementation and User Interface Architecture.* In this paper, the foundations of HCI most relevant are the *usability, the observation and empirical data* and the *representation and analysis,* because those concepts are the more widely used in the content retrieved within the LR scope. Following are commented:

- Usability is "the extent to which a product can be used by specified users to achieve specified goals with effectiveness, efficiency and satisfaction in a specified context of use" (ISO 9241–11). The concept is applied from the lowest level the visual layout -the information and controls displayed on a screen and the user immediate behavior- to the higher level that includes social and organizational contexts – people who uses the system, their beliefs and values, and the purpose and constraints of the design-.
- Observation and Empirical Data where can be featured the main the methods to evaluate and observe the HCI, the *laboratory experiments* and *field studies.* The *laboratory experiments* are where users perform a task or interact under controlled conditions, and the *field studies* are those performed where users are use technology without controlled conditions (in the workplace, outside, in their homes, etc.) [22].

3   Literature Review

As previously presented, the aim of this Literature Review is to find out how software architectures support the HCI analysis processes, with special attention on the different approaches followed in HCI analysis, how are designed the software architectures and to discover if there is a relationship in the literature with the HCI analysis and eLearning fields (through the application of these software architectures). Following these goals, the LR was conducted by the following questions:

Question 1: What is the current state of the art of software architectures in the field of HCI analysis?

Question 2: Are there trends or mechanisms in software engineering that cover the field of software architectures supporting HCI analysis?

Question 3: Are there a specific trend in the software architectures designed to support HCI analysis related specifically to its application in eLearning?

3.1   Methodology

The literature review presented in this paper is part of a wider literature review centered in the research areas of software architectures. For that reason, authors present in this paper a literature review only of scientific works indexed in the Web of Science and Scopus databases, ensuring that the papers, books and book chapters reviewed are relevant and represent high quality content.

The search was not restricted by time periods, and terms used to perform the literature review were the following:

- In the Web of Science: *TS = ("software architecture" AND (HCI OR "Human-Computer Interaction") AND analy*)*
- In Scopus: *TITLE-ABS-KEY ("software architecture" AND (HCI OR "Human-Computer Interaction") AND analysis)*

The results retrieved from these query terms were 8 documents in the Web of Science and other 55 in the Scopus database, as shows the Fig. 1. These 63 (55 in fact, due 8 documents are coincident in both databases) results were reviewed initially by reading their abstract, and later by reading the full paper; evaluating by this way if the content fitted in the questions posed and building the classification shown in the Table 1 and in the Subsect. 3.3. The spreadsheet available in https://goo.gl/Mq0nmd resumes the filtering done, exposing how were selected or rejected the papers retrieved from the databases regarding to their title, abstract or full text.

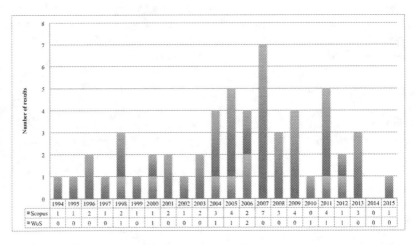

	1994	1995	1996	1997	1998	1999	2000	2001	2002	2003	2004	2005	2006	2007	2008	2009	2010	2011	2012	2013	2014	2015
Scopus	1	1	2	1	2	1	1	2	1	2	3	4	2	7	3	4	0	4	1	3	0	1
WoS	0	0	0	0	1	0	1	0	0	0	1	1	2	0	0	0	1	1	1	0	0	0

Fig. 1. Results of the query - distribution over the time (results excluding coincidences among both databases).

3.2   Results

After the selection of the papers regarding their titles, abstracts or full text, 16 papers [23–38] result to be the most relevant for the defined Literature Review purposes.

These papers selected papers were published among 1998–2013 (https://goo.gl/Mq0nmd). As follows, the papers analyzed were categorized depending on what questions answer each one.

Q1: What is the current state of the art of software architectures in the field of HCI analysis?

Regarding this question, all the papers [23–38] fulfilled a minimal answer, because each one of them provides its point of view of the current state of the art. For example, many of them provide application approaches, explaining the devices and physical contexts that could appear in the HCI analysis, among the different devices and contexts, appear in the review the personal computers, wearables, mobile/smartphones, servers, domotics or robots. On the other hand, there papers that focus its content to certain aspects related to software architectures and HCI analysis process. For example, there are some papers retrieved that feature the contents on the Software Engineering contents related to this kind of software (as explained in the following question), or in the HCI aspects.

Regarding the HCI aspects and the context application of the analysis, there is a broad range: there are papers that present contents on HCI analysis regarding astronauts training (Mackin et al. [23]), in humanoid robots that analyze HCI and react to users and environment (Kato *et al.* [33]; Fujita *et al.* [34]), in HCI analysis observing the body and physical reactions of users and not only analyzing the behavior in front the software (Sulzmann et al. [29]; Ardizzone et al. [36]), in HCI related to hardware (Mackin et al. [23]; Biel et al. [25]; Sulzmann et al. [29]; Doswell [32]; Kato *et al.* [33]; Fujita *et al.* [34]; Ardizzone et al. [36]) or software elements (Eelke and Jan [24]; Grill and Gruhn [25]; Folmer et al. [26]; Pinheiro et al. [27]; Bouchrika *et al.* [28]; Juárez-Ramírez *et al.* [30]; Ko *et al.* [31]; Doswell [32]; John and Bass [35]; Gundy, et al. [37]; and Bass and John [38]), etc. Also there is a trend among the results in software architectures that support HCI analysis to improve the *usability* of the software/hardware systems; some papers that cover directly this issue are: Eelke and Jan [24]; Biel et al. [25]; Juárez-Ramírez *et al.* [30]; or Bass and John [38].

In general the results retrieved provide good insights about the current state of the art in this topic, representing varied application context, approaches, methodologies, and well-balanced distribution of theoretical-practical contents.

Q2: Are there trends or mechanisms in software engineering that cover the field of software architectures supporting HCI analysis?

The papers that answer in any way this question were [24–28, 30, 32, 35]. The common issues that cover these papers more related to the software engineering are related to software patterns to model properly the behavior and functionality of the software components (Eelke and Jan [24]; Biel et al. [25]; Folmer et al. [26]; Pinheiro et al. [27]; Bouchrika *et al.* [28]; Juárez-Ramírez *et al.* [30]; Doswell [32]; and John and Bass [35]), the correct description of the software architecture system through using UML (Unified Modeling Language) or ADL (Architecture Description Language) [24–28, 30, 32, 35]. Also there are references to some trends in software engineering and related areas that can be relevant for the topic apart of those previously described, like the requirements engineering, or even in other papers not selected finally for the final Literature Review, topics like information fusion, visualization of HCI interaction, etc.

Singularly in those paper more focused on software engineering, there is a lack of description about how these components that collaborate to achieve the common goal of the software architecture communicate between them: there are only 3 papers that explain it (Mackin et al. [23]; Bouchrika *et al.* [28]; and Sulzmann et al. [29]). Also authors find lacks in descripting the technologies used in those papers that present practical test of the architectures, as well as a serious lack describing or using standards in the software architectures description or designing.

Q3: Are there a specific trend in the software architectures designed to support HCI analysis related specifically to its application in eLearning?

The unique paper resultant of the search performed in the Literature Review scope that answer this question (at least in a partial way) was the paper [32] written by Doswell. In this paper, Doswell present a software architecture that includes commu-nication with wearable and mobile devices in order to measure the HCI regarding to eLearning processes and how it could be used in the future to find out engagement, etc. However, the paper do not deepen in features like standards (in any aspect) or in formal specifications. There is another paper [33], written by Kato *et al.*, that points out implicitly a possible use of humanoid robots in physical learning processes, but only as an possibility of use, with no concretion.

Despite of that, authors consider that there are many key points, features and approaches presented in the papers that could serve to develop software architectures that help learning processes through the analysis of HCI in the context of students' interaction with eLearning systems and contents.

3.3 Analysis and Discussion

In order to summarize the main features retrieved from the software architecture, HCI analysis processes and eLearning properties of each paper retrieved during the Liter-ature Review, authors have built a category classification (presented in Table 1 or available online in https://goo.gl/3TJvbY) with the common properties observed (24):

1. Physical context /devices (included in the analysis)
   (a) Personal computers
   (b) Wearables
   (c) Mobile/smartphones
   (d) Servers
   (e) Domotics
   (f) Robots
2. Software Engineering specifications
   (g) Components' communication: details on how the software architecture com-ponents communicate among them, etc. (strategies, format, standards).
   (h) Information collectors: details on how the system collects the information about HCI processes.

Table 1 Classification of the LR regarding the main common features observed. E – explicit feature, I – implicit feature, U – unavailable feature. Available also in https://goo.gl/3TJvbY

    (i)   Architecture diagrams (ADL, UML, etc.)
    (j)   Design details (patterns, use cases, etc.)
    (k) Technologies, languages: description about the software/hardware properties, the technologies, frameworks or languages used.
    (l)   Standards: is the architecture presented based on standards?
3. Human-Computer Interaction specifications
    (m) Measurement process description
    (n) React to users' interaction: is the HCI analysis intended to allow the software architecture reacts to the interaction?
    (o) Centered on usability: is the HCI analysis presented centered mainly on usability?
    (p) HCI – software elements: is the HCI analysis based on interaction with software elements?
    (q) HCI – hardware elements: is the HCI analysis based on interaction with hardware elements?
    (r) Laboratory experiments: is the HCI analysis performed in a laboratory experiment?
    (s) Field study: is the HCI analysis performed in a field study?
    (t) Standards: uses standards in the HCI analysis?
4. Learning
    (u) Purpose of analysis: the paper describes the learning purpose/goals/intentions of the HCI analysis?
    (v) Standards: are involved eLearning standards in HCI analysis or in the software architecture?
    (w) Potential users: it describes the potential users/beneficiaries of the HCI analysis related to eLearning?
    (x) Mobile learning: is the eLearning application of the HCI analysis related to mobile learning?

In the Table 1 can be observed how each of the items and categories described is included or not in the content: E (explicit) the item is mentioned or commented explicitly in the document, I (implicit) the item is implicit in the contents analyzed, U (unavailable) the item is not mentioned in any way.

Regarding the Table 1 and the results presented before, it is clear that the software architectures that support HCI analysis is not the most popular subject in the Web of Science and Scopus databases, i.e. the same search terms without "analysis" provides 38 results in the Web of Science instead of 8. Although could be possible that the term "analysis" restrict so much the search, and trying with other search terms related to the same topics could lead researchers to get better outcomes.

Despite of the number of papers that fit outstandingly the goal planned for this Literature Review, is clear that the software architectures can have a determinant role in HCI analysis processes, due their design can improve significantly the measurement, analysis and feedback of the interaction. Also is clear, that many approaches presented in the papers reviewed suffer a lack of rigor regarding standards, proper specifications of goals, designs and methodologies, as well as not much of them present real cases tested with real users in real contexts.

Regarding the results, also is significant that only one paper focuses its research on software architectures and HCI analysis on the application of these approaches to the eLearning field; authors agree on this kind of software systems can help to develop new complex systems that comprise several applications and systems (conforming true learning ecosystems) where different applications, systems, devices and methods benefit learners by working together in a proper way to help and improve the learning process.

Despite of these considerations, can be a real opportunity of improvement, authors believe that could exist a niche in publications regarding to software architectures, HCI processes analysis (and, of course, its application to eLearning processes); today, the research on software architectures, decentralized or complex systems and ecosystems represent the future in several fields, where there is a need of tools, systems and applications working together to achieve more complex goals than current ones.

4 Conclusions

This paper presents a Literature Review on software architectures that support Human-Computer Interaction analysis. In the final phase of the LR have been fully reviewed 15 software architectures proposals, analyzing if them answer one of the 3 research questions proposed (What is the current state of the art of software architectures in the field of HCI analysis?; Are there trends or mechanisms in software engineering that cover the field of software architectures supporting HCI analysis?; Are there a specific trend in the software architectures designed to support HCI analysis related specifically to its application in eLearning?) and classifying them according to 24 features proposed by the authors due their common use in this research area and topics. Regarding the results of the LR, there are some key points that can be featured:

- According to the results retrieved from the search in the Web of Science and Scopus database, there are not a lot of content related to the subject of this paper, or at least, not categorized in the same way paper does. This could represent an opportunity in publishing in this research area.
- Authors consider that could be a niche for publication is in the context of software architecture and HCI analysis and its application in eLearning contexts; only one paper deals with this issue of those retrieved. Despite this low number, has been observed that many of the software architectures and approaches reviewed have principles that could be applied to improve eLearning.
- There are some trends in software engineering proper for this kind of software architectures, but they are not massively used in the papers reviewed. Authors remarked lacks on the papers about specific content on standards, communication protocols and strategies among software components, or in describing the specific technologies and technical details of those architectures presented that have been tested in real experiments. These considerations also could be applied to the HCI topics presented in the papers, authors find out that there is not enough content on how the experiments were conducted, what standards were followed, etc. and there are many issues and approaches that can be improved in further research.

Authors assume that in some cases the research that cover all of these areas are an unexplored territory, and there are some papers that begin to cover them, but there is an opportunity for further research that could lead to improve the future complex systems, ecosystems and sets of varied applications that work for common goals.

Acknowledgments. The author Juan Cruz-Benito would like to thanks the European Social Fund and the *Consejería de Educación of the Junta de Castilla y León* (Spain) for funding his predoctoral fellow contract.

References

1. Agah, A.: Human interactions with intelligent systems: research taxonomy. Comput. Electr. Eng. **27**, 71–107 (2000)
2. Patil, D.J.: Data Jujitsu: The Art of Turning Data into Product. O'Reilly, Sebastopol (2014)
3. Patil, D.J., Mason, H.: Data Driven. Creating a Data Culture. O'Reilly, Sebastopol (2014)
4. Ball, P.: Why Society is a Complex Matter: Meeting Twenty-First Century Challenges With a New Kind of Science. Springer Science & Business Media, Berlin (2012)
5. Brown, J., Marshall, S.: Sharing human-computer interaction and software engineering design artifacts. In: Proceedings of 1998 Australasian Computer Human Interaction Conference 1998, pp. 53–60. IEEE (1998)
6. Shen, J., Pantic, M.: A software framework for multimodal humancomputer interaction systems. In: IEEE International Conference on Systems, Man and Cybernetics, 2009. SMC 2009 , pp. 2038–2045. IEEE (2009)
7. Wu, C.-L., Fu, L.-C.: Design and realization of a framework for human–system interaction in smart homes. IEEE Trans. Syst. Man Cybern. Part A: Syst. Hum., **42**, 15–31 (2012)
8. Cockburn, A.: The interaction of social issues and software architecture. Commun. ACM **39**, 40–46 (1996)
9. Albert, W., Tullis, T.: Measuring the User Experience: Collecting, Analyzing, and Presenting Usability Metrics. Newnes, Australia (2013)
10. Heer, J., Agrawala, M.: Software design patterns for information visualization. IEEE Trans. Vis. Comput. Graphics **12**, 853–860 (2006)
11. Keim, D.A.: Information visualization and visual data mining. IEEE Trans. Vis. Comput. Graphics **8**, 1–8 (2002)
12. Cruz-Benito, J., Maderuelo, C., García-Peñalvo, F.J., Therón, R., Pérez-Blanco, J.S., Zazo, H., Martín-Suárez, A.: Usalpharma: a software architecture to support learning in virtual worlds. IEEE Revista Iberoamericana de Tecnologias del Aprendizaje (2016, in press)
13. Cruz-Benito, J., Therón, R., García-Peñalvo, F.J., Pizarro Lucas, E.: Discovering usage behaviors and engagement in an educational virtual world. Comput. Hum. Behav. **47**, 18–25 (2015)
14. García-Peñalvo, F.J., Cruz-Benito, J., Maderuelo, C., Pérez-Blanco, J.S., Martín-Suárez, A.: Usalpharma: a cloud-based architecture to support quality assurance training processes in health area using virtual worlds. Sci. World J. **2014**, 1–10 (2014)
15. Gómez Aguila, D.A., García-Peñalvo, F.J., Therón, R.: Analítica visual en elearning. El Profesional de la Información **23**, 233–242 (2014)
16. Fidalgo-Blanco, Á., Sein-Echaluce, M.L., García-Peñalvo, F.J., Conde, M.Á.: Using learning analytics to improve teamwork assessment. Comput. Hum. Behav. **47**, 149–156 (2015)

17. Gómez-Aguilar, D.A., Hernández-García, Á., García-Peñalvo, F.J., Therón, R.: Tap into visual analysis of customization of grouping of activities in eLearning. Comput. Hum. Behav. **47**, 60–67 (2015)

18. Kumar, V., Chattaraman, V., Neghina, C., Skiera, B., Aksoy, L., Buoye, A., Henseler, J.: Data-driven services marketing in a connected world. J. Serv. Manag. **24**, 330–352 (2013)

19. Alier, M.F., Guerrero, M.J.C., Gonzalez, M.A.C., Penalvo, F.J.G., Severance, C.: Interoperability for LMS: the missing piece to become the common place for e-learning innovation. Int. J. Knowl. Learn. **6**, 130–141 (2010)

20. Kruchten, P.: The Rational Unified Process. Addison-Wesley, Boston (1998)

21. Bass, L., Clements, P., Kazman, R.: Software Architecture in Practice. Addison-Wesley Professional, Boston (2012)

22. Dix, A.: Human-computer interaction. In: Liu, L., Özsu, M.T. (eds.) Encyclopedia of Database Systems, pp. 1327–1331. Springer, Boston (2009)

23. Mackin, M.A., Gonia, P.T., Lombay-Gonzalez, J.A.: An information system prototype for analysis of astronaut/computer interaction during simulated EVA. In: Aerospace Conference, 2012 IEEE, pp. 1–8 (2012)

24. Eelke, F., Jan, B.: Experiences with software architecture analysis of usability. Int. J. Inf. Technol. Web Eng. (IJITWE) **3**, 1–29 (2008)

25. Biel, B., Grill, T., Gruhn, V.: Exploring the benefits of the combination of a software architecture analysis and a usability evaluation of a mobile application. J. Syst. Softw. **83**, 2031–2044 (2010)

26. Folmer, E.: Welie, M.v., Bosch, J.: Bridging patterns: an approach to bridge gaps between SE and HCI. Inf. Softw. Technol. **48**, 69–89 (2006)

27. Pinheiro, V., Furtado, E., Furtado, V.: A unified architecture to develop interactive knowledge based systems. In: Bazzan, A.L., Labidi, S. (eds.) SBIA 2004. LNCS (LNAI), vol. 3171, pp. 174–183. Springer, Heidelberg (2004)

28. Bouchrika, I., Ait-Oubelli, L., Rabir, A., Harrathi, N.: Mockup-based navigational diagram for the development of interactive web applications. In: Proceedings of the 2013 International Conference on Information Systems and Design of Communication, pp. 27–32. ACM, Lisboa, Portugal (2013)

29. Sulzmann, F., Blach, R., Dangelmaier, M.: An integration framework for motion and visually impaired virtual humans in interactive immersive environments. In: Stephanidis, C., Antona, M. (eds.) UAHCI 2013. LNCS, vol. 8011, pp. 107–115. Springer, Heidelberg (2013)

30. Juárez-Ramírez, R., Gómez-Ruelas, M., A. Gutiérrez, A., Negrete, P.: Towards improving user interfaces: a proposal for integrating functionality and usability since early phases. In: 2011 International Conference on Uncertainty Reasoning and Knowledge Engineering (URKE), pp. 119–123 (2011)

31. Ko, A.J., Lee, M.J., Ferrari, V., Ip, S., Tran, C.: A case study of post-deployment user feedback triage. In: Proceedings of the 4th International Workshop on Cooperative and Human Aspects of Software Engineering, pp. 1–8. ACM, Waikiki, Honolulu, HI, USA (2011)

32. Doswell, J.T.: Context-aware mobile augmented reality architecture for lifelong learning. In: 2006 Sixth International Conference on Advanced Learning Technologies, pp. 372–374 (2006)

33. Kato, S., Ohshiro, S., Itoh, H., Kimura, K.: Development of a communication robot Ifbot. In: Proceedings of 2004 IEEE International Conference on Robotics and Automation, ICRA 2004, vol. 691, pp. 697–702 (2004)

34. Fujita, M., Kuroki, Y., Ishida, T., Doi, T.T.: Autonomous behavior control architecture of entertainment humanoid robot SDR-4X. In: Proceedings of 2003 IEEE/RSJ International Conference on Intelligent Robots and Systems (IROS 2003), vol 961, pp. 960–967 (2003)
35. John, B.E., Bass, L.: Usability and software architecture. Behav. Inf. Technol. **20**, 329–338 (2001)
36. Ardizzone, E., Chella, A., Pirrone, R.: An architecture for automatic gesture analysis. In: Proceedings of the Working Conference on Advanced Visual Interfaces, pp. 205–210. ACM, Palermo, Italy (2000)
37. Grundy, J., Hosking, J., Mugridge, W.B.: Inconsistency management for multiple-view software development environments. IEEE Trans. Softw. Eng. **24**, 960–981 (1998)
38. Bass, L., John, B.E.: Linking usability to software architecture patterns through general scenarios. J. Syst. Softw. **66**, 187–197 (2003)

Development of Virtual Reality (VR) as an Affordable Learning Method with Species of Nature

O.L.F. Gil[(✉)] and V.J. Cardozo[(✉)]

Universidad Nacional de Colombia, Palmira, Colombia
{lfgilo, jjcardozov}@unal.edu.co

Abstract. Virtual reality (VR) has been implemented in developed countries to facilitate visual, experimental, and sensory communication; in this project a test was performed to evaluate the interaction, acceptance and experience of users with the VR as a tool for learning in Colombia by building a lower cost simulator VR affordable to the community which enables teachers, students or any user interested in environmental issues to interact with 4D models and experience physical and psychological immersion in natural environments. The methods used for data collection were the survey and the panel of users, yielding data supportive to the conclusion that this technology can be replicated in the region to improve the quality of learning adapted to local conditions, which strengthens the knowledge of fauna and flora of Colombia.

Keywords: Virtual reality · Experience design · Interaction · Learning methods · Sensory experience · Industrial design · Affordable costs

1 Introduction

Virtual reality (VR) is defined as the representation of an environment or space by capturing high-definition video and 3D modeling, described by its ability to provide physical and psychological immersion (Gutierrez 2002); the concept of "immersion" refers to the degree to which a user is isolated from the real world and is transported to a situation or environment, in order to exert influence on his feelings and sensations. A research concerning the issue of VR is the study by Reilly (1991), in which the potential of this technology applied to archeology is extolled, by enhancing factors such as interactivity, visualization and realism transmitted to observers immersed then, in a multi-sensory experience to enjoy the works of art and archaeological finds. This project intended to explore possibilities of wide implementation of the method for learning purposes in Colombia.

2 Hypothesis

Virtual reality generating a multi-sensory experience by virtual immersion can be implemented at affordable costs as a learning tool in developing countries.

© Springer International Publishing Switzerland 2016
P. Zaphiris and A. Ioannou (Eds.): LCT 2016, LNCS 9753, pp. 137–144, 2016.
DOI: 10.1007/978-3-319-39483-1_13

3   Methodology

The methodology used in this research is explorative, with phases of design and construction, data collection and analysis of results, keeping in mind the needs of a developing country with the requirement of accessibility and affordability of technology. A method to evaluate the VR system was developed starting from the study of the methods of usability and user-centered design, with a cycle of interaction between the simulator, the stimuli generated for user experimentation, feedback and developed experiences that the learning of a topic contribute, which resulted in the user's physical and psychological immersion in a virtual environment (Fig. 1).

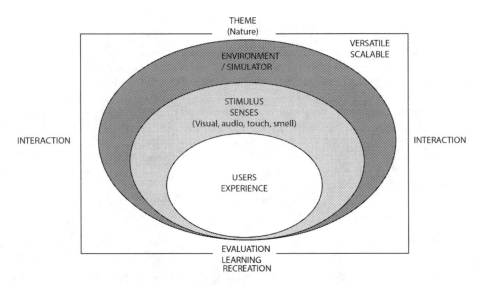

Fig. 1. Methodology interaction (VR). Immersive environment to evaluete the user experience.

In this project, a test was conducted in the department of Valle del Cauca, south-west Colombia, where an experience on the topic: Birds and their habitat, is implemented due to the high diversity of species found in this area of the country since according to Echeverry-Galvis (2013), more than 817 species are identified here; this richness of information can generate the user interaction with technology and nature. The project was developed in 6 phases: data collection in actual environment, design and construction of prototype, preliminary test, an interaction test measured by survey and panel of users, analysis of results and conclusions. In the first phase the data of nature were collected and an immersion took place in the wooded area of the hamlet Chicoral of the township Dapa in the Valle del Cauca, Colombia, the photographic and video recording was made through the capture of high definition images of the area to be simulated, observing the characteristics of the space in terms of scents, sounds more frequently sensed, and most constant climate temperature; the information obtained was edited and suited to be projected in the simulator, which was built with easy access resources in the region and at lowest cost to existing solutions in the market. The instruments used for data collection are a survey to thirty persons designed with 5 questions in Likert scale 1–5, through which experience, learning species and acceptance of the technology is measured, and the method of panel of users carried out with 9 persons to debate on usability, interaction and experience in the acceptance of VR as a learning tool. The tests were conducted in the Laboratory of Human Factors of the National University of Colombia in Palmira and included the voluntary participation of students and professors.

4 Preliminary Analysis

A collection of preliminary information was obtained. This information was edited and adapted to improve communication between user and VR simulator, evaluating comfort, ease of use and affordability through the method of collecting survey data.

In the design of the simulator, this project studied works by Ju-Ling Shih et al. (2014) and Okita et al. (2013), which enabled the identification of the main elements of these experiences. To construct the first simulator 1.0 various materials that generate stimuli on the senses and easily accessible were evaluated by performing an initial test designed for the interaction of a person with the system. The simulator 1.0 is built in PVC coated in black satin fabric, its measures are 1 m wide and 2 m high to accommodate a person in bipedal position; the structure can be assembled and disassembled in an estimated span of 15 min and the technologies used to stimulate the senses are affordable for the Colombian context: For visual transmission a Smart TV 49 inches, diagonal measurement 123.2 cm, digital tuner DVB cooler - T2 response speed 120 Hz and 4 K resolution was used, for the aural stimulus a 4 speakers RMS power 500 W home theater was handy, the sense of touch (haptic perception) was stimulated by a water mist spray, the temperature control was implemented by means of a 3 in 1 air cooler - heater - purifier fan flowing 800 m^3/h, which has the ability to control the temperature in an area of 28 m^2 and a humidifier with forest and pine oil scents; the spatial distribution shown in Fig. 2.

The next phase was data collection in which test 1.0 of interaction was measured by means of a survey and a panel of users; the results pointed out that 76.47 % of users had an immersive experience in a virtual environment, with an effectiveness of the impact of the stimulus on the senses of 41.18 %. The learning experience of bird species was measured with a test of 5 questions rated according to the scale: Excellent-Outstanding-Fair-Insufficient-Deficient: 48.79 % of users answered questions correctly.

From the results obtained in the test 1.0, changes arise to enhance the experience of immersion in the virtual environment simulator, reduce costs of the simulator, and improve ease of assembly by developing a simulator and a test 2.0 which will allow the data comparison.

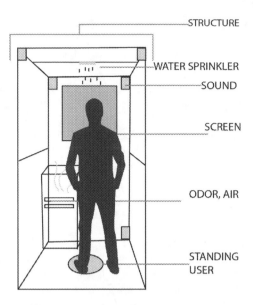

Fig. 2. Scheme first proposal simulator

5   Test 2.0

To carry out the test a simulator with dimensions 1.80 M high by 1.50 M wide and 1.30 M deep was designed and constructed for 2 users in sitting position. The materials used for the structure were industrial double wall cardboard waterproofed with sealing lacquer, the whole structure can be assembled and disassembled in an estimated lapse of 10 min. Two methods were implemented to stimulate the sense of sight: 1. Using Google virtual reality glasses (Google cardboard), consisting of a cardboard-based viewer, Velcro, magnets and lenses to give a feeling of depth, to transmit the image from a smartphone with a high concentration of pixels per inch the Smartphone maximum size should be 163 mm long and 83 mm high. 2. VR goggles VRBOX compatible with smartphone screens: 4.7–6.0 inches. For the aural stimulus a dome type earphone of 30 mm to guarantee a balanced sound was used, neodymium magnets of high power offered a powerful sound with a frequency range between 12 Hz and 22 kHz, the sense of touch was stimulated by a spray of water mist, the temperature control was implemented with an air cooler - heater - purifier fan flowing 800 m^3/h, that controls the temperature in an area of 28 m^2 and a humidifier scented pine and forest; distribution within the simulation space is shown in Fig. 3.

6   Users Panel

Carried out in the city of Palmira Valle del Cauca with nine users to bring about debate as to the experience, usability and learning resulting from the interaction with the VR simulator. Students and other persons interested in the subject of nature were convened

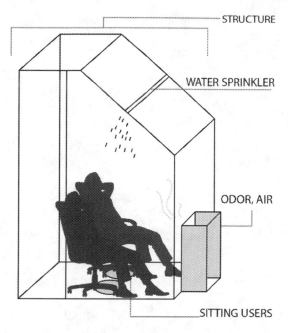

Fig. 3. Scheme second proposal simulator

to interact voluntarily with the simulator and undergo the VR experience; it was recorded by videos and photographs of the body and facial gestures of these persons during the test to measure the reactions to sensory stimuli. A single survey was conducted after the experience in the simulator. Later on all users assembled to debate about the recent experience with each of the objects within the simulator with questions about interaction and involvement of their senses, the learning phase was measured through remembrance of the information and acceptance with the frequency of use provided.

The total number of valid questionnaires was 29. The survey measured the variables experience, learning, and acceptance of the technology.

7   Analysis of the Data

7.1   Survey Results

The analysis of the data was performed by means of descriptive statistical methods calculating the average ($\bar{x}$), and the standard deviation (σ) is studied by VR simulator used in test 2.0.

Demographic data collected are sex and age and are studied twelve variables of simulation of the 4D environment are: V1. Immersive experience; V2. Aural test; V3. Visual test; V4. Touch test; V5. Smell test; V6. Environment experience; V7. Audio volume; V8. Projected video; V9. Temperature; V10. Essence smell V11. Experienced

Table 1. Studied variables

Variable	N	$(\bar{x})$	%	(σ)	Minimum	Maximum
V1. Immersion experience	29	3.41	68.2 %	.78	2.00	5.00
V2. Aural test	29	3.59	71.8 %	1.05	1.00	5.00
V3. Visual test	29	4.41	88.2 %	.91	1.00	5.00
V4. Touch test	29	3.38	67.6 %	1.40	1.00	5.00
V5. Smell test	29	3.79	75.8 %	1.18	1.00	5.00
V6. Environment experience	29	2.79	55.8 %	.41	2.00	3.00
V7. Audio volume	29	2.41	48.2 %	.82	1.00	3.00
V8. Projected video	29	2.79	55.8 %	.41	2.00	3.00
V9. Temperature	29	2.83	56.6 %	.38	2.00	3.00
V10. Essence smell	29	2.38	47.6 %	.68	1.00	3.00
V11. Experienced with VR	29	1.38	27.6 %	.49	1.00	2.00
V12. Factors nonuse RV	29	2.10	42.0 %	.94	1.00	4.00

with VR, and V12. Factors nonuse VR; Table 1 shows the results of the survey for the set of variables.

Analysis of the results indicates that, overall immersive experiences developed in the VR simulator proposed were perceived as outstanding (68.2 %), according to the results of $(\bar{x})$ 3,41 y $\sigma = 0,46$ in the V1 variable: Immersion Experience; however it is important to note that this result is based on dimensions visual (V3: $(\bar{x})$ 4,41 y $\sigma = 0,91$), aural (V2: $(\bar{x})$ 3,59 y $\sigma = 1,05$) and olfactory (V5: $(\bar{x})$ 3,79 y $\sigma = 1,18$); which yielded much higher results in $(\bar{x})$ and low relative values of σ.

The variables V7, V8, V9, V10, V11 and V12; yielded evaluations close to 50 %, and high coincidence in the responses is noted by the low values of σ. These results suggest the need to go on improving the quality of sensory stimuli to provide a better immersive experience, given that these variables focus on the technical quality of the means used in the VR simulator.

7.2   User Panel Results

An agreement was voted out by users for the analysis of qualitative data recorded in the panel discussion the ease of use of the simulator was positive for seven out of nine users. The evaluation of each element of the simulator showed that google cardboard generates discomfort in the area of the nose after five minutes of use. The RV box are more comfortable for eight out of nine users who said that it is more dynamic to interact with the video information by comparison with Google Street view application; the temperature had a positive rating, the space felt fresh and was related to the information transmitted in the video, the smells applied for the test were voted positive by six users and negative by four users, which suggested it would be interesting to have variety of odors according to everything in the video broadcast. It was discussed if it would be of interest for the users to know other places in Colombia by means of the VR system starting from four options: Amazonas, Nevado del Ruiz, Santa Marta, and Medellin;

Amazonas was most voted and the main reasons mentioned were interest in learning culture, and diversity.

The VR system simulator was associated with four main aspects of life: fun, relaxation, medicinal, and learning. Users related the simulator to three main variables: learning was voted favorably by four users, three users chose fun and two users favored relaxation.

8 Conclusions

The main contribution of this work is to approach the immersive experience of users in a low-cost simulator as a learning tool in culture and biodiversity through user-simulator interaction. The data obtained support the conclusion that this technology generates in 82.64 % of users sensory experiences that facilitate communication and learning; the simulator design and experience-based information on the diversity of birds allowed the users to discover a new learning methodology of nature and added new vitality to the mechanism of cultural transmission through the support of digital technology. Acceptance is a 68.79 % of users stating that they would use VR to learn about topics of interest and propose new areas of use, such as tourism businesses and advertising campaigns that attract the attention of young audiences in Colombia.

9 Future Lines of Research

For the project's progress the simulator must be modified according to the results found in test 2.0 in order to potentiate immersion capabilities mainly in controlling temperature and stimulating touch and smell. It should further investigate which are the most optimal elements to enhance stimuli and interaction continuing with the requirement of affordability.

References

Martinez, D., Kieffer, S., Martinez, J., Molina, J.P., Gonzalez, B.P.: Usability evaluation of virtual reality interaction techniques for positioning and manoeuvring in reduced, manipulation-oriented environments. Vis. Comput. **26**(6), 619–628 (2010)

Shih, J.-L., Jheng, S.-C., Tseng, J.-J.: A simulated learning environment of history games for enhancing (2014)

Obadiora, A.J.: Comparative effectiveness of virtual field trip and real field trip on students' academic performance in social studies in Osun State Secondary Schools. Mediterr. J. Soc. Sci. **7**(1), 467 (2016)

Malinvaud, D., Londero, A., Niarra, R., Peignard, o.: Auditory and visual 3D virtual reality therapy as a new treatment for chronic subjective Doctor (2015)

Yao, H.-P., Liu, Y.-Z., Han, C.-S.: Application expectation of virtual reality in basketball teaching. Procedia Eng. **29**, 4287–4291 (2012)

Burrows, C.N.: Using Video Games to Communicate Health Messages: The Role of Psychological Immersion (2015)

Häfner, P., Häfner, V., Ovtcharova, J.: Teaching methodology for virtual reality practical course in engineering education. Procedia Comput. Sci. **25**, 251–260 (2013)

Wei, X., Weng, D., Liu, Y., Wang, Y.: Teaching based on augmented reality for a technical creative design course. Comput. Educ. **81**, 221–234 (2014)

Okita, S.Y., Turkay, S., Kim, M., Murai, Y.: Learning by teaching with virtual peers and the effects of technological design choices on learning. Comput. Educ. **63**, 176–196 (2013)

Fracchia, C., Armiño, A.A., Martins, A.: Realidad Aumentada aplicada a la enseñanza de Ciencias Naturales (2015)

Quintana, M.G.B.: A pedagogical model to develop teaching skills. The collaborative learning experience in the Immersive Virtual World TYMMI. Comput. Hum. Behav. **51**, 594–603 (2015)

Gutierrez, J.: Aplicaciones de realidad virtual en psicologia clínica (2002)

Pujol, L.: Archaeology, museums and virtual reality (2004)

Reilly, P.: Towards a virtual archaeology (1991)

Reilly, P., Rahtz, S.P.Q.: Three-dimensional modelling and primary archaeological data (1992)

Echeverry-Galvis, Á.: Listado actualizado de las aves endémicas y casi-endémicas de Colombia. Biota Colomb. **14**(2), 235–272 (2013)

Natural Interaction and Movement Paradigms. A Comparison of Usability for a Kinect Enabled Museum Installation

Luis A. Hernández-Ibáñez$^{(\boxtimes)}$, Viviana Barneche-Naya,
and Rocío Mihura-López

VideaLAB, Universidade da Coruña, A Coruña, Spain
{luis.hernandez,viviana.barneche,rocio.mihura}@udc.es

Abstract. In this paper, the authors evaluate and compare two different paradigms of natural interaction, one metaphorical and one natural, in order to control the movement of the user inside a virtual model of an archaeological reconstruction. This work measures the two paradigm's usability in order to use this installation in a museum environment. The system was implemented on a game engine enabling the use of a Kinect 2 depth camera to obtain user input by means of body gesture analysis.

Keywords: Natural interaction · Usability · System Usability Scale · Kinect · Game engine · Virtual archaeology · Museum · Virtual museum

1 Introduction

With the dawning of the new museology, in the early 1970's, museums began a process of change in their methods of communication with their users, now encouraging them to interact more with the exhibition thus making them abandon their classical role as passive spectators, to become the agents of their own learning experience in a proactive and entertaining way. For this purpose, many different emerging technologies have been applied, from multimedia content to virtual reality environments.

Nowadays, game engines are becoming popular as a mean to develop high-end, real-time presentations of virtual environments not necessarily related to the game industry. Many examples of their use in the field of architectural and urban visualization can be found. Therefore, virtual reconstruction of historical heritage using these engines has been the logical next step in the direction of their use in virtual archaeology and the application of such technology in the field of museology.

Natural interaction is another emerging trend with direct application for museum installations. It is also used in the game industry to enhance the gaming experience by means of specialized hardware designed to obtain information of the user's intention without using traditional devices such as a computer mouse or a gamepad. Depth cameras, such as the Kinect family, allow the computer to be aware of the user's movements.

© Springer International Publishing Switzerland 2016
P. Zaphiris and A. Ioannou (Eds.): LCT 2016, LNCS 9753, pp. 145–155, 2016.
DOI: 10.1007/978-3-319-39483-1_14

Many interesting examples showing how game engines, sometimes with the use of a depth camera, displays visual recreations of archaeological reconstructions can be found today [1–6].

Despite that, few studies can be found that takes into respect the usability of the different paradigms for movement and actuation that are implemented in those systems. There is a variety of interaction mechanism to transform the user gestures into computer commands, some of them more easy to use and intuitive than others. Their functioning mechanic ranges from a single user gesture to control one specific action, such as forward displacement, to a complex set of user gestures to control a wide variety of movements and actions.

Natural interaction paradigms trend to provide the user with the confidence of using familiar, everyday actions to control the functioning of the computer application. These actions mimic gestures and behaviors utilized in the real life to achieve different goals in the virtual realm. Depending on the conceptual relations to the everyday gestures that they mirror, these actions can be classified as follows:

- *Natural:* The user applies gestures for the exact same action in the real world. (i.e. the action of grabbing to handle a virtual object.)
- *Metaphoric:* Actions that evokes the desired behavior of the system by the existence of a correspondence and similarity. In a metaphoric interface there is a mapping of concepts and operations between to domains, in this case the virtual world and the reality so that an interaction suggested by the metaphor source domain corresponds to the execution of the application implementing the metaphor target domain [7] (i.e. moving a hand left and right in the air to browse a sequence of pictures in a projection screen).
- *Symbolic:* In symbolic natural interaction the objects are represented by their visual, aural, and maybe in the future touch sensitive clones. They are naturally manipulated, but they are still representations and not real things [8] (i.e. driving a virtual car by moving hands to control a virtual steering wheel).

In the exploration of architectural reconstructions of archaeological remains, the user movement inside the model is the most important interaction. The examples aforementioned found in museums and exhibitions present different approaches to translate the visitor intentions to the movement of his or her representation in the virtual world but there are not enough case studies that supports either the preference of one over the others, nor the simple adequacy of a paradigm for what is intended. Indeed, the authors' experience on the use of some of these installations is that they are sometimes too cumbersome for the visitor to understand.

2 Objectives

The experiment we present here has the general objective of testing and evaluating the advantages and limitations of two different paradigms of movement inside an archaeological example in terms of engagement and usability in order to be used in a museum environment.

The test was done on a virtual model of a 4th century Roman villa [9, 10], constructed as a virtual installation for an interpretation center near Seville (Spain).

The virtual model was intended to accomplish two objectives. On the one hand, it was to display a complete recreation of the mosaics found in the nearby excavation, allowing the visitors to contemplate the appearance of the pavements in their full size instead of just fragments. On the other hand, the villa model was designed to act as a built-in environment that could provide context for the interpretation of the mosaics (Figs. 1, 2 and 3).

Fig. 1. Atrium entrance with "The Judgment of Paris" mosaic put in place

Fig. 2. Atrium with the central *impluvium*

Fig. 3. *Lararium*

The digital reconstruction was implemented to be explored by means of natural interaction schemes. To achieve this goal, a Kinect sensor for Xbox One also known as Kinect V2 was used, a device designed for videogame interaction that detects the presence and motion of players (Fig. 4).

Fig. 4. Kinect interaction

The virtual representation of the *domus* can be fully visited. The user can walk freely throughout all of the complex, enjoying not only the architecture of the building, but also the wall paintings, furniture, mosaics, and other elements of material culture (amphorae for oil and wine, *tegulae*, oil lamps, etc.). The setting of the different spaces (atria, *peristila, lararium, triclinium, tablinium*, etc.) helps interpreting daily life in such facilities. The main focus is the mosaic of the "Judgement of Paris" since this piece is unique in Hispania, being one of only five known cases found in all of the Roman Empire depicting this theme [11].

In line with attaining a quality evaluation of the user experience, we should consider various aspects in terms of usability, effectiveness and satisfaction. This evaluation can be carried out by means of interviews regarding the ease or difficulty of its use during the visit to the virtual museum. The questions included aspects about the environment and the main objects, including the mosaics.

The collected results should contribute to the study of paradigms of navigation inside virtual architectural environments such as those used in the field of virtual archaeology.

3   Movement Paradigms. Implementation

The installation captures the user's gestures by means of a Kinect depth camera attached to the system. The game engine that is used to visualize the virtual model (Unreal engine 4) incorporates a Kinect 4 Unreal library developed by Opaque Multimedia. The authors used that library to code the different gestures and actions that users perform to move and interact inside the virtual building.

The Kinect system is capable to feed the game engine with a continuous flow of data describing the body configuration of a user in front of the device. This data contains the location of a set of characteristic points in the user's body, called joints, together with their topological relations that describe a simple skeleton that depicts the user's pose. The Kinect for Unreal libraries can be queried to obtain both position and orientation of some joints related to other joints and to the Kinect device.

The two different interaction schemes described in this paper have been implemented as described below.

- **Metaphorical. Rise-hand scheme:** This approach uses the movement of the user's arm to control both displacement and orientation. The player controller analyses how much the user lifts his or her hand (Fig. 4) and measures the angle formed by the wrist and the elbow, both in the horizontal plane (yaw) relative to the direction to the Kinect Device, which is used for turning, and in the vertical plane (pitch) relative to the vertical, which is used to move forward and control speed. An idle arm, pointing to the floor means a zero angle in both directions.

    The pitch angle may be negative, thus allowing for backward displacement by pointing the arm just slightly backwards.

    The user can change his or her orientation at the same time by pointing sideways with the same arm. Hence, the user can turn and control the displacement speed simultaneously.

- **Natural. Step/Twist scheme:** This second approach is designed to offer the user a way to explore the virtual building by using movements similar to those used when walking. In this scheme, users can increase or decrease the virtual walkthrough speed by stepping forward or backward and perform turns by twisting the upper body clockwise for a right turn and counterclockwise for a left turn.

Marks in the ground depicting the usual arrow icons used in audio and video playback indicated locations for the start, move forward at slow pace, move forward quickly and move backward commands. Users were placed in the starting position to begin the test and were then given a brief description of the movement scheme prior to letting them move alone.

4   Usability Test

The authors applied a qualitative, user-centred methodology, based on measurement and systematic analysis of the values used by ISO 9241-11 to define usability; namely effectiveness, efficiency and satisfaction [12].

4.1   Methodology

The authors chose to apply a custom methodology in this experiment which could combine the measure of the perception of the user of the mechanical aspects of the system with their experience of the virtual visit of the virtual villa. This second aspect was studied both from the perspective of the accessibility of the subject to the architectural environment as well as their satisfaction as a museum visitor. Aside from collecting data, users were filmed while performing the tests. This allowed the authors to gather useful information to be applied in future enhancements of the system.

The experiment was organized as follows: First, users gave their usual demographic data as well as a self-assessment of their skills as videogame players. Then, they received a general explanation of the Roman villa and walked through it using both paradigms, first trying to accomplish a task and then moving freely afterwards.

Subjects were interviewed to evaluate their perception of the architecture of the building, the objects and signs placed inside it and their perception regarding the attention consciously employed in the use of each movement scheme. Next, in order to concentrate the study to a specific user profile, namely the museum visitor, the authors applied the System Usability Scale SUS [13]. SUS is a Likert scale that gives great importance to the subjective opinion of the users, and at the same time being a reliable[1] method to obtain usability measurements.

---

[1] Appointed by Lewis and Sauro [14]. While the typical minimum target for the usability polls used in research is 0.7 [15, 16], the alpha coefficient for SUS gives a value of 0,85, or even as high as 0.91 as it was recently verified by Bangor, Kortum and Miller [17]. Tullis and Stetson [18] demonstrated that reliable results can be obtained from a sample composed by 8 to 12 users and also that this method discriminates better for small sized samples than CSUQ y QUIS [12].

4.2   Selection of the Data Sample

The data sample for this experiment was defined through a selection of key informers marked as potential museum visitors. A pilot test carried out previously used a convenience sample close to this profile. In order to stablish the percentages that define the profile of a museum visitor, the authors applied the data obtained by a study performed by the Spanish *Laboratorio Permanente de Público de Museos* [19]. The result of this distribution of statistical variables, from a combinatory optimization perspective gives optimum results for a sample size of 38 individuals. For the case described here, and considering that the SUS methodology has demonstrated to be reliable for a sample size of 8–12 people, the sample was recalculated and the number 13 was used as the next confidence value for the aforementioned percentages. This resulted in the following distribution is as follows.

– Number of individuals 13 (mean error: 1.29 pp)
– Gender: 6 males, 7 females
– Age: less than 25:2; 26 to 45: 6; 46 to 65: 4; 66 and older: 1
– Education: Primary: 1; High school: 6; University: 4: PhD: 2

5   General Results

The results of the test carried out for both paradigms of movement yielded the following results, collected in Table 1, expressed in a value range from 0 to 10.

Table 1. General results

	Rise hand		Step/Twist	
	Mean	σ	Mean	σ
1. Easiness to appreciate the Architecture of the place	8,69	1,49	8,42	2,48
2. Easiness to read signs	2,77	2,69	4,77	3,26
3. Easiness to contemplate objects	8,46	1,55	8,15	1,51
4. Easiness to contemplate mosaics	6,46	3,18	7,92	2,23
5. Conscious attention put to control the movement	6,65	3,32	6,04	2,73
6. Conscious attention put on the museum experience	6,42	1,62	6,88	2,39
7. SUS (max 100)	81,92	11,36	79,81	16,80

Regarding SUS, both paradigms yielded a result over 70, which placed them in the interval between Good and Excellent in the adjective rating elaborated for SUS by Bangor et al. [17].

Table 1 shows a comparison between both paradigms regarding their effectiveness for the visitor of a virtual museum. They show that architecture of the place is appreciated easily in both paradigms. On the other hand, both paradigms presented problems when users tried to get to a place to read signs with descriptive text, which is a task that requires a more precise placement in front of the sign and the right distance. That points to a clear necessity to improve the system in that regard.

The easiness of contemplating the objects placed in the scene received a good valuation in both paradigms. Contemplation of the mosaics, which are located on the floor presented more difficulties for the rise-hand paradigm than for the step/twist paradigm (Fig. 5).

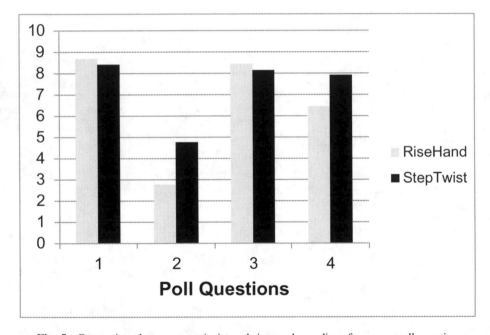

Fig. 5. Comparison between step/twist and rise-rand paradigm for every poll question

It is interesting to note the ratio of attention consciously invested in enjoying the museum compared to the attention that is consciously invested in controlling the movement (Fig. 6). We can tell that the step/twist paradigm shows to be more appropriate behavior for a museum installation, displaying the need of less attention invested in controlling movements and more attention could be invested in the experience.

The analysis of the SUS from a gender perspective presents a good valuation for both paradigms, but females give specially good grades to the step/twist scheme (Fig. 7). The standard deviation for females is also smaller, indicating a clear agreement in that sense.

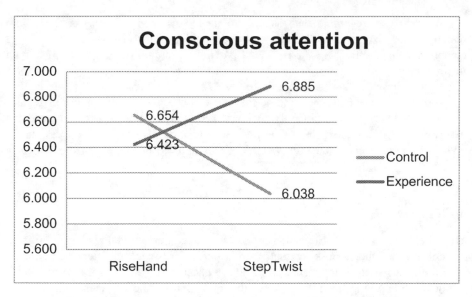

Fig. 6. Comparison of conscious attention invested in both paradigms

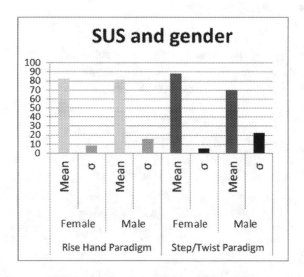

Fig. 7. Gender comparison of SUS results

6 Discussion

6.1 Effectiveness

The effectiveness of both of the paradigms can be measured by analyzing their suitability to contribute to the installation in order to achieve its purpose as a virtual museum.

In this sense, regarding the easiness to perceive the virtual environment, both paradigms offered good results in the architectural aspect (question 1), and object contemplation (question 3). The rise-hand paradigm presents slightly better results in this regard.

A clear drawback appears when it comes to the task of reading informative signs (question 2), the rise-hand seems to be the worse of the two paradigms in this regard. Two users remarked their difficulty to reach a proper location in order to read the descriptive signs correctly. Regarding the contemplation of the mosaics (question 4), both paradigms receive a medium valuation, although the step/twist scheme is clearly superior.

6.2 Efficiency

The efficiency in this case can be described as the use of attentional resources invested in achieving a concrete task or goal. In this particular aspect, the step/twist scheme surpasses the rise-hand scheme since it allows the user to move in the virtual environment while giving more attention to the enjoyment of the experience than to the control of the movement in the digital space (Fig. 6).

6.3 Satisfaction

The SUS results permits the measuring of the global satisfaction for a museum user profile that utilizes the system. Both paradigms are valuated in the range of Good to Excellent. That offers a positive support for the implementation of this kind of installations in a museum environment.

7 Conclusions

This experiment concludes the suitability of Kinect based natural interaction for museum installations both for natural and metaphorical paradigms, specifically for rise-hand and step/twist movement schemes. In this regard, results yield very good valuations for both schemes in regard of effectiveness, efficiency and satisfaction when the experiment is applied on a museum user profile sample. The system is good for experiencing digital architectural environments and for contemplating objects such as those present in the virtual museums seen in the field of virtual archaeology. Nevertheless, some effort has to be invested in the design aspect of the virtual signs located on those environments, which are somehow difficult to reach and read by users.

In general, the step/twist scheme gave better results, which points in the direction that natural paradigms of natural interaction could be more adequate than metaphoric ones for museum installations.

References

1. Sheng, W., Ishikawa, K., Tanaka, H.T., Tsukamoto, A., Tanaka, S.: Photorealistic VR space reproductions of historical kyoto sites based on a next-generation 3D game engine. J. Adv. Simul. Sci. Eng. **1**(1), 188–204 (2015)
2. Lercari, N., Mortara, M., Forte, M.: Unveiling California history through serious games: Fort Ross Virtual Warehouse. In: De Gloria, A. (ed.) GALA 2013. LNCS, vol. 8605, pp. 236–251. Springer, Heidelberg (2014)
3. Pietroni, E., Adami, A.: Interacting with virtual reconstructions in museums: the Etruscanning project. J. Comput. Cult. Heritage (JOCCH) **7**(2), 9 (2014)
4. Richards-Rissetto, H., Robertsson, J., von Schwerin, J., Agugiaro, G., Remondino, F., Girardi, G.: Geospatial Virtual Heritage: a gesture-based 3D GIS to engage the public with Ancient Maya Archaeology. In: Archaeology in the Digital Era, pp. 118–130 (2014)
5. Cappelletto, E., Zanuttigh, P., Cortelazzo, G.M.: 3D scanning of cultural heritage with consumer depth cameras. Multimedia Tools Appl. **75**, 1–24 (2014)
6. Huyzendveld, A., Di Ioia, M., Ferdani, D., Palombini, A., Sanna, V., Zanni, S., Pietroni, E.: The virtual museum of the Tiber Valley project. Virtual Archaeol. Rev. **3**(7), 97–101 (2012)
7. Celentano, A., Dubois, E. (2014). Metaphors, analogies, symbols: in search of naturalness in tangible user interfaces. In: Proceedings of the 6th International Conference on Intelligent Human Computer Interaction, Paris, France (2014)
8. Sperka, M. Past and future of human-computer interaction. In: Proceedings of the International Conference on Current Issues of Science and Research in the Global World. Viena Austria (2014)
9. Blázquez Martínez, J.M.: Mosaicos romanos del Campo de Villavidel (León) y de Casariche (Sevilla). Archivo Español de Arqueología **58**, 115–117 (1985)
10. De la Hoz Gandara, A., Jimenez, J.C.: Informe de la Segunda Campaña de Excavaciones en la Villa Romana de El Alcaparral. Anuario Arqueológico de Andalucía **3**, 371–379 (1987)
11. Blázquez Martínez, J.M.: Mosaicos romanos del Campo de Villavidel (León) y de Casariche (Sevilla). Archivo Español de Arqueología **58**, 115–117 (1985)
12. Brooke, J.: SUS: a retrospective. JUS J. Usability Stud. **8**(2), 29–40 (2013)
13. Brooke, J.: SUS-a quick and dirty usability scale. Usability Eval. Ind. **189**(194), 4–7 (1996)
14. Lewis, J.R., Sauro, J.: The factor structure of the system usability scale. In: Kurosu, M. (ed.) HCD 2009. LNCS, vol. 5619, pp. 94–103. Springer, Heidelberg (2009)
15. Landauer, T.: Behavioral research methods in human-computer interaction. In: Helander, M., Landauer, T., Prabhu, P. (eds.) Handbook of Human-Computer Interaction, pp. 203–227. Elsevier, Amsterdam (1997)
16. Nunnally, J.: Psychometric Theory. McGraw-Hill, New York (1978)
17. Bangor, A., Kortum, P., Miller, J.T.: An empirical evaluation of the system usability scale. Int. J. Hum. Comput. Inter. **24**, 574–594 (2008)
18. Tullis, T., Stetson, J.: A comparison of questionnaires for assessing website usability. In: UPA 2004 Conference, Minneapolis, Minnesota pp. 7–11 (2004)
19. Laboratorio permanente de público de museos: Conociendo a nuestros visitantes. Estudio de público en museos del Ministerio de Cultura. Secretaría General Técnica del Ministerio de Cultura, Madrid (2011)

Pseudo-Haptics Presentation for Promoting Historical Understanding

Takumi Horiguchi[✉] and Akihiro Kashihara

Graduate School of Informatics and Engineering,
The University of Electro-Communications,
1-5-1 Chofugaoka, Chofu, Tokyo 182-8585, Japan
horiguchitakumi@uec.ac.jp,
akihiro.kashihara@inf.uec.ac.jp

Abstract. In learning history, it is important to promote historical thought, which involves understanding causal relationships among historical events and a chain of the relationships. This paper proposes a method to allow the learners to compose a causal map, in which historical events are represented as nodes, and the causal relationships are represented as links between the nodes. It can visualize the causal relationships and the causal chains. However, it is not necessarily easy to become aware of them during the map generation. The causal map proposed in this paper accordingly aims to allow the learners to become aware of not only the causal relationships between historical events but also the causal chains with pseudo-haptics on tablet media such as iPad. This paper also demonstrates a tablet tool on iPad, which helps learners compose a causal map from instructional text about history.

Keywords: Pseudo-haptic feedback · Causal map generation · History learning · Tablet media

1 Introduction

In learning history, it is important to promote historical thought, which involves understanding causal relationships among historical events and a chain of the relationships [1]. In general, learners are expected to learn such causal relationships and their chains from an instructional material such as textbook. However, historical learning is not easy for the learners. It is particularly hard to find out the causal relationships embedded in the material. In addition, the learners often finish learning without becoming aware of the causal chains, which is necessary for understanding the suitability of the causal relationships.

In this paper, we propose a causal map, in which historical events are represented as nodes, and the causal relationships are represented as links between the nodes. It can visualize the causal relationships and the causal chains. In order to promote understanding of the causal relationships, related work on historical learning support has proposed a method of helping learners generate a map including the causal relationships from instructional text [2]. However, it is not necessarily easy to become aware of them during the map generation. It also seems hard to find out the causal chains

© Springer International Publishing Switzerland 2016
P. Zaphiris and A. Ioannou (Eds.): LCT 2016, LNCS 9753, pp. 156–164, 2016.
DOI: 10.1007/978-3-319-39483-1_15

embedded in the text to understand the suitability of the causal relationships. The causal map proposed in this paper accordingly aims to allow the learners to become aware of not only the causal relationships between historical events but also the causal chains with pseudo-haptics on tablet media such as iPad.

Pseudo-haptics is illusion about the tactile sense caused by uncomfortable feeling between physical manipulation of an object and its visual movement. We have already ascertained that pseudo-haptic feedback for manipulating a concept map representing knowledge learned from an instructional text could promote an awareness of important concepts or important relationships embedded in the text [3]. In this work, we attempt to introduce the pseudo-haptics into historical understanding.

In this paper, we demonstrate a method to present pseudo-haptic feedback in composing a causal map. In operating the nodes corresponding to the key historical events and the links included in a causal chain, the learners are provided with the visual movements, which intend to bring about pseudo-haptic senses such as heaviness and tension. In case the learners operate a link included in the causal chain, a pseudo-haptic feedback involving tensile strength is transmitted among all the links in the chain, which would allow them to become aware of the causal chain. Such cognitive awareness would also allow the learners to understand the suitability of the causal relationships between the original cause and the end effect of the chain.

This paper also demonstrates a tablet tool on iPad, which helps learners compose a causal map from instructional text about history. This tool prepares a text and the corresponding correct causal map including all causal relationships embedded in the text. The learners are required to compose a causal map corresponding to the correct map in the following two steps. In the first step, they are expected to compose an overview map, which includes only the key historical events. In the second step, they are required to complete the causal map with WHY-questions, which includes several intermediate events between the primary events necessary for representing the causal chains.

In the following, we first describe historical learning. Second, we describe a causal map used in historical learning, and how it is composed. Third, we describe how pseudo-haptic feedback from touch operations is presented and what kind of cognitive effects is obtained from it. Let us finally demonstrates a tablet tool on iPad, which helps the learners compose a causal map from an instructional text.

2 Historical Learning

In social studies, learners are expected to learn social events/phenomenon and the principles involved in them, which can be often used for explaining why and how the events occur. With such principles, the learners can explain the similar events/phenomenon. In learning history, historical events could be also explained with the principles. It is particularly important to explain why and how one historical event brings about another event. The learners should accordingly learn the explanatory principles to understand the historical events.

However, it is quite difficult to find out the principles from the social events described in instructional text. In learning history, there is another method for understanding the events, which allows the learners to find out the causal relationship between one event as a cause and another event as an effect, and its suitability. The causal relationship also involves several intermediate events between the cause and the effect. This method allows the learners to explain a chain of the causal relationships between the intermediate events to understand the suitability of the relationship between the cause and the effect.

2.1   Related Work

[4] proposed a model for explaining causal relationships between social events, which includes three variables representing causes, effects, and their intermediates. This model allows the learners to build up a theory for explaining the causal relationship between the cause and effect from WHY-question that indicates why the cause brings about the effect by means of the intermediate events. For example, let us consider the following WHY-question:

"Why did the Mongolian invasion bring about the Einin Order for Benevolent Government issued by Kamakura Shogunate?"

Such a question could prompt the learners to build up the theory for explaining the causal relationship between the Mongolian invasion as a cause and the Einin Order as the effect. They are expected to find out the intermediate events to answer the question. This allows them to more deeply understand the causal relationship between the cause and the effect. In case they do not know the intermediates, on the other hand, they would fail to explain. It is accordingly necessary to provide the learners with some aids for uncovering the intermediate events.

Another related work proposed the method for providing learners with a number of WHY-questions in gradual detail [5], which gradually ask the intermediate events and their causal relationships. This allows the learners to understand the causal relationship between the cause and the effect, and the suitability. However, the learners could not fully find out intermediate events to explain, which would result in insufficient understanding of the causal relationship.

This paper accordingly proposes a method to allow the learners to fully pick up the mediated events as follows.

2.2   Causal Map-Based Approach

This paper proposes a method to allow the learners to compose a causal map, in which historical events are represented as nodes, and the causal relationships are represented as links between the nodes. It can visualize the relationships between the events and their causal chains. However, it is difficult to extract the events from an instructional text and to compose the causal map. In addition, the learners finish learning with insufficient understanding of the causal relationships. In order to resolve this issue, we propose the causal map composition in two steps. In the first step, the learners are expected to compose a map with the prepared events that are extracted as key events in advance from the text. In this step, they could understand an overview of the causal map to be composed.

In the second step, the learners are expected to pick up the intermediate events from the text to make their chain including the original cause and the end effect. The candidates for the intermediates are underlined in advance in the text. When they get stuck, they are also given the WHY-questions that intend to promote picking up the intermediates. When the learners operate the nodes as key events or the nodes included in the chain of the intermediate events, in addition, pseudo-haptic feedback is provided so that they can become aware of the key events or the chain. In this step, they could deeply understand the causal relationship between the original cause and the end effect, and its suitability with the intermediate events.

3   Causal Map Composition

Let us demonstrate the causal map composition with Fig. 1. Figure 1(A) shows an instructional text, which describes "Decline of Kamakura Shogunate". Figure 1(B) shows the causal map to be composed from Fig. 1(A). This map includes the original causes of decline of Kamakura Shogunate, which are indicated by the three nodes, *the Mongolian invasions*, *the division succession*, and *the infiltration money economy*. However, it would be generally difficult for the learners to understand the suitability of the causal relationship between the original causes and the end effect without the intermediate events and the causal chain.

The causal map composition in this paper has two steps. In the first step, the learners are expected to compose a map shown in Fig. 2, which includes the key events prepared from the text. The map represents an overview of the causal relationships embedded in "Decline of Kamakura Shogunate". In the second step, the learners are expected to pick up the events as intermediate ones between the key events from the parts underlined in the text shown in Fig. 1(A). The events picked up are inserted between the key events.

On the other hand, the learners cannot always pick up the intermediate events fully to complete the causal map shown in Fig. 1(B). In this case, WHY-questions are presented to them. If the learners do not pick up any events between the node *the division of succession* and *poverty of vassals in the Kamakura*, for example, the following question is presented:

"Why was *poverty of vassals in the Kamakura* caused by *the division of succession?*"

They would attempt to search for the reasons in the text to understand it is because "the estate of the vassals decreased". They are then expected to locate the node between *the division of succession* and *poverty of vassals in the Kamakura*, and to make the links. They are required to continue such map composition and WHY-question answering until they complete the causal map shown in Fig. 1(B).

In addition, the two types of pseudo-haptic feedback are provided on a causal map composition in the second step. When the learners operate the initial nodes as key events located in the first step, they first have the pseudo-haptic feedback that feels heavy. It intends to remind them that the nodes are the key events. When they operate

Kamakura Shogunate forced the vassals to make lots of sacrifices due to the Mongolian invasions. However, the Shogunate could not pay plenty of reward for the vassals, and the vassals were furthermore forced to have the roles of guardians against the foreign countries. In addition, the estates of the vassals decreased due to the division of succession, and the vassals who got into debt increased due to the infiltration of the money economy. These caused poverty of the vassals in the Kamakura, which also brought about the decrease of vassals who were appreciated to Kamakura Shogunate. In order to resolve it, the Shogunate issued Einin Order for Benevolent government, which intended to prevent the vassal system in Kamakura from collapsing. But, it did not prevent the poverty of the vassals. The lenders who lent money and land to the Shogunate were taken in and lost them. From these, the Shogunate lost the trust, and then declined.

(A)

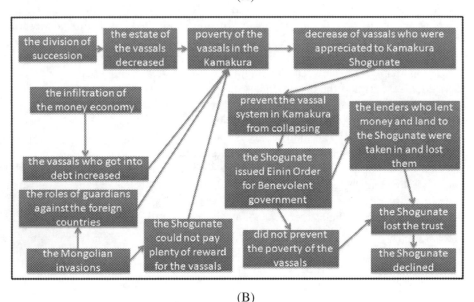

(B)

Fig. 1. A causal map of decline of the Kamakura Shogunate

the intermediate nodes and links in the chain from the original cause node to the end effect node, they have the pseudo-haptic feedback that presents the propagation of tensile force in the chain. For example, let us consider the chain of the original node *the division of succession*, *the estates of the vassals decreased*, and the end effect *poverty of vassals in the Kamakura*. The three events have the causal relationships. When the learners move the intermediate node *the estates of the vassals decreased*, the following visual information is demonstrated: the node *the division of succession* pushes the

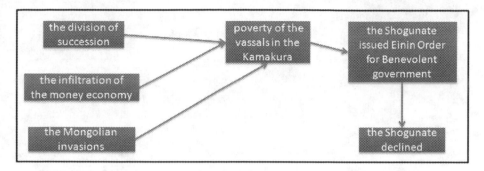

Fig. 2. A causal map of first step

linked node *the estates of the vassals decreased*, then the pushed node next pushes the node *poverty of vassals in the Kamakura*. The pushed movement visualizes the propagation of the force from the original cause to the end effect, which suggests the causal chain.

4   Map Composition with Pseudo-Haptic Feedback

4.1   Pseudo-Haptic Feedback and Cognitive Effects

Pseudo-haptic is illusion about the tactile sense caused by uncomfortable feeling between physical manipulation of an object and its visual movement. When an object on the tablet is operated via finger, for example, it moves with a delay in comparison with the finger movement. Learners would feel that the object is heavy [6]. We have already ascertained that pseudo-haptic feedback for manipulating a concept map representing knowledge learned from an instructional text could promote an awareness of important concepts and relationships embedded in the text [3]. Presenting a heavy feeling could give an indication of an important concept. Presenting a tension could also give an indication of a strong relationship. As a result, it is possible to give cognitive effects to learner by presenting pseudo-haptic feedback. In addition, it can be expected to promote an understanding of the corresponding concept or relationship.

4.2   Causal Map with Pseudo-Haptic Feedback and Propagation of Force

The learners are provided with pseudo-haptic feedback and the propagation of force as shown in Table 1. In addition, the table shows cognitive awareness that is obtained from the pseudo-haptic feedback. For example, let us consider the second line shown in Table 1 with Fig. 3. When a learner operates the node *poverty of vassals in the Kamakura*, it moves with a delay in comparison with the touch operation. The visual movement represents heaviness of the node as the pseudo-haptic feedback, which suggests the key event.

In addition, let us also consider the third line shown in Table 1. When the learner moves the intermediate node *prevent the vassal system in Kamakura from collapsing*,

Table 1. Pseudo-haptic feedback and the propagation of the force from operation

Operation on causal map	Pseudo-haptic feedback	The propagation of the force	Cognitive awareness
Node operation	Node heaviness	N/A	Key event
Intermediate node operation	N/A	The original causal node pushes the linked the intermediate node, then the pushed node next pushes the end effect node	Causal chain

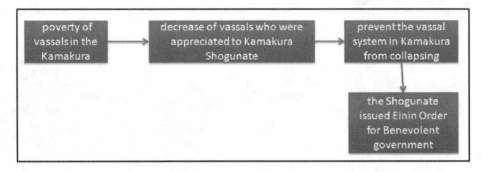

Fig. 3. Part of a causal map of the decline of the Kamakura Shogunate

the following visual information is demonstrated: the node *poverty of vassals in the Kamakura* pushes the linked node *decrease of vassals who were appreciated to Kamakura Shogunate*, then the pushed node next pushes the node *prevent the vassal system in Kamakura from collapsing*, and then the pushed node pushes the node *the Shogunate issued Einin Order for Benevolent government*. The pushed movement visualizes the propagation of the force from the original cause to the end effect, which suggests the causal chain. It can be expected to promote the historical understanding.

5   Causal Map Composition on Tablet Tool

We have developed a tablet tool on iPad, which can provide the learners with pseudo-haptic feedback according to Table 1. Figure 4 shows the user interface of the tool. Let us here describe the framework of the tablet tool, the causal map composition on the tool, and the learning process with the tool.

5.1   Framework

This tool prepares a text and the corresponding correct causal map including all causal relationships embedded in the text. The learners are required to compose a map corresponding to the correct map. The learners are expected to compose the map in the two steps. In the first step, they would use the prepared node to link and to compose an overview map. When they think the map is completed, they can push the button "Answer" that is prepared in the user interface.

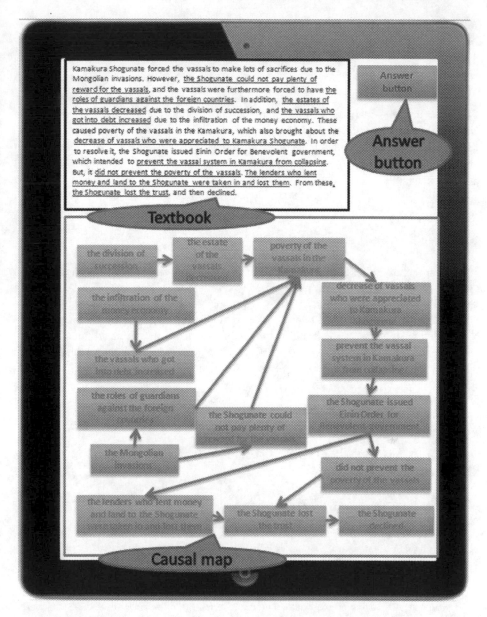

Fig. 4. User interface

If the learners complete the overview map, they are expected to move to the second step. In this step, the learners are expected to touch the underlined characters in the text to locate the intermediate nodes. They are then expected to refine the overview map using the located nodes to complete the correct map. In case the learners push the "Answer" button and the map is incomplete, the tool presents the WHY-questions that induce them to complement the incomplete causal relationships and chains. In addition, when the learners move the nodes that embed the pseudo-haptic feedback, the learners are provided with the corresponding feedback.

5.2   Map Operations

This tool provides learners with the map operations: movement of node, generation of node/link and delete of node/link. Movement of node is operated by drag on the node. The learners can touch and drag the node with fingers they want to move. Generation of link is operated by tap and draw. The learners can tap a node to become the starting point of the link. Then, they can draw the link to another node. Delete of link is operated by long tap. The learners can do long press on the links they want to delete.

6   Conclusions

This paper has described the causal map composition in learning history with pseudo-haptic feedback. It can be expected to promote the historical understanding. We have also demonstrated a causal map generation tool on iPad, which could produce pseudo-haptic feedback including the propagation of the force on touch operations.

In future, we will evaluate the potential of pseudo-haptic feedback and the propagation of the force in the causal map on tablet tool. In addition, we will confirm whether the tablet tool can promote historical understanding.

Acknowledgment. This work is in part supported by JSPS KAKENHI Grand Number 15K12408.

References

1. Lee, P.: Historical literacy: theory and research. Int. J. Hist. Learn. Teach. Res. **5**(1), 29–41 (2005)
2. Nate, Y., Tokutake, K., Kojiri, T.: Creation support for causal relationship graph of historical events based on state transition map. IEICE Tech. Rep. **115**(127), 43–48 (2015). (in Japanese)
3. Kashihara, A., Shiota, G.: Knowledge construction with visual and pseudo-haptic senses. IEICE Trans. **J98-D**(1), 104–116 (2015). (in Japanese)
4. Funada, J.: Developing lesson plans for social studies in junior high school to explain historical causality: using an explanatory model to teach the unit on "Rise of the Samurai and Formation of the Samurai Administration". J. Res. Educ. Soc. Stud. Dept. **24**, 61–70 (2012). (in Japanese)
5. Yoshizaki, Y.: Development of social studies lessons aimed at elaborating the structure of knowledge by children through focusing on causal relationships, as well as divisions and chain of "why" questions. J. Res. Edu. Soc. Stud. Dept. **26**, 71–80 (2014). (in Japanese)
6. Lecuyer, A.: Simulating haptic feedback using vision: a survey of research and applications of pseudo-haptic feedback. Teleoperators Virtual Environ. **18**(1), 39–53 (2009). (MIT Press)

The Many Voices of Audiobooks: Interactivity and Multimodality in Language Learning

Emanuela Marchetti[1] and Andrea Valente[2(✉)]

[1] Lillebaelt Academy, University of Applied Sciences, Odense, Denmark
emma@eal.dk
[2] Maersk Mc-Kinney Moller Institute, University of Southern Denmark (SDU),
Odense, Denmark
anva@mmmi.sdu.dk

Abstract. A case study is presented, aimed at making audiobooks interactive in the context of English teaching in Danish high-school. Social interaction was chosen as key feature to allow high-school students and teachers to annotate audiobooks, then share and comment on the annotations. This new work is supported by unpublished data from two other studies, which provided insights on the potential of interactive audiobooks. All case-studies were conducted in a user-centred fashion and build on social semiotics, in which interactive audiobooks are seen as providing new ways to receive, interpret and share literary texts within the social context of the English language class. Local primary and secondary schools were involved in ethnographic user studies and qualitative evaluations with semi-functioning prototypes. The findings and technical solutions explored in the three studies are the basis for design guidelines aiming at making audiobooks interactive and better integrated in learning contexts.

Keywords: E-Learning · Multimodal interaction · Information presentation · Knowledge management

1 Introduction

In recent years audiobooks have become increasingly more accessible, both in the market and in free, often publicly supported, streaming sites and apps[1]. Denmark follows this trend and many local schools (primary and secondary) consider free audiobook repositories as part of their resources. However, our data suggest that integration of audiobooks in the class poses many challenges. In our observation of primary and secondary school classes we noticed that audio resources are often used in a 'passive' way, for instance fruition of audiobooks takes more time than reading, often audiobooks offer a shorter version of the original text, finally audiobooks are perceived as more passive than regular books as it is not possible to take notes and mark specific passages as with books and e-readers. We noticed a lack of active uses of audio content for example in relation to generation and editing of audio content, and virtually no audio-based interactivity.

---

[1] Danish primary school site: https://www.folkeskolen.dk/504367/det-skal-vaere-nemmere-for-laerere-at-finde-relevante-e-og-lydboeger (last seen 25th February 2016).

© Springer International Publishing Switzerland 2016
P. Zaphiris and A. Ioannou (Eds.): LCT 2016, LNCS 9753, pp. 165–176, 2016.
DOI: 10.1007/978-3-319-39483-1_16

In the past two years we have conducted three case-studies to explore the untapped potential of audio in the context of learning of English as a foreign language in primary and secondary schools. Our studies suggest that textual and video modalities are predominant in classes practice, even when most of the orchestration (Prieto et al. 2015) of learning activities is oral. We consider the lack of interactive audio as a missed opportunity to promote richer use of multimodal resources in class, especially since many available technologies (e.g. smartphones) easily support creation, fruition, and efficient storage of audio content. Moreover, audio contents might support learners with special needs, such as: visually impaired people or pupils affected by dyslexia or when learning a foreign language ordering commutes for occasional, non-formal learning.

In the following sections we present related work (Sect. 1.1), our three case-studies (Sects. 2 and 3), discussions (Sect. 4) and conclusions (Sect. 5).

1.1   Related Work

Several studies have already explored use of audiobooks as tools for creative engagement with literary stories and tools for learning foreign languages. For instance Furini (2007) and Huber et al. (2007) challenged the typical use of audiobooks, which was found to be passive with respect to books. Both studies argue in fact that readers of audiobooks might gain a more passive experience, being constrained to listen to the story, therefore, they have explored possibilities to enable users to interact with non-linear narratives creating their own stories. The study conducted by Furini aims at turning the passive reader of audiobooks into the "director of the story" (Furini 2007, p. 1). In developing his system he looks at the use of audiobooks through a cinematic metaphor, imagining the experience of editing new stories as if the reader was editing video sequences, referring to movies like *Sliding Doors* and *Pulp Fiction* as displaying non-linear stories. The system targets three main use cases: entertainment, education, and game applications. The design focuses on two main principles: transparency, as the book file should be standard and easily handled by the system, and security, as only the owner of the audiobook file should be able to play it and she should not be able to alter the original media files from which the audiobook was created. The article discussing Furini's studies, however, focuses on the technical aspects of the design of the system and does not discuss in details the expected user experience or results from testing.

Huber et al. (2007) take a similar approach and discuss the evolution of audiobooks into interactive media, suitable for editing non-linear stories. The authors propose to combine elements from computer games with the experience of listening to oral presentations, which are defined by Huber et al. as immersive and entertaining. Moreover, sonification was used as a resource for interaction, in order to enable the users to interact with the system mainly through sound, but this interaction style was found difficult by the users.

A relevant study has been conducted by Alcantud-Díaz and Gregori (2014), who propose an extensive review of the use of audiobooks in foreign language learning and two projects named *Tales of the World* and *The Power of Tales: Building a Fairer World*. The authors claim that even though in their country, Spain, audiobooks are not commonly used, they can see great potentials in supporting English learning in relation to the five skills listed in the Common European Framework of Reference for language learning: listening, reading, spoken interaction, and writing. The two projects discussed by Alcantud-Díaz and Gregori aim at spreading awareness of languages as scaffolding for intercultural values and respect for human rights in the educative community. The outcome from both projects were collections of tales, for the *Tales of the world* project 40 tales were gathered from underprivileged countries, for *The Power of Tales* 15 tales against violence were collected. All the tales were edited into free downloadable audiobooks. The format of audiobooks was chosen in order to give access to pupils with learning and visual difficulties; moreover, audiobooks were seen as a mean to improve learners' English pronunciation. The other studies discussed in the review (Alcantud-Díaz and Gregori 2014) focus on the use of audiobooks for primary school pupils dealing with language learning, such as Wilde and Larson (2007) who argue that audiobooks enabled children 8 to 12 years of age to find more time to read, hence reading more books. Moreover, Baskin and Harris (1995) found that use of audiobooks supported students with learning difficulties, who find it challenging to interpret written text, in making sense of written texts and improving their reading fluency in English as first language.

Moving away from the learning context, we can find another form of interactive audio: audio walks or audio tours (van Zeijl 2013). Similar to the audio material offered by museum, audio walks are usually implemented as mobile apps where users can follow predefined audio commentary while moving around a city or a building. An interesting commercial product of this kind is yapQ's "Worldwide city guides"[2], a mobile app that offers audio walks in multiple languages and for many cities; the application uses geolocation and text-to-speech to generate interactive audio guides. The contents in this case are not user-generated. SoundCloud[3] instead is an example of user-generated and socially shared resources: *"SoundCloud is [...] social sound platform where anyone can create sounds and share them everywhere"*. Among other sound collections, SoundCould offers a selection of audio walks.

In the following sections we will show more possible ways in which audio can be made interactive and we will explore the possibilities offered by social creation and sharing of audio data.

2   Two Supporting Case Studies

The main case study described in this paper is supported by unpublished data from 2 other case studies conducted in the past two years, which provided insights on the advantages of interactive audiobooks. All the three case studies adopted the User Centred Design method supported by qualitative methods. Our students had to conduct a full design iteration consisting of: a field study investigating the practice, in which users participate in; a phase of analysis in which design requirements are formulated; a phase

---

[2] Freely available on GooglePlay.

[3] List of popular audio walk on SoundCloud: https://soundcloud.com/tags/audio%20walk.

of conceptualization through brainstorming and prototyping techniques; testing in which a semi-functioning prototype is evaluated with the users. The testing was conducted as a play test session with focus groups, involving users in demonstration of the prototypes. Qualitative methods were chosen for several reasons: first of all our students engaged with a limited number of users, either high-school, primary school classes, or focus groups. Second, the students' goal was to closely explore current user experience and opportunities for improvement, also enabling the users to propose possible ideas. Specifically, for the main use case, our students adopted visual ethnography in situ, semi-structured interviews for which they were requested to prepare a minimum set of pre-defined questions for the users (Yliriksu and Buur 2007). The students were therefore required to analyze the gathered video recordings scrutinizing how users interacted during class activities and how they talked about their practice (verbal and non-verbal language) during the interviews, with the goal of identifying aspects that needed improvements or support. Semi-structured interviews and observations were also adopted in the two supporting studies. Given that our students were still learning about UCD and qualitative methods, we took part in many of the phases of the 3 studies, complementing their field work with our notes and reflections. The findings discussed in the following sections are the result of this process.

2.1 Audio Deliverables

The audio deliverables application originated from the supervision of 4 groups of students attending the Software Engineering and IT bachelor at the University of Southern Denmark (SDU); the semester long project, run in fall 2014, was about developing user-centered software solutions to better support English teachers in 2 Danish primary schools. The field study started with observations of 2 classes of 4th graders learning English, one in each school. After a preliminary visit and meeting with the 2 teachers who agreed to participate in this study, the groups of SDU students visited the school repeatedly and proceeded by defining requirements and producing a few prototypes, from low-fidelity ones to partially working horizontal prototypes (created using MIT's AppInventor[4]).

The 2 teachers, here called Anders and Britta for anonymity, were also interviewed; they showed very different approaches of using technology in their teaching. Anders can be considered a designer of content. He states openly that he has limited IT skills but he is very creative in the design and generation of new content. In the first visit he showed us how he wrote a short dialogue with 4 roles, for his students to read aloud. In fact, spoken interaction and comprehension are the main goals for the 4th grade English curriculum. The dialogue was about 3 friends who interact with the waiter (the other role) in a British restaurant, and have to order, confirm their orders, eat and pay the waiter, who in turn has asks typical questions about their choice of food, beverages and how they want to settle their check. It was clear that Anders compensates the lack of interactivity in his material (which was not given to the pupils in digital format, but

---

[4] AppInventor's official page: http://appinventor.mit.edu/explore/.

written at his computer and then printed) with role play and social interaction. Britta is much more in touch with IT and in particular likes to use what is available online, but she re-contextualizes it according to her pupils' needs. She has a toolbox approach and often uses tools that are not originally pedagogical, like video editing, comics authoring tools and online audiobooks in English. In our first visit Britta brought her class to the IT lab for the English lecture; the pupils kept switching from audiobooks to cartoon editing, to chats with the teacher and each other.

We found these two approaches very intriguing and believe they should be further studied. However, in this paper we are mostly interested in user-generated audio contents, therefore, we will focus on the group of SDU students working with Anders' class. They noted the various problems he had orchestrating the class with his printed material: the pupils were divided in groups of 3 to 4, and had to read the text a few times, waiting for Anders to drop by, listen to them and provide feedback. The result was the audio deliverable application, a mock-up mobile app that allowed pupils to read an English text aloud in group, and deliver it to the teacher as an audio recording. These audio deliverables afford good peer interaction and make the communication with the teacher more asynchronous. Moreover, they represent a form of audio content generation that is natural and very easy to master for 4th grade pupils who are typically proficient in the use of smart phones; the focus was mainly on reading skills.

The development and testing of the audio deliverable application, together with the feedback we received from Anders and his class convinced us that audio content can be easier to generate than written English (for Danish 4th graders). Recordings enable more asynchronous teacher/pupils interaction, they open for peer reflection and can be preserved to serve as a learning diary to make students more aware of their progress.

2.2 Carbooks

This study demonstrates the versatility of audio as a communication modality, by mapping gamebooks into mobile-friendly, interactive audiobooks. The goal of this project was to offer an entertaining and relaxing experience to kids who often get car-sick in long car trips, and have problems reading or watching videos while traveling. In this case playing videogames using mobile devices is not an option; audiobooks instead can offer relief and help passing the time in a fun or perhaps educational way. However, audiobooks provide a passive experience and can become boring in long trips, so we wanted to investigate how non-linear narrative can be used in audiobooks, to create interactive and enjoyable experience for kids and young adults. A focus group was created to play-test the interactive audiobooks, composed of 10 young adults (age 19 to 25) and 2 kids (10 and 12); the family of the 2 kids was among the other stakeholders involved in the project. The Carbook bachelor project tested various ideas, running in the fall 2015 semester and through 3 iterations, with the central focus to develop an audio-only interactive application for android platform. The main tools were Unity[5] and Google Text-To-Speech.

---

[5] Unity3d website: https://unity3d.com/.

Removing the graphical user interface while retaining the interactivity typical of digital games proved one of the major challenges; the project also explored possibly mappings between input modalities and choice in the non-linear narrative. A mobile phone offers gestures, microphone and orientation/motion detection. Typical gestures we considered are touch, hold and swipe. As for microphone input, voice recognition was too complex to work in practice and it would have been mostly limited to English language, so volume level was used instead; microphone input was used in the second iteration of the interactive audio book prototype, but turned out to be unreliable and difficult to use by the players, who got frustrated by the experience. In the third (and final) prototype microphone was replaced by orientation (basically reading the state of the phone's gyroscopes). These input modalities were to be used in steering the narrative of the interactive audio book, mostly without the player looking at the screen, and that required some analysis too; background audio clues were also used (in version 2 of the prototype) to help players orient themselves while exploring the locations in the story. In printed gamebooks the player is often faced with 3 to 6 options to select from, but in Carbooks we had to break down the player options in sequences of binary choices. This restructuring of the choices made it easy to map input events with binary alternatives, but it could be argued that it has limited the non-linearity of the narrative (reducing de facto the branching factor of the multi-linear plot).

The Carbooks project shows that interactivity can work in audio-only (or audio-first) applications, and that the user experience is similar to that of slow-paced exploration/adventure video games, such as classic text-based games of the 1980s. Smart phones, with their current computing power, audio support and their wide range of input modalities, proved a reasonable choice of platform for audio-only interactive applications. The main limitation of the project however, was that it did not focus on content creation, so while we have evidence that interactivity and audio work for simple, fun non-linear stories, we have to progress further with our studies before we can directly link interactive audio books to language learning.

3   The Main Case Study: Social Audiobooks

The last and main case study was conducted in relation to an elective course in Media Sociology, the course lasted for five weeks in the fall semester of 2015, and focused on e-learning with students from the Multimedia Design program (MMD for short) at the Lillebaelt Academy in Odense, Denmark. The 21 students had to work on a mini-project in groups of three or four, in cooperation with Nyborg gymnasium, a high-school located in Nyborg a small town on the island of Funen, Denmark. From the point of view of the Lillebaelt Academy, the learning goal of the mini-projects was to create conditions for the MMD students to conduct a rigorous user centered design process, actively involving users, to adopt a contextual perspective on the design of learning technologies, and to critically reflect on how their new solution contributes to teaching and learning practices in the gymnasium. On the other hand the gymnasium in Nyborg was eager to explore and test together with MMD students new interactive solutions, which could enrich the current learning and teaching practices.

In their Media Sociology course, the MMD students were introduced to five research articles applying a specific learning theory to learning contexts and to the design of a digital solution. One particular group of three MMD students explored the design of an application to support interactivity with audiobooks, these students chose to work with the studies conducted by Hattie and Gan (2011) in visible learning and by Marchetti and Petersson Brooks (2012) in the sociocultural theory. Hattie and Gan (2011) explain how visible learning can affect learning practice, discussing the role of teachers in enabling the students in formulating learning goals and success criteria, in providing descriptive feedback, which enables students to improve their skills, and formative assessment, aimed at collecting evidence of the student's achievement. Marchetti and Petersson Brooks (2012) instead adopt the sociocultural theory in the design of a digital exhibit, aimed at enriching the social interaction between guides and visitors during guided tours. The study aims at enriching the interaction between guides and visitors, looking into guided tours as a sociocultural activity, which is influenced by the traditions and practices of museum contexts. The project of our students aimed at designing an interactive solution to enrich learning practice and social interaction in English language class of the Nyborg gymnasium.

3.1   Audook: Social Experience of Audiobooks Social

The Audook mini-project by one group of three MMD students explored how interactive fruition of audiobooks could enrich learning practice in classes of English literature and language, with the cooperation of a gymnasium teacher (here called Sanne) and her class, 15 students of approximately 15–16 years of age. The outcome of the Audook mini-project represents an attempt of transduction of reading assignments from the visual to audio mode. Transduction is defined in social semiotics as a translation, in which meaning-material is moved from one mode to another, for instance "from speech to image, from writing to film" (Kress 2010, p. 125). Since each mode has specific material qualities and entities to be manipulated, for instance speech has words and images have colors, each mode has also a different history of social use. This in turn has implications on how the same meaning-material is formulated and transmitted by the sender, and on how the message is received and interpreted by the audience, so that the same message might be slightly altered in its meaning through the transduction process. Audiobooks represent for instance a case of transduction from the visual book format into an auditive one. As showed by related studies (Alcantud-Díaz and Gregori 2014) the fruition of the same story both through reading and in audio form affects significantly how learners experience reading, in some cases even enabling them to improve their skills.

Through their field study the three MMD students found that English classes in Nyborg, involved mostly reading and analyzing texts. The English teacher Sanne was concerned with choosing samples of English literature that the students could find interesting to "motivate her pupils to read and analyze the texts". For this reason she said: "I am trying to look for novels that can be interesting, handling topics about social relations and adventures". Her strategy involves "books that have become popular in recent years, often because they were adapted into movies, so that they have heard about them". During our study for instance the class was reading "The Beach" by Alex Garland, which is also the subject of a popular Hollywood movie starring Leonardo Di Caprio. In this way the teacher was already encouraging a multimodal fruition and analysis of the assigned novel. We found that the Nyborg students are typically assigned a set of pages or entire chapters to read for a certain date. While in class they are asked to discuss in groups the read chapters and to fill a form with questions or aspects to reflect upon, such as the maturation of a character, the social conflicts, or narrative techniques adopted by the writer; afterwards, a group discussion is conducted in class. The students also watch the movie based on the novel they are reading, together with the teacher. This is supposed to keep them motivated to read and reflect on how the novel could be interpreted, and Sanne added with satisfaction "they often prefer the novel to the movie!" as the students notice that in the movie many elements were omitted or the actors representing specific characters do not match their imagination.

The gymnasium students complained, however, that reading requires a "total" involvement; several of them said that they can read mostly while on the bus or at home, but unfortunately they cannot read while running or walking in town. Reading is also perceived as isolating, so that for sharing impressions on specific passages they have to either meet or write through social media.

The design process that led to the creation of *Audook*, an application aimed at providing an alternative fruition of literary texts. The central idea was to operate a transduction of novels into audio, and create a gesture-based app for mobile phones. The requirements involved being able to use a hand gesture to add a bookmark on a specific passage, while listening to an audiobook; users should also be able to add comments in spoken and in written forms by opening a visual interface, and share their comments and bookmarks through social media.

The resulting prototype mobile application (visible in Fig. 1) offers a richer, multimodal experience than just reading and showcases the extension of annotating and sharing comments from a book to an audiobook. A summative evaluation provided criticisms and positive feedback. For example it was noted that audiobooks take longer to "read" than books. Both we and the group developing Audook agree that it is not a good idea to substitute visual reading because of the importance of seeing the text, especially in language learning. There were also concerns on the quality of the voices obtained via text-to-speech, with respect to those of actors and native speakers reading the texts. Concerns were raised by the teacher in relation to how she could fetch audiobooks for her students; the fully developed application should be able to connect with the collection of audiobooks of the school or of the local library, which is already available online, enabling the teacher and her students to easily get the novels they need.

On the positive side, audiobooks can be "read" also while doing sports, walking or running; they can be easier to access than books (and e-books) while travelling on public transportation with less chances of motion sickness. Using Audook, books critique and commentaries could be shared electronically in preparation for group discussion in class. It was also asked by a few students if it was possible to listen to an audiobook while watching the e-book version (a scenario similar to existing karaoke applications): in this way users could learn more effectively how to pronounce new

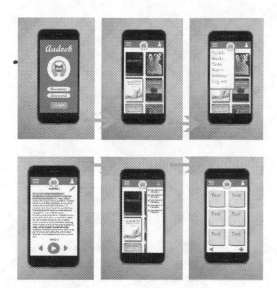

Fig. 1. Overview of the interface of Audook. The top row shows the log-in screen and the initial access to the audiobooks library. The second row shows how the text can be visualized by the reader, and the sharing and annotation features.

words. Finally, the Audook app was positively evaluated as an interactive alternative to normal reading, expanding opportunities for multimodal fruition of novels and for sharing personal reflections on texts. In general the social aspect of the application and the possibility to listen to the story while engaging in outdoor activities were particularly appreciated as if they were making the experience of reading less isolating.

4 Discussion

The main case study and the 2 supporting studies show the wide spectrum of opportunities offered by audiobooks in language learning, from content generation to social and game-like interactivity. The main contributions of this paper are design insights to make audiobooks interactive and better integrated in the social interaction emerging in learning contexts, between learners and teachers but also among peer learners. At the same we aim at exploring how the transduction of literary texts could foster different experiences, when moving from the visual and tangible modes associated to the experience of physical books and e-readers, to the auditory modality enhanced by interactivity.

Comparing the three case studies, we can see that interactive audiobooks are preferred to non-interactive ones by potential users, who in our testing consistently described typical audiobooks as eliciting passive experiences. Interactivity with the text was evaluated positively both in relation to exploring non-linear stories, but also in contexts of language learning (Alcantud-Díaz and Gregori 2014). As pointed out in Kress (2010) the transduction of literary text into an auditory format can significantly alter how readers relate to the text. The auditory modality can make the reading activity more flexible and accessible for learners, for instance the possibility to create audio deliverables can support adoption of pedagogical approaches like visible learning (Hattie and Gan 2011), in which learners and their teachers can afford longitudinal monitoring of spoken language competences. The recordings created during language learning open the possibility to apply analysis techniques and data mining on audio content. This is valid also for learners who have a busy day and see in the auditory fruition of novels a better support for multi-tasking, enabling them to "read" also when traveling and reading might get them sick and when engaging in outdoor activities. Moreover, the audio modality can better support children who are still in the progress of developing writing skills in their own or in a foreign language, as well as learners with linguistic difficulties. Finally, the study in Nyborg provides new insights on how interactive audiobooks could contribute to turn reading into a social experience, as according to sociocultural theories in learning. Adopting a sociocultural perspective (Rogoff 1990), learning is seen as a social practice in which learners are facilitated by an expert adult, the teacher, but can also support each other, in a persistent and asynchronous way. Enabling learners to share their thoughts and bookmarks with each other, Audook can contribute to the emergence of a shared understanding of the text at hand enriching the process of textual analysis and reflection.

Building on these case studies, we propose insights on how audiobooks could be turned into an interactive medium:

1. Support generation of audio as well as fruition. Audio just requires a bit of technical support, for example, Google docs can be extended to allow voice comments on texts, by using add-on like Kaizena[6].
2. Leverage on social and asynchronous communication between teachers and students, and provide support for peer-learning.
3. Consider multiple storylines in audiobooks. Multiple storylines can allow for experiential learning (Furini 2007; Alcantud-Díaz and Gregori 2014) and support case-based reasoning. A major drawback of authoring non-linear narrative is the need to create multiple, potentially modular storylines; non-linear audiobooks in particular have always been human-intensive. Our Carbooks project, however, shows that text-to-speech technology is currently widely available (on laptops and even mobile devices) and good enough at least for English. All teachers in the schools we visited have at least basic IT skills, hence they have no problem in generating English texts and potentially create written non-linear narrative; our experience with Carbooks convinced us that by leveraging on text-to-speech and gesture-based non-visual interfaces, non-linear audiobooks in English can potential be created by the teachers themselves, in this way supporting language learning.
4. Socially generated audio content as a kind of social media data. We suggest to consider the audio content generated by a group of students learning English as similar to the content produced in a social media. Since voice data-mining is still very complex and dependent upon pronunciation, often imprecise and typically works for English and very few other languages, we consider social media

---

[6] Kaizena's webpage: https://kaizena.com/.

approaches like user-created tags as the best option to classify and search through audio contents.

5. Audio as a complement to visual modality. Based on our studies we do not aim at replacing the visual modality of reading, but at providing complementary auditory alternatives that could enrich how people experience literary texts.

The exploration of interactive audiobooks is not new, as we can see in current research, however, we may argue that these studies have taken a limited perspective, mainly supporting the authoring of non-linear stories. On the other hand, when coming to learning these studies seem eager to argue that audiobooks can offer better support to learners in acquiring linguistic as well as intercultural competences (Alcantud-Díaz and Gregori 2014). In our studies we take instead a more cautious position, as results from our testing suggest that visual reading is perceived as more personal and active, as readers can decide for themselves how quickly they want to read, they can imagine for themselves the features of a character or a setting. At the same time audiobooks do not allow for that freedom, as they impose a specific timing and the voice of the reader, which could be found unpleasant or expressing feelings in an inappropriate way for the sensitive of the listener.

Audiobooks have many faces (or *voices*) and seem to us to possess untapped potential. The students from Nyborg gymnasium appeared eager to identify both the new possibilities offered by the Audook application, but were also aware of some intrinsic limitations of audiobooks.

5   Conclusion

The main contributions of this paper are insights on how to make audiobooks interactive and better integrated in learning contexts, in particular when learning English as a foreign language. The three case studies discussed show the large spectrum of opportunities offered by audiobooks in language learning, from content generation to social and game-like interactivity. Our prototypes provide evidence that audiobooks can help in documenting learning (thanks to audio deliverables), in supporting different learning experiences and styles, and in complementing visual information when exploring non-linear narrative.

We believe that the experience obtained in the three studies and the insights we gained can be used as design guidelines to develop more interactive audiobooks and audio-enabled applications. A fully functional mobile application based on the outcome of the main case study is currently under development.

References

Alcantud Díaz, M., Gregori Signes, C.: Audiobooks: improving fluency and instilling literary skills and education for development. Tejuelo (Trujillo) **20**, 111–125 (2014)

Baskin, B.H., Harris, K.: Heard any good books lately? The case for audio books in the secondary classroom. J. Read. **38**(5), 372–376 (1995)

Furini, M.: Beyond passive audiobooks: how digital audiobooks get interactive. In: IEEE Consumer Communication and Networking, pp. 971–975. IEEE Press, New York (2007)

Hattie, J., Gan, M.: Instruction based on feedback. In: Mayer, R.E., Alexander, P.A. (eds.) Handbook of Research on Learning and Instruction, pp. 249–271. Routledge, New York and London (2011)

Huber, C., Röber, N., Hartmann, K., Masuch, M.: Evolution of interactive audiobooks. In: 2nd Conference on Interaction with Sound (Audio Mostly 2007), pp. 166–167. Fraunhofer Institute for Digital Media Technology IDMT (2007)

Kress, G.: Multimodality: A Social Semiotic Approach to Contemporary Communication. Routledge, London and New York (2010)

Marchetti, E., Petersson Brooks, E.: From lecturing to apprenticeship. In: Fourth International Conference on Mobile, Hybrid, and On-Line Learning, pp. 225–224. IARIA (2012)

Prieto, L.P., Sharma, K., Dillenbourg, P.: Studying teacher orchestration load in technology-enhanced classrooms. In: Conole, G., et al. (eds.) EC-TEL 2015. LNCS, vol. 9307, pp. 268–281. Springer, Heidelberg (2015). doi:10.1007/978-3-319-24258-3_20

Rogoff, B.: Apprenticeship in Thinking. Cognitive Development in Social Context. Oxford University Press, Oxford (1990)

van Zeijl, M.: The soundwalker in the street: location-based audio walks and the poetic re-imagination of space. In: De Michelis, G., Tisato, F., Bene, A., Bernini, D. (eds.) ArtsIT 2013. LNICST, vol. 116, pp. 17–24. Springer, Heidelberg (2013)

Wilde, S., Larsson, J.: Listen! It's Good for Kids. AudioFile Magazine, 23–25 (2007). April/May issue. http://www.audiofilemagazine.com/content/uploaded/media/listen-goodforkids.pdf

Yliriksu, S., Buur, J.: Designing with Video. Focusing the User Centred Design Process. Springer, London (2007)

On the Integration of Tangible Elements with Multi-touch Surfaces for the Collaborative Creation of Concept Maps

Gustavo Salvador-Herranz[1], Jorge D. Camba[2], Ferran Naya[3],
and Manuel Contero[3(✉)]

[1] Dpto. Expresión Gráfica, Proyectos y Urbanismo,
Universidad CEU Cardenal Herrera, Valencia, Spain
gsalva@uch.ceu.es
[2] Gerald D. Hines College of Architecture and Design,
University of Houston, Houston, TX, USA
jdorribo@uh.edu
[3] Instituto de Investigación en Bioingeniería (I3B),
Universitat Politècnica de València, Valencia, Spain
{fernasan,mcontero}@upv.es

Abstract. Collaborative creative work in small groups can significantly improve learning, particularly when supported by concept maps. Although useful in collaborative environments, most applications for the development of concept maps are designed for personal or small tablet computers, which can limit student communication in a team setting. In addition, the use of these applications usually requires training periods that may reduce the time allotted for regular learning activities. In this context, digital tabletops can effectively promote collaboration and face-to-face communication by providing a large horizontal interactive surface. However, despite its large size, a single tabletop cannot accommodate more than three or four students. Therefore, collaborative learning spaces and work groups with multiple devices become necessary. In such scenarios, the exchange of information between groups is critical. In this paper, we propose the use of tangibles, as a natural mechanism to exchange information by using a distributed collaborative concept map application.

Keywords: Tabletops · Multi-touch surfaces · Tangibles · Concept maps · Collaborative work

1   Introduction

Collaborative learning is an effective educational method that plays an essential role in theories such as Constructivism and Knowledge Building [13, 18]. Studies have shown that collaborative creative work in small groups can significantly improve learning when supported by concept maps [11]. Concept maps are tools to organize, represent, and structure knowledge relationships in a graphical format. Although useful in collaborative environments, most applications for the development of concept maps are

© Springer International Publishing Switzerland 2016
P. Zaphiris and A. Ioannou (Eds.): LCT 2016, LNCS 9753, pp. 177–186, 2016.
DOI: 10.1007/978-3-319-39483-1_17

designed for personal or small tablet computers, which can limit student communication in a team setting. In addition, the use of these applications usually requires training periods that may reduce the time allotted for regular learning activities.

Studies suggest that large horizontal interactive surfaces can effectively promote collaboration and face-to-face communication [2, 6, 14]. These surfaces often provide multi-touch interfaces that implement common hand gestures for basic operations such as zoom, pan, and rotate. In this paper, we present a software tool for developing concept maps that combines tangible interactive controls with multi-touch and multi-user capabilities. Tangible controls provide a richer and more direct interaction mechanism than plain visual representations on the computer screen normally do [3–5, 20]. Multi-touch surfaces make interactions more natural and intuitive.

Our interactive surface is designed around an optical infrared frame mounted on a commercial large screen high-definition TV set. The optical frame supports the simultaneous detection of a large number of contact points, which allows the use of physical objects (which can be 3D printed) to reproduce various touch patterns, similar to those performed by explicit hand gestures on the table. These patterns are then recognized by our system and used to identify what tangible element is being used as well as to calculate its position and orientation on the surface. As a result, specific functionalities can be assigned to physical elements based on its position and orientation on the surface (i.e. to simulate the physical interaction with a rotating knob).

Our application uses tangible elements as a method to manage information locally on an interactive surface and as a natural mechanism to exchange information between different surfaces to support distributed collaborative design work. A preliminary usability evaluation shows that the application is intuitive and provides sufficient functionality and resources to build large concept maps of relatively high complexity.

2 Distributed Concept Maps

Tabletop systems offer a large interactive surface on which several users can work collaboratively and communicate face-to-face. In this regard, some researchers have used tabletops to create concept maps in collaborative digital work spaces [9].

Although the work space of a tabletop system is large, it is difficult for more than three or four users to work simultaneously in a comfortable and productive manner. In collaborative work scenarios with many users, it is possible to define a distributed model where a set of tabletop devices connect to a common digital work space. In [16], an implementation of this model is described. The model allows the extension of the local collaborative workspaces that are established around a physical interactive surface, into a distributed setting that allows the interconnection of remote devices. Therefore, a common virtual workspace is generated, similar to the concept of cloud. The interaction with the system is based on Natural Interfaces. Unlike other solutions, our technology allows designing complex schemes of classroom orchestration in a natural and simply manner.

Fig. 1. Representation of a distributed collaborative work space

A software application for the construction of concept maps was developed based on the distributed collaborative work space model [16]. The system allows the construction of concept maps in this digital space, so each tabletop connected to the system acts as an interactive window to the common space (Fig. 1). The system provides a natural interface that minimizes learning curves and allows the addition of new information through BYOD mechanisms (Bring Your Own Device). For example, users can use their smart phones to send text and images to the system or by e-mail or through the social network Twitter.

In collaborative environments, the exchange of information between groups is especially important. Our system facilitates these tasks by implementing operations such as copy/cut/paste, which propagate hierarchically through the directed graph defined by the concept map. Thus, a user can copy part of a concept map by selecting the root node of a subtree and clicking the appropriate option on the context menu provided by the system. By using zooming and panning operations, users can "virtually" move over to the working area of a different group of users and perform a "paste" operation.

However, this mechanism can become confusing to some users in environments where several working groups are distributed in a room. In this scenario, where users carry their devices around the room, the fact that information can only move virtually without involving a physical displacement of users, may be perceived as unnatural.

These impressions are reflected in the usability test performed in [16]. The results of this study (using a Likert [8] scale of 5 values) are shown in Table 1. While results were positive in all cases, teamwork (question 6) received the lowest score.

Subsequent interviews with users who participated in the experiment revealed difficulties in tasks related to the exchange of information among different working groups.

The integration of new mechanisms based on physical manipulators of information can simplify the exchange and manipulation of digital information between working cores, making it more natural for users.

Table 1. Evaluation test questions and results from previous study [16]

	Question	x	σ
1	Using the tool is easy	4.60	0.50
2	Understanding the system is easy	4.20	0.70
3	Learning to operate the system is easy	4.70	0.47
4	Learning to operate the system is fast	4.90	0.31
5	Remembering to operate the system is easy	4.65	0.49
6	Teamwork is easy	3.90	0.64
7	Overall, I found the system easy to use	4.60	0.50
8	Overall, I found the system useful	4.35	0.49

3   Tangible Interface

A Tangible User interface (TUI) is a user interface where users can interact with digital information through a physical medium. Natural interfaces give digital information a physical form, which simplifies user interaction by becoming metaphors for handling physical objects and materials (actions that are performed instinctively).

TUIs have been widely used in teamwork and collaborative learning environments [3–5, 20]. In our previous work, we used tangible items over tabletop systems to improve collaborative work in teams [1]. Our system used tangible elements to represent conceptual map nodes, while transitions were represented graphically by the tabletop. Similar systems were described in [12, 19]. For instance, in [19], both nodes and transitions are represented digitally, and tangible manipulators are used as tools to perform actions (create and move nodes, create and label links, etc.). Other studies use tabletops for the implementation of concept maps without the use of tangible items [9]. From the standpoint of collaborative work, results are satisfactory at the local level, where multiple users work simultaneously over a single interactive surface.

In this paper, we propose the use of tangible manipulators to implement information exchange operations in a distributed scenario between different tabletop devices of different working groups. Therefore, the transfer of information becomes a physical action, similar to what happens in a traditional work environment, where the physical transfer of information involves the movement of users.

3.1   Using Tangibles to Exchange Information

The information exchange between tabletops using tangible elements is implemented as cut/copy/paste operations. For these tasks, two tangible marks are used, the first one associated with the 'cut' operation and the second one associated to the 'copy' operation. The two operations are similar. Only 'cut' deletes information from the source tabletop. In both cases, the information is temporarily stored in the clipboard (supported by the application server). Placing a 'cut' tangible on a concept map node will copy the node and its hierarchically dependent child nodes to the clipboard and delete it from the source working area. The 'copy' operation is similar, but the original information will not be deleted from the source. By placing the 'tangible manipulator' on a different tabletop system (or on a different location on the same tabletop), the hierarchical structure stored in the clipboard will appear, with the root node directly under the manipulator.

3.2   Additional Operations with Tangibles

Tangible manipulators are also designed for zooming and panning operations. For zooming, the tangible manipulator must be placed on the tabletop surface and rotated. Clockwise rotation implies a positive zoom, while counterclockwise rotation implies a negative zoom. Similarly, by moving the tangible associated with the panning operation, it is possible to move the displayed area of the work plane.

4   Implementation Details

4.1   Tabletop System

Since the appearance of the first tabletop devices, several types of solutions and technology implementations have been used [10, 17]. The use of infrared optical frames [1] allow to convert any flat screen into a multi-touch tabletop device. Currently, the affordability and availability of this type of frames has increased significantly, even for very large screens formats, reaching high resolutions and high rates (>=200 Hz) in the detection of touches. The type of tangible interaction described in this paper is not common in optical frame based tabletops.

4.2   Tangible Marks

In our previous work [15], we developed a system of tangible manipulators based on the use of physical objects that were completely passive. The position and orientation of these manipulators could be identified and calculated in real time when placed on the working surface to reproduce various touch patterns, similar to those performed by specific hand gestures on the interactive table.

An example of the developed tangible passive manipulators (corresponding to id's 2, 3 and 5) is shown in Fig. 2. If necessary, the physical marks can be labeled according to its functionality. The basic element consists of a cylindrical base with three pins, which describe an isosceles triangle. This basic element corresponds to the handler with ID = 0. Since the three pins form a triangle, the element is stable on the surface of the tabletop and its circumcenter defines the XY position of the manipulator. Additionally, the orientation of the mark (an isosceles triangle) can be easily determined.

Fig. 2. Example of passive tangible manipulators placed on an optical frame surface

The codification of the different IDs is performed by adding additional pins between the two pins that define the short side of the isosceles triangle according to a binary encoding in base 2 arrangement. Therefore, the number of different manipulators can be 2^n, where 'n' is the maximum number of pins that can be placed between the two pins that define the short side of the triangle. This number depends on the resolution of the optical frame and size (radius) of the manipulator. An example of eight possible encodings using three pins is shown in Fig. 3.

Fig. 3. Codification of eight manipulators using three pins

Once the markers are placed on the interactive surface, a set of single touches are detected, which are treated as point clouds and segmented into clusters. Subsequently, for each cluster the system calculates in real time the XY position of its centroid, its orientation, and ID, and encapsulates this information in respective TUIO frames [7]. The set of points detected on the interactive surface to the situation presented in Fig. 2 is illustrated in Fig. 4.

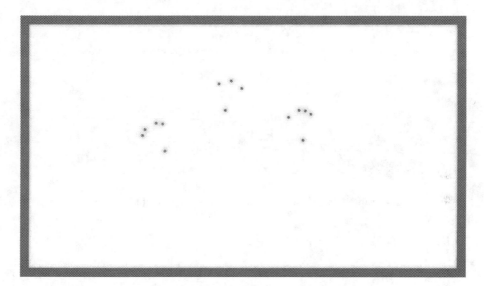

Fig. 4. Points detected on an interactive surface from the three tangible marks shown in Fig. 2

4.3   System Architecture

The Distributed Concept Map system is an application that consists of a server and several local nodes (tabletop systems) connected via a TCP/IP network (Fig. 5).

Both local and server applications were implemented using the Unity engine, which provides extensive support for developing graphical and networking applications. The entire virtual workspace is managed by the server and each client has a view of it. Any action performed by a client is transmitted to the server, which immediately updates the scene and, in return, sends the changes back to the clients. The operation is similar to a network video game, where a common virtual world is stored on a server, and each player connects to it as a client.

Using the API provided by the optical frame manufacturer, a daemon process was developed to continually sample touches on the interactive tabletop and return them as XY point coordinates. With this information, a middleware application computes the number of marks placed on the surface as well as their respective IDs, position and orientations, and encapsulates this information in TUIO frames that are sent via UDP to the local application. All points that are not classified into any cluster (and thus do not belong to any mark) are sent as single points in single TUIO "point" frames. This feature allows compatible interaction with the multi-touch table using both tangible marks and hand gestures.

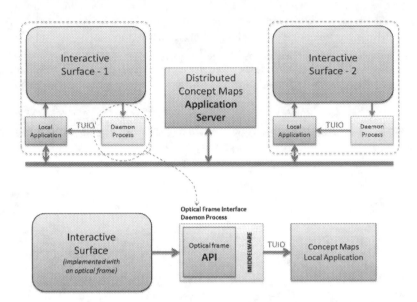

Fig. 5. Architecture of the distribute concept maps with tangible elements interface

5 Preliminary Usability Evaluation

A preliminary test was conducted to study the impact of tangible manipulators in a collaborative work scenario where eight students distributed in two tabletops worked on the construction of concept maps on a common theme. The session was conducted by teachers to encourage situations where both groups of students needed to exchange knowledge, and experiences to build a complete concept map. Such situations caused the physical movement of students and information. The questionnaire and results of the 5-point Likert scale used in the evaluation are shown in Table 2.

Table 2. Questions and results of the preliminary usability evaluation test using tangibles

Question		x	Σ
1	Using the tool is easy	4.75	0.46
2	Understanding the system is easy	4.38	0.52
3	Learning to operate the system is easy	4.75	0.46
4	Learning to operate the system is fast	4.63	0.52
5	Remembering to operate the system is easy	4.88	0.35
6	Teamwork is easy	4.63	0.52
7	Overall, I found the system easy to use	4.63	0.52
8	Overall, I found the system useful	4.63	0.52
9	I found the mechanism for information exchange between groups easy and simple	4.75	0.46

6 Conclusions and Future Work

Based on the results of the preliminary usability test, the use of tangible manipulators has been shown beneficial in tasks related to the exchange and management of information between different workgroups. Comparing these results with those obtained in our first usability test (Table 1), we can observe an improvement in question 6.

From interviews with students who participated in the first test, it was concluded that the low scores obtained in the question 6 were mainly due to the difficulty of exchanging information between groups. In this regard, it appears that the addition of tangibles for handling information simplifies this task and makes it more natural. This conclusion is reinforced by the scores from question 9, which confirm that tangible markers are easy to use for information exchange activities. Moreover, a natural flow of students between the two work groups was observed during the experiment. The virtual information transfer between the two tabletops mimics the physical transfer of information media in traditional work environments.

The use of tabletop systems implemented with optical frame technology combined with the use of the proposed passive tangible manipulators, results in a tool with a reasonable price/performance ratio that has proven useful in distributed collaborative learning environments. In the future, more comprehensive testing usability evaluations involving a larger number of users and tabletop stations will be conducted.

References

1. Bhalla, M.R., Bhalla, A.V.: Comparative study of various touchscreen technologies. Int. J. Comput. Appl. **6**, 12–18 (2010)
2. Dillenbourg, P., Evans, M.: Interactive tabletops in education. Int. J. Comput.-Support. Collaborative Learn. **6**, 491–514 (2011)
3. Falcão, T.P., Price, S.: What have you done! the role of 'interference' in tangible environments for supporting collaborative learning. In: Proceedings of the 9th International Conference on Computer Supported Collaborative Learning, vol. 1, pp. 325–334 (2009)
4. Ishii, H.: Tangible User Interfaces. CRC Press, Boca Raton (2007)
5. Ishii, H., Ullmer, B.: Tangible bits: towards seamless interfaces between people, bits and atoms. In: Proceedings of the ACM SIGCHI Conference on Human Factors in Computing Systems, Atlanta, Georgia, USA, pp. 234–241 (1997)
6. Jackson, A.T., Brummel, B.J., Pollet, C.L., Greer, D.D.: An evaluation of interactive tabletops in elementary mathematics education. Educ. Tech. Res. Dev. **61**, 311–332 (2013)
7. Kaltenbrunner, M., Bovermann, T., Bencina, R., Costanza, E.: TUIO: a protocol for table-top tangible user interfaces. In: Proceedings of the 6th International Workshop on Gesture in Human-Computer Interaction and Simulation, pp. 1–5 (2005)
8. Likert, R.: A technique for the measurement of attitudes. Arch. Psychol. **22**(140), 1–55 (1932)
9. Martínez Maldonado, R., Kay, J., Yacef, K.: Collaborative concept mapping at the tabletop. In: ACM International Conference on Interactive Tabletops and Surfaces, pp. 207–210 (2010)

10. Müller-Tomfelde, C.: Tabletops-Horizontal Interactive Displays: Horizontal Interactive Displays. Springer Science & Business Media, Heidelberg (2010)
11. Novak, J.D., Cañas, A.J.: The theory underlying concept maps and how to construct and use them (2008)
12. Oppl, S., Stary, C.: Tabletop concept mapping. In: Proceedings of the 3rd International Conference on Tangible and Embedded Interaction, pp. 275–282 (2009)
13. Perkins, D.: The many faces of constructivism. Educ. Leadersh. **53**, 6–11 (1999)
14. Piper, A.M., Hollan, J.D.: Tabletop displays for small group study: affordances of paper and digital materials. In: Proceedings of the SIGCHI Conference on Human Factors in Computing Systems, pp. 1227–1236 (2009)
15. Salvador-Herranz, G., Contero, M., Camba, J.: Use of tangible marks with optical frame interactive surfaces in collaborative design scenarios based on blended spaces. In: Luo, Y. (ed.) CDVE 2014. LNCS, vol. 8683, pp. 253–260. Springer, Heidelberg (2014)
16. Salvador-Herranz, G., Contero, M., Dorribo-Camba, J.: Management of distributed collaborative learning environments based on a concept map paradigm and natural interfaces. In: Frontiers in Education Conference, IEEE, pp. 1486–1491 (2013)
17. Schöning, J., Hook, J., Bartindale, T., Schmidt, D., Oliver, P., Echtler, F., Motamedi, N., Brandl, P., Zadow, U.: Building interactive multi-touch surfaces. In: Müller-Tomfelde, C. (ed.) Tabletops-Horizontal Interactive Displays, pp. 27–49. Springer, Heidelberg (2010)
18. Tam, M.: Constructivism, instructional design, and technology: implications for transforming distance learning. Educ. Technol. Soc. **3**, 50–60 (2000)
19. Tanenbaum, K., Antle, A.N.: Using physical constraints to augment concept mapping on a tangible tabletop. In: Proceedings of the International Conference on Education and Information Technology, pp. 539–547 (2008)
20. Zuckerman, O., Arida, S., Resnick, M.: Extending tangible interfaces for education: digital montessori-inspired manipulatives. In: Proceedings of the SIGCHI Conference on Human factors in Computing Systems, pp. 859–868 (2005)

Studying Children's Navigation
in Virtual Reality

Aimilia Tzanavari[1]([✉]), Chris Christou[2], Kyriakos Herakleous[3],
and Charalambos Poullis[3]

[1] PROTOIO Inc., San Francisco, USA
aimiliatzanavari@gmail.com
[2] Department of Design and Multimedia, University of Nicosia, Nicosia, Cyprus
christou.ch@unic.ac.cy
[3] Immersive and Creative Technologies Lab, Concordia University,
Montreal, Canada
kyriakosv2005@hotmail.com, charalambos@poullis.org

Abstract. Navigation in large-scale virtual environments is composed of locomotion and wayfinding. We compared two locomotion techniques in an immersive CAVE-like display in order to determine which one promotes better performance in children in a wayfinding task. A 'treasure hunt' game scenario was devised in which participants had to navigate to various houses of a virtual village that was previously seen only on a map. The 2D coordinates of paths taken by participants were recorded together with their success rates in finding the targets, and the time taken to reach their destination. Children showed that although the pointing method allowed them better control in locomotion, neither method was preferred in terms of success rates and timing.

Keywords: Navigation · Virtual reality · CAVE · Children

1 Introduction

Navigation in virtual environments consists of two components: Locomotion and wayfinding [1, 2]. The aim of all locomotion (travel) methods is to allow the user to explore virtual environments easily and naturally while supporting spatial awareness and reducing cognitive load [3]. Maintaining spatial awareness is especially important for wayfinding, which in itself is a cognitively challenging task. Knowing where one is in relation to a destination is essential for effective wayfinding.

The most natural techniques of simulating locomotion are ones in which the user receives proprioceptive and vestibular inputs from their body movements. In this respect Slater et al. [4] devised a technique whereby the user walks in place and makes normal head movements. Their movements were interpreted by a neural network classifier in order to update their viewpoint in the scene. A similar method was employed by Adamo-Villani and Jones [5] in a comparison between different immersive travel methods designed for children. More recently there have been developments in omnidirectional treadmills (e.g. [6, 7]), which can be used mainly in

© Springer International Publishing Switzerland 2016
P. Zaphiris and A. Ioannou (Eds.): LCT 2016, LNCS 9753, pp. 187–197, 2016.
DOI: 10.1007/978-3-319-39483-1_18

conjunction with HMDs. These allow the user to walk normally on the treadmill and these movements are monitored in order to update the view of the virtual world.

The importance of real walking in spatial cognition was highlighted by a series of experiments by Ruddle and Lessels [8] in which participants performed a search task in a room-sized virtual environment. The experiments compared gaze-directed travel using either a desktop display, a HMD with joystick or physical walking using a HMD. They found that only in the latter condition (real walking with HMD) was performance comparable to the same task conducted in the real world. The other two methods produced more errors with around 50 % of real-world performance. Their conditions differed in the amount of body-based information provided: In the first scenario (desktop display) no body-based information was provided, whereas gaze-directed travel with HMD provided rotational body information only and the free walking with HMD condition provided both rotational and translation body information.

These results were interpreted as supporting the use of physical walking interfaces in navigation through virtual environments. However, walking devices have limited scope and applicability. For example, they are large because they have to provide an area for the user to walk, they are difficult to physically move around, and it may not always be appropriate to have physical walking during exploration: larger virtual environments are more easily explored using simulated translation. Addressing these issues Riecke et al. [9] performed the same experiment but requiring all participants to wear a HMD to navigate. Again body-based information was none, rotation only or rotation and translation (real walking). They found that although walking with a HMD produced the best results, rotation only performance was comparable to real walking and better than no body-based information at all. This suggests that allowing a user to perform physical rotations in a virtual environment is more important than providing physical translation.

The results of Riecke et al. [9] suggest that a combination of head-tracked orientation changes with translation controlled using a joystick may be the most versatile method of locomotion which still supports spatial awareness. This can be accomplished using a steering method. Two steering methods commonly used are the *gaze-directed* method and the *pointing* method [10]. Bowman et al. [11] identified these two as the most general and efficient for spatial navigation. They allow for rotational head movements while enabling translation using a hand-held device. They differ only in that the gaze-directed method couples the translation direction with the viewing direction. The pointing method allows the user to pick the translation direction by pointing (with a tracked hand or pointing device).

These two methods have also been the subjected to comparative evaluations to find which is preferred by users. Asking users to walk along a line to a target object Bowman et al. [12] found that the gaze-directed method produced slightly better performance in terms of speed and accuracy (staying close to the line). However, this difference was not statistically significant. In another task in which participants had to move to a point relative to an object they found that the pointing method produced better performance using the same metrics. These experiments utilized a sparse virtual environment consisting of rectangular spaces defined only by concentric lines. Each method appeared to have its advantages and disadvantages (listed in Table 1). They noted that more significant differences between the two motion techniques might be found with more complex navigation tasks and in richer 3D contexts. Such a scenario for example might involve someone steering themselves along a city street with all the visual cues that we normally experience in the real world.

Table 1. Advantages and disadvantages of gaze-directed and pointing methods of travel. From [12]

	Advantages	Disadvantages
Gaze-directed	Steering and view are coupled	User's head can stay relatively still
	Ease of use/learning	More comfortable
	Easier to travel in a straight line	Can look and move in different directions
	Slightly more accurate	
Pointing	User's head can stay relatively still	Can lead to overcorrection
	More comfortable	More cognitive load
	Can look and move in different directions	Harder to learn for most users
		Slightly less accurate

In other studies Suma et al. [13] compared real walking with gaze-directed and pointing motion control in spatial cognition tasks using a HMD. They found a trend for better performance with real walking but no difference between the other two methods. Adamo-Villani and Jones [5] reported a study in which child participants had to navigate to fixed targets in a virtual environment displayed in a CAVE. They compared travel using either a wand device (pointing method with uncoupled gaze) with a gesture-based interface consisting of a pair of tracked data gloves and a body-centered interface utilizing a dance platform which used stepping as a locomotion metaphor. They found that, in terms of time to reach the targets, the wand and gesture conditions produced the fastest results. The wand method also yielded the lowest error-rate (incorrect turns en route to the target).

These latter findings may indicate that performance with gaze-directed and pointing methods may be dependent on the type of display used. All of the comparative studies above used a HMD except for Adamo-Villani and Jones [5] which took place in a CAVE-like display. Theoretically, the display device may have an impact as the HMD with its limited field of view will have different requirements and entail different user strategies than, say, a CAVE display which can provide a wider field of view.

2   Motivation and Objectives

Our aim was to determine whether there exists a preference for either the gaze-directed and pointing methods of travel implemented in a CAVE environment displaying a realistic scene, taking the special user group of children as participants. Although Bowman et al. [12] found minor differences between these methods under certain circumstances, we hypothesized that the reason for this was the sparseness of the environment they used, the nature of their tasks and the limited field of view available. We decided to test these methods using a realistic task requiring spatial awareness and high cognitive load while maintaining precise control of locomotion. Wayfinding requires that decisions be constantly made according to where the subject believes they are in the environment and in relation to their goal. It is also a common task that is easily comprehensible to children. Our experiment therefore differs from previous studies in the following respects:

- Using a CAVE-like display that provides peripheral visual information.
- A natural yet complex task of wayfinding under cognitive load.
- A more realistic environment where destinations are shielded from the start position.

These three factors may all influence preference for motion control. The CAVE display provides peripheral vision that was not available in traditional HMDs. Bowman et al. [12] for example, used a HMD with a field of view of 60 degrees. A CAVE display provides a field of view of 200 degrees. A complex environment will also result in obstructions of the line of sight between the subject and their destination, forcing them to store their route in working memory. An efficient motion control technique would not interfere with this information and allow them to find their target successfully.

3   Experimental Design

The virtual setting for our experiments was a village populated with distinctive buildings serving different social functions such as a school and a bakery. We placed signs around the village to identify the direction to various places (excluding buildings that served as targets in the experiment). The task involved a wayfinding exercise in which users were initially shown a map of their current location in the village and the location of a building that contained a large gold treasure chest (Fig. 1). Their task was to proceed as quickly as possible to the building while staying on the path. Travel speed was kept constant for all trials.

Fig. 1. The maps presented during the four trials

The two travel modes used in these tests differed only in that the pointing method allowed gaze in a direction independent of the direction of travel. From previous experiments described in the literature we identified accuracy, efficiency and control as often used parameters that encompass Bowman et al.'s [12] guidelines for travel methodologies. Accuracy in our case was measured by the number of times participants found the treasure. Efficiency was determined by the time it took to reach the target destination. Finally, control was measured by asking participants to keep to the center of the paths running between the buildings.

4 Experiment

The wayfinding ability in children and their development of mental representations of routes has been studied extensively (see [14] for review). However, relatively few studies have been conducted regarding map use in larger-scale environments. Developmental psychologists have suggested that children's abilities to represent environments follow a developmental sequence from egocentric representations to abstract allocentric representations [15, 16]. Recent studies have shown that there is a developmental progression in children aged 6 to 10 in route learning with younger children's wayfinding being more dependent on landmarks [17]. These developmental studies suggest that by 12 years of age children are able to encode a route procedurally. Comparison of way-finding ability between children of this age and adults of 22 years of age have shown no appreciable difference between them in real world experiments [18].

We were motivated to see how children navigate in VR. Interaction methods should be inclusive if VR technology is to benefit a wide range of societal needs. Even though children at the age of 11 can find their way in the real world using directions it remains to be seen if navigating in a virtual environment with the added cognitive load of using a motion control device is as straightforward.

We used a between-subjects design and each child participant had four trials using one or other of the two travel modes.

4.1 Participants

We contacted a local school to organize a class visit to the CAVE facility in order to test whether children demonstrated any preference for either one of the two travel methods described. Twenty-six (26) children (13 male and 13 female) aged between 11 and 12 years of age took part in the study. The children's parents signed informed consent forms that had been forwarded to them a week before the visit.

Summarizing the demographic data, in terms of computer use the majority of children (54.2 %) said they used a computer several times daily and 29.2 % said they used a computer during each week. In terms of computer games 45.8 % said they played computer games sometime during each week and 45.8 % said they played several times daily. None of the children had been in a CAVE display before. 80 % of the children owned either a Nintendo Wii or Sony Playstation. It is therefore reasonable to assume that the majority had experience with some form of game control device.

4.2 Design

We used a between-subjects design to test the two travel modes with the routes depicted in Fig. 1. Thus each child performed 4 trials using one of the two travel modes on an alternately assigned basis. The accuracy metric was the number of successful trials. Efficiency being measured by the time taken to complete a route. Control of movements was assessed by the mean square deviation from the center of the path during travel. Recording terminated when the participant reached within a fixed distance of the target entrance or after 80 s, in which case the trial was considered unsuccessful.

4.3 Procedure

The children completed an adult-supervised pre-test questionnaire and were alternately assigned to one of the two travel modes. They were individually familiarized with the CAVE, fitted with the stereo glasses and instructed as to the use of the wand according to their prescribed condition. They were allowed a short time to familiarize themselves with the motion control device and the experiment commenced when they were ready.

4.4 Results

Data from 2 children (1 male, 1 female) was discarded owing to inability to complete all four trials. Figure 2(a) shows the mean time taken to traverse each route for each mode of travel (for both successful and unsuccessful trials). On inspection, the average trial times appear to correlate with the length of each route although, interestingly, the travel times for routes 1 and 3 appear longer than routes 2 and 4. In these trials the participant's start point and direction violates Levine's (1984) forward-up equivalence principle and indicates perhaps an increased cognitive effort required to encode and traverse the route.

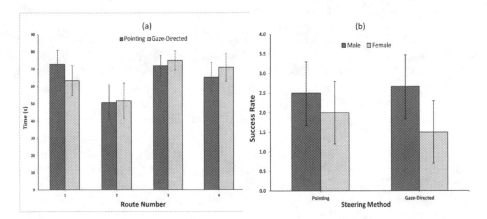

Fig. 2. (a) Children's mean trial duration (for all trials) for each treasure route. N = 12 for each condition, error bars are 0.95 confidence intervals. (b) Mean number of successful trials for children according to gender as function of steering mode. Error bars denote 0.95 confidence intervals.

In terms of the two motion control methods under consideration, trial times appear similar for the two travel conditions. We performed a repeated measures ANOVA with mode of travel as between subject's factor. This showed that there was no significant difference between the modes of travel in terms of trial time [F $(3, 22) = 1.77$, $p = 0.16$]. In terms of timeouts (time limit being reached before reaching target) the pointing condition produced 21 in total (relative frequency $= 0.44$) and the gaze-directed condition produced 23 (relative frequency $= 0.48$).

We summed the number of successful trials for each participant and performed a factorial ANOVA. Since we had a balanced design with equal numbers of males and females performing each of the primed searches with both modes of travel we could take gender into account. The ANOVA therefore consisted of two factors (Gender and Travel Mode) with number of successful trials as the dependent variable. Figure 2(b) shows the mean number of successful route traversals as a function of travel mode for the two genders. Results of the ANOVA show that gender was significant [F $(1, 20) = 4.55$, $p < 0.05$] with boys having greater success than girls. The mode of travel was not significant [F $(1, 20) = 0.18$, $p = 0.67$] and the interaction between these two factors was not significant [F $(1, 20) = 0.73$, $p = 0.4$].

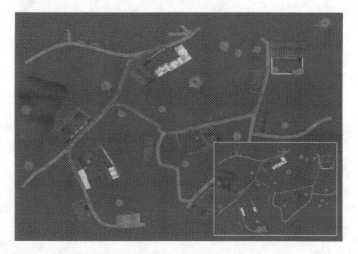

Fig. 3. The routes taken by child participants. Large deviations have been removed. Inset picture shows all data. (Color figure online)

Finally, we look at the level of control afforded by each of the two travel methods. We found that some participants used at least one 'illegal' route to reach the primed destination (see inset in Fig. 3). These trials were removed from the comparison data. We see from the overlays of the paths followed in Fig. 3 that the pointing method allowed participants to stay closer to the center of the path. Figure 4 shows the mean square deviation (from the ideal path) for all 24 children. For all routes participants had lower mean deviations when using the pointing method of steering. A repeated measures ANOVA with 4 levels (corresponding to each route) and steering method (pointing, gaze-directed) as between-subjects factor showed that this difference was significant [F (1, 22) = 5.72, p < 0.05].

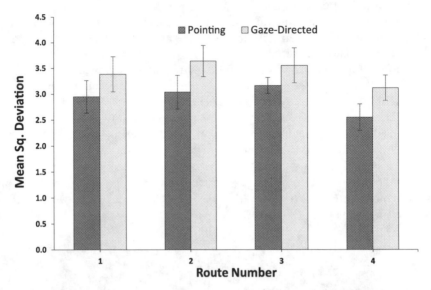

Fig. 4. Mean square deviations from the center of the path (in virtual world units) derived from children's navigation data. Error bars show standard error of the mean, N = 12 for each condition.

Because of the elevated number of timeouts we considered that this may have masked any difference between mode of travel and if enough time was given a preference for one method or the other would have been revealed. In order to further compare the two methods, regardless of whether participants reached the treasure location, we subdivided each route into a series of 10 equidistant waypoints and counted the number of waypoints reached for each route. A waypoint was considered to be reached if the user came within 15 world units of it (corresponding to 3 times the width of the path). Averaging across routes, we found that children using the pointing method reached 7.56 (SD = 1.45) waypoints and children using the gaze-directed method reached 7.79 (SD = 1.54). A t-test for independent samples by group showed no significant difference between the number of waypoints reached [t(22) = −0.37, p = 0.7].

4.5   Summary and Discussion

In terms of our measure of accuracy using each travel method we found no difference between the pointing method and the gaze-directed method. Similarly there was no significant difference between trial times for the two groups. However children were able to control their movements better with the pointing method than with the gaze-directed method.

The increased number of timeouts initially suggests that children did not have enough time to complete the path traversals, although a closer look at the data in terms of the waypoints covered regardless of whether they reached their target similarly suggested no difference between the two travel modes. The increase in timeouts reduced the amount of available data and so the results remain inconclusive. The fact that children found the task difficult may be explained by one of two possibilities. Firstly, it may be that children required more time to complete the routes and the time allowed was insufficient to do so. Secondly, it may be the case that children in many cases did not encode their route through the environment sufficiently to allow them to reach the target and got lost. In the former case the mode of travel may have made a difference, but not in the latter. Our analysis of waypoints reached for both groups shows that travel mode was not a significant factor regardless of the time allowed. Furthermore, visual inspection of path traversal behaviour of individual participants who did not complete their routes showed that they had good control over their navigation but simply made wrong turns and got lost. Nevertheless, further experiments would be required to investigate this more comprehensively.

5 Conclusion

In this experiment we compared two commonly used steering methods in a wayfinding task where the participants were children. In the gaze-directed method movements through the environment occur along the direction in which the user is looking. In the pointing method movement occurs in the direction of a hand-held pointing device allowing independent head movements. Both methods have their advantages. For example, the pointing method allows the users' head to stay relatively still making it more comfortable. On the other hand, the gaze-directed method allows changes in direction simply by rotating one's head and the user does not have to point with an interaction device which may reduce arm strain.

Previous comparisons of these two methods have measured accuracy, efficiency and control by measuring time to complete particular tasks correctly and the ability of users to follow paths. These tasks however were carried out using head mounted displays and have involved rather contrived tasks in non-realistic immersive environments. We were motivated to carry out experiments in a CAVE display that does not restrict the users head movements and in which the peripheral vision of the user is much greater. We also used a realistic wayfinding task requiring the user to make head-movements to assess where they were and where they were going. Wayfinding is a cognitively challenging task in itself and any intrinsic benefits of either travel mode would be reflected in the objective measures that we made. We were principally concerned with timing to reach a destination, the number of successful route completions and the ability to maintain trajectories along fixed paths. These measures, as well as the wayfinding task itself, can be seen as encompassing the several parameters identified by Bowman et al. [12] as the qualities of an effective motion control method; namely accuracy, spatial awareness, ease of learning, ease of use and information gathering.

From our own subjective impressions the task was surprisingly difficult considering the simplicity of the topology. The main confounding factor in navigation through a large-scale environment is that buildings can obscure the line of sight and the task becomes one of using a cognitive map to encode where one is in relation to one's destination and to control how to get there. On presentation of the map we found that the best strategy was to imagine facing the direction of travel and then navigating the intended route by encoding which way to turn at each junction.

The data from our child participants shows that they found wayfinding in VR difficult. They reached the target destination on approximately half of their trials using either control method. Also, data from two children had to be discarded and this inevitably made the comparison between the two travel modes difficult. However, with the data available we can at least draw the conclusion that the pointing method allowed greater control in path following.

The fact that our sample of children found this task difficult is intriguing. However, on a trial by trial basis child participants appear more likely not to have had enough time to reach the target destination suggesting that they either found motion control more difficult in general or they did not encode their route sufficiently. The latter would conflict with, for example, the results of Cornell et al. [18] who compared wayfinding behaviour between 11 and 22 year olds. In Cornell's experiment, children were walked through a campus grounds and asked to find their way back. They therefore had prior exposure to the scene they had to navigate. The cognitive demands of our task were somewhat greater. The children had no prior exposure to the environment they had to navigate in. They were shown a map and asked to navigate from one location to another. A more suitable paradigm might have shown participants the routes to be traversed in advance, perhaps using a virtual fly-through, rather than a map. This would have provided them with additional information such as landmarks, which appear to be important for children's wayfinding [17] and thus a fairer comparison between travel methods is possible.

Acknowledgements. The research presented in this paper was made possible with the use of the VR CAVE equipment, at the Immersive and Creative Technologies Lab (http://www.theictlab. org). The acquisition and establishment of the equipment was part of the IPE/NEKYP/0311/02 "VR CAVE" project http://www.vrcave.com.cy) and was financially supported by the Cyprus Research Promotion Foundation and the European Structural Funds.

References

1. Montello, D.R.: Navigation. In: Shah, P., Miyake, A. (eds.) The Cambridge Handbook of Visuospatial Thinking, pp. 257–294. Cambridge University Press, Cambridge (2005)
2. Wiener, J.M., Büchner, S.J., Hölscher, C.: Taxonomy of human wayfinding tasks: a knowledge-based approach. Spat. Cogn. Comput. **9**(2), 152–165 (2009)
3. Bowman, D.A., Kruijff, E., LaViola Jr., J.J., Poupyrev, I.: 3D User Interfaces: Theory and Practice. Addison-Wesley, Boston (2004)
4. Slater, M., Usoh, M., Steed, A.: Taking steps: the influence of a walking technique on presence in virtual reality. ACM Trans. Comput. Hum. Interact. (TOCHI) **2**, 201–219 (1995)
5. Adamo-Villani, N., Jones, D.: Travel in immersive virtual learning environments: a user study with children. IADIS Int. J. Comput. Sci. Inf. Syst. **2**(2), 151–161 (2007)

6. Souman, J.L., Giordano, P.R., Schwaiger, M., Frissen, I., Thümmel, T., Ulbrich, H., Ernst, M.O.: CyberWalk: enabling unconstrained omnidirectional walking through virtual environments. ACM Trans. Appl. Percept. (TAP) **8**(4), 25 (2011)
7. Giordano, P.R., Souman, J., Mattone, R., De Luca, A., Ernst, M., Bulthoff, H.: The CyberWalk platform: human-machine interaction enabling unconstrained walking through VR. In: Paper Presented at the First Workshop for Young Researchers on Human-Friendly Robotics (2008)
8. Ruddle, R.A., Lessels, S.: The benefits of using a walking interface to navigate virtual environments. ACM Trans. Comp. Hum. Interact. (TOCHI) **16**(1), 5 (2009)
9. Riecke, B.E., Bodenheimer, B., McNamara, T.P., Williams, B., Peng, P., Feuereissen, D.: Do we need to walk for effective virtual reality navigation? Physical rotations alone may suffice. In: Hölscher, C., Shipley, T.F., Olivetti Belardinelli, M., Bateman, J.A., Newcombe, N.S. (eds.) Spatial Cognition VII. LNCS, vol. 6222, pp. 234–247. Springer, Heidelberg (2010)
10. Mine, M.: Virtual environment interaction techniques. In: SIGGRAPH 1995, Course, No. 8 (1995)
11. Bowman, D., Johnson, D., Hodges, L.: Testbed evaluation of virtual environment interaction techniques. Presence: Teleoper. Virtual Environ. **10**(1), 75–95 (2001)
12. Bowman, D., Koller, D., Hodges, L.F.: Travel in immersive virtual environments: an evaluation of viewpoint motion control techniques. In: Proceedings of the Virtual Reality Annual International Symposium, pp. 45–52. IEEE (1997)
13. Suma, E.A., Babu, S., Hodges, L.F.: Comparison of travel techniques in a complex, multi-level 3D environment. In: IEEE Symposium on 3D User Interfaces. 3DUI 2007. IEEE, March 2007
14. Blades, M.: Research paradigms and methodologies for investigating children's wayfinding. In: Foreman, N., Gillet, R. (eds.) A Handbook of Spatial Research Paradigms and Methodologies. Spatial Cognition in the Child and Adult, vol. 1, pp. 103–130. Psychology Press, Hove (1997)
15. Piaget, J., Inhelder, B.: The Child's Conception of Space. W.W. Norton, New York (1967)
16. Siegel, A.W., White, S.H.: The development of spatial representations of large-scale environments. In: Reese, H.W. (ed.) Advances in Child Development and Behavior, vol. 10, pp. 9–55. Academic Press, New York (1975)
17. Lingwood, J., Blades, M., Farran, E.K., Courbois, Y., Matthews, D.: The development of wayfinding abilities in children: learning routes with and without landmarks. J. Environ. Psychol. **41**, 74–80 (2015)
18. Cornell, E.H., Heth, C.D., Rowat, W.L.: Wayfinding by children and adults: response to instructions to use look-back and retrace strategies. Dev. Psychol. **28**(2), 328–336 (1992). http://dx.doi.org/10.1037/0012-1649.28.2.328
19. Levine, M., Marchon, I., Hanley, G.: The placement and misplacement of you-are-here maps. Environ. Behav. **16**(2), 139–157 (1984)

Learning Performance

Evaluation of the CTMTC Methodology for Assessment of Teamwork Competence Development and Acquisition in Higher Education

Miguel Á. Conde[1]([⊠]), Ángel Hernández-García[2],
Francisco J. García-Peñalvo[3], Ángel Fidalgo-Blanco[4],
and Marisa Sein-Echaluce[5]

[1] Department of Mechanics, Computer Science and Aerospace Engineering,
Robotics Group, University of León, Campus de Vegazana S/N,
24071 León, Spain
miguel.conde@unileon.es
[2] Departamento de Ingeniería de Organización,
Administración de Empresas y Estadística, Universidad Politécnica de Madrid,
Av. Complutense 30, 28040 Madrid, Spain
angel.hernandez@upm.es
[3] Faculty of Science, Computer Science Department,
Research Institute for Educational Sciences, GRIAL Research Group,
University of Salamanca, Plaza de los Caídos S/N, 37008 Salamanca, Spain
fgarcia@usal.es
[4] Laboratory of Innovation in Information Technologies, LITI,
Universidad Politécnica de Madrid,
Calle de Ríos Rosas 21, 28003 Madrid, Spain
angel.fidalgo@upm.es
[5] Department of Applied Mathematics, University of Zaragoza,
Campus Rio Ebro, Calle de María de Luna 3, 50018 Saragossa, Spain
mlsein@unizar.es

Abstract. The majority of tasks and processes at the workplace involve the collaboration of two or more people, which explains that teamwork competence acquisition has become a priority for educational institutions. In project-based learning, student assessment is complex and generally focuses on the final outcome delivered by the group, without paying attention to the contribution of each individual or to the complete process. CTMTC is a methodology that facilitates teamwork competence acquisition and individual and group assessment in collaborative learning. This study describes and evaluates the application of CTMTC for student assessment in group project-based learning in Higher Education. The study also shows a particular case scenario of application of CTMTC and evaluates the benefits derived from the use of CTMTC. The results suggest that the methodology should be tailored to students' needs and course characteristics, and reveal a positive perception from students about the application of the CTMTC methodology.

Keywords: Teamwork competence · CTMTC · Moodle · Individual assessment · Group assessment

© Springer International Publishing Switzerland 2016
P. Zaphiris and A. Ioannou (Eds.): LCT 2016, LNCS 9753, pp. 201–212, 2016.
DOI: 10.1007/978-3-319-39483-1_19

1   Introduction

Development and acquisition of the teamwork competence (TWC) is essential in educational and professional contexts because: (1) teamwork involves sharing of information and discussion among students to build mental models in a cooperative way, ultimately contributing to the improvement of students' learning [1,2]; (2) companies seek that prospective employees have developed the TWC because members of an organization are working together in groups to achieve common goals [3]; (3) the application of the Bologna process positions TWC as a key competence that student should develop in Higher Education.

Despite all the institutional efforts to promote and foster TWC, assessment of TWC acquisition is a difficult task. Most of the time, the assessment of TWC is determined by the final result or work that teams deliver, ignoring what happens during the different stages of the process, variability between the amount and relevance of individual contributions, or without any consideration about the different stages of the teamwork process.

From the above, a systematic and scientific study and assessment of TWC requires methodologies that facilitate quantitative assessment. The present work describes the application and evaluation of a methodology (CTMTC, Comprehensive Training Model of the Teamwork Competence) that both improves TWC and facilitates its objective assessment. CTMTC takes into account the group results and how each individual has acquired the competence. The methodology relies on the analysis of learning evidences from data generated by the use of IT-based learning tools by student teams during a project development [4]. The application of the methodology entails that teams develop the project in several stages adapted from the International Project Management Association (IPMA) [5, 6].

The objectives of this research are to present and compare the tools used in courses following the CTMTC methodology, to evaluate students' perception about the implementation of the CTMTC, and to show how the CTMTC contributes to improve TWC and student assessment in teamwork-based courses. In order to do so, the study presents the application of the CTMTC methodology to three degree and one masters' courses, describes the implementation of the CTMTC on those courses, and compares the results with previous editions of the courses that did not incorporate the CTMTC.

The study is structured as follows. Section 2 describes the CTMTC methodology. Section 3 explains the practical implementation of CTMTC in the courses. Section 4 illustrates in more detail one of these implementations. Section 5 compares the implementation described in Sect. 4 with outcomes from previous editions of the course and evaluates the methodology implementation from a qualitative perspective. Finally, Sect. 6 summarizes the main results and the conclusions derived from the research.

2   The CTMTC Methodology

TWC assessment is complex, especially when examining how the individual acquires this competence. There are several methods to assess TWC acquisition but they focus mainly in the assessment of group outcomes. Such methods evaluate the individual acquisition of the competence relies on observation of students' perceptions through opinion surveys, self-evaluation questionnaires or peer evaluations to measure individual evidences [7–9]. Ultimately, these methods evaluate the knowledge students have about their task, their peers' tasks, and project goals and milestones. However, this approach may not be the best, because other elements have a high impact in group outcomes: leader behavior, cooperation between peers, problems between team members, performance of each member, etc. [10]. It is difficult to collect this kind of information, which requires a continuous monitoring of how the group carries out the activity. In order to ease and streamline this process, this study presents CTMTC and its associated tools.

CTMTC is a proactive method that draws on three aspects of group-based learning: teamwork phases (mission and goals, responsibility maps, planning, implementation and organization of documentation), collaborative creation of knowledge, and cloud computing technologies (wikis, forums, social networks and cloud storage systems) [4]. In the CTMTC, faculty continuously monitors team members' collaboration and individual evidences along the teamwork phases. Monitoring also enables teachers to guide students' individual learning. CTMTC allows teachers to do partial summative assessments of TWC [11]. This method has been tested in prior settings [10–13].

Assessment of students' individual learning evidences requires a continuous exploration of what they are doing during the learning experience, and a global analysis once the course finishes. Controlled environments with a small number of students allow teachers to easily perform monitoring and analysis but in courses with higher number of students, it requires the use of automated tools due to its time-consuming nature. This study includes one of these applications, designed as a learning analytics tool that accesses, analyzes and structures the information about students' interactions stored in Learning Management Systems (LMS). Analysis and presentation of the information follows the requirements of CTMTC: the learning analytics tool presents the information about the group members' forum interaction organized by course, group, thread and person. This information allows instructors to check the evolution of the group, average interaction of its members and the level of cooperation between them. The tool also shows each member's individual participation in a thread, if the leader is acting as expected, etc. The main benefit of the application of this tool is that it reduces the effort of assessing group and individual interaction and it makes it easier to apply CTMTC [13–15]. As next section shows, the application of the methodology and the technologies used in each of the courses vary from one to another.

3   Implementation of the CTMTC Methodology

All the courses under examination follow the CTMTC, with teamwork occurring online along the course (using forums and wikis/Dropbox to communicate and share contents/files, respectively). Every four weeks the students must make a presentation of their work. Apart from interacting with other group members, students interact with the different technological systems used. These interactions leave traces that teachers may use as evidences, such as forum posts and WhatsApp messages, achievement of the CTMTC phases (mission and goals, map of responsibility, planning, etc.) and outcomes (final deliverables). At the end of the process, students must publish the final result of their work. Optionally, they can record a video (with a maximum length of 10 min) to present the result, describe the way the team organized and coordinated, and show individual and group work evidences.

One of the main benefits of the CTMTC is its flexibility. For this study, the authors adapted it to the specific needs and features of each of the courses where CTMTC implementation was decided at the University of León (4 completed courses, with 5 more ongoing courses using CTMTC at this moment). The four completed courses are part of the Bachelor of Science and Master of Science degrees on Computer Science. Each course has a different number of students and specific course goals, and therefore the CTMTC methodology needs adaptation to adhere to the requirements of each course.

- Operating Systems. It is a second year course of the Bachelor of Science on Computer Science degree, with a total of 110 students. The application of CTMTC focuses on one activity that has a weight of 22 % of the final score. Although choice of team members and coordinators is open, the group must choose one of the three possible topics for the work. Groups have 3 or 4 members, who use the LMS forums to interact between them; additionally, some of the students also use instant messaging tools such as WhatsApp. Each group publishes its partial outcomes in the LMS wiki and deliver their final outcome using Moodle LMS assignment block.
- Accessibility. It is a fourth year course of the Bachelor of Science on Computer Science degree, with a total of 71 students. In this course, the application of the CTMTC focuses on one activity with a 60 % weight of the final grade. The instructor determines the composition of the groups, but students can freely designate their coordinator/leader and choose the topic between different possible projects. Team members use the LMS forums and Wiki for interaction and publication of final results, respectively. Optionally, they may also send partial results of their work to the teacher.
- Dedicated and Embedded Architectures. This is a fourth year course of the Bachelor of Science on Computer Science degree, with a total of 15 students. CTMTC covers all course activities. Groups consist of a number of members between 2 and 4, for a total of 6 groups. Students can freely choose their group and their coordinator. The project involves the same task for all groups. Students interact through a forum, use the wiki to publish their results and Moodle assignment block to deliver the final project.
- High Performance Computing. It is a first year course of the Masters in Computer Science degree, with a total of 8 students. CTMTC is applied to a task with a weight of 60 % of the final grade. Given the low number of students, they were all included in one group, and student tracking did not require the use of learning analytics tools. Group members freely choose their coordinator. The choice of tools to use to complete the project is also open. The application of CTMTC includes GitHub as a repository, Moodle Wikis as a means to publish group results and gitter as a space for communication and interaction.

The above list shows the adaptation of CTMTC to the specific characteristics of each course. The following section describes with a higher level of detail one of the courses and compares the outcomes after application of CTMTC with those of previous editions of the course.

4 The Application of CTMTC in the Operating Systems Course

Operating Systems is a first semester course in the second year of the Bachelor of Science on Computer Science degree. In the past five years, there were more than 100 students enrolled per year. The course duration is 60 face-to-face hours (20 of them are theory and the remaining 40 h correspond to lab classes). The objective of the course is the acquisition of basic knowledge about how an operating system works, and therefore it is strongly oriented to practice. The main topics covered include abstraction of process, and analysis of problems related with concurrency and process scheduling. Completion of tasks requires the use of C Programming Language and processes and threads libraries.

Students' final grade comprises two parts: theory (35 % of the final grade) and practice (65 % of the final grade). Practice includes two assignments: the interim assignment (35 % of the final practice grade) and the final assignment (65 % of the practical grade). The application of the CTMTC focuses on the interim assignment (with a total weight of 22.8 % over the final grade). Interestingly, the interim deliverable is not mandatory (in other words, students can pass the course regardless of completing it or not).

The 106 participating students freely formed groups (a total of 28 groups), with 3–4 members per group, and they named the person in charge of group coordination.

The teachers proposed three possible activities/projects for the groups to choose, and thus different groups could have the same project as final assignment. Each of these groups that completed the interim assignment had to follow the phases of the CTMTC methodology, using Moodle Forum as main space for interaction. In the Moodle Forum a group member can only read messages and threads created by their group partners, and teachers may read all the messages in every group, and also read them on a per group basis (as an example, Fig. 1 shows the list of threads for group 16). When the interaction between students takes place in other systems, such as WhatsApp for instant messaging, students have to upload the conversation as attached files in forum posts.

Students display the outcomes of the activities they complete on a wiki. The wiki is private for group members and teachers. The work done in the wiki has to incorporate the phases described in CTMTC, information about the activity and the name of the group coordinator. Each phase is associated to a particular page in the wiki and a link to the forum thread where the discussion about the issue took place. Figure 2 shows one of these wikis. Finally, the students deliver the final result of their project through a Moodle assignment block.

For an effective development of the course, teachers need not only to assess the final outcomes of each group, but also the outcomes of each member of the group. In order to do so the teachers can use the forum to see group members' interaction, and the wiki and a Moodle assignment to see the outcomes of the group work. The vast amount of data available makes it difficult to analyze these evidences. For example, this course has 28 wikis (with more than 4 pages each) and a forum with 245 threads and 1520 posts. Manually analyzing the work of a group and its group members is a time-consuming task for instructors. For example, a manual inspection of each group's

Fig. 1. Group 16 interactions in the Moodle Forum

Fig. 2. Wiki including group 16's CTMTC outcomes

activity takes lasted between 40 min and 1 h (this time does not include assessment). That is, it requires between 19 and 28 h to complete the inspection of every group in the course.

In order to face this problem, course teachers use a learning analytics tool that provides a quick and effortlessly way to retrieve the information required for assessment of groups' and individuals' outcomes (Fig. 3 depicts general information about course and groups returned by the learning analytic tool for the interim assignment).

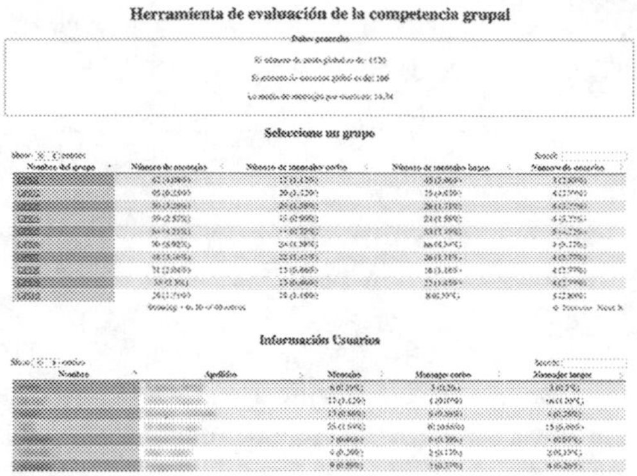

Herramienta de evaluación de la competencia grupal

Datos generales

Número de posts global es de 4130
El número de sesiones global es de 106
La media de mensajes por sesión es 38,74

Seleccione un grupo

Nombres del grupo	Número de sesiones	Número de mensajes cortos	Número de mensajes largos	Número de sesiones

Información Usuarios

Nombres	Apellidos	Mensajes	Mensajes cortos	Mensajes largos

Fig. 3. Information returned by the learning analytics tool in the Operating Systems course

Two rubrics enable student assessment of both group and individual work. The rubric for group work assessment builds on prior studies using the CTMTC [4, 10, 12, 13], while the rubric for individual assessment focuses on individual acquisition of TWC and takes into account previous research related to teamwork behavior [10, 12, 13]. In this sense, teamwork behaviour refers to performing individual activities that contribute to the team work process: interpersonal behaviours (conflict and problem solving, collaboration, communication) and management behaviours (assuming leadership, establishing goals, planning tasks, coordinating the other members in the group) [16, 17].

The next section evaluates the application of CTMTC in the Operating Systems course, quantitatively (final grades) and qualitatively (student perceptions about CTMTC), and compares the results with those obtained in previous editions of the course that did not incorporate CTMTC.

5 Case Study

Table 1 shows participation, average assignment grades and average course grades in the last three editions of the course (the most recent being the one implementing CTMTC). Regarding participation, Table 1 reveals high participation levels in the interim assignment in previous editions (around 80 %), rising to nearly complete participation (96.36 %) after application of the CTMTC. The observation of assignment average grade returns interesting results because the value in the 2014/15 edition of the course is much higher than the one from the previous year and the one from the CTMTC course; however, it is worth noting that the cause of this unexpected result might be that the 2014/15 edition used peer-review methods. Finally, Table 1 also shows that average course grade is higher in the course using CTMTC. A possible explanation is that the phases defined by CTMTC (i.e., definition of the mission and goals, planning, etc.) may help to better plan and manage the group project. Because the study only includes one edition of the course using the CTMTC, future editions of the course using the CTMTC would confirm these results.

Table 1. Participation, average assignment grade and average course grade of the last three editions of the course Operating Systems.

	2013/2014	2014/2015	2015/2016
Participation (Pct.)	88/110 (80 %)	100/128 (78.12 %)	106/110 (96.36 %)
Assignment Avg. Grade (Std. Dev.)	48.60/100 (37.1)	75.90/100 (26.59)	59.88/100 (21.1)
Course Avg. Grade (Std. Dev.)	34.62/100 (23.71)	46.81/100 (16.30)	49.30/100 (19.68)

As mentioned earlier, a qualitative evaluation of the CTMTC in this study also entails students' perception about the application of the methodology. In order to collect this information participants were asked three open questions:

Q1. "In your opinion, what are the main advantages of the CTMTC?"
Q2. "What are the main problems you have encountered with the use of CTMTC?"
Q3. "'What additional tools/systems (not included in the CTMTC) have you used in the course?"

The qualitative analysis consists of an examination of the text from the responses given by participants. This procedure includes grouping responses based on topic-proximity criteria for Q1 (advantages of the application of the methodology or the tools employed by CTMTC), Q2 (problems with application of the methodology), and Q3 (tools used for assignment completion). After classification, we combined the results in a matrix in order to extract conclusions [18]. Table 2 shows the first 20 (out of 106) responses to the three questions.

Even though Table 2 just shows 20 results, most of the students perceive the methodology as something positive, highlighting advantages related to teamwork behaviors, as described by Tasa et al. [17]. Some responses correspond to interpersonal behaviors (communication, problem solving, collaboration, organization, knowledge sharing, helping other group members, etc.) and other have to do with management behavior (distribution of tasks, deadlines, publication of results, planning, leadership, etc.).

Students perceive that under the CTMTC they actually work as a group, and therefore the methodology helps them to successfully complete the project. Interestingly, participants are second year degree students with no prior knowledge about project management, and thus they perceive the idea of working together and organizing their work as something positive. On the other hand, a group of students do not find the methodology useful, showing a preference for individual work – three of them were part of a group where they did not had any prior relationship with the rest of the group members–, and only 9 out of 106 students (8.49 %) have negative opinions regarding the usefulness of the methodology.

More than a third of participants (34.5 %) state that they do not encounter any problem with CTMTC, while 44 % of students claim they have problems related to the communication tools used in the course. The latter group finds that forums cannot accurately represent actual interaction between group members, and express their preference for integration of instant messaging tools (messaging tools are allowed as group work evidence on the condition that students upload their conversations to the

Table 2. Students' perception about the use of CTMTC (truncated to N = 20 students)

	Advantages	Problems	Tools
S1	Forces all group members to contribute	Documentation	None
S2	Includes project planning and management	None, problems with other group members	None
S3	Facilitates knowledge sharing	None	None
S4	Planning for development	Time to define scheduling	Instant messaging
S5	Lesser complexity	Application of the methodology in general	GIT Repositories
S6	Induces collaborative work	Use of forums to register participation	Chat
S7	Project management for goal achievement	Methodology application harder than development	WhatsApp, Telegram
S8	Too much organization required for a simple assignment	Distribution of tasks	Google drive
S9	Enables working as team	Problems with partners	None
S10	Facilitates coordination	Communication via forums	None
S11	Eases work	Other means of communication preferred	None
S12	Improves communication	Demands lots of work for short tasks	Dropbox
S13	Helps problem solving	None	Google code
S14	Facilitates distribution of tasks	None	None
S15	Grading does not only include final result	Forum use for interaction	Communication tools
S16	None	Problems with other group members (distribution of tasks)	None
S17	Includes planning and deadlines	Leadership implies more work	None
S18	Improves organization	Publication of results is time-consuming	None
S19	Publication of results forces members to work	Agreement among group members	None
S20	Emphasizes importance of leadership	Phases	None

forum, an option that only 2 of the 28 groups chose). Some students (13 % of the total) report problems with other members of the group. The main causes of these problems are perception of different levels of implication between members, unfair/uneven distribution of tasks, and missing or nearly missing deadlines. These are all common problems related to coordination and teamwork. Other problems mentioned include higher complexity and difficulty to apply the methodology than project difficulty, unfair grade weighing for leadership because group leaders have more workload, or lack of knowledge about what they should publish on the wiki.

Concerning the use of tools, 73.6 % of participants report satisfaction with the tools that application of CTMTC demands. A majority of the rest suggest the use of instant messaging tools that provide information about real time interaction instead of using the forum for interaction reporting. A reason for this perception might be that the University of Leon's Moodle instance does not publish the post immediately after students post it, and therefore there is a delay that slows down communication. Finally, six students propose the use of code repositories for each group member to upload their code so teachers may check out individual contributions.

6   Conclusions

TWC is essential for educational institutions and in order to improve the employability of students. This study describes and evaluates the application of the CTMTC methodology for student assessment in group project-based learning in Higher Education.

The study is part of a research project aiming to compare the effectiveness of different methodologies applied to courses that involve work group and collaborative learning. The research focuses on the application of CTMTC and reveals how its flexibility enables adaptation to courses with very different characteristics (e.g. number of students, types of assignments) by allowing the integration of different tools. The research details a case study of one specific context of application of the CTMTC.

The case study suggests that application of CTMTC helps increasing students' participation and final grades. Furthermore, students have a positive perception of the application of CTMTC, and they feel that it helps them improve project management, planning, distribution of tasks, and setting of deadlines and milestones. This perception suggests that CTMTC may help developing teamwork behaviors that students shall require in other courses and in their jobs in the future [17]. Some students report that some of the problems related to teamwork, such as communication, collaboration, and motivation, are not solved by the application of CTMTC. Even though most of the students claim that the tools used in the course are appropriate for the methodology, some of them point out problems that relate directly to the tools required for the application of CTMTC. From a course design view, instructors should find ways to find complementary technical solutions that cover this gap and address this issue in following editions of the course.

This study is part of an ongoing and constantly evolving line of work on course design and implementation of methodologies to improve collaborative project-based learning. Future avenues of research should address the influence of project selection, a characterization of how students use the tools (and which ones best suit their knowledge and abilities), or teachers' perception of the application of CTMTC. It would also be of interest to establish a comparison between the results returned by the learning analytics system and other tools used for TWC assessment, such as self-perception questionnaires and peer review techniques [7–9].

Acknowledgements. This work is partially supported by *Cátedra Telefónica – Universidad de León* and Spanish Ministry of Economy and Competitiveness under grant DPI2013-40534-R.

References

1. Leidner, D.E., Jarvenpaa, S.L.: The use of information technology to enhance management school education: a theoretical view. MIS Q. **19**, 265–291 (1995)
2. Vogel, D.R., Davison, R.M., Shroff, R.H.: Sociocultural learning: a perspective on GSS-enabled global education. Commun. Assoc. Inf. Syst. **7**, 9 (2001)
3. Iglesias-Pradas, S., Ruiz-de-Azcárate, C., Agudo-Peregrina, Á.F.: Assessing the suitability of student interactions from Moodle data logs as predictors of cross-curricular competencies. Comput. Hum. Behav. **47**, 81–89 (2015)
4. Lerís, D., Fidalgo, Á., Sein-Echaluce, M.L.: A comprehensive training model of the teamwork competence. Int. J. Learn. Intellect. Cap. **11**, 1–19 (2014)
5. NCB – Bases para la competencia en dirección de proyectos. http://www.lpzconsulting.com/images/CP-_Trabajo_en_Equipo.pdf. Accessed 24 Feb 2016
6. NCB – Bases para la competencia en dirección de proyectos. http://aeipro.com/index.php/es/mainmenu-publicaciones/mainmenu-publicaciones-libros/223-ncb-30-bases-para-la-competencia-en-direccion-de-proyectos. Accessed 24 Feb 16
7. Strom, P.S., Strom, R.D., Moore, E.G.: Peer and self-evaluation of teamwork skills. J. Adolesc. **22**, 539–553 (1999)
8. De-los-Ríos-Carmenado, I., Figueroa-Rodríguez, B., Gómez-Gajardo, F.: Methodological proposal for teamwork evaluation in the field of project management training. Procedia Soc. Behav. Sci. **46**, 1664–1672 (2012)
9. Poblete, M., García Olalla, A.: Análisis y Evaluación del Trabajo en Equipo del alumnado universitario. Propuesta de un modelo de Evaluación de Desarrollo del Equipo. In: Conference Análisis y Evaluación del Trabajo en Equipo del alumnado universitario. Propuesta de un modelo de Evaluación de Desarrollo del Equipo (2014)
10. Fidalgo-Blanco, Á., Sein-Echaluce, M.L., García-Peñalvo, F.J., Conde, M.Á.: Using learning analytics to improve teamwork assessment. Comput. Hum. Behav. **47**, 149–156 (2015)
11. Séin-Echaluce, M.L., Fidalgo Blanco, Á., García-Peñalvo, F.J., Conde, M.Á.: A knowledge management system to classify social educational resources within a subject using teamwork techniques. In: Zaphiris, P., Ioannou, A. (eds.) LCT 2015. LNCS, vol. 9192, pp. 510–519. Springer, Heidelberg (2015)
12. Fidalgo, A., Leris, D., Sein-Echaluce, M.L., García-Peñalvo, F.J.: Indicadores para el seguimiento de evaluación de la competencia de trabajo en equipo a través del método CTMT. In: Congreso Internacional sobre Aprendizaje Innovación y Competitividad - CINAIC 2013 (2013)
13. Fidalgo-Blanco, Á., Sein-Echaluce, M.L., García-Peñalvo, F.J.: Students' knowledge sharing to improve learning in academic engineering courses. Int. J. Eng. Educ. (IJEE) (in press)
14. Fidalgo Blanco, Á., Conde, M.Á., Sein-Echaluce, M., García-Peñalvo, F.J.: Diseño y desarrollo de un sistema basado en Learning Analytics para evaluar la competencia de trabajo en equipo. In: Conference AISTI - Asociación Ibérica de Sistemas y Tecnologías de Información (2014)

15. Conde, M.Á., Hérnandez-García, Á., García-Peñalvo, F.J., Séin-Echaluce, M.L.: Exploring student interactions: learning analytics tools for student tracking. In: Zaphiris, P., Ioannou, A. (eds.) LCT 2015. LNCS, vol. 9192, pp. 50–61. Springer, Heidelberg (2015)
16. Martinez, J.E.P., Garcia Martin, J., Alonso, A.S.: Teamwork competence and academic motivation in computer science engineering studies. In: 2014 IEEE Global Engineering Education Conference (EDUCON), pp. 778–783. IEEE, Istanbul (2014)
17. Tasa, K., Taggar, S., Seijts, G.H.: The development of collective efficacy in teams: a multilevel and longitudinal perspective. J. Appl. Psychol. **92**, 17–27 (2007)
18. Miles, M.B., Huberman, A.M.: Qualitative Data Analysis: An Expanded Sourcebook. Sage Publications, Thousand Oaks (1994)

Mixed Method Assessment for BIM Implementation in the AEC Curriculum

Jose Ferrandiz[1(✉)], David Fonseca[2], and Abdulaziz Banawi[1]

[1] Department of Architectural Engineering, United Arab Emirates University,
Al Ain, United Arab Emirates
jose.ferrandiz@uaeu.ac.ae
[2] GRETEL - Grup de Recerca en Technology Enhanced Learning,
La Salle Universitat Ramon Llull, Barcelona, Spain
fonsi@salle.url.edu
[3] Department of Architectural Engineering, King abdulaziz university,
Rabig, Saudi Arabia
abanawi@kau.edu.sa

Abstract. This paper aims to design a mixed-method evaluation study. The target of this study is to analyze the implementation of the Building Information Modeling/Management technology in the Architectural Engineering Curriculum. We will use the mixed-method evaluation process based on quantitative and qualitative approaches to measure the level of motivation, satisfaction and performance of the students with Building Information Modeling/Management (BIM) technology and obtaining the proper feedback to optimize the implementation of BIM in the Architectural, Engineering and Construction Management (AEC) curriculum.

Keywords: BIM · AEC · Curriculum · Higher education · Mixed methods · Enhanced learning · User centered evaluation · Motivation · Satisfaction · User profile

1 Introduction

BIM will be a milestone at the AEC programs in the near future. The AEC Industries nowadays face an inflection point, as scholarship describes it: "twenty years ago, AutoCAD pushed designers into a new era; BIM represents a new generation of virtual model already widely accepted it by the industry [1] BIM's multi-dimensional approach allows to see how the pieces of their project fit together in real time" [2], that gives the students the opportunity to understand how all the knowledge acquired through the different courses fit together and the relation between them. The students will use BIM technologies to create a model which contains all the information in a single file to produce all the documentation that other-wise would be created in isolation and duplication [3].

The purpose of this paper is to explain the design of the methodology to obtain the data to analyze the implementation of BIM Technology in the AEC curriculum taking into consideration these factors: The motivation of the students towards computer tools technologies and the usability of BIM applications in their studies and career; the

© Springer International Publishing Switzerland 2016
P. Zaphiris and A. Ioannou (Eds.): LCT 2016, LNCS 9753, pp. 213–222, 2016.
DOI: 10.1007/978-3-319-39483-1_20

student proficiency with the tools required; the adaptability of these technologies to the course where it will be introduced; and the students future intentions towards the different software used after this experience.

The methodology of this study will be a mixed-method quantitative/qualitative, where the student interaction with the BIM tools will be analyzed. The research will be done in several courses related to the areas of design, construction and computer tools where BIM is included. The analysis will quantify the motivation, and satisfaction of the students and determine the reasons after this data.

2 Related Work

2.1 Enhanced Learning: Increasing the Motivation and Satisfaction of the Students

The use of ICTs (Information Communication Technologies) in educational methods is defined in the curricula of many undergraduate and master's degrees, including the architecture degree, the focus of this study [4]. These descriptions indicate that the student be able to acquire both personal and collaborative competencies and skills related to active learning, as well as information management, through applications and devices that enable the adoption of Project Based Learning (PBL) approaches. These methods should allow students to work using specific and effective roles much more quickly than with traditional systems and should be able to apply them in their work environment in the future. For all of these reasons, it is necessary to propose and implement new methods through PBL and BIM systems, including the use of appropriate technologies that enable the student to more optimally dedicate him/herself to project and time management.

We must approach the world and teaching of architecture as a component of traditional teaching, which also includes law, medicine, the fine arts and politics. From this perspective, drawing, painting and photography would be precursors to the main technological innovation incorporated at the educational and professional levels: the computer and the use of CAD (Computer-Assisted Design) applications [5, 6]. The following evolution is much more recent and is, in a sense, the cause of the current changing landscape and great need for much broader training in all types of technologies: the appearance of BIM (Building Information Modelling) [7]. Traditional proposals, CAD, the more recent BIM, and other techniques, such as digital sketching (DS) and digital infographics (also known as digital graphics, DG), are all aimed at solving one of the main problems in architecture: the modelling and visualization of complex elements. The acquisition and representation of data associated with land are complex and incompletely documented aspects of modelling [8]. From an academic viewpoint, these systems are used to improve the acquisition of skills and spatial competencies to analyse the visual impact of any building or architectural project.

Numerous types of studies have linked the use of ICTs with improved student motivation and, correspondingly, academic performance [9]. While focusing on the study of user behaviour and emotions, we cannot forget its connection with the area of widely documented knowledge corresponding to user experience and usability (UX). These areas are historically related to the field of human-computer interaction (HCI).

From that perspective, it would be interesting to analyse any innovation that involves the use of new computer systems or technologies [10].

2.2 Building Information Modelling (BIM), in the Curriculum of the Student

The implementation process of BIM in schools revealed that it should not be simply to create a new course in the curriculum because, as claim Taylor et al. [11]: *"BIM has the potential to be introduced throughout the program"*. Some schools in the AEC sector are exploring BIM applications in their disciplines and struggling to integrate them with other ones. This is what all the schools should do, in the opinion of Camps [12]. The schools can maintain the strengths of traditional education based on disciplines and become multidisciplinary [13]. A separate integrative approach, in which the subjects are divided into separate courses, but try to collaborate with each other, ensures no insulation [14].

Thus the principles of BIM can be first introduced into a subject and then between disciplines [15]. The first two years would focus on the individual skills of modelling and analysis of the model [16] (BIM Course and DGR). The subsequent years could focus more on teamwork and complexity through collaboration [16]. (BIM Course, Design Studio and Building Technology). The last year could deal with actual construction projects in collaboration with companies [16] (BIM Course and Management) [17].

As the great study cited [17] above explains, the BIM implementation at the AEC curriculum has a lack of data. Our study will provide the methodology to collect scientific data about the students' motivation, satisfaction and performance after the implantation of BIM technology in the courses of Design, Construction and Modeling and Simulation. This data will be a perfect tool to analyze and design a solid BIM implementation.

2.3 Mixed Methods Assessment in Educational Environments

Quantitative methods are vital for rapidly assessing the key factors from the design perspective that are to be evaluated at the beginning, during, or at the end of the development process. By characterizing and providing detail to the quantitative data, however, qualitative methods provide a point of view that is more subjective and, at times, complementary to the user. Whereas quantitative studies have traditionally been linked to statistical and sociological studies, qualitative approaches have been used in the social sciences and usability research, especially due to the personal input that can characterize highly detailed responses. A combination of both approaches generates what is commonly known as mixed-methods research, which has been widely tested and continues to produce study results, filling gaps in each model and refining the obtained results [18].

To analyze the proposed methods and assess the degree to which they were accepted, we used a formula for data extraction that was previously validated in other educational studies in the same field [19]. An initial pre-test was conducted to obtain the student's profile and starting level of motivation/knowledge about the use of selected technologies. At the end of the course, a post-test was conducted to assess the level of satisfaction and completed use of each system, also a personal interview was conducted using the Bipolar Laddering (BLA) technique [20], which allows us to identify and quantify the strong and weak points of the proposed methods. The current proposal has a clear line of continuation in future iterations because it reveals correlations between statistical results and final grades in a way that allows us to evaluate the relationships between different variables in the study and the student's improvement. This proposal also allows us to form conclusions in the future that can be extrapolated and validated in other areas of knowledge. Likewise, the mixed approach will allow us to extract data and identify noteworthy and adaptable aspects in future applications of the proposed system.

3 The Case Study

This section presents the development of the methodology to collect the data for the analysis of the BIM technology implementation in the Architectural Engineering Curriculum. This methodology has to deal with the difficulty of being applied in different courses of the design, construction and computer tools areas of the architectural engineering program. Every course has its own different teaching methodology, criteria and objectives.

The main objectives of the study are to create a methodology to collect mixed data; to measure the students motivation and satisfaction in the courses where we apply the new proposal; to create a new method to collect samples of the student's marks, from the course designed; and finally, to create a method to analyze the performance of the students.

3.1 Methodology

This research is based on a mixed-method research methodology. As Johnson et al. [21] define it, mixed-methods research "is an intellectual and practical synthesis based on qualitative and quantitative research; it is the third methodological or research paradigm (along with qualitative and quantitative research). It recognizes the importance of traditional quantitative and qualitative research but also offers a powerful third paradigm choice that often will provide the most informative, complete, balanced, and useful research results". The research that we are developing aims to provide real quantitative and qualitative data as a tool for the AEC schools to decide how to introduce BIM in their curriculum.

The methodology design in this paper will be applied during three semesters. In the first semester it will be considered as preliminary, and we will use it to validate or improve the final methodology for the study.

The study will have two main elements the tests and the exercises delivered by the students. These two elements will provide us the data to evaluate the motivation, satisfaction and performance of the students.

3.2 Test Design

The design of the "test of user" is a common topic inside the scientific research and experimentation based on user's responses that will provide us the data. The main objective of these tests is to assess the usability of the new learning environment. In this specific case, the learning environment change is due to implementation of BIM technology in the courses of design, construction and computer tools.

In the university framework there are successful studies to design the survey process that we will take into account to develop this methodology. These studies analyze the implementation of new technologies at the curriculum based on the user profile. The focus of these studies is the efficiency and effectiveness of the course, and the level of satisfaction and students preferences [22]. The most common parameters considered in this type of survey are, the degree of knowledge of the technologies, the use made of social networks, computer tools application level and theoretical knowledge of the course applying the new technology studied that will be implemented [23].

For this specific research which is based on the implementation of the BIM technology at the architecture, engineering and construction management curriculum, we will develop a two test survey; the pre-test to know the students proficiency and expectations; and the post-test to know their motivation, and satisfaction.

We will develop a cyclical process in order to validate or improve the test methodology for this study. This cyclical process is composed of three phases. The first phase is the development, validation or improvement of the test. The second phase is the extraction of the data for the main research. The third phase is the analyses of the results of the survey looking for unnecessary and lost data that we should collect for the main research.

To begin the research with a solid foundation, we developed the first test from the one published at [23]. This test is used in several upstanding studies like [24, 25], and already tested and validated. The first step was to analyze their test and check which chapters could be useful and which ones we should replace for our specific research.

There were six chapters in their initial profile test, new technologies; Internet social network and other tools; applications; computers and laptops; mobiles; and augmented reality. After the analysis of the questions we decided that the last chapter would focus on the technology they were implementing which is not the same as we were testing. All the others are used to create a user profile that will be useful to realize a better analysis of our results. For this reason we decided to change the augmented reality chapter, creating a new chapter to analyze the students' proficiency and expectations of BIM technology applied to the courses. The chapters that we used from their test where rewritten for an easier understanding of our students.

The BIM chapter that we developed aims to extract three main items: their level on BIM before starting the course; their expectations towards BIM technology and finally their technology preferences to be applied in the construction, design and other type of courses.

The pre-test will be run during before the fourth week of the course, after the students finalized their registration. This item will provide us the student profile of each course that we are studying. It will help us to adjust and personalize the course to our students (Fig. 1).

NEW TECHNOLOGIES					Mobile				
How keen are you on Computer tools, Software and technology?					**Do you have mobile?**				
Nothing	Few	Some	Much	A lot	**Brand:**		Modelo:		
Which of these technologies do you usually use?					**Internet:**	3G	4G	Wifi	
A- Mobile	B- Camera	C- MP3/4	D- PC		**Other: Screen:**	<4"	4.-5	5-6	
E- Laptop	F- Game	G- Smartph	H- Tablet		≥6				
Console					**Which options of your mobile do you usually use?**				
Which of these technologies do you own?: How many hours a day do you use the laptop?					Internet	SMS	MMS	APPS Music	Video
<1	1-2	2-4	4-8	>8	Camera	Others:			
What do you use your PC/Laptop for:					**Type of contract?**				
Study	Work	Enterteinemt	Oters:		Pay as you go	Contract			
INTERNET & SOCIAL MEDIA					**Which company do you usually use:**				
Which device do you usually use for internet?					Etisalat	Du	Other:		
Mobile	Laptop	PC	Tablet	Smartph	**BIM**				
how many hours do you spend on internet?					**Do you know what is BIM? How did you know about BIM?**				
<1	1-2	2-4	4-8	>8	**Which is your level in BIM**				
Where do you usually connect to internet?					**Do you think that BIM will be useful in your studies?**				
Home	Univ.	Work	Ciber		**Do you think that BIM can be useful in your construction learning?**				
Public WIFI	Mobile	Oters:			**How:**				
which conecction do you usually use?					**Do you think that BIM can be useful in your design?**				
WI-FI	ADSL	3G	TV	Others:	**Do you think that would be difficult to apply BIM to your projects?**				
What do you usually use?					**Do you think that BIM will be a limitation in your designs?**				
E-mail	Chats	Search tools	games		**DEVICES**				
Architecture	Blogs	Sports	News	Others	**Which learning platform would you like to use?**				
Do you usually use social media? What do you use the social media for?									
Professional	studies	Friendship	Otrers:				Construction	Design	Other courses
TOOLS					Hand drawing		☐	☐	☐
Which social media tools do you use?					Autocad		☐	☐	☐
Facebook	Twitter	Tuenti	Linkedin	Taringa	Computer tools:		☐	☐	☐
MySpace	H5	Orkut	Other:		0 Autocad		–	–	–
Which tools do you use to share files? (photos, video, text, CAD, etc.)					0 Revit		–	–	–
Dropbox	mega	Rapidshare	yousendit		0 Other:		–	–	–
Picasa	Flickr	Other:			Tablet		☐	☐	☐
Which photo-editor and CAD programs do you use?					Mobile		☐	☐	☐
Tell us your level in the programs: 0-None, 1-Low, 2-Medium, 3-High					On line		☐	☐	☐
AutoCAD	REVIT	MicroStation	Rhinoceros	Ilustrator	Other:		☐	☐	☐
MAX	M Design	SketchUP	Adobe	Other:					
Do you play video games?									
What video game system do you use? Which kind of games do you use?									
PC & LAPTOP									
Do you own a PC or Laptop?									
Brand:									
Model:		Processor:							
Which software do you use to develop and show up your design proyects?									
AutoCAD	REVIT	MicroStation	Rhinoceros	Ilustrator	**COURSE NAME:**				
MAX	M Design	SketchUP	PhotoShop	Other:					

Fig. 1. Pre-test example design

The cyclical process to improve the methodology will be done for the whole process as a set of elements. This process will be right after the results analysis of both tables. This process aims to validate or modify the questionnaires to improve the data collected. To develop the second test, we review the mixed-methods research literature and choose the test from [19] as the base. We decided to implement their general assessment part of the questionnaires, and create two specific new chapters about the BIM technology.

The first chapter will test the satisfaction of the students in relation to the BIM technology contribution in their studies and future career. During this first chapter we will ask questions as: how useful will BIM be in your studies, and do you think that BIM will improve your grades.

The second chapter will test the users' perception of the BIM tools in the different areas of the AEC (architecture, engineering and construction management) and the usability of these technologies to improve the AEC curriculum. We will ask questions as: Evaluate Revit as a tool to understand the building systems, components and joints; and evaluate Naviswork as a tool to review your projects using clashes and comments. With all these questions we will have a map of the students' understanding and perception towards the BIM tools and the courses where it is applied.

This second questionnaire will be delivered to the students during the last two weeks of lectures before the final exams. We have developed the tests using Excel and Google forms. The second tool gives us the possibility to run the survey online.

3.3   Performance Data, Collection and Analysis Design

As part of the methodology for our research, we develop criteria to collect the samples of the exercises from the courses. This criterion is one of the key points for our research. To provide it with the proper importance, we set up several attributes as a must. The process to collect the exercise samples ruled by our criteria has to be reproducible, measurable, objective, methodological, scheduled, and organized. All these attributes of the criterion will give us a solid scientific foundation to begin our research, and creates a common framework where the researchers will be able to share, compare and validate the results.

To begin the solid foundation of our research we need samples from the courses before the implementation of the new technology we are going to test. To collect these samples, as stated before, we have created the following rules.

The first criteria to establish will be the type of samples that will be collected. The samples from the previous courses will be graded exercises, which we will document by PDF. To be methodological, standardized and organized we will add to these exercises several pieces of information: the name of the institution where the course is done (United Arab Emirates University), the country (United Arab Emirates), the semester (Spring, Fall or Summer), the year of the course (2016), the course name (Intermediate Design Studio), the number of students on each group (1, 2, 3…), the grade accomplish (A+, A…), and the grading criteria if it is available.

The second criteria will be from where we will take these samples. The samples will be collected from the official course file. This will create the possibility for any other researcher to collect the same information to validate our experiment.

The third criteria will be the number of samples to collect. We will collect three graded-samples, one from a very poor student, another one from an average student and the last one from an outstanding student. When a very poor sample is not available, we will collect only the average and good student samples.

The fourth criteria will be from when these samples can be taken. The samples will be taken from the previous three semesters before the technology that we want to try is implemented (Fig. 2).

To collect the samples from the actual course, we will follow the first three criteria stated before. For the first one, we will collect graded-samples of the exercises in PDF, adding all the relevant information. For the second one, we will do it in the opposite direction, so the new graded exercises done with the new technology implementation that we will use to compare with the old ones, will be the exercises that we will add in our course file. For the third, we will collect the three graded-samples as explained before.

As this methodology is set up to be used by any course that wants to implement and test a new technology, the criteria of evaluation will be defined by elements which are stated in the syllabus of the courses. For this reason the evaluation, analysis and comparison of the graded samples already collected will be done by following the

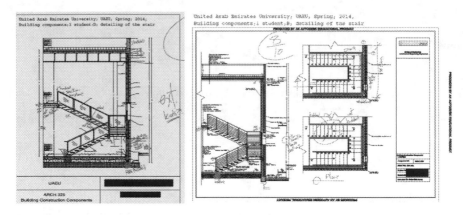

Fig. 2. Samples of previous graded exercises from the course building components

criteria of the course that is written in the syllabus. The evaluation will use the outcomes, milestones or objectives and grades given by the professor as the three different resources to test the samples. We will test all the samples three times, evaluating the level of accomplishment at each criterion. These criteria are set up by the professor in the syllabus of the course. We are going to lay out one sample for each of the outcomes and milestone criteria, understanding that it is a partial view of the real analysis. The outcome and milestone criteria used as samples for the article was developed by assistant professor Abdulaziz Banawi of the United Arab Emirates University, for the intermediate course syllabus in the Spring of 2015.

The first analysis that we are going to introduce will be the outcomes analysis. "Outcome 1: Students demonstrate proficiency in designing and developing detailed construction drawings for their proposals including design of integrated profiles, material selection and systems design [C, E, J]". These letters makes reference to the ABET accreditation program outcomes (A-K): http://www.abet.org/wp-content/uploads/2015/05/E001-15-16-EAC-Criteria-03-10-15.pdf.

The analysis of this outcome as a criteria to analyze the graded-samples, gives us this set of rules to evaluate the exercises of intermediate design studio. We should look for detailed construction drawings, the integration of the elements in the design, applied criteria to select the materials and systems alternatives, and selection criteria. It is very clear from the outcome, so it can be analyzed and compared.

The second type of analysis that we will run, will be the milestones or objectives of the course. The sample that we brought is a milestone that states what should be target by the exercises, "Building Design Research: design issues, site factors analysis, spatial analysis, case studies, design intent". As stated in the milestone, we will look in the samples for the site, spatial and case studies analysis, as well as the design approach. As we can see, the outcomes and the milestones give us a totally different analysis approach.

The third and last analyses will synthesis of the other two previous analyses introducing the variable of the grades given by the professor.

4   Conclusions

As a result of this paper, we have created a mixed-method methodology to analyze the motivation, satisfaction and performance of the students at a course that is implemented with a new ICT technologies. This methodology gives everyone, the opportunity to perform the same experiment and validate or discuss our data. In this paper we have presented two separate methodologies, a test-based one that provides us the motivational and satisfaction analysis, and another one based on graded sample exercises that test the performance of the students.

The test-based methodology is a mixed-method survey that gives us the "user profile", their motivation, and satisfaction based on two tests that are performed at the beginning and at the end of the course and is specifically designed for the implementation of BIM.

We created a graded-sample methodology to analyze the performance and improvement of the students in the course which is implementing a new innovative teaching methodology. This methodology developed in this paper provides: a research common framework based on available and official data; and a reproducible, measurable, objective, methodological, scheduled, and organized system to collect and analyzed the samples.

The combination of the test-based and the graded-sample methodologies provides realistic and more accurate data about the implementation of BIM in the AEC curriculum which has not been done before. This study will provide new insights and the proper feedback to optimize the implementation of BIM in the (AEC) curriculum.

References

1. Sabongi, F.J.: The integration of BIM in the undergraduate curriculum: an analysis of undergraduate courses. In: Proceedings of the 2009 ASC International Conference (2009)
2. McFarlane, B.: How a major design firm adapted to a paradigm shift. Healthc. Des. **8**, 12 (2008)
3. Thompson, D., Miner, R.G.: Building information modeling-BIM: contractual risks are changing with technology (2006). http://www.aepronet.org/ge/no35.html
4. Rabee Reffat, K.F.U.P.M.: Revitalizing architectural design studio teaching using ICT: reflections on practical implementations. Int. J. Educ. Dev. using ICT, **3**(1) (2007)
5. Mitchell, W.J.: Computer-Aided Architectural Design, 573 p. Ill. Mason Charter Publishers, Inc., New York (1977)
6. Ullman, D.G., Wood, S., Craig, D.: The importance of drawing in the mechanical design process. Comput. Graph. **14**(2), 263–274 (1990)
7. Sanguinetti, P., Abdelmohsen, S., Lee, J., Lee, J., Sheward, H., Eastman, C.: General system architecture for BIM: an integrated approach for design and analysis. Adv. Eng. Inform. **26** (2), 317–333 (2012)
8. Fassi, F.: 3D modeling of complex architecture integrating different techniques – a critical overview. Int. Arch. Photogrammetry Remote Sens. Spat. Inf. Sci. Zurich **XXXVI-5/W47**, 11 (2007)

9. Fonseca, D., Martí, N., Redondo, E., Navarro, I., Sánchez, A.: Relationship between student profile, tool use, participation, and academic performance with the use of Augmented Reality technology for visualized architecture models. Comput. Hum. Behav. **31**, 434–445 (2014)
10. Hassenzahl, M., Tractinsky, N.: User experience a research agenda. Behav. Inf. Technol. **25** (2), 91–97 (2006)
11. Taylor, M.J., Liu, J., Hein, M.F.: Integration of Building Information Modeling (BIM) into an ACCE Accredit Construction Management Curriculum (2007). https://fp.auburn.edu/heinmic/Pubs/ASC%202008-Integration.pdf
12. Camps, H. L.: BIM: education and the global economy. JBIM **2,** 33–37. (2008). Spring, Washington, www.wbdg.org/pdfs/jbim_spring08.pdf
13. Bronet, F., Cheng, R., Eastman, J., Hagen, S., Hemsath, S., Khan, S., Regan, T., Ryan, R., Scheer, D.: Draft: the future of architectural education. In: AIA TAP 2007 (2007)
14. Techel, F., Nassar, K.: A sustainability design perspective. In: Proceedings of ASCAAD 2007, Alexandria, Egypt (2007). www.ascaad.org/conference/2007/050.pdf
15. Hietanen, J., Drogemuller, R.: Approaches to university level BIM education. In: IABSE Conference, Helsinki, Finland (2008)
16. Kymmell, W.: Building Information Modeling: Planning and Managing Construction Projects with 4D CAD and Simulations. McGraw Hill, New York (2008)
17. Barison, M.B., Santos, E.T.: BIM teaching strategies: an overview of the current approaches. In: Proceedings of ICCCBE 2010 International Conference on Computing in Civil and Building Engineering (2010)
18. Fonseca, D., Redondo, E., Villagrasa, S.: Mixed-methods research: a new approach to evaluating the motivation and satisfaction of university students using advanced visual technologies. Univ. Access Inf. Soc. **14**(3), 311–322 (2015)
19. Fonseca, D., Valls, F., Redondo, E., Villagrasa, S.: Informal interactions in 3D education: citizenship participation and assessment of virtual urban proposals. Comput. Hum. Behav. **55**, 504–518 (2016)
20. Pifarré, M., Tomico, O.: Bipolar laddering (BLA): a participatory subjective exploration method on user experience. In: Proceedings of the 2007 Conference on Designing for User eXperiences (DUX 2007), p. 12. ACM, New York, NY, USA (2007). Article 2
21. Johnson, R.B., Onwuegbuzie, A.J., Turner, L.A.: Toward a definition of mixed methods research. J. Mixed Methods Res. **1**(2), 112–133 (2007)
22. Martín Gutiérrez, J.: Estudio y evaluación de contenidos didácticos en el desarrollo de las habilidades espaciales en el ámbito de la ingeniería (2010)
23. Redondo, E., Fonseca, D., Sánchez, A., Navarro, I.: Augmented reality in architecture degree. New approaches in scene illumination and user evaluation. Int. J. Inf. Technol. Appl. Educ. (JITAE) **1**(1), 19–27 (2012)
24. Fonseca, D., Villagrasa, S., Valls, F., Redondo, E., Climent, A., Vicent, L.: Engineering teaching methods using hybrid technologies based on the motivation and assessment of student's profiles. In: Frontiers in Education Conference (FIE). 2014 IEEE, pp. 1–8 (2014)
25. Fonseca, D., Villagrasa, S., Valls, F., Redondo, E., Climent, A., Vicent, L.: Motivation assessment in engineering students using hybrid technologies for 3D visualization. In: 2014 International Symposium on Computers in Education (SIIE), pp. 111–116 (2014)

Learning and Performance Support - Personalization Through Personal Assistant Technology

Jean-Francois Lapointe[(✉)], Heather Molyneaux, Irina Kondratova, and Aida Freixanet Viejo

Human-Computer Interaction Team, National Research Council of Canada, Information and Communications Technologies, Ottawa, Canada
{jean-francois.lapointe,heather.molyneaux, irina.kondratova,aida.freixanetviejo}@nrc-cnrc.gc.ca

Abstract. Personalization is important for online learning due to the ever changing needs of online learners and because of its potential to reach a wide variety of users. This paper describes the results of a literature review about the personalization of online learning systems. It also describes results of user studies of the prototype of a learning and performance support (LPSS) platform developed at the National Research Council of Canada. Main findings are that personalized learning systems can enhance learning effectiveness and motivate learners, and that learners are looking for ways to better explore their learning context through social network.

Keywords: Personal learning environment · Personalization · Collaborative learning · Learning and performance support

1 Introduction

The National Research Council of Canada's (NRC) Learning and Performance Support Systems (LPSS) program is developing a personal learning and performance support platform that crosses organizational boundaries to create a collaborative learning network. The LPSS platform provides individuals with access to their own learning resources and their learning records, allowing for job preparation and continued learning. LPSS is built around the Personal Learning Record (PLR) which contains the user's learning records. The personalization of the LPSS is achieved via the Personal Learning Assistant (PLA).

This paper is based on the findings of a literature review on Personal Learning Environments (PLEs) including current learning needs analysis, and on the results of LPSS user feedback studies. Selected articles were reviewed by researchers in order to assess the state of the art functionality of existing PLEs, where the users personally customize a framework to enhance their learning. The articles on Personal Learning Assistants (PLAs) that involve the discovery, annotation and access to learning resources within PLEs were also reviewed in order to validate future work on LPSS. In the paper, we summarize the role of personalization in PLEs and provide a brief

© Springer International Publishing Switzerland 2016
P. Zaphiris and A. Ioannou (Eds.): LCT 2016, LNCS 9753, pp. 223–232, 2016.
DOI: 10.1007/978-3-319-39483-1_21

overview of the LPSS, including user feedback and evaluations related to personalization. Future work on LPSS platform and on the Personal Learning Assistant is also discussed in the conclusion.

2 User Learning Needs

Learning needs have changed over time due to the proliferation of instant communication and access to information [1]. Increased connectivity has led to a blurring of both work and personal lives, especially with younger employees, who turn to social media for professional and personal communication [2]. As a result of this change we need to rethink how we learn; from traditional models of learning to digital education through personalized learning paths [1] which include a wide variety of collaboration tools for communication, team collaboration, writing/editing and engaging/networking [2]. There is a need to connect and support people with a broad range of technologies, processes and content as well as a need for on demand learning that doesn't disrupt workflow and productivity [3].

In traditional e-learning content, the learning units and the order in which they are taken is decided by the provider. Learning management systems are course-centric. Current trends in learning include: learners moving into different and potentially unrelated fields over their lifetime; the rise of informal learning; lifelong learning – learning as a continual process; and know-how being replaced with know-where as a result of exponentially growing knowledge [4]. Trends in learning and communication point towards the need for personal learning environments (PLE) where the learners choose the content, their learning path and work at their own pace [5, 6].

PLE is a learner-centric ideology rather than a software application [6]. A PLE system is: decentralized; places the individual at the center; grants user access to LMS systems as well as other sources of information; allows for direct connections to collaborative environments separate from LMS; and connects individuals with LMSs (which are centralized). Within the PLE the individuals' data is theirs to manage and share as they see fit and the data goes with them as they change jobs or training programs [7].

The literature on personalization shows a need to move beyond traditional systems, as well as a shift towards lifelong learning that is not just personalized but also personal: this is why LPSS was designed. LPSS is a single point of access for development and training needs, and ultimately, career development and enhancement. The main objective of the NRC's LPSS program is to design, deploy, refine and commercialize an online system for improving people's learning and work performance [8]; however, LPSS goes beyond the limitations of traditional systems. LPSS emphasizes an individualized learning path with context-aware support. The platform places emphasis on personal learning through self-guided learning (including the use of simulations and simulation data), and will use social networks to create personal knowledge and learning through a variety of different communication systems [9].

3 Personalization

In the context of learning, personalization is an evolution of the concepts of differentiation and individualization. There is no single shared definition of the meaning of personalization; we define it as systems and methods that incorporate technology to differentiate resources and processes, based on each learners' skills, interests, needs and learning profile in order to accelerate and deepen learning [10, 11]. The next step after personalization learning is personal learning, which implies a custom-built learning system for each user [12].

The need for personalization is not something new; in the paper *Learning for Mastery*, the author writes "the basic task in education is to find strategies which will take individual differences into consideration but in such a way as to promote the fullest development of the individual" [13]. Personalization is important because online learning reach a much wider variety of users than traditional environments and also because users work with the system individually [14]. Personalized learning systems can enhance learning effectiveness [14, 15] and help learners to feel more motivated [16].

We identify two main categories of research on personalization and learning. One category focuses on structured learning in a specific context, like the Protus system designed to help to learn specific programming languages which work with a predefined set of learning contents [17]. The other category focuses on Personal Learning Assistants (PLA) or other Personal Learning Environments (PLE), some examples are the TRAILER where the main objective is to help learners manage competences acquired through informal learning [18] and the LPSS project [8] shown in this paper. These two categories are not exclusive, as more structured and formal learning can also be provided through PLA or PLE; and both also have some common points, like the type of variables that are considered to personalize the learning experience (learning style, performance level, etc.). Personalization within PLEs can be achieved in different degrees and in different ways depending on the nature of the system, the data gathered or its purpose. The main concepts that are related to personalization in PLE are described below.

Recommendation systems are a main point of research in relation to personalization, and different variables are used to leverage the recommendations: learning styles, performance, learner's activities, browsing behaviors, learner's interests or social connections among others. Some research points to the value of considering context (computing, location, time, physical conditions, resources, user and social relations) to "better predict and anticipate the needs of users, and act more efficiently in response to their behavior" [19]. Recommender systems are a crucial part of personalizing learning as they aim to provide suitable resources to learners. The output of the recommenders is usually in form of a list of resources (content, user actions, people) and in some cases the learner can give feedback about the usefulness of the recommendations proposed in order to improve future recommendations [14].

Collaboration is used as a mechanism for personalizing the learning experience through different techniques. For example, a collaborative voting approach is used to find the average difficulty of specific course contents [20] or a combination of social network data and learner's learning context is used in E-SoRS to provide the best connections to solve questions emerged while researching or studying [14]. Collaboration is strongly related to the concepts of social connections and community [19].

The importance of defining the user model is emphasized in the research on personalization. The model could be inferred from behavioral data, as found in eTeacher [21], or extracted from tests and surveys answered by the learner, like in Protus [17]. Learning styles are considered one of the most important factors influencing e-learning and personal academic competence [16]. To personalize learning, one needs to personalize learning objects, learning activities and learning methods, which are all interconnected with the learning style of the learner [22].

In PLEs there is a shift in control which comes from the move from institutionalized learning environments to learning spaces centered on the user. In this new space, users control the process of learning and create their own environment by searching, aggregating, creating and sharing contents [23]. Research indicates that learning styles can vary depending on the task or the learning content so the learner needs to be able to change this information at any time [17]. To personalize the experience, the learner should have control over the information and organization of the system.

Strongly related to the shift in user control, there is also the adaptation aspect, which refers to the ability of the system to learn from its own use. The user controls the system when he actively modifies it, but to empower the adaptation, the system needs to use behavioral data, activities, paths, explicit feedback or other data collected for the improvement of the system. For example, the system uses the feedback provided by the user in order to suggest future actions [21].

The use of affective information is also a part of the research on personalization [19]. Influence of emotions on learning and how they can be used to improve learning experience [24], and the importance of using strategies to motivate learners, like providing the opportunity for a second formative assessment [25] are relevant for this subject.

4   LPSS and Personalization

Since the launch of the pre-release in 2014, the National Research Council of Canada (NRC) is continually developing the LPSS platform, a system that shifts the learning perspective from classroom learning to personal learning. LPSS creates a personalized, dynamic and ongoing learning environment with access to enhanced learning resources on demand. This learning platform goes beyond personalized learning towards personal learning. Rather than offering a customized version of a generic offering, the goal of LPSS is to enable each learner to develop their own custom learning program from the ground up [26]. The LPSS pre-release version that was launched on October 21, 2014 (www.lpss.me):

> provides individual learners with the tools and support necessary to access learning from any number of providers – not just educational institutions, but also their friends and mentors, their current and future employers, community and social programs, and much more. Built on current and evolving learning technology standards, it is designed to provide access to MOOCs, to traditional learning management systems, to stand-alone courses and software, and even to the world of the Internet of things [26].

Within the LPSS platform, a personal instance is created for each learner, designed to keep track of everything related to learning – exercises followed, tests taken, games and simulations attempted, web pages accessed, etc. LPSS stores all that in a single location within the Personal Learning record (PLR). Unlike a learning management system, LPSS plans to combine data from the user's learning environment, the work environment and the social environment, thus enabling adaptive learning software to close the loop between learning and performance, and capture both formal and informal learning. PLR manages user's learning and training records, credentials and badges over a lifetime, making it easier for employers to identify qualified candidates and for prospective employees to identify skills gaps.

The LPSS platform aims at enabling features such as an automated recognition of competencies and analysis of workflow and job skills, as well as contextual assistance and access to references and learning materials on demand from any device. In addition, LPSS aims to improve the personal learning experience by providing more insight into user's learning patterns [27]. A snapshot of a personal LPSS dashboard is provided in Fig. 1.

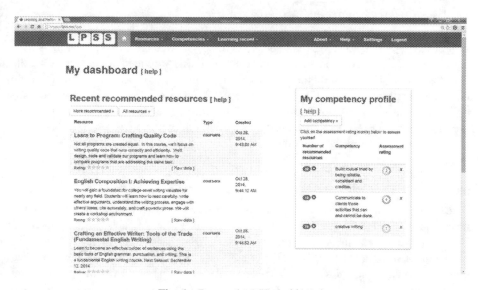

Fig. 1. Personal LPSS dashboard

In the process of designing the LPSS platform, the NRC team conducted an in-depth literature review on the personalization of adaptive learning systems [8]. This study found the analysis of user characteristics to be an essential part of an adaptive system development process and identified features that have been successfully employed in many adaptive systems. Individual user characteristics are crucial to consider in designing features that are relevant for the system's adaptation, for advancing personal learning experiences beyond the one-size-fits-all approach and to ensure that user individual characteristics are taken into account to accomplish quality learning with proper performance support mechanisms in place.

Since LPSS is a networked personal learning platform, user studies involving collaborative learning spaces are relevant as well. For example, Höver et al. [28] looked at various ways to link, share and filter learning resources; provide visualization; archive resources and provide detailed levels of anchors for linking learning resources, including the need for referencing paragraphs, sentences, words, timestamps, and annotations. Other researchers [29] have also looked at linking course data to allow for different recommendations for users with different educational backgrounds. This is of particular relevance for the design of the LPSS personal recommender and a toolkit, both designed to provide enhanced access to resources, activities and credentials in a dynamic personal learning environment.

Since the launch of the LPSS pre-release, the research team has conducted various user studies to collect information on system use, perceived usefulness, perceived ease of use, and user satisfaction with the various tools and functionalities available within LPSS. The parts of these studies relevant to personalization are described in the next section of the paper.

5 LPSS User Feedback and Evaluations

In order to gather user feedback and evaluate the LPSS website, NRC researchers used three methods. Firstly, a feedback email address was provided to the users of the website to allow them to send their comments and suggestions. Secondly, surveys were conducted with the users. Finally, an internal review of the lpss.me website was conducted in the form of a usability study. This section provides details on the methods used to obtain user feedback, followed by a discussion of personalization feedback and recommendations from the users themselves.

5.1 Feedback Email

Since the launch of lpss.me, users have been able to communicate with NRC researchers via a feedback email provided via a link at end of each lpss.me webpage. Overall, 34 feedback emails were received since the launch of the system. These emails can be divided in three categories: (1) promotion, which included emails that promoted the user's own technical skills or the skills of the company they work for; (2) improvements suggestions for the LPSS research team on what the system should do; and (3) bug reporting, where the users email LPSS researchers when a feature isn't operating as it should. The second category of feedback emails (improvement suggestions) yielded several user comments related to the personalization of the LPSS system, and will be discussed in the results section.

5.2 Survey

An invitation to participate in a survey was sent to 232 people who registered into the LPSS platform. Between November 2014 and December 2015, 49 users responded to the survey. The majority of respondents were male, from between 40 to 69 years old, involved in online learning and highly educated. As a result, the findings from the survey cannot be seen as representative of the general population, but are sample viewpoints from power users within the online learning community.

A total of 24 questions were asked, ranging from demographics questions (e.g. age, gender, education, and familiarity with online learning, etc.) to more specific questions about the LPSS system. Questions that elicited responses concerning personalization of the system included the open ended text question: "What would you like a learning and performance management system (like LPSS) to do for you? How would you like to use it?"

5.3   Internal Review

An internal review of the website was conducted during the fall of 2015. This review was designed as a usability study of the LPSS platform conducted with NRC employees. It is the first step before conducting an external review of the platform.

When doing usability studies, the number of participants matter and the maximum benefit/cost ratio comes from testing four users [30]. Therefore, four persons (3 men and 1 woman) were recruited to participate in the internal review. They all had graduate degrees and were employees of the NRC involved in the LPSS program.

Participants were asked to complete eight tasks within the LPSS platform while thinking aloud in the presence of a researcher. The tasks were:

1. Log into the website, scan the information provided and report on what you think it is offering and how you can benefit from it.
2. Go to the dashboard and look at it. Report on what you think is the purpose of the different sections that you see.
3. Think about a topic/domain/skill you would like to improve and add it to your competency profile.
4. Without looking at the system, report where you think you could find relevant information about this topic.
5. Proceed to one credential you have in the learning record section and convert it to a pdf.
6. Log into the system, access the dashboard and explain what you see. How do you think it can be used? Would you like more/less or different information?
7. How would you filter the resources by type or keyword?
8. Now that you know more about the system, could you explain in your own words what you think it does? Would you use it? Why?

The internal review was conducted on regular laptops running the Morae 3.3.3 usability testing software. The screen display, mouse clicks and the webcam recordings (user's face and voice) were recorded for later review and analysis.

Before the study the users were given a short introduction to the study and its methodology. They were then provided with a computer and asked to perform eight tasks using the think aloud protocol. For some of the tasks, test accounts were created to avoid spending time on the sign up process that was not in the scope of the test.

5.4   Results

Some useful feedback on the platform was collected using the above mentioned methods. Given the focus of this paper, we are reporting only the results that relate to the personalization of the LPSS site.

Feedback emails. One user gave the following advice for improving the recommendation system: "It may be convenient to allow for the rating of resources in terms of relevance to the user. That may make the recommendations more intelligent. For example, I like the recommendations by the aggregation website http://www.elearninglearning.com/."

Survey. Respondents were asked what they would like LPSS to do for them. The answers related to personalization were:

- Provide a way to network around competencies; learn from what others interested in similar competencies are studying.
- Highlight things of interest based on personal profile and activities.
- It could be interesting to browse competencies with the users profile associated, to optimize the network effect.

Internal review. One issue reported was that the user expected his competencies level would be determined by a third party organization, instead of having the user manually adding his competencies.

Another reported issue was that users would appreciate an increase in the number of options to filter and narrow their searches.

A third reported issue was that when you create a credential in the Learning Record section, the system should automatically add your name, since the LPSS.me account is personal.

A fourth reported issue was that when exporting his credentials to a pdf, a user would have liked to have the option to tailor what is shown in the pdf, by selecting specific credentials.

Beyond the need for additional tailoring, the users revealed via email, survey and internal review responses the importance of social learning and the usefulness of rated resources. Users wanted to see what others with similar competencies and interests are learning in order to further their own learning. Also users wanted to see resources rated, both automatically and by other users who have used the resources, as well as easier filtering in the system.

6   Conclusion

This paper presented research and development underway at the National Research Council of Canada to develop personalized learning technology for learning and performance support. The paper provides an overview of the importance of personalization in online learning and in the context of LPSS, demonstrates that personalization can be applied in different ways within the learning platform.

The paper demonstrates the importance of understanding end-user needs, expectations and doubts when gathering personalization requirements, which can be accomplished through different methods like feedback emails, surveys and internal reviews. In the initial phase of LPSS development, considering the user feedback received, the main personalization findings are related to the social aspect of competencies (exploring what others in the same context are doing), better filtering capabilities and more options in relation to resources or user searches.

Future work on the LPSS platform will continue its focus on personalized learning by strengthening the social network aspects of the platform, further allowing learners to create and share information. External reviews will also be conducted to get user feedback from external users. User interactions will be captured in order to allow data analytics on them. Finally, researchers working on LPSS will continue exploring the challenges and opportunities for creating a truly personal learning environment, customized for and created by each user.

References

1. Swartzberg, C., Swartzberg, R.: Digital Education Gets Smart with Personalized Learning Paths. Bizcommunity. Education and training (2015)
2. Sarrrazin, H., Sprague, K., Huskins, M.: Enabling Enterprise Collaboration. McKinsey & Company, New York (2013)
3. Rosenberg, M.J., Foreman, S.: Learning and Performance Ecosystems: Strategy, Technology, Impact and Challenges. White paper. The eLearning Guild (2014)
4. Siemens, G.: Connectivism: A Learning Theory for the Digital Age. eLearnspace (2004)
5. Dascalu, M., Bodea, C., Moldoveanu, A., Mohora, A., Lytras, M., Pablos, P.O.: A recommender agent based on learning styles for better virtual collaborative learning experiences. Comput. Hum. Behav. **45**, 243–253 (2015)
6. Ali, S.M., Ghani, I., Latiff, M.S.A.: Interaction-based collaborative recommendation: a personalized learning environment (PLE) perspective. KSII Trans. Internet Inf. Syst. **9**(1), 446–464 (2015)
7. Downes, S.: LMS vs PLE. YouTube. https://www.youtube.com/watch?v=zDwcCJncyiw (2012)
8. Fournier, H., Molyneaux, H.: Learning and Performance Support Systems: Personal Learning Record: User Studies White Paper. NPARC #: 21275411, p. 19. doi: http://doi.org/10.4224/21275411 (2015)
9. Downes, S.: Design Elements in a Personal Learning Environment. Lecture presentation delivered to Invited Talk, Guadalajara, Mexico (2015)
10. Pane, J.F., Steiner, E.D., Baird, M.D., Hamilton, L.S.: Continued Progress: Promising Evidence on Personalized Learning. RAND Corporation, Santa Monica, CA (2015). http://www.rand.org/pubs/research_reports/RR1365.html
11. Grant, P., Basye, D.: Personalized Learning. International Society for Technology in Education, Arlington (2014)
12. Downes, S.: When U.S. air force discovered the flaw of averages. http://www.downes.ca/post/64908 (2016)
13. Bloom, B.: Learning for Mastery. Evaluation Comment v1 n2. Center for the Study of Evaluation of Instructional Programs, University of California, Los Angeles, USA (1968)

14. Akbari, F., Taghiyareh, F.: E-SoRS: a personalized and social recommender service for e-learning environments. In: 8th National and 5th International Conference on e-Learning and e-Teaching (ICeLeT), Tehran (2014)
15. Chen, W., Su, M., He, X., Chen, Y.: Personalized learning instant support service. J. Convergence Inf. Technol. (JCIT) **8**(1), 578–587 (2013)
16. Dascalu, M.-I., Bodea, C.-N., Moldoveanu, A., Mohora, A., Lytras, M., de Ordóñez Pablos, P.: A recommender agent based on learning styles for better virtual collaborative learning experiences. Comput. Hum. Behav. **45**, 243–253 (2015)
17. Klašnja-Milićević, A., Vesin, B., Ivanović, M., Budimac, Z.: E-learning personalization based on hybrid recommendation strategy and learning style identification. Comput. Educ. **56**(3), 885–899 (2011)
18. García-Peñalvo, F.J., Zangrando, V., García Holgado, A., Gónzalez Conde, M.Á., Seone Pardo, A.M., Alier Forment, M., Janssen, J., Griffiths, D., Mykowska, A., Ribeiro Alves, G., Minovic, M.: TRAILER project overview: tagging, recognition and acknowledgment of informal learning experiences. In: 2012 International Symposium on Computers in Education (SIIE). Institute of Electrical and Electronics Engineers, IEEE Catalog Number CFP1286T-ART, Andorra la Vella (2012)
19. Verbert, K., Manouselis, N., Ochoa, X., Wolpers, M., Drachsler, H., Bosnic, I., Duval, E.: Context-aware recommender systems for learning: a survey and future challenge. IEEE Trans. Learn. Technol. **5**(4), 318–335 (2012)
20. Chen, C.-M., Lee, H.-M., Chenb, Y.-H.: Personalized e-learning system using item response theory. Comput. Educ. **44**(3), 237–255 (2005)
21. Schiaffino, S., Garcia, P., Amandi, A.: eTeacher: providing personalized assistance to e-learning students. Comput. Educ. **51**(4), 1744–1754 (2008)
22. Kurilovas, E., Kubilinskiene, S., Dagiene, V.: Web 3.0-based personalisation of learning objects in virtual learning environments. Comput. Hum. Behav. **30**, 654–662 (2014)
23. Saadatmand, M., Kumpulainen, K.: Content aggregation and knowledge sharing in a personal learning environment. iJET **8**(S1), 70–77 (2013)
24. Shen, L., Wang, M., Shen, R.: Affective e-Learning: using "emotional" data to improve learning in pervasive learning environment. Educ. Technol. Soc. **12**(2), 176–189 (2009)
25. Huang, M.-J., Huang, H.-S., Chen, M.-Y.: Constructing a personalized e-learning system based on genetic algorithm and case-based reasoning approach. Expert Syst. Appl. **33**, 551–564 (2007). Science Direct
26. Downes, S.: This is the next era of learning. http://www.online-educa.com/OEB_Newsportal/stephen-downes-learning-support-systems/ (2014)
27. National Research Council of Canada: Social, Technical and Economic Realities Collide: The Perfect Storm for Personal Learning. NRC, p. 13. http://nparc.cisti-icist.nrc-cnrc.gc.ca/npsi/ctrl?action=shwart&index=an&req=21275106&lang=en (2015)
28. Höver, K.M, Hartle, M., Rößling, G., Mühlhäuser, M.: Evaluating how students would use a collaborative linked learning space. In: Proceedings of the 16th Annual Joint Conference on Innovation and Technology in Computer Science Education, 27 June 2011, pp. 88–92. ACM 2011
29. He, L., Wu, C., Wu, J., Xie, M., Huang, L., Ye, G.: Linked course data-based user personal knowledge recommendation engine. J. Comput. Inf. Syst. (2013)
30. Nielsen, J., Landauer, T.K.: A mathematical model of the finding of usability problems. In: CHI 1993 Proceedings of the INTERACT 1993 and CHI 1993 Conference on Human Factors in Computing Systems, pp. 206–213 (1993)

An Instrument for Measuring Students' Perceived Digital Competence According to the DIGCOMP Framework

Leo A. Siiman, Mario Mäeots, Margus Pedaste[✉],
Robert-Jan Simons, Äli Leijen, Miia Rannikmäe, Külli Võsu,
and Maarja Timm

University of Tartu, Ülikooli 18, 50090 Tartu, Estonia
{leo.siiman,mario.maeots,margus.pedaste,
ali.leijen,miia.rannikmae}@ut.ee,
prjsimons@gmail.com, kyllivosu@gmail.com,
maarja.timm@gmail.com

Abstract. The ability to use digital technologies to live, work and learn in today's knowledge-based society is considered to be an essential competence. In schools, digital technologies such as smart devices offer new possibilities to improve student learning, but research is still needed to explain how to effectively apply them. In this paper we developed an instrument to investigate the digital competences of students based on constructs from the DIGCOMP framework and in the contexts of learning science and mathematics in school and outside of school. Pilot testing results of 173 students from the 6th and 9th grades ($M = 12.7$ and 15.7 years of age, respectively) were analyzed to remove unnecessary items from the instrument. The pilot study also showed preliminary smart device usage patterns that require confirmation by a large-scale study. Digitally competent use of smart devices may help facilitate widespread use of computer-based resources in science education.

Keywords: Digital competence · Mobile learning · Use of smart devices · ICT in education

1 Introduction

The ability to use digital technologies to live, work and learn in today's knowledge-based society is considered to be so essential that in 2006 the European Parliament and Council specifically acknowledged digital competence as one of eight key competences necessary for personal fulfilment, active citizenship, social cohesion and employability [1]. More recently, a report commissioned by the European Commission entitled *DIGCOMP: A Framework for Developing and Understanding Digital Competence in Europe* identified 21 digital competences and grouped them into 5 areas: Information, Communication, Content Creation, Safety and Problem Solving [2]. The DIGCOMP framework was developed based on a review of the literature on the concept of digital competence [3], an analysis of 15 different case-studies [4] and consultations with 95 experts [5]. In the context of the DIGCOMP framework the term 'digital competence' is defined to be a set

© Springer International Publishing Switzerland 2016
P. Zaphiris and A. Ioannou (Eds.): LCT 2016, LNCS 9753, pp. 233–244, 2016.
DOI: 10.1007/978-3-319-39483-1_22

of knowledge, skills and attitudes needed by citizens to use ICT to achieve goals related to work, employability, learning, leisure, inclusion and/or participation in society [2].

In Estonia the DIGCOMP framework was used as a basis for introducing a new general competence (digital competence) into the national curriculum in August 2014. This general competency requirement defines digital competence as:

the ability to use new digital technology to cope in a rapidly changing society when studying, acting and communicating as a citizen; to find and store information through digital tools and judge its relevance and credibility; to participate in digital content creation, including making and using text, pictures and multimedia; to use digital tools and strategies to solve problems; to interact and collaborate in digital environments; to be aware of risks and protect one's privacy, personal information and digital identity in online environments; to abide by the same morals and values in online environments as in everyday life [6].

Now that education policy in Estonia explicitly expects schools to play a major role in developing students' digital competence [7], there is a need to understand digital competence as it is defined in the national curriculum and study how it informs teaching and learning. Since the DIGCOMP framework served as the basis for defining digital competence in the Estonian national curriculum it is important to investigate how that framework can be practically applied in schools to develop the various digital competences listed in the curriculum requirements. At a practical level the suitability of the DIGCOMP framework for school-age students has not been established. The framework describes individual competences using analogous terms (e.g., *I can browse for, search for and filter information online*) that may be perceived by some to actually address separate competences. Unlike survey items about digital skills found in the *Eurostat Community Survey on ICT Usage in Households and by Individuals* [8], which asks respondents whether they perform specific activities (e.g., *Do you use the Internet to read online news sites?*), the DIGCOMP self-assessment items tend to be more abstract (e.g., *I can browse the Internet for information*; *I can search for information online*). Therefore, there is a need to study whether the relatively abstract terms used to describe digital competences in the DIGCOMP framework are understood in a consistent manner by school-age students.

Especially important nowadays is to engage young people in science and mathematics. These subjects are fundamental for building the next generation of innovators in today's technology-driven economy. However, studies show that students in Europe [9], including Estonia [10], have low motivation towards learning science and mathematics. A potential solution is to seize upon the interest young people show with smart devices (smartphones, tablet computers) and integrate new pedagogies such as BYOD (Bring Your Own Device) in the science and mathematics classroom [11]. Computer-based science resources, such as those found in the online learning environment Go-Lab [12], offer opportunities for students to learn science through personalized experiments and apply a scientific inquiry methodology using their smartphone or a tablet. Initial results of implementing Go-Lab science scenarios on Wi-Fi enabled tablets have shown positive results with 15-year-old students [13]. Further uptake of Go-Lab resources for large-scale use in education can benefit from a better understanding of the digital competence of today's students. There is still a lack of research about the use of smart devices by students to learn science and mathematics

[14]. The instrument developed in this study is a first step towards collecting accurate data about the use of smart devices by students and provides data to make preliminary inferences about the digitally competent use of smart devices by students to learn science and mathematics.

2 Method

The instrument in this study aimed to collect data from school-age students about their use of smart devices and their digitally competent use of smart devices to learn science and mathematics. It adopts some useful layout formats and scales from the survey instrument used by PISA to investigate use of ICT by students [15], and similarly uses a self-report questionnaire to collect data about how often students perform certain activities in specific contexts. The activities in this instrument are related directly to the digital competences described in the DIGCOMP framework. The contexts include in school and outside of school learning, as well as a context to measure use of smart devices for activities not related to school learning.

2.1   Designing and Developing the Instrument

The DIGCOMP framework [2] was examined closely to determine which constructs related to digital competence to study. The DIGCOMP framework identifies five main areas of digital competence (Information, Communication, Content Creation, Safety and Problem-Solving) which are interpreted in this study as our main constructs. The 21 individual digital competences in the DIGCOMP framework are then taken to be subscales of these main constructs. Selection of which digital competences to include in the instrument was influenced by our choice to employ a self-report questionnaire. Maderick et al. [16] concluded that self-assessment of digital competences that can be otherwise assessed through criterion-referenced tests are not accurate or valid. They reported that participants in their study (preservice teachers) overestimated their digital competence through self-assessment [16]. We decided that the constructs Safety and Problem-Solving can be better assessed by tests and therefore excluded these two main constructs from this instrument. Likewise, 6 of the 13 subscales in the remaining three main constructs were also judged to be more appropriately measured by assessing actual performance on a task rather than with a self-report usage survey. These subscales were likewise excluded. The remaining 7 digital competences included in this instrument were: browsing, searching and filtering information; storing and retrieving information; interacting through technologies; sharing information and content; collaborating through digital channels; developing content; and integrating and re-elaborating.

Definitions given in the DIGCOMP framework for each of the 7 digital competences under consideration appear to include similar and perhaps redundant terminology. For example, the digital competence *Browsing, searching and filtering information* is described to be "To access and search for online information, to articulate information needs, to find relevant information, to select resources effectively, to navigate between online sources, to create personal information strategies." [2, p. 17]. Within that definition there are 6 separate clauses and even the title of the digital competence includes three similar terms (browsing, searching and filtering). Hence, to create items for our instrument based on the 7 selected digital competences we decided to write three versions of each digital competence and test them in a pilot study. The three variations were generated by looking at the terms used in the DIGCOMP definition and choosing those believed to be most readily understood by our target audience (school-age students). Table 1 gives an overview of the instrument items that were developed. The item order was chosen such that each version of a digital competence is asked once before asking alternative versions of the same digital competence.

The question format and frequency scale for presenting the item in our instrument are similar to the survey instrument used by PISA to investigate use of ICT by students [15]. However, an important difference is that we were interested in studying how often a student performs a certain activity in four differing contexts. These contexts not only give information about the use of smart devices in school, where current teaching practice may not yet apply such digital technology to a wide extent, but also on the use of smart devices outside of school where usage may be more prevalent. The four differing contexts are: (1) at school for tasks assigned by a science or mathematics teacher, (2) outside of school for tasks assigned by a science or mathematics teacher (e.g., homework), (3) outside of school for learning additional science or mathematics information not required by a teacher, and (4) outside of school for activities not related to school learning. These four contexts describe possible ways students are currently using smart devices. Table 2 summarizes the structure of the instrument and shows how a question about a single digital competence item is presented in a matrix layout for the four differing contexts.

2.2   Implementing the Instrument

Considering the age of our target audience, the need to maintain their interest in completing the questionnaire, our desire to record analytics data such as time spent per question, our need for flexible styling and formatting options of content and a solution that would be scalable for large numbers of respondents, it was decided that the instrument should be administered electronically on tablet computers. In addition, electronic administration of the instrument needed to work offline to ensure that locations with poor or no Wi-Fi coverage would still permit data collection. Given all the needs of this instrument we proceeded to create the technical solution ourselves.

The technical solution for administering the instrument on tablet computers is based on saving an HTML file to a tablet computer's internal memory and running the file locally in the tablet's web browser. The HTML file was created using the hypertext markup language to define the layout and style of the instrument and the JavaScript programming language to add interactivity to the instrument.

Figure 1 shows how the instrument appears on both iPad and Android tablets. The interactive functionality in the HTML file included forward and backward buttons to navigate between different items, checks to ensure only one response to single-choice questions, checks for nonresponse and an alert message to a respondent that they cannot continue until all questions are answered, calculation of a unique timestamp when a

Table 1. Development of instrument items corresponding to 7 digital competences (construct subscales) found in the DIGCOMP framework and grouped under three areas of digital competence (i.e. main constructs in this instrument).

Main construct	Construct subscales	Instrument items (item number in parentheses)		
		Version 1	Version 2	Version 3
Information	Browsing, searching and filtering information	(1) I use a smart device to browse the Internet and find information …	(8) I use a smart device to search the Internet for information …	(15) I use a smart device to search and find information on the Internet …
	Storing and retrieving information	(2) I use a smart device to save files and content (e.g., texts, pictures, music, videos, or web pages) …	(9) I use a smart device to store files and content for later retrieval (e.g., texts, pictures, music, videos, and web pages) …	(16) I use a smart device to organize digital files and content (e.g., texts, pictures, music, videos, and web pages) …
Communication	Interacting through technologies	(3) I use a smart device to communicate with others …	(10) I use a smart device to chat online …	(17) I use a smart device to communicate with others using online social networks …
	Sharing information and content	(4) I use a smart device to share web links with others …	(11) I use a smart device to send files via email attachments …	(18) I use a smart device to upload digital files and share them with others …
	Collaborating through digital channels	(5) I use a smart device to participate in group work …	(12) I use a smart device to collaborate with others …	(19) I use a smart device to contribute to the outcome of group work …
Content creation	Developing content	(6) I use a smart device to create digital files and content (e.g., texts, presentations,	(13) I use a smart device to edit my own digital content (e.g., texts, presentations,	(20) I use a smart device to improve my own digital content (e.g., texts, presentations,

(Continued)

Table 1. (*Continued*)

Main construct	Construct subscales	Instrument items (item number in parentheses)		
		Version 1	Version 2	Version 3
		pictures, audio, video) ...	pictures, audio, video) ...	pictures, audio, video) ...
	Integrating and re-elaborating	(7) I use a smart device to modify the digital content of others (e.g., texts, presentations, pictures, audio, video) ...	(14) I use a smart device to refine the digital content of others (e.g., texts, presentations, pictures, audio, video) ...	(21) I use a smart device to improve the digital content of others (e.g., texts, presentations, pictures, audio, video) ...

Table 2. Format and layout of a single question in the instrument. The question corresponds to a single digital competence item and respondents answer for four differing contexts.

The question is first structured in a form that asks about frequency of smart device use in various contexts that are found in the below matrix. How often do you use a smart device to [*insert digital competence item here*] in the following situations?					
The question is rephrased in the 1ˢᵗ person and ellipses used to connect the question to the four differing contexts. I use a smart device to [*insert digital competence item here*] ...	*A 5-point frequency scale*				
	Never or hardly ever	Once or twice a month	Once or twice a week	Almost every day	Every day
The four differing contexts are presented to respondents. (a) ... at school for tasks assigned by my science or mathematics teacher.	O	O	O	O	O
(b) ... outside of school for tasks assigned by my science or mathematics teacher (e.g., homework)	O	O	O	O	O
(c) ... outside of school for learning additional science or mathematics information not required by my teacher.	O	O	O	O	O
(d) ... outside of school for activities not related to school learning.	O	O	O	O	O

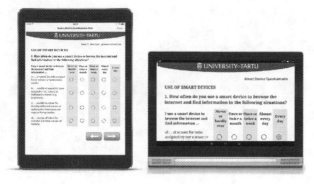

Fig. 1. Appearance of the instrument on iPad and Android tablets. The instrument allows us to gather responses offline, store the data locally and at a later time upload the data to an online spreadsheet file.

respondent selects their first response, and calculation of the time spent per question. A submit button at the end of the instrument was also created and when pressed saved all the data into a format that could be easily read by a spreadsheet application for data analysis. Another HTML file was used to upload (when it was possible to establish a Wi-Fi Internet connection with the tablet) all the data (multiple respondent data may have been collected on a single tablet) to an online spreadsheet file.

2.3 Pilot Study

A pilot study was organized to test the instrument with the target audience and gather data to improve the reliability, practicality and conciseness of the instrument. Recall that three potentially redundant items were created for each digital competence construct (see Table 1). Statistical analysis and feedback from the pilot study suggested shortening the instrument via removal of unnecessary items.

A total of 173 students from the 6th and 9th grades (12.7 and 15.7 years of age, respectively) from 2 urban and 2 rural schools participated in the pilot study.

The instrument was completed voluntarily by students who had returned an informed consent form (the form required parental approval for participation and was distributed at least one week before administration of the instrument). Two trained university students familiar with the questionnaire traveled to schools on separate occasions to administer the instrument. They were available to answer questions about the instrument from students.

3 Results

The results of data collection from the pilot study were analyzed and used to remove ineffective items from the instrument. Analysis of the pilot study data also revealed some interesting preliminary usage patterns of smart devices by students.

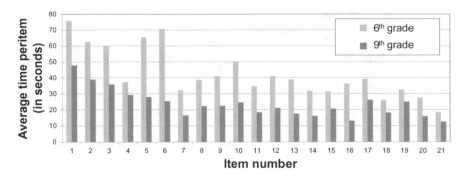

Fig. 2. Average time spent to complete an item by 6th and 9th grade students

3.1 Time Spent Per Item

Included in the data collection was analytics dealing with the time spent per item. Since each item appeared separately on the tablet screen it was possible to record the time spent completing that particular item. Figure 2 shows the average time spent per item (in seconds) for each of the 21 items. The figure distinguishes between 6th and 9th grade students. It can be seen that in the beginning there is a learning curve to get familiar with the questionnaire structure and format. After the first few questions the students in general answer subsequent items more quickly. One concern of the instrument was response burden. However, we see that even by the end of the questionnaire the average time spent per item remains above 10 s. Thus, it does not appear that students get tired or start rapidly making responses on the final items.

It should be noted that before students began answering these items related to digital competences there was a section asking them to enter data about their background (name, age, gender, grades, etc.) and a section about availability of smart devices. These sections together took 6th graders an average time of 3.34 min to complete and 9th graders an average time of 2.95 min to complete.

3.2 Final Version of the Instrument

Two stages of analysis were used to remove ineffective items from the instrument. The first stage relied on calculating internal consistency using Cronbach's alpha correlation coefficient. The items were grouped under the three main constructs (see Table 1) and analyzed to see if their removal improves the internal consistency (reliability) of the instrument. Items 1, 2, 3, 6, 12, 13, 16, and 18 showed an increase in Cronbach's alpha correlation coefficient in at least one of the four contexts studied. All of items that showed an increase in Cronbach's alpha were removed except for item 6. Unlike the other items, the frequency distribution for item 6 showed a greater number of 'every day' responses compared to its two alternative versions. It also showed the least number of 'never or hardly ever' responses compared to its alternatives. This suggested that students better understand item 6 and were able to answer that they performed the activity more often, in contrast to the alternate item versions where confusion may have prevented students from answering that they performed the activity as often as their responses to item 6.

After the first stage of item removal there remained 3 items in the Information construct, 6 items in the Communication construct, and 5 items in the Content Creation construct. It was decided to perform another stage of item removal with the aim of

Table 3. Pilot study results of items selected to be in the final version of the instrument and organized according to main construct, context* and grade level.

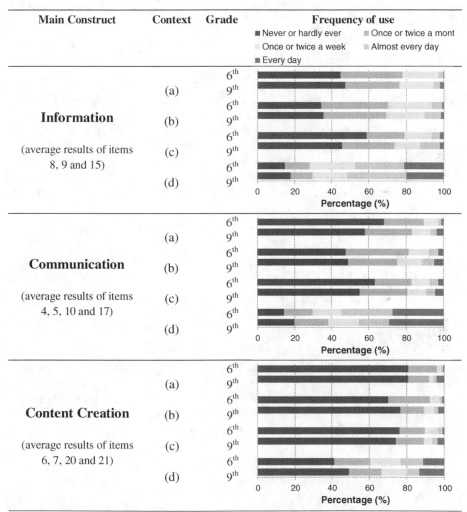

Note. Contexts in the above table refer to: (a) at school for tasks assigned by a science or mathematics teacher, (b) outside of school for tasks assigned by a science or mathematics teacher (e.g., homework), (c) outside of school for learning additional science or mathematics information not required by a teacher, and (d) outside of school for activities not related to school learning).

obtaining 3 to 4 items in each construct. For the second stage of item removal it was also decided that there must be at least one item representing each of the 7 digital competences in the instrument. The second stage of item removal relied in part at looking at levels of skewness in the distribution of responses to the items as well as on consideration of item wording. Two researchers compared the remaining items using this criterion and concluded that items 11, 14 and 19 should be removed. Thus, the final instrument was reduced from 21 items to 11 items. Each of the of 7 digital competences measured by our final instrument is represented by at least one item: browsing, searching and filtering information (items 8 and 15); storing and retrieving information (item 9); interacting through technologies (items 10 and 17); sharing information and content (item 4); collaborating through digital channels (item 5); developing content (items 6 and 20); and integrating and re-elaborating (items 7 and 21).

3.3   Smart Device Usage Patterns of 6th and 9th Grade Students

Although space limitations prevent a detailed presentation and discussion of the pilot study results, some preliminary patterns are apparent. Table 3 presents the pilot study results categorized by main construct, context and student grade level. It can be seen that use of smart devices outside of school for purposes other than school learning result in the highest frequency responses. Also, it is evident that use of smart devices for Content Creation is considerably less than use of smart devices for Information or for Communication. These results begin to show that the developed instrument is useful for extracting usage patterns of students' smart device use. More detailed analysis with a larger representative sample size is needed to make generalizable conclusions as well as to indicate which background characteristics of students can explain the smart device usage patterns.

4   Discussion

Applying this instrument on a large scale in schools is expected to give us an overview of the current situation of how students use smart devices and provide data to assess the digital competence of primary and secondary school students. It is important to keep in mind that this initial instrument is based on a self-report survey. Research shows that the accuracy of self-evaluation instruments cannot always be assumed because students tend to be overconfident in rating their skills [17]. It is also important to note that some of the digital competences might not be assessed with high validity in self-report tests [16]. For this reason we did not focus in our study on assessing two competence areas of the DIGCOMP framework, namely the areas of Safety and Problem Solving. International assessments of computer and information literacy, such as ICILS [18], use computer-based interactive tasks to assess how well students can solve problems. In order to ensure that students can solve problems with ICT or problems in using ICT they actually need to face these problems and come up with solutions. The solutions they present should then be evaluated (how appropriate the solution is and how fast was it obtained). For the same reason, it is not reasonable to ask if a student is able to use his or her smart device safely or can avoid safety issues like viruses. It is something that needs actual testing or observation of students' behavior in action. The tests and/or observations are also needed to increase the validity of self-report surveys in the competence areas of Information, Communication and Content Creation. Therefore, we see a need for future studies to evaluate the validity of the results of the current study by triangulation while using other methods to characterize students' digital competence. It is also noted that assessment of digital competences appears to have logical links to computer-based assessment, since demonstration of task-based performance of digital competence is most reasonably done in digital environments. Computer-based assessment of problem solving skills has been used by the PISA test since 2006, and more recently in 2015 PISA began assessing collaborate problem solving skills using virtual computer agents [19]. Thus, the assessment of digital competences in a computer-based environment seems to be feasible and warrants further study.

Nevertheless, the instrument developed in the current study is an important first step towards understanding the learning opportunities offered by smart technologies in science and mathematics classrooms. It provides an essential overview of how students are currently using smart devices. The next step is to integrate data collection tools in smart devices so that automatic data collection can serve approaches for learning analytics and support students in improving their digital competence. A better understanding of students' digital competence will help facilitate quicker uptake of computer-based science resources such as those provided by the Go-Lab project [12]. Initial results of implementing Go-Lab science scenarios on Wi-Fi enabled tablets have shown positive results [13].

5   Conclusion

In conclusion, a self-report questionnaire was developed, pilot tested, refined and is now ready for large-scale implementation. The instrument surveys how often students use a smart device to perform a digitally competent activity in four differing contexts. The contexts relate to in school and out of school learning of science and mathematics, as well as a context about using smart devices outside of school for activities not related to school learning. The results of a pilot study with 173 students from the 6th and 9th grades were analyzed to select which items from the DIGCOMP framework are best understood by school-age children. Implementation of this instrument on a large scale will allow us to accurately determine how often, in which ways and for what digital competent activities students use smart devices. Moreover, it is expected that data analysis of large-scale data will reveal which background characteristics of students best explain their smart device use.

Acknowledgments. This study was partially funded by the Estonian Research Council through the institutional research funding project "Smart technologies and digital literacy in promoting a change of learning" (Grant Agreement No. IUT34-6). This study was also partially funded by the European Union in the context of the Go-Lab project (Grant Agreement No. 317601) under the Information and Communication Technologies (ICT) theme of the 7th Framework Programme for R&D (FP7). This document does not represent the opinion of the European Union, and the European Union is not responsible for any use that might be made of its content.

References

1. European Parliament and the Council: Recommendation of the European parliament and of the council of 18 December 2006 on key competences for lifelong learning. Official Journal of the European Union, L394/310 (2006)
2. Ferrari, A.: DIGCOMP: A Framework for Developing and Understanding Digital Competence in Europe. Publications Office of the European Union, Luxembourg (2013)
3. Ala-Mutka, K.: Mapping Digital Competence: Towards a Conceptual Understanding. Publications Office of the European Union, Luxembourg (2011)
4. Ferrari, A.: Digital Competence in Practice: Analysis of Frameworks. Publications Office of the European Union, Luxembourg (2012)
5. Janssen, J., Stoyanov, S.: Online Consultation on Experts' Views on Digital Competence. Publications Office of the European Union, Luxembourg (2012)
6. *Põhikooli riiklik õppekava*: [National curriculum for basic schools]. Riigi Teataja I, 29.08.2014, 20 (2014). https://www.riigiteataja.ee/akt/129082014020. Accessed 26 Feb 2016
7. Republic of Estonia Ministry of Education and Research: The Estonian Lifelong Learning Strategy 2020. Tallinn (2014). https://hm.ee/en/activities/digital-focus
8. European Schoolnet and University of Liege: Survey of schools: ICT in education. Benchmarking access, use and attitudes to technology in Europe's schools. Final Report (ESSIE). European Union, Brussels (2013). http://ec.europa.eu/digital-agenda/sites/digital-agenda/files/KK-31-13-401-EN-N.pdf
9. Sjøberg, S., Schreiner, C.: The ROSE project. An overview and key findings (2010). http://roseproject.no/network/countries/norway/eng/nor-Sjoberg-Schreiner-overview-2010.pdf
10. Teppo, M., Rannikmäe, M.: Paradigm shift for teachers: more relevant science teaching. In: Holbrook, J., Rannikmäe, M., Reiska, P., Ilsley, P. (eds.) The Need for a Paradigm Shift in Science Education for Post-Soviet Societies: Research and Practice (Etonian Example), pp. 25–46. Peter Lang GmbH, Frankfurt (2008)
11. Song, Y.: Bring your own device (BYOD) for seamless science inquiry in a primary school. Comput. Educ. **74**, 50–60 (2014)
12. de Jong, T., Sotiriou, S., Gillet, D.: Innovations in STEM education: the Go-Lab federation of online labs. Smart Learn. Environ. **1**, 1–16 (2014)
13. Mäeots, M., Siiman, L., Kori, K., Eelmets, M., Pedaste, M., Anjewierden, A.: The role of a reflection tool in enhancing students' reflection. In: Proceedings of the 10th International Technology, Education and Development Conference (INTED), 7th–9th March 2016, Valencia, Spain (2016, in press)
14. Crompton, H., Burke, D., Gregory, K.H., Gräbe, C.: The use of mobile learning in science: a systematic review. J. Sci. Educ. Technol. (2016). doi:10.1007/s10956-015-9597-x, (Published online before print 14 Jan 2015)
15. OECD: PISA 2012 ICT Familiarity Questionnaire. OECD, Paris (2011)
16. Maderick, J.A., Zhang, S., Hartley, K., Marchand, G.: Preservice teachers and self-assessing digital competence. J. Educ. Comput. Res. (2015). doi:10.1177/0735633115620432, (Published online before print 24 Dec 2015)
17. Dunning, D., Heath, C., Suls, J.: Flawed self-assessment: implications for health, education, and the workplace. Psychol. Sci. Publ. Interest **5**, 69–106 (2004)
18. Fraillon, J., Schulz, W., Ainley, J.: International Computer and Information Literacy Study: Assessment Framework. IEA, Amsterdam (2013)
19. OECD: PISA 2015: Draft Collaborative Problem Solving Framework (Web-Based Material) (2013). http://www.oecd.org/pisa/pisaproducts/Draft%20PISA%202015%20Collaborative%20Problem%20Solving%20Framework%20.pdf. Accessed 29 Sept 2015

Searching Interactions and Perceived Learning

Xiangmin Zhang[(⊠)]

Wayne State University, 106 Kresge Library, Detroit, MI 48202, USA
Ae9101@wayne.edu

Abstract. This research investigates the user's learning during interactive searching process, to find out what search behaviors would be associated with the user's perceived learning, and whether or not the user's perceived learning could be reflected in the existing search performance measures, so that such measures could also be used for indicating learning during searching process. The research used a data set collected by a research project on searching, which involved 35 participants at a major US university. The results show that the number of documents saved is significantly correlated with perceived learning for all search topics. None of the search performance measures is correlated with perceived learning in general. However, for specific topics, one of the performance measures, Recall, is significantly correlated with perceived learning. The results and the implications of the findings are discussed.

Keywords: Searching interactions · Learning by searching · Perceived learning · Searching behavior · Search performance

1 Introduction

The use of information technologies has dramatically changed the way people learn. Online courses are now widely available to remote learners, who maybe students enrolled in a formal education program for a degree or certificate, or maybe informal learners who just want to learn something new.

In the meantime, information, including learning materials, has increased explosively on the Web that is open to the public. Learning objects [3] have been created specifically for supporting learning, and various digital libraries consolidate information resources on the Internet in supporting learning [13]. Many people now learn directly from internet sources for different learning objectives [7]. Because of the support of information technologies and the accessible information on the Internet, self-directed learning, informal learning, life-long learning, as well as formal education in higher education, can happen as elearning in a technology-rich environment, which is more convenient for learners.

This research considers search systems as an IT tool that can play an important role in supporting learning. While it is not difficult to find literature on the use of technology in general to support learning (e.g., [5, 6, 11, 14]), there has not been much research yet on learning while conducting interactive searches. In this research, we investigated into this emerging and important aspect of the learner's use of searching systems such as web search engines. Today's web search systems provide fast access to the vast amount of

© Springer International Publishing Switzerland 2016
P. Zaphiris and A. Ioannou (Eds.): LCT 2016, LNCS 9753, pp. 245–255, 2016.
DOI: 10.1007/978-3-319-39483-1_23

information on the Web. Naturally, searching has become a common activity in both formal classroom and in other informal learning settings. The combination of searching and learning has created the phenomena that is referred to as "learning by searching" [16]. For this research, specifically, we are interested in the relationships between online searching and learning: whether there would be any user search behaviors that could be indicative of learning, and whether or not learning during searching could be assessed by using the existing search performance measures. While learning is a task by people at a wide span of ages, the population that is considered in this study is adult learners.

2   Searching and Learning

Searching and learning behaviors have traditionally been two separate areas of studying. To lay a foundation for the current research, a discussion on learning and searching, and the relationship between the two, is necessary.

2.1   Searching is Part of Learning Process

Searching is a process of information seeking, in particular, for digital information. Because search always starts with an information need or statement, which represents the user's intended information, searching also involves the evaluation or judgement on the search results to see if the search results are indeed related to the search objectives. A complete search process normally includes the following steps: forming the search query (or transforming the internal information need into a formal, explicit search statement); submitting the search query to the search system; evaluating the search results; if not satisfied or the information need changed, revising the search query and resubmitting it, and reevaluating the results. This information searching process has long been recognized as part of the learning process because the information retrieved is used as the input for learning. In [10] the author developed an information search process model, describing different stages during the search process that people seek information to learn the world around them. This model is part of people's learning process. If the search system could not provide the needed information in the learning process, problems may arise which would hinder learning.

Despite the recognition of the importance of searching or information seeking for learning, searching and learning have traditionally been viewed as two separate things: searching is to collect information for learning, and learning is another process that uses the information being collected.

2.2   Learning by Searching

Searching is not just part of learning process. Searching has become more than just finding pieces of information: it shares learning activity features. People, particularly students, often employ explicit search as part of the learning process in studying of a specific topic. [12] argued that learning was a key process within the common activity of exploratory search, among three kinds of search activities: lookup (finding a fact, etc.), learning (acquisition of knowledge, etc.), and investigation (analysis, evaluation, discovery, etc.). As more primary materials go online, searching to learn is increasingly viable. Exploratory search systems are needed to support the full range of users' search activities, especially learning and investigation, and not just lookup, which usually can be completed by one iteration of query-results. This inseparability of learning and searching is also promoted by "informed learning" [2], in which it is argued that information activities and learning are simultaneous processes.

Further evidence to support that searching is learning process is provided by [9], based on the cognitive processes involved. The cognitive processes involved in learning are summarized in the "Taxonomy Table" in [1], which includes six major categories of cognitive processes: remember, understanding, apply, analyze, evaluate and create, in the order of from simple to complex. Based on these cognitive processes, [9] classified 426 searching tasks according to cognitive process features in [1]. Seventy-two participants were asked to perform these tasks in a laboratory experiment. The results showed that information searching was a learning process with searching behavior characteristics specific to particular cognitive levels of learning. The results indicated that applying and analyzing, the middle two of the six categories, generally took the most searching effort in terms of queries per session, topics searched per session, and total time searching. The lowest two learning cognitive processes, remembering and understanding, exhibited searching characteristics similar to the highest order learning cognitive processes of evaluating and creating. Based on the findings, [9] suggested that a learning theory may be better to describe the information searching process. Such a theory, however, will need to be based on more understanding of learning during the search process.

In the present research, "learning (by searching)" means acquiring new knowledge about a topic through interactive searching activities. "Learning by searching" can be evidenced by the use of digital content as well as search engines in classrooms: students often employ searching as part of their classroom learning process when studying a specific topic. In this scenario, learning happens during the search process, not *after* searching.

There has been some research on learning by searching. To support learning by searching, [16] designed a system that could do automatic analysis on the search results for a particular course. This system combined searching and learning automatically, and helped address the fundamental issue of supporting learning while searching.

The factors (other than the behaviors) that may be associated with perceived learning were investigated in [17]. These factors include the user's prior knowledge, prior search skills/experience (because the searches were on genomics documents, search skills/experience was restricted to Medline database search experience), search task characteristics such as general/specific, and the user satisfaction with the search results they found in relating to a specific search topic. The results showed that in general (without considering the task characteristics), all three factors: prior knowledge, prior search experience, and satisfaction, were significantly correlated with perceived learning.

3   Research Questions

Based on the previous work, the current work seeks to extend the scope of previous research to the understanding of how users learn by investigating the relationships between users' learning and their search behavior and between learning and their actual search performance in terms of search outcome. Although searching and learning share common cognitive processes and are considered inseparable in this study, the learning tasks are normally not explicitly defined, but are implied in searching tasks or topics. Therefore, when investigating learning during searching process, instead of using some actual learning tasks, this study uses "perceived learning," i.e., the user's feelings about their knowledge gains from the searching process. Two research questions are addressed in this research:

1. What search behaviors are associated with perceived learning?
   Users' behaviors on a search system have been studied for decades. These include querying behaviors, search result accessing behaviors, and so on. Behaviors which are significantly associated with perceived learning need to be identified. This identification will help understand when and how when users conduct interactive searching, they are actually learning.
2. Are user's learning correlated with the search success as measured by typical search performance measures, so that learning during searching could also be indicated by using such measures?
   For learning during interactive searching process, one possible solution for learning assessment would be using the existing measures for search performance to assess learning. Search performance has traditionally been evaluated using the classic measures of Precision and Recall. These "relevance" based measures test the user's ability to find relevant documents using the search system. They do not relate to learning directly. It is unknown if these measures would be able to be used for assessing learning by searching. [4] demonstrated the correlation between users' knowledge, represented by a pre-knowledge score, and search performance, represented by a search score. Participants took a knowledge test before searching and were scored by the proportion of items correctly answered. The same test was applied after searching. It was found that the score after searching was positively correlated with the pre-search knowledge score. Their study [4], however, did not explicitly evaluate the difference between the search score and knowledge score. This study will compare these measures with the user's perceived learning, hoping to find out if the measures could also be applied to assess learning in searching.

By answering the above research questions, the current research seeks to further the understanding of learning by searching, and to provide evidence for developing needed search technologies to support learning.

4 Methods

This research used the data collected and shared by a large research project on user's information searching behavior at a major US research university. A detailed and complete description of the research design and the user experiment for the data collection can be found in [17]. In this article, we describe the resulting data and the measures that are used in this study.

4.1 Data Set

The data was collected through a laboratory user experiment in which 35 participants performed four search tasks using the standard Text Retrieval Conference (TREC) Genomics Track data, which are PubMed documents. The search topics were also adopted from the Genomics Track dataset [8]. The search topics are classified into two categories: general and specific, based on each topic's relation to the National Library of Medicine's controlled vocabulary, Medical Subject Headings (MeSH) tree. The participants' search behaviors were recorded by the system. Before and after each searching task, participants were also asked to fill out the pre- and post-task questionnaires. The logged behavior data and the completed questionnaires consisted of the primary data used in this research.

Based on the original research design [17], the collected data set included the following types of data on two sets of search topics: general and specific topics:

- Users' search behavior data, such as the number of queries submitted to the system for a search topic, the average query length for a topic, the time spent on a topic, the documents selected from the search results pages (SERPs), and so on.
- Users' search performance data, mainly the number of documents judged and saved by the user as relevant for a topic, and
- The questionnaire data, from both the pre- and post-task questionnaires, which included questions on demographic data and a question of if the user felt that new knowledge was learned through the search on a topic.

4.2 Measures

The following measures were used in the study:

- Perceived Learning
  This was a user self-reported rating on a 7 point scale in the post-task questionnaire, to the question if new knowledge was learned from the search, from 1 for Not at all, 4 for Somewhat, and 7 for Learned a lot (Extremely).
- Search Interaction behaviors/activities
  In total, 11 behavior variables, as listed in Table 1, were analyzed in this study.

These behavior variables have been frequently used in information seeking research.

Table 1. Behavior variables

Behavior variables	Description
#ofQs	The total number of queries submitted to the search system for a specific search task
q-Length	Query length is the number of words contained in a query. Here query length is the average length of multiple queries for a search task
#ofDocs-Saved	Number of documents/abstracts saved form the search results for a task
#ofDocs-viewed	Number of documents/abstracts opened and viewed from the search results for a topic
Ratio-of-DocsSaved/Viewed	The ratio of documents saved and the documents opened/viewed
#ofActions-task	The total number of actions during working on a search topic. The actions include both keyboard and mouse actions
#ofSERPs-viewed	Number of search result pages viewed or checked that were returned by the search system
Time-for the task	The total time spent on tasks
Ranking-on-SERPs	The average ranking position of the documents opened in SERPs. "1" is the top ranking, most related by the system and the larger the number, the lower the ranking is
Average-dwell-time	Average time spent on viewing document/abstract
Querying time	Average time spent on working on queries

- Search performance measures

  The classical performance measures, Precision and Recall [15], were used in the study. Precision is the number of correct search results divided by the number of all retrieved results, and Recall is the number of correct search results divided by the number of all possible relevant results in the search system.

  Each participant's performance measures are included in the dataset. These performance measures were calculated based on the participants' evaluation of search results. In the experiment that generated the data set, Participants were asked to conduct searches on the experimental system and to find and save as many relevant documents as possible. After finishing their search activities, they evaluated all saved documents. Participants rated the relevance of the saved documents using a five point scale ranging from "not relevant" to "highly relevant" with "somewhat relevant" as the mid-point.

4.3 Data Analysis

Pearson correlation analysis and GLM/ANOVA procedures were the main statistic methods used in the study. The data analyses were performed using SPSS.

5   Results and Discussion

5.1   Search Behaviors and Perceived Learning

The results of correlation analysis are presented in Table 2.

Table 2. Correlations between perceived learning and behavior measures

Behavior variables	Correlation with perceived learning (n = 140)
#ofQs	r = −.085 (.320*)
q_length	r = .060 (.482)
#ofDocs_Saved	r = .180 (**.034**)**
#ofDocs_opened/viewed	r = .082 (.336)
Ratio_of_DocsSaved/Viewed	r = .311 (**.000**)**
#ofActions_task	r = .107 (.206)
#ofSERPs_viewed	r = .086 (.314)
Time_for_Task	r = .031 (.714)
Ranking_on_SERPs	r = .168 (**.047**)**
Average_dwell_time	r = −.047 (.584)
Query_time	r = −.049 (.567)

*Numbers in parenthesis are significance (p) value of the correlation.
**Correlation is significant (2-tailed).

As presented in Table 2, among all the 11 behavior variables investigated, only three variables have significant correlations with perceived learning: the number of documents saved, the ratio of the number of saved documents and the number of documents opened or viewed, and the average ranking position of the documents opened.

Of the three variables, the ratio of the documents saved from all viewed is significant at $p < 0.01$ level. The other two are significant at the 0.05 level ($n = 140$). All correlations are positive. The results indicate that when more relevant documents are being saved, without viewing too many documents, it is more likely the user will report that they have learned. Since the number of documents opened alone does not have a significant correlation with perceived learning, it seems that the significance of the ratio mainly comes from the contribution of the number of documents saved. The significant correlation between the ranking position and perceived learning indicate that the lower (the larger the number) the mean rank of the opened documents in SERPs, the more likely the user will feel they have gained new knowledge.

A follow-up GLM/ANOVA analysis identified that the ratio was the only variable that had a significant effect on perceived learning ($F = 10.838$, $p = .001$). All other behavior variables do not show significant effect on perceived learning.

The results show that stronger perceived learning is associated with more document savings and lower ranking in the SERP list, which imply that more effort is needed during the search interaction process. These two factors could be indicators of a user's

Table 3. Correlations between perceived learning and performance measures

Performance measures	Correlation with perceived learning (n = 140)
Precision	r = −.069 (.416*)
Recall	r = .052 (.545)

*Numbers in parenthesis are significance (p) value of the correlation.

learning. The finding sheds light on how the system may predict how much users gain knowledge through observable search behaviors.

No significant correlations are found between perceived learning and other user behaviors or efforts, such as the amount of time spent on the task, time spent on each page, number of pages viewed, number of queries issued, etc. Intuitively, learning might be associated with some of these behaviors. Future work will need to continue examining the relations between learning and these behaviors. If some additional important behaviors could be identified, it will help the system infer users' learning, and adapt search accordingly for the user.

5.2   Perceived Learning vs. Performance

The correlation analysis found that perceived learning is not necessarily associated with any of the search performance measures: Precision and Recall. There are no significant correlations between the two sets of measures. The results are listed in Table 3. A follow-up GLM/ANOVA analysis found no significant effect on perceived learning from any of the performance measures.

One possible explanation for the result could be that a document judged relevant to the search topic does not necessarily add new knowledge to the user, i.e., the relevant document is not connected to the users' knowledge status. "Learning" new knowledge is a goal different from finding "related" documents. A document could be "relevant" in many ways.

5.3   Effects of Topic Characteristics on Perceived Learning

The analyses described in the above sections did not consider the search task characteristics, i.e., the difference between general topics and specific topics, which intuitively is related to learning.

The data was further separated into two subsets, one for general topics and the other one for specific topics. The same statistical analyses were conducted separately for each of the two types. The number of participants included in the data set for the general topics is different from that of specific topics, due to the unbalanced number of topics in each category. The correlations between perceived learning and search behaviors are presented below first, which is followed by the results of correlation analysis on search performance.

Search Behaviors. The results here are slightly different from the results in Sect. 5.1. Table 4 presents the correlations between the three behavior variables (that are discussed

Table 4. Correlations between perceived learning and behavior measures for general and specific topics separately.

Behavior variables	Correlation with perceived learning	Specific topics (n = 50)
	General topics (n = 90)	
#ofDocs_Saved	.126 (.235)	.338 (**.016****)
Raio_of_DocsSaved/Viewed	.248 (**.018****)	457 (**.001****)
Ranking_on_SERPs	.192 (.069)	.122 (.399)

*Numbers in parenthesis are significance (p) value of the correlation.
**Correlation is significant (2-tailed).

below) and perceived learning, under the two conditions separately: one for general topics and one for specific topics. All other behavioral variables that did not change from the previous analysis are excluded from the table.

As Table 4 shows, for both general and specific topics, the average ranking on SERPs is no longer a significant factor that is associated with perceived learning. One direct consequence of slitting the data into two subsets is that the sample size in either subset is much smaller than that in the whole data set. It is possible that while checking down the search result list may be associated with perceived learning in large samples, it may not be the case for smaller samples. Given that one individual user's data size is normally small, a document's ranking position in SERPs may not be an important factor to consider.

Interestingly, the number of saved documents was found significantly correlated with perceived learning in the whole data set. But this further analysis found that it actually is significant only for the specific topics, not for general topics. It could be the case that specific topics are easier to learn than general topics because specific topics are relatively clearer than general ones, which normally are vaguer than specific ones.

The ratio is still significantly correlated with both general and specific topics. However, different from the test results from the whole data set where a significant effect is found with the ratio on perceived learning, a GLM/ANOVA analysis does not found significant effect of this variable. Again, it may be because the samples are not big enough to draw the results. In fact, none of the behavior variables is found to have an effect on perceived learning in either the general or specific topic case.

Performance Measures. A GLM/ANOVA analysis was first conducted to examine if the search topic characteristic would have significant effect on participants' perceived learning, if a given topic is general or specific. Similar to the result from the analysis on the whole data set, no significant effect is found on perceived learning from performance measures in either general or specific topic case.

While the result is not significant from the GLM/ANOVA analysis, the correlation analysis found some meaningful results that show significant correlations with perceived learning. The results are presented in Table 5, which shows that Recall score has significantly positive correlation with perceived learning for specific tasks, at p = 0.037, which for some reason the GLM/ANOVA was unable to detect. This finding is different

Table 5. Correlations between perceived learning and different types of topics

Performance measures	Perceived learning	Specific (n = 50)
	General (n = 90)	
Precision	$r = -.083$ (.439*)	$r = -.040$ (.785)
Recall	$r = .021$ (.842)	$r = .296$ ($p = $ **.037**)

*Numbers in parenthesis are significance (p) value of the correlation.
**Correlation is significant (2-tailed).

from the result with the whole data set, where no significant correlations were found with either performance measures, despite a larger sample size of whole data set. It shows that when searching for specific topics, whether or not to find as many as possible all the relevant documents does seem to be related to whether or not the user would feel having learned new knowledge.

It could be that in the case of specific topics users are able to gain more concrete ideas and, thus, are more capable of identifying the relevant documents, are thus are able to learn. In general topics, users may not be able to learn much in abstract terms on the general topic. They might also have difficulty in gaining a clear idea of how much they had learned about a general topic than from working on a specific topic.

6 Conclusion

In response to the two research questions, the research found that:

- Perceived learning is only associated with limited types of search behaviors: the number of documents saved (as relevant). The more the saved documents, the strong feeling of having learned. The ranking position of the documents opened in SERPs can also significantly correlate with perceived learning, but only if the sample size is large: the lower ranking positions of the documents opened, the more the user would perceive learning. But when the sample size is smaller, the correlation is not strong. Realistically for an individual user, this perhaps means the ranking position is not a strong behavior factor to consider as an indicator of learning.
- Perceived learning does not show, in general, significant correlation with search performance, measured by the classical information retrieval metric: Precision, Recall and F_2 measures. However, considering the search topic characteristics and focusing on specific topics, Recall is significantly correlated, at $p = 0.05$ level, with perceived learning. This result suggests that for a specific search topic, a user's learning is related to the number of relevant documents the user can find: the more relevant documents found the more the user may learn. Recall may be used as an indicator of the user's learning, if the search topic's specificity could be determined.

It should be admitted that the study focuses on a narrow domain: genomics. Therefore, the findings may not be appropriate to generalize to other subject areas. Similar research is need in other areas to collect empirical evidences.

The results of the study have significant implications for search-based technological support for elearning. Supporting learning has been the major goal and in the meantime a great challenge for the design of many information systems, particularly digital libraries. Such systems need to develop and incorporate new, learning supportive functions.

Acknowledgement. The author thanks the Personalization of the Digital Library Experience research team (supported by IMLS grant LG 06-07-0105-07) who collected and shared the data, without which this work would not have been accomplished.

References

1. Anderson, L.W., Krathwohl, D.A.: A Taxonomy for Learning, Teaching, and Assessing: A Revision of Bloom's Taxonomy of Educational Objectives. Longman, New York (2001)
2. Bruce, C., Hughes, H.: Informed learning: a pedagogical construct attending simultaneously to information, use and learning. Libr. Inf. Sci. Res. **32**(2010), A2–A8 (2010)
3. Downes, S.: Learning objects: resources for distance education worldwide. Int. Rev. Res. Open Distance Learn. **2**(1), 1–35 (2001)
4. Duggan, G.B. Payne, S.J.: Knowledge in the head and on the web: using topic expertise to aid search. In: Proceedings of the SIGCHI 2008, pp. 39–48 (2008)
5. Edelson, D.C., Gordin, D.N., Pea, R.D.: Addressing the challenges of inquiry-based learning through technology and curriculum design. J. Learn. Sci. **8**(3&4), 391–450 (1999)
6. Farwick, R., Hester, O.J.L., Teale, W.H.: Where do you want to go today? Inquiry-based learning and technology integration. Read. Teach. **55**(7), 616–625 (2002)
7. Goldman, S.R., Braasch, J., Wiley, J., Graesser, A., Brodowinska, K.: Comprehending and learning from Internet sources: Processing patterns of better and poorer learners. Read. Res. Q. **47**(4), 356–381 (2012)
8. Hersh, W., Voorhees, E.: TREC genomics special issue overview. Inf. Retrieval **12**(1), 1–15 (2009)
9. Jansen, B.J., Booth, D., Smith, B.: Using the taxonomy of cognitive learning to model online searching. Inf. Process. Manag. **45**(2009), 643–663 (2009)
10. Kuhlthau, C.: Seeking Meaning, 2nd edn. Libraries Unlimited, Westport (2004)
11. MacGregor, S.K., Lou, Y.: Web-based learning: how task scaffolding and web site design support knowledge acquisition. J. Res. Technol. Educ. **37**(2), 161–175 (2005)
12. Marchionini, G.: Exploratory search: from finding to understanding. Commun. ACM **49**(4), 41–46 (2006)
13. Marchionini, G., Maurer, H.: The roles of digital libraries in teaching and learning. Commun. ACM **38**(4), 67–75 (1995)
14. Shih, J.-L., Chuang, C.-W., Hwang, G.-J.: An inquiry-based mobile learning approach to enhancing social science learning effectiveness. Educ. Technol. Soc. **13**(4), 50–62 (2010)
15. Van Rijsbergen, C.J.: Information Retrieval, 2nd edn. Butterworth, Newton (1979)
16. Yin, C., Sung, H.-Y., Hwang, G.-J., Hirokawa, S., Chu, H.-C., Flanagan, B., Tabata, Y.: Learning by searching: a learning environment that provides searching and analysis facilities for supporting trend analysis activities. Educ. Technol. Soc. **16**(3), 286–300 (2013)
17. Zhang, X., Liu, J., Liu, C., Cole, M.: Factors influencing users' perceived learning during online searching. In: Proceedings of the 9th International Conference on e-Learning (ICEL-2014), pp. 200–210 (2014)

Web-based, Mobile
and Ubiquitous Learning

Evaluating Usability of M-Learning Application in the Context of Higher Education Institute

Aijaz Ahmed Arain[1], Zahid Hussain[1(✉)], Wajid H. Rizvi[2], and Muhammad Saleem Vighio[1]

[1] Science and Technology, Quaid-E-Awam University of Engineering, Science and Technology, Nawabshah, Pakistan
{aijaz, zhussain, saleem.vighio}@quest.edu.pk
[2] Institute of Business Administration, Karachi, Pakistan
wrizvi@iba.edu.pk

Abstract. In a system development process, usability evaluation is a crucial part of the process. The purpose of this paper is to test the usability of new developed application called "DARSGAH" for getting optimum outcomes from m-learning (Mobile Learning) technology. This application provides learning opportunities to University students. Initially, pilot test was conducted with 10 participants. After slight word refinement and minor changes in the application full scale usability test was conducted with other 100 participants who were selected randomly from the University by generating random numbers (student IDs) using SPSS. The data was collected using System Usability Scale (SUS) questionnaire immediately after the test, to obtain students' overall perception about the application. The findings revealed that the application is user friendly, effective, and efficient and the users were satisfied as the overall average score of SUS is 84. The total task completion rate was 100 % which means that the application was very effective.

Keywords: M-learning · Usability testing · System Usability Scale (SUS) · Usefulness · DARSGAH · Mobile application

1 Introduction

1.1 M-learning

M-learning technology provides learning opportunities offered by mobile technologies when user is not at predetermined location. By ubiquitous technology user can take advantages to learn from anywhere at any time with the use of mobile devices [1].

The schools, colleges, universities and other educational institutions have been motivated to switch towards m-learning due to omnipresent access through wireless technologies to enhance learning and teaching methods [2].

GSM/2.5G technology had a limitation as lower speed caused slower adoption of the m-learning technology. But recently 3G & 4G technology has been introduced in

© Springer International Publishing Switzerland 2016
P. Zaphiris and A. Ioannou (Eds.): LCT 2016, LNCS 9753, pp. 259–268, 2016.
DOI: 10.1007/978-3-319-39483-1_24

Pakistan so now there is a strong need to utilize the higher speed for adopting the m-learning technology.[1]

The rest of the paper is divided into following sections: Subsects. 1.2 and 1.3 describe usability and SUS, respectively. Section 2 is about related work while Sect. 3 provides details about the application. Methodology has been described in Sect. 4 while results and statistical analysis are given in Sect. 5 and finally in Sect. 6 conclusion is given.

1.2   Usability

Usability is a degree of ease to use software technology and having user friendly interface (UI). Common qualities regarding usability that define the degree of ease are labeled as ease of use, efficiency, effectiveness, learnability, and user satisfaction.

For developers, the purpose of usability testing is to point out the interface characteristics of the product, minimize the cost of development and support, and raise its market attractiveness [3].

There is empirical evidence to suggest that usability testing is very compulsory to eliminate usability problems [4–6].

1.3   System Usability Scale

The measurement of the usability is very complex; however, a simple, quick and dirty usability scale has been developed by Brooke [7]. There is a suggestion that the SUS survey questionnaire should be conducted immediately after the usability test. The SUS scale consists of 10 usability items; these items are used to assess the ease of use, efficiency, learnability, and satisfaction of an existing system. Each item of SUS scale consists of 5 point Likert Scale. All odd items are phrased positively and to obtain the result 1 has to be subtracted from participant's response and all even items are negatively phrased questions where to obtain the result participant's response has to be subtracted from 5, which scales each item from 0 to 4. The total score is multiplied by 2.5 to provide a score out of 100, which is interpreted as a percentile ranking and not as a percentage.

Tullis and Stetson state that 68 SUS average score is threshold. If the score is above 68, it will be considered more than average and if the score is below 68, then score is considered less than average [8].

2   Related Work

Fetaji et al. have introduced "Mobile Learning Usability Attribute Testing" (MLUAT) which is the usability evaluation method and they performed the comparison of MLUAT with two other usability evaluation methods. The goal was to test e-learning

---

[1] www.pta.gov.pk/annual-reports/ptaannrep2013-14.pdf (Last accessed on: 20-11-2015).

and m-learning. The results of comparison showed that MLUAT is more efficient usability evaluation method [9].

Alelaiwi and Hossain have conducted a practical usability evaluation study on specific e-learning tools. They formed two groups of real users, one group has HCI knowledge and other without HCI knowledge. Usability evaluation questionnaires were distributed to both groups. They concluded that the group without HCI knowledge was more satisfied than the group with HCI knowledge because HCI knowledge group has more expectations with e-learning tool [10].

Two alternative approaches were adopted by Summers and Watt are: 1. Mobile applications are created and tested by students; and 2. Existing products are modified by students using instructions/documentation rather than creating a new one from the scratch. The Results were successfully achieved through both approaches and it was recommended that both approaches could be easily adopted and adapted [11].

Lee and Salman have used Mobile Collaborative Learning (MCL) which is a mobile learning application and it has more importance in educational environment. They have presented both theoretical and technical fundamentals for designing and developing an effective Mobile Collaborative Learning environment. They have also introduced a new approach for building a mobile learning application. Finally, using Android operating system they have designed and constructed a prototype with a suggestive infrastructure for MCL [12].

The impact of a screen size of mobile phones on users' efficiency, effectiveness and ease of use was measured by Raptis et al., using System Usability Scale. They conducted an experiment using same brand (Samsung) with three different screen sizes. Sixty participants were involved in the experiment [13].

Baillie and Morton have tested two mobile applications; both applications are designed on same concept, one application is designed with HCI other is designed without HCI principles. Both applications were tested with users in a field to see which was the simplest and most intuitive to use. Its usability was measured by using System Usability Scale [14].

3   Introduction to DARSGAH Application

The name of the m-learning application developed is "DARSGAH" which means "Place of Learning" in English. DARSGAH is a web based application and it is accessible with native Android based mobile app. The core purpose for developing the DARSGAH application is to test if the learning outcomes of (Higher Education Institute) students can be enhanced. The application has been developed at Quaid-e-Awam University, Nawabshah, Pakistan. The application has five features: Lecture wise videos, Lecture wise notes, Lecture wise MCQ (Multiple Choice Questions) tests, Chat room for group chatting and Forum for discussion about videos, Notes and MCQ tests.

Figure 1 shows three screens, first screen (a) is a login screen for authentication, second screen (b) is a video lecture screen with Like, Rating and Total viewed options. Users can also make notes about video and save permanently in their account for future reference. Users can write comments about current video for other users. Third screen (c) shows complete lecture wise notes.

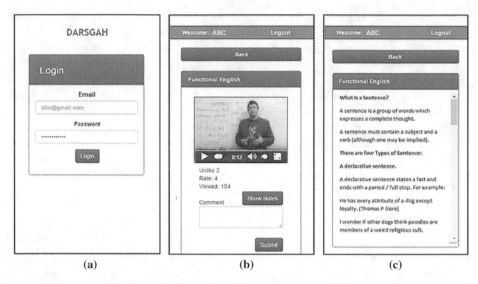

Fig. 1. Screenshots of (a) Login screen (b) Video lecture (c) Lecture wise notes

The application also has lecture wise MCQ tests for practice and students can rate each question and they can write comments as well. The application also has chat room for group chatting of online users. All chatting messages will be stored in database and can be viewed by any student for a reference. Another feature of the application is a forum, where Students can put questions and can also give answers for any question.

4 Methodology

Before conducting usability test of DARSGAH the m-learning application, pre and post-test questionnaires were developed. After the pilot study by ten representative users, minor changes were incorporated in the application and minor word refinement was also carried out in the questionnaires. In addition to that System Usability Scale questionnaire was used to get user perception on the m-learning application. In the full scale test, hundred (n = 100) participants from the university students were selected randomly having smartphones where 70 % are male and 30 % are female participants who took part in the usability test. All the participants were university students having smartphone usage experience and most of them had experience of internet use on smartphone.

Among several usability evaluation methods, formal experiment was used due to its wide spread use. Before performing usability tasks, all participants filled pre-test questionnaire for collecting demographic information. During usability test all the participants performed 5 given usability tasks one by one in the office of the university lab on same smartphone and on same internet bandwidth. The model of smartphone was Samsung Galaxy Grand Prime. The time duration and the tasks completion rate were recorded for each participant. After performing the usability tasks, the test participants filled the post-test questionnaire to collect their opinion about the DARSGAH m-learning application and System Usability Scale questionnaire has also been filled by the same participants for general perception about the DARSGAH application.

5 Results

The results are presented below in the subsections.

5.1 Demographic Data

Figure 2(a) shows that all the participants are graduate studying in different departments and there is no participant studying in post-graduate studies. Figure 2(b) shows three age groups from range 16–20 years having 65 % participants, from range 21–25 years having 35 % participants and from range 26 years and above having no participant at all. Figure 2(c) shows male and female ratio of the participants.

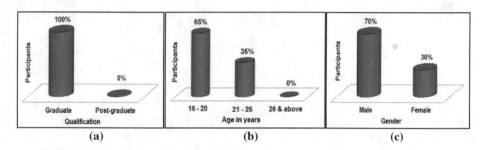

Fig. 2. (a) Qualification (b) Age in years (c) Gender of participants

Figure 3(a) shows 100 % participants using smartphone where 73 % participants using smartphone from 1 to 5 years, and 27 % from 6 to 10 years. Similarly Fig. 3(b) shows 51 % test participants using internet on daily bases, 29 % weekly, 4 % monthly, 14 % occasionally and only 2 % participants never used the internet on their smartphones.

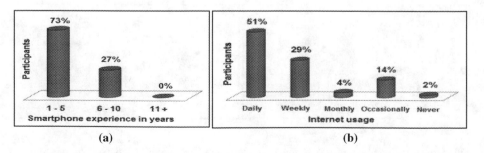

Fig. 3. (a) Smartphone experience in years and (b) Internet usage frequency

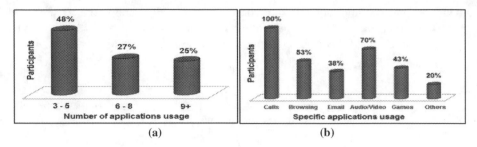

Fig. 4. (a) Number of apps usage frequency and (b) Specific apps usage frequency

Figure 4(a) shows three groups of users (1) 48 % users are using 3 to 5 applications on daily basis, (2) 27 % users are using 6 to 8 applications and (3) 25 % users are using 9 or more than 9 applications daily. Figure 4(b) shows 100 % participants use their smartphones for calls, 53 % for browsing, 38 % for emails, 70 % for Audio/Video (Entertainment), 43 % for games and 20 % participants used other applications on their smartphones.

5.2 Usability Test

In the usability test there were total five tasks to be performed by the participants. Effectiveness was measured by the task completion rate. The total task completion rate was 100 % which means that the application was so easy and effective that all the participants completed all the five given tasks.

Efficiency was measured by task completion time, Fig. 5(a) shows male and female participants' performance time in seconds and Fig. 5(b) shows the overall result of the tasks completion time with 5 given usability tasks. The performance ratio of male and female participants is approximately equal. Task No. 2 has depth level 1 that's why the participants took less time to complete it while Task No. 1, 3 & 5 have same depth (depth level 2) that's why the participants took almost the same time for completion. Task No. 4 has depth level 3 that's why the participants took more time than other tasks which shows that overall the application is efficient.

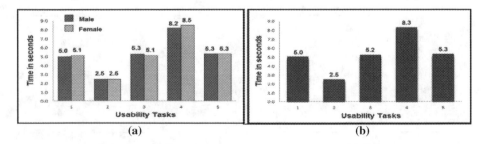

Fig. 5. (a) Average time of tasks completion by male & female (b) Total average time of tasks completion

5.3 System Usability Scale

System Usability Scale (SUS) is most widely useable scale in HCI world.

Figure 6(a) shows average score of male which is 85, while for female is 83 and mean is 84 which is more than average SUS score (68). Figure 6(b) shows 100 participants' score graph. It means m-learning application is very easy to use for new users. This figure also shows participants may use this m-learning application efficiently and almost all participants are satisfied.

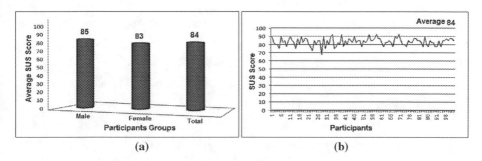

(a)　　　　　　　　　　　　(b)

Fig. 6. (a) Average SUS score of male, female & total (b) SUS score of 100 participants

Table 1 shows that the 91.7 % participants' given response is 3 or 4 score (4 is the best) that means the application is user friendly and efficient. Only 3 % participants' response is towards 0 or 1, and 5.3 % participants' response are neutral.

Table 1. Ten SUS items' response from score 0 to 4

SUS score from 0–4	Q1	Q2	Q3	Q4	Q5	Q6	Q7	Q8	Q9	Q10	Participants' response in %
0	1	0	0	1	0	1	0	0	0	0	0.3 %
1	0	4	0	10	0	9	0	1	2	1	2.7 %
2	0	12	0	6	7	14	2	3	1	8	5.3 %
3	51	50	34	35	69	52	32	32	53	53	46.1 %
4	48	34	66	48	24	24	66	64	44	38	45.6 %

Results of Q1 & Q9 of SUS questionnaire show that almost all the participants are satisfied. The result of Q5 shows that the application's design is good and the application is well integrated. Q6 shows that the application is consistent; Q4 & Q10 show application's learnability which is good and Q2, 3 & 8 show that the application is very user friendly.

5.4 Statistical Analysis

SUS Score. The results were extracted using SPSS v.20. Table 2 shows group differences on SUS scores.

Table 2. Group differences

Group	Category	Mean and SD
Smartphone use	1 to 5 years	(M = 83.34, SD = 4.24)
	6 to 10 years	(M = 83.42, SD = 6.01)
Number of apps use	3 to 5 Apps	(M = 83.96, SD = 6.96)
	6 to 8 Apps	(M = 82.67, SD = 5.39)
	9 + Apps	(M = 83.96, SD = 6.96)

Table 3 shows effects of smartphone use and number of Apps use on SUS scores.

Table 3. Independent T-test and one-way ANOVA

Independent T-test	Smartphone use years	t(90) = −0.07	p = 0.944
One-way ANOVA	Number of Apps use	F (2,97) = 0.610	p = 0.545

The result shows that there was no effect of smartphone use in years and number of apps used on a smartphone on perceived usability. There was no statistical significant difference across the groups on SUS scores. Since SUS mean score across the groups was around 84 suggesting that the perceived usability is high across the group.

Task Completion Time. Table 4 shows mean and standard deviation of completion time of each task.

Table 4. Descriptive statistics

Task	Mean	Std. deviation
1. Play video of lecture no. 2	5.0300	1.00960
2. Enter into the chat Room	2.4800	0.62732
3. Open Notes of lecture no. 3	5.2100	1.02784
4. Add a New question into the forum	8.2900	1.42343
5. Take test of lecture no. 4	5.3300	1.03529

Table 5 shows effect of smartphone use in years and number of Apps used on total task completion time.

Table 5. Independent T-test and one-way ANOVA

Independent T-test	Smartphone use years	t(98) = -0.1.8	p = 0.06
One-way ANOVA	Number of apps use	F (2,97) = 1.009	p = 0.368

The results are consistent to the SUS scores; there was no statistically significant difference across the groups on total task completion time as well.

6 Conclusions

This study investigated the DARSGAH application for testing the efficiency, effectiveness and user satisfaction with two usability evaluation methods (a) Formal experiment (b) System Usability Scale questionnaire. Both the methods show that the application is very user friendly, efficient and effective and can be utilized for the m-learning purpose. The total task completion rate for all the participants was 100 % which means that the application was very effective. The application was equally user friendly and efficient for the across the groups (smartphone use in years/number of Apps use) on both SUS score and total task completion time.

References

1. Ko, E.H., Chiu, D.K., Lo, P., Ho, K.K.: Comparative study on m-learning usage among LIS students from Hong Kong, Japan and Taiwan. J. Acad. Librariansh. **41**(5), 567–577 (2015)
2. Althunibat, A.: Determining the factors influencing students' intention to use m-learning in Jordan higher education. Comput. Hum. Behav. **52**, 65–71 (2015)
3. Gong Chao.: (2009) Human-computer interaction: the usability test methods and design principles in the human-computer interface design. In: 2nd IEEE International Conference on Computer Science and Information Technology, ICCSIT 2009, pp. 283–285, 8–11 August 2009
4. Bandi, A., Heeler, P.: Usability testing: a software engineering perspective. In: 2013 International Conference on Human Computer Interactions (ICHCI), pp. 1–8. IEEE (2013)
5. Cheng, J., Zhu, Y., Zhang, T., Zhu, C., Zhou, W.: Mobile compatibility testing using multi-objective genetic algorithm. In: 2015 IEEE Symposium on Service-Oriented System Engineering (SOSE), pp. 302–307. IEEE (2015)
6. Zhang, T., Gao, J., Cheng, J., Uehara, T.: Compatibility testing service for mobile applications. In: IEEE Symposium on Service-Oriented System Engineering, pp. 179–186 (2015)
7. Brooke, J.: SUS-A quick and dirty usability scale. Usability Eval. Ind. **189**(194), 4–7 (1996)
8. Tullis, T., Stetson, J.: A comparison of questionnaires for assessing website usability. In: Proceedings of the Usability Professionals Association (UPA) 2004 Conference, pp. 7–11 (2004)
9. Fetaji, B., Ebibi, M., Fetaji, M.: Assessing effectiveness in mobile learning by devising MLUAT (Mobile Learning Usability Attribute Testing) methodology. Int. J. Comput. Commun. **5**(3), 178–187 (2011)
10. Alelaiwi, A., Hossain, M.S.: Evaluating and testing user interfaces for e-learning system: blackboard usability testing. J. Inf. Eng. Appl. **5**(1), 23–30 (2015)
11. Summers, S., Watt, A.: Quick and dirty usability testing in the technical communication classroom. In: Professional Communication Conference (IPCC), 2015 IEEE International, pp. 1–4. IEEE (2015)
12. Lee, K.B., Salman, R.: The design and development of mobile collaborative learning application using android. J. Inf. Technol. Appl. Educ. **1**(1), 1–8 (2012)

13. Raptis, D., Tselios, N., Kjeldskov, J., Skov, M.B.: Does size matter?: investigating the impact of mobile phone screen size on users' perceived usability, effectiveness and efficiency. In: Proceedings of the 15th International Conference on Human-Computer Interaction with Mobile Devices and Services, pp. 127–136. ACM (2013)
14. Baillie, L., Morton, L.: Designing quick & dirty applications for mobiles: making the case for the utility of HCI principles. In: Proceedings of the ITI 2009 31st International Conference on Information Technology Interfaces, ITI2009, pp. 293–298. IEEE (2009)

Using Mobile Learning in Formal and Non-formal Educational Settings

Débora N.F. Barbosa[1]([⊠]), Patrícia B.S. Bassani[1],
Rosemari L. Martins[1], João B. Mossmann[2], and Jorge L.V. Barbosa[3]

[1] Feevale University, Novo Hamburgo, Brazil
{deboranice,patriciab,rosel}@feevale.br
[2] Digital Games, Feevale University, Novo Hamburgo, Brazil
mossmann@feevale.br
[3] University of Vale dos Sinos, São Leopoldo, Brazil
jbarbosa@unisinos.br

Abstract. This paper presents experiences on mobile devices in formal and non-formal educational settings based on the relation among different ongoing research projects involving the use of mobile devices, such as tablets in educational processes. The experiences addressed in this work are interconnected through a common objective: to use of mobile devices as tablets in education to enhance teaching and learning processes. Therefore, this paper presents our experiences in two educational settings, regarding the challenges and issues we face when including the use of mobile devices in educational processes. The study uses a qualitative approach with results indicating three relevant aspects, apart from the educational setting. Therefore, we concluded that the use of mobile technologies in educational processes involve: the training of teachers or educators; the selection, organization and planning of digital resources; and, the profile of the students implicated in the educational process.

Keywords: Mobile learning · Formal education · Non-formal education

1 Introduction

The rapid technological and social changes, which are characteristic of our society, bring technological advances that provide support for new social norms [1]. Education is one of the areas impacted by this technological society [2]. In this way, the proliferation of mobile computing devices and social networks are impacting on social and educational habits [1–3]. Mobile technologies allow the user to take with him/her the object of study or to access it from anywhere, intensifying the use of mobile devices in education – it is called Mobile Learning [4–7]. The use of mobile technologies in education facilitates the development of personalized educational processes, focused on the needs and learning profile of the subject [8–10].

To keep up with technological and social changes, formal and non-formal education spaces need to constantly reinvent themselves [11–16]. Formal education corresponds to a systematic, organized educational model, structured and administered

© Springer International Publishing Switzerland 2016
P. Zaphiris and A. Ioannou (Eds.): LCT 2016, LNCS 9753, pp. 269–280, 2016.
DOI: 10.1007/978-3-319-39483-1_25

according to a given set of laws and norms, a curriculum with objectives, content, and methodology, which necessarily involves the teacher, the students, and formal institutions, such as schools or universities [11, 14]. According to Eaton [8], Non-formal Education is an educational process that involves flexible curriculum and methodology, capability of adapting to the needs and interests of students, for whom time is not a pre-established factor but is contingent upon the student's work pace. Generally, this educational process takes place in non-formal educational institutions and a qualified teacher or a leader with more experience may conduct the learning process.

This paper presents experiences on mobile devices in formal and non-formal educational settings based on the relation among different ongoing research projects involving the use of mobile devices such as tablets in educational processes. We understand that there is an interconnection between these types of educational processes, which can improve the learning processes in both cases and increase the use of mobile technologies in educational settings. In Brazil, previous work has reported on the benefits of the use of mobile devices in formal education [9, 12, 13, 17–19] and also for students undergoing oncological treatment (non-formal education) [20]. The interconnect way in the process education in both cases can increase the use of mobile technologies in educational processes.

The researches are developed in the region of Vale do Sinos, in the state of Rio Grande do Sul, Brazil. With a focus on formal education, the research aims to investigate different opportunities of using tablets in the classroom in order to encourage innovative educational practices. The study is conducted in two different elementary schools involving teachers and students. With a focus on non-formal education, the research aims to identify how mobile devices, as tablets, can be used to assist in tutoring children and adolescents receiving treatment for cancer. The study is conducted in partnership with the Support Association in Oncopediatrics (AMO), which assists children and teenagers with cancer and a vulnerable social situation.

Therefore, this paper presents our experiences in two educational settings, regarding the challenges and issues we face when including the use of mobile devices in educational processes. The study uses a qualitative approach with results indicating three relevant aspects, apart from the educational setting. The methodology research is classified as applied, involving case studies and informal interviews and observation methods. Therefore, we concluded that the use of mobile technologies in educational processes involve: the training of teachers or educators; the selection, organization and planning of digital resources; and, the profile of the students implicated in the educational process.

This paper is organized as follows. In Sect. 2, we present the research context, the methodology proposal for applying mobile devices and the proposal for the selection and organization of mobile technologies for tablets. In Sect. 3 we present our experiences with the use of mobile devices in formal and non-formal context educational and a reflection about the results. Finally, in Sect. 4, we present the research conclusions and future works.

2 Research's Organization

2.1 Understanding Research's Context

Considering the formal educational setting this study presents experiences in using tablets in the classroom based on three different projects[1]. The *Educanet project* happens in a private school and aims to enhance educational practices with the use of ICT. The project *Teaching and learning on the web: the architecture of participation of web 2.0 in the context of face-to-face education*, already finished, happened articulated along with *Educanet*, and was focused on the investigation of the use of social software in the final years of elementary school. Finally, the ongoing project *Pedagogical practices in cyberspace* is involving students and teachers from the first years of an elementary public school.

Considering the non-formal educational setting, this study presents experiences in using tablets based on *Mobile Learning project*, conducted in partnership with the Support Association in Oncopediatrics (AMO). AMO assists children and teenagers with cancer besides having a vulnerable social situation and it offers a range of activities involving cancer patients and their families, including a computer workshop and tutoring. In order to accomplish this, AMO relies on social educators and a pedagogical educator. One of the main difficulties faced by those receiving assistance from AMO is that of keeping up with the school curriculum during and after periods of hospitalization or low immunity. So, the study seeks to identify how mobile devices can be used to assist in tutoring for children and adolescents receiving treatment for cancer and their families. The study involves subjects from the fourth and ninth of elementary school.

2.2 Applying Mobile Technologies

The proposal for applying mobile technologies in formal and non-formal education follows the Information and Communication Technology (ICT) Competency Framework for Teachers, developed by Unesco [21]. The Framework is arranged in three different approaches to teaching (three successive stages of a teacher's development): Technology Literacy, Knowledge Deepening, and Knowledge Creation.

It is also important that students develop competencies for the use of technology in learning. In this paper, the proposal for applying mobile devices follows Unesco's framework including the student perspective (Fig. 1). Figure 1 shows how Technology Literacy, Knowledge Deepening and Knowledge Creation are articulated for the mobile learning perspective in Formal and Non-formal Education.

The first approach involves **Technology Literacy**. During this stage, the discovery and free exploration of technologies is developed. For the teacher, this step is necessary

---

[1] The educational system in Brazil is organized into basic education and higher education. Basic education involves the elementary school (9 years – children from 6 to 14 years old) and the high school (3 years – from 15 to 17). The beginning years of elementary school involve 5 grades (children from 6 to 10 years old) and the final years of elementary school involve 4 grades (children 11 to 14).

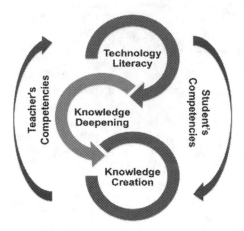

Fig. 1. Framework for applying mobile technologies

in order to appropriate the technology and consider and plan methods to integrate the use of ICT in the standard school curriculum, pedagogy and classroom structures. From the students' perspective, this involves the acquisition and recognition of devices and applications, the usability and development of the various necessary elements, such as registration, profile, navigability, etc.

The second approach involves **Knowledge Deepening**. At this stage, from the teacher's perspective, the changes should be broad and have more impact on learning, creating opportunities to develop skills in order to use more sophisticated methodologies and technologies, driving change into the curriculum. From the students' perspective, this step enables students to acquire in-depth knowledge of their school subjects and apply it to complex, real-world problems.

The third approach involves **Knowledge Creation**, which includes the 21st century skills that are needed to create new knowledge and engage in lifelong learning – i.e. the ability to collaborate, communicate, create, innovate and think critically [21]. From the teacher's perspective, the use of technology must be understood in terms of cultural artefacts, surrounding both the subject student and the subject teacher. From the students' perspective is necessary to be prepared for the development of pedagogical activities that will require the effective use of virtual communities, collaborative applications, teamwork, tools for communication and creation and problem solving.

2.3   Selecting and Organizing Mobile Digital Resources

One of the fundamental issues for the use of mobile devices in education is the selection and organization of applications. In this sense, frameworks or methodologies can be sought in the literature for the selection of applications for mobile devices in education. Most studies, in addition to addressing the pedagogical issue, analyze the function of applications and their potential use [5, 18, 22]. In the other hand, the online stores (Google Play and iTunes - Apple Store), considering Android and iOS/Apple platforms, use categories to allow specific applications to be found easily, according to the needs of users. Considering these studies, we tried to select applications that were focused on assisting teaching and learning processes in formal education, as well as in tutoring in a non-formal setting. Firstly, applications were organized according to their organization in the online store. However, during development of the experiments, we identified the need for a categorization that supported the selection and organization of applications on the devices, assisting in the planning of pedagogical activities. Considering this, the following categories were proposed for classification of the applications in our researches:

- **Support:** The *Native* applications already available on the devices and applications used to assist and support pedagogical activities. These applications are, in general, not the focus of the process, but rather support the use of other applications or activity. The applications in this category are widely used in the Technology Literacy phase, in which subjects adapt to using the devices. This category includes many different applications. So, it is possible to create a subcategory in order to group the applications according to their features. For Example, it can be **subcategorized** into *Media Option* group application voice recognition, audio files, video, etc.;

- **Education:** Applications specifically focused on the themes to be developed within the pedagogical proposal being applied. These are **subcategorized** according to the themes to be worked on, such *as Literacy, Portuguese, Mathematics, Spanish, English, Music, Arts, etc.* The applications in this category can be widely used in the Knowledge Deepening phase;

- **Entertainment:** These may also include an interdisciplinary approach with respect to other categories and involve applications used in a less restrictive approach to take advantage of the devices. At the same time, they are fundamental to the process of technology literacy the subjects undergo in order to use the devices. These can be **subcategorized** into *Action and Adventure; Sports; Casual, etc.*

- **Collaborative:** Applications that make use of mobility, encouraging exchange of knowledge and teamwork among subjects, involving activities focused on their social interaction. This category can be **subcategorized** into applications for *Social Networking, Virtual Learning Community and Environment, Collective Writing, Blogs, Creativity/Multimedia, etc.* The applications in this category can be widely used in the Knowledge Deepening and in the Knowledge Creation phase;

In our classification we do not explicitly use a *Games category*. In this paper, a game, when applied with an educational goal, is considered to have the aim of involving the player-student in a playful and entertaining, although formal, universe, with an educational objective to be achieved. In this way, we conclude that the game concept is incorporated across categories. For example, a game can be classified as a *Collaborative* as well as an *Entertainment* or *Education* resource.

3 Using Mobile Learning in Education

3.1 Experiences in Formal Education

The use of tablets in education, in the context of the *Educanet* project, began in 2012, when the school purchased 20 iPads. These are currently used in early childhood education and in the initial years of elementary education, totaling 177 students and 9 teachers (in the third stage of the second cycle/fifth year of the double teaching system). The teachers involved in the project were accompanied on a subject basis and/or in small groups for studies on the use of tablets in the classroom. In the first phase of using the iPads, focusing on technology literacy (2012/1st semester), student activities involved entertainment and the use of several applications for tutoring. Entertainment activities were performed for the first few occasions in order to assess students' knowledge of the devices and to enable teachers to become familiar with the dynamics of using iPads in the classroom. In this stage were used mainly applications from the categories **Education** and **Entertainment**. In the second phase, focusing on knowledge deepening (2012/2nd semester and 2013), the teachers began to use the tablets in the classroom without any monitoring by the training staff. The activities proposed for students involved the use of applications in order to reinforce the school curriculum in development. The activities in this stage sought coordination between the applications and the proposed lesson, but activities were still very much focused on the applications. In this stage were used mainly applications from the category **Support**, especially photography, video and text editing. The third stage, involving knowledge creation, in development this year, seeks to explore pedagogical practices through the use of tablets from the perspective of the digital cultural artefact. In this perspective, we seek to overcome the emphasis on applications and create opportunities for activities effectively integrated into content and the daily lives of students. Therefore, in this stage, applications from **Support** and **Collaborative** categories were the most used.

The research called *Teaching and learning on the web: the architecture of participation of web 2.0 in the context of face-to-face education* has begun in 2013 with the acquisition of 17 tablets with Android. This research was developed during two years (2013–2014) using the action-research methodology involving teachers and students in the final years of elementary school. We understand that changes in the pedagogical practices can't be mandatory. This way, involving the teacher in the research process and turning him the actor of his educational process could provide significant changes through new teaching practices. The approach used in the teacher educational process was based in according to the three phases of framework for applying mobile technology (Fig. 1). The first phase involved the **Technology Literacy** of the teacher. This phase, which occurred in the first semester of 2013, involved experiences with the use of tablets and with mobile applications with the purpose of allowing the teachers to know the potential of mobile devices and the possibilities of the use of social software in the classroom. The **Knowledge Deepening** phase was developed in the second semester of 2013. During this phase we worked with the teachers in order to develop class planning and to help them in the activities with the tablets and with the use of social software in the classrooms. The third and more complex phase is the knowledge creation. This phase occurred during 2014, when the teachers were challenged to use the tablets and the social software without the overseeing of the research team. This proposal involved mainly applications categorized as collaborative like Evernote and Pinterest. However, applications from the **Support** category also were necessary, especially video, photography, and audio applications.

The research called *Pedagogical practices on ciberspace* has begun in 2014 with the acquisition of 15 tablets with Android. The research is happening in a public school involving students and teachers of the first years of elementary school. This school is part of the One Laptop per Child program. In this program each student has his own laptop to study. The school also has a laboratory with 15 computers, and wifi internet access in the whole school. During the first semester of 2014, the activities involved the organization of tablets, installation of applications, and teachers' education in the technological literacy perspective. In the second semester of 2014 the activities with students began. The activities were conducted in partnership with the teachers. The students' first experience with tablets aimed to observe their previous knowledge in the use of mobile devices. The students could freely explore the different applications installed. We perceived that they chose applications from entertainment and collaborative categories such as Facebook and Youtube. We understand that this free activity can also be understood as a time when teachers could explore, along with the students, the different possibilities of the tablets, and to learn more about the applications. From the second semester of 2014 until the present many activities were conducted with students. The most used applications were those, which allow the production of students, such as text applications (Bamboo Paper), photography (camera, Paper Artist), video (VideoShow), and others. Therefore, in this stage, applications from **Support** category were the most used.

It is important to highlight that in all the three-presented cases the proposal of the activities and the selection of applications were guided by the learning goals.

3.2 Experiences in Non-formal Education

The research called *Mobile Learning Project* has begun in the first semester of 2013 with the acquisition of 7 tablets with Android. In the case of this research the tablet devices are shared.

During 2013 year, twelve subjects in the age range of eight to sixteen participated in this research, which also involved the AMO. Of these, seven subjects are undergoing cancer treatment and the others are family members. Seven of them were patients, while the others were family members. The patients were undergoing medical treatment for cancer problems such as leukemia, lymphoma and bone cancer. The work has been developed through weekly classroom-based workshops in according to the three phases of framework for applying mobile technology (Fig. 1) and was integrated with the basic computer course offered to patients and families. The educator responsible for the course was involved in the process and assists researchers in the proposed activities.

In the **Technology Literacy** phase, free entertainment and appropriation workshops were held for use of the mobile devices. During this phase, the subjects were observed to have no great difficulty using the devices. In this stage, applications from **Support** category were the most used. The **Knowledge Deepening** phase took place from April to October 2013. Planning is conducted for each workshop, in which subjects are asked to develop the proposed activities, according to the themes to be addressed. The workshops to use the applications related to the teaching Mathematics, Portuguese, Entertainment, as well as basic computer and office tools. For example, we used an educational application called "Jogo da Forca" (hangman game) that improves Portuguese skills. As a result of using the applications in this phase, we realized the need to develop mobile educational games that addressed more specific content focused on the needs of the subjects – in Portuguese and Mathematics. Accordingly, the project team developed two games, called "Corrida Gramatical" (Grammar Race) and "Navegática" [10]. These applications are also used in the workshops and are continually updated. Therefore, in this stage, applications from **Education** and **Entertainment** category were the most used. The **Knowledge Creation** phase began in the second semester of 2013 and made use of collective and collaborative writing with Evernote. During this phase, each subject created a note in the Evernote. In this note, they wrote about things that they liked, as music, sports, friends, etc. So, in this stage, **Collaborative** category was the most used.

During the second semester of 2014, five subjects in the age range of six to fourteen participated in this research. The subjects were students from the fourth to ninth year of elementary school. The subjects used tablets containing applications for entertainment and for stimulating skills of the reading, the writing and the logical reasoning. During this year the workshops were developed only by the researcher's team. Sometimes AMO's educator (a pedagogue) used to observe the work being developed. The educator did use tablets or participated in the activities.

The activity that all of them developed was a Fanzine. The objective of this activity was to stimulate skills of reading, writing and text structure. This activity also was chosen because it provided the authors expressing their interests on various subjects such as music, toys, drawings and hobbies. Each workshop had a plan, which was required to subject them to develop the proposed activities, as the project developed. First the subjects passed the **Technology Literacy** phase where the tablet and its resources were used freely. During this phase the subjects were motivated to use the applications that involve Mathematics and Portuguese, as well as explore device capabilities, surf the Internet and access to Google Play to suggest new applications. Therefore, in this stage, applications from **Support**, **Education** and **Entertainment** category were the most used. In the **Knowledge Deepening** phase, the Fanzine project was development. For this, we used the Supernote application, which allowed the inclusion of images, audio and drawings, as well as written with keyboard and hand.

The subjects also used the device features such as the camera, to photograph objects and put in the magazine. The teachers pointed out areas for improvement and the correction during the writing, so that participants were able to learn rules and apply them appropriately in their texts. They also play during this phase the games that the project team developed ("Corrida Gramatical" (Grammar Race) and "Navegática"). We evaluated these games during workshops and we used the information for update them. As the first phase, applications from **Support**, **Education** and **Entertainment** category were the most used. The Knowledge Creation phase was development interchanging with the **Knowledge Deeping**, because during the workshops, the participants also used the browser to process the information on the Internet and capture images, manipulated through the photo application. They used e-mail to share their fanzines with each other, using for this applications classified in **Collaborative** category. So, it was observed that the fanzines' productions reflected the personality of each author.

3.3 Analysis

The autonomy becomes an important element in the meaning of learning for the subject. The subject, responsible for their own education, develop and redevelop the elements of the learning, making choices and interacting and selecting meaningful elements to assist in their learning. This process of meaningful learning and the subject's engagement with teaching and learning are present in both formal and nonformal education settings. In the formal setting, we realize that the more the teacher coordinates the technology with the curriculum and pedagogical practices, the more students engage and perceive meaning in pedagogical activities, including relating with other areas of knowledge. In the non-formal setting, we see that coordinating technology with the pedagogical objective to be achieved, together with the social context and health of the subject (in the case of this study, considering the stage of cancer treatment of the subject) is fundamental to the proposed objectives. In addition, regardless of the context, we observe students exploring the potential of tablets, making choices and using resources and applications beyond those proposed for the pedagogical activity, collaborating to achieve the proposed objectives. In many cases, teachers or educators find themselves learning new tools that had not been considered in the context of the proposed activity. It can therefore be seen that the effective use of technology in an educational context involves the training of teachers or educators and the appropriation of technologies by students, with the involvement of both subjects as active players in the educational process.

Pedagogical actions that involve meaningful learning and student autonomy have specific characteristics in formal and non-formal education settings. In formal education, the fact activities are aimed at organized groups, with similar ages, interests and knowledge, which is a facilitating factor. For example, the activities generally involve classes of students who are in the same school year and have been together for a longer period of time – usually one year. In addition, teachers often have a "history" of the student or class since they have attended the school for a long time. Accordingly, this scenario is seen to facilitate the planning of pedagogical activities involving technologies and the evaluation of results, impacting new activities to be proposed. In a nonformal educational setting, planning, observing and evaluating educational activities with the aid of technologies involves a broad diversity of subjects and interests. Generally, groups are heterogeneous both in terms of interests and knowledge. For example, in the same group we have subjects from the fourth, fifth and ninth years of elementary education. Consequently, the same activity needs to involve different subjects, content and objectives.

Whether in a formal or non-formal context, we observed that the student subject truly perceives and uses technology, to a greater or lesser degree, as a part of their culture. So, the subjects in school or in social projects today were born and live in a digital culture in which digital technological artefacts, according to Bassani [9], are natural elements, embedded in the lives of these subjects, to a greater or lesser degree. From the perspective of the subject teacher or educator, technology is an element to be understood, explored and reworked, given that it is not a "natural" part of the culture. According to Prensky [16], these subjects, who are generally teachers or educators, tend to speak a digital language with an "accent" and may demonstrate difficulty in understanding and expressing themselves digitally, need to adapt to this new digital culture and appropriate digital technological artefacts. In both research settings, we clearly see the differences related to digital culture among teachers or educators and students. For the teacher or educator, considering the use of technology in the educational process always involves knowledge of this technology and a level of comfort with the resources to be used. This aspect limits use of the available resources, even if a team of experienced researchers supports the teacher. This occurs more clearly in a formal setting since the teacher has responsibilities with regard to the formal school process and needs to reinvent and rework the educational process. The teacher therefore needs to deal with the new and the unknown. In the context of non-formal education, although researchers also support educators, they feel less restricted to experiment with technological resources, learning along with the student and changing the pedagogical activity during the process. In addition, since this occurs in a more informal setting with more varied subjects, it naturally creates an environment in which living with diversity is natural. The autonomy of the student in this case is fundamental since it the educator needs to take account of the different objectives and needs present in the same class, within the context of a single activity. The same activity can therefore achieve the objectives of one group, but needs to be adjusted for another. Accordingly, both the student subject and the educator subject are more comfortable in exploring the proposed digital resources.

4   Conclusions and Future Works

This article presented the relation between the formal and non-formal educational settings regarding the challenges and issues we face when including the use of mobile devices as tablets in both educational processes. The experiences were interconnected through a common objective: to use mobile devices, as tablets, in education to enhance teaching and learning processes. According to our studies, we identified that the main issues regarding the use of mobile technologies in educational processes are related to three aspects: (1) *The training of teachers or educators*. The use of technology in the educational process always involves knowledge of this technology and a level of comfort with the resources to be used. It is important that teachers or educators make use of mobile technology and identify how this technology can support learning process. For this, the training for the use of technology in teaching is necessary; (2) *The selection, organization and planning of digital resources*. It is important to identify and organize the mobile application considering the learning objective. So, teachers and educators need to be updated about applications and its possibilities; (3) *The profile of the students involved in the educational process*. Pedagogical actions that involve meaningful learning and student autonomy have specific characteristics in formal and non-formal education settings. Therefore, it is necessary that teaching and learning process take this into consideration.

The research has not been concluded yet. We are analyzing the data collected considering the learning process. Regarding formal education, it is necessary to identify how the tablets have improved the pedagogical practices of teachers and how students were involved in the proposed activities. On the other hand, considering the non-formal education, it is necessary to analyze how the activities with the use of tablets have assisted tutoring and how the reading and logical reasoning skills have been developed.

Moreover, it is important to review the proposal for the selection and organization of applications in mobile devices. During the research we concluded that there are different needs in formal and non-formal educational settings. In addition, we must evaluate effectively if this proposal helps teachers and educators in the applications' selection.

Acknowledgments. We thank the National Council for Scientific and Technological Development – CNPq/Brazil (http://www.cnpq.br) for providing financial support for this study. Finally, we would like to thank Feevale (http://www.feevale.br) and Unisinos (http://www.unisinos.br) for embracing this research.

References

1. Castells, M.: A Sociedade em Rede - A Era da Informação [Network Society - The Information Age], 1–6 edn. Editora Paz e Terra, são paulo (1999)
2. Kearney, M., Schuck, S., Burden, K., Aubusson, P.: Viewing mobile learning from a pedagogical perspective. Res. Learn. Technol. **20**, 14406 (2012)
3. Traxler, J.: Distance education and mobile learning: catching up, taking stock. Distance Educ. **31**(2), 129–138 (2010)
4. Saccol, A.I.C.Z., Schlemmer, E., Barbosa, J.L.V.: M-learning e Ulearning: Novas Perspectivas da Aprendizagem Móvel e Ubíqua [New Perspectives of Mobile and Ubiquitous Learning], vol. 1, 1st edn, p. 162. Pearson Prentice Hall, São Paulo (2010)
5. Deegan, R., Rothwell, P.A.: Classification of m-learning applications from a usability perspective. J. Res. Cent. Educ. Technol. **6**(1), 6–27 (2010)
6. Severín, E., Capota, C.C.: La computación uno a uno: nuevas perspectivas [One-to-one computing: new perspectives]. Revista Iberoamericana de Educación **56**, 31–48 (2011)
7. Barbosa, J.L.V., Barbosa, D.N.F., Wagner, A.: Learning in ubiquitous computing environments. Int. J. Inf. Commun. Technol. Educ. **8**(3), 1–14 (2012). doi:10.4018/jicte.2012070108
8. Reychav, I., Dunaway, M., Kobayashi, M.: Understanding mobile technology-fit behaviors outside the classroom. Comput. Educ. **87**, 142–150 (2015). http://dx.doi.org/10.1016/j.compedu.2015.04.005
9. Bassani, P.B., Barbosa, D.N.F.: Experiences with the use of personal learning environments in school settings: mobility and web 2.0 in the final grades of elementary education. In: Proceedings of 5th Personal Learning Environments (PLE) (2014)
10. Barbosa, D.N., Bassani, P.B., Mossmann, J.B., Schneider, G.T., Reategui, E., Branco, M., Meyrer, L., Nunes, M.: Mobile learning and games: experiences with mobile games development for children and teenagers undergoing oncological treatment. In: Göbel, S., Wiemeyer, J. (eds.) GameDays 2014. LNCS, vol. 8395, pp. 153–164. Springer, Heidelberg (2014)

11. Jones, A.C., Scanlon, E., Clough, G.: Mobile learning: two case studies of supporting inquiry learning in informal and semiformal settings. Comput. Educ. **61**, 21–32 (2013). http://dx.doi.org/10.1016/j.compedu.2012.08.008

12. Martin, F., Ertzberger, J.: Here and now mobile learning: an experimental study on the use of mobile technology. Comput. Educ. **68**, 76–85 (2013). http://dx.doi.org/10.1016/j.compedu. 2013.04.021

13. Dresselhaus, A., Shrode, F.: Mobile technologies academics: do students use mobile technologies in their academic lives and are librarians ready to meet this challenge? Inf. Technol. Libr. **31**(2), 82–101 (2012)

14. Eaton, S.E.: Formal, Non-formal and Informal Learning: The Case of Literacy, Essential Skills and Language Learning in Canada. Eaton International Consulting Inc., Canada (2010). Ainsworth, HL., (Ed.)

15. Palfrey, J., Gasser, U.: Born Digital: Understanding the First Generation of Digital Natives. Basic Books, New York (2008)

16. Prensky, M.: Digital natives digital immigrants. In: Prensky, M. (ed.): On the Horizon, vol. 9, no. 5, (2001). http://www.marcprensky.com/writing/. Accessed 15 June 2015

17. Bassani, P.B.S., Barbosa, D.N.F., Eltz, P.T.: Práticas Pedagógicas com a Web 2.0 no Ensino Fundamental [Pedagogical Practices with Web 2.0 in Elementary Education]. Revista Espaço Pedagógico **20**, 286–300 (2013)

18. Ipads for Learning project. Getting Started: classroom ideas for learning with the iPad, State of Victoria, Department of Education and Early Childhood Development, Melbourne (2011). http://www.ipadsforeducation.vic.edu.au. Accessed Jan 2015

19. Yin, C., Ogata, H., Tabata, Y., Yano, Y.: Supporting the acquisition of Japanese polite expressions in context-aware ubiquitous learning. Int. J. Mobile Learn. Organ. **4**(2), 214–234 (2010). doi:10.1504/IJMLO.2010.032637

20. Barbosa, D.N.F., Sarmento, D.F., Barbosa, J.L.V., Geyer, C.F.R.: Em direção a Educação Ubíqua: aprender sempre, em qualquer lugar, com qualquer dispositivo [Towards Ubiquitous Education: always learning, in any place, with any device]. Revista Novas Tecnologias na Educação **6**, 1–10 (2008)

21. UNESCO. ICT Competency Framework for Teachers 2009. http://unesdoc.unesco.org/images/0015/001562/156209por.pdf. Accessed 15 Mar 2015

22. Patten, B., Sánchez, I.A., Tangney, B.: Designing collaborative, constructionist and contextual applications for handheld devices. Comput. Educ. **46**, 294–308 (2006)

Towards Understanding the MOOC Trend: Pedagogical Challenges and Business Opportunities

Fisnik Dalipi[✉], Sule Y. Yayilgan, Ali S. Imran, and Zenun Kastrati

Faculty of Computer Science and Media Technology, Norwegian University
of Science and Technology (NTNU), Gjøvik, Norway
{fisnik.dalipi, sule.yildirim, ali.imran,
zenun.kastrati}@ntnu.no

Abstract. Undoubtedly, MOOCs have the potential to introduce a new wave of technological innovation in learning. In spite of the great interest among the educators and the general public MOOCs have generated, there are some challenges that MOOCs might face when it comes to examining and determining the best pedagogical approaches that MOOCs should be based on. Moreover, MOOCs are facing also challenges towards building a consistent business model. The main objective of this paper is to shed more light on the MOOCs phenomenon, by analyzing and discussing some benefits and drawbacks of MOOCs from the pedagogical and business perspectives. Therefore, in this paper we provide an in-depth analysis of MOOCs challenges and opportunities towards determining pedagogical innovations. We also analyze current trends of MOOCs expansion to create new educational markets by overpassing the bricks-and-mortar educational institutions. To do so, we conduct a SWOT analysis on MOOCs. Finally, we provide possible directions and insights for future research to better understand how MOOCs can be improved to lead to greater innovations in the higher education landscape to answer the needs of a knowledge-based economy.

Keywords: MOOC · SWOT · Pedagogy · Business model · Challenges · Opportunities

1 Introduction

Massive Open Online Courses (MOOCs) represent online courses aimed at unlimited participation and are open access on the Internet. In particular, MOOCs represent a stage that led to dramatic changes in the development of web-based education systems, which have been enabled by the rapid growth of Internet use, and increase in bandwidths over the past decade [1]. MOOCs remained relatively unknown until 2011 when a number of the most prestigious universities in the United States started to offer MOOCs by putting their courses online and by setting up open learning platforms, such as edX, Coursera and Udacity. That year will be remembered as the year of disruptive innovation, when Internet technology enabled the popularity of MOOCs, a form of disruptive or transformative education, currently growing at an alarming rate. Besides

© Springer International Publishing Switzerland 2016
P. Zaphiris and A. Ioannou (Eds.): LCT 2016, LNCS 9753, pp. 281–291, 2016.
DOI: 10.1007/978-3-319-39483-1_26

Coursera, edX, and Udacity, many other companies providing different platforms have emerged, such as Course Builder, Khan Academy, iVersity, and every month there seems to be a new platform available. They all claim they are committing their best resources to making education freely available to anyone who seeks it.

Nevertheless, all these platforms are still facing various challenges in many directions, most importantly towards building consistent business models and determining best pedagogical approaches. What is common to each of the platforms is that they are not offering qualifications or degree level programs. Whether MOOCs will achieve the level of success within next five years as some educators are predicting depends entirely on how well the new technology based method of teaching clear some very high hurdles [2]. These hurdles to some extent are remaining unsolved completely in recent times. We address them below with the following questions:

How to manage teaching a course effectively with hundreds or thousands of students? How to pedagogically design courses for such enrollment? How to assess the learning outcomes? How to combat the low completion rate with MOOCs? How to know that a student taking exams and quizzes is really the student enrolled in the course? How does social media like Twitter or Facebook play role in this? How does the big data and learning analytics influence higher education, and how to address this issue? Will MOOCs replace accredited curriculums? How to build financial models for MOOCs? How to understand what the costs are? Shall MOOCs be designed in-house or be outsourced completely? How does open education resources relate to MOOCs?

In this paper, we address some of these challenges in developing and utilizing MOOCs, by providing a thorough analysis of each challenge. Consequently, we believe MOOCs offer the potential to influence the traditional universities in providing improved education even though there are the stated concerns and questions surrounding MOOCs and their use in higher education.

The rest of the paper is structured as follows. Section 2 covers the related work. The SWOT analysis is provided in Sect. 3. Section 4 addresses some of the pedagogical approaches and challenges of MOOCs. In Sect. 5, we discuss the current developments with MOOCs from the business model viewpoint. Section 6 concludes this paper.

2 Related Work

MOOCs have been in eLearning business for a while now but whether they are as effective as face-to-face pedagogy and how MOOC affordances such as interactive exercises, social networks, and rich multimedia content can be harnessed in face-to-face education are some of the questions that have intrigued many of the researchers recently.

To understand the effectiveness of MOOCs, which is measured as "meeting the user's learning goals," Gamage et al. has proposed a framework to analyze the effectiveness of eLearning in MOOCs from a learner's perspective [3] using a Grounded Theory (GT) methodology [4]. In their study, the authors have proposed a ten-dimensional framework consisting of pedagogy, usability, motivation, interactivity, collaboration, network of opportunity, support for learner, content, technology, and assessment. They found that participants showed a keen interest in collaboration and interactivity, and that careful attention to pedagogy and the assessment is an effective support to their learning in MOOC. MOOC affordances are other criteria to measure the usefulness of the system studied by Delgado et al. in their research [5]. The authors have shared some of their experiences combining MOOC-like content in on-campus courses in this study. According to the authors, the effectiveness of the MOOC affordances depends upon the composition of curriculum mode such as interleaved or sequential and the specific needs of the subject. Even though the efficacy and the affordances of MOOCs are an alternative to face-to-face pedagogies [4, 5], other challenges influencing blended learning experience include student's attitude to learning, learner group dynamics, interactions among learners and a lack of well-known learning script [6].

The authors conclude that MOOC technologies hardly support blended learning experiences due to the lack of social interaction, monitoring, and intervention by instructors. There is a general perception and to some extent the expectation that learning technology will be able to solve the problem of worldwide demand for higher education [7]. Having said that, requiring MOOC to be part of learning technology poses another challenge in the field of learning design (LD) i.e. how to design pedagogies to support students on a large scale. This requires addressing all the attributes of the field which were set out in the Larnaca Declaration, as suggested by Laurillard [7]. These include: "the focus on pedagogy in all its forms; the description of LD as computational objects; the sharing of ideas; the scope across all sectors and subject areas; the pedagogic categorization of learning designs; the attention to what students do in order to learn; the mapping to implementations, and the focus on effectiveness". In another study by Goto et al., MOOCs were used to increase pre-service teachers' knowledge about LD [8]. The authors using a case study showed how the reflections of pre-service teachers inform (via LEAP21) the teachers' understanding of LD after going through a 3rd-year bachelor level MOOCs module themselves.

Shang and Zue argue that "the size of the learner population and the heterogeneity of the learner's backgrounds make conventional one-size-fits-all pedagogies inappropriate" [9]. They propose a conceptual model where educational resource linking with the goal of satisfying various learning needs are addressed, by building a rich platform integrating abundant and open online resources. This work is similar to the one presented in [10].

Subbian in his research has identified the key elements of MOOCs that can influence pedagogy and learning in STEM disciplines [11]. Iwamoto, studied the learning infrastructures on businesses in service industries [12]. The authors in [13] have introduced the design of a MOOC for Entrepreneurship education in the form of Serious Games (SGs). In another study, the same authors analyzed the entrepreneurship skills developed in a Game-Based Learning MOOC (GBL MOOC) according to five assessed activities developed during the course [14]. According to them, the GBL MOOC for entrepreneurship studies resulted in an acceptable overall degree of satisfaction with the use of SGs during the MOOC.

3 SWOT Analysis: A Way to Understand the Logic Behind MOOCs

We use a SWOT analysis to identify, describe and analyze some of the advantages and limitations of MOOCs, in terms of strengths, weaknesses, opportunities and threats, presented as in Fig. 1.

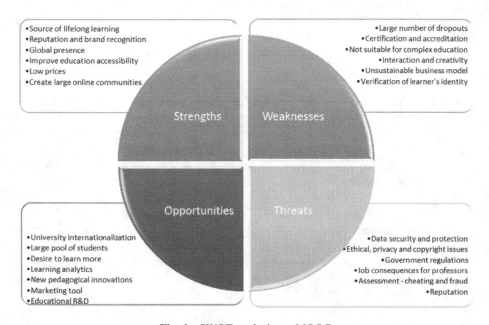

- Source of lifelong learning
- Reputation and brand recognition
- Global presence
- Improve education accessibility
- Low prices
- Create large online communities

- Large number of dropouts
- Certification and accreditation
- Not suitable for complex education
- Interaction and creativity
- Unsustainable business model
- Verification of learner's identity

Strengths   **Weaknesses**

Opportunities   **Threats**

- University internationalization
- Large pool of students
- Desire to learn more
- Learning analytics
- New pedagogical innovations
- Marketing tool
- Educational R&D

- Data security and protection
- Ethical, privacy and copyright issues
- Government regulations
- Job consequences for professors
- Assessment - cheating and fraud
- Reputation

Fig. 1. SWOT analysis on MOOCs

3.1 Strengths

In the strength section, we have identified the following characteristics of MOOCs: source of lifelong learning, reputation and brand recognition, global presence, improving education accessibility, low prices, and creating large online communities.

Taking a MOOC offers a major benefit particularly to lifelong learners. People from a wide range of age categories and backgrounds from all over the world can engage in learning via MOOCs. They provide an advantage to universities to develop a more strategical approach to online learning and to improve reputation by enhancing classroom teaching practices and developing new revenue models. MOOCs represent a fantastic international recruiting tool for the universities having audience from every corner of the world. Additionally, the teachers get an opportunity to reach people around the world like never before and continue to grow themselves through crowd-sourced feedback about their teaching styles and lesson plans, content, and learning outcomes. MOOCs will make knowledge and quality education more accessible for people who would never be able to attend a prestigious educational institute. Classes can be followed at any time, without a transportation cost and there is no need to participate physically in the classroom. They are generally free of charge [15].

3.2 Weaknesses

The weaknesses that we see as significant are: large number of dropouts, certification and accreditation, not suitable for complex education, interaction and creativity, and verification of the learner's identity. Unlike MOOCs are able to enroll more students than the traditional universities, they suffer from much larger drop-out rates [16, 17]. Some of the reasons for the low graduation rates are course methodology, lack of social interaction and creativity. Furthermore, certifications that MOOC companies deliver are not accredited by any relevant quality assurance organization. As suggested by Daniel [18], special organizations with extensive experience in accrediting web based learning should be engaged to certify the acquired knowledge. Teaching a complex engineering class to thousands of students requires professors and teaching assistants to perform labor-intensive tasks such as preparing laboratory experiments, examining project demonstrations and assessments, and performing workshops and consultation with students. Due to the demanding aspects of these activities, there raises the question of the adequacy of MOOCs to meet these specific needs of MOOCs courses.

Various control mechanisms are required for incorporation into MOOCs platforms to ensure and verify correct identity of learners. Formal exams also demand a connection between student and exam and makes institutions responsible for issuing certificates only to persons actually taking exams. In this context, Coursera applies biometric identification methods to verify students through photos and text samples [19]. The challenge here is on managing and administering biometric data while preserving the privacy of people whom provide such data.

3.3 Opportunities

Through developing MOOCs, universities have the possibility to extend reachability and accessibility of their teaching activities globally. Having the ability to create large online communities MOOCs allow capturing large amounts of data. Such data may bring useful information to institutions in many different ways. For instance, having early access to global talent pool can help employers in their recruitment process in finding desired profiles. Companies may also see MOOCs as flexible and cheap options to train their most enthusiastic workers with desire to advance their knowledge. MOOCs also can help higher education institutions to enhance learning outcomes, thanks to new pedagogical innovations and research. Besides, advertisers can also benefit by having access to these platforms. Due to the large amount of time that learners spend on such platforms, advertisers can simultaneously receive more clicks on their ads.

Finally, the abundance of data collected on MOOC platforms enable institutions to identify and facilitate various learning patterns of learners. Collection and analysis of data about learning patterns and contexts is referred to as learning analytics process.

3.4   Threats

While there are many positive aspects that MOOCs can offer, there are also ethical and privacy implications arising from various initiatives. Some of these concerns are listed by Marshall [20], including commercial exploitation of learners, as well as research ethics concerns arising from analysis done by academics and institutions. The lack of quality and standards can damage the reputation of an institution. Consequently, this brings a false picture of MOOCs as being the best e-Learning choices for universities. Moreover, new technological and policy solutions are required in practice in order to protect and secure learner's data, to maintain anonymity of such data, and to ensure data is not shared or served as a subject of commercial purposes.

Since MOOCs are massive and open, it is difficult to maintain copyright laws. So far, definitive answers and solutions are lacking in terms of having proper copyright laws in place. The authors in [21] give the suggestion of shared copyright vision to best allocate and manage copyrights in online courses. The assessment of learning and cheating in MOOCs is also a major remaining challenge, and mature solutions to address this issue are still lacking [22].

4   Pedagogical Challenges and Novel Teaching Approaches

The MOOC phenomena has produced a lot of interesting information and experiences about course design and delivery in online context. The most popularized categorization of MOOCs is based upon two distinct pedagogical foundations: connectivism (cMOOCs) and behaviorism (xMOOCs) [23]. The literature reports that in MOOCs development, to some extent, all the three learning theories, behavioristic, cognitive, and sociocultural theories have been taken into consideration. Regardless of this, we believe that the sociocultural component, which puts emphasis on the interaction between lecturers and learners, cannot be fully applied here. MOOCs pedagogy is lacking in innovation since it is limited to video-watching, testing knowledge via multiple choice questions and provides little guidance to the students. Up to now, research is very scarce towards examining and determining the best pedagogical approaches that MOOCs should be based on [24–26]. In this context, there are numerous factors and challenges we have identified:

- MOOCs platforms, from the technological point of view are still not close to replicate the interaction and community building, taking place in the traditional higher education sector, which represent the heart of the education.
- Due to large number of audiences, such massive learning is not suitable for focusing on the particular needs of each learner. Limited feedback is provided to learners on individual basis.
- New instructional design is required for assessment and promotion of interaction with the MOOCs content.
- Application of social learning is necessary to take advantage of online collaborative learning tools and to keep learners motivated.
- In spite of interactive user and discussion forums MOOCs provide, students need to use learning content as a context to engage in intellectual discussions, to debate,

to argue and to develop critical thinking skills. New methodologies of utilizing MOOCs in blended learning need to be examined.

- Students are offered continuous support in terms of guidance, mentoring, and providing instructions in traditional education. This support cannot be fully emulated by MOOCs.
- Quite a low number of students actually take assessment exams at the end of a MOOC which makes it difficult to assess whether students joining a MOOC are actually learning the content, and hence whether the MOOC is achieving its goal.

Among research proposals towards identifying significant opportunities for using new alternative pedagogical approaches that would take full advantage of MOOCs, we consider the work by [27], where authors address pedagogical opportunities and learners' choices. Some of the novel aspects offered by MOOCs in this context are given in Table 1. However, there is not much research work related to using MOOCs as a basis for developing novel teaching approaches.

Table 1. Pedagogical approaches [27]

Pedagogic dimension	Dominant	Emergent opportunities
Academic role	Lecturer	Instructional designer, facilitator and co-learner
Assessment	Teacher assessed examinations and essays	Automated assessment and peer and teacher validated portfolio
Teaching design	Content focused, teacher controlled, specified tasks	Learner determined curriculum with full use of open educational resources and online communities

As far as blended learning is concerned, we believe that the integration of MOOCs with classroom teaching as part of blended learning, rather than full replacement for traditional courses, will be an interesting and innovative pedagogical alternative. Research initiatives towards this issue are in very early phases [28] and little information exists on using MOOCs for blended learning.

5   Are Business Models for MOOCs Sustainable?

The creation of consistent business models for MOOCs is one of the most discussed issues that has arisen so far in MOOCs history [29, 30]. From the early stages of their development, commercial MOOCs adhere to what is known as 'freemium to premium' business model. This model offers core services and products to a large group of users being initially free of charge. Once a consumer base has been established, a fee is then charged for premium or advanced services and products to a smaller portion of this user base. In the context of funding, MOOCs were established by funds originating from venture capitalists, universities and foundations, which aim to generate revenues by taking advantage of the innovative approach these platforms provide.

As is usually the case for Internet start-ups, where there is no "one-fits-all" business model for the sector, MOOCs are also facing challenges on adopting business models in order to generate revenues in a sustainable manner. In addition, only few potential business models of MOOCs are proposed in literature. Recently, Fischer et al. [31] analyze the business model of Coursera, edX and Udacity by applying the business model concept of [32]. They propose this model to be used as a conceptual framework while analyzing and comparing business models in order to extrapolate a best practice business model. Belleflamme and Jasqmin [15] see MOOCs as multi-sided platforms by identifying four groups or sides that are likely to gravitate around MOOCs, i.e., students, professors, universities, and private actors. Moreover, authors describe five potential business models to monetize the value of these platforms: certification model, freemium model, advertising model, job-matching model, and subcontractor model. The most promising way that authors suggest to monetize MOOCs businesses is the subcontractor model, potentially combined with some elements from the other models. In his work of potential future business models for MOOCs [33], Kalman refers to the sale of learners' data, advertising, and income from "superstar faculty" giving video lectures. Van Dijck and Poell [34] go further to acknowledge that the freemium model will cause a disruption of the entire educational system, also considering that it may not be long before MOOCs implement personalized ads in online educational environments and sell the learners' data to businesses competing for global talent.

Presently, three of the most preferred motivations for introducing and offering MOOCs include charging for certificates, linking students with potential employers, and charging for additional services. Table 2 provides a broader overview of current business models by three of the most famous xMOOCs, i.e. Coursera, edX and Udacity.

Table 2. Variety of xMOOCs business models

Coursera	edX	Udacity
Certificate fee	Certificate fee	Certificate fee
Sale of participant data	Self-service fee	Recruiter program for companies
Sharing learners CV with companies	edX-supported fee	Sponsorships or fees for high-tech courses from employers
Secure assessments		Job match services
Training courses for employees		
Course sponsorships		
Tuition fees		
Advertisements		

Despite all the mentioned research efforts carried out towards establishing business models for MOOCs, we still lack coherent and systematic knowledge on creating a fully-fledged business model, which will overcome the uncertainties about how to monetize MOOCs platform businesses and qualify them as a valid alternative to traditional higher education institutions.

6 Conclusions

The aim of this paper was twofold. Firstly, it provided a SWOT analysis on MOOCs in general. Secondly, it aimed at identifying and analyzing the MOOCs challenges and opportunities from pedagogical and business standpoint. The analysis also includes the current trends of MOOCs expansion to create new educational markets for both supporting and sometimes overpassing the traditional educational institutions. Nevertheless, in doing so, MOOCs providers face challenges that need to be overcome even if partially to benefit from the foreseen opportunities of MOOCs. Such challenges include the sociotechnical aspect, since MOOCs are still not close to replicate the interaction, and community building taking place in the traditional higher education sector. As far as learning challenges are concerned, we see that learning is not customized for individual needs and differences, and feedback provided to learner is limited. New instructional designs are required to promote interaction. Social learning needs also to be promoted where students will engage in intellectual discussions, debate, argue and develop critical thinking skills. More guidance and mentoring, continuous support and instructions should be offered to learners. Furthermore, encouraging more learners to take assessment exams and when necessary understanding the reasons for learners to avoid taking exams is required. Considering the business challenges, developing business models in order to monetize MOOCs is another challenge to overcome since MOOCs business models are far from being sustainable.

Currently, as regards achieving pedagogical innovations with a basis in using MOOCs, a lot of research is underway on applying machine learning approach on building assessment techniques followed by smart and interactive interfaces. In this context, big data learning analytics is another flourishing area as the candidate for promoting pedagogical innovation.

References

1. Allison, C., Miller, A., Oliver, I., Michaelson, R., Tiropanis, T.: The Web in education. Comput. Netw. **56**, 17 (2012)
2. Hayman, P.: In the year of disruptive education. Commun. ACM **55**(12), 20–22 (2012)
3. Gamage, D., Perera, I., Fernando, S.: A framework to analyze effectiveness of eLearning in MOOC: learners perspective. In: 8th International Conference on Ubi-Media Computing (UMEDIA), pp. 236–241, 24–26 August 2015
4. Gamage, D., Fernando, S., Perera, I.: Factors leading to an effective MOOC from participants perspective. In: 8th International Conference on Ubi-Media Computing (UMEDIA), pp. 230–235, 24–26 August 2015
5. Delgado K.C., Munoz-Merino, P.J., Alario-Hoyos, C., Estevez Ayres, I., Fernandez-Panadero, C.: Mixing and blending MOOC technologies with face-to-face pedagogies. In: IEEE Global Engineering Education Conference (EDUCON), pp. 967–971, 18–20 March 2015
6. Claros, I., Echeverria, L., Cobos, R.: Towards MOOCs scenarios based on collaborative learning approaches. In: IEEE Global Engineering Education Conference (EDUCON), pp. 989–992, 18–20 March 2015

7. Laurillard, D.: Designing the pedagogies for student support on the large scale. In: IEEE 63rd Annual Conference International Council for Educational Media (ICEM), p. 1, 1–4 October 2013

8. Goto, J., Batchelor, J., Lautenbach, G.: MOOCs for pre-service teachers: their notions of 21st century learning design. In: IST-Africa Conference, pp. 1–9, 6–8 May 2015

9. Li, S.-W., Zue, V.: Would linked MOOC courseware enhance information search? In: IEEE 15th International Conference on Advanced Learning Technologies (ICALT), pp. 397–399, 6–9 July 2015

10. Imran, A.S., Kowalski, S.J.: HIP – a technology-rich and interactive multimedia pedagogical platform. In: Zaphiris, P., Ioannou, A. (eds.) LCT 2014, Part I. LNCS, vol. 8523, pp. 151–160. Springer, Heidelberg (2014)

11. Subbian, V.: Role of MOOCs in integrated STEM education: a learning perspective. In: IEEE Integrated STEM Education Conference (ISEC), pp. 1–4, 9 March 2013

12. Iwamoto, T.: Effects of learning infrastructures on businesses in service industries. In: 2014 Portland International Conference on Management of Engineering and Technology (PICMET), pp. 3339–3343, 27–31 July 2014

13. Margomero, R., Mireia U.: Serious games integration in an entrepreneurship massive online open course (MOOC). In: Proceedings of 4th International Conference, SGDA 2013, Trondheim, Norway, 25–27 September 2013

14. Mireia U., Margarida R.: Entrepreneurship competence assessment through a game based learning MOOC. In: Second International Conference, GALA 2013, Paris, France, 23–25 October 2013

15. Belleflamme, P., Jasqmin, J.: An economic appraisal of MOOC platforms: business models and impacts on higher education. In: LAMETA, Unite Mixte de Recherche, October 2014

16. Bruff, D.: Online learning ecosystems: what to make of MOOC dropout rates? (2013). http://derekbruff.org. Accessed 18 Dec 2015

17. Gallagher, S., Garrett, G.: Disruptive education: Technology Enabled Universities. Sydney, Australia: United States Studies Centre, University of Sydney (2013). http://ussc.edu.au. Accessed 27 Dec 2015

18. Daniel, J.: Making sense of MOOCs: musings in a maze of myth, paradox and possibility. J. Interact. Media Educ. (2012). http://jime.open.ac.uk/article/2012-18/pdf. Accessed 6 Jan 2016

19. Coursera: How to earn your verified certificate, Signature Track Guidebook. (2016). https://www.coursera.org/signature. Accessed 16 Jan 2016

20. Marshall, S.: Exploring the ethical implications for MOOCs. Distance Educ. 35(2), 250–262 (2014)

21. Educause Brief, Copyright Challenges in a MOOC Environment, EDUCAUSE (2013). https://net.educause.edu/ir/library/pdf/pub9014.pdf. Accessed 11 Jan 2016

22. Northcutt, C., Ho, A.D., Chuang, I.L.: Detecting and Preventing "Multiple-account" Cheating in Massive Open Online Courses. eprint arXiv:1508.05699. August 2015

23. Chadaj, M., Allison, C., Baxter, G.: MOOCs with attitudes: insights from a practitioner based investigation. In: IEEE Conference Frontiers in Education, Madrid (2014)

24. Chew, L.K.:Instructional Strategies and Challengings in MOOCs. Adv. sch. Teach. Learn. 2(1) (2015)

25. Lebron, D.: Comparing MOOC-based platforms: reflection on pedagogical support, framework and learning analytics. In: International Conference on Collaboration Technologies and Systems, Atlanta, USA (2015)

26. Lackner, E., Ebner, M., Khalil, M.: MOOCs as granular systems: design patterns to foster participant activity. eLearning Papers, No. 42, June 2015. ISSN 1887-1542

27. Yuan, L., Powell, S., Olivier, B.: Beyond MOOCs: Sustainable Online Learning in Institutions. http://publications.cetis.ac.uk/2014/898. Accessed 21 Jan 2016
28. Israel. M.J.: Effectiveness of integrating MOOCs in traditional classrooms for undergraduate students. Int. Rev. Res. Open Distrib. Learn. **16**(5) (2015)
29. Attis, D., Koproske, C., Miller, C.: Understanding the MOOC trend: the adoption and impact of massive open online courses. The Education Advisory Board, Washington, DC (2012). http://www.eab.com. Accessed 25 Jan 2016
30. Young, J.R.: Revenue-sharing models between edX and university partners. The Chronicle of Higher Education, 21 February 2013. http://www.chronicle.com
31. Fischer, H., Dreisiebner, S., Ebner, M., Kopp, M., Koehler, T., Franken, O.: Revenues vs. costs of MOOC platforms. Discussion of business models for xMOOC providers, based on empirical findings and experiences During implementation of the Project iMOOX. In: 7th International Conference on Education, Research and Innovation. Seville, pp. 2991–3000 (2014)
32. Euler, D., Seufert, S., Zellweger, F.: Geschäftsmodelle zur nachhaltigen Implementierung von eLearning an Hochschulen. In: Breitner, M., Fandel, G. (eds.) E-Learning Geschäftsmodelle und Einsatzkonzepte, pp. 85–103. Gabler, Wiesbaden (2006)
33. Kalman, Y.: A race to the bottom: MOOCs and higher education business models. Open Learn. **29**(1), 5–14 (2014)
34. Van Dijck, J., Poell, T.: Higher Education in a networked world: European responses to U.S. MOOCs. Int. J. Commun. **9**, 2674–2692 (2015)

ICT for Older People to Learn about ICT: Application and Evaluation

Camino Fernández[✉], Gonzalo Esteban, Miguel Á. Conde,
and Francisco J. Rodríguez-Lera

Department of Mechanics,
Computer Science and Aerospace Engineering, Robotics Group,
University of León, Campus de Vegazana S/N, 24071 León, Spain
{camino.fernandez,gestc,miguel.conde,
fjrodl}@unileon.es

Abstract. Information and communication technologies are becoming a common instrument of daily life. They are available to more and more people everyday, but that does not imply that they are usable and useful for everyone. There are specific groups such as older people, with specific characteristics, such as motor control problems or reduced vision, that affect both the way they use these technologies and also how they learn how to use them. In this paper, we propose to use massive open online courses in order to show older people how to take advantage of the resources available through new technologies. This proof of concept shows that the use of ICT for learning about ICT can be an adequate solution for older people.

Keywords: ICT · Older people · MOOC · Usability · Mobile devices

1 Introduction

Information and Communication Technologies (ICT) have emerged and their use is affordable for almost everyone. That involves a change in individuals' daily lives. Internet use has become popular, mobile devices are used with different aims and not only as phones. It is essential to be always online and connected with friends and family by using social networks. We are continuously using texting tools to contact people, sending pictures, microblogging, etc. However, this landscape is not the same for everyone. People with disabilities or older people do not always see technology in the same way as other users do [1, 2]. In fact, this last collective, that is continuously growing, use ICT in a different way and pursue different aims [3, 4]. Older people were not born in an ICT context but they have to use it because of its high popularity. In this case, ICT, which has, as one of its goals, to promote integration and enhance relationships between people, is not having the expected effect with them. For older people, the use of technology can become something exclusive instead of inclusive [4]. The main problem is that technology has been developed in many cases without taking into account the special needs of older people, and that they have no previous training in this kind of technologies [5].

Given this context, the paper presents a project developed at the University of León that aims to define a learning program about ICT use for older people. The key issue of

© Springer International Publishing Switzerland 2016
P. Zaphiris and A. Ioannou (Eds.): LCT 2016, LNCS 9753, pp. 292–302, 2016.
DOI: 10.1007/978-3-319-39483-1_27

this project is that, instead of teaching older people in face-to-face sessions, what we have done is using ICT to teach ICT. As this learning program should have the higher dissemination possible, we have used MOOCs (Massive Open Online Course) as the way to deliver this knowledge. MOOCs allow an undefined number of students, are carried out in online contexts and the contents are available by using the Internet [6]. These type of courses provide significant benefits for older people such as that they can easily access new knowledge, contact with peers with similar aims and reuse and see the contents as many times as needed. Moreover, this type of courses has a key element for older people: Videos. This type of users are used to watch TV, so videos are not something strange to them so that learning can be focused on how to do the things and not only on the concepts. With this in mind, in the University of León, a MOOC experience was developed.

This MOOC shows to older people how to use iOS and Android devices. The researchers explore the main functionalities used by older people, and based on them, they developed the videos and activities to include in the MOOC. The contents are deployed in a learning platform of the University of León and have been tested by an older people group (with individuals with ages from 60 to 85).

This paper is structured as follows. In the following section, the background of this research is described. Later on, in Sect. 3, the contents development and how they have been deployed in a MOOC platform are described. In Sect. 4, a pilot carried out as a proof of concept is presented and the results of that pilot are discussed. Finally some conclusions are posed.

2   Research Background

This section aims to describe what can be understood as older people and their relationship with technology. After that, some learning experiences are commented, with special attention to those related to older people and MOOCs.

2.1   Older People and ICT

As commented above, ICTs can help people during their daily life. However, not everyone use the technology in the same way, and this is especially noticeable when talking about older or disabled people. But what do we mean by older people, also known as elderly people or senior citizens? This depends on issues such as the life expectancy or quality of aging that are related to the context. This context can have different levels of development; can have different quality of health services, etc. For instance, in Europe, an older person is not the same as in Africa. Most developed countries set the age of 65 years to define when a person is older.

At the moment, there is not a United Nations (UN) standard numerical criterion, but the UN agreed the cut-off is 60+ years to refer to the older population [7]. For this research, this will be the age used to define an older person. However, we should not forget that older people is a very heterogeneous group and for this research we will take also into account the following categories inside the older people group [8]: 1. Age more or less close to retirement (period of pre-retirement); 2. Autonomous age as a pensioner (period of independent living); 3. Age with increasing handicaps (start of period of dependent living) and 4. Dependent pensioners' age (period of dependent living up to the end of life).

It should be noted that older people is a collective that is continuously growing. An example of this can be observed in the European Union (EU). Due to the dynamics in fertility, life expectancy, and migration, the age structure of the EU population will change strongly in the coming decades. The overall size of the population is projected to be slightly larger by 2060 but much older than it is now [9].

Older people have special features and use ICT in a different way from people that have grown surrounded by ICT [3, 5, 10, 11]. This means that there is an important gap between them [12, 13]. In order to bridge this gap between older persons and digital natives, the different countries and institutions have developed several initiatives. For instance, the European Commission funds research and applied research under The Seventh Research Framework Programme [14] and its successor, Horizon 2020 [15]. For instance, with Member States, the European Commission participates in the Active and Assisted Living Joint Programme (with a grant of 700 million euros) [16]. In 2011 the Commission started the European Innovation Partnership on Active and Healthy Ageing that promotes several projects.

But, is so much money needed to make ICT more accessible and useful for older people? The answer is obviously yes. ICT has a high potential for inclusion of older people but it can also be associated to exclusion. ICT can be inclusive because it promotes social interaction, gives them lots of helpful apps for their daily lives, provides them with new ways to keep contact with family and friends, etc. [17, 18]. However, there are several issues that make difficult for older people to use ICT [3, 11, 19, 20]:

- The older people group is not an homogeneous one concerning education, income or even the different types of disabilities often associated with age. Elderly people as a group are the ones at the greatest risk of being excluded from the benefits of the Information Society.
- They have not directly been involved in the evolution of ICT or the Internet, and they have to learn to use something that has been developed without taking into account their specific needs.
- Older people have problems to use the technology and learn how to use it because, ICT does not always take into account their age-related sensory, physical and cognitive features, and neither possible motor control and cognitive impairment.
- The affordability of ICT. Older people income can be a limitation for using and accessing ICT.
- The availability of ICT services is also a problem because of geographical restrictions. For instance, people with a limited access to Internet in rural areas.
- Accessibility and usability issues are essential for the success of any ICT solution and especially critical with older persons that, as mentioned above, have age-related special features.

A clear example of how this issues influence older people can be how they use mobile devices. This kind of ICT solutions has high penetration and acceptation in our society. By the end of 2015, there are more than 7 billion mobile cellular subscriptions in the world and more than a mobile device per person in the developed countries [21]. These devices provide access to a complete set of services that can be employed with different purposes. A high percentage of older people in developed countries owns one of these devices, however they use only mobile phones for very limited purposes, such as for calling or texting in emergencies. This is mainly caused because the devices are not adapted to their needs, because they need to learn how to use the device and such tools have not been designed thinking of their special features [2, 3].

Given this context, and in order to reduce this exclusion, several initiatives have been defined. For this research, the most relevant ones are those related to learning activities for older people.

2.2   Older People and ICT Learning

As commented above, older people need to use ICT and these persons have several constraints that make it hard for them. Learning initiatives are essential to address this problem, and to make ICT something inclusive for older people, learning is something that does not only happen linked to an institution (university, high school, etc.). People can also learn in non-formal contexts and during their daily life [22–24]. The European Commission, through the lifelong learning program, has defined different initiatives to help older people to learn [25, 26] and also the different countries are enhancing this kind of learning actions [3].

Older people are quite interested in participating in these learning activities. They value the role of ICTs for keeping them in touch with family and friends, using the Internet for information searching, for hobbies and interests, and to make the mechanics of daily life easier [10].

However, older people present also difficulties to learn about ICT. Some common problems are: lack of confidence and fear of using ICTs (they are worried about doing something wrong or break something); the absence of support after the learning action; the high cost of training (although learning initiatives are addressing this problem); memory problems; problems with understanding technical jargon; etc. Some of these barriers are reduced with growing familiarity with ICT's, but some persist and some others are affected by aging constraints (physical and cognitive changes, motor control problems, reduced vision, etc.) [8, 10].

Given these barriers, what is clear is that older people has to be considered in the definition of ICT-based learning solutions and learning activities [11]. Moreover, learning plans should be flexible enough to support technology evolution and the change of older people conditions due to their age [8].

With this constraints, what has resulted to be a good solution is the use of visual contents that older people can see as many times as they want to, and demonstrative videos are specially useful [27]. In Spain, *Fundación Telefónica* and the regional governments have carried out several initiatives in this sense [28], such as courses about how to use an iOS or/and Android smartphone [29].

However, lots of these courses are carried out in face-to-face modality, and for the online courses, a learning platform is not always used [29]. In those cases, the interaction of older people with their peers is missed, and this issue is important in learning activities. Keeping this in mind, a possible solution would be the use of a learning platform that supports video based contents, facilitate older people evaluation and interaction with their peers.

This solution could be the MOOCs (Massive Open Online Course). This kind of courses can be easily accessible for older people, provide them with tools to interact with others and with contents based mostly on videos that can help them to learn how to use different systems [30]. MOOC courses bring great opportunities to enhance the quality of life of elderly people by enabling lifelong learning and inclusion in learning communities [31]. There are several initiatives of MOOCs for older people, for instance, the ones proposed by some regional governments of Spain such as CyLDigital [32].

However, the use of a MOOC is not necessarily associated to learning success, it is necessary to take into account that each user is different and the contents should be adapted to their specific needs (in what can be known as an adaptive MOOC). In this way, it is possible to mitigate several traditional problems of MOOCs such as: dropout rate; low number of cooperative activities; and the continuity of learning communities beyond the MOOC [33]. Moreover, with older people also MOOC platforms should be adapted considering accessibility issues.

Taking this into account, in the present research several contents were developed and they were deployed on a learning platform as part of a MOOC. This is done with the aim to test if this kind of courses can help old people to learn about ICT.

3 Development and Deployment of a MOOC

Once decided to apply a MOOC solution for older people learning, the next decision was which contents to use as a proof of concept. Taking into account the popularization of mobile devices, our idea was to develop a MOOC about smartphones, including both iOS and Android as the most common operating systems. The main aim of this course was to introduce the use of a smartphone to people that was not using it, or to improve the use of those persons that only use a very limited set of functionalities. This means that: (1) It was necessary to know if the course student uses the smartphone or not; (2) Define contents for both beginners with smartphones, and older people with some previous experience; (3) Deploy the contents in a learning platform and present them depending on the student profile, that is, in an adaptive way.

Regarding the first issue, the MOOC included, as the first module, a learning guide with information about the course and a questionnaire. It asks older people about their age, about their experience with smartphones, and about their smartphone operating system (Fig. 1). With this information, two different learning pathways were proposed; a simple one and an advanced one.

The definition of the contents requires to decide which functionalities would be described and what would not. In order to do this, the researchers of this project use studies such as [5, 34] and initiatives such as [29, 32] and the list of functionalities considered were: physical management of the device (buttons and touch-based movements); Basic Settings (main screens, icons management, alarms, apps installation, etc.); Contacts and email management; SMS (management and delivery of SMS);

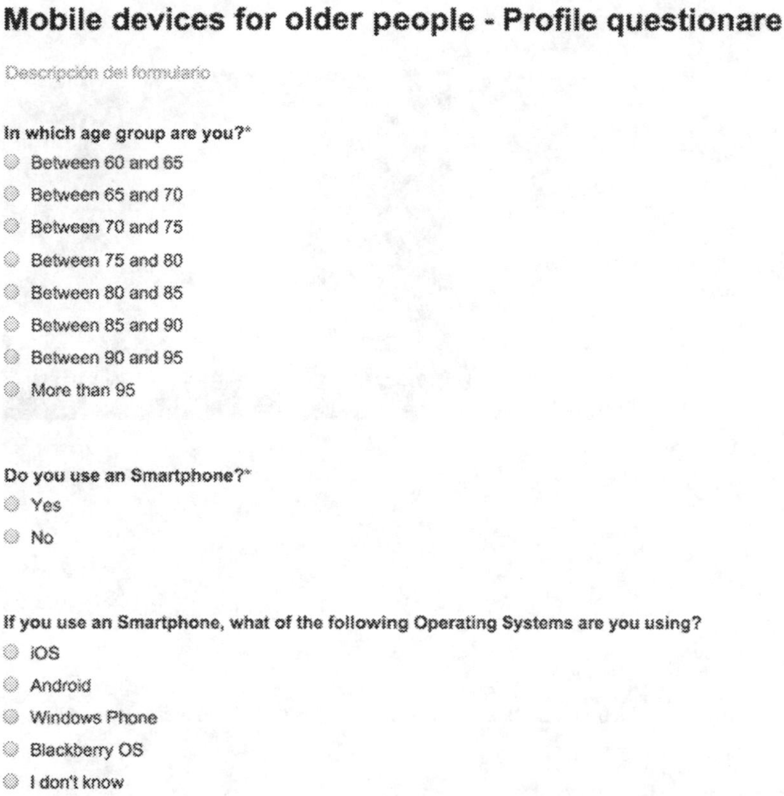

Mobile devices for older people - Profile questionare

Descripción del formulario

In which age group are you?*

○ Between 60 and 65

○ Between 65 and 70

○ Between 70 and 75

○ Between 75 and 80

○ Between 80 and 85

○ Between 85 and 90

○ Between 90 and 95

○ More than 95

Do you use an Smartphone?*

○ Yes

○ No

If you use an Smartphone, what of the following Operating Systems are you using?

○ iOS

○ Android

○ Windows Phone

○ Blackberry OS

○ I don't know

Fig. 1. Questionnaire to gather information about older people profile

Instant Messaging Systems (Whatsapp is used as an example); Web Browsing; and Integrated Camera Usage (take photos, make videos, store and manage media files). The authors carried out a presentation video for each of those functionalities and at least two additional videos describing the specific functionality for iOS and Android (although some functionalities are divided into several videos). Each video lasts up to five minutes and has some tasks associated that students can carry out and assess by themselves. Moreover, the student has always a jargon glossary available. In order to evaluate the acquired knowledge, the MOOC is finished with an evaluation questionnaire.

Finally, once the contents were developed, they were deployed in a learning platform. The best option would have been a MOOC platform, but the university did not have a contract with any MOOC platform. Given this situation, the authors decided to use Moodle as a MOOC platform (only for the proof of concept) and its lesson tool, and Google Forms to gather the information about the user and provide them with proper content (Fig. 2 shows the content once deployed).

Contacts Mangement

The following video shows how contacts are managed.

Task 1

1. Create a contact from scratch

2. Find the contact

3. Send a SMS to the contact

4. Phone him/her

3. Create a contact from a phone call

Fig. 2. Video and associated task for the Agenda Management in iOS

4   Experiment

In order to check the solution proposed, an experiment with a group of older people has been carried out. It involves 10 individuals that will be considered the experimental group, and 10 individuals that would be the control group. The experimental group members answered a questionnaire after carrying out the MOOC. The control group members did not participate in the course but most of them have a smartphone. 8 of the 10 older persons form the experimental group are between 60 and 75 years old and all of them have a smartphone (7 Android and 1 iOS). Besides, in the experimental group there are 2 older persons with an age between 75 and 85 that do not have a smartphone but aim to learn how to use it before buying one. The control group consists of 7 persons with an age between 60 and 75 and 3 more with an age between 75 and 85 that have not a smartphone.

From this experiment it is possible to explore students' perception taking into account the usability of the system (in this case the mobile device).

4.1   Methodology

The methodology aims to explore if the perception of the mobile device usability changes when participating in the MOOC.

Usability evaluation may involve the study of several issues such as: the user satisfaction, the perception of use, the efficiency of the system, etc. In this case the issue to consider was satisfaction. It was analysed using a System Usability Scale (SUS). SUS is a simple ten-item scale that gives a global view of subjective assessments of usability [35]. In the experiment, the members from both the experimental and the control groups fulfil the SUS form. In this way, it was possible to compare those that participate in the course and those that do not. Moreover, it would be possible to compare those older persons with a smartphone to those that do not have one.

4.2 Results and Discussion

As commented above, SUS form was applied to the experimental and the control group so that different results were expected.

The results for SUS in the experimental group was a 76,4 %, which is above the acceptable satisfaction level of 68 % described by Sauro [36]. It could be higher but the contents have been deployed in a platform that is not defined specifically for MOOCs, and there are only 10 students involved in the course, while a MOOC usually has hundreds or thousands. That is, the interaction with peers was poor in this proof of concept.

The results in the control group were of 39,4 %. That can be normal because this group is formed by older people that, although have a smartphone, do not usually use all the functionalities of the device. They perceive the smartphone as a complex device to use and they require the support of expert people in order to use it properly [3, 5].

Figure 3 shows a comparison in the average values of each answer for the experimental and control groups.

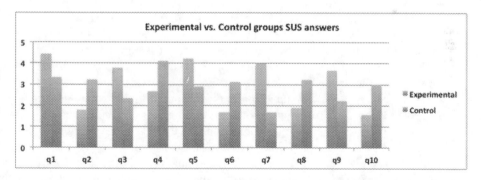

Fig. 3. Comparison between the average answers for each question of the SUS questionnaire (Color figure online)

It should be noted that there are differences of 1 or more Likert scale level for all questions except for question 1 (q1). This question is "I think that I would like to use this system frequently". These answers can be similar because both the people of the experimental and control groups would like to use the system frequently, mobile devices are something they use and want to use everyday although in this question is not defined how easy is to use it. From this comparison, it is also possible to see that there is a special difference for question 7 (q7). That is, "I would imagine that most people would learn to use this system very quickly". People in the experimental group think that it is easy to learn to use the system, but the persons in the control group have not carried out the course, so they have a very different perception.

From this experiment it is also interesting to compare the SUS average score for the older persons with ages between 75 and 85 years old and that have not a smartphone. These persons in the experimental group have an average score of 71,2 % with a difference of 5,4 % from the average value for the group. This kind of older persons in the control group has a score of 22,5 % with a 16,9 % of difference from the average value of their group. This could be caused because the persons without a smartphone in the experimental group have learned to use it after the course and they have a similar perception of satisfaction with the device; while those in the control group have even more difficulties than their peers because they have not a smartphone to interact with.

5   Conclusions

The present research has dealt with an issue as learning ICT by using ICT, but in this case the students involved in this learning activity are older people. People from this collective have very specific needs and special features related to their age. In order to guarantee a successful use of ICT it is necessary to carry out learning actions oriented to them and to take their reality into account.

This paper has explored some of the problems that older people has regarding the use of ICT, and also while carrying out online learning activities. Given this context, we consider that the best learning strategy can be MOOCs because they are oriented to video-contents, are usually free and allow older people to interact with peers with similar problems and/or motivations. In order to test this MOOCs about ICT for older people, we have carried out an implementation as a proof of concept. After assessing the usability of the action, it was possible to see that the satisfaction of the older people was higher in those students that have participated in the MOOC.

However, the pilot carried out has several limitations, most of them because it is only a proof of concept. These limitations are: (1) It should include more older people, because a population of 20 persons is not very meaningful; (2) With only 10 older persons in the experimental group, the interaction into the MOOC is not high; (3) We should use a MOOC oriented platform to achieve all the expected benefits of this kind of courses; (4) The platform was not adapted taking into account usability issues [31] because we were using an institutional environment that can not easily be changed.

As future research lines, it would be useful to explore, in a qualitative way, students perceptions after the learning activity. Moreover, the deployment and publication of the contents in a MOOC platform could be interesting to analyze the results in real contexts.

Acknowledgments. This work is partially supported by *Cátedra Telefónica – Universidad de León* and Spanish Ministry of Economy and Competitiveness under grant DPI2013-40534-R.

References

1. García-Peñalvo, F.J., Conde, M\'{.A}., Matellán-Olivera, V.: Mobile apps for older users – the development of a mobile apps repository for older people. In: Zaphiris, P., Ioannou, A. (eds.) LCT. LNCS, vol. 8524, pp. 117–126. Springer, Heidelberg (2014)
2. Kurniawan, S.: Older people and mobile phones: a multi-method investigation. Int. J. Hum.-Comput. Stud. **66**, 889–901 (2008)
3. Fundación-Vodafone-España: TIC y Mayores (2012)
4. Fundación-Orange: eEspaña 2014, Madrid (2015)
5. Fundación-Vodafone-España, Red.es: Tecnologías orientadas a la movilidad: valoración y tendencias, Madrid (2014)
6. Pappano, L.: The Year of the MOOC. The New York Times 2 (2012)
7. Definition of an older or elderly person. Proposed Working Definition of an Older Person in Africa for the MDS Project. http://www.who.int/healthinfo/survey/ageingdefnolder/en/. Accesed 03 Feb 2016
8. Ala-Mutka, K., Malanowski, N., Punie, Y., Cabrera, M.: Active ageing and the potential of ICT for learning. European Commission, Seville, Spain (2008)
9. European-Commission: The 2015 Ageing report - Economic and budgetary projections for the 28 EU Member States (2013–2060). Publications Office of the European Union, Luxembourg (2015)
10. Sandhu, J., Damodaran, L., Ramondt, L.: ICT skills acquisition by older people: motivations for learning and barriers to progression. Int. J. Educ. Ageing **3**, 25–42 (2013)
11. Amaro, F., Gil, H.: ICT for elderly people: "Yes, They Can!". In: Conference ICT for Elderly People: "Yes, They Can!", pp. 3792–3803 (2011)
12. Prensky, M.: Digital natives, digital immigrants. On the Horizon **9**(5), 1–6 (2001)
13. Prensky, M.: Digital natives, digital immigrants, part II: do they really think differently? On the Horizon **9**(6), 1–6 (2001)
14. European Union's Research and Innovation funding programme for 2007–2013. https://ec.europa.eu/research/fp7/. Accessed 26 Jan 2016
15. HORIZON 2020 - The EU Framework Programme for Research and Innovation. http://ec.europa.eu/programmes/horizon2020/. Accessed 26 Jan 2016
16. The Active and Assisted Living Joint Programme (AAL JP). https://ec.europa.eu/digital-agenda/node/50829. Accessed 26 Jan 2016
17. White, H., McConnell, E., Clipp, E., Bynum, L., Teague, C., Navas, L., Craven, S., Halbrecht, H.: Surfing the net in later life: a review of the literature and pilot study of computer use and quality of life. J. Appl. Gerontol. **18**, 358–378 (1999)
18. Weatherall, J.W.A.: A grounded theory analysis of older adults and information technology. Educ. Gerontol. **26**, 371–386 (2000)
19. Czaja, S.J., Lee, C.C.: Designing computer systems for older adults. In: Julie, A.J., Andrew, S. (eds.) The human-computer interaction handbook, pp. 413–427. L. Erlbaum Associates Inc., Hillsdale, NJ, USA (2003)
20. European-Commission: Active Ageing in the Information Society: e-Inclusion – Be part of it!, Brussels (2007)
21. ITU: ICT Facts and Figures, Geneva, Switzerland (2015)
22. García-Peñalvo, F.J., Colomo-Palacios, R., Lytras, M.D.: Informal learning in work environments: training with the social web in the workplace. Behav. Inf. Technol. **31**, 753–755 (2012)
23. Halliday-Wynes, S., Beddie, F.: Informal Learning. At a Glance. National Centre for Vocational Education Research Ltd., Adelaide (2009)

24. Otero, M.S., McCoshan, A., Junge, K.: European inventory on validation of non-formal and informal learning. ECOTEC Research and Consulting Limited (2005)
25. COM: COM(2001) 678 final. Making a European area of lifelong learning a reality. Communication from the Commission (2001). http://eur-lex.europa.eu/LexUriServ/LexUriServ.do?uri=COM:2001:0678:FIN:EN:PDF
26. Davie, R.: Older people in Europe - EU policies and programmes. European Parliamentary Research Service, European Union (2014). http://www.europarl.europa.eu/RegData/bibliotheque/briefing/2014/140811/LDM_BRI(2014)140811_REV1_EN.pdf
27. Struve, D., Wandke, H.: Video modeling for training older adults to use new technologies. ACM Trans. Access. Comput. **2**, 1–24 (2009)
28. European Regional Development Fund. http://ec.europa.eu/regional_policy/en/funding/erdf/. Accesed Feb 2016
29. Fundación Vodafone con los Mayores - Curso smartphone. http://www.fundacion vodafoneconlosmayores.com/. Accessed 2 Feb 2016
30. Arguel, A., Jamet, E.: Using video and static pictures to improve learning of procedural contents. Comput. Hum. Behav. **25**, 354–359 (2009)
31. Sanchez-Gordon, S., Lujan-Mora, S.: Web accessibility of MOOCs for elderly students. In: Conference Web Accessibility of MOOCs for Elderly Students, pp. 1–6 (2013)
32. CyL Digital. https://www.cyldigital.es/formacion/formacion-on-line. Accessed 02 Feb 2016
33. Fidalgo-Blanco, Á., García-Peñalvo, F.J., Sein-Echaluce, M.: A methodology proposal for developing adaptive cMOOC. In: Proceedings of the First International Conference on Technological Ecosystem for Enhancing Multiculturality, pp. 553–558. ACM, Salamanca, Spain (2013)
34. Strengers, J.: Smartphone interface design requirements for seniors. Master Information Studies - Program Human Centered Multimedia, University of Amsterdam (2012)
35. Brooke, J.: SUS: a quick and dirty usability scale. In: Jordan, P.W., Thomas, B., Weerdmeester, B.A., McClelland, I.L. (eds.) Usability Evaluation in Industry. pp. 107–115. Taylor & Francis, Abingdon (1996)
36. Sauro, J.: A Practical Guide to the System Usability Scale: Background, Benchmarks and Best Practices. CreateSpace (2011)

The Design and Implementation
of a Cross-Platform Teaching System

Songfeng Gao and Yonghao Xie[⊠]

Beijing University of Civil Engineering and Architecture, No. 1 Museum Road,
Xicheng district, Beijing, People's Republic of China
gaosongfeng@bucea.edu.cn, 2418636274@qq.com

Abstract. With the development of computer technology and network technology, the traditional test mode is not able to fully meet digital, standardized test requirements. Traditional exam modes include artificial test paper, artificial marking, several processes statistics and performance analysis papers, results statistics, papers analysis etc., The whole process is cumbersome and inefficient. Moreover, with the change of examination techniques and carrier landmark, we can say the traditional examination method is no longer suitable for today's exam. Now appears online examination system is an extension of the traditional examination and change, with its own efficient and convenient, flexible benefits, widespread concern various institutions. On the other hand, with the rapid development of mobile communication technology and intelligent portable device innovation, appearing more and more sophisticated intelligence products, marking the arrival of the mobile Internet era. As a smart phone operating system, Android platform by virtue of its open source, openness and stability, it has become the current most users, the fastest growing mobile smartphone operating system.

In summary, The campus of the previous examination system is applied to the mobile client, not only can make full use of space, anytime, anywhere to exam, not too much limited by time and space. And greatly simplifies the examination process, reducing the onerous test management work, which is a mobile Internet application development model better.

In order to make the examination system to have flexible scalability and cross-platform portability, At the same time convenient for each subsystem integration, based Android platform and application software technology Web application server communication, combined with the actual traditional examination process, design the overall structure and function of the system to achieve the main module, in order to develop versatility, flexibility, ease of maintenance of the mobile phone side of the school examination system. The system includes system settings, test status, clear examination, re-examination, the online exam, the student information maintenance and queries, bank maintenance, query results, review papers, exit multiple module systems, it can enter their own questions and its related the freedom to create and delete, save students answer timely information, the system uses a manual marking and automatic scoring combination to provide a more objective reference points.

The system uses Android as an operating system, using J2EE as a development framework, JAVA as the system development language, using the B/S structure of the network architecture model, applicating SQL Server2005 database management system to store student information and questions as to

© Springer International Publishing Switzerland 2016
P. Zaphiris and A. Ioannou (Eds.): LCT 2016, LNCS 9753, pp. 303–309, 2016.
DOI: 10.1007/978-3-319-39483-1_28

achieve different people, from different locations (such as LAN, WAN, Internet/Intranet), with different access methods to access and manipulate a common database. It can effectively protect data platform and access manage-ment, as well as its own security server database, to better improve the overall security of the system.

In this paper, based on the Android platform school examinations system design, development and related technology is described and discussed. First of all, the analysis shows that schools in the past exam mode, so as to define the overall layout of the system and its related processes. Secondly, using the JAVA language for the completion of the layout of the main module for development, implementation steps are discussed in detail. Finally, the system is optimized and the relevant contents are summarized. After the completion of the system development, the function of each function should be checked to ensure that the system can achieve the expected purpose, better guarantee the availability and safety of the system.

The realization of the Android platform of school examination system, not only to meet the school standardized tests of functional requirements, and well solves the shortcoming of lack of portability of the original system. It is able to improve the flexibility and practicality of the system, teachers and students can use and search examination system related information anytime and anywhere, to a greater extent save time and space occupancy. In the implementation of the Android examination system, there are still many problems, but also need to continue planning and design. But the whole process of its development, this is a familiar and the process of exploration, and it is proved that this is an effective research and development process, at the same time,, it has important guidance and reference for the future development of a more excellent and more efficient system.

Keywords: JAVA · Examinations · System · Android

1   Introduction

1.1   Research Background

With the development of mobile Internet technology, not only changing our way of life, but also changing the traditional test pattern. In the forefront of mobile Internet wave Android mobile intelligent operating system, more and more widely be applied to today's test model.

Past the traditional examination mode after artificial group volume, manual marking, score statistics and papers and tests, analysis process, often need to spend a lot of manpower and material resources and financial resources, the whole process cumbersome and inefficient. So the traditional examination way has not fully meet the needs of education informatization construction and modern teaching [1]. Now college students for mobile Internet cognitive degree is self-evident, the traditional exam mode and the combination of mobile networking, developed an Android based smartphone operating system under the test program, can reduce the test cost, easing the burden on teachers, greatly improve the work efficiency, ensure the quality of the exam. At the same time, based on the test pattern under the Android mobile intelligent operating system, has become a trend of assessment of students' academic level of higher education, the examination is the original way of development and innovation, conform to the requirements for the development of the information age [2], will also was welcomed by college students.

1.2   The Development of Mobile Internet

Today is the era of Internet, the Internet has become the essential element in life, in almost every corner around us. Especially in recent years, the popularity of cell phones and other portable devices, especially the rapid development of mobile smart phones, mobile Internet concept of thorough popular feeling, is bound to lead a new wave of technology.

From the user perspective, the so-called Mobile Internet refers to the way the application of mobile, portable tablet PCs and other mobile devices to access the Internet over a wireless connection, although it seems that only the access equipment has changed, and in fact has prompted the Internet occurred a lot of fundamental change. Acceleration in the pace of life, people today need to be more precise and more direct service, "small and light" and "Communication and convenient" determined by the characteristics of the mobile Internet and PC Internet fundamentally different place, and trends associated with the Department.

First of all, the mobile Internet, its biggest feature is the characteristics of easy to carry, compared to the massive PC or laptop, mobile phone and tablets and weight are more appropriate people carry in the body. Especially mobile phones, today's mainstream contact tools, mobile phone is almost 24 h a day with people around you. Mobile phones as a tool of mobile Internet access, to search information resources required for people at any time, make full use of the fragmented time in the life, work, accept and deal with all kinds of Internet information.

Second, different from the PC model of human-computer interaction process, the mobile Internet in the unique way of human-computer interaction, since mobile portable devices have small screens, and no keyboard input devices such as external, shown to result in the user's information or controls are relatively few. While the terminal capabilities by the terminal size, processing power, battery capacity and other limitations. This requires that mobile Internet devices will be needed to refine the content as much as possible, to reduce the user's input operation. However, in general, for a large number of formal jobs, people will still choose PC. Therefore, mobile communications equipment to provide users with more entertainment and communication. So when making interactive users prefer the multi-touch and gestures, body feeling.

Finally, because of the mobile Internet business has received the network and terminal capacity constraints, therefore, its content and form also needs to be suitable for a particular network technical specifications and terminal type, therefore, when using mobile Internet business, the use of content and services more intimate, especially in mobile phone as the client access to the Internet, including users mobile phone number, real information and user directories contain user information at any time are likely to leak, social relations, therefore, mobile Internet users for its information security requirement is extremely high, generally do not reveal information risks install new applications.

1.3   The Android Platform Development

Android is an Open source mobile devices operating system based on Linux, mainly used for smart phones and tablets and other mobile devices, set up by Google's Open Handset Alliance (smaller companies, Open Handset Alliance) continued leadership and development.

Android was originally founded by Andy rubin, originally developed the purpose of this system is to create a digital camera's advanced operating system; But it was found that the market demand is not big enough, and the fast-growing smartphone market, so the Android was transformed into an operating system for smartphones. In August 2005 to be bought by Google technology businesses in the United States. In November 2007, Google and 84 manufacturers, developers and telecom operators set up the Open Handset Alliance to jointly develop improved Android system, then Google to Apache free open source license authorization way, released the source code, Android allows producers running Android smartphone, then gradually expand to tablets and other fields.

On the one hand, the development of the Android system in the country mainly for secondary development on the Android system, based on the Android source code, and the depth of the customized version of the operating system.

Second, the openness of the Android platform allows any mobile terminal manufacturers to join the Android alliance, significant openness can make its have more developers, with users and applications is growing, more and more get the welcome of the masses, the Android platform.

1.4   JAVA EE Platform

Java EE (Java Platform, Enterprise Edition) is the sun's Enterprise application version. This version is formerly known as J2EE, can help us develop and deploy a portable, robust, scalable and secure Java application server.

Along with the rapid development of science and technology, Java EE has evolved into the current enterprise development is actually one of the standard platform, Java EE application because of its high degree of development, stable performance, high safety etc., by the enterprise spirit domain relevant personage, the more the more enterprises to choose the Java EE as a development platform.

The advantages of Java EE platform is more outstanding, such as: JUnit and TestNG to test code (including unit, integration and function test) write created conditions; The implementation of continuous integration can rely on the continuous integration server, and so on. Now existing Java EE technology is very mature, the vendor containers tend to be more homogeneous, so the Java EE is the mainstream of development enterprise Web application frameworks technology, in today's enterprise project development and Microsoft's MS.NET together form the two core framework technology.

1.5   Study the Significance of School Examinations System Design Based on the Android System

Because previous test mode after artificial group general volume, manual marking, score statistics and papers and tests, analysis process, the whole process is complicated and inefficient, already can not fully meet the demand of digital and standardized test. Not only that, as the school examination technology and carrier of epoch-making change, to say the traditional way of examination is no longer suitable for today's exam.

And now with the rapid development of mobile communication technology and intelligent portable device of continuous innovation, the emergence of more and more intelligent and advanced products, marks the arrival of the era of mobile Internet. As a smartphone operating system, Android platform, with its open source, openness and stability, has become the current user, most of the fastest growing mobile smartphone operating system.

So to school examinations system based on the Android system design of the related research and implementation, not just to satisfy the functional requirement of standardized tests in school, and very good solve the disadvantage of the lack of portability of original system, to improve the flexibility and practicability of the system, the teachers and students can use anytime and anywhere, processing, search relevant information in the test system, more save the time and space.

2 System Builds Related Technologies

2.1 JAVA

Java is a simple, cross-platform, object-oriented, distributed, explains, the robust security, the structure of the neutral, portable, performance is very excellent multi-threaded, dynamic languages. Suitable for large enterprise applications and Internet applications, especially application system based on B/S agency.

2.2 B/S Structure Mode

Structure B/S (Browser/Server), is one of the Web after the rise of the network structure model, a Web Browser is one of the main client application software, the model unified the client, will be the core of the system function realization part focus on the Server, simplify the development, maintenance and use of the system. Client only need to install a browser and Server installation, such as SQL Server database, the browser can interact through the Web Server and database data.

B/S mode is divided into three levels [3]: the first layer is the client browser, for the presentation layer. The second layer is a Web server, it is the business logic layer. The third is the database server, this layer is the data access layer.

2.3 The Database

Database designer performance evaluation, the basis of information management information system implementation to do try to use the least amount of data table, the optimization to realize the function of demand, and the retrieval database to be simple and colleges and universities. The test system based on Android system under application of the database is SQL Server2005. The database is easy to use, good scalability, high and related software integration degree, etc.

3 System Overall Design

According to the requirements in the test, the system needs to be done function module mainly includes:

Test information. After the examinee input information in school, to the system, the query to participate in the test project, choose to take an examination after entering the examination. Exam questions from the backstage database according to the format of the list, and prompt the exam time. Candidates can submit after finish the test paper, if the test time, test paper automatically submit.

Course maintenance. The examinee exam content according to the courses for the progress and questions from the backstage database and maintenance related.

Query. Examination after landing, can query before the test information, through this function, the examinee can query the corresponding standard answer questions.

Test condition. The examinee when log in problem solving, according to the length of the examinee answer the time required for each question and problem of simple and easy degree, corresponding to the examinee state judge, for students in terms of which type of class, to make a more objective basis.

Re-exam. Test for examination, unqualified candidates system will give the chance of the second test, students can login, you can test.

Paper review. The examinee answer all the questions, under the condition of the test time allowed, can choose paper review. According to test yourself to answer to determine degree, choose the check part of the paper.

Teachers' information management. Management teacher after login, can undertake maintenance of examinee's information, including adding information, query, modify the examinee information candidates on the history of the exam and reply to the original information and password.

Demand analysis of the test, can design the overall structure of this system include two aspects: the examination system at the front desk and the background system.

Examination system at the front desk includes: login, examinee examination, the exit examination, scores query, information query. Exam system background include: the examinee information management, test management and test question management.

In short, the system of separating performance and the database, the examinee users through the Android client input and query information, from all walks of life to get the data in the database.

4 Summarizes

Due to the limitation of research time and ability, the system is the basis of the examination system module, the design of the other modules such as question bank is not very standard, and automatic marking function in volume and stay in the most basic level, the examination process confidentiality also need to be better improved. To sum up, this system still has many problems, its need to improve, need to accumulate experience in practice, in turn, strengthen perfect, I hope one day, can truly implement such a system, provide convenience for future examination.

References

1. Boschmann, E.: Teaching chemistry via distance education. J. Chem. Educ. **80**(6), 704 (2003)
2. Qing, S.,: The Choice of paperless network test system. Sci. Technol. Innov. Herald **8** (2008)
3. Jian, H., Jia L., Yong, Z.: Web-based online examination system. Xi'an University of Science and Technology

Heuristic Evaluation for Serious Immersive Games and M-instruction

Neil Gordon, Mike Brayshaw$^{(\boxtimes)}$, and Tareq Aljaber

Department of Computer Science, University of Hull, Hull HU6 7RX, UK
{n.a.gordon,m.brayshaw}@hull.ac.uk,
t.aljaber@2013.hull.ac.uk

Abstract. Two fast growing areas for technology-enhanced learning are serious games and mobile instruction (M-instruction or M-Learning). Serious games are ones that are meant to be more than just entertainment. They have a serious use to educate or promote other types of activity. Immersive Games frequently involve many players interacting in a shared rich and complex – perhaps web-based - mixed reality world, where their circumstances will be multi and varied. Their reality may be augmented and often self-composed, as in a user-defined avatar in a virtual world. M-instruction and M-Learning is learning on the move; much of modern computer use is via smart devices, pads, and laptops. People use these devices all over the place and thus it is a natural extension to want to use these devices where they are to learn. This presents a problem if we wish to evaluate the effectiveness of the pedagogic media they are using. We have no way of knowing their situation, circumstance, education background and motivation, or potentially of the customisation of the final software they are using. Getting to the end user itself may also be problematic; these are learning environments that people will dip into at opportune moments. If access to the end user is hard because of location and user self-personalisation, then one solution is to look at the software before it goes out. Heuristic Evaluation allows us to get User Interface (UI) and User Experience (UX) experts to reflect on the software before it is deployed. The effective use of heuristic evaluation with pedagogical software [1] is extended here, with existing Heuristics Evaluation Methods that make the technique applicable to Serious Immersive Games and mobile instruction (M-instruction). We also consider how existing Heuristic Methods may be adopted. The result represents a new way of making this methodology applicable to this new developing area of learning technology.

Keywords: Heuristic evaluation · Serious games · M-instruction · M-learning

1 Introduction

Throughout education, there is a growing focus ways to improve student engagement [2], which may be through utilising different pedagogic approaches [3] or technologies [4–8]. Serious Games are one approach to improve engagement through the benefits of a typically fun based, interactive environment where the learning is embedded within playful activity; the game has the aim of delivering some knowledge and/or skill as the student progresses through the game [4].

© Springer International Publishing Switzerland 2016
P. Zaphiris and A. Ioannou (Eds.): LCT 2016, LNCS 9753, pp. 310–319, 2016.
DOI: 10.1007/978-3-319-39483-1_29

The technological developments – primarily through computer and related IT – have led to Technology Enhanced Learning (TEL) [9], which encompasses software of computer based learning approaches, as well as the internet based eLearning.

One particular approach to technology enhanced learning is to utilise immersive environments – ones in which the learner is placed in a simulation of the real world [10], so that the student behaves as though in a real world context which is identified as improving learning in various ways. Combining the notion of serious games and immersive learning, serious immersive games utilise game-like (or actual game) environments to provide learning opportunities.

Computer Based Instruction in its general sense leads on to the more specific concept of Mobile-instruction (M-instruction) - also known as mobile learning (M-learning). In this paper, we consider such M-instruction as learning that utilises mobile devices [11]. As these have become increasingly sophisticated, the distinction between M-instruction and other e-learning is reducing. An example of the convergence of eLearning and M-instruction is that tablet and mobile devices can now routinely access server-based material. Modern learning environments support mobile friendly formats and interfaces. However, there are some distinct characteristics – particularly when considering the interface specific elements of eLearning designed for a computer (desktop or laptop), as opposed to the types of interaction that are more suited to mobile devices.

The game based and mobile approaches to software to support learning are examples of ubicomp. Ubiquitous computing and applications (also known as pervasive computing, or as ubicomp) relates to the concept that computing (and in particular, computer science and software engineering) appears everywhere [12]. Users may interact with this in a variety of forms, and the issue of evaluating such ubicomp applications becomes complex – since there are a myriad of platforms and instances of use. Moreover, as noted by Gordon [13], where ubicomp is applied to give students choice (i.e. flexible education), the location and time of study, so the context of use, will vary. Thus, the issue of evaluation becomes a multi-dimensional one. One potential approach that is explored in this paper is heuristic evaluation.

To support changes and innovations in teaching and learning, software and systems have been, and continue to be, developed. For software and system development, there are a number of potential ways to help in designing and evaluating them, from functional behaviour through to the acceptability to the users. Regarding the learning software considered in this paper, this may be evaluated as general software, through usability requirements, or, as considered in Brayshaw et al. [1], may be evaluated through heuristic evaluation. Usability testing is well established in software engineering, that focusses on the user interaction with the system [14]. This typically requires that a scenario be created for the users to work within, carrying out specific activities, which can be observed and measured to indicate the usability of the system. The clear difficulty here, when considering ubicomp – is that there is a multitude of possible scenarios, and each may have its own characteristics.

Heuristic Evaluation [14] offers an approach that uses evaluators to identify potential issues in the system, in relation to a set of identified principles that reflect usability characteristics.

2 Utilising Heuristic Evaluation as an Approach to Evaluation Pedagogic Software: An Empirical Application

Heuristic Evaluation is an informal method of usability analysis that lends itself to domains like serious games and M-instruction. Whilst we strongly support the use of more traditional, empirical methods there are circumstances when this is not always possible. The use of traditional evaluation methodologies presupposes that we have access to the end users. In an education context, this could be in a direct classroom scenario or by bringing learners into a laboratory under controlled conditions. However, with modern computer connectivity our "end users" can literally be anywhere. Indeed the underlying presupposition of M-instruction is that they are anywhere and mobile to boot! Therefore, we have to develop ways of evaluating our solutions before they go out. Heuristic evaluation allows pedagogical solutions to be tested at source – before they are shipped – by getting experts to evaluate the solution ahead of time.

2.1 Benefits of Heuristic Evaluation

Four major advantages of Heuristic Evaluation are

- Heuristic Evaluation, as opposed to a traditional evaluation, is cheap and providing the relevant expertise is readily to hand, easy to perform.
- The task is itself easy to grasp and once explained the required expertise from the identified cognoscente is usually happily given.
- The planning and control of conventional evaluation is not needed, something we will exploit in the work outlined here.
- It is useable through the project development lifecycle. It thus does not need a completed system. From first design, to iterative prototyping stages, the final deliverables it is a usable evaluation methodology.

2.2 Heuristics for Software Design

The most received version of Heuristic Evaluation is by Neilson [15–17]. It consists or a series of heuristics or rules of thumb that advise on design. They are as follows

- Transparency of system status – can the user see what state they are in?
- Correlation between the system and the real world – the desktop metaphor is frequently used here as a good example. It gives a good mapping between the computer and what they are trying to achieve in the real world.
- User Control and Freedom.
- Consistency and Standards. Consistency in a user interface is clearly vital as are the application of relevant standards.
- Error Prevention. Can errors be anticipated and designed out of the equation.
- Recognition rather than recall. Having to remember or recall is problematic. If users can work things out live - this is better.
- Flexibility and Efficiency of Use.

- Aesthetic and Minimalist Design.
- Help Users Recognise, diagnose, and recover from errors.
- Help and Documentation.

2.3   Heuristics for Educational Applications

In the context of educational evaluation, [18, 19] added the following:

- Feedback and designer/learner models (Squires and Preece):- In an education context, feedback is incredibly important. It needs to be cogent and timely.
- Cosmetic authenticity (Squires and Preece):- avoid interface components that the learner could misinterpret.
- Representational forms (Squires and Preece):- The interface should place a "low cognitive demand on the learner and functionality should be obvious" (Squires and Preece). The system should be transparent and encourage learning.
- Multiple views/representations (Squires and Preece):- does the learning software support different forms of learning? Is there one content model or can others be supported?
- Interaction flow (Squires and Preece):- extrinsic feedback e.g. error messages can cause distractions. Is there a consistent and uninterrupted flow to learning?
- Navigation (Squires and Preece):- can the learner easily navigate through their learning episodes with appropriate feedback given at critical points on this journey?
- Learners Control and Self-Directed learning (Squires and Preece):- can learners express their autonomy and ownership of their journey?
- Subject Content [19]:- The preamble and context setting should be relevant to the questions and tutorials and to the appropriate skill level. Is choice of media delivery right and addresses targeted learning outcomes?
- Assessment (Benson et al.):- is self-assessment available and the feedback to that assessment at the correct level. In what terms can we look at the quality and content of the assessment and feedback?

These heuristics are the starting point to evaluation. Based up these we are in a position to reflect critically upon what would otherwise be hard to evaluate empirically software solutions.

2.4   Existing Work Utilising Heuristic Evaluation

As reported in [1] we have used Heuristic Evaluation extensively and successfully in the past. In particular, we have used it to evaluate a Semantic Web Based Personalised VLE [20] that looked to semantically synthesize multiple sources of media to produce a personalized learning experience for evaluating software for those with disabilities [21]; and as a design tool in an evolving iterative prototyping tutoring system for teach computer programming [22]. Each time it provided a flexible tool to evaluate and reflect upon the work undertaken. It is in this context that we sought to again use this technique and apply it in contexts where simple end user evaluation is less straightforward.

3   Technology Enhanced Learning Through

3.1   Serious Immersive Games

Introduction to Serious Immersive Games. Serious games are games intended to do more than simply entertain; they have a serious use to educate or promote other types of change [23]. This approach is known as edutainment – and offers the potential to motivate learners by making learning a fun experience [24]. Whilst the games may be based on human-to-human interaction, card or other activity based, the arrival of computer video games in the 1960's onwards has enabled the richer and more varied set of interaction and automatic gameplay to enable different approach. A variant of utilising games to teach is to utilise game mechanics in other areas – such gamification [25] can offer benefits in designing learning material. In this paper, serious games will focus on computer-based games for teaching.

One particular approach, as computer graphics and sound have evolved, has been the rise of immersive games, that can use 2D or 3D graphics and stereo sound, frequently involving many players interacting in a shared rich and complex (often web-based) mixed reality world, where the player circumstances will be multi and varied. The player reality may be augmented and often self-composed, as in a user-defined avatar in a virtual world. The technology for this can range from the 2D representation on a traditional monitor -where the immersion is more limited though with modern large curved screens can still effective – through to a CAVE (Cave Automatic Virtual Environment) where the player is surrounded on multiple sides giving a more complete illusion.

In this context, education and training can overlap – the value of many immersive environments is in the ability to simulate a real world scenario so that the player can learn from the experience, whether the focus is on learning knowledge, developing physical skills, or a mix of the two.

Challenges in Evaluating Immersive Games. Evaluating serious games can be considered in several dimensions. As a game, there is the question of how fun and playable the game is. As an educational platform, the attention is on how effectively the learner engages and learns. Finally, as a piece of software, the focus is on how well the software achieves the functional requirements – for both gameplay and learning. Assessing the learning functionality is beyond the scope of the current work; instead, we focus on the engagement as we can measure it through the usability of the software. There are numerous HCI approaches, but as noted above, typical usability testing depends on being able to create typical user scenarios. The key benefit of serious immersive games is that the user – the player – may be in a wide variety of contexts. Moreover, in the case of multi-player games, the gameplay and experience will vary depending on a wide set of variables. Where serious games are used outside of a controlled educational setting, the variables will include not knowing the nature or profile of the user, nor their own motivation. Where players are joining and leaving the game environment because of their other commitments, it is difficult to monitor their experience of using the system. Monitoring of their activity may be useful in indicating engagement and the apparent success of the system – but too late to improve it.

3.2   M-instruction

Introduction to M-instruction. M-instruction, also known as mobile learning is about being able to learn on the move [26]. An increasing amount of modern computer use is via smart devices, pads, and laptops – indeed, in some contexts this is the preferred and main route for access to computing. People use these devices in a wide variety of places and contexts, giving them flexibility in when and where they access content; thus it is a natural extension to want to use these devices to learn: M-instruction encompasses the concept of utilising mobile computer devices to support teaching and learning anywhere.

Mobile technologies allow for a wide variety of learning support, from static content (web pages, course notes through PDF etc.), with interactive content, and apps and internet based material.

M-instruction is of particular relevance to lifelong learners who are not situated in a traditional learning environment [28]. However, it can also allow more choice for students on traditional courses, enabling blended learning, with some traditional on-site provision, supplemented and complemented by mobile.

What Challenges Are There When Evaluating M-instruction? Whilst M-instruction has its own characteristics, it shares some of the challenges of serious games when considering how to evaluate it; if the aim is to evaluate the effectiveness M-instruction, then the first issue is how to measure that value. The dimensions to consider for M-instruction are around the usefulness of the material for users to access, and to what extent the material is effective in enabling the user to learn.

We have no way of knowing their situation, circumstance, education background and motivation, or of the customisation of the final software they are using. Getting to the end user itself can also be problematic as these are learning environments that people will dip into at opportune moments. As with serious games, we will not consider the effectiveness of the learning itself here, but rather how to attempt to ensure the system is providing suitable functionality, enabling and encouraging engagement and use.

3.3   Ubiquitous or Pervasive Computing Solutions for Learning

Ubicomp and Pervasive Computing. The previous two sections have illustrated two areas where computer science has enabled new opportunities for established learning (game based and more general teaching) to take new forms – with computer games and mobile as platforms. As noted, these share characteristics in what they offer – flexible access, the ability to choose if and when to use them, and for how long. Indeed, the two examples overlap where virtual environments are accessed via mobile devices – with technologies such as Google Glass and Oculus Rift showing that the convergence of these is accelerating.

Evaluating Ubicomp. As software and systems become more pervasive, integrated and sometimes hidden, the challenge of how to evaluate them grows. The features already noted in the two examples of this paper show certain commonality – with varied users, in a wide variety of potential use scenarios. Amongst the toolkit of evaluation techniques, user focussed approaches [29] and frameworks [30] rely on being able to identify and observe users. For the serious immersive games and the M-: Learning examples considered in this paper, the problem remains that identifying users and being able to monitor and measure their use to evaluate the system. Here we propose a hybrid approach of usability and heuristic evaluation.

4   Heuristic Evaluation as an Approach to Meet the Challenges in Evaluating Serious Immersive Games, M-Instruction and Ubicomp

4.1   Heuristic Evaluation

If access to the end user is hard because of location and user self-personalisation, then one solution is to look at the software before it goes out. Heuristic Evaluation allows us to get User Interface (UI) and User eXperience (UX) experts to reflect on the software before it is deployed. As summarised above, we have demonstrated before its use with pedagogical software [1]. In this paper, we propose an extension to existing Heuristics Evaluation Methods that make this technique applicable to Serious Immersive Games and M-instruction. We will also propose how existing Heuristic Methods may be adopted. The result represents a new way of making this methodology applicable to a new developing area of learning technology.

4.2   A Hybrid Evaluation Approach

The system proposed here utilises elements of traditional usability testing - selecting the categories for measurement and evaluation – but then uses a heuristic approach where expert users then evaluate their experience against these measures. This combination approach has been developed for health M-instruction applications [27], which is a more specialised form of M-instruction. Evaluation here – as in the cases described in the case studies considered in [1], is carried out through a process of questionnaire and interview of the experienced and expert users.

This type of approach – with a selective set of usability metrics, evaluated through use by experts – benefits from the utilisation of specialised users, where the general interface and environment can be assessed in the light of longstanding relevant experience.

In an ideal world, it would be desirable to triangulate this approach with experimental based empirical work. This is possible where we can produce an experimental design with clearly identified variables, sufficient balance control and numbers to carry this off in a defensible scientific manner. Running this study alongside a heuristic evaluation would give a way of adding confidence to a heuristic evaluation story. Indeed comparing the two approaches would be insightful. However, it is the very nature of the topic of this paper that make this approach very problematic. The end-users of serious immersive games and M-instruction technology are going to be hard to get into the lab. If you did manage to do this, it would still be such an unnatural environment for them to engage in their normal interaction it is not clear what would be actually learnt. If we want to study, serious immersive games and M-instruction in the large, other triangulating techniques need to be investigated. Heuristic Evaluation gives a handle on looking, from a designers and experts perspective, on the software solutions we have made. The actually experience of the users out there in cyberspace is a harder thing to judge.

5 Conclusions and Future Work

5.1 Outcomes and Conclusions

What have we learned from this effort so far is that the identification of suitable metrics and usability measures is non-trivial, but can lead to a more rapid evaluation in the process of development, and so can aid the software engineer in developing the user side functionality? Of course, the heuristic evaluation is just part of the picture, and that user-based evaluation is still needed as a part of the entire process, especially when it comes to evaluating the learning benefits of the serious games and mobile systems. Some raw data might be gained from usage metrics and performance. The trouble with M-Instruction is that people often only use an online tutorial to find the information that they need. They do not intend to finish the tutorial – they will quit it when they have found what they were after. Therefore, a metric that looks to completion rates or final marks is going to be wide of the mark on many occasions. The social interactions and social computing aspects also means that in a game scenario what can be learnt from scores or levels is also not going to tell the full story. They may however give us a limited part of the picture – so as means of triangulating our data there is some potential here.

5.2 Future Work

To the future - Serious Games and M-Instruction are just two instances of Pervasive and Ubiquitous Computing. Further work is needed to evaluate how effective Heuristic Evaluation is as a tool in evaluating these applications where the end users are at a distance and we cannot monitor them closely by traditional usability terms. One area of particular interest here is the potential to gather information on usage patterns – time, place, duration – and utilise big-data to attempt to gauge the effectiveness. The importance of Big Data to this endeavour is that it has the potential to look at users in the large. Larger samples will give a better broad-grained picture of user behaviour from which to judge what typical behavioural patterns are. If we have these more general views, we can then compare and contrast them with the insights that heuristic evaluation have given us and potentially confirm our views.

Another area for further work is that of embedding formative and diagnostic assessment within the game environment (for serious games), and within the learning pathway for M-instruction, to attempt to address the question of how to determine the effectiveness of these systems in teaching. Thus, the act of engaging in the use of the software will give us valuable data. By placing implicit performance, gathering spies within an application we have target the questions we want answered. This way the insights that we need into learning experience can be made to flow from our software as a natural consequence of use.

References

1. Brayshaw, M., Gordon, N., Nganji, J., Wen, L., Butterfield, A.: Investigating heuristic evaluation as a methodology for evaluating pedagogical software: an analysis employing three case studies. In: Zaphiris, P., Ioannou, A. (eds.) LCT 2014, Part I. LNCS, vol. 8523, pp. 25–35. Springer, Heidelberg (2014)
2. Zyngier, D.: (Re) conceptualising student engagement: doing education not doing time. Teach. Teach. Educ. **24**(7), 1765–1776 (2008)
3. Gordon, N.: Enabling personalised learning through formative and summative assessment. In: Technology-Supported Environments for Personalized Learning: Methods and Case Studies, pp. 268–283. Information Science Publishing, Hershey (2009)
4. Susi, T., Johannesson, M., Backlund, P.: Serious games: An overview. Technical report, School of Humanities and Informatics, University of Skövde, Sweden (2007)
5. Anderson, J.R.: Learning to program in LISP. Cogn. Sci. **8**, 87–129 (1984)
6. O'Shea, T., Self, J.: Learning and Teaching with Computers: Artificial Intelligence in Education. The Harvester Press Limited, Brighton (1983)
7. Papert, S.: MIND-STORMS: Children, Computers, and Powerful Ideas. The Harvester Press, Brighton (1980)
8. Skinner, B.F.: The technology of teaching. Proc. R. Soc. Ser. B **162**, 427–443 (1965)
9. Spector, J.M., Davidsen, P.I.: Designing technology enhanced learning environments. In: Instructional and Cognitive Impacts of Web-Based Education, pp. 241–261 (2000)
10. Dede, C.: Immersive interfaces for engagement and learning. Science **323**(5910), 66–69 (2009)
11. Quinn, C.: mLearning: Mobile, Wireless, in your Pocket Learning. LineZine, Fall 2000 (2000). http://www.linezine.com/2.1/features/cqmmwiyp.htm
12. Greenfield, A.: Everyware: The Dawning Age of Ubiquitous Computing. New Riders, Berkeley (2010)
13. Gordon, N.: Flexible Pedagogies: technology-enhanced learning. Higher Education Academy, NIACE (2014). http://www.heacademy.ac.uk/resources/detail/flexible-learning/flexiblepedagogies/tech_enhanced_learning/main_report
14. Nielsen, J.: Usability inspection methods. In: Conference Companion on Human Factors in Computing Systems. ACM (1994)
15. Nielsen J.: How to conduct a Heuristic Evaluation (Online) (2015). http://www.useit.com/papers/heuristic/heuristic_evaluation.html
16. Nielsen, J., Mack, R.L.: Heuristic Evaluation. Usability Inspection Methods, pp. 25–62. Wiley, New York (1994)

17. Nielsen, J., Molich, R.: Heuristic evaluation of user interfaces. In: Proceedings of ACM CHI 1990 Conference, Seattle, WA, 1–5 April, pp. 249–256 (1990)

18. Benson, L., Dean, E., Grant, M., Holschuh, D., Kim, B., Kim, H., Lauber, E., Loh, S., Reeves, T.: Heuristic Evaluation Instrument and Protocol for E-Learning Programs (Online) (2001). http://it.coe.uga.edu/~treeves/edit8350/HEIPEP.html

19. Squires, D., Preece, J.: Predicting quality in educational software: evaluating for learning, usability and the synergy between them. Interact. Comput. **11**, 467–483 (1999)

20. Wen, L., Brayshaw, M., Gordon, N.: Personalized content provision for virtual learning environments via the semantic web. Innovations Teach. Learn. Inf. Comput. Sci. **11**, 14–27 (2012)

21. Nganji, J.T., Brayshaw, M.: Designing and reflecting on disability-aware e-learning systems: the case of ONTODAPS. In: IEEE 14th International Conference on Advanced Learning Technologies (ICALT), Athens, Greece (2014). http://ieeexplore.ieee.org/stamp/stamp.jsp? tp=&arnumber=6901543&isnumber=6901368, doi:10.1109/ICALT.2014.167

22. Butterfield, A.M., Brayshaw, M.: A pedagogically motived guided inquiry based tutor for C#. In: Gordon, N.A., Graham, D. (eds.) Proceedings of the HEA STEM (Computing) Learning Technologies 2014 Workshop, University of Hull (2014). https://www.researchgate.net/publication/263213733_Proceedings_of_the_HEA_STEM_%28Computing%29_Learning_Technologies_2014_Workshop

23. Michael, D.R., Chen, S.L.: Serious Games: Games that Educate, Train, and Inform. Muska & Lipman/Premier-Trade, New York (2005)

24. Egenfeldt-Nielsen, S.: Beyond edutainment: Exploring the educational potential of computer games. Lulu.com (2005)

25. Gordon, N., Brayshaw, M., Grey, S.: Maximising gain for minimal pain: utilising natural game mechanics. Innovation Teach. Learn. Inf. Comput. Sci. **12**(1), 27–38 (2013)

26. Taylor, J.: Towards a task model for mobile learning: a dialectical approach. Int. J. Learn. Technol. **2**(2), 138–158 (2006)

27. Aljaber, T., Gordon, N., Kambhampati, C., Brayshaw, M.: An evaluation framework for mobile health education software. In: Proceedings of the 2015 Science and Information Conference (2015)

28. Holzinger, A., Nischelwitzer, A., Meisenberger, M.: Lifelong-learning support by M-instruction example scenarios. eLearn **11**, 2 (2005)

29. Korn, M., Bødker, S.: Looking ahead: how field trials can work in iterative and exploratory design of ubicomp systems. In: Proceedings of the 2012 ACM Conference on Ubiquitous Computing. ACM (2012)

30. Silva, J.L., Campos, J., Harrison, M.: Formal analysis of ubiquitous computing environments through the APEX framework. In: Proceedings of the 4th ACM SIGCHI Symposium on Engineering Interactive Computing Systems. ACM (2012)

Evaluation of the New Outdoor Study Scheme Using Mobile Phone Based on the Zeigarnik Effect

Yuko Hiramatsu[1(✉)], Kumiko Kanbayashi[2], Atsushi Ito[3], and Fumihiro Sato[1]

[1] Chuo University, 742-1 Higashinakano, Hachioji, Tokyo 192-0393, Japan
{susana_y, fsato}@tamacc.chuo-u.ac.jp
[2] Kyowa Exeo Corporation, 3-29-20 Shibuya, Shibuya, Tokyo 150-0002, Japan
k.narita@isd.exeo.co.jp
[3] Utsunomiya University, 7-1-2 Yoyo, Utsunomiya, Tochigi 321-8505, Japan
at.ito@is.utsunomiya-u.ac.jp

Abstract. Many devices using ICT seem to bring students much information. They look up a lot of information and feel as if they already know the places or things using their PC. However, it is not all of the objects or is much for students to select high quality ones. Some cannot find interesting points among too much information. On the other hands, human beings take an interest in uncompleted or interrupted tasks. Using this human disposition, we create new application for outdoor studying in order to make some remarkable points using the Zeigarnik Effect. A little lack of information becomes a trigger to their interesting study. According to the effective results of our trials, we put it to practical use. In addition, we verified the safety mobile phone's usage during walking by EEG measurement for practical application.

Keywords: Outdoor study · Application · Mobile phone · Zeigarnik effect · BLE beacon · EEG measurement

1 Introduction

Many devices provide information through information and communications technology (ICT). Using Internet, ordinary life style expands into sightseeing areas by some navigation, SNS etc. Such information makes tourists safety. However, Some attractive points of the travel are beyond the ordinary life. Visiting unknowing place or finding new things makes us pulsate. It is a new experience. Therefore ICT always does not make trips attractive to people.

In addition, information on traditional themes information is not so enough. There is a huge numbers of information. However, many of them are written by new tourists who don't know the place well.

In Japanese schools, history and nature learning is supplemented by several day trips, which provide a more positive learning experience than the classroom. For this purpose, 87.3 % of junior high schools allow students to walk around the area by themselves in small groups [1]. Prior to the trip, students study the visited area in the

© Springer International Publishing Switzerland 2016
P. Zaphiris and A. Ioannou (Eds.): LCT 2016, LNCS 9753, pp. 320–331, 2016.
DOI: 10.1007/978-3-319-39483-1_30

classroom using books and the Internet. However, they find more information than what can be processed and remembered, and often fail to extract the important information. As a result, their interest may be diminished when visiting the area.

To overcome this problem, we have developed a new learning model for outdoor studies based on the Zeigarnik effect [2], i.e., the positive effect of incomplete or interrupted tasks on human interest. This paper examines our learning model for outdoor study, our original application system, and the practical evaluation of the system in outdoor trials.

To gratify teachers and parents, who are responsible for students' safety, we must also verify the safety functionality of the device. The learning tools are selected by teachers and purchased by parents. Therefore, the device must not only satisfy the students but also include safety functions that reassure teachers and parents.

We focus on two applications of our model. One is a Bluetooth low energy (BLE) Beacon system in Nikko, the world heritage site in Japan. And the other is an application using GPS. Both applications exploit the Zeigarnik effect. Section 2 of this paper presents some essential background, and Sect. 3 discusses related works. Sections 4 and 5 present our original system and the results of three trials, respectively. The third trial evaluates the safety of using a mobile phone while walking, and is accompanied by electroencephalography (ECG) measurements. In the concluding section, we discuss the effectiveness of our scheme as an outdoor learning tool and further issues of mobile studying.

2 Background

2.1 Mobile Phone Usage by Children in Japan

Japan's Ministry of Internal Affairs and Communications has stated the importance of incorporating ICT into the learning environment. When used effectively, the distinctive features of ICT are expected to foster the required abilities of children living in the 21st century, a period of drastic changes [3]. Governmental guidelines were enacted and digital contents and instruments are now being integrated into school curricula.

On the other hand, to halt the rising incidence of mobile phone crimes, the Ministry of National Education stipulated in 2009 that children should not bring mobile phones to school [4]. This rule remains valid in 2015. There are over 1 million mobile phone subscribers in Japan. According to the Internal Affairs Ministry of Research (2015), 94.5 % of Japanese households have mobile phones and 67.4 % of households have smartphones. Smartphones are especially popular among the younger demographic. 94.1 % persons from 20 to 29 years old have smartphones and 68.6 % persons from 10 to 19 years old have their own smartphones [5].

As an ICT instrument, the mobile phone is considered to be of dubious value [6]. Whereas the use of digital textbooks and tablets is encouraged, the use of smartphones is disfavored for several reasons. Therefore, despite being the most familiar ICT instrument, smartphones are not being used for learning in schools.

However, students sometimes contact their teachers through mobile phones during outdoor study. Before visiting the area, students learn the history, art, architecture and special features of the area in the classroom. Students conduct Internet searches on the area through their personal computers, and record the important points in their note-books. They might create a leaflet for the school trip. When visiting the area, they are provided with a map and the leaflet, but they seldom consult this documentation. Students bring their mobile phones for emergency contacts.

After the large 2011 earthquake at Fukushima, Japan, many parents hoped that their children's schools would allow mobile phones with GPS during the school trip. Telephone numbers, e-mail addresses and location technologies on mobile phones provide essential information in disasters. However, such specialized use means that mobile phones are merely safety boxes while students are in school. We propose that mobile phones not only ensure students' safety, but could also enhance their formal learning.

3 Related Works

In 2009 the Ministry of Education, Culture, Sports, Science and Technology (MEXT) issued a notification forbidding school children to take mobile phones to elementary schools in Japan.

In a randomized study called Project ABC, Aker and co-authors investigated the effectiveness of mobile phone learning in Niger, Africa [7]. Besides the experimental results, they discussed the price and mobility of mobile phone learning. The results suggested that mobile phones can serve as an effective and sustainable learning tool. However, the study subjects were adult students rather than children.

Many schools have adopted tablets as a learning tool. For example, all secondary school students in Saga Prefecture (Japan) are required to use tablets. Some elementary schools in Takeo (a city of Saga Prefecture) have also introduced tablet learning [8].

We suggested that 21 skills can be acquired by mobile phones, the most popular instruments [9]. Mobile phone learning can be especially effective in outdoor study [10]. The present paper is a continuation of this study.

Evidence of the Zeigarnik effect was reported by Schiffman and Greist-Bousquet in 1992 [11]. The subject has also been studied from an environmental psychology and tourism perspective. Pearce and Stringer [12] investigated the Zeigarnik effect in physiology, cognition and individual variation. Similar studies were conducted by Fridgen [13], van Raaij [14], and Sasaki [15]. Sasaki proposed that a trip can be divided into 3 scenes: before the trip, during the trip, and after the trip [15]. Our new system focuses on the experiences before and during the trip.

4 Our Research and Original System for Outdoor Studying in the School Trip

4.1 Our Research About ICT Instruments at Junior High School and High School in Tokyo Area

We questioned teachers on the use of ICT instruments in junior and senior high schools in the Tokyo area, Japan. From 10th to 18th February, 2015, we disseminated questionnaires to 300 schools and received responses from 85 teachers (response percentage

28.33 %) and valid responses are 83. According to the results of these questionnaires, we found some characteristic points.

(1) During ordinary lessons

Teachers considered that ICT instruments should be used in classroom lessons. However, 42.17 % of the respondents felt uneasy about using ICT instruments in their own classes. PCs and projectors are the main learning tools at present, but many teachers would adopt digital texts and tablets for classroom learning. Despite the governmental guidelines, tablets were used by only 20.48 % of respondents. Some of the teachers, while understanding that ICT instruments will become mandatory learning tools in the near future, reported on the poor quality of ICT contents. Some teachers regarded paper and pencils as the best current learning implements, and did not feel competent in making ICT contents. Mobile phones are prohibited in public junior high schools, but are permitted in some private schools outside of class hours (for family contact purposes only).

(2) During outdoor study (school trips)

Neither teachers nor students do not use tablets at all on school trips. However, 59.04 % of the schools permit students to bring their mobile phones (future phones or smart phones) on the school trips, in order to contact to teachers when they walk around the area with 4–6 persons.

4.2 Our Original System for Outdoor Studying on the School Trips

Our aim is to develop an active learning system for students. ICT instruments inclosing smartphone are important tools to live in the 21th century. Students must appreciate the strengths and weaknesses of smartphone use.

According to our questionnaire results (Sect. 4.1), the majority of students take mobile phones on their school trips. Therefore, we considered that our mobile phone-based system would be widely accepted during school trips. Our system is described below and summarized in Fig. 1.

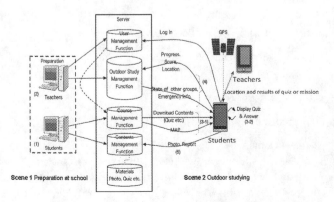

Fig. 1. Overview of our outdoor study system

There are 2 main scenes: before the trip and on the trip. Students prepare for their outdoor studies as an incomplete experience. Before the trip, they learn the history and specific arts in the area and prepare quizzes for their classmates on their PCs. The prepared quizzes are unknown to the other students. In other cases, teachers prepare missions for the students and inform them that the tasks will be completed at the visited site. Such incomplete experiences rouse human interest in the topic. One version of the Zeigarnik effect maintains that completed tasks are less well recalled than uncompleted tasks. Whereas some engineers have created detailed navigation systems for trips, we deliberately exploit the Zeigarnik effect to create incomplete experiences for students. During the trip, students undertake tasks using their smartphone or tablet. In addition, teachers can easily locate the students. The sense of safety of teachers is an important aspect of the system in practical use.

We created this system (Fig. 1). Then Kyowa Exeo Inc. attempted to create such system in practical stage. We collaborated this company and continued researches. In addition, we made a quiz course in the application of SCOPE (Strategic Information and Communications R&D Promotion Programme) project [16] in Nikko.

5   Trials Using the System

5.1   The Trial at a High School in Hawaii

(1) Summary of the trial

We had a trial with tablets at a high school class using new application by Kyowa Exeo Inc. In this application, the moving information of the present position can is captured by GPS accessible via the Internet. Students (n = 29) ordinary used tablets in their class and were issued with questionnaires before and after using the system. The functions of the application were map, mission, quiz, photo, video and chat.

- Before the school trip (November 2014)

Students learned about Hawaii and input their walking root by each group. In addition they tried to walk around the school using the application. Finally, they answered the first questionnaire.

- During the trip to Hawaii (December 2014)

Completing the missions specified in the application, students walked for half a day in Hawaii.

- After the trip (December 2014)

Students answered the second questionnaire.

(2) Results of questionnaires

The questionnaire results were evaluated on four-level scales. The missions and quizzes yielded very interesting results. Students favorably anticipated the mission and quizzes before the trip (3.1). After the trip, their evaluations were lower than before (2.9), but many of the students recorded their interest in the mission and quizzes in their free comments. The contents of the missions and quizzes in the Hawaii trip may not have fully engaged the students, although the functions were interesting and they would like to write comments freely. These results suggest that we should reconsider the contents of the mission and quizzes.

Students rated Map high in Hawaii, too. Map with direction made students at ease in the first visiting place. Comparing before and after the trip, they enjoyed the application more in Hawaii. However, group cooperation was lower during the trip (see Fig. 2).

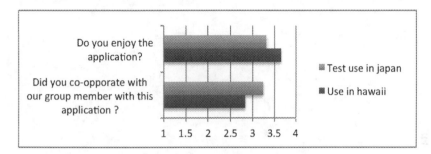

Fig. 2. Example of evaluations before and after the Hawaii trip

After the school trip, 26 students (90 %) assessed the application as useful. Although 16 students did not anticipate special use of the application before the trip, 28 students (96 %) answered that they would use this application again after the trip, and 28 students would highly recommend its use to juniors. However, some students and one teacher reported that the tablet was overly large and heavy.

5.2   A Trial in Nikko, the World Heritage Site in Japan

We implemented another trial in Nikko, a world heritage site in Japan. Setting BLE beacons on the poles by the roadside, we constructed course quizzes and applied them on iPhones on September 26–27, 2015. An application screen and a BLE beacon on a roadside pole are presented in Figs. 3 and 4, respectively. This system is designed not only for Japanese students but also for foreigners with limited access to Wi–Fi. The application can be installed at Wi–Fi-providing hotels and cafés, enabling its use without the Internet (see Fig. 5).

Twenty-eight students participated in the trial. Twenty-three students were required to complete 10 quizzes on the road, whereas 5 students walked without the application for comparison. Before looking at some important objects, students were provided with quizzes on the nearby locality, which they answered by viewing objects at the sites. Memory is thought to be largely visual [17]. Therefore, besides answering the questionnaires, students were requested to draw a map and to check some points on the map.

After the walking exercise, students answered the questionnaires and drew their maps of the area [18]. The answers of the application users were more concrete than those of the 5 students not provided with the application. On average, the application

Fig. 3. Beacon on a pole

Fig. 4. Map and quiz screen of the application

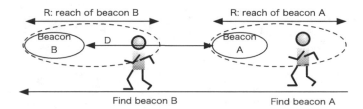

Fig. 5. Distance between beacons

users placed 9.18 objects on the map from the station to the shrine, whereas the non-application participants placed an average of 5.80 objects. The application users tended to remember not only the answers to the quizzes but also the shops around the beacons where they answered the quizzes.

After one month, the same students answered another questionnaires and checked 3 points in each photograph of the area walked in Nikko. We then constructed heat maps from the students' checks.

Figure 6 is a heat map of the way to the main shrine in Nikko. Architectures on the road were scarcely recalled by the students. Students recognized the street as the way to the main shrine and examined the local signs. A small BLE beacon, on which no letters were visible in the photograph, was remembered by the students. For comparison with

Fig. 6. A heat map on the way to the main shrine (by application users)

users viewing the same photographs without having visited the area, we also recruited unrelated third parties (n = 19). The heat map of the unrelated subjects exhibited no warm areas on the way to the main shrine.

As shown in Fig. 7, students noticed the architectures in the shrine, especially the upper right section, which was quizzed in the application.

Fig. 7. A heat map in the shrine (by application users)

The same photo is used as Figs. 7 and 8. Figure 8 is a heat map of unrelated third parties. Comparing Fig. 7 with Fig. 8, we can conform that the application users remembered the quiz point. The unrelated students focused main structure as same as application users. However, they seldom paid attention to right one. The application users paid special attention to the section on which they were quizzed.

Fig. 8. A heat map in the shrine (by unrelated students)

According to the results, we confirmed that our quizzes' application using Zeigarnik effects is effective for memory. Students remembered BLE beacon and the object at the quizzes. The results confirmed that the use of the quizzes exploiting the Zeigarnik effect improves recall.

In addition, the evaluation of the questionnaires showed us important points. Students evaluated the quiz when traditional object in front of them linked to their daily life. Students who evaluated quiz contents kept higher score than students who evaluated interface of the application after 2 months. It is assumed as the Zeigarnik effect.

5.3   For the Practical Use -Safety-

(1) For safety in the case of disaster

Although learning is the most important purpose of the proposed application, its introduction to schools requires further consideration. In most cases, the purchasers are the parents, not the students. Therefore, the use of mobile phones on students' school trips is financed by parents and decided by teachers. The merits of mobile phone usage must be considered from the viewpoints of students, teachers and parents. The basic requirement of school trips is safety (Table 1).

Table 1. Targets and required functions

Target	Important Factor	Function
Perents	Safety asistance	Shelter information
Students	Study, Fun	Quiz, Mission, Map, Photo, Chat
Teachers	Location of students, Communication	GPS, Telephone, SMS

According to our research (4.1), tablets are not currently employed in school trips. Teachers need to know the locations of small groups of students separately walking around the visited area. The system must accommodate these demands. The system developed by Kyowa Exeo [19] has a new function that directs students to the nearest shelter when disaster strikes. This functionality has been recommended by parents and teachers. (See Fig. 9.) Students use the right side of the mobile as a chat space. The emergency announcements are indicated the space in the time of disaster.

(2) Safety evaluation of walking with a mobile phone by EEG measurement

Walking with a mobile phone may be dangerous. In addition, students and one of the teachers reported that tablets were large and heavy in the Hawaii trial. To assess the practical use of mobile phone learning, we experimentally tested the safety of mobile phone use using a simple EEG measuring instrument (head set type). We tested two differently sized tablets; an iPad mini (200 mm × 134.7 mm) and an iPad2 (240 mm × 167.5 mm). The subjects (2 male, 2 female, aged in their 20's) walked around an area in Tokyo for approximately 3 h, while using the application installed on the tablets. The experiment was conducted on March 12, 2015.

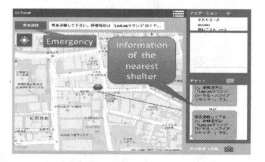

Fig. 9. The screen of emergency

Figure 10 presents the brain waves of one subject (male). When he arrived at the point, he was relaxed and carried out the mission with attention. There were sudden changes several times. When he walked across the road, walked in the crowded street, found the favorite things and arrived at the destination. Another 3 persons showed same tendency. However, the brain waves of 2 women were often lacked (missing value). The points of high attention and sudden changes indicate awareness of potential danger.

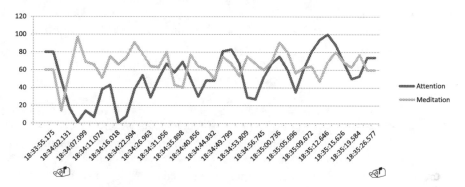

Fig. 10. A part of brain waves patterns of one subject

After the walking exercise, the subjects were presented with questionnaires. The questionnaire evaluations are summarized in Fig. 11. The usefulness and interest of the application were highly rated, but the safety was ranked lower than the other factors, especially on the iPad 2 (average rating 2.75 out of 5). Subjects judged that the iPad 2

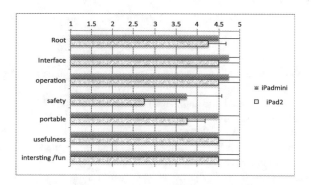

Fig. 11. Evaluation results of the 20th user trial (5-point Likert scale)

was too large for the exercise and compromised their safety.

According to the result, we have to consider about safety walking with mobile phone. To improve the safety of mobile phone learning applications, we could equip an accelerometer that notifies students of potential danger when walking with the mobile phone.

6   Conclusions

In several trials, we demonstrated the effectiveness of our outdoor study scheme based on ICT. Although ICT provides numerous information, much of that information is superfluous or uninspiring. We need to trigger students' interest in their studying. When students were required to seek unknown information, they became actively engaged with the target objects. Students using the application looked around the area, noted the architectures, and identified site-specific arts more positively than students not using the application. We hope to design opportunities for students to learn about and appreciate objects.

To realize such services, the functions and targets of the application must satisfy not only students but also their teachers, whose requirements may differ from those of students.

Our outdoor study scheme was highly rated in the trials, but several issues have yet to be resolved. For safety purposes, students could be equipped with an accelerometer that notifies them or switches off the screen in potentially dangerous situations. The small screen of the mobile phone narrows the viewing angle of users. We will also research the quality of the missions and quizzes installed in the device, and consider the suitability of ultra-modern functionalities, such as augmented reality (AR), for outdoor study.

Mobile internet use is increasing annually around the world. We intend to introduce Japanese culture to students in other countries, too. Mobile phone is suitable device to connect their classroom and real outdoor study.

Acknowledgments. This research was performed as a cooperative research with Kyowa Exeo and as a SCOPE (Strategic Information and Communications R&D Promotion Programme) project funded by the Ministry of Internal Affairs and Communications.

References

1. The Travel News, 30 July 2010. http://www.travelnews.co.jp/news/kankou/1007301042.html
2. Zeigarnik, B.V.: On finished and unfinished tasks. In: Ellis, W.D. (ed.) A Sourcebook of Gestalt Psychology. Humanities Press, New York (1967)
3. Ministry of Internal Affairs and Communications, "Future School Promotion Research Society" to be opened (2011). http://www.soumu.go.jp/main_sosiki/joho_tsusin/eng/Releases/Telecommunications/110720_a.html
4. Ministry of Education, Culture, Sports, Science and Technology HP (2009). http://www.mext.go.jp/b_menu/hakusho/nc/1234695.htm
5. Ministry of Internal Affairs and Communications: 2015 WHITE PAPER Information and Communications in Japan (Outline) (2015). http://www.soumu.go.jp/main_content/000380937.pdf
6. Ito, A., Hiramatsu, Y., Shimada, F., Sato, F.: Designing education process in an elementary school for mobile phone literacy. J. Green Eng. **3**, 307–324 (2013). River Publishers

7. Aker, J., Ksoll, C., Lybbert, T.J.: ABC, 123: The Impact of a Mobile Phone Literacy Program on Educational Outcomes - Working Paper (2010). http://www.cgdev.org/publication/abc-123-impact-mobile-phone-literacy-program-educational-outcomes-working-paper-223

8. Report of Education in Takeo City Using ICT, June 2015 (2015). https://www.city.takeo.lg.jp/kyouiku/docs/20150609kyouiku01.pdf

9. Hiramatsu, Y., Ito, A., Inagaki, K., Shimada, F., Sato, F.: A study to activate communication by using SNS on mobile phone: an essay lesson at the elementary school. In: HCII 2015, Los Angeles (2015)

10. Hiramatsu, Y., Ito, A., Fuii, M., Sato, F.: Development of the learning system for outdoor study using Zeigarnik effect. In: HCII 2014, Greece (2014)

11. Schiffman, N., Greist-Bousquet, S.: The effect of task interruption and closure on perceived duration. Bull. Psychon. Soc. 30(1), 9–11 (1992)

12. Pearce, P.L., Stringer, P.F.: Psychology and tourism. Ann. Tourism Res. 18, 136–154 (1991)

13. Fridgen, J.D.: Environmental psychology and tourism. Ann. Tourism Res. 11(1), 19–39 (1984)

14. Van Raaij, W.E.: Consumer research on tourism: mental and behavioral constructs. Ann. Tourism Res. 13, 1–9 (1986)

15. Sasaki, T: Kankoo-Ryoko no Sinrigaku, p. 38. Kitaoji Shobo (2007)

16. The Ministry of Internal Affairs and Communications, Strategic Information and Communications R&D Promotion Programme, 22 August 2015. http://www.soumu.go.jp/main_sosiki/joho_tsusin/scope/

17. Haber, R.N., Standing, L.G.: Direct measures of short-term visual storage. Q. J. Exp. Phycol. 21, 43–54 (1969)

18. Thorndyke, P.W., Hayes-Roth, B.: Individual differences in spatial knowledge acquired from maps and navigation. Cogn. Phycol. 14, 560–589 (1982)

19. Emergency Evacuation Information System, the Patent Number 2016-8851 (P2016-8851A)

An Analysis of Social Collaboration and Networking Tools in eLearning

Ali Shariq Imran[1(✉)], Krenare Pireva[2], Fisnik Dalipi[1], and Zenun Kastrati[1]

[1] Faculty of Computer Science and Media Technology,
Norwegian University of Science and Technology (NTNU), Gjøvik, Norway
{ali.imran,fisnik.dalipi,zenun.kastrati}@ntnu.no
[2] Faculty of Computer Science, University of Sheffield, Sheffield, UK
kpireva1@sheffield.ac.uk

Abstract. Many online learning websites and learning management systems (LMS) provide social collaboration and networking tools to aid learning and to interact with peers for knowledge sharing. The benefit of collaborating with each other is certainly undeniable, such tools, however, can be a distraction from the actual tasks for learners. The paper presents a study on social media tools supported by various eLearning systems to understand the impact on students learning activities. A survey questionnaire is designed for this purpose. The data is collected from students who have had experience using different massive open online course (MOOC) eLearning platforms and LMS from various universities. The results of the survey indicate that more than 95 % of the participants use at least one of the social tools in their daily life activities, and almost 84 % of them have used these tools in connection with the eLearning systems. It is also interesting to note that 92 % of the participants intend to use social tools for study purposes. The results indicate that there is a need to integrate more of these social media tools into eLearning systems.

Keywords: Social media · Networking tools · Collaborative tools · eLearning

1 Introduction

The emergence of web 2.0 in 2004 lead to the development of interactive social media tools that allows users to indulge in a social discussion. These tools aid pedagogy by utilizing social media on the web and facilitate the learning process further through interaction among users, making education more convenient and widespread. The social media tools including collaboration tools and networking tools help learners and instructors indulge in a formal and informal way of knowledge acquisition. These tools recently have become an integral part of today's educational system, including learning management systems (LMS), such as Moodle, Blackboard, Atutor, Fronter, and massive open online course (MOOC) eLearning platforms such as Coursera, edX, Udacity, Khan Academy.

© Springer International Publishing Switzerland 2016
P. Zaphiris and A. Ioannou (Eds.): LCT 2016, LNCS 9753, pp. 332–343, 2016.
DOI: 10.1007/978-3-319-39483-1_31

The social tools not only provide an easy way of communication between users to collaborate on various tasks, but they also are a good way to share knowledge by promoting distance and blended education.

Social media is a broader term that can be defined as a collection of communication, networking, sharing, and collaboration tools on the web 2.0 [1]. As shown in Fig. 1, social media encompasses social networking platforms such as Facebook and Google+; collaboration tools such as blogs and wikis; and communication tools such as discussion forums and chats - among others. Social media, therefore, provides an umbrella of services, from posting ideas on the web to collaborative group tasks. In this paper, we categorize social media into two categories: (i) social collaboration tools; i.e. those tools which provide some collaboration work among peers such as discussion forums, wikis, blogs, virtual classroom, and (ii) social networking tools; i.e. those tools which provide networking capabilities including file sharing such as chats, Facebook, Twitter, SMS feature. In the rest of the paper, we collectively refer social collaboration tools and social networking tools as 'social media'.

With the advancement of web 2.0 technology, particularly of social media, many eLearning systems are competing to offer social tools and other collaboration and networking services keeping in view today's educational needs. With this growing trend, the use of open-source educational platforms (such as Moodle),

Fig. 1. Social Media and its components

freely available educational resources (such as Wikipedia, Youtube videos), online collaboration utilities (such as Google apps), and the use of a variety of social tools especially those that are offering personalized services through recommender systems [2] and other artificial intelligence techniques [3], are becoming very popular. These personalized features are being integrated into eLearning systems to facilitate the learning process by promoting collaboration among peers and interaction between learners and teachers while performing all in one service.

The social media, despite the socialization, are extensively used for collaboration work on different education topics in addition to commenting, sharing, liking, discussing and interacting with each other. Table 1 shows a list of social tools provided as part of various LMS and MOOC platforms.

Table 1. Support for social tools provided by various LMS and MOOC

Social collaboration and networking tools	eLearning Systems							
	LMS				MOOC			
	Moodle	Blackboard	Atutor	Fronter	Coursera	edX	Udacity	Khan Academy
Discussion Forum	✓	✓	✓	✓	✓	✓	✓	✓
Wiki	✓	✓	✓	✓	✓	✓	✓	✓
Blog	✓	✓	✓	✓	✓	✓	✓	✓
Chat	✓	✓	✓	✓	✓	✓	✓	✓
Quiz	✓	✓	✓	✓	✓	✓	✓	✓
Virtual classroom	✓	✓	X	✓	X	✓	X	✓
Twitterfeed	✓	✓	X	X	X	X	X	X
SMS feature	✓	✓	✓	✓	X	X	X	X
Facebook integration	✓	✓	✓	X	X	X	X	X
Peer assessment	✓	✓	X	✓	X	✓	X	✓

Social tools such as discussion forums, wikis, blogs, and chats are used widely by almost all the eLearning systems. Most LMS have also seamlessly integrated fully featured social networking tools such as Facebook for collaborative learning while the MOOC platforms mostly rely on the discussion forums.

In this paper, we focus our attention on identifying and evaluating such educational systems which use social media tools to aid collaboration, knowledge sharing and group activities. This, in turn, helps us determine the impact of these social tools in today's eLearning systems, and to understand better whether these tools are helping students learn better or are just diverting them from their principal objective.

The rest of the paper is structured as follows. In Sect. 2 we present literature review. Section 3 gives an overview of the survey followed by analysis and results discussion in Sect. 4. The last section presents conclusion and some insight into future directions.

2   Literature Review

Social media has been investigated as a promotional tool for higher education, as the print and broadcasting media is fading out [4], and more and more universities are adopting social media tools to reach out to a bigger number of audience. Could this mean that the social collaboration and networking tools provided by social media are going to play a significant role in education in years to come? Also, what impact they are going to have on the learners' activities? This section explores some of the recent research works concerning social media and use of social collaboration and networking tools in education to find out the answers.

Most social media are developed for promoting socialization through collaboration, social interaction, content sharing and discussion. An extra push for enhancing the use of social media in education was a result of the advances in mobile data usage, the high penetration of internet [5], and the high percentage possession of smartphones [6]. The portability of smart devices has increased the use of social media in everyday life, giving users the opportunity not only to access the educational content from anywhere and anytime but also to interact and collaborate on the educational tasks via social interaction tools through different eLearning systems. The benefit of using social media for communication and collaboration has influenced the idea of integrating the social tools in education, by pushing the class discussion further, through social platforms, such as Facebook, LinkedIN, GoogleApps, YouTube, and Twitter among others.

Some work has been reported in recent years about social platforms and eLearning, and how the first component is affecting the learning process [7–10]. For instance Hitrec et al. conducted a survey and analyzed how the use of social software (such as wikis, blogs, VoIP, social bookmarks) in combination with social networks have modernized the way of learning, and how their usage determined the group approach toward the accomplishment of their goals [7]. Tulaboev and Oxley presented a study to explore the factors that affect the acceptability and effectiveness of using web 2.0 social networking tools as an aid to learning [11]. In a similar study by Kaeomanee et al., investigation of the use of social software for knowledge sharing among students in Malaysia is carried out [12]. Roreger in [9] emphasized the importance of integrating learning content management with online social platforms, and how this can impact education in the longer run. Klimova et al. discussed the potential contribution of social networks to learning. Eight people took the survey via a focused interview for their study on five social networks. The results emphasized that Facebook is a preferable social network choice by participants among other tools, and mainly students with ICT background uses the social networks for education purposes [13]. Whereas [9], concluded that even learners with a strong background in ICT are not utilizing the opportunities offered by social platforms such as better collaboration and interaction services, which brings an added value to eLearning systems. However, in paper [14] authors have raised another issue, they thought that social networks and the collaboration through them have grabbed learners concentration and attention by diverting them toward non-educational activities, and concluded that this could affect the education in a bad sense.

There is no denying that these social media tools are going to play a significant role in the teaching in years to come - be it the distance and blended education or face-to-face. This is evident from the fact that more and more universities are incorporating social media tools into their educational activities, as the popularity of social networks combined with social tools is increasing with the advancement of web 2.0. Seeing this growing trend, in this paper, we try to figure out how often student across different universities uses these social tools for education purposes and how satisfied are they with these tools. This study will help us better understand how important it is to integrate a diversity of social tools within eLearning systems, and what impact they could have on the learning activities. For this purpose, we conducted a survey asking participants about their experience of using social media tools for educational activities. The next section highlights the survey.

3   Methodology

An online survey was conducted for this study. Students from 13 different institutes in 12 countries participated in the survey. A country-wise distribution of participants is shown in the Fig. 2. The survey consists of 20 questions, out of which first five questions focused on the personal and background information of the participants while the rest focused on the use of social media tools. The survey questionnaire is designed in a way to identify the extent of social tools involvement in personal life, as well as in educational activities. The following are some of the questions asked in the questionnaire:

1. Are you familiar with social networking tools? Yes/No.
2. Are you using any social tools supported by the eLearning systems in the learning process? (If Yes, answer following questions)/No (go to question 3)
   2.1. Which one is your preferred communication tool?

2.2. What are the main purposes of using it?

2.3. How long have you been using it?

2.4. How useful do you find it?

2.5. Do you counter any problems or difficulties using it?

2.6. Will you invite your friends/colleagues to use one of these communication tools?

3. Do you intend to use them?

4. To what extent do you think that social collaborative tools could contribute to learning process within an eLearning platform?

5. What are the barriers to using these tools?

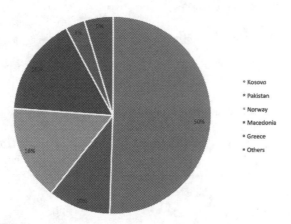

Fig. 2. Country wise distribution of participants

4   Analysis and Results

This section presents the survey results and their analysis. The survey data is collected from 218 students in total out of which 198 are enrolled in bachelor's program, 17 are in masters, and 3 are doing Ph.D. There were 163 male and 55 female participants with an average age of 24. As many as 183 students are from computer science domain, 19 from engineering while the rest of them are from social sciences group.

The social networking tools are currently very much popular and in use by almost everybody. Students use these tools quite frequently on a regular basis as shown in Fig. 3.

This reflection is in line with the findings of our questionnaire which shows that more than 95 % (207) of the respondents are familiar with the social networking tools as shown in question 8 of Fig. 4. Apart from Facebook, the preferred social networking tools of users are those which are supported by the

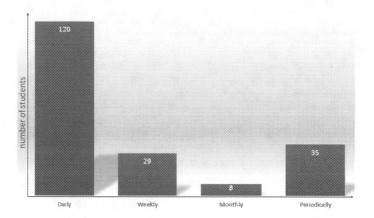

Fig. 3. How often users use the social tools

MOOC eLearning platforms such as discussion forums and blogs while tools backed by other systems including most LMS such as virtual classroom, built-in chat, SMS are not that popular. This finding is reflected in Fig. 5 and is also evident from the answers to question 9 and question 12 in Fig. 4, where around 84 % of users use the tools supported by MOOC eLearnig platforms while only 53 % of them use the tools supported by LMS or other platforms.

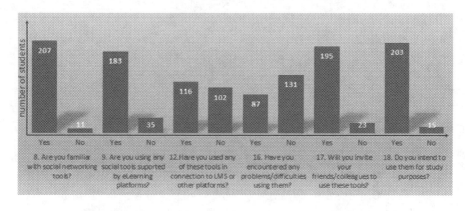

Fig. 4. Students feedback on the usage of social tools

Even though these tools are widely used by students in their daily activity, however, some of the students find difficulties using these tools for learning. The difficulties students usually faces include keeping up pace with group discussions and ongoing activities, keeping track of tasks on multiple forums, lack of fully integrated social tools, and distractions caused by some tools. In connection with this, around 39 % (87) of the respondents claim that they have encountered such difficulties using the social networking tools.

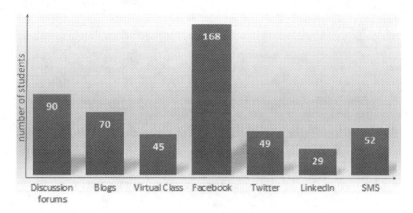

Fig. 5. Preferred communication tools

Despite encountering difficulties, many students favored these tools for eLearning activities and would love to use them for study purposes, as can be seen in question 17 and question 18 of Fig. 4. They believe that using social networking and collaborative tools will help them to further enhance learning, as also claimed in a study performed by [15]. Additionally, the 195 'yes' answers out of 218 that responded to the question of whether they will invite friends/colleagues to using these tools enforce further the idea of integrating the social tools in the educational system.

Facebook without any doubt stood out as the excellent communication, networking and socializing tool for education purposes, as it allows students to create close and open groups with similar interests, freely share documents, discuss ideas and be in touch with each other all the time. The students realized that they can easily use and adapt to the social media tools for learning since they communicate, search for information and socialize in everyday life through the same platforms [6]. Figure 5 shows this trend, where 168 of total participants said that they prefer Facebook as an extra social collaborative tool within eLearning platforms, followed by the traditional discussion forum and blog.

Not surprisingly many students use social tools to study these days, and it is encouraging to see that the trend in the use of social media has shifted towards education. This is most likely because many educational activities make use of social media and social tools in one form or the other. As is shown in Fig. 6, almost more than $2/3^{rd}$ of the participants today use social tools to study in their universities.

On a scale of 1 to 5, where 1 being extremely dissatisfied and 5 being extremely satisfied, 42 of the total participants were extremely satisfied. 90 were very satisfied while around 65 of them were neutral and only a bunch of the total participants were not satisfied at all with these tools for studying, as shown in Fig. 7. Almost same number of participants found these tools useful as well.

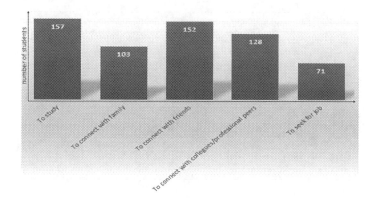

Fig. 6. The main purpose of using social tools

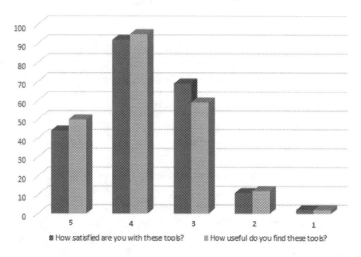

Fig. 7. The satisfaction and usefulness of social tools

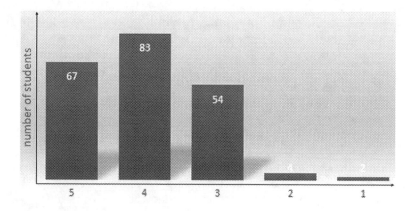

Fig. 8. The contribution of social tools in learning process

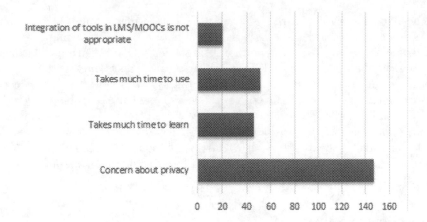

Fig. 9. The barriers faced using social tools

The results are more or less the same on the question of 'contribution of social tools in learning process' as can be seen in Fig. 8. As many as 150 participants think that the social collaborative tools could contribute to learning process within an eLearning platform while 54 took a neutral stance and only 6 disagree. The graph uses a scale of 1 to 5, where 1 being no contribution at all and 5 being the highest contribution.

Using and being familiarized with new social tools usually have prejudices of different nature. Most of the students opted for 'concerned about the privacy issue' from four given options when they were asked about the barriers they face in the use of social tools for education, as shown in Fig. 9.

5   Conclusions

This paper sheds some light on the use of social collaboration and networking tools provided as an integral component of today's eLearning systems and the impact of such tools for the learning activities. For this study, students of various institutes were asked a series of questions to share their experience of working with different eLearning systems, and whether they have used any of the social tools in connection with educational activities. The study indicates that almost 84 % (157 of 218) of the participants have used at least one of the social media tools in connection with learning. Since these tools have become an essential part of today's lifestyle and students are familiar with them, so most of the participants recommended to make use of them for educational activities.

Almost 60 % of the participants were satisfied and extremely satisfied with the usage of social media tools in eLearning while nearly $1/3^{rd}$ of the participants were neutral, and only 10 % disagree. More than half of the participants also agree that social media tools could contribute effectively to learning process within eLearning systems, although many of them showed concern about their privacy when using these tools in connection with educational activities.

Facebook as evident is the preferred choice for many followed by discussion forums and blogs. Facebook is mostly supported by LMS while discussion forums and blogs are features commonly found in MOOC eLarning platforms. Incorporating more of these tools in today's educational systems is going to help students collaborate on various educational tasks better, however, how effective these tools can be for study purpose is a question that needs to be answered.

By examining the impact and evaluating the advantages and disadvantages of such social media tools in educational activities, better 'personalized services' can be provided to learners. Such as, artificial intelligence based pedagogical chat bots that can mimic the responses of a live instructor for one to one communication with learners.

References

1. Kaplan, A.M., Haenlein, M.: Users of the world, unite! the challenges and opportunities of social media. Bus. Horiz. **53**(1), 59–68 (2010)
2. Lu, J.: Personalized e-learning material recommender system. In: International Conference on Information Technology for Application, pp. 374–379 (2004)
3. Pireva, K., Kefalas, P.: The use of multi agent systems in cloud e-learning. In: Doctoral Student Conference on ICT, pp. 324–336 (2015)
4. Almadhoun, N.M., Dominic, P., Woon, L.F.: Social media as a promotional tool in higher education in Malaysia. In: National Postgraduate Conference (NPC 2011), pp. 1–7. IEEE (2011)
5. Redecker, C., Ala-Mutka, K., Punie, Y.: Learning 2.0-the impact of social media on learning in Europe. Policy brief. JRC Scientific and Technical report. EUR JRC56958 EN (2010). http://bit.ly/cljlpq. Accessed 6 Feb 2016
6. Alabdulkareem, S.A.: Exploring the use and the impacts of social media on teaching and learning science in Saudi. In: Procedia-Social and Behavioral Sciences, vol. 182, pp. 213–224 (2015)
7. Hitrec, I., Pogarcic, I., Suman, S.: eLearning: a social software in higher education learning. In: Proceedings of the 34th International Convention, MIPRO, pp. 1207–1212. IEEE (2011)
8. Li, X., Ganeshan, K., Xu, G.: The role of social networking sites in e-learning. In: Frontiers in Education Conference (FIE), pp. 1–6. IEEE (2012)
9. Roreger, H., Schmidt, T.C.: Socialize online learning: why we should integrate learning content management with online social networks. In: International Conference on Pervasive Computing and Communications Workshops (PERCOM Workshops), pp. 685–690. IEEE (2012)
10. Ternauciuc, A., Mihaescu, V.: Use of social media in MOOC-integration with the moodle LCMS. In: The International Scientific Conference on eLearning and Software for Education, vol. 4, p. 298. "Carol I" National Defence University (2014)
11. Tulaboev, A., Oxley, A.: A case study on using web 2.0 social networking tools in higher education. In: International Conference on Computer & Information Science (ICCIS), vol. 1, pp. 84–88. IEEE (2012)
12. Kaeomanee, Y., Dominic, D.D.P., Rias, R.M.: Investigating social software usage for knowledge sharing purpose among students: a Malaysian higher education perspective. In: Symposium on E-Learning, E-Management and E-Services (IS3e), pp. 1–6. IEEE (2012)

13. Klimova, B., Poulova, P., Sucharda, O.: Social networks and their use in Education. In: 12th International Conference on Emerging eLearning Technologies and Applications (ICETA), pp. 233–237. IEEE (2014)
14. Tariq, W., Mehboob, M., Asf, M., Khan, Y., Ullah, F.: The impact of social media and social networks on education and students of Pakistan. In: IJCSI, vol. 9, pp. 407–410 (2012)
15. Azam, S., Wang, F., Ng, J.: Investigation of the utilisation of social networks in e-learning at Universities. In: International Conference on TALE, pp. 441–446. IEEE (2014)

A Micro-Web Involving Learning Scenario Generation with Linked Open Data for Web-Based Investigative Learning

Yasuhiro Kakinuma[✉] and Akihiro Kashihara

Department of Informatics, Graduate School of Informatics and Engineering,
The University of Electro-Communications,
1-5-1 Chofugaoka, Chofu, Tokyo 182-8585, Japan
y.kakinuma@uec.ac.jp, akihiro.kashihara@inf.uec.ac.jp

Abstract. In investigative learning with Web resources, learners need to define the relationship between the topic and sub-topics through the creation of learning scenario. However, the Web space is not well-structured for learning. It is accordingly difficult for the learners to construct a learning scenario by themselves. The main purpose of this paper is to build up Micro Web inheriting the characteristics of the Web, which involves automatic generation of learning scenario by means of DBpedia Japanese as Linked Open Data (LOD) for Wikipedia. Such generated scenario enables an adaptive support for the learning scenario creation.

Keywords: Micro web · LOD · Learning scenario · Investigative learning

1 Introduction

On the Web, there are currently a great number and variety of existing information resources suitable for learning. These Web resources allow learners to investigate any topics to learn, which would promote learning in a wider, deeper, and timely way [1, 2]. Such investigative learning involves navigating the Web pages in the resources to construct knowledge about a topic investigated. In recent years, investigative learning with Web resources has been introduced into primary and secondary education classes [3].

In the investigative learning process with Web resources, the learners need to reconstruct the contents to be learned by themselves since most Web resources are not well structured for learning. In addition, these resources do not always provide a learning scenario indicating the topics and the sequences to be learned. It is accordingly necessary for the learners to create their own learning scenario while investigating learning process. In investigating a topic with Web resources, the learners are expected not only to integrate and construct knowledge learned at each resource, but also to find out related topics to be further investigated that can be viewed as the sub-topics. In this way, investigative learning process involves decomposing the topic into the sub-topics, which is regarded as creating a learning scenario. Such topic decomposition would make the investigative learning process more structured. However, it is not so easy for the learners to conduct the topic decomposition concurrent with the navigation and knowledge construction process.

© Springer International Publishing Switzerland 2016
P. Zaphiris and A. Ioannou (Eds.): LCT 2016, LNCS 9753, pp. 344–355, 2016.
DOI: 10.1007/978-3-319-39483-1_32

We have accordingly developed a system called interactive learning scenario builder on iPad (iLSB-tablet for short), which scaffolds learning scenario creation. iLSB-tablet follows the model of Web-based investigative learning we have built up. This model expects learners to search for Web resources with search engine to navigate the Web pages and construct knowledge and to create a learning scenario. The results of the case study with iLSB-tablet suggest that the learning scenario creation can be promoted while investigative learning process, and also that it is not so easy for the learners to create more proper scenario by themselves.

The main issue addressed in this paper is how to help learners create a proper learning scenario. Our approach to this issue is to design a micro-Web, which is a micro-world for the Web. The micro-Web provides learners with a scaffold for their investigative learning where they can be supported by means of a scenario suitable for learning a topic. It also prepares a limited number and kinds of Web resources related to the topic. A challenge in this work is how to generate such learning scenario from the unstructured hyperspace provided on the Web.

In this paper, we propose a promising method of the learning scenario generation with Linked Open Data (LOD for short) of Wikipedia, which is provided by DBpedia Japanese. It is possible to use SPARQL queries to get the data (or keywords) linked to a topic, which are found in the Wikipedia pages. The procedure of generating a learning scenario involves the following four steps. In the first step, an instructor is expected to select an initial topic and its related topics to provide a topic set involving the related topics. The second step is to generate a SPARQL query with the initial topic to obtain the related data that includes a lot of related keywords. The third step is to extract the topics commonly included in the obtained data and the topic set, which correspond to the sub-topics. In the fourth step, the part-of link between the initial topic and each sub-topic is generated. Generating the SPARQL query with each sub-topic and repeating from the second step to the fourth step, a learning scenario is automatically generated.

This paper also describes a case study with the learning scenario generation, which involves several trials of generating scenarios for learning different topics. The results would suggest its effectiveness. In addition, we will discusses how to build up the micro-Web involving the learning scenario generation in detail, and how to use iLSB-tablet on the Micro-Web.

2 Model of Web-Based Investigative Learning

Let us first introduce the model of Web-based investigative learning proposed in our previous work [4]. As shown in Fig. 1, this model includes three phases, which are phase of search for Web resources, navigational learning phase, and phase of learning scenario building.

In the phase of search for Web resources, learners would use the search engine such as Google with a keyword (called topic keyword) that represents an initial topic, and explore the Web resources. In the navigational learning phase, the learners would navigate across the Web resources to investigate the topic and learn the contents of the

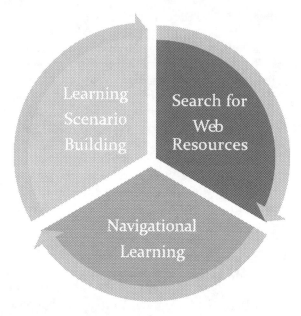

Fig. 1. Model of Web-based investigative learning

Web resources. Such navigational learning involves constructing knowledge that they have learned from the Web resources.

In the phase of learning scenario building, the learners would find out related topics from their knowledge constructed, which can be considered as sub-topics of the initial topic. They would build the learning scenario by decomposing the topic into sub-topics and relating the topic and the sub-topics. The learning scenario building is continued until the topic decomposition does not occur anymore.

3 Learning Scenario Generation for Micro-Web

This paper proposes an automatic method to generate a learning scenario for the Micro-Web. Toward building the Micro-Web from the unstructured Web, we use LOD of Wikipedia presented by DBpedia Japanese.

3.1 Micro-Web

The Micro-Web is viewed as a micro-world [5] for the Web. It provides learners with a scaffold for their investigative learning where they can be supported by means of a scenario suitable for learning a topic. The Micro-Web could also include unstructured and unreliable Web resources in addition to the ones useful for learning.

In general, the learners have difficulties in finding out the resources necessary for investigating the topic because of the enormous ones on the Web, and often finish learning with insufficient knowledge. In contrast, the Micro-Web allows an instructor to beforehand restrict the number of Web resources. The instructor is also allowed to choose the sub-topics to assume the learning scenario that the learners should follow in investigating the topic. The learners are accordingly allowed to construct their knowledge appropriate to the topic.

In this way, the Micro-Web provides learners with a structured micro-world for the Web, which includes the Web resources useful for their investigative learning process.

3.2 Learning Scenario Generation with LOD of Wikipedia

Our approach to automatic generation of learning scenario is to use LOD of Wikipedia provided by DBpedia.

– Linked Open Data (LOD)

LOD provides the method to publish and share the data on the Web, and link the data each other to represent Web information. It is generally under the open license.

Representative LOD services include DBpedia and Freebase [6]. In this work, we use DBpedia Japanese [7] presented by the national information science research institute [8]. This LOD processes the data of Japanese Wikipedia such as infobox, category information, images, geographical coordinate, and links to the outside Web pages. Such information is structured and converted into linked data, which is also represented with RDF (Resource Description Framework). RDF is a machine-readable data model for describing the Web information. In RDF, data is described by means of triplet form such as subject-predicate-object. More specifically, it means resource (as subject), property (as predicate), and resources (as object). The RDF triplets describing the data in LOD is obtained with query language SPARQL [9].

Figure 2 shows an example of RDF triplet description. This triplet describes a property "wikiPageWikiLink" of DBpedia Japanese as the predicate in a resource of "Global Warming" as the subject, and describes a resource of "Kyoto Protocol" as the object. The property "wikiPageWikiLink" means the link from a certain Wikipage to different one [10]. In this triplet, the predicate means that there is a link from the resource "Global Warming" to the resource "Kyoto Protocol". All resources dealt with by DBpedia Japanese have the corresponding Wikipedia pages. As shown in Fig. 2, we can search many resources including "Global Warming" (such as greenhouse gas, carbon dioxide, etc.) when we put the query about the "Global Warming" into the SPARQL endpoint [11] to get the information of relevant words.

– Procedure of the learning scenario automatic generation

Let us next explain the basic steps for the automatic generation of learning scenario from SPARQL query.

1. An instructor is expected to select an initial topic and its related topics to be learned, and to provide a topic set involving the related topics.
2. A SPARQL query with the initial topic is generated and sent to DBpedia Japanese. The related keywords are then obtained from the LOD.

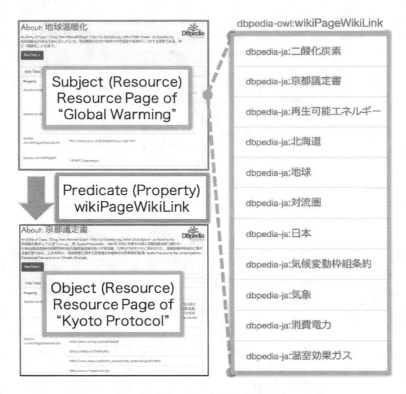

Fig. 2. Example of RDF description

3. The topics commonly included in the obtained keywords and the topic set are extracted as the sub-topics.
4. The part-of link between the initial topic and each sub-topic is generated.

The SPARQL query with each sub-topic is continuously generated, and the process from the second step to the fourth step is repeated. Then, a learning scenario is automatically generated.

As shown in Fig. 3, for example, consider the case where the instructor selects "Global Warming" as an initial topic. He/she also prepares "Greenhouse Effect Gas", "Kyoto Protocol", "Carbon Dioxide", etc. as related topics that the learners should investigate about the "Global Warming". These related topics will be included in an automatic generated scenario. Then, a SPARQL query about "Global Warming" is generated, and the Wikipedia resources linked from "Global Warming" are obtained as the related keywords from the LOD by means of the property "wikiPageWikiLink". If there are common keywords included in the related topics and obtained keywords, they are extracted as the sub-topics. In Fig. 3, "Greenhouse Effect Gas" and "Abnormal Weather" are extracted as the sub-topics of "Global Warming". In the same manner, the next SPARQL queries including "Greenhouse Effect Gas" and "Abnormal Weather" are generated and the related keywords are obtained from the LOD. As shown in Fig. 3, the sub-topics for "Greenhouse Effect Gas" are detected as "Kyoto Protocol" and "Carbon Dioxide". Repeating these processes, we can obtain a topic tree structure representing a learning scenario about "global warming".

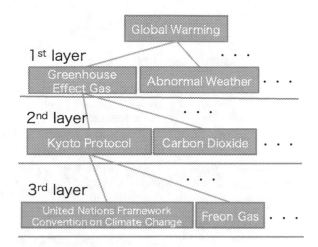

Fig. 3. Example of topic keywords acquisition every hierarchy

− Framework of the Micro-Web

Figure 4 shows a framework of the Micro-Web involving the automatic learning scenario generation. In this framework, an instructor selects a topic and related topics necessary for the automatic scenario generation. The learning scenario is generated with the LOD provided by the DBpedia Japanese.

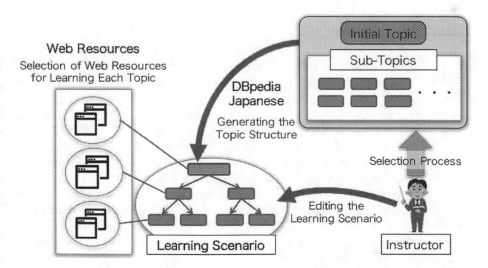

Fig. 4. Framework of the Micro-Web

If the generated scenario structure does not satisfy the instructor, he/she could edit it to re-generate the appropriate scenario. After the scenario is decided, the instructor could integrate the Web resources, which are contributory to investigative learning with all the topics included in the scenario.

3.3   Topic Keyword Extraction by SPARQL Query

Figure 5 shows an example of a query that queries the SPARQL endpoint of DBpedia. The resource (subject) in this example is represented as "dbp:global warming", and the property (predicate) corresponds to "dbp-owl:wikiPageWikiLink". The resource (object) to be extracted is represented as "?thing1", which is a variable in the query. The results of the query are stored in this variable. The "prefix" in the query is used for shortening the description of the URI. The names of the resources stored in "?thing1" are shown in the property "rdfs:label". The resources is also stored in the variable "?thing2".

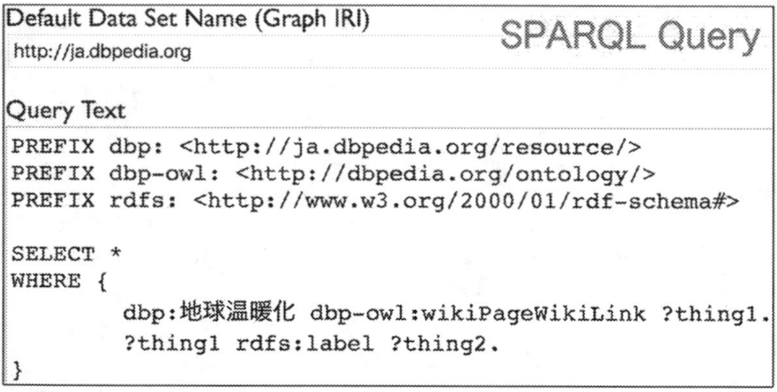

```
Default Data Set Name (Graph IRI)              SPARQL Query
http://ja.dbpedia.org

Query Text

PREFIX dbp: <http://ja.dbpedia.org/resource/>
PREFIX dbp-owl: <http://dbpedia.org/ontology/>
PREFIX rdfs: <http://www.w3.org/2000/01/rdf-schema#>

SELECT *
WHERE {
        dbp:地球温暖化 dbp-owl:wikiPageWikiLink ?thing1.
        ?thing1 rdfs:label ?thing2.
}
```

Fig. 5. An Example of SPARQL query

Figure 6 shows an output of the query in Fig. 5, which includes the URLs obtained. After the SPARQL query is inputted, the JSON format of the keyword data is extracted as the output.

Figures 7 and 8 show examples of learning scenario generation. In Fig. 7, 16 topics out of 20 related ones are extracted as the sub-topics from the initial topic "Global Warming". 12 topics of these 16 topics are also extracted at the first layer, and there are only the 3 sub-topics that have the sub-topics at the second or third layers. The remaining 4 related topics are not extracted in the scenario.

In Fig. 7, most related topics are extracted at the first layer because there are the links between these topics and "Global Warming" in Wikipedia. In order to avoid such topic decomposition, we need to update the learning scenario generation method. We currently consider the update as follows. First, we will beforehand classify the related topics into several groups. We will then refine the automatic scenario generation method so that one keyword is extracted from each group at the same layer.

thing1	thing2
http://ja.dbpedia.org/resource/11世紀	"11世紀"@ja
http://ja.dbpedia.org/resource/12月29日	"12月29日"@ja
http://ja.dbpedia.org/resource/1850年	"1850年"@ja
http://ja.dbpedia.org/resource/1860年	"1860年"@ja
http://ja.dbpedia.org/resource/1896年	"1896年"@ja
http://ja.dbpedia.org/resource/1900年	"1900年"@ja
http://ja.dbpedia.org/resource/1979年	"1979年"@ja
http://ja.dbpedia.org/resource/1988年	"1988年"@ja
http://ja.dbpedia.org/resource/1992年	"1992年"@ja
http://ja.dbpedia.org/resource/19世紀	"19世紀"@ja
http://ja.dbpedia.org/resource/1世紀	"1世紀"@ja
http://ja.dbpedia.org/resource/2001年	"2001年"@ja
http://ja.dbpedia.org/resource/20世紀	"20世紀"@ja
http://ja.dbpedia.org/resource/7月6日	"7月6日"@ja
http://ja.dbpedia.org/resource/9月29日	"9月29日"@ja
http://ja.dbpedia.org/resource/アル・ゴア	"アル・ゴア"@ja
http://ja.dbpedia.org/resource/メタン	"メタン"@ja
http://ja.dbpedia.org/resource/二酸化炭素	"二酸化炭素"@ja
http://ja.dbpedia.org/resource/京都議定書	"京都議定書"@ja
http://ja.dbpedia.org/resource/再生可能エネルギー	"再生可能エネルギー"@ja

Fig. 6. Example of SPARQL query output (HTML Format)

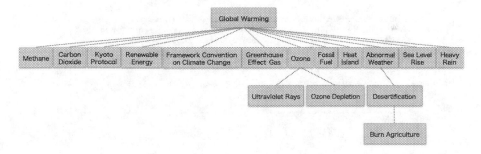

Fig. 7. Example of learning scenario generation

In grouping the related topics about "Global Warming", we introduce three viewpoints which are "Cause", "Effect", and "Countermeasure". Following these viewpoints, we classified the related topics into three groups and simulate the automatic scenario generation. Figure 8 shows the learning scenario to be generated. We do not currently implement the updated method. In future, we need to refine the learning scenario automatic generation method.

On the other hand, there is another approach to generating a structured scenario with the categories used in Wikipedia, which classifies the Wikipedia articles by fields.

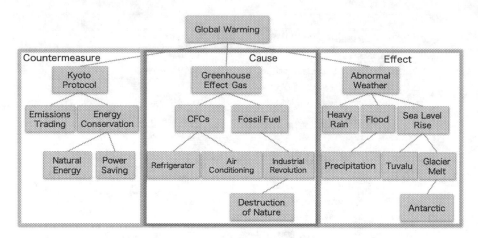

Fig. 8. Example of learning scenario by grouping related topics

In this approach, the sub-topics to be investigated are selected from the categories. Figure 9 shows an example of a query to the SPARQL endpoint. This asks what category belongs to "global warming" indicated by "category-ja:" Fig. 10 shows the result, which includes the categories belonging to "global warming".

```
Default Data Set Name (Graph IRI)
http://ja.dbpedia.org                          SPARQL Query

Query Text
PREFIX rdfs: <http://www.w3.org/2000/01/rdf-schema#>
PREFIX category-ja: <http://ja.dbpedia.org/resource/Category:>
PREFIX skos: <http://www.w3.org/2004/02/skos/core#>

SELECT *
WHERE {
        category-ja:地球温暖化 ^skos:broader ?thing1.
        ?thing1 rdfs:label ?thing2.
}
```

Fig. 9. Example of query to acquire the lower category

Figure 11 shows a learning scenario generated with the category names extracted from the Wikipedia. In this example, the category name of "global warming" is given as the initial topic. From the "global warming" category, the category names such as "fossil fuel", "greenhouse gas", etc. are extracted. As we have confirmed, there are currently some cases where important topics such as "Kyoto Protocol" in learning "global warming" are missing in this method. In order to resolve such problems, it is necessary to use the property "dbp-owl:wikiPageWikiLink" as discussed in Fig. 5.

thing1	thing2
http://ja.dbpedia.org/resource/Category:化石燃料	"化石燃料"@ja
http://ja.dbpedia.org/resource/Category:温室効果ガス	"温室効果ガス"@ja
http://ja.dbpedia.org/resource/Category:気候変動に関する政策	"気候変動に関する政策"@ja
http://ja.dbpedia.org/resource/Category:気候変動関連組織	"気候変動関連組織"@ja
http://ja.dbpedia.org/resource/Category:気候変動の影響	"気候変動の影響"@ja
http://ja.dbpedia.org/resource/Category:反地球温暖化論	"反地球温暖化論"@ja
http://ja.dbpedia.org/resource/Category:気候変動の原因	"気候変動の原因"@ja
http://ja.dbpedia.org/resource/Category:気候変動防止	"気候変動防止"@ja
http://ja.dbpedia.org/resource/Category:気候変動防止活動	"気候変動防止活動"@ja

Fig. 10. Example of category output results of SPARQL query

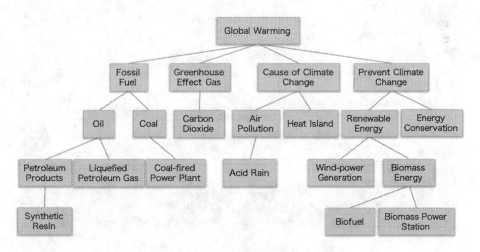

Fig. 11. Example of learning scenario by categorizing

4 iLSB-Tablet

In this work, we have developed interactive Learning Scenario Builder on iPad (iLSB-tablet for short), which is a Web-based investigative learning support system [12]. Figure 2 shows the user interface of iLSB-tablet.

This system follows the model of Web-based investigative learning as shown in Fig. 1, and provides learners with the functions that are search engine, keyword repository for storing keywords representing the contents learned about the topics, and learning scenario builder. In addition, the system presents a list of attributes representing the relationships between topics, which functions as a scaffold for the learners to pick the important topic keywords up from the Web pages or the keyword repository

[12]. This allows them to decompose the topic into the sub-topics to generate the meaningful scenario.

In the future, we will plan to develop a function for comparing the learning scenario generated by the learners with the scenario automatically generated by the system. Presenting the difference between the scenarios promotes the investigative learning process. The comparison function could also provide some foundation for adaptation of investigative learning on the Micro-Web (Fig. 12).

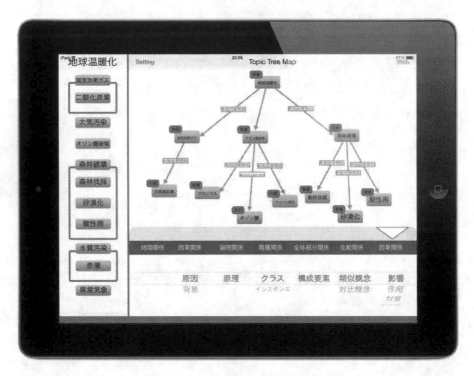

Fig. 12. User interface of iLSB-tablet

5   Conclusion

In this paper, we have proposed the Micro-Web and learning scenario generation with LOD provided by DBpedia Japanese. As future work, we need to implement iLSB-tablet with automatic scenario generation and with the comparison function for adaptive investigative learning. We will also evaluate the proposed method in detail and refine it base on the results.

Acknowledgment. This work is in part supported by JSPS KAKENHI Grand Number 26282047.

References

1. Kashihara, A., Hasegawa, S.: A model of meta-learning for web-based navigational learning. Int. J. Adv. Technol. Learn. **2**(4), 198–206 (2005)
2. Land, S.M.: Cognitive requirements for learning open-ended learning environments. Educ. Technol. Res. Dev. **48**(3), 61–78 (2000)
3. Ministry of Education, Culture, Sports, Science and Technology (MEXT)," the Period for Integrated Studies" (in Japanese)
4. Kashihara, A., Akiyama, N.: Learner-created scenario for investigative learning with web resources. In: Lane, H., Yacef, K., Mostow, J., Pavlik, P. (eds.) AIED 2013. LNCS, vol. 7926, pp. 700–703. Springer, Heidelberg (2013)
5. Matsubara, Y.: Simulation Virtual reality system, Knowledge base, The Institute of Electronics, Information and Communication Engineers, group S3 part 11 "Education support system". In: Education/Learning Support System, Chap. 4, pp. 17–22 (2011). http://www.ieice-hbkb.org/files/S3/S3gun_11hen_04.pdf
6. Freebase. https://www.freebase.com
7. DBpedia Japanese. http://ja.dbpedia.org
8. National Institute of Informatics. http://www.nii.ac.jp
9. For RDF query language SPARQL. http://www.asahi-net.or.jp/ ~ ax2s-kmtn/internet/rdf/rdf-sparql-query.html
10. About: Link from a Wikipage to another Wikipage – DBpedia. http://dbpedia.org/ontology/wikiPageWikiLink
11. SPARQL Endpoint: Virtuoso SPARQL Query Editor. http://ja.dbpedia.org/sparql
12. Kinoshita, K., Kashihara, A.: Scaffolding topic decomposition in investigative learning with web resources. In: Proceedings of ICCE 2014, Nara, Japan (2014)

E-Learning 3.0 Framework Adoption: Experts' Views

Paula Miranda[1(✉)], Pedro Isaias[2,3], Carlos J. Costa[4], and Sara Pifano[5]

[1] Escola Superior de Tecnologia de Setúbal, IPS,
Campus do IPS, Estefanilha, 2910-761 Setúbal, Portugal
paula.miranda@estsetubal.ips.pt
[2] Universidade Aberta, Palácio Ceia, Rua da Escola Politécnica,
nº 141-147, 1269-001 Lisbon, Portugal
pisaias@uab.pt
[3] ADVANCE Research Center – ISEG, University of Lisbon,
Rua do Quelhas, 6, 1200-781 Lisbon, Portugal
[4] University Institute of Lisbon (ISCTE-IUL),
Adetti-IUL, Avenida Forças Armadas, 1649-026 Lisbon, Portugal
carlos.costa@iscte.pt
[5] ISR Lab – Information Society Research Lab, Lisbon, Portugal

Abstract. The pervasiveness of the Semantic Web in educational contexts is acquiring a growing importance also at the level of e-Learning. The improvements it promises to introduce in online education are causing interest and curiosity in terms of its implementation and practical repercussions for learning. Since it is in its early stages it becomes important to explore the conditions that will favor its adoption. In order to delineate its prosperous deployment, this paper presents the outline of a Critical Success Factors framework. The purpose of this paper is to collect the point of view of e-Learning experts with regards to this framework. The experts were presented with the framework via semi-structured interviews and they were asked to review its core elements. The results of the data collection provide a substantial validation of the framework and reiterate its relevance in delimiting the proliferation of e-Learning 3.0.

Keywords: e-Learning 3.0 · Semantic web · Critical success factors · Educational technology

1 Introduction

Web 3.0 comes with a pledge for the revolution of e-Learning, namely via increased personalization and machine understandable content. The affordances of the Semantic Web to online learning are at the origin of a new stage for electronic learning, e-Learning 3.0 (EL 3.0).

EL 3.0 is at the centre of several research ventures and it is inspiring interest among researchers and practitioners. The proliferation of EL 3.0 is dependent on a multiplicity of facilitating conditions that will maximize the positive impact of the Semantic Web. Web 3.0 will represent an improvement of some of the technology that was made available by Web 2.0, but given that the learning process requires a multidisciplinary

© Springer International Publishing Switzerland 2016
P. Zaphiris and A. Ioannou (Eds.): LCT 2016, LNCS 9753, pp. 356–367, 2016.
DOI: 10.1007/978-3-319-39483-1_33

intervention, pedagogy and technology are expected to represent a united front [31]. The application of the Semantic Web to an online learning context has the potential to address some of e-Learning's limitations, specifically the lack of data accuracy, information overload and the fact that content is not prepared to be read by machines [46].

The outline of a framework of Critical Success Factors (CSFs) for EL 3.0 provides a substantial support for framing the evolution and prospective adoption of this third phase of online learning. The framework that this paper proposes derives from the initial work of Miranda et al. [30], who suggested a preliminary CSFs framework specifically for EL 3.0 systems. This framework was composed of five categories: technology, content, students, professors and educational institutions. This paper will provide a reorganisation of this framework that is divided into three domains: technology, content and stakeholders.

The first part of the paper provides a brief examination of what defines EL 3.0 and presents the suggested CSFs framework for EL 3.0. The next section addresses the methods that were used and prefaces the third part of the paper that presents and discusses the results of the semi-structured interviews with e-Learning experts.

2   The Successful Adoption of EL 3.0

Web 3.0 introduces a variety of benefits to e-Learning, more specifically the enhancement of personalised learning environments, a growing interoperability among applications, the employment of semantic annotation, the dissemination of domain ontologies [26], the growing application of 3D visualisation, distributed computing, interaction [43] and more self-organisation [18]. One of the precepts of EL 3.0 is the effective management of information to answer the users' questions. It is similar to a personal assistant who gathers data on the user and accesses and links resources on the internet to better meet their needs [54]. This is also what is at the foundation of customised searches for learning resources, which can through semantic annotation be constantly improved [48]. On the other hand, the main challenges of EL 3.0 include the fact that it requires a significant effort in terms of ontology development, the educational entities' lack of willingness to share data, the need to develop standards for data and content exchange, data privacy and security and trust [26].

2.1   EL 3.0 CSF Framework

The successful adoption of EL 3.0 is dependent on the reunion of a multiplicity of factors that are transversal to diverse domains of e-Learning [13]. The framework that is proposed in this paper intends to depict a fundamental structure of those factors. The general outline of its categories was inspired by the work of Selim [45] who advocated that e-Learning's critical success factors could be divided into four areas: the teacher, the learner, information technology and institutional support. Furthermore, it derives from a reorganisation of the CSFs framework that Miranda et al. [30] proposed for EL 3.0 systems, which was divided into technology, content, students, professors and educational institutions. Thus, in essence, the critical success factors' framework for EL

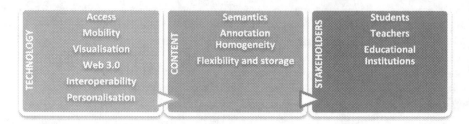

Fig. 1. Outline of EL 3.0 CSFs framework

3.0 encompasses three core categories portrayed in Fig. 1: technology, content and stakeholders.

The technology category includes a series of CSFs that will facilitate the more technical aspects of EL 3.0 and allow the transposition of learning to online scenarios: access, mobility, visualisation, Web 3.0, interoperability and personalization. Access is related to the fundamental premise that technology's unavailability has a negative effect on e-Learning's acceptance [3]. Its core requirements consist in hardware equipment both its availability [38] and its reliability [45], a fast internet connection [38], that can be effective [45] and the existence of user-friendly interfaces and applications [13, 22, 32, 56]. Mobility, in the form of mobile technology, will be essential for ubiquitousness [33] and it will demand mobile apps [5, 35], and smart mobile technology [7, 23, 42]. Visualisation accounts for the sensorial element of EL 3.0 and the variety of formats [7] and it needs visualisation tools [8, 40], 3D and immersive Web [33, 35] and 3D visualisation and interaction [12, 23]. As to Web 3.0 it is a valuable resource to EL 3.0 [56] and it demands semantic features [10, 53], ontology-based tools [19, 21], ontology creation [13] and maintenance [51] and intelligent search engines [47, 52]. Interoperability relates to the challenge of the integration of different applications [19] and to be promoted it requires semantic interoperability [17, 44] and interoperability of web-based educational systems [6, 18]. Finally, personalisation represents a solution for dealing with a vast amount of online materials [23] and it requests the use of user profiling techniques [26, 54], Artificial Intelligence [34, 43, 47] and intelligent e-Learning systems [9, 41].

Content is an essential aspect of EL 3.0 and it subsumes three CSFs, semantics, annotation homogeneity and flexibility and storage. Semantics account for a greater access to significant content [17], requiring big data management [15, 23], machine-understandable learning material [9, 44], semantic web ready content [11, 12], metadata [19, 47] and semantic markup [16, 24]. With respect to annotation homogeneity its value lies in its capacity to enable different computers to understand and exchange data with each other [53] and it demands semantic homogeneity [25, 50] and a widely spread ontology structure [19, 26]. Finally, flexibility and storage relates to the need for content to be dynamic [46] and the need for effective storage capacity. In order to be accomplished, this CSF demands cloud computing [4, 18], open data [39, 54], personalised content [27, 57] and learning objects [29, 57].

The final category, stakeholders, accounts for the human and institutional aspect of EL 3.0 and it comprises three CSFs: the students, the teachers and the educational institutions. The students' contribution to the success of EL 3.0 relates to their engagement in collaboration [1, 7], active participation [3, 20] and their personal and technical skills [18, 28]. The teachers, on the other hand are required to have ICT training [34, 49] and to be creators of meaning [24, 48]. The educational institutions have a fundamental part in the availability of infrastructures [55] and institutional assistance [45]. Hence, their capacity of being a CSF for EL 3.0 is intrinsically connected with infrastructural development [1, 50], providing training for e-learning [33, 37], the inter-connectedness among institutions [26, 36], the development of learning methods based on real [2, 33] and the provision of large repositories of linked data [7, 54].

3 Methodology

The validation of the proposed framework was done via the use of semi-structured interviews with experts in the field of e-Learning. The interviews were designed to last around 40 min and they were divided into four sections. The first section was comprised of general questions on the definition and reach of EL 3.0, while the remaining parts focused on each of the categories of CSFs, technology, content and stakeholders, respectively. Two pilot interviews were conducted to test and perfect the initial script.

In total 10 experts were interviewed, 3 female and 7 male. The experts were from the USA, Brazil, Australia, Germany, Dubai, Greece and the UK and they were either involved in research, teaching or both. They were invited to participate in the interviews due to their experience with education technology. From the total of 10 interviews, 2 were conducted in person, 2 were done via Skype and 6 were delivered through email.

The main purpose of the interviews was the assessment of the EL 3.0 CSFs framework. The use of semi-structured interviews facilitates the fluidity of a conversation that is framed by an initial alignment of questions. They allow the use of a script to lead the interview, but at the same time they provide the opportunity to more liberally insert different topics or explore subjects that may surface during the interviews [14].

4 Results and Discussion

In general, all the interviewees agreed with the framework and recognized the importance of the CSFs for the proficient development and adoption of EL 3.0 at a wider scale.

4.1 EL 3.0 and Its Reach

The objective of the first part of the interviews was to examine the experts' opinions about the definition of EL 3.0, its reach and the opportunities and challenges that Web 3.0 would introduce in e-Learning. In terms of defining EL 3.0, since it is a recent concept, some of the respondents were hesitant in providing a specific description of the term. Nonetheless, the majority was able to associate it with learning analytics, extraction of knowledge, seamless learning, the integration of big data, artificial intelligence, Web 3.0 and semantic tools, interactive learning, machine associated meaning, personalization and anytime/anywhere learning. Despite this knowledge of what EL 3.0 stands for, when asked about its current reach, all the respondents stated that it is still at an early age and that it has an experimental and speculative nature, which is in line with other studies [36].

Concerning the benefits that Web 3.0 will represent for e-Learning, the participants mentioned the increase of social interaction, communication and the personalization of learning, namely through artificial intelligence. Also, they reported changes at the level of the relationship between the students and the teachers and the recommendation of more pertinent learning material, brought by the assistance of machines and semantics. Finally, they associated Web 3.0 with data merging and processing, intelligent machines, the acceleration of learning and the mitigation of the workload of the teacher. The fundamental precepts that the experts mentioned were coherent with previous research [26, 43]. While they were quick to see the advantages that Web 3.0 introduces, they were equally able to point out the challenges of the implementation of EL 3.0, namely privacy and security concerns with regards to the access to data sources, just as it's been previously reported [26]; the restrictions of learning analytics and big data; issues of a technological and infrastructural nature; and the adaptation of teachers to this new stage of e-Learning. Other challenges included the extensive creation and development of semantic tools, the lack of close partnerships, the existence of ontologies that cannot be reused, the insufficient training of professionals and good pedagogical proposals.

4.2   Technology

In relation to access, as much as hardware and internet connectivity have become widespread, the respondents still highlighted some problems with the access to sustainable internet connections, mainly in rural areas and also issues with the availability of hardware equipment in schools. Some of the solutions that the participants presented for improving access consist in shared access to technology among students that don't have their own devices, enhance access to mobile technology to simplify internet connection, the integration of tools in the every-day life, top-down promotion and use, inclusion of technology training in the curriculum and making application as intuitive as possible, as advocated also by Ahmud-Boodoo [1].

With respect to mobile technology itself and reiterating the literature [23], all the participants agreed that it is important for EL, with one of the interviewees stating that "It's almost inevitable to think of education of the future without thinking about mobility" (R9). According to the participants mobile technology is important in the sense that it collects more data from more sources for learning analytics and the offering of more personalized solutions, mobile learning is more integrated in the real world, it allows students to have continuous access to the world around them, it enables the students to import what they learn to their everyday life, it broadens the scope of the technology that teachers can use. Furthermore a 24/7 access has become a regular expectation. One of the aspects that was also mentioned was the necessity of creating learning scenarios that are attuned with mobile learning.

Visualisation was one of the elements that was assessed in the technology category and it was overall validated by the participants. One of the interviewees said that visualization "is the crux of web 3.0 and will to a greater extent differentiate it from its earlier generations of web and or EL" (R6). Some of the tools that the participants underline subsume virtual reality and augmented reality interfaces to assist learning in real-life scenarios, and graphical renderings to provide innovative insight into data. Visualisation offers a stimulus for different parts of the user's cognition. Also, as Banciu and Florea [7] argued it promotes the use of the visual as teaching and learning material which enhances the acquisition of skills, competences and knowledge.

Similarly to what was defended in previous studies [42, 56], the respondents believe that Web 3.0 is an integral part of EL 3.0, but given the more technical requirements of this question, some respondents found it difficult to state which of its main features should be used in e-Learning. The remaining interviewees highlighted the characteristics that they deemed as being important, namely semantics for data merging and processing and for the intelligent processing of data by machines, customized and context-specific help to students in real-life environments, mobile web, data analytics, semantic meaning, knowledge extraction, information visualisation based on annotation, personalisation tools or algorithms and intelligent tutoring systems and intelligence.

The promotion of interoperability for the advancement of EL 3.0, that was argued in previous research [19, 26], was reiterated by the answers of the interviewees. In conformity with the participants, this support of interoperability can be done through common data formats between authoring tools; information repositories and learning management tools; the development of APIs (application programming interfaces); standardization; pertinent organizations to work with tech enterprises; creation of tools that education stakeholders can integrate in their educational practice routines; EU standardization to enable platforms and frameworks for shared practice; good vocabularies and reusable ontologies that can be used across different environments.

Personalisation was the final CSF in the technology category to be reviewed by the participants, who agreed with the literature [23] in term of its importance for EL 3.0. As reported by one of the respondents, some platforms are already offering several personalisation solutions, for example Carnegie Learning, MeuTutor, Grockit and Aleks, but Moodle which is the most widely used system is not able to integrate them. Also, another respondent argued that EL 3.0 will introduce personalization to scale. In accordance to the interviewees, there are several aspects that will contribute to personalization: the monitoring of the progress of learners to tailor content based on their peculiarities, the use of Latent Semantic Analysis, AI, namely algorithm called BKT - Bayesian Knowledge Tracing (Tree); Educational Data Mining; Knowledge Representation; machine learning; and a greater alignment among critical learning design factors such as learning objectives, learning content, pedagogical dimensions and learning assessment.

4.3   Content

In line with previous studies [17], semantically annotated content was deemed as essential to the progress of EL 3.0. Nonetheless not all the respondents were able to identify ways of increasing it. The respondents cited the significance of the interoperability and interconnectedness of tools and the need for an agreement on interoperability and common standards. Also, one of the respondents highlighted the fact that people can learn by themselves by reorganizing material or indexing it on different ways. Semantic annotation of conversations, learning paths, content reviewed, EL systems will be able to identify what information is relevant to be displayed. In that sense it is necessary to develop frameworks to provide this annotation. Another participant, named a few challenges related to semantic annotation: the need for good repositories that allow communication between languages and vocabularies; the lack of good, reusable annotations; the issue of the training of the people who are producing the annotation; and the technology in itself, the need for good authoring tools to assist annotation. Further to this CSF, the participants were asked to provide their viewpoint on the importance of big data management techniques and to suggest the most appropriate ones for educational settings. This was again a question where some of the participants (4) were not comfortable answering. While most agreed with research that argues that big data management techniques are important for EL 3.0 [15, 23], the majority was not able to suggest specific techniques. The few participants that did recommend some techniques, mentioned the management of links, cloud storage, Sequential Data Analysis, Natural Language Processing and Latent Semantic Analysis. Some interviewees recognized that in the future these techniques will be important in managing the information that results from millions of students using LMS, such as Moodle and in sorting all of the information that is available on the Web for learning. Moreover, the data that was previously regarded as being trivial or too extensive to be used, pertaining to user activity on the web is now seen as valuable.

With respect to annotation homogeneity, three of the interviewees did not answer this question. Overall the respondents conveyed its importance for creating common ground, enabling exchange, interoperability, the reusability of data and e-Learning systems' analysis and process, which corroborated the work of Vera et al. [53]. Furthermore, standardization was deemed an important condition to promote the widespread use. One of the experts stated that the issue with annotation is the definition of context. In situations where there is knowledge about the context under which an annotation was made, then the semantics will not be lost. Hence, it is not about homogeneity, but knowing the foundational ontology and describing the context. Another participant believed that annotation homogeneity was only important for subjects which are very specific and have enormous amounts of data.

The flexibility of content and the importance of having suitable storage capacity were the two last aspects to be reviewed in the content category. The respondents focused more on the storage perspective and with relation to flexibility they only mentioned open data, the fact that content should be readily available, compact and affordable and that indexing strategies are necessary to ensure the flexibility of content across different systems and platforms. Generally speaking they all agreed that the existence of good storage solutions is crucial and provided some suggestions:

combining hard drive storage with cloud computing, increasing bandwidth on both wired and wireless networks, real-time streaming media, cloud computing and triple stores tools. In the context of this CSF, the experts were also questioned as to the importance of cloud computing and if they (or their students) used it. The majority stated that they did use cloud computing, namely Google Drive and Dropbox and that it is important, which is also supported by the literature [4, 18]. A fundamental aspect of using cloud computing seemed to be security, thus backups should be ensured. Also, one of the participants said that contrary to what is advertised, cloud computing is not unlimited. Some of the advantages of cloud computing that participants highlighted have to do with the possibility of having a few storage locations that can be access from anywhere and the fact that it enables interoperability, reusability and scalability.

4.4   Stakeholders

The stakeholders' category was comprised of students, teachers and educational institutions.

With respect to the students, it was important to assess the viewpoints of the experts in terms of their role in this new stage of e-Learning. An essential perspective for the part that students are expected to play has to do with participation: "So actually I think that the only thing that should be expected of the student is interacting. Their inter-action, nothing more than that, this is my view. So basically you must have those interactions so that EL3.0 can indeed happen." (R9). According to the interviewees, besides their participation, in order to thrive in EL 3.0, students need to have more interaction; to innovate, engage in problem solving and to collaborate; to connect with anywhere/anytime learning; to be interested in using technology for the purpose of learning; to be creative and willing to generate content; and to be digitally literate as defended by some researchers [18, 28].

The participants' views on the expectations for the teachers portray a multifaceted and polyvalent position. Overall, the interviewees stated that the teachers should act as knowledge facilitators, as co-learners and as collaborators. They should be open to using digital tools and to present them to the students, to engage in the creation of different learning materials, as was argued by [24, 48], to use flipped, blended and constructivist teaching methodologies and to be ready to embrace, learn and integrate new technologies. Moreover, it is crucial that they are capable of being both peda-gogical and technical experts. One of the respondents also underlined the fact that some teachers do not have the necessary ICT skills to engage with technology and while there are some teacher that are very enthusiastic about technology in learning, there are others that create difficulties. This need for ICT training had already been mentioned by previous studies [34, 49].

Finally, when looking at stakeholders it is crucial to examine the role of the edu-cational institutions. Some of the respondents mentioned the insufficient support that the institutions provide, namely in terms of offering appropriate technological conditions and ensuring their quality and adequacy, which is one the main responsibilities that researchers [1, 50, 55] attribute to them. According to the interviewees, educational entities need to embrace the era of digitalization, to guarantee students access to hardware, software and connectivity, to provide both technical and administrative infrastructures, to assist the teachers in the development of their competences and methodologies and practice openness and collaboration rather than competitiveness.

5 Conclusion

With EL 3.0 still in its early stages it becomes imperative to examine how its adoption should be guided and by which means it should be accomplished. The delimitation of a framework to define its CSFs will assist the contextualization of this phenomenon and it will provide a framing structure to encourage its development.

The results of the semi-structured interviews with e-Learning experts demonstrated that while there is a general notion of the importance of Web 3.0 for e-Learning, the specific contours of EL 3.0 are still unknown for some researchers and practitioners. There was a higher difficulty for the respondents to answers technology related questions or to offer very detailed information about certain CSFs, especially if they were mainly technical. Generally speaking all the CSFs were validated by the experts in their interviews, which reiterates the significance of the CSF framework.

Prospective research ventures are to focus on a further validation of these CSFs and to concentrate on using this validation to explore interdependence relations between the CSFs. Also, future studies would be required to extend this validation to other stake-holders namely the students and the educational institutions.

References

1. Ahmud-Boodoo, R.B.: E-learning and the semantic web: a descriptive literature review. In: Issa, T., Isaías, P. (eds.) Artificial Intelligence Technologies and the Evolution of Web 3.0, pp. 66–100. IGI Global, Hershey (2015). doi:10.4018/978-1-4666-8147-7.ch004
2. Alsultanny, Y.A.: E-learning system overview based on semantic web. Electron. J. e-Learn. 4(2), 111–118 (2006)
3. Amit, C.: Web 3.0 and e-learning: the empowered learner. In: Issa, T., Isaías, P. (eds.) Artificial Intelligence Technologies and the Evolution of Web 3.0, pp. 101–123. IGI Global, Hershey (2015). doi:10.4018/978-1-4666-8147-7.ch005
4. Andrea, G., Mauro, G.: Adoption of e-learning solution: selection criteria and recent trends. LISP Informatic Lab for Pedagogical Sperimentation, University of Milan-Bicocca, Milan, Italy (2012)
5. Armstrong, K.: From IA Richards to web 3.0: preparing our students for tomorrow's world. World Acad. Sci. Eng. Technol. 58, 954–961 (2009)
6. Aroyo, L., Dicheva, D.: The new challenges for e-learning: the educational semantic web. Educ. Technol. Soc. 7(4), 59–69 (2004)
7. Banciu, D., Florea, M.: Information quality–a challenge for e-Learning 3.0. Revista Română de Informatică și Automatică 21(3), 75 (2011)
8. Bidarra, J., Cardoso, V.: The emergence of the exciting new web 3.0 and the future of open educational resources. In: Proceedings of the EADTU's 20th Anniversary Conference (2007)

9. Bucos, M., Dragulescu, B., Veltan, M.: Designing a semantic web ontology for e-learning in higher education. Paper presented at the 9th International Symposium on Electronics and Telecommunications (ISETC) (2010)
10. Castellanos-Nieves, D., Fernández-Breis, J.T., Valencia-García, R., Martínez-Béjar, R., Iniesta-Moreno, M.: Semantic web technologies for supporting learning assessment. Inf. Sci. **181**(9), 1517–1537 (2011). doi:10.1016/j.ins.2011.01.010
11. Ciravegna, F., Chapman, S., Dingli, A., Wilks, Y.: Learning to harvest information for the semantic web. In: Bussler, C.J., Davies, J., Fensel, D., Studer, R. (eds.) ESWS 2004. LNCS, vol. 3053, pp. 312–326. Springer, Heidelberg (2004). doi:10.1007/978-3-540-25956-5_22
12. Damiano, R., Gena, C., Lombardo, V., Nunnari, F., Suppini, A., Crevola, A.: 150 Digit_Integrating 3D into a web 3.0 learning-oriented. Paper presented at the 2011 International Conference on Broadband and Wireless Computing, Communication and Applications (BWCCA) (2011)
13. Devedžić, V.: The setting for semantic web-based education. In: Devedžić, V. (ed.) Semantic Web and Education. Integrated Series in Information Systems, vol. 12, pp. 71–99. Springer, New York. doi:10.1007/978-0-387-35417-0_3
14. Dicicco-Bloom, B., Crabtree, B.F.: The qualitative research interview. Med. Educ. **40**(4), 314–321 (2006). doi:10.1111/j.1365-2929.2006.02418.x
15. Foroughi, A., Yan, G., Shi, H., Chong, D.: A web 3.0 ontology based on similarity: a step toward facilitating learning in the big data age. J. Manag. Analytics, 1–17 (2015). doi:10.1080/23270012.2015.1067154
16. Ghaleb, F., Daoud, S., Hasna, A., ALJa'am, J.M., El-Seoud, S.A., El-Sofany, H.: E-learning model based on semantic web technology. Int. J. Comput. Inf. Sci. **4**(2), 63–71 (2006)
17. Gladun, A., Rogushina, J., García-Sanchez, F., Martínez-Béjar, R., Fernández-Breis, J.T.: An application of intelligent techniques and semantic web technologies in e-learning environments. Expert Syst. Appl. **36**, 1922–1931 (2009). doi:10.1016/j.eswa.2007.12.019
18. Goroshko, O.I., Samoilenko, S.A.: Twitter as a conversation through e-learning context. Revista de Informatica Sociala **15** (2011)
19. Gupta, V., Dubey, S.M.: Automatic collaboration and analysis of semantic web information for electronic learning environment (2013)
20. Halimi, K., Seridi-Bouchelaghem, H., Faron-Zucker, C.: An enhanced personal learning environment using social semantic web technologies. Interact. Learn. Environ. **22**(2), 165–187 (2014)
21. Holohan, E., Melia, M., McMullen, D., Pahl, C.: Adaptive e-learning content generation based on semantic web technology (2005)
22. Hsu, I.-C.: Intelligent discovery for learning objects using semantic web technologies. Educ. Technol. Soc. **15**(1), 298–312 (2012)
23. Hussain, F.: E-Learning 3.0 = E-Learning 2.0 + Web 3.0? Paper presented at the IADIS International Conference on Cognition and Exploratory Learning in Digital Age (CELDA 2012) (2012)
24. Ivanova, M., Ivanova, T.: Web 2.0 and web 3.0 environments: possibilities for authoring and knowledge representation. Revista de Informatica Sociala **12**(7), 7–21 (2009)
25. Karadimce. A: Quality Estimation of E-learning Semantic Web Ontology (2013)
26. Kaur, G., Chaudhary, D.: Semantic web: a boon for E-learning. Int. J. Adv. Res. Comput. Commun. Eng. **4**(7) (2015)
27. Kurilovas, E., Serikoviene, S., Vuorikari, R.: Expert centred vs learner centred approach for evaluating quality and reusability of learning objects. Comput. Hum. Behav. **30**, 526–534 (2014)

28. Loureiro, A., Messias, I., Barbas, M.: embracing web 2.0 & 3.0 tools to support lifelong learning - let learners connect. Procedia Soc. Behav. Sci. **46**, 532–537 (2012). doi:10.1016/j.sbspro.2012.05.155

29. Memeti, A., Imeri, F., Xhaferi, G.: Reusing learning objects and the impact of web 3.0 on e-learning platforms. Int. J. Comput. Distrib. Syst. **4**(3), 64–68 (2014)

30. Miranda, P., Isaias, P., Costa, C.J.: From information systems to e-Learning 3.0 systems's critical success factors: a framework proposal. In: Zaphiris, P., Ioannou, A. (eds.) LCT 2014, Part I. LNCS, vol. 8523, pp. 180–191. Springer, Heidelberg (2014)

31. Miranda, P., Isaias, P., Costa, C.J.: The impact of web 3.0 technologies in e-Learning: emergence of e-Learning 3.0. In: Proceedings of EDULEARN 2014, pp. 4139–4149 (2014)

32. Naeve, A., Lytras, M., Nejdl, W., Balacheff, N., Hardin, J.: Advances of the semantic web for e-learning: expanding learning frontiers. Brit. J. Educ. Technol. **37**(3), 321–330 (2006)

33. Norman, H., Din, R., Nordin, N.: A preliminary study of an authentic ubiquitous learning environment for higher education. Learning **3**(4), 89–94 (2011)

34. Noskova, T., Pavlova, T., Iakovleva, O.: Web 3.0 technologies and transformation of pedagogical activities. In: Tomayess, I., Pedro, I. (eds.) Artificial Intelligence Technologies and the Evolution of Web 3.0, pp. 16–36. IGI Global, Hershey (2015). doi:10.4018/978-1-4666-8147-7.ch002

35. Oake, K.: Web 3.0: Transforming Learning. Training Industry Quarterly. A Training Industry, Inc. Ezine (2011)

36. Ohler, J.: The semantic web in education. EDUCAUSE Q. **31**(4), 7–9 (2008)

37. Paechter, M., Maier, B., Macher, D.: Students' expectations of, and experiences in e-learning: their relation to learning achievements and course satisfaction. Comput. Educ. **54**(1), 222–229 (2010)

38. Pocatilu, P., Alecu, F., Vetrici, M.: Using cloud computing for E-learning systems. In: Proceedings of the 8th WSEAS International Conference on Data Networks, Communications, Computers (DNCOCO 2009), pp. 7–9 (2009)

39. Powell, M., Davies, T., Taylor, K.C.: ICT For or Against Development_an intro to Web 3.0. IKM Working Paper (16):1–34 (2012)

40. Rajiv, M.L.: Web 3.0 in Education & Research. BVICAM's Int. J. Inf. Technol. **3** (2011)

41. Rashid, S., Khan, R., Ahmed, F.: A proposed model of e-learning management system using semantic web technology (2013)

42. Rego, H., Moreira, T., Morales, E., Garcia, F.: Metadata and knowledge management driven web-based learning information system towards web/e-Learning 3.0. Int. J. Emerging Technol. Learn. (iJET) **5**(2) (2010)

43. Rubens, N., Kaplan, D., Okamoto, T.: E-learning 3.0: anyone, anywhere, anytime, and AI. In: International Workshop on Social and Personal Computing for Web-Supported Learning Communities (2011)

44. Schaffert, S., Bürger, T., Hilzensauer, W., Schaffert, S.: Underlying concepts and theories of learning with the semantic web. In: TSSOL, pp. 67–83 (2008)

45. Selim, H.M.: Critical success factors for e-learning acceptance: confirmatory factor models. Comput. Educ. **49**(2), 396–413 (2007). http://dx.doi.org/10.1016/j.compedu.2005.09.004

46. Shah, N.K.: E-learning and semantic web. Int. J. e-Education e-Business e-Management e-Learning **2**(2), 113–116 (2012)

47. Shaltout, M.S.A.-F., Salamah, B.: The impact of web 3.0 on e-Learning. In: 2013 Fourth International Conference on e-Learning "Best Practices in Management, Design and Development of e-Courses: Standards of Excellence and Creativity", pp. 227–232. IEEE (2013)

48. Sheeba, T., Begum, S.H., Bernard, M.J.: Semantic web to e-Learning content. Int. J. Adv. Res. Comput. Sci. Softw. Eng. **2**(10), 58–66 (2012)

49. Sue, G.: The impact of web 2.0 and web 3.0 on academic roles in higher education. In: Issa, T., Isaías, P. (eds.) Artificial Intelligence Technologies and the Evolution of Web 3.0, pp. 1–15. IGI Global, Hershey (2015). doi:10.4018/978-1-4666-8147-7.ch001
50. Tiropanis, T., Davis, H., Millard, D., Weal, M.: Semantic technologies for learning and teaching in the web 2.0 era: a survey of UK higher education. In: The Proceedings of the Web Science 2009 Conference, WebSci (2009)
51. Torniai, C., Jovanovic, J., Gasevic, D., Bateman, S., Hatala, M.: E-learning meets the social semantic web. In: Eighth IEEE International Conference on Advanced Learning Technologies, ICALT 2008, pp. 389–393. IEEE (2008)
52. Tresp, V., Bundschus, M., Rettinger, A., Huang, Y.: Towards machine learning on the semantic web. In: Costa, P.C.G., d'Amato, C., Fanizzi, N., Laskey, K.B., Laskey, K.J., Lukasiewicz, T., Nickles, M., Pool, M. (eds.) URSW 2005–2007. LNCS (LNAI), vol. 5327, pp. 282–314. Springer, Heidelberg (2008). doi:10.1007/978-3-540-89765-1_17
53. Vera, M.M.S., Breis, J.T.F., Serrano, J.L., Sánchez, M., Espinosa, P.P.: Practical experiences for the development of educational systems in the semantic web. NAER: J. New Approaches Educ. Res. 2(1), 23–31 (2013)
54. Virtič, M.P.: The role of internet in education. Paper presented at the 9th International Scientific Conference on Distance Learning in Applied Informatics (DIVAI 2012), Štúrovo, Slovakia (2012)
55. Wagner, N.L., Hassanein, K., Head, M.M.: Who is responsible for e-Learning success in higher education? A stakeholders' analysis. Educ. Technol. Soc. 11(3), 26–36 (2008)
56. Wang, J.: Education 3.0: effect learning style and method of instruction on user satisfaction. Eur. Acad. Res. I 1(5), 755–769 (2013)
57. Watson, W.R., Watson, S.L., Reigeluth, C.M.: Education 3.0: breaking the mold with technology. Interact. Learn. Environ. 23(3), 332–343 (2015)

Mobile Quality of Social Web Applications Designed for Collaborative Writing

Tihomir Orehovački[1(✉)] and Snježana Babić[2]

[1] Department of Information and Communication Technologies,
Juraj Dobrila University of Pula, Zagrebačka 30, 52100 Pula, Croatia
tihomir.orehovacki@unipu.hr
[2] Polytechnic of Rijeka, Trpimirova 2/V, 51000 Rijeka, Croatia
snjezana.babic@veleri.hr

Abstract. Social web applications are nowadays commonly employed in all fields of human endeavor. It is therefore of a high importance that they meet requirements of as many quality dimensions as possible. This paper reports findings of an empirical study which was carried out with an aim to examine quality of social web applications when they are used in a mobile environment. Participants in the study were students from two Croatian higher education institutions who carried out predefined scenario of interaction with two social web applications for collaborative writing on their smartphones and afterwards evaluated their perceived quality by completing the post-use questionnaire. The analysis of collected data uncovered the relevance of pragmatic and hedonic facets of mobile quality in the context of evaluating social web applications for collaborative writing.

Keywords: Mobile quality · Social web application · Collaborative writing · Questionnaire · Empirical findings

1 Introduction

The quality of applications that are running on mobile devices is one of the essential predictors of their acceptance by end users and thus their success. More specifically, some particular features of mobile technology (such as connectivity, convenient user interface, touch screen, context awareness, supported devices, etc.) affect users' satisfaction and loyalty and should therefore take part in the process of evaluating the quality of mobile applications [36]. Compared to personal computers, several additional characteristics of mobile devices have to be considered in that context, including mobility, screen size, virtual keyboard, and social interconnectivity [1]. According to Huang [15], both hardware and software related challenges need to be tackled when designing mobile devices. While challenges related to hardware encompass limited input facilities (like keyboard, touch screen, and scroll wheel), limited output facilities (such as small screen size, audio output, etc.) and design for mobility, software related challenges mainly cover navigation, search engine, images and icons. As one of the outcomes of their study, Flora et al. [9] found that more than 75 % of respondents strongly believe that positive user experience (e.g. feeling comfortable in interaction

© Springer International Publishing Switzerland 2016
P. Zaphiris and A. Ioannou (Eds.): LCT 2016, LNCS 9753, pp. 368–379, 2016.
DOI: 10.1007/978-3-319-39483-1_34

with gadget and feeling smart while performing assignments without tutorials or other types of assistance) importantly contributes to the perceived mobile quality.

Kang et al. [20] distinguish two types of mobile applications: (1) web-based applications composed of pages optimized for mobile devices, and (2) native applications originally developed for different mobile devices like smartphones and tablets. An important effect on quality of native and web-based mobile applications has user experience that can be considered within following two categories: the context (hardware affordances, platform capabilities and user interface conventions, and an environment in which an application is used), and the implementation (performance, design, and integration with platform features) [3]. The use of social web applications on mobile devices offer new opportunities for interaction and collaboration among users that are continuously connected [10]. Web 2.0 applications (such as wikis, blogs, microblogs, social bookmarking sites, social networking sites, mashups, podcasting applications, e-portfolios, virtual worlds, online office suites, and knowledge management applications) support various breeds of interaction among users as well as creation, sharing, organization and integration of different artefacts [30]. In the ecosystem of social web applications, the users are no longer the consumers of content but contribute both actively (by creating content in their diverse forms) and passively (by using services that are available to the community of users) to the development of Web 2.0 applications [37]. In addition, the authors pointed out that the ability to use Web 2.0 applications on multiple platforms (PC, smartphone, PDA, etc.) represents an additional challenge to the design of a user experience and is therefore important to identify user needs in a timely manner. Li and Choi [21] stated that due to particularities of mobile devices (such as smaller screen and limited input methods) users have a number of issues (e.g. they can see only small part of the document) with the employment of applications meant for collaborative writing (e.g. Google Docs and Zoho Docs, etc.) when used on them. In that respect, the authors concluded that the use of social web applications on mobile devices is limited to chat, making group discussions, brain storming or informal collaborative writing. Drawing on a feedback received from students, Cochrane and Bateman [4] concluded that the choice of a smartphone type represents a key factor in the acceptance and use of social web applications on mobile devices as well as their integration in educational context with the collaboration as the main objective.

Considering all the aforementioned, quality attributes proposed in recent standard on software quality assessment (e.g. ISO/IEC 25010 [18]) cannot be used as guidelines for the design and development of high quality mobile applications [38]. Apart from user experience which reflects hedonic dimensions of quality, usability is focused on pragmatic facets of quality [2]. It is therefore important to introduce novel quality models that will be consisted of dimensions related to both usability and user experience. The main objective of this paper is to identify factors that significantly affect mobile quality in the context of social web applications.

The remainder of the paper is organized as follows. Next section offers a brief overview of prior studies focused on the assessment of particular dimensions of mobile quality. Proposed framework for measuring mobile quality of social web applications is introduced in the third section. Employed research methodology and study findings are presented in the fourth section. The key contributions, limitations of the study and future research directions are discussed in the last section.

2   Related Work

Baharuddin et al. [2] emphasize that for the purpose of designing and evaluating mobile applications, one should take into account specific properties and limitations of following four contextual factors: user, environment, technology, and task/activity. By understanding mentioned factors, it is possible to determine which usability dimensions (effectiveness, efficiency, satisfaction, usefulness, aesthetic, learnability, simplicity, intuitiveness, understandability, and attractiveness) should be considered when designing mobile applications. The same authors also stated that the use of web applications on mobile devices which have not been initially designed for them makes users weary and eventually affects the extent to which mobile usability of those applications is perceived by users.

According to Zamfiroiu [39], there are two groups of factors that contribute to the quality of mobile application. Battery life, RAM memory of a mobile device, CPU processing power, users' expectations, the distribution way of applications, level of the developer's involvement, and memory on hard disk of the mobile device are external factors because they have indirect impact on quality of mobile applications. The group of internal factors is related to specificities of mobile applications including the source code, used technologies, the information volume provided, commands rapidity, and testing level. As relevant quality characteristics of a mobile application Rabi'u et al. [35] pointed out battery life, navigation, robustness of operating system, and screen size. They also suggested that the usability of mobile applications should be measured by means of following attributes: understandability, learnability, operability, and attractiveness.

Based on the analysis of prior empirical studies, Coursaris and Kim [6] found that usability of mobile applications is most commonly measured with following attributes: efficiency, errors, ease of use, effectiveness, satisfaction, and learnability. As a follow up, Harrison et al. [12] proposed PACMAD model meant for evaluating usability of mobile application that includes following 7 attributes: effectiveness, efficiency, satisfaction, learnability, memorability, errors, and cognitive load. They also pointed out that the first three of mentioned attributes must be evaluated while remaining four can be hard for measuring.

By adapting scales from the Information System Success Model [8], Özata [34] discovered that system quality, information quality and perceived enjoyment are important determinants of users' satisfaction in the context of using Facebook as a mobile application for smartphones and tablets. However, it appeared that construct flow (the extent to which an individual becomes deeply absorbed in an activity) do not have direct significant influence on users' satisfaction. Results of the study carried out by Hussain and Kutar [16] uncovered that features of mobile devices have strong effect on users' satisfaction related to mobile applications. More specifically, the users expressed higher level of satisfaction when they used iPhone than when they employed O2 Orbit device. The rationale behind this results is that users experienced a greater number of issues when they used OS2 Orbit (e.g. font size, navigation, and interface design) than when they had an interaction with iPhone (e.g. hypersensitivity of virtual keyboard). Gikas and Grant [10] have investigated the use of social media and Web 2.0 applications on smartphones for learning purposes in higher education institutions and found that students had difficulties with data entry due to too small virtual keyboards. By combining adapted scales from TAM model [7] and an expectancy - confirmation theory [23], Ohk et al. [22] confirmed that perceived usefulness, interactivity, and perceived ease of use have positive impact on consumer satisfaction while in turn consumer satisfaction positively affects consumers' intentions to continuously use mobile applications. Results of the research conducted by Hsiao et al. [14] revealed that users' satisfaction, tight connection with others, and hedonic motivation significantly contribute to continuance intention of social applications as well as that users' satisfaction and habit have full mediation effects between perceived usefulness and intention to continue use social applications. Based on the analysis of data collected from 330 KakaoTalk and 311 Facebook users, Ha et al. [11] discovered that users' attitude towards mobile social networking sites is influenced by hedonic, integrative, and mobile convenience gratifications while cognitive, hedonic, integrative, and social interactive gratifications are affected by mobile convenience.

Jung and Yim [19] have found indirect effect of user interface design on the perceived usability of smartphone applications by means of following mediating variables: learnability of applications and interactions between users and smartphone applications. In addition, they discovered that user interface design has direct effect on learnability of applications and interactions between users and smartphone applications which in turn have direct impact on perceived usability of smartphone applications. Taking the aforementioned into account the authors concluded that mobile applications will be easy to use and learnable only if their user interface is simple and consistent.

Ickin et al. [17] conducted qualitative and quantitative study on the sample of three types of smartphones (Motorola, HTC, and Samsung) that all had preinstalled Android operating system. The study participants employed mentioned mobile devices in order to use 13 different categories of mobile applications including social network applications (OkCupid, Cooliris, Foursquare, Facebook, Twitter, Tumblr, and Touiteur). Analysis of collected data has shown that application's interface design contributes to the quality of experience because the users reported number of issues related to this construct including the position and location of the keys on the smartphone screen, difficulty with resizing, web-page scrolling, inefficient manual input (e.g., "fat finger" problem). According to the same authors, the second relevant construct is application performance because users commonly used expressions such as "freeze", "sloppy", "sluggish", "speed", "performance", "usage of memory", and "sdcard" when they wanted to emphasize that particular application has not met requirements of this construct to the acceptable extent. They also found that users who previously used these applications on their personal computers reported lower level of quality of experience because they had much higher expectations. Apart from application's interface design and application performance, the quality of experience is also affected by battery, phone features, apps and data connectivity cost, user's routine, and user's lifestyle [17].

Hoehle and Venkatesh [13] uncovered that usability of mobile applications accounts for 47 % of variance in continued intention to use social media on mobile devices. According to the outcomes of their study, relevant predictors of continued intention to use mobile social media applications are following six usability attributes: application design (branding, data preservation, instant start, orientation), application utility (collaboration, content relevance, search), user interface graphics (aesthetic graphics, realism, subtle animation), user interface input (control obviousness, de-emphasis of user settings, effort minimization, fingertip-size controls), user interface output (concise language, standardized user interface element, user-centric terminology), and user interface structure (logical path, top-to-bottom structure). It should be noted that application design, application utility, and user interface graphics have the strongest impact on loyalty related to the use of mobile social media applications.

The aforementioned findings indicate that current studies on the assessment of mobile quality are mainly focused on exploring its usability dimensions whereas measuring hedonic facets of mobile quality is rather rare. In addition, there is a lack of studies which consider both pragmatic and hedonic attributes when evaluating mobile quality. All the set forth motivates us to introduce a framework that would enable assessment of all relevant attributes related to usability and user experience of social web applications and in the same time take into account particularities of their use on mobile devices. Details on the proposed framework are provided in the following section.

3   Research Framework

As a follow up to the initial set of quality attributes proposed by Orehovački [27], evaluation methodology introduced in [24], their validation on the representative sample of various Web 2.0 applications when they have been used in their native environment [26, 31–33] as well as games [28], and their refinements [25, 29], a novel evaluation framework adapted to the context of using social web application on mobile devices was proposed. The adapted version of the conceptual model is comprised of five quality categories which are further decomposed into 37 quality attributes.

System quality refers to attributes that measure the extent to which social web application: provides various navigation mechanisms (navigability); has uniform interface structure, design, and terminology (consistency); is similar to previously used applications (familiarity); can be customized to meet users' needs (customizability); has implemented mechanisms that protect created artefacts from unauthorized use (security); operates properly with different types of devices and among different environments (compatibility); can exchange files with other applications and use files that were exchanged (interoperability); can adapt to the environment in which it is used (responsiveness); is usable on mobile devices (mobile-friendliness).

Service quality relates to attributes aimed for evaluating the degree to which social web application: provides various forms of help to users (helpfulness); is available every time users need it (availability); facilitates management of created artefacts (artefacts management); contains mechanisms that prevent errors to emerge (error prevention); is dependable, stable, and bug-free (reliability); can quickly recover from errors and operational interruptions (recoverability); notifies users with appropriate and useful messages (feedback); supports teamwork and enables different types of communication among users (interactiveness).

Performance refers to attributes that measure the extent to which the use of social web application: enables users to execute tasks accurately and completely (effectiveness); enables users to quickly perform tasks (efficiency); responds promptly to users' actions (response time); is capable to operate under an increased or expanding work-load (scalability); is usable within and beyond initially intended contexts of use (context coverage).

Effort relates to attributes dealing with the evaluation of the degree to which: the interaction with social web application consumes small amount of physical and mental energy (minimal workload); social web application is usable to people with the widest range of characteristics and capabilities (accessibility); users have full freedom in executing tasks by means of the social web application (controllability); is simple to operate the social web application (ease of use); is easy to become proficient in interacting with the social web application (learnability); is simple to memorize how the social web is used (memorability); the interaction with social web application is unambiguous (understandability).

User experience refers to attributes meant for measuring the extent to which: the social web application has visually appealing user interface (aesthetics); the social web application is beneficial in the context of tasks execution (usefulness); the interaction with the social web application holds the users' attention and stimulates their imagi-nation (playfulness); users have positive perception about the use of social web application (attitude towards use); the social web application has met users' expecta-tions (satisfaction); the social web application arouses users' emotional responses (pleasure); the social web application is distinctive among applications with the same purpose (uniqueness); users have the intention to continue to use the social web application and recommend it to others (loyalty).

4   Results

Participants. A total of 162 respondents (53.70 % male, 46.30 % female), aged 20.73 years (SD = 3.879) on average, participated in the study. At the time study took place, majority of the sample (74.07 %) were enrolled to one of the undergraduate study programs at Polytechnic of Rijeka (POLYRI) whereas remaining 25.93 % were third-year undergraduate students of Informatics at the Department of Information and Communication Technologies, Juraj Dobrila University of Pula (UNIPU). Most of them (77.78 %) were full-time students. All of them had been loyal consumers of mobile Internet on a daily basis. More specifically, 82.72 % of students had been accessing the Internet via their smartphones more than three times a day while 59.26 % of them have been spending more than ten hours a week on using the Internet via their smartphones. In most cases (88.89 %), students had been employing their smartphones for accessing social networking sites like Facebook which was followed by other activities such as making and receiving calls (80.86 %), Web browsing (71.60 %), synchronous messaging and exchange of multimedia content by means of services such as Viber (69.14 %), listening to music (66.05 %), sending SMS messages (66.05 %), taking photos (55.56 %), mobile learning (35.80 %), playing installed games (29.63 %), mobile banking (25.93 %), and taking and sharing selfies (19.14 %). When the use of mobile Internet was considered, the students reported they have been employing it most frequently (88.89 %) for social networking and subsequently for the purpose of synchronous messaging and exchange of multimedia content (73.46 %),

Web browsing (71.60 %), watching videos on services such as YouTube (67.90 %), accessing the educational content published on learning management system such as Moodle (56.79 %), reading news on web portals (51.23 %), mobile learning (37.65 %), accessing educational content located outside the learning management system (31.48 %), mobile banking (24.07 %), online shopping (19.75 %), and playing online games (17.90 %).

Procedure. The study was conducted in controlled lab conditions and was composed of two main parts: (1) interaction with two social web applications for collaborative writing on participants' mobile devices and (2) evaluation of their perceived mobile quality by means of the post-use questionnaire. Upon arriving to the lab, the participants were welcomed and briefly informed about the quality evaluation study. At the beginning of the scenario performance session, each participant received the form containing a list of 46 representative steps of interaction. Participants were asked to conduct all scenario steps twice – first with Google Docs and then using the Zoho Docs (both depicted in Fig. 1). After completing all the scenario steps with both social web applications, the participants were asked to fill out the post-use questionnaire. At the end of the study, respondents were debriefed, and thanked for their participation. The duration of the study was three hours.

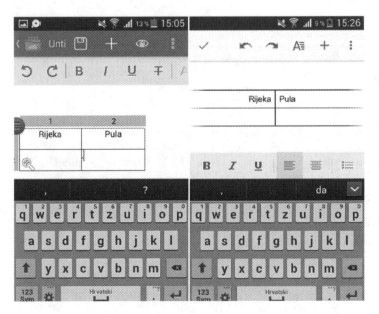

Fig. 1. Screenshots of mobile versions of evaluated social web applications for collaborative writing (left: Zoho Docs, right: Google Docs).

Apparatus. The study adopted a within-subjects design comparing two social web applications. Majority of participants (80.86 %) completed scenario of interaction with social web applications on smartphones that run Android operating system whereas 79.01 % of them employed Google Chrome web browser to carry out particular steps of the scenario. Data was gathered with the use of the post-use questionnaire which was administrated online by means of the KwikSurveys[1] questionnaire builder. The questionnaire comprised 12 items related to participants' demography and 137 items meant for measuring pragmatic and hedonic dimensions of mobile quality. Responses to the questionnaire items were modulated on a four point Likert scale (1 – strongly agree, 4 – strongly disagree). The sum of responses to items assigned to corresponding attribute was used as a composite measure which reflects particular facet of mobile quality. Differences between Google Docs and Zoho Docs were examined with Wilcoxon Signed-Rank Tests. The rationale behind the choice to employ this nonparametric equivalent to the dependent t-test relies on the outcomes of Shapiro-Wilk Tests which revealed that at least one of the variables in a pairwise comparison violates the assumption of normality in data ($p < .05$). In that respect, all the reported results are expressed as the median values. The effect size (r) was estimated as a ratio of Z-value and the square root of number of observations. According to Cohen [5], the values of .10, .30, and .50 indicate small, medium, and large effect size, respectively.

Findings. The analysis of collected data revealed that mobile quality of Google Docs is significantly higher ($Z = -9.756$, $p = .000$, $r = -.54$) than those of Zoho Docs. More specifically, it appeared that at the level of quality attributes the aforementioned applications do not differ significantly only in terms of the degree to which they are usable every time users want to interact with them ($Z = -1.171$, $p = .242$) nor to the extent to which they facilitate management of created artefacts ($Z = -1.580$, $p = .114$). It was also found that the degree to which Zoho Docs has met requirements of eight quality attributes (recoverability, loyalty, reliability, attitude toward use, response time, customizability, responsiveness, and pleasure) is medium worse than those achieved by Google Docs. In the case of remaining 27 quality attributes, Google Docs proved to have slightly better scores than Zoho Docs. When the mobile quality of evaluated social web applications is considered at the level of categories, it appears that they differ mainly by the extent to which they met requirements related to system quality ($Z = -11.039$, $p = .000$, $r = -.61$). The set forth is mostly caused by determined differences between Google Docs and Zoho Docs in the extent to which users can personalize them ($Z = -5.679$, $p = .000$, $r = -.32$) as well as to the degree to which they are able to adapt their features to the specificities of the device on which they are employed ($Z = -5.404$, $p = .000$, $r = -.30$). On the other hand, it was found that two social web applications differ at least with the respect to the amount of effort users have to employ in order to complete tasks by means of their interface functionalities ($Z = -5.724$, $p = .000$, $r = -.32$). This is mainly caused by the fact that there is small difference ($Z = -2.453$, $p = .000$, $r = -.14$) in the quantity of physical and mental load users have to invest to complete tasks with evaluated social web applications. Results of data analysis are summarized in Table 1.

---

[1] https://kwiksurveys.com.

Table 1. Outcomes of data analysis

Quality categories and attributes	Z	Effects in size (r)	Median values	
			Google Docs	Zoho Docs
Perceived mobile quality	**−9.756**	**−.54**[a]	**266.50**	**303.50**
System quality	**−11.039**	**−.61**[a]	**66.00**	**84.50**
Navigability	−4.090	−.23[a]	11.00	12.00
Consistency	−4.375	−.24[a]	6.00	7.00
Familiarity	−4.443	−.25[a]	8.50	9.00
Customizability	−5.679	−.32[a]	10.00	11.00
Security	−5.114	−.28[a]	16.00	17.00
Compatibility	−3.551	−.20[a]	8.00	8.00
Interoperability	−4.619	−.26[a]	6.00	6.00
Responsiveness	−5.404	−.30[a]	8.00	8.00
Mobile-friendliness	−4.299	−.24[a]	6.00	6.00
Service quality	**−6.874**	**−.38**[a]	**57.00**	**63.00**
Helpfulness	−5.150	−.29[a]	10.00	11.00
Availability	−1.171	N/A	4.00	4.00
Artefacts management	−1.580	N/A	10.00	9.00
Error prevention	−3.066	−.17[a]	5.00	6.00
Reliability	−6.300	−.35[a]	5.00	6.00
Recoverability	−6.941	−.39[a]	4.00	6.00
Feedback	−4.933	−.27[a]	10.00	10.00
Interactiveness	−2.749	−.15[a]	9.00	10.00
Performance	**−6.162**	**−.34**[a]	**43.00**	**47.00**
Effectiveness	−4.534	−.25[a]	11.00	12.00
Efficiency	−3.654	−.20[a]	9.00	10.00
Response time	−5.807	−.32[a]	5.00	6.00
Scalability	−4.723	−.26[a]	11.00	11.00
Context coverage	−4.156	−.23[a]	6.00	6.00
Effort	**−5.724**	**−.32**[a]	**42.00**	**45.00**
Minimal workload	−2.453	−.14[a]	7.00	7.00
Accessibility	−3.957	−.22[a]	6.00	6.00
Controllability	−3.957	−.22[a]	6.00	6.50
Ease of use	−4.780	−.27[a]	6.00	7.00
Learnability	−4.488	−.25[a]	6.00	6.00
Memorability	−5.100	−.28[a]	5.50	6.00
Understandability	−4.485	−.25[a]	6.00	6.00
User experience	**−6.466**	**−.36**[a]	**54.50**	**63.50**
Aesthetics	−4.717	−.26[a]	5.00	6.00
Usefulness	−4.330	−.24[a]	6.00	7.00
Playfulness	−4.708	−.26[a]	8.00	9.00
Attitude toward use	−6.158	−.34[a]	6.00	6.00

(*Continued*)

Table 1. (*Continued*)

Quality categories and attributes	Z	Effects in size (r)	Median values	
			Google Docs	Zoho Docs
Satisfaction	−4.489	−.25[a]	6.00	8.00
Pleasure	−5.350	−.30[a]	8.00	10.50
Uniqueness	−4.057	−.23[a]	7.50	8.00
Loyalty	−6.667	−.37[a]	7.00	9.50

[a] Google Docs > Zoho Docs

5   Conclusions

The aim of this paper was to determine which attributes are relevant for evaluation of quality in the context of social web applications for collaborative writing when they are employed on mobile devices. For that purpose, an empirical study was carried out during which the participants performed scenario-based assignments with two applications (Google Docs and Zoho Docs) and subsequently evaluated their perceived mobile quality by means of the post-use questionnaire.

According to the results of data analysis, when evaluation of mobile quality in the context of social web applications designed for collaborative writing is concerned, one should first pay attention to measuring all relevant dimensions of system quality followed by assessing facets of service quality, user experience, performance, and eventually effort. When study results are taken into account at the level of mobile quality attributes, they can be, with respect to their relevance, classified into four categories: (1) essential attributes ($r > |−.29|$) whose requirements social web application has to meet because otherwise its overall perceived mobile quality will be significantly decreased; (2) sufficient attributes ($|−.20| < r < |−.29|$) which are also very important but failing to meet their requirements will be penalized less severe than in the case of essential attributes; (3) desired attributes ($r < |−.20|$) whose relevance is significantly lower than those of previous two types of quality attributes but social web application still needs to comply with their requirements to some extent; and (4) not relevant ($r = N/A$) which does not have to be taken into account when measuring mobile quality of social web applications for collaborative writing. All the aforementioned indicates that proposed mobile quality model and corresponding post-use questionnaire are capable to determine significant differences between very similar representatives of social web applications for collaborative writing.

As in the case of most empirical studies, this one also has its limitations. The first one is related to homogeneity of participants. Although students are representative users of social web applications for collaborative writing because they employ them for educational purposes, heterogeneous group of users could have perceived particular dimensions of mobile quality in a different manner. The second limitation deals with the interpretation of reported findings because they are generalizable only to social web applications for collaborative writing. In order to explore the robustness of presented results, further studies should be carried out. In that respect, our future work will be focused on exploring the robustness of reported findings on a various types of mobile applications evaluated by heterogeneous sample of users.

References

1. Alshehri, F., Freeman, M.: User experience of mobile devices: a three layer method of evaluation. In: Proceedings of the 25th Australasian Conference on Information Systems, pp. 1–10. ACIS, Auckland (2014)
2. Baharuddin, R., Singh, D., Razali, R.: Usability dimensions for mobile applications - a review. Res. J. Appl. Sci. Eng. Technol. **5**, 2225–2231 (2013)
3. Charland, A., Leroux, B.: Mobile application development: web vs. native. Commun. ACM **54**(5), 49–53 (2011)
4. Cochrane, T., Bateman, R.: Smartphones give you wings: pedagogical affordances of mobile Web 2.0. Australas. J. Educ. Technol. **26**(1), 1–14 (2010)
5. Cohen, J.: A power primer. Psychol. Bull. **112**(1), 155–159 (1992)
6. Coursaris, C.K., Kim, D.J.: A meta-analytical review of empirical mobile usability studies. J. Usability Stud. **6**(3), 117–171 (2011)
7. Davis, F.D.: Perceived usefulness, perceived ease of use, and user acceptance of information technology. MIS Q. **13**(3), 319–340 (1989)
8. DeLone, W.H., McLean, E.R.: Information systems success: the quest for the dependent variable. Inf. Syst. Res. **3**(1), 60–95 (1992)
9. Flora, H.K., Wang, X., Chande, S.V.: An investigation on the characteristics of mobile applications: a survey study. Int. J. Inf. Technol. Comput. Sci. **6**(11), 21–27 (2014)
10. Gikas, J., Grant, M.M.: Mobile computing devices in higher education: student perspectives on learning with cellphones, smartphones & social media. Internet Higher Educ. **19**, 18–26 (2013)
11. Ha, Y.W., Kim, J., Libaque-Saenz, C.F., Chang, Y., Park, M.C.: Use and gratifications of mobile SNSs: Facebook and KakaoTalk in Korea. Telematics Inform. **32**(3), 425–438 (2015)
12. Harrison, R., Flood, D., Duce, D.: Usability of mobile applications: literature review and rationale for a new usability model. J. Interact. Sci. **1**(1), 1–16 (2013)
13. Hoehle, H., Venkatesh, V.: Mobile application usability: conceptualization and instrument development. MIS Q. **39**(2), 435–472 (2015)
14. Hsiao, C.H., Chang, J.J., Tang, K.Y.: Exploring the influential factors in continuance usage of mobile social Apps: satisfaction, habit, and customer value perspectives. Telematics Inform. **33**(2), 342–355 (2016)
15. Huang, K. Y.: Challenges in human-computer interaction design for mobile devices. In: Proceedings of the World Congress on Engineering and Computer Science, pp. 20–22. IAENG, San Francisco (2009)
16. Hussain, A., Kutar, M.: Apps vs devices: can the usability of mobile apps be decoupled from the device. Int. J. Comput. Sci. Issues **9**(3), 11–16 (2012)
17. Ickin, S., Wac, K., Fiedler, M., Janowski, L., Hong, J.-H., Dey, A.K.: Factors influencing quality of experience of commonly used mobile applications. IEEE Commun. Mag. **50**(4), 48–56 (2012)
18. ISO/IEC 25010:2011. Systems and software engineering - Systems and software Quality Requirements and Evaluation (SQuaRE) - System and software quality models (2011)
19. Jung, W., Yim, H.R.: The mediating effects of learnability and interaction on the perceived usability of smartphone applications. Int. J. Softw. Eng. Appl. **9**(9), 1–8 (2015)
20. Kang, B., Lee, J., Kissinger, J., Lee, R.Y.: A procedure for the development of mobile applications software. In: Kang, B., et al. (eds.) Software Engineering Research, Management and Applications. SCI, vol. 570, pp. 141–150. Springer, Heidelberg (2015)
21. Li, M., Choi, Y.M.: An exploration of mobile collaborative writing interface design. In: Zaphiris, P., Ioannou, A. (eds.) LCT 2015. LNCS, vol. 9192, pp. 97–105. Springer, Heidelberg (2015)
22. Ohk, K., Park, S.B., Hong, J.W.: The influence of perceived usefulness, perceived ease of use, interactivity, and ease of navigation on satisfaction in mobile application. Adv. Sci. Technol. Lett. **84**, 88–92 (2015)

23. Oliver, R.L.: A cognitive model for the antecedents and consequences of satisfaction. J. Mark. Res. **17**(4), 460–469 (1980)
24. Orehovački, T.: Development of a methodology for evaluating the quality in use of web 2.0 applications. In: Campos, P., Graham, N., Jorge, J., Nunes, N., Palanque, P., Winckler, M. (eds.) INTERACT 2011, Part IV. LNCS, vol. 6949, pp. 382–385. Springer, Heidelberg (2011)
25. Orehovački, T.: Methodology for Evaluating the Quality in Use of Web 2.0 Applications, Ph. D. thesis. University of Zagreb, Faculty of Organization and Informatics, Varaždin (2013)
26. Orehovački, T.: Perceived quality of cloud based applications for collaborative writing. In: Pokorny, J., et al. (eds.) Information Systems Development – Business Systems and Services: Modeling and Development, pp. 575–586. Springer, Heidelberg (2011)
27. Orehovački, T.: Proposal for a set of quality attributes relevant for web 2.0 application success. In: Proceedings of the 32nd International Conference on Information Technology Interfaces, pp. 319–326. IEEE Press, Cavtat (2010)
28. Orehovački, T., Babić, S.: Inspecting quality of games designed for learning programming. In: Zaphiris, P., Ioannou, A. (eds.) LCT 2015. LNCS, vol. 9192, pp. 620–631. Springer, Heidelberg (2015)
29. Orehovački, T., Babić, S., Jadrić, M.: Exploring the validity of an instrument to measure the perceived quality in use of web 2.0 applications with educational potential. In: Zaphiris, P., Ioannou, A. (eds.) LCT 2014, Part I. LNCS, vol. 8523, pp. 192–203. Springer, Heidelberg (2014)
30. Orehovački, T., Bubaš, G., Kovačić, A.: Taxonomy of web 2.0 applications with educational potential. In: Cheal, C. et al. (eds.) Transformation in Teaching: Social Media Strategies in Higher Education, pp. 43–72. Informing Science Press, Santa Rosa (2012)
31. Orehovački, T., Granić, A., Kermek, D.: Exploring the quality in use of web 2.0 applications: the case of mind mapping services. In: Harth, A., Koch, N. (eds.) ICWE 2011. LNCS, vol. 7059, pp. 266–277. Springer, Heidelberg (2012)
32. Orehovački, T., Granić, A., Kermek, D.: Evaluating the perceived and estimated quality in use of web 2.0 applications. J. Syst. Softw. **86**(12), 3039–3059 (2013)
33. Orehovački, T., Granollers, T.: Subjective and objective assessment of mashup tools. In: Marcus, A. (ed.) DUXU 2014, Part I. LNCS, vol. 8517, pp. 340–351. Springer, Heidelberg (2014)
34. Özata, F.Z.: Determinants of user satisfaction with mobile applications: case of facebook as a mobile app in Turkey. In: Proceedings of Business and Management Conferences, pp. 262–282. IISES, Vienna (2015)
35. Rabi'u, S., Ayobami, A.S., Hector, O.P.: Usability characteristics of mobile applications. In: Proceedings of the 1st International Conference on Behavioural and Social Science Research, pp. 1–5 (2012)
36. Schweighofer, T., Heričko, M.: Mobile device and technology characteristics' impact on mobile application testing. In: Proceedings of the 2nd Workshop of Software Quality Analysis, Monitoring, Improvement, and Applications, pp. 103–108. CEUR, Novi Sad (2013)
37. Vaananen-Vainio-Mattila, K., Vaataja, H., Vainio, T.: Opportunities and challenges of designing the Service User eXperience (SUX) in web 2.0. In: Saariluoma, P., Isomäki, H. (eds.) Future Interaction Design II, pp. 117–139. Springer, Heidelberg (2009)
38. Zahra, S., Khalid, A., Javed, A.: An efficient and effective new generation objective quality model for mobile applications. Int. J. Mod. Educ. Comput. Sci. **5**(4), 36–42 (2013)
39. Zamfiroiu, A.: Factors influencing the quality of mobile applications. Informatica Economică **18**(1), 131–138 (2014)

iMOOC Platform: Adaptive MOOCs

María Luisa Sein-Echaluce[1](✉), Ángel Fidalgo-Blanco[2],
Francisco J. García-Peñalvo[3], and Miguel Ángel Conde[4]

[1] University of Zaragoza, Zaragoza, Spain
mlsein@unizar.es
[2] Technical University of Madrid, Madrid, Spain
angel.fidalgo@upm.es
[3] GRIAL Research Group, University of Salamanca, Salamanca, Spain
fgarcia@usal.es
[4] GRIAL Research Group, University of León, León, Spain
miguel.conde@unileon.es

Abstract. Massive Open Online Courses or MOOCs presents low completion rates, they are massive thus the participants' profile is too much heterogeneous regarding origin, capacitation, motivation and learning aims. The number of studies that propose using adaptive techniques to resolve the problems above is increasing. This work presents the logistic, methodological and technological models of an adaptivity-based framework. This framework includes the basic elements of adaptive learning using a learning management system as core technology and expanding the adaptive possibilities in the logistics of the courses. The proposed model is implemented in an adaptive platform so called iMOOC that currently has a campus composed by four adaptive MOOCs. Also, a study about the participants' perception of usefulness and their needs for the adaptive processes is presented.

Keywords: Adaptive learning · Massive open online course · Online learning · Learning management system

1 Introduction

MOOC (Massive Open Online Course) means the last social advance in open education. Millions of users around the world make this type of courses offered by teachers of the most prestigious universities. The number of MOOCs continues growing and also the people who join them. Along with this growth, debates and studies have arisen including social issues (change of the university model), economic issues (new revenue for universities), technological issues (MOOC specific online platforms) and methodological issues (new pedagogical models).

Along with the reviews about the history and the specific characteristics of MOOCs (mass use, heterogeneity and multi-profiles/preferences/learning objectives) [1–4] there are future recommendations to improve the low completion rates [5] and the learning outcomes, including the application of adaptive learning techniques among their strategies [6–8]. Daniel et al. say [9] "A possible, but still undeveloped, solution that will probably be available in the near future is to implement adaptive learning techniques to

© Springer International Publishing Switzerland 2016
P. Zaphiris and A. Ioannou (Eds.): LCT 2016, LNCS 9753, pp. 380–390, 2016.
DOI: 10.1007/978-3-319-39483-1_35

make MOOC courses more personalized", also point some of adaptivity "Agents analyzing the learner's profile could customize a course as follows: adjusting course content according to the participants' pre-requisites or educational background; changing course content according to the participant's location or country of origin, for example language, units of measure, currency symbol, seasons, etc.; and showing relevant case studies or further readings according to the country or region of origin/interest", and about the required collaboration among the involved agents "There is a need to develop sophisticated adaptive learning mechanisms that will require the establishment of MOOC working partnerships between educators, instructional designers, and programmers".

In this sense, the hypermedia systems, which were initially developed several years ago [10–12], jointly with other technologies that are starting to be used in the MOOC deployment in order to follow the users' behavior in this kind of courses, such as semantic web [13] and learning analytics [14, 15]. This way recommendations to the participants may be done [16] or detecting possible dropouts, for example through the participation in the for a [17].

There exist several frameworks that allow the inclusion of adaptive techniques in MOOCs. Sonwalkar [19] proposes, using web services and a computer architecture, an Adaptive Learning Systems (ALS) that adapts itself to five learning styles throughout diagnostic assessments about the participants' preferences and goals. Onah & Sinclair [19] use recommendation systems "The framework supports users in creating their own paths, allowing them to make informed choices about appropriate resources based on their expression of current objectives and preferences". This framework focuses on capturing the users' knowledge using concept-based quizzes. Teixeira [20] adds to his MOOC pedagogical model, so called iMOOC, the content adaptation taking into account the participants' prior knowledge and the device they use to access the course.

In this paper an adaptive framework is proposed. It has been tested in the intelligent MOOC (i-MOOC) platform [21–24]. Most of MOOCs are xMOOC type, that means they are based on similar models of the traditional Learning Management Systems (LMS). This kind of MOOCs forces students to adapt themselves both learning strategy and resources. Also, some of these MOOCs incorporate cooperative learning tools, usually Web 2.0 tools and social networks. i-MOOC platform improves this classical model combining the best elements of xMOOCs and cMOOCs types with adaptive capabilities in the same online system [25–28].

This paper covers three of the four aspects mentioned above: logistic, methodology and technology (apart from the economics models MOOCs). A specific experience with the proposed framework has been developed, including characteristics of the related frameworks cited, but adding more capabilities regarding the logistic part and simplifying the technology used.

The main goals of this paper are:

- Describing a logistic, methodological and technological proposal based on a platform that allows for adaptive MOOCs.
- Identifying the adaptive processes that can be associated to a MOOC.
- Measuring the perception of the participants in a MOOC about the adaptive characteristics thereof.

The rest of paper is organized as follow. Section 2 presents the proposed model to integrate adaptive MOOCs (aMOOC). Section 3 introduces the experience done. Section 4 presents the results, including the participants' characteristics and their perception about the adaptive activities that a MOOC should incorporate. Finally, the conclusion section closes the paper with the discussion of the experience and the obtained results.

2 An Adaptive Model for MOOCs

The proposed model is based on the authors' framework [28] that has been tested with a real case its effectiveness to reduce the MOOC dropout ratio [5] and to improve the users' satisfaction. This framework is based on a learning ecosystem [23, 29–32] composed by a Learning Management System (LMS) plus several own services for adaptivity and learning analytics and web 2.0 tools for knowledge management and gamification [33].

This work is focused on the applied adaptive methodology and the support learning ecosystem. In the following subsections the adaptive characteristics of the proposed model regarding logistic, methodology and technology are presented.

2.1 Logistic Model

The i-MOOC platform [21] is used. It has been developed throughout a collaboration agreement between Tech University of Madrid and University of Zaragoza in 2013. In 2015 the University of Salamanca joined to this agreement.

Figure 1 shows the logistic model that is proposed in this work. The platform may be composed by "n" virtual campuses, and each virtual campus includes by a set of aMOOCs.

The adaptive characteristics are:

- Against a classic MOOC, with fixed starting and ending dates and specific week timetable (all is oriented to users adapt themselves to the MOOC), this proposal has a wide period of learning that supports different schedules and plans. During this period the enrolment process is open and every participant decides, from an individual point view, the number of aMOOCs that wants to do, also the intensity and the working schedule.
- Virtual campus definition, each one composed by aMOOCs sharing a common topic or knowledge field. Each specific aMOOC is independent from the others, but it can be joined with other aMOOCs in order to create a greater pedagogical unit and optimize common resources. The interconnection is based on sharing resources, activities and itineraries (learning paths).
- The training from other aMOOCs is recognized. Common parts to other made aMOOCs are identified, this way the shared part is validated. For example, if in the "A" aMOOC a student develops an activity to acquire a specific skill, this student will not to do the activities related to the same skill in the same virtual campus.

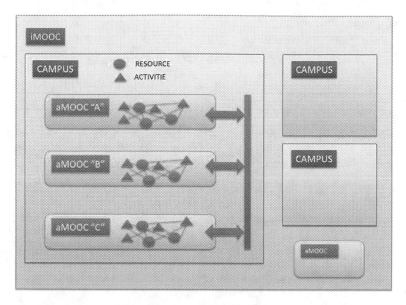

Fig. 1. Logistic model

2.2 Methodological Model

The experience gathered by the authors in previous works about adaptive learning in online environments [34–36] is used. The research conducted previously has led to discover basic needs deficiencies that teachers find in their day to day and require contributions by teachers adapted to each student. In previous experiences the following "adaptive pills" merged to satisfy different needs of adaptivity [37]:

- P_1. Self-assessment training.
- P_2. Adapted advance to the student's learning speed.
- P_3. Adaptation of learning to different profiles/skills/interests.
- P_4. Contributing and sharing resources among a set of users with a common interest/profile.
- P_5. Adapted learning to the acquired knowledge (the results of the activities to be carried on).
- P_6. Monitoring student's progress.

The combination of these "adaptive pills" are included in the aMOOCs, allowing to create different learning pathways and other actions that personalize learning.

2.3 Technological Model

For this experience no technological development is needed, because of Moodle [38] LMS is used. Moodle has more personalization capabilities than other platforms such as edX regarding educative tools, analysis and SCORM compliance. Also, Moodle is friendly enough for both instructional designers and students, due to it eliminates some barriers for creating MOOCs in some specialized platforms. On the other hand, Moodle fulfill the accessibility standards, has mobile access and the allowed resources may be youtube videos and accessible formats (html, pdf, etc.), which permit the users' access from a huge number of devices. The platform has been tested with a vey large number of students [39].

The large and active developer Moodle community ensures improved versions (continually updated) including increasingly useful tools. Also external plugins complement the basic installation. All this makes it possible to carry out the methodological requirements, putting technology at the service of the methodology. Some tools provided by Moodle are described below, which provide solutions, respectively, to the needs of adaptivity (adaptive pills P_i) listed above:

- S_1 (P_1) Quizzes with feedback and hints.
- S_2 (P_2) Activity completion and Restrict access options.
- S_3 (P_3) Groups and groupings. Group Choice plugin.
- S_4 (P_4) Forums (grouping mode).
- S_5 (P_5) Activity completion and Restrict access options. Lesson.
- S_6 (P_6) Table of Activity completion.

3 Research Context

The proposed framework has been implemented in the i-MOOC platform [21] through the "Educational innovation MOOC campus" composed by four aMOOCs. The first edition of this campus was opened during four months (from November 23rd, 2015 to February 28th, 2016). The available aMOOCs in this first edition were:

- aMOOC Practical fundamentals of educational innovation (15 h) [40].
- aMOOC Flip Teaching (20 h) [41].
- aMOOC Learning communities (15 h) [42].
- aMOOC Teamwork competence development (30 h) [43].

The used LMS, Moodle 2.8, includes, as elements for adaptivity facilitators, access restrictions, finalization conditions, groups and groupings, as well as several plugins to choose the group and to generate certificates, for example. These tools have been used to make visible the resources done by the students in previous activities (several resources at the same time or in sequence), to share the works done by the participants with their peers with the same profile (same interest, same educational level), to offer different resources depending on the participants' preferences or previous knowledge, to offer different learning paths depending on participants' profile (for example, in the aMOOC of teamwork competence the chosen profiles are teacher, student and researcher) and to follow the participant progress.

The evaluation has been made using quizzes and Q&A fora in Moodle with automatic feedback and faculty feedback. According to the framework proposed in [28], fora have been used fora to promote discussion between participants and with the faculty, also throughout the fora participants may upload new resources. Besides, Google+ "Innovación Educativa Aplicada" social net has been used to share resources and information.

The results of an initial survey to detect participants' profiles and their preferences with respect to certain adaptive actions to be implemented in a MOOC are presented in the following section.

4 Results of Implementation

At the date of 19.02.2016 the Educational Innovation MOOC Campus had 870 enrolled people (the campus closes at the date of 28.02.2016); 519 of them had fulfilled the initial survey about the participants' characteristics and their perception about the possible adaptativity options in future aMOOCs.

Regarding the countries of origin, slightly more than half of the participants are Spanish; the rest are distributed in 27 Spanish-speaking countries (official language of the course). The top ten countries are: Spain (53.86 %), Mexico (10.62 %), Argentina (6.18 %), Peru (5.41 %), Colombia (5.02 %), Venezuela (4.25 %), Ecuador (3.67 %), Brazil (1.74 %), Dominican Republic (1.35 %) and Bolivia (1.16 %).

With respect to gender, 53.95 % are women. Tables 1, 2 and 3 show the obtained data about participants' professional profile, educational innovation previous experience and motivation for enrolling in the MOOC Campus.

Table 1. Professional profile

Self-employed	5.59
K12 teacher	10.02
Secondary teacher (13–18 years)	24.08
Vocational education teacher	10.79
University teacher	22.54
Employee (non teacher)	5.97
Student (non university)	0
University student (education area)	6.55
University student (non education area)	1.93
Other	12.52

Table 2. Educational innovation previous experience

I have not previous experience	21.00
I only have seen information in Internet	30.25
I have applied or apply educational innovation	38.34
I have occupied or occupy a position related to educational innovation	10.40

The questions about participants' preferences regarding adaptivity characteristics that they will like to find in the aMOOCs, using a Likert scale 1–4, (1- Completely disagree; 2- Somewhat agree; 3- Sufficient agree; and 4- Strongly agree) are gathered in Table 4.

Table 3. Motivation for enrolling in the MOOC Campus

Expanding my education in general	53.37
Knowing what the educational innovation is, but for now I will not apply	12.72
Starting to apply educational innovation	35.65
Having a new vision of educational innovation	44.12
Researching in educational innovation	46.63
Knowing how the course is organized and/or accessing to the materials	19.27

Table 4. Perception about adaptivity aspects

	1	2	3	4
F_1- Proposing of different activities depending on my choice or the results of my evaluation	0.58	4.43	47.98	47.01
F_2- Accessing the contents/activities following my learning speed of work, without a specific timetable to do that	0.58	5.78	27.55	66.09
F_3- Choosing between different difficulty levels in the contents/activities to reach different learning objectives	0.39	5.59	41.62	52.41
F_4- Organizing interest groups by the same area or the same experience level to discuss in specific fora	0.77	13.68	43.93	41.62
F_5- Choosing different evaluation methods (self-evaluation, peer review, etc.)	0.96	7.90	45.47	45.66
F_6- Organizing peer evaluation also by interest groups/same area/same level of experience	2.31	10.02	47.98	39.69

5 Discussion

The proposed framework includes the adaptive elements that Sonwalkar [18] establishes the ALS should have, including adaptive logistic in the way to set up the MOOC campuses with the aMOOCs and simplified technology to develop the adaptive learning in each aMOOC, which mean a significant advance in comparison with the above mentioned proposals [18–20]. The proposed model has been implemented in the "Educational Innovation MOOC Campus".

It has been confirmed the heterogeneity of the participants in this experience based on variables: country of residence (27 different), gender (just over half of women), professional profile (teachers, students, freelancers and other professions), previous experience in educational innovation and motivation for the course [28].

Campus participants have given a high valorization to the adaptive processes, with a value greater that 86 % (including 3- Sufficient agree; and 4- Strongly agree answers). The perception of usefulness of the logistic proposal in the adaptivity has been confirmed, with a special focus on the bigger period to make the course and the methodology of each aMOOC, where the navigation adaptation of the contents according their own learning speed received a 93.64 % of valorization. Regard to learning processes embedded in aMOOCs, 94.03 % indicates that they would like to choose between different levels of difficulty and different learning objectives. It also indicates that it is advantageous to use the adaptivity so that they can form homogeneous groups for the development of the same activity or to discuss between them (85.55 %). However, there is a 2.31 % that is not agree that peer review is conducted by homogeneous groups. We should discern whether this rejection is not specifically directed to the activity of peer review that does not please itself to all participants. All this supports the general recommendations applying adaptability in MOOCs [6–9].

6 Conclusions

As a general conclusion, it has been shown that the logistic, methodological and technological model offers new options to the previous frameworks; it may be implemented in a particular product and the campus users of this experience accept adaptivity on eLearning platforms, in MOOCs and in cooperative activities.

Future work is devoted to process the final data about participation in the campus, as well as the final satisfaction surveys that validate the model. These actions will make possible improvements such as:

- Creating new learning pathways within each aMOOC, which fit the profiles of the participants and the course subject (because of they are related).
- Improving the automatic feedback to perform activities.
- Sending recommendations for other aMOOCs depending on the results of certain activities.
- Generating different certificates for different purposes within the same aMOOC and campus certificates.

Acknowledgements. We would like to thank the GATE Service of the Technological University of Madrid, the Government of Aragón, the European Social Fund and the Ministry of Education of the Region of Castilla-León for their support. Finally, the authors would like to express their gratitude to the research groups (LITI, http://www.liti.es; GIDTIC, http://gidtic.com and GRIAL, http://grial.usal.es).

References

1. Daniel, J.: Making sense of MOOCs: musings in a maze of myth, paradox and possibility. J. Interact. Media Educ. 3 (2012). Accessed 18 Feb 2016. http://www-jime.open.ac.uk/jime/article/viewArticle/2012-18/html
2. Fidalgo Blanco, Á., Sein-Echaluce Lacleta, M.L., Borrás Gené, O., García-Peñalvo, F.J.: Educación en abierto: Integración de un MOOC con una asignatura académica. Educ. Knowl. Soc. (formerly Revista Teoría de la Educación: Educación y Cultura en la Sociedad de la Información), **15**, 233–255 (2014)
3. Martínez Abad, F., Rodríguez Conde, M.J., García-Peñalvo, F.J.: Evaluación del impacto del término "MOOC" vs "eLearning" en la literatura científica y de divulgación. Profesorado. Revista de currículum y formación del profesorado, **18**, 185–201 (2014)

4. Chiappe Laverde, A., Hine, N., Martínez Silva, J.A.: Literatura y práctica una revisión crítica acerca de los MOOC. Comunicar **44**, 09–18 (2015)
5. Jordan, K.: MOOC completion rates: the data (2015). http://www.katyjordan.com/MOOCproject.html. Accessed 18 Feb 2016
6. BIS.: the maturing of the MOOC: literature review of massive open online courses and other forms of online distance learning. BIS Research Paper, 130 (2013). https://www.gov.uk/government/uploads/system/uploads/attachment_data/file/240193/13-1173-maturing-of-the-mooc.pdf. Accessed 18 Feb 2016
7. Hollands, F.M., Tirthali, D.: MOOCs: expectations and reality. Full report. Center for Benefit-Cost Studies of Education, Teachers College, Columbia University, New York (2014). http://cbcse.org/wordpress/wp-content/uploads/2014/05/MOOCs_Expectations_and_Reality.pdf. Accessed 18 Feb 2016
8. Fidalgo Blanco, Á., García-Peñalvo, F.J., Sein-Echaluce Lacleta, M.L.: A methodology proposal for developing adaptive cMOOC. In: García-Peñalvo, F.J. (ed.) Proceedings of the First International Conference on Technological Ecosystems for Enhancing Multiculturality (TEEM 2013), pp. 553–558. ACM, New York (2013)
9. Daniel, J., Vázquez Cano, E., Gisbert, M.: The future of MOOCs adaptive learning or business model? RUSC. Univ. Knowl. Soc. J. **12**(1), 64–74 (2015). http://dx.doi.org/10.7238/rusc.v12i1.2475
10. Brusilovsky, P.: Methods and techniques of adaptive hypermedia. User Model. User-Adap. Inter. **6**(2–3), 87–129 (1996). http://doi.org/10.1007/BF00143964
11. Berlanga, A.J., García-Peñalvo, F.J.: Learning design in adaptive educational hypermedia systems. J. Univ. Comput. Sci. **14**, 3627–3647 (2008)
12. Berlanga, A.J., García-Peñalvo, F.J.: IMS LD reusable elements for adaptive learning designs. J. Interact. Media Educ. **11**, 1–16 (2005)
13. Berlanga, A., García-Peñalvo, F.J.: Learning technology specifications: semantic objects for adaptive learning environments. Int. J. Learn. Technol. **1**, 458–472 (2005)
14. Gómez-Aguilar, D.A., Hernández-García, Á., García-Peñalvo, F.J., Therón, R.: Tap into visual analysis of customization of grouping of activities in eLearning. Comput. Hum. Behav. **47**, 60–67 (2015)
15. Gómez-Aguilar, D.A., García-Peñalvo, F.J., Therón, R.: Analítica Visual en eLearning. El Profesional de la Información **23**, 236–245 (2014)
16. Bousbahi, F., Chorfi, H.: MOOC-Rec: a case based recommender system for MOOCs. Procedia- Soc. Behav. Sci. **195**, 1813–1822 (2015)
17. Xing, W., Chen, X., Stein, J., Marcinkowski, M.: Temporal predication of dropouts in MOOCs: reaching the low hanging fruit through stacking generalization. Comput. Hum. Behav. **58**, 119–129 (2016)
18. Sonwalkar, N.: The first adaptive MOOC: a case study on pedagogy framework and scalable cloud architecture—Part I. In: MOOCs Forum, 1(P), pp. 22–29 (2013). http://online.liebertpub.com/doi/pdf/10.1089/mooc.2013.0007. Accessed 18 Feb 2016
19. Onah, D.F.O., Sinclair, J.E.: Massive open online courses- an adaptive learning framework. In: 9th International Technology, Education and Development Conference, IATED, Madrid, Spain, 2–4 March, pp. 1258–1266 (2015). http://www2.warwick.ac.uk/fac/sci/dcs/people/research/csrmaj/daniel_onah_inted2015.pdf
20. Teixeira, A., Garcia-Cabot, A., García-López, E., Mota, J., de-Marcos, L.: A new competence-based approach for personalizing MOOCs in a mobile collaborative and networked environment. RIED. Revista Iberoamericana de Educación a Distancia **19**(1), 143–160 (2016). http://dx.doi.org/10.5944/ried.19.1.14578
21. i-MOOC Platform (2016). http://gridlab.upm.es/imooc/

22. García-Peñalvo, F.J., Cruz-Benito, J., Borrás-Gené, O., Blanco, Á.F.: Evolution of the conversation and knowledge acquisition in social networks related to a MOOC course. In: Zaphiris, P., Ioannou, A. (eds.) LCT 2015. LNCS, vol. 9192, pp. 470–481. Springer, Heidelberg (2015)
23. Cruz-Benito, J., Borrás-Gené, O., García-Peñalvo, F.J., Fidalgo-Blanco, Á., Therón, R.: Extending MOOC ecosystems using web services and software architectures. In: Proceedings of the XVI International Conference on Human Computer Interaction, Vilanova i la Geltrú, Spain, 07–09 September 2015, Article 52. ACM, New York (2015)
24. Cruz-Benito, J., Borrás-Gené, O., García-Peñalvo, F.J., Fidalgo Blanco, Á., Therón, R.: Detección de aprendizaje no formal e informal en Comunidades de Aprendizaje soportadas por Redes Sociales en el contexto de un MOOC Cooperativo. In: Rodrigues, M.R., Nistal, M.L., Figueiredo, M. (eds.) Atas do XVII Simpósio Internacional de Informática Educativa (SIIE 2015), Setúbal, Portugal, 25 a 27 de Novembro de 2015, pp. 410–418, Escola Superior de Educação do Instituto Politécnico de Setúbal, Setúbal, Portugal (2015)
25. Fidalgo-Blanco, Á., Sein-Echaluce Lacleta, M.L., García-Peñalvo, F.J.: MOOC cooperativo. Una integración entre cMOOC y xMOOC. In: Fidalgo Blanco, Á., Sein-Echaluce Lacleta, M.L. (eds.) Actas del II Congreso Internacional sobre Aprendizaje, Innovación y Competitividad, CINAIC 2013, Madrid, 6–8 de noviembre de 2013, pp. 481–486. Fundación General de la Universidad Politécnica de Madrid, Madrid, España (2013)
26. Fidalgo-Blanco, Á., Sein-Echaluce, M.L., García-Peñalvo, F.J., Esteban Escaño, J.: Improving the MOOC learning outcomes throughout informal learning activities. In: TEEM 2014. ACM International Conference Proceedings Series (ICPS), New York, USA, pp. 611–617 (2014). http://dl.acm.org/citation.cfm?id=2669963
27. García-Peñalvo, F.J., Fernández Hermo, V., Fidalgo Blanco, Á., Sein-Echaluce, M.L.: Applied educational innovation MOOC: learners' experience and valorization of strengths and weaknesses. In: TEEM 2014. ACM International Conference Proceedings Series (ICPS), New York, USA, pp. 139–145 (2014). http://dl.acm.org/citation.cfm?id=2669892
28. Fidalgo-Blanco, A., Sein-Echaluce, M.L., García-Peñalvo, F.J.: Methodological approach and technological framework to break the current limitations of MOOC model. J. Univ. Comput. Sci. 21(5), 712–734 (2015)
29. García-Peñalvo, F.J., Seoane-Pardo, A.M.: Una revisión actualizada del concepto de eLearning. Décimo Aniversario. Educ. Knowl. Soc. 16, 119–144 (2015)
30. García-Peñalvo, F.J., Hernández-García, Á., Conde-González, M.Á., Fidalgo-Blanco, Á., Sein-Echaluce Lacleta, M.L., Alier-Forment, M., Llorens-Largo, F., Iglesias-Pradas, S.: Learning services-based technological ecosystems. In: Alves, G.R., Felgueiras, M.C. (eds.) Proceedings of the Third International Conference on Technological Ecosystems for Enhancing Multiculturality (TEEM 2015), Porto, Portugal, 7–9 October 2015, pp. 467–472. ACM, New York (2015)
31. Berthelemy, M.: Definition of a learning ecosystem. Learning Conversations. Thoughts, ideas and reflections from Mark Berthelemy (2013)
32. García-Holgado, A., García-Peñalvo, F.J.: Architectural pattern for the definition of eLearning ecosystems based on Open Source developments. In: Sierra-Rodríguez, J.L., Dodero-Beardo, J.M., Burgos, D. (eds.) Proceedings of 2014 International Symposium on Computers in Education (SIIE), Logrono, La Rioja, Spain, 12–14 November 2014, pp. 93–98. Institute of Electrical and Electronics Engineers, USA (2014)
33. Borrás Gené, O., Martínez Núñez, M., Fidalgo Blanco, Á.: Gamification in MOOC: challenges, opportunities and proposals for advancing MOOC model. In: García-Peñalvo, F. J. (ed.) Proceedings of the Second International Conference on Technological Ecosystems for Enhancing Multiculturality (TEEM 2014), pp. 215–220. ACM, New York (2014)

34. Lerís, D., Sein-Echaluce, M.L.: La personalización del aprendizaje: Un objetivo del paradigma educativo centrado en el aprendizaje. Arbor **187**(Extra_3), 123–134 (2011). http://dx.doi.org/10.3989/arbor.2011.iExtra_3
35. Berlanga, A.J., García, F.J., Carabias, J.: Authoring adaptive learning designs using IMS LD. In: Wade, V.P., Ashman, H., Smyth, B. (eds.) AH 2006. LNCS, vol. 4018, pp. 31–40. Springer, Heidelberg (2006)
36. Lerís-López, D., Vea-Muniesa, F., Velamazán-Gimeno, M.Á.: Aprendizaje adaptativo en Moodle: tres casos prácticos. Educ. Knowl. Soc. **16**(4), 138–157 (2015)
37. Sein-Echaluce, M.L., Aguado, P.M., Esteban-Escaño, J., Esteban-Sánchez, A., Gracia-Gómez, M.C., Florentin, P., Leris, D., Vea, F., Velamazán, M.A.: Design of adaptive experiences in higher education through a learning management system. In: TEEM 2015. ACM International Conference Proceedings Series (ICPS), New York, USA, pp. 159–164 (2015)
38. Moodle (2016). http://moodle.org
39. MoodleMOOC. Teaching with Moodle MOOC (2016). https://learn.moodle.net/?lang=es
40. FPIE. Video presentation (2016). https://prezi.com/glu0pwhpnbc3/fundamentos-practicos-de-la-innovacion-educativa/. Accessed 18 Feb 2016
41. FT. Video presentation (2016). https://www.youtube.com/watch?v=h3W1nOD3FRo&feature=youtu.be. Accessed 18 Feb 2016
42. CA. Video presentation (2016). https://innovacioneducativa.wordpress.com/2015/11/10/como-utilizar-una-red-social-para-construir-una-comunidad-de-aprendizaje/. Accessed 18 Feb 2016
43. TE. Video presentation (2016). https://innovacioneducativa.wordpress.com/2015/11/03/como-formar-y-evaluar-en-la-competencia-de-trabajo-en-equipo-de-forma-sencilla-el-metodo-ctmtc/. Accessed 18 Feb 2016

Usability Evaluation of a Dynamic Geometry Software Mobile Interface Through Eye Tracking

Serap Yağmur$^{(\boxtimes)}$ and Murat Perit Çakır

Graduate School of Informatics,
Middle East Technical University, Ankara, Turkey
{yagmur, perit}@metu.edu.tr

Abstract. The use of information technology in mathematics education has become popular due to the increasing availability of software applications designed for constructing mathematical representations. In this study, we conducted a usability evaluation of GeoGebra, which is a commonly used math education tool that provides dynamic geometry, spreadsheet and algebra features. This study reports the findings of a usability experiment where we employed an eye tracker to evaluate the mobile version of GeoGebra. Our findings suggest that the mobile version primarily replaced the function of the mouse cursor in the desktop version with the fingertip, and did not take advantage of the gestures supported by the multi-touch screens of new generation tablet computers. Based on the empirical findings of the study, design ideas for improving the usability of the existing GeoGebra mobile interfaces are proposed.

Keywords: Usability · GeoGebra · Eye tracking · Mobile usability

1 Introduction

Over the last few decades, Information and Communication Technologies (ICT) have assumed an increasingly important role in the teaching of mathematics and science. Computers in the classroom have become an indispensable tool for supporting teaching and learning [14]. Innovations in ICT have made computing a ubiquitous phenomenon where devices such as computers, tablets, and smart phones are widely adopted in our daily lives as well as in educational activities.

Advances in computing and multimedia have enabled students to visualize and engage with mathematical concepts that were not possible with earlier systems or with the traditional resources such as textbooks. There are several kinds of software applications that can be used to aid math education [1]. Main types of mathematics education software that are popularly used by practitioners are predominantly Dynamic Geometry software, spreadsheets and Computer Algebra Systems (CAS) [5]. Many pedagogical environments for math education have been developed, such as Cinderella (www.cinderella.de), Geometer's Sketchpad (www.keypress.com/sketchpad), Cabri geometre II+ (www.cabri.com), and GeoGebra (www.GeoGebra.org), sampled among

© Springer International Publishing Switzerland 2016
P. Zaphiris and A. Ioannou (Eds.): LCT 2016, LNCS 9753, pp. 391–402, 2016.
DOI: 10.1007/978-3-319-39483-1_36

many other applications. This study focuses on GeoGebra, because it is a free Dynamic Geometry Software (henceforth DGS) that also provides basic features of a Computer Algebra System to bridge the gap between math domains such as geometry, algebra and calculus [4] and is freely available at www.geoegebra.org. This software combines geometry, algebra and calculus into a single and easy package for teaching and learning mathematics from elementary to university level [6].

According to Hohenwarter and Preiner [6], GeoGebra appears to be a user-friendly software that can be operated intuitively and does not require advanced skills to get started. It is easily accessible from home as well as from school via multiple platforms. Students can practice, do homework, prepare for their lessons and revise from home. It also supports multiple languages and is a great asset for classrooms that have multilingual learners. They can create and share their constructions by using the GeoGebraWiki tool or use the templates provided to customize the tool for their learning needs. There is a user forum where students and teachers can share ideas and discuss math problems [7].

Domènech [4] stated that students encounter many types of difficulties when learning mathematical concepts and solving such problems often require coordinated reasoning over symbolic expressions and visualizations. Although students can face structural and visualization problems when learning geometry, developing deductive reasoning skills can be considered as the biggest challenge for the students. In particular, students may have difficulty moving from geometry based on shallow visual properties to a geometry based on a deeper understanding of the structural patterns that bring together primitive objects such as points and lines for constructing more complex geometric representations [4]. For example, students can observe how changing the radius of a cylinder changes the side area both graphically and symbolically in an environment like GeoGebra. In other words, students can observe the implications of a visual action on the quantities and vice versa, which will help them understand the relationships among different ways to represent the same mathematical concept. Realization of such connections among different representations is considered as an indication of deep learning of mathematical concepts, and dynamic geometry software has the potential to stimulate and facilitate the development of such deep level of understanding.

The realization of such benefits depend on to what extent the interface effectively supports students to construct and manipulate dynamic representations. Systems such as GeoGebra requires users to add and manipulate basic primitive constructs such as points, angles, lines, and circles. These primitives need to be combined in specific ways to construct even more complex objects that are typically used in the math classroom, and combining objects often involve specific interface actions such as selecting two points to combine with a line, or dragging a point to change its coordinates. Although these interface actions are based on traditional mouse-based gestures used for desktop applications, learning appropriate use of the features for building math representations may not necessarily be a trivial matter for the students. Consequently, usability issues involved with the design of the interface elements and gestures acting on them have important educational consequences. However, systematic usability studies of primitive interface elements provided by dynamic geometry tools are not widely covered in the literature. Existing evaluations tend to focus more on pedagogical aspects, with the exception of a few studies focusing on usability concerns.

To the best of our knowledge, there are two main studies focusing on the usability of similar DGS software. In the first study, Hohenwanter and Lavizca [8] evaluated the difficulties encountered by the participants while using basic GeoGebra tools through a questionnaire. This study was carried out with the participation of 44 mathematics teachers, where they were asked to rate the GeoGebra tools from 0 = very easy to 5 = very difficult. According to the results, Hohenwanter and Lavizca classified the tools in terms of their difficulty of use, and stated that "easy-to-use" tools can be discovered via individual experimentation at home or school, the "middle" difficulty tools should be demonstrated by the instructor, and the "difficult-to-use" tools require both guidance and planned exercises to master their use [8]. The second study was conducted by Konterkamp and Dorhman [9], where they used a prototype of Cinderella to investigate the affordances of multi-touch screens for constructing geometric objects. In particular, they evaluated how Cinderella supports multi-touch features. Their findings pointed out that existing interfaces do not adequately take advantage of multi-touch features and function primarily as an extension of pen-based single touch interfaces [9].

Given the recent proliferation of mobile DGS applications and their increasing potential for widespread use, this study aims to explore to what extent the recently released table version of the popular GeoGebra system makes effective use of the affordances of mobile user interfaces. In particular, the purpose of this study is to explore the effectiveness of the iPad version of GeoGebra, and to suggest interaction design ideas to improve upon the detected usability issues.

2 Methodology

In this study, we conducted a usability evaluation of the recently released iPad version of GeoGebra by using a Tobii X2-60 eye tracker mounted mobile stand. The study aims to identify usability issues in the present mobile interface in an effort to explore ways to improve students' engagement with geometric reasoning by constructing, manipulating and reflecting upon geometric objects. Based on the ISO 9241-11 [2] definition of usability, the evaluation focused on efficiency, effectiveness and satisfaction dimensions.

2.1 Design of the Study

Participants. Our sample included 10 participants who are graduate students at a local university, which presents one of the target user groups for the developers of dynamic geometry software. The average age of the participants was 26.5 (range: 24–31). The majority of the participants were female (7 female, 3 male). Subjects from several different specialty areas in field participated. 5 of the participants had an Engineering Sciences background, 3 participants were enrolled in Basic Sciences (Math & Statistics), and two participants were majoring in Educational Sciences. Before the experiment participants were asked to rate their basic math and computer skills between 1–9. On average the participants rated their computer skills and basic math skills as 7.8 and 6.2 respectively. None of the participants had any prior experience with GeoGebra or a similar dynamic geometry application (Fig. 1).

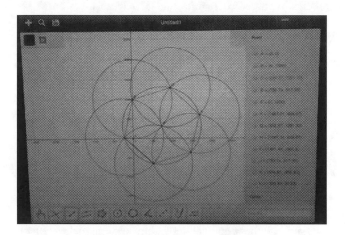

Fig. 1. GeoGebra Tablet Interface

Materials, Apparatus and Software. The first data collection instrument employed is a scaled down version of the System Usability Scale (SUS) questionnaire developed by John Brooke from Digital Equipment Corporation [3]. This scale allows researchers to carry out a quick and practical usability evaluation of a given user interface. As Sauro argued SUS can be used on very small sample sizes (as few as two users) and still generate reliable results [10].

In this study, a Tobii X2-60 eye tracker was used together with a special stand for mobile devices (Fig. 2). This eye tracker device can track both eyes of the participants at a rate of 60 Hz to gather information about the duration and the location of their gaze movements by using infrared cameras [13]. The Tobii X2-60 is a small and portable eye tracker, so it can be used for usability studies conducted with different interfaces such as laptops, mobile devices, as well as real word interfaces and TV screens [12].

2.2   Data Collection Procedure

During the usability study, a set of geometric construction problems that could be completed within an hour were given to each subject (Table 1). The tasks were adapted from the tutorials prepared by the Virtual Math Teams (VMT) project team [11]. Before the experiment, frequently used GeoGebra tools while solving geometry problems were introduced together with an example for constructing an equilateral triangle by using dynamic circles. The tasks we used in this study were related to the use of basic features of the system. We did not expect the users to reach perfect solutions to the given

Table 1. Tasks of the study

Task 1:	Draw any triangle, show its angle and edge length and add any edge length of this triangle.
Task 2:	Draw a straight line passing through the points A (5, 0) and B (0, 2) and indicate the equation of the line.
Task 3:	Without using the polygon tool form a square. Prove that the shape is a square.
Task 4:	Draw a graph of the equation y = 3 × 2 + 5.
Task 5:	Draw three parallel lines and form an equilateral triangle, which should touch the parallels at its corners.
Task 6:	Using only circles and line segments draw a hexagon. Prove that the shape is a hexagon.

problems in this study. We just sought to find out if they could construct an acceptable dynamic geometry presentation and, if yes, how much effort they put in constructing it.

2.3   Data Analysis

In this study a mixed methods approach was employed for the analysis of usability issues involved with the tablet version of GeoGebra. After the experiments, data gathered from the eye-tracker were analyzed quantitatively. For this analysis, areas of interest (AOI) over the GeoGebra interface were defined, and then various eye tracking measures were extracted such as time to total visit, mouse click count, percentage of time spent on an AOI, number of fixations prior to first fixation on an AOI, percentage of participants who fixated the target at least once by using the Tobii Studio Software. In addition to this, a task analysis was conducted to guide the statistical analysis of the eye tracking data. The overall SUS rating for the Geogebra mobile system is calculated based on the participants' responses to the questionnaire they filled after the experiment. Finally, participants were asked open-ended questions after the experiment about the difficulties they had while using the GeoGebra mobile interface.

3   Results

3.1   SUS Evaluation

Table 2 summarizes the SUS scale ratings of the participants collected after the experiment. The SUS score (47.0) was found to be below average.

3.2   Task Analysis

The analysis of task performance is carried out in 3 steps. First, overall measures of accuracy and completion times are provided for all tasks. Next, the analysis is elaborated further via a hierarchical task analysis, where the sequence of actions performed by subjects in each task is compared with respect to expected solution steps. Finally, the analysis is further developed with eye tracking measures, which aim to provide

Table 2. SUS scores of the study

	1	2	3	4	5	Score
1- I think that I would like to use this system frequently.	5	3	2	0	0	5
2- I found the system unnecessarily complex.	1	3	4	1	1	22
3- I thought the system was easy to use.	2	1	4	3	0	18
4- I think that I would need the support of a technical person to be able to use this system.	2	3	1	3	1	22
5- I found the various functions in this system were well integrated.	1	3	2	4	0	19
6- I thought there was too much inconsistency in this system.	3	2	3	2	0	26
7- I would imagine that most people would learn to use this system very quickly.	2	0	4	4	0	20
8- I found the system very cumbersome to use.	2	3	1	3	2	21
9- I felt very confident using the system.	2	3	2	3	0	16
10- I needed to learn a lot of things before I could get going with this system.	2	2	1	3	2	19
Total						188
SUS Total	188 * 2.5 =					470
SUS (Average)	470/10					47

further insights regarding the attentional resources participants used while attempting the construction tasks.

First, we identified the number of correctly solved and unsolved cases for each task. All participants were able to complete tasks 1, 2 and 4. Participants seemed to struggle the most with tasks 5 and 6. One participant failed to complete task 3. On average subjects took more time to complete tasks 5 and 6. The length of the interquartile range is also higher for tasks 5 and 6, which indicate a higher level of variability among participants as compared to other tasks. Since the task completion values were not normally distributed, a non-parametric Friedman's ANOVA test was used for statistical comparison. Friedman's ANOVA showed that there is a significant difference among the tasks in terms of their completion times, $\chi2 = 24.19$, $p < .01$. Follow up pair-wise comparisons with Wilcoxon Signed Rank tests found that the difference between tasks 1 and 4 ($z = -2.70$, $p < .01$), 1 and 5 ($z = -2.19$, $p < .05$), 1 and 6 ($z = -2.37$, $p < .05$), 2 and 3 ($z = 2.19$, $p < .05$), 2 and 4 ($z = 2.80$, $p < .05$), 2 and 5 ($z = 2.20$, $p < .05$), 2 and 6 ($z = 2.37$, $p < .05$), 3 and 5 ($z = 2.20$, $p < .05$), 4 and 5 ($z = 1.99$, $p < .05$), 4 and 6 ($z = -2.37$, $p < .05$) were statistically significant.

In order to further analyze the task performance of the participants, transcripts that capture the sequential list of actions performed by each participant while attempting the geometric construction problems from the eye tracking videos. These transcripts capture a short description of each move, its time-stamp or time duration, the total number of fixations and the average fixation duration logged during that move. Each line of action in the transcript is classified into three basic categories; visual search, construction actions, and actions that indicate failure or repair. Visual search refers to those segments where the user visually scans the interface without tapping on any items, indicating that he/she is searching for the relevant system features. Construction actions refer to drawing new objects such as adding a point, line, etc., Repair or failure actions include cases when the user performs an undo, erases an existing part of the dynamic drawing, or decides to quit the task. A total number of 1373 action descriptions were categorized.

When we investigate the transcripts, we see that participants spent 22 % of their total time on searching for relevant drawing features that they may use to solve the task at hand, 58 % of their total time while constructing drawings, and 20 % on repairing or erasing existing parts of a drawing.

For each segment categorized as visual search or construction, average fixation duration and the number of fixations were also recorded as indicators of efficiency and cognitive workload. Since undo and erasing actions took on average small amount of time, those segments were not subjected to fixation analysis. Figure 2 shows the distribution of average time duration for each visual search and construction action. A two way ANOVA analysis showed that the average time spent on visual search was significantly higher than average time spent on construction actions, $F(1,1013) = 10.093$, $p < 0.05$. There was also a significant interaction effect, $F(5, 1013) = 2.655$, $p < 0.05$. This is due to the fact that the time spent on visual search is especially higher than construction in tasks 3 and 6, which indicates that subjects had more difficulty finding related drawing features during these tasks. There are also cases such as tasks 1 and 5 where visual search and construction actions had similar average time.

Figure 2 shows the distribution of total fixation counts for each segment type across all tasks. A 2-way ANOVA showed that the visual search segments have significantly higher number of fixations as compared to construction segments, $F(1,1008) = 13.472$, $p < 0.01$. The difference was particularly high for tasks 3 and 6, which suggest that subjects searched the interface more vigorously in these tasks. The interaction of segment type and task was also significant, $F(5,1008) = 2.280$, $p < 0.05$, which is due

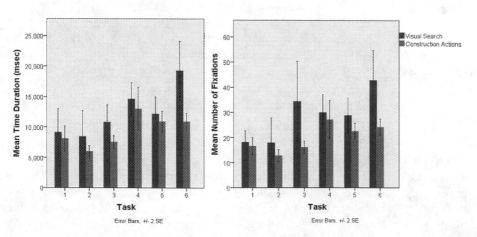

Fig. 2. Average time spent and mean number of fixations during visual search and construction episodes across all tasks.

to the fact that some tasks such as 1 and 4 had almost equal mean fixation counts for search and construction segments.

Figure 3 shows the distribution of average fixation duration values observed in search and construction segments for all tasks. A 2-way ANOVA conducted on average fixation duration values showed a significant effect of segment type, $F (1, 1008) = 9.372$, $p < 0.01$. Construction segments have higher average fixation values than visual search segments. The interaction effect was not significant, $F (5, 1008) = 0.991$, $p > 0.05$, so the pattern of relationship is preserved across different tasks. This suggests that the fixations that guide the construction of dynamic figures tend to elicit higher average duration values than fixations that guide the search process.

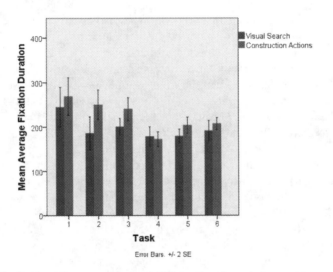

Fig. 3. The distribution of average fixation duration values in each segment type across all tasks

4   Discussion

Our first research question is concerned with the usability issues involved with the tablet version of GeoGebra. Our main findings regarding this question are discussed under the sub-titles of effectiveness, efficiency and satisfaction.

4.1   Effectiveness

In order to evaluate the effectiveness of the GeoGebra interface, we focused on the task accuracy statistics. Tasks 1, 2 and 4 were accurately completed by all participants, whereas tasks 3, 5 and 6 were not accurately completed by 1, 4 and 3 of the participants respectively. Tasks 3, 5 and 6 included additional problem solving steps, whereas other tasks could be considered more routine application of the drawing tools. However, the main goal of GeoGebra is to help students explore geometry through building such dynamic constructions, so we believe such tasks are still relevant within the context of a usability study.

The highest number of failures in the experiment occurred while participants attempted Task 5. There were two important issues in Task 5. The first one was to draw 3 parallel lines by using the parallel line tool. The other was to construct an equilateral triangle. The problem mostly faced by the participants who used the parallel line tool was for them to put points instead of drawing a line. To use the parallel line tool in GeoGebra, it was necessary to choose another line firstly and then to draw another line parallel to it. In other words, after clicking the parallel line tool, firstly the line targeted would be clicked and then the screen would be clicked to draw the desired parallel line. The participants who did not know at first that they needed another line faced this problem, and then formed a line to solve this problem, but this time they went on putting points as they did not know the order of clicking. Although the drawing of an equilateral triangle, which is another element of the task, was easy for some participants, it proved difficult for others. Unable to notice that an equilateral triangle could be drawn by using the regular polygon tool, the participants lost time using the other polygon tools.

4.2   Efficiency

We considered the time and the number of steps each task took as indicators of efficiency in this study. The box-plot in Fig. 3 shows the distribution of completion times measured in seconds for each successfully completed task. The box-plot shows that on average subjects took more time to complete tasks 5 and 6. The length of the interquartile range is also higher for tasks 5 and 6, which indicate a higher level of variability among participants as compared to other tasks.

When the number of steps it took participants to complete each task was examined, we found that Task 6 took the most number of steps as compared to all other tasks, which on average took 40 steps to complete. While completing this task, most of the participants had difficulty forming circles with the same radius that intersect with each other. To intersect them accurately, they were required first to draw a circle with center A and passing through point B, and then click on point B to select it as the center of the second circle and then select point A to let the new circle pass through A. Participants ended up drawing two intersecting circles that did not share the same radius. Another case in which the participants had difficulty was to form new intersecting points on these intersecting circles. Most of the participants searched for the intersection tool for a long time. It did not occur to them that the point tools could be in the subtitle. Considering the task and the way the tool is used, they seemed to ignore the possibility that the point tools would be in the subtitle, and so they looked for them at different parts of the interface for a long time. Participants also had problems with using the intersect tool. This was probably because the expected way to use the intersect tool requires users first to click on one of the circles and then on the other circle. Those who tried to put the intersecting point immediately without doing these two steps process failed. Another problem frequently faced by the participants was the accidental deletion of all existing constructions on the screen. The users, therefore, had to redraw the circles which they had already formed previously.

4.3   Satisfaction

Participants' satisfaction with the tool was investigated through the SUS scale results as well as the post interview comments obtained via open-ended interview questions after the experiment. Table 2 summarizes the SUS scale ratings of the participants for the Tablet version of GeoGebra as 47.0, which was below average according to Sauro's criterion [8]. This suggests that there are important usability issues limiting users' overall satisfaction with the interface.

Participants' post interview comments provided further insights into their level of satisfaction with the GeoGebra interface. For instance, Participant 2 reported that she was bored because of not being able to do what she has done in GeoGebra in one time. Noticing the input bar and finding "double click to open input bar" message was difficult. Moreover, she stated that she could not put the points in specific places with precision. The necessity of selecting the targeted object or the drawing tool at every time was boring. The undo button sometimes undoes everything to the initial state. Similarly, participant 3 stated that typing a function into the input bar makes it harder to select the points that are not in the axes and the use of the Erase tool was not very clear. Participant 4 reported that priorities can be given while two different things such as point or line are input. Participant 5 stated menus in which some geometry shapes are provided together with text descriptions of the functions was not user-friendly. Moreover, he also commented that input area where functions are written was hard to see. Participant 6 reported that she could not get used to touch pad since her hands sweat. She could not understand what the slider tool really does. She emphasized she could not draw a triangle by entering 3 in the Regular Polygon tool as input. Moreover, she stated that it was not easy to understand what can be done in the input bar. Participant 7 also commented that the Input bar was not user friendly. Furthermore, she reported it was hard for her to draw 2 intersecting circles and it was so difficult to mark a desired point. Participant 8 stated that Pictures (Icons) do not indicate the purpose of the button. She suggested that any help of the system will make it easier to be used. Participant 9 reported that while he was drawing a polynomial curve, it takes time to find that the function should be inserted in the input area.

4.4   Suggestions for Improvement

Our usability analysis highlighted some of the difficulties users faced when they were given the task of making specific constructions with minimal supervision. Some of the issues we found could be detrimental to the broader educational adoption of the tool, so we also aimed to suggest some interface design improvements that may help mitigate some of the usability issues we found out.

A peculiar issue our participants had with the angle tool was to put the angles in the desired part of the drawing. In the current interface you need to click on three points in either clock-wise or counter-clockwise direction to mark an internal or external angle. Alternatively, the system could allow users to select the location of the angle with a hand gesture similar to how we draw angles on paper by drawing a small arc connecting two existing line segments. In this new feature, after the user selects the angle button, he will draw a short arc touching on both segments between which the angle should appear. Until the user lifts his finger from the screen, the system can display a visual feedback by highlighting the line segments implicated and the anticipated area where the angle will appear. Such a feature would simplify defining angles by eliminating the need to identify 3 points in a specific order, and providing a more naturalistic method based on a familiar with drawing.

Given the limited display size, it is generally difficult to make precise drawing or editing actions on a tablet window. There are existing solutions for guiding text editing movements over mobile interfaces where users can hold and drag to open a zooming lens, which allows them to make more precise movements such as inserting the carat or highlighting a specific portion of the text. Intersecting geometric objects, placing points at specific places may benefit from such guidance as well.

Participants also experienced difficulty with managing text input via interfaces such as the Input Bar and the Redefine window. The fact that GeoGebra is making use of the standard keyboard of iPad seems to be contributing to this issue. A keyboard that is optimized for the math notation expected by GeoGebra would make such interfaces easier to use for the users.

Problems faced by the participants with moving and deleting existing objects on the interface motivated another possible design improvement. In the current interface, before moving an object one needs to click on a button to switch the cursor into the selection mode, which requires an additional step almost always forgotten by the users. In such cases users ended up moving only a part of the construction, which distorted the overall structure, and required the use of the undo button. Since the moving operation requires clicking on and dragging the object, when the user clicks on the object for a brief amount of time, a context menu may open (e.g. like a right click does on most operating systems) which may present a few alternative actions such as Move or Delete.

5   Conclusion

In this study we conducted a usability evaluation of the recently released iPad version of GeoGebra, which is one of the first dynamic geometry applications that allow users to construct and view dynamic figures on mobile devices. Overall, we aimed to identify if GeoGebra is effectively taking advantage of touch-based gestures to support the construction of dynamic geometry objects, and to explore in what ways the interface can be explored to make abstract geometry concepts more tangible for students.

Our findings suggest that the mobile version primarily replaced the function of the mouse in the desktop version with the finger, and did not take advantage of the gestures supported by the multi-touch screens of new generation tablet computers. GeoGebra should take better advantage of the unique affordances of multi-touch features, such as the ones proposed by Konterkamp [9] in the context of dynamic geometry over smart boards, where users can draw a line by using two fingers at the same time, or draw a circle by having one finger as the center together with an arc gesture circling around the center. We believe recognizing such gestures will contribute to the overall usability of the GeoGebra mobile interface and its further adoption by the educational community.

In addition to this general lack of support for multi-touch actions, we identified other usability issues and offered possible interface design ideas that may help users overcome such issues.

The existing GeoGebra platform is mathematically very versatile and comprehensive, and it holds great potential for transforming math education at all levels starting from elementary school to graduate level education. However, making those versatile features difficult to access will inevitably hamper the general adoption of the tool and the effective use of dynamic constructions for math learning. We hope that the open source community supporting the development of GeoGebra will address the issues identified in this study in the near future.

References

1. Bakara, K.A., Ayuba, A.F., Luanb, W.S.: Exploring secondary school students' motivation using technologies in teaching and learning mathematics. Procedia Soc. Behav. Sci. **2**, 4650–4654 (2010)
2. Battleson, B., Booth, A., Weintrop, J.: Usability testing in academic libraries: a case study. J. Acad. Librarianship **27**(3), 188–198 (2001)
3. Brooke, J.: SUS - A quick and dirty usability scale. United Kingdom: Digital Equipment Co. Ltd. (1986). http://cui.unige.ch/isi/icle-wiki/_media/ipm:test-suschapt.pdf. Accessed 23 Jan 2014
4. Domènech, N.I.: Influence of dynamic geometry software on plane geometry problem solving strategies. Doctoral dissertation, Universitat Autònoma de Barcelona (2009)
5. Drijvers, P., Trouche, L.: From artifacts to instruments - a theoretical framework behind the orchestra metaphor. In: Heid, M.K., Blume, G.W. (eds.) Research on Technology in the Learning and Teaching Mathematics: Syntheses and Perspectives (2007)
6. Hohenwarter, M., Preiner, J.: Design guidelines for dynamic mathematics worksheets. In: The Proceedings of the CADGME Conference (2007)
7. Hohenwarter, M., Jarvis, D., Lavicza, Z.: Report of the First Meeting of the International GeoGebra Institute. University of Cambridge, Faculty of Education (2008)
8. Hohenwarter, J., Hohenwarter, M., Lavicza, Z.: Evaluating difficulty levels of dynamic geometry software tools to enhance teachers' professional development. Int. J. Technol. Math. Educ. **17**(3), 127–134 (2010)
9. Kortenkamp, U., Dohrmann, C.: User interface design for dynamic geometry software. Acta Didactica Napocensia **3**(2), 59–66 (2010)
10. Sauro, J.: Measuring Usability with the System Usability Scale (SUS). Measuring Usability (2011). http://www.measuringusability.com/sus.php. Accessed 2014
11. Stahl, G., The VMT Team: Dynamic - Geometry Activities with GeoGebra for Virtual Math Teams. The Math Forum at Drexel University, Philadelphia (2012)
12. Tobii X2-60 Eye Tracker User Manual. Tobii. http://www.tobii.com/Global/Analysis/Downloads/User_Manuals_and_Guides/Tobii_X2-60_EyeTrackerUserManual_WEB.pdf. Accessed 2014
13. Uzunosmanoğlu, S.D.: Examining Computer Supported Collaborative Problem Solving Processes Using the Dual Eye-Tracking Paradigm. Metu Library, Ankara (2013)
14. Wenglinsky, H.: Does it compute? The relationship between educational technology and student achievement in mathematics. ETS Policy Information Center Report (1998)

Intelligent Learning Environments

Learning Analytics and Spelling Acquisition in German - A First Prototype

Markus Ebner[1]([⊠]), Martin Ebner[2], and Konstanze Edtstadler[3]

[1] Institute of Information Systems and Computer Media,
Graz University of Technology, Graz, Austria
markus.ebner@tugraz.at
[2] Educational Technology, Graz University of Technology, Graz, Austria
martin.ebner@tugraz.at
[3] University College of Teacher Education Vienna/Krems,
Vienna, Austria
konstanze.edtstadler@kphvie.ac.at

Abstract. Data-driven learning in combination with emerging academic areas such as Learning Analytics (LA) has the potential to tailor students' education to their needs [1]. The aim of this article is to present a web-based training platform for primary school pupils who struggle with the acquisition of German orthography. Our objective is the improvement in their writing and spelling competences. The focus of this article is on the development of the platform and the details concerning the requirements and the design of the User Interface (UI). In combination with Learning Analytics, the platform is expected to provide deeper insight into the process of spelling acquisition. Furthermore, aspects of Learning Analytics will help to develop the platform, to improve the exercises and to provide better materials in the long run.

Keywords: German orthography · Technology-enhanced learning · Learning analytics · Educational media

1 Introduction

This article introduces the workflow and the interface design of a prototype development in the field of German orthography with a strong approach on LA. The platform, IDERBLOG[1], which is described in Sect. 3, aims to solve this issue by combining Technology Enhanced Learning (TEL) and LA with the acquisition of German orthography [2, 3]. The platform, which will be released in the course of 2016, will serve as a motivating innovation for children to acquire German orthography more easily. Teachers and researchers will benefit from the application which supports their decision-making process by providing them with possible educational interventions [3, 4].

The platform is based on Learning Analytics. The amount of data produced in the field of education is used by various kinds of institutions worldwide [5]. This kind of interaction leaves traces behind so that the learners' behavior can be analyzed [6].

---

[1] Platform IDERBLOG, available online: http://iderblog.eu/ (German language only, last visited December 7, 2015).

© Springer International Publishing Switzerland 2016
P. Zaphiris and A. Ioannou (Eds.): LCT 2016, LNCS 9753, pp. 405–416, 2016.
DOI: 10.1007/978-3-319-39483-1_37

The students' interactions with the learning platform are captured for analysis as well in order to gain further understanding, knowledge and insights about a learners' learning process [7]. This information can then be used for early detection of learning issues and enables teachers to actively intervene [8, 28]. The platform IDERBLOG will use this information in order to enhance the acquisition of German orthography, since problems in the field of German orthography affect primary school pupils' as well as university students' in everyday life situations [2].

1.1 Outline

The next section gives a short overview of the German orthography as well as LA. The subsequent sections are concerned with the planned workflow of the platform development, its prospects for self-learning and the process of interface designing. The last section will focus on the outlook and benefits of the platform.

2 Related Work

2.1 German Orthography

As the German orthography uses an alphabetic writing system, it is characterized by the fact that the phonemic structure of spoken language is mirrored in written language [9]. This leads to the assumption that words are spelled as they sound. Although the German orthography is much more transparent than the English one, where "the alphabet contains just 26 letters [which] correspond to 44 phonemes associated with 102 functional spelling units" [10], it is not as transparent as, for example, the Turkish one. The reason for unreliable correspondences lies in the missing 1:1 phoneme-grapheme-correspondences of the phonological principle, which is often caused by interfering principles of the semantic principle [2]. In contrast to the overall opinion, the majority of correct spellings can be systematically explained.

The co-existence of these principles has a huge impact on spelling instruction and acquisition [2]. One problem is, that the German orthography is often not taught systematically due to the missing knowledge of the orthographic system and its theoretical foundation. Consequently, many students experience spelling instructions as boring and formal, despite the fact that correct spelling is considered rather prestigious within the German-speaking world [11]. "In contrast to other areas of language learning, there is hardly space to argue about the correct or incorrect spelling of a word. This orthographical stiffness can probably serve as an explanation for its importance" [2]. Spelling competence is often reduced to a person´s knowledge of the correct spelling of given words and the rules of orthography. However, it is important to understand that it includes also being sensitive to misspelled words, knowing how to correct them, using spelling aids and applying strategies to prevent spelling errors in the long run [2, 13]. The consideration of this definition of spelling competence is fundamental for the applied approach in the project IDERBLOG.

2.2   Learning Analytics (LA)

LA focuses on "the measurement, collection, analysis and reporting of data about learners and their contexts, for purposes of understanding and optimizing learning and the environments in which it occurs" [31]. According to Campbell et al. [16], an analysis process has five steps: capture, report, predict, act and refine. Clow [17] used these five steps as a basis for his iterative learning analytics cycle which states that the loop should be closed. Khalil and Ebner [7] added stakeholders to the cycle according to their visions and missions. In addition, they spot the light on some of the ethical issues of LA and proposed an anonymization framework to preserve privacy of students [32]. The learners' data have to be processed in a specific mode in order to conduct scientific analysis and in order to support teachers and students with the adaption of their teaching and learning approach [26]. As a part of the previous frameworks, an adequate visualization has to be applied to present the feedback as simple and informative as possible to the stakeholders [14, 15]. Furthermore, analytical approaches to model a learner's profile based on their answering behavior and the analysis of different error types can lead to findings that help to enhance the whole learning process [18, 19].

3   The Platform

3.1   The Concept

The platform IDERBLOG tries to combine the development of writing skills, the acquisition of orthographic competence and the use of modern means of communication and digital instruments [2]. The aim is not to replace handwriting with the keyboard, but rather take advantage of the digital age: On the one hand, a text written on the platform can be published on a blog. Thereby, the platform is "providing relevant reasons and audiences for writing" [20]. On the other hand, the text is first analyzed automatically regarding spelling mistakes based on Learning Analytics and can consequently be edited several times. It is expected that the motivation to formulate a text and to revise it many times with the prospect of publishing it, is higher compared to typical essay writing in a classroom [2].

The analysis is conducted by the core of the platform, the *intelligent dictionary*, which also serves as the basis for training orthographic skills. By this, the children should be encouraged to reflect and think about the language to become aware of the structure of words [24]. It categorizes mistakes in order to offer specific feedback and hints for correcting the misspelled word. Based on the mistakes it also provides a qualitative analysis of orthographic problems for teachers. Additionally, these categories of mistakes are connected with a number of exercises in a training database [2].

The platform for the project is currently under development and not available for public presentation yet (rollout in 2016). However, the planned workflow and the general concept to ensure good age-appropriate usability and interface design [3] will be described briefly in the following sections.

3.2   Intelligent Dictionary and Feedback

The main idea behind the *intelligent dictionary* is that in case of a spelling mistake hints for corrections are provided. This stands in contrast to conventional autocorrection systems, which only give the information that something is wrong and/or immediately provide the correct word. The intelligent feedback system is based on the findings, that it is important to offer exercises and hints that allow the autonomous correction in a motivating context, in order to acquire correct spelling [30]. Therefore, the hint for correcting a mistake is given by a feedback that is formulated in a way that the learner has to think about the spelling [2].

For example, due to the morphological principle of the German orthography a word/morpheme is always spelled in the same way. Because of the phenomenon of terminal devoicing, there is a difference in the pronunciation, depending on the position of the obstruent (e.g. the written <g> is pronounced devoiced in /tak/ 'day' because it is at the end of the word, but voiced in /tage/ 'days' because it is at the beginning of the syllable). Therefore, children often spell /tak/ due to the phoneme-grapheme-correspondences incorrectly <*Tak> instead of <Tag>. In case these kinds of mistakes happen, the *intelligent dictionary* gives feedback that encourages the pupil to contemplate on a longer form of this word in order to decide which letter is the correct one.

The different categories for mistakes in the *intelligent dictionary* are based on the theory of German orthography e.g. [12]. Furthermore, various approaches as well as requirements for qualitative analysis of misspellings are considered [2, 29].

For teachers and parents, the platform will offer overall feedback of the student's performance. In combination with LA we plan to: (a) make in-depth analysis [26] of occurred misspellings for better understanding of the process of spelling acquisition; (b) predict the performance of students; (c) make recommendations for personalized exercises; (d) offer a reflection about recommended exercises and changing performance in the student's spelling acquisition; (e) benchmark possible weak points of the platform.

3.3   General Workflow for Text Creation and Correction

The students, as shown in Fig. 1, can write their texts on the provided platform (1). First, the text will be analyzed orthographically by the *intelligent dictionary* (2) [2]. Proper feedback, based on the error type and category, will be provided to the students. Then they have the choice to either try to correct the text (3) or submit directly (4). This intermediate step encourages pupils to correct misspelled words independently and self-reflexively [21]. After submission, the teacher gets a notification (5) and inspects the text for further correction and/or improvements as well as personal notes for the student (6). The result is then delivered back to the students for inspection (7). After this step, the text may be published in the provided class blog (8). Based on the recommendations made by the system, the student can choose between different exercises (9) and/or take the exercises suggested by the teacher (10).

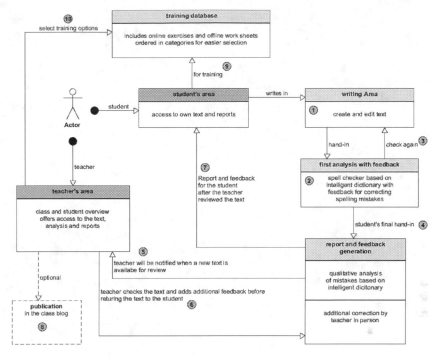

Fig. 1. General workflow of the text creation and correction [2]

3.4 Student's Workflow

Figure 2 shows the detailed workflow of a student. After the Login an overview over all submitted texts will be provided with the feedback given by the teacher as well as further information and hints for possible self-study exercises, provided by the training database. The process of text creation is outlined in Fig. 2 as well. The process is designed to be as simple as possible in order to ensure an easy usability and can be directly started with one click after the Login.

3.5 Teacher's Workflow

Figure 3 shows the workflow of the teacher. In order to offer schools, classes and students an easy registration a separate usermanager is provided. The system also allows the administration of the classes. In case a student loses his/her password it can be easily reset. The teacher area gives an overview over all texts of the classes in which the teacher is active. A separate area will inform the teacher if there are new texts available for correction. An overview of occurred mistakes and suggested exercises will be provided for the class as well as for the individual student. This information can then be used for early detection of learning issues and enables teachers to undertake a proper intervention [8, 28].

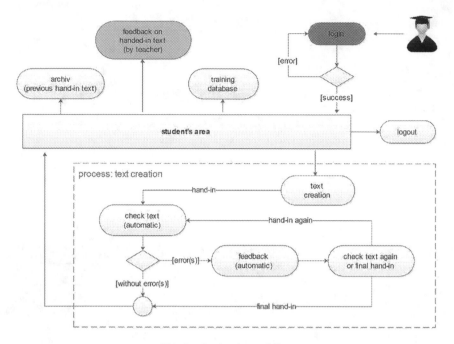

Fig. 2. Student's workflow

If there is a new text available, the teacher can further inspect the text and correct it if necessary. Additionally, errors which may not have been detected and categorized by the *intelligent dictionary* can be categorized. This ensures a qualitative analysis of all misspelled words of a given text by the teacher. Consequently, the system will recognize and categorize the error correctly in future submissions.

3.6   Training Database

A training database is provided by the platform. It contains selected existing online and offline exercises (currently 260). Online exercises that are exclusively developed for the project will also be added. The preselection of exercises helps teachers to support students with the improvement of the performance in problematic/challenging areas identified by LA. For a better overview, these exercises and worksheets are congruently ordered in categories and sub-categories of spelling mistakes [2]. All exercise types are available to teachers and students for free [25].

4   Interface Design

The platform is designed for primary school children, aged 8 to 12. The focus lies on a graphically appealing and age-appropriate web interface [22]. As suggested in the NMC Horizon Report [1], we reviewed the possibility to include the pupils as

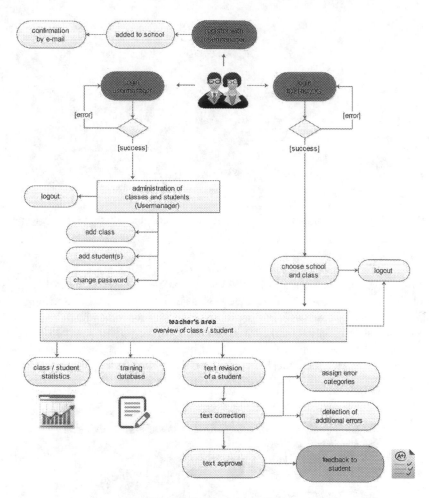

Fig. 3. Teacher's workflow

co-designers in the process. A graphic designer created drafts and color schemes for the project that have been examined and rated by students from different schools and classes. The favored design by the majority has then been developed further and integrated into the platform. The process is shown in Fig. 4.

To guarantee easy usability of the platform, we had to ensure that the students can reach the most important parts of the platform in less than five clicks. This convenient accessibility in combination with attractive figures should ensure high motivation in fulfilling the task of writing texts. In ongoing usability tests [23] we continue to improve the concept step by step [2].

In the next subsections, interesting areas are presented in form of mockups with a brief description.

Fig. 4. Figure creation: first prototypes (left) and final figures on the webpage (right)

4.1   Student's Writing Area

After the login, the student may start the writing process, as described in Fig. 2, with one click. Figure 5 shows the first review stage with information concerning wrong written words (in this case two). Further information on how to handle this error will be displayed by clicking on the marked word. With this information, it should be possible for the student to correct the word and submit the text for another check, if necessary. This intermediate step facilitates independent and self-reflexive corrections among pupils [21].

Fig. 5. Student's writing area

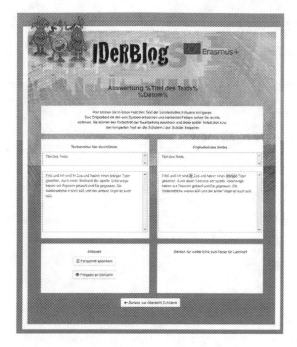

Fig. 6. Teacher's correction area

4.2   Teacher's Correction Area

After the students' final submission, the teacher will be informed about it. She or he has then the possibility to review the different steps of contributions by the student (if there has been more than one) in order to examine the independent correction abilities. Furthermore, as shown in Fig. 6, the teacher is able to correct the text, give notes and make it ready for the publication in the blog. Additionally, errors which may not have been detected and categorized by the *intelligent dictionary* can be categorized in this step. Once the teacher has finished the review, the student will be informed and can inspect the text and take further actions, e.g. look into online courses or exercises recommended by either the teacher or the system to improve her or his own abilities in writing.

5   Outlook

This article introduces a platform for children aged 8 to 12 with the goal to motivate them to improve their spelling skills via writing and publishing texts in a blog. During the text creation process, students benefit from automatic feedback provided by the *intelligent dictionary*. This feedback is based on categories with age-appropriate responses for mistakes. Furthermore, the platform provides a qualitative analysis for the teacher, who can use the results to help pupils with the improvement of word spelling. A training database provides teachers and students with proper exercises for supervised and unsupervised learning. LA is used for in-depth analysis [26] of the occurred misspellings and will help to understand the process of spelling acquisition in detail. The results and an overview of possible systematically made mistakes will be presented to students, teachers and parents in an appropriate way. This allows the measurement of a student's performance in the long run [27]. It is expected that this unique combination in one platform has a positive impact on didactic approaches, education and science [2].

Acknowledgements. This research project is supported by the European Commission Erasmus+ program in the framework of the project IDERBLOG. For more information about the project IDERBLOG and its project partners: Hugo Adolph[2], Christian Aspalter[3], Susanne Biermeier[4], Sandra Ernst[5], Sonja Gabriel[6], Gabriele Goor (See footnote 5), Michael Gros (See footnote 2), Mike Cormann (See footnote 5), Anneliese Huppertz (See footnote 5), Kathrin Irma (See footnote 4), Susanne Martich (See footnote 3), Nina Steinhauer (See footnote 2), Behnam Taraghi[7] and Marianne Ullmann (See footnote 3), please visit our homepage http://iderblog.eu/ (German language only).

References

1. Johnson, L., Adams Becker, S., Estrada, V., Freeman, A., Kampylis, P., Vuorikari, R., Punie, Y.: Horizon Report Europe: 2014 Schools Edition. Publications Office of the European Union, Luxembourg, The New Media Consortium, Austin (2014)
2. Edtstadler, K., Ebner, M., Ebner, M.: Improved German spelling acquisition through learning analytics. eLearning Papers 45, pp. 17–28 (2015)
3. Ebner, M., Taraghi, B., Ebner, M., Aspalter, C., Biermeier, S., Edtstadler, K., Gabriel, S., Goor, G., Gros, M., Huppertz, A., Martich, S., Steinhauer, N., Ullmann, M., Ziegler, K.: Design für eine Plattform zum Schreibenlernen im Grundschulalter. In: Rathmayer, S., Pongratz, H. (eds.) Proceedings of the DeLFI Workshops 2015 co-located with 13th e-Learning Conference of the German Computer Society (DeLFI 2015), Munich, Germany, 1 September 2015, pp. 118–122 (2015)
4. Ebner, M., Taraghi, B., Saranti, A., Schön, S.: Seven features of smart learning analytics-lessons learned from four years of research with learning analytics. eLearning Papers 40, pp. 51–55 (2015)
5. Piety, P.J.: Assessing the Educational Data Movement. Teachers College Press, New York (2013)

---

[2] LPM Saarland, Beethovenstraße 26, 66125 Saarbrücken, Germany.

[3] University of Teacher Education Vienna, IBS/DiZeTIK, Grenzackerstraße 18, 1100 Vienna, Austria - Europe.

[4] Albert-Weisgerber School St. Ingbert, Robert-Koch-Straße 4, 66386 St. Ingbert, Germany.

[5] School of Raeren, Hauptstraße 45, 4730 Raeren, Belgium - Europe.

[6] University College of Teacher Education Vienna/Krems, Mayerweckstraße 1, 1210 Vienna, Austria - Europe.

[7] Graz University of Technology, Department Educational Technology, Münzgrabenstraße 35a, 8010 Graz, Austria - Europe.

6. Duval, E.: Attention please! learning analytics for visualization and recommendation. In: Proceedings of the 1st International Conference on Learning Analytics and Knowledge, LAK 2011 (2011)
7. Khalil, M., Ebner, M.: Learning analytics: principles and constraints. In: Proceedings of the World Conference on Educational Multimedia, Hypermedia and Telecommunications, EdMedia 2015, pp. 1326–1336. AACE, Waynesville (2015)
8. Siemens, G., Long, P.: Penetrating the fog: analytics in learning and education. EDUCAUSE Rev. **46**(5), 30 (2011)
9. Katz, L., Frost, R.: The reading process is different for different orthographies: the orthographic depth hypothesis. Haskins Laboratories Status Report on Speech Research, pp. 147–160 (1992)
10. Snowling, M.J.: Developmental dyslexia: a cognitive developmental perspective. In: Aaron, P.G., Joshi, R.M. (eds.) Reading and Writing Disorders in Different Orthographic Systems, pp. 1–23. Kluwer Academic Publishers, Dordrecht (1989)
11. Küttel, H.: Probleme des Erwerbs der Orthographie. In: Nerius, D. (ed.) Deutsche Orthographie, pp. 417–451. Georg Olms, Hildesheim, Zürich, New York (2007)
12. Nerius, D. (ed.): Deutsche Orthographie. Georg Olms, Hildesheim, Zürich, New York (2007)
13. Naumann, C. L.: Zur Rechtschreibkompetenz und ihrer Entwicklung. In: Bremerich-Vos, A., Granzer, D., Köller, O. (eds.) Lernstandbestimmung im Fach Deutsch, pp. 134–159. Beltz, Weinheim & Basel (2008)
14. Baker, R.S.J.D., Duval, E., Stamper, J., Wiley, D., Buckingham Shum, S.: Panel: educational data mining meets learning analytics. In: Buckingham Shum, S., Gasevic, D., Ferguson, R. (eds.) Proceedings of the 2nd International Conference on Learning Analytics and Knowledge (LAK 2012), New York, USA, p. 20 (2012)
15. Neuhold, B.: Learning Analytics-Mathematik Lernen neu gedacht. BoD–Books on Demand, Norderstedt (2013)
16. Campbell, J.P., DeBlois, P.B., Oblinger, D.G.: Academic analytics: a new tool for a new era. EDUCAUSE Rev. **42**(4), 40 (2007)
17. Clow, D.: The learning analytics cycle: closing the loop effectively. In: Buckingham Shum, S., Gasevic, D., Ferguson, R. (eds.) Proceedings of the 2nd International Conference on Learning Analytics and Knowledge (LAK 2012), New York, USA, pp. 134–138 (2012)
18. Taraghi, B., Saranti, A., Ebner, M., Müller, V., Großmann, A.: Towards a learning-aware application guided by hierarchical classification of learner profiles. J. Univ. Comput. Sci. **21**(1), 93–109 (2015)
19. Taraghi, B., Frey, M., Saranti, A., Ebner, M., Müller, V., Großmann, A.: Determining the causing factors of errors for multiplication problems. In: Ebner, M., Erenli, K., Malaka, R., Pirker, J., Walsh, A.E. (eds.) EiED 2014. CCIS, vol. 486, pp. 27–38. Springer, Heidelberg (2015)
20. Government of South Australia (Department of Education and Children's Services): Spelling: from beginnings to proficiency: a spelling resource for planning, teaching, assessing and reporting on progress (2011). http://spellandvocab.weebly.com/uploads/3/8/3/1/38315669/spelling_-_from_beggining_to_proficiency.pdf
21. Bartnitzky, H.: Individuell fördern–Kompetenzen stärken. Grundschule aktuell **9**, 6–11 (2010)
22. Liebal, J., Exner, M.: Usability für Kids. Springer Fachmedien Wiesbaden, Wiesbaden (2011)

23. Holzinger, A., Errath, M., Searle, G., Thurnher, B., Slany, W.: From extreme programming and usability engineering to extreme usability in software engineering education (XP+ UE→ XU). In: 29th Annual International Conference on Computer Software and Applications, COMPSAC 2005, vol. 2, pp. 169–172. IEEE (2005)
24. Tsesmeli, S.N., Seymour, P.H.K.: Derivational morphology and spelling in dyslexia. Read. Writ. **19**(6), 587–625 (2006)
25. Gros, M., Steinhauer, N., Ebner, M., Taraghi, B., Ebner, M., Aspalter, C., Martich, S., Edtstadler, K., Gabriel, S., Huppertz, A., Goor, G., Biermeier, S., Ziegler, K.: Schreiben – Rechtschreiben lernen und Lesen mit der Plattform Individuell Differenziert Rechtschreiben mit Blogs – kurz IDeRBlog. In: LA-Multimedia, vol. 4, pp. 22–24 (2015).
26. Siemens, G.: Learning analytics: envisioning a research discipline and a domain of practice. In: Proceedings of the 2nd International Conference on Learning Analytics and Knowledge, pp. 4–80. ACM (2012)
27. Schön, M., Ebner, M., Kothmeier, G.: It's just about learning the multiplication table. In: Proceedings of the 2nd International Conference on Learning Analytics and Knowledge, pp. 73–81. ACM (2012)
28. Greller, W., Drachsler, H.: Translating learning into numbers: a generic framework for learning analytics. J. Educ. Technol. Soc. **15**(3), 42–57 (2012)
29. Edtstadler, K.: Qualitative Fehleranalyse im Schriftspracherwerb. Kritik und Kriterien. In: Lindner D., Beer, R., Gabriel, S., Krobath, T. (eds.) Dialog Forschung – Forschungsband 2015, pp. 169–178. Lit-Verlag, Vienna (2016)
30. Klicpera, C., Schabmann, A., Gasteiger-Klicpera, B.: Legasthenie. Reinhardt Utb Verlag, Stuttgart (2003)
31. Siemens, G., Gasevic, D.: Guest editorial - learning and knowledge analytics. Educ. Technol. Soc. **15**(3), 1–3 (2012)
32. Khalil, M., Ebner, M.: De-identification in learning analytics. J. Learn. Anal. **3**(1), 129–138 (2016)

An Approach to Measuring the Difficulty of Learning Activities

Francisco J. Gallego-Durán$^{(\boxtimes)}$, Rafael Molina-Carmona, and Faraón Llorens-Largo

Cátedra Santander-UA de Transformación Digital, Universidad de Alicante, Alicante, Spain
{fgallego,rmolina,faraon}@dccia.ua.es

Abstract. In any learning environment, training activities are the basis for learning. Students need to practice to develop new skills and improve previously acquired abilities. Each student has specific needs based on their previous knowledge and personal skills. The allocation of a proper activity for a particular student consists in selecting a training activity that fits the skills and knowledge of the student. This allocation is particularly important since students who are assigned a too hard training activity will tend to leave it rather than making the necessary effort to complete it. Moreover, when the activity is too easy it does not represent a challenge for the student and the learning outcomes will tend to be very limited. An motivating activity, suitable for a given student, should be neither too easy nor too difficult. The problem arises when trying to measure or estimate the difficulty given any training activity. Our proposal is a definition of difficulty of a learning activity that can be used to measure the learning cost of a general learner. As a first step, the desirable features and the intrinsic limitations of a difficulty function are identified, so that a mathematical definition can be obtained quite straightforward. The result is an intuitive, understandable and objectively measurable way to determine the difficulty of a learning activity.

Keywords: Difficulty estimation · Learning activity

1 Introduction

Learning is a fascinating event that happens in nature as the maximum expression of adaptation. Having the ability to learn means being able to remember past events and associate them with present situations to take decisions. Although quite a few low-level mechanisms of learning remain unknown, life experience suggests that there is a strong correlation between the activities any individual performs and learning. This is the basis for training and education: creating experiences to make learners' brains adapt and remember. In fact, learning experiences designed by the teachers in order to generate concrete learning outcomes on learners are often referred to as Learning Activities.

© Springer International Publishing Switzerland 2016
P. Zaphiris and A. Ioannou (Eds.): LCT 2016, LNCS 9753, pp. 417–428, 2016.
DOI: 10.1007/978-3-319-39483-1_38

The space of possible learning experiences is huge so, which experiences are more suitable for a learning objective and a particular learner? Among others, the concept of difficulty has a very important role to play in this context.

Difficulty is a widespread concept and it can be intuitively defined as the abilities and cost for a learner to successfully complete a given learning activity. In spite of being subjective, it is considered among the main factors determining learners' motivation [4,5,13,26,27]. In order for optimize learning, difficulty of any given exercise should match abilities of the learner [12,14,19,24,28]. Matching the abilities means being so difficult as to be an interesting challenge, at the same time as being so easy to be reachable with a limited amount of effort in time.Therefore, correctly estimating the difficulty of learning activities is the first step to be able to optimize the learning process.

The main objective of this research is creating a definition of difficulty of a learning activity that can be used to measure the learning cost for a general learner. A general learner would be any individual that performs learning activities and improves its results, as a consequence of learning.

A brief background about the research context is presented in Sect. 2. Section 3 identifies the information sources available for measuring difficulty. The desired properties and the limitations of difficulty measures are presented in Sects. 4 and 5. Section 6 is devoted to design some mathematical functions that meet the properties and give useful outcomes as well as analysing their usefulness for learning activities. Finally, the conclusions and future work are presented in Sect. 7.

2   Background

To understand the relation between difficulty, motivation and learning, let us focus on the notion of *Flow Channel* (Fig. 1) [7,25]. The Flow Channel represents the way difficulty and skills of the learner relate to each other:

- When difficulty is much higher than learners' skills, anxiety appears. This is psychologically explained by learners perceiving their skills as insufficient, thus getting demotivated. They normally feel that the activity requires too much effort compared to their perceived capabilities. This often leads to early abandon.
- On the contrary, if learners' skills already include what the activity provides as learning outcome, boredom shows up. Having to invest time and/or resources to get an already possessed outcome is interpreted as lost time. Interest vanishes, motivation decreases and boredom appears.
- When skills and difficulty are balanced, learners enter a state of Flow. In Schell words [25], Flow is sometimes defined as *a feeling of complete and energized focus in an activity, with a high level of enjoyment and fulfilment.*

This research assumes The Flow Channel theory as a key point for improving the design and selection of learning activities.

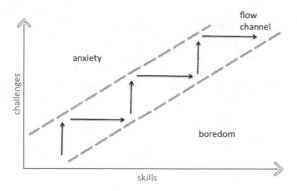

Fig. 1. Representation of the flow channel, by Csikszentmihalyi [3]

Some research work has been carried out calibrating difficulty by analysing student historical data [21], or using linear regression to estimate difficulty based on user data [2] or even on generating exercises automatically with a given established difficulty [20,22]. But these studies are spread, discontinued and seem to be disconnected from each other. In general, the concept of difficulty within the academic world does not seem to capture too much attention.

More studies related to difficulty can be found changing the focus to the field of Computer Games. The parallelism with academic learning is complete: if a level of a game is too difficult or too easy, players tend to stop playing the game. Therefore, it is vital for a game to have a well designed progression of difficulty, if willing to catch the attention of the players. Most studies in this field try to develop methods to dynamically adjust difficulty to match player's skills [9,10,15,16]. All these studies use existent levels of difficulty proposed in present Computer Games and focus on selecting the most appropriate for each player and game being played. Hunicke and Chapman [9,10] take measures of performance of the player and tries to predict if the player is going to fail to anticipate and adjust the level of difficulty. The proposal is completely specific to First Person Shooter (FPS) games [23], as measures are defined for this specific type of gameplay. Mladenov and Missura [16] use data collected from previously played games to analyse a set of gameplay characteristics and input this data to a supervised Machine Learning algorithm. The goal is to have an offline prediction of the level of difficulty players are going to select in their next game. Missura and Gartner [15] take a different approach for automatically selecting difficulty for a given player among a set of finite difficulty levels. They divide the game into play-review cycles. They measure the performance of the player in the play cycles, and change difficulty level on review cycles accordingly to their estimations.

Herbrich et al. [8] present a very interesting work on measuring players' skills comparatively. Their system, called TrueSkill, is based on chess' Elo rating system [6]. Just like the Elo rating system, players have a 1-dimensional value ranking that predicts their probability of winning against other players by logistic comparison. Although this work is not directly based on difficulty, it is indirectly valuing players' skill with similar intention: match players against those with similar abilities to foster balanced games.

Another interesting work is that proposed by Mourato and dos Santos [17]. Their goal is to procedurally generate content for Platform Games similar to Super Mario Bros [18]. The problem with this kind of content is how to classify the generated content with respect to difficulty. They propose a way to measure difficulty in Platform Games by measuring players' probability of failing after each individual obstacle in the game. The concepts are interesting but they lack a practical result with actual players and ready-to-be-played generated content.

Finally, Aponte et al. [1] present one of the most interesting reviewed works. In their work they state that their goal is "to evaluate a parameter or a set of parameters that can be considered as a measure of a game difficulty". They start by measuring the difficulty of a reduced Pacman game with 1 ghost. In their Pacman game, speed of the ghost is a configurable parameter to make the game more difficult at will. They measure the score of a synthetic player as number of eaten pellets and then show a graph with the evolution of this value depending on the speed of the ghost. This approach lets them show the progression of difficulty depending on the selected level (speed of the ghost). Based on that result, they define a set of properties that a general definition of difficulty should have, and propose a general theoretic definition of difficulty as the probability of losing at a given time t. They only propose this definition, but do not perform any kind of test or mathematical proof. It ends up as a simple proposition based on their arguments.

All these previous works demonstrate the incipient interest of the research community for measuring difficulty. This trend is confirmed by the growing focus on measuring learning in general. The NMC Horizon Report: 2016 Higher Education Edition [11] states that there is a renewed interest in assessment and the wide variety of methods and tools to evaluate and measure the elements related to the learning process.

3   Sources for Measuring Difficulty

Let us consider difficulty as a cost: in order to successfully finish an activity, any learner has to pay a cost in time and effort. Measuring time is trivial from a conceptual point of view. The problem comes from measuring effort. How can we measure effort? Do we have an objective definition of what effort is?

It will be considered that effort is indirectly related to progress. The more progress is achieved, the less effort is required to finish. Although this logic consideration is not a concrete definition of effort, it has many advantages:

- For many kinds of activity, progress is relatively easy to define and measure objectively.
- A measure for progress is also closely related to learning outcomes: most activities yield learning outcomes even when not fully completed. In fact, that learning outcomes become clear when success ratio increases out of repeating the activity.
- As progress to success is one of the key factors in motivation, measures taking progress into account also foster motivation.

Therefore, this research will consider "more difficult" an activity when less progress is done. In the sake of rigour, progress will be considered with respect to time: progress percentage per unit of time will be an inverse measure for difficulty. So, an activity being "more difficult" will imply that less progress is made per time unit. This will let us measure difficulty in an intuitive, understandable and objectively measurable way.

4   Desired Properties for Difficulty

There are several ways of defining difficulty as a relationship between time and progress. It is important to have guidance for selecting an appropriate measure from such a huge set of potential definitions. So, establishing a set of desired properties will ensure that the selected definition is useful under defined criteria. These desired properties will act as restrictions, reducing the search space.

Let us consider the next set of properties, having present that measuring and comparing learning activities is the final goal:

- Difficulty should always be positive. Progress and time are always positive or 0 values when measuring a learning activity. A negative difficulty coming out of these two values is impossible and would have no meaning.
- Difficulty should have a minimum value. A difficulty value of 0 would mean that no time/effort is required to finish a given activity. That would correspond to an activity that is already done.
- Difficulty should also have a maximum value. Making difficulty unbound would imply that any value could be "not so difficult" compared to infinite. Having a maximum value lets us fix impossible activities, which is desirable. An unbound upper limit that should be labelled as infinity makes formulation more complicated and has no advantage on comparisons.
- Fixing 1 as the maximum value for difficulty has advantageous properties. That bounds difficulty in the range $[0, 1]$, which lets us consider it as a probability. That makes sense and is compatible with previous considerations. Moreover, that enables the probability theory as a valid set of tools for working with difficulty, which is very desirable.
- Difficulty should not be a unique value but a function over time. While an activity is being done, difficulty keeps changing as progress is being made.
- Difficulty must be a continuous function over time. It makes no sense for a moment in time not to have a difficulty associated.
- Difficulty must be a non-strictly decreasing function. Every time a learner makes progress on a given learning activity, difficulty decreases by definition as less progress is required to meet success.

Let us consider an example of activity: "scoring five 3-point shots in a basketball court, in less than 5 min". This is a training activity whose expected learning outcome is an improvement in shooting precision to basket[1]. This activity will take

---

[1] Although other learning outcomes can be considered from this activity, let us consider it just as a precision improvement exercise.

at most 5 min, and at least the time required to shot 5 times: time cost is straight-forward. Regarding to effort, it will depend on previous conditions. A trained, muscular player may complete the activity fast, without much effort, whereas a weak novice could require many attempts to finish it successfully. Moreover, novice players may waste much more energy because they lack adequate technique. This could also be considered more effort.

The activity could be analysed many times and from different perspectives, and many definitions for "effort" could be found. Before entering an endless debate on what "effort" is or should be, let us consider a useful point of view with respect to our goal of measuring difficulty. An indirect measure for "effort" could be derived from the intrinsic failure/success measures of the activity. When 5 min are over, a player that scored 4 baskets is closer to success than other who only scored 1. It can be considered that having scored 4 baskets leaves out less progress to be done for succeeding than scoring just 1. Under this consideration, there is less effort pending to succeed when more percentage of the activity has been completed.

Let us compose a function with this properties, for the basketball example. Let us imagine a player that scores 5 baskets at times $t_i \in \{15, 40, 62, 128, 175\}$, $i \in \{1, 2, 3, 4, 5\}$ in seconds. Difficulty could be represented as shown in Fig. 2: whenever player scores baskets, difficulty decreases. Decreasing difficulty can be considered as a step function, maintaining its value except on scoring events. It also can be considered as a linear function, resulting on a much smooth shape. Moreover, a linear function seems to inform better about the pace of the player.

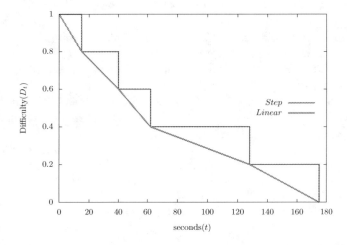

Fig. 2. Manually constructed difficulty function for basket example. Difficulty decreases as player progresses, scoring baskets in this example.

As it can be deduced from Fig. 2, these properties configure a very powerful definition of difficulty: it goes far beyond a simple scalar quantity, defining a representative function. This function represents progress of the player over time which gives much more information about the process. This new information will also be useful for visual comparison of activity profiles as well as individual or group profiles.

5   Intrinsic Limitations

The selected properties limit the way activities should be defined. Not every possible activity will fit for this model. This is both a limitation and a design guide. Activities designed for this model of difficulty will have a set of properties:

– Activities require progress to be measurable (i.e. they should have a score). For instance, an activity defined as "selecting the proper answer from a set of 4" has no way of measuring progress. Although time to answer and success can be measured, there is no progress towards success. Resulting functions would represent either a full square or a line, depending on model selected.
– Score (i.e. progress) has to be non-strictly increasing function over time. As score is measuring progress to an end it does not make sense for it to decrease. General score measures having punishments or negative score events would not be appropriate. However, almost any score measure could be transformed in an equivalent non-strictly increasing measure for this purpose.
– Activities must have a measurable success status or, at least, a maximum score. This is required to define difficulty within its limits. Progress can be measured in unbounded activities, but cannot be scaled to a $[0, 1]$ range.
– Activities must be considered over time. For instance, an activity about creating a program cannot be considered just as its final result. Having a single point of evaluation is similar to not being able to measure progress. It is also very important to measure time required to do the activity. If all the learners hand the result of an activity at the same time and no measures have been taken previously, no data will be available for the model.

These intrinsic limitations are part of the selected set of properties and shall be assumed. However, it can be seen positively. Having activities where progress is measurable over time and with well defined score limits or success status is very interesting for learners. Progress informs learners about the status of their evolution to success, and also remove their doubts about their skills being enough for the activity. Although these design impositions are not easy to achieve on every activity, they are definitely desirable from educational point of view.

6   Mathematically Defining Difficulty

With all desired properties and limitations clarified, a working mathematical definition of difficulty can be constructed. Let A be the set of all possible activities, and L the set of all possible learners. Let $\alpha \in A$ be a concrete learning activity. As an activity, α can be performed by any learner $l \in L$. Each l performs α a number of times $N_l \in \mathbb{N}$. So let $\alpha_l^i, l \in L, i \in \mathbb{N}, i \leq N_l$ represent the i-th realization of the activity α by the learner l.

Each α_l^i takes an amount of time $t_l^i \in \mathbb{R}$, measured in seconds. Let us consider, for simplicity, that each α_l^i starts at time 0 and ends at t_l^i. Then, let $S_t(\alpha_l^i) \in \mathbb{R}$ be a function that measures the score got by learner l, at time t on its i-th realization of α. So, $S_t(\alpha_l^i)$ is the function that measures the progress towards success of a learner that performs an activity.

The score function is expected to be explicitly defined for each activity. In fact, many different score functions can be defined for each activity. Therefore, let us assume that activities and their score functions are defined by activity designers. Also, for clarity reasons, let us assume that activities and score functions meet desired properties and limitations exposed on Sects. 4 and 5.

In previous sections, difficulty has been defined as the inverse of progress. However, this cannot be defined exactly this way. Difficulty must be defined in $[0,1]$ range, and the score function could have a much broader range. However, the score function should be non-strictly increasing, and should have an upper limit. Therefore, the score function could be safely assumed to start at 0, because the actual range of the function can always be moved to start at 0. Let $S^\star(\alpha)$ be the maximum score value for the activity α,

$$S^\star(\alpha) \in \mathbb{R}, S^\star(\alpha) \geq S_t(\alpha_l^i) \quad \forall l \in L, i \in N_l \tag{1}$$

This lets us define the "easiness function" as a scaled version of the score function over time in the $[0,1]$ range:

$$E_t(\alpha_l^i) = \frac{S_t(\alpha_l^i)}{S^\star(\alpha)} \tag{2}$$

The function defined in Eq. 2 is called "easiness function" as it is exactly the inverse of the initial definition of difficulty. Therefore, the definition of difficulty follows:

$$D_t(\alpha_l^i) = 1 - E_t(\alpha_l^i) \tag{3}$$

This definition of difficulty is tied to the concept of progress. It represents an advantage over estimating difficulty with just a single scalar value: the resulting graph shows an evolution over time which informs of the whole realization of the activity. It also yields instant values for difficulty at any time of the realization. This values intrinsically represent the percentage of progress remaining to finish the activity. They could also be interpreted as the probability of failing the activity[2].

However, these values are quite plain: they are instant values that do not capture information on the progress by themselves. The result is similar to considering any instant t to be independent from the others that compose the timeframe of the activity. For instance, this is like considering in the basketball example that scoring at first shot is equally probable to scoring after 4 baskets, or at a last attempt, when time is finishing. Nevertheless, a more accurate definition should consider that events occurring at time t are influenced by all events happened in the range $[0,t]$.

---

[2] This interpretation is bound to discussion about its real meaning as a probability.

Experience shows that influence of a timeframe over next time steps is strong on humans. It is convenient to consider how human factors relate over time: psychological status, strength, fatigue, motivation, etc. Time steps in the timeframe of any learning activity, performed by a human learner, are best considered to be strongly interdependent. Therefore, can be improved by making D_t depend on a function of all $t' \in [0, t]$, to make final values express this interdependency.

There are many approaches to make D_t dependent on the set of all past values of difficulty $\{D_{t'}/t' \in [0, t]\}$. Moreover, there is no theoretical way to determine the appropriate way to weight all the possible factors. What is more, different activities and learners will have different influence factors. This makes extremely difficulty, if at all possible, to design a theoretical relation covering such a chaotic landscape. This suggests using an experimental approach instead. Therefore, this research starts modelling influence in a very simple way. This first model can be used as a benchmark to test other different approaches and experimentally determine better ways of defining difficulty.

Assuming that $D_t, \forall t$ should depend on $\{D_{t'}/t' \in [0, t]\}$ and $0 \leq D_t \leq 1$, let us define D_t as the area of the curve above E_t related to the maximum possible area up to the instant t,

$$D_t(\alpha_l^i) = 1 - \frac{1}{t} \int_0^t E_t(\alpha_l^i) dt \qquad (4)$$

Equation 4 defines difficulty D_t as a value depending on all previous history of the i-th realization of an activity α by a learner l. The dependency is made indirect, using the easiness function as a proxy for difficulty. This makes definition easier, eliminating recursive references and associated problems.

Using the new definition stated at Eq. 4 the graphical layout of D_t varies greatly, as Fig. 3 shows. Compared to Fig. 2, the new definition for D_t results in a function that responds much smoothly to score events. This new behaviour shows an interesting feature. Let us assume that $t \in [0, t^\star]$. Using Eq. 4, $D_{t^\star}$ will directly depend on the performance shown by the learner during the realization of the activity (being $D_{t^\star} > 0^3$). In the basketball example, the faster baskets get scored, the lower $D_{t^\star}$ will be, and vice-versa. Therefore, after completing an activity, the lower the residual difficulty value $D_{t^\star}$, the greater the performance shown by the learner.

The interesting property shown by $D_{t^\star}$ is a direct consequence of its cumulative definition. So, this property will be shown by $D_{t'}, \forall t' \in [0, t^\star]$. Therefore, D_t can now be used as a performance measure with more information than E_t, as it integrates information about score and time/frequency in one single value. Careful analysis of D_t for different learners and realizations of the same activity could lead to establishing correlations with abilities learnt and degree of mastery.

---

[3] Unless $D_0 = 0$, which would only happen on activities completed at start time. That is a degenerate case with no interest in practice. Thus, it can be safely ignored.

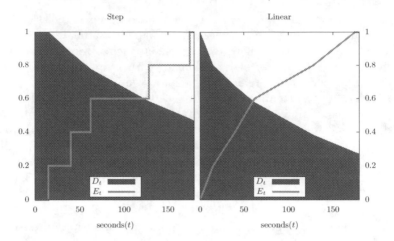

Fig. 3. Behaviour of D_t using Eq. 4 with data from the basketball example from Sect. 4. Left, exact definition for E_t with step value changes. Right, linear interpolation for E_t.

7 Conclusions and Further Work

In this paper a general definition for difficulty has been presented. This new definition has been designed on the bases of a list of desired properties. By using this proposed definition, difficulty becomes measurable, can be compared and visualized, and is related to effort over time. Effort is modelled as required time to achieve a specific score value. Therefore, proposed definition of difficulty takes into account progress towards solving a learning activity, based on the score an agent achieves when performing the activity.

This proposed definition of difficulty has limitations in the sense that activities have to meet some requirements to be measurable under this definition. The activity should be performed over time and a score function to measure progress should be available. The score function should have upper and lower boundaries and be non-strictly increasing: there should be no possibility of losing score over time.

But this proposed definition has also many interesting advantages. Most of its advantages come from being drawable: this confers it the ability to show its progress over time, so that it transmits characteristics of the learner and the learning activity graphically. Different parts of the learning activity can be identified: for instance, most difficult parts will produce valleys in the graph that will permit not only their identification, but also their measurement. Activities can be compared using their difficulty graphs, yielding a much accurate knowledge about which ones require more effort, and the differences in the distribution of the effort over time. These advantages make the proposed definition of difficulty a powerful tool for analysing and comparing learning activities.

The formal definition of difficulty has other implications: it is possible to take it as a starting point to build adaptive learning systems that could automatically assign the suitable learning activities to students. As a further step, we plan to analyze the behaviour of the difficulty definition in real learning activities with different features, as well as to make a deeper study about the meaning of the proposed charts.The final aim is maintaining learners in the state of flow or, in other words, motivating them.

References

1. Aponte, M.-V., Levieux, G., Natkin, S.: Scaling the level of difficulty in single player video games. In: Natkin, S., Dupire, J. (eds.) ICEC 2009. LNCS, vol. 5709, pp. 24–35. Springer, Heidelberg (2009)
2. Cheng, I., Shen, R., Basu, A.: An algorithm for automatic difficulty level estimation of multimedia mathematical test items. In: Eighth IEEE International Conference on Advanced Learning Technologies, ICALT 2008, pp. 175–179, July 2008
3. Csikszentmihalyi, M.: Flow: The Psychology of Optimal Experience. Perennial Modern Classics. Harper Perennial Modern Classics, New York (1990)
4. D'Mello, S., Olney, A., Williams, C., Hays, P.: Gaze tutor: a gaze-reactive intelligent tutoring system. Int. J. Hum.-Comput. Stud. **70**(5), 377–398 (2012)
5. Domínguez, A., Saenz-De-Navarrete, J., De-Marcos, L., Fernández-Sanz, L., Pagés, C., Martínez-Herráiz, J.J.: Gamifying learning experiences: practical implications and outcomes. Comput. Educ. **63**, 380–392 (2013)
6. Elo, A.E.: The Rating of Chess Players, Past and Present. Arco Pub, New York (1978)
7. Getzels, J., Csíkszentmihályi, M.: The Creative Vision: A Longitudinal Study of Problem Finding in Art. A Wiley-Interscience publication, Wiley (1976)
8. Herbrich, R., Minka, T., Graepel, T.: Trueskill^{TM}: a bayesian skill rating system. In: Schölkopf, B., Platt, J., Hoffman, T. (eds.) Advances in Neural Information Processing Systems, vol. 19, pp. 569–576. MIT Press (2007)
9. Hunicke, R.: The case for dynamic difficulty adjustment in games. In: Proceedings of the 2005 ACM SIGCHI International Conference on Advances in Computer Entertainment Technology, ACE 2005, NY, USA, pp. 429–433 (2005)
10. Hunicke, R., Chapman, V.: AI for dynamic difficulty adjustment in games (2004)
11. Johnson, L., Adams Becker, S., Cummins, M., Estrada, V., Freeman, A., Hall, C.: NMC Horizon Report: 2016 Higher Education Edition. New Media Consortium; EDUCAUSE Learning Initiative, Austin Texas; [S.l.] (2016)
12. Koster, R., Wright, W.: A Theory of Fun for Game Design. Paraglyph Press, Pittsburgh (2004)
13. Lee, J.J., Hammer, J.: Gamification in education: what, how, why bother? Acad. Exch. Quart. **15**(2), 2 (2011)
14. Ley, T., Kump, B.: Which user interactions predict levels of expertise in work-integrated learning? In: Hernández-Leo, D., Ley, T., Klamma, R., Harrer, A. (eds.) EC-TEL 2013. LNCS, vol. 8095, pp. 178–190. Springer, Heidelberg (2013)
15. Missura, O., Gartner, T.: Predicting dynamic difficulty. In: Shawe-Taylor, J., Zemel, R., Bartlett, P., Pereira, F., Weinberger, K. (eds.) Advances in Neural Information Processing Systems, vol. 24, pp. 2007–2015. Curran Associates, Inc. (2011)
16. Mladenov, M., Missura, O.: Offline learning for online difficulty prediction (2010)
17. Mourato, F.J., dos Santos, M.P.: Measuring difficulty in platform videogames. In: 4a Conferencia Nacional em Interacao Pessoa-Mquina, pp. 173–180. Grupo Portugues de Computaao Grfica/Eurographics (2010)

18. Pedersen, C., Togelius, J., Yannakakis, G.N.: Modeling player experience in Super Mario Bros. In: Proceedings of the 5th International Conference on Computational Intelligence and Games, CIG 2009, Piscataway, NJ, USA, pp. 132–139. IEEE Press (2009)
19. Petkovic, D., Okada, K., Sosnick, M., Iyer, A., Zhu, S., Todtenhoefer, R., Huang, S.: Work in progress: a machine learning approach for assessment and prediction of teamwork effectiveness in software engineering education. In: Frontiers in Education Conference (FIE), pp. 1–3, October 2012
20. Radošević, D., Orehovački, T., Stapić, Z.: Automatic on-line generation of student's exercises in teaching programming. In: "Automatic On-line Generation of Students Exercises in Teaching Programming", Central European Conference on Information and Intelligent Systems, CECIIS (2010)
21. Ravi, G., Sosnovsky, S.: Exercise difficulty calibration based on student log mining. In: Mšdritscher, F., Luengo, V., Lai-Chong Law, E., Hoppe, U. (eds.) Proceedings of DAILE 2013: Workshop on Data Analysis and Interpretation for Learning Environments. Villard-de-Lans. France, January 2013
22. Sadigh, D., Seshia, S.A., Gupta, M.: Automating exercise generation: a step towards meeting the MOOC challenge for embedded systems. In: Proceedings of Workshop on Embedded Systems Education (WESE), October 2012
23. Saldana, J.M., Marfia, G., Roccetti, M.: First person shooters on the road: leveraging on aps and vanets for a quality gaming experience. In: Wireless Days, pp. 1–6. IEEE (2012)
24. Schalk, P., Wick, D., Turner, P., Ramsdell, M.: Predictive assessment of student performance for early strategic guidance. In: Frontiers in Education Conference (FIE 2011), pp. S2H-1–S2H-5, October 2011
25. Schell, J.: The Art of Game Design: A Book of Lenses. Morgan Kaufmann Publishers Inc., San Francisco (2008)
26. Verdú, E., Regueras, L.M., Verdú, M.J., Leal, J.P., de Castro, J.P., Queirós, R.: A distributed system for learning programming on-line. Comput. Educ. **58**(1), 1–10 (2012)
27. Wang, A.Y., Newlin, M.H.: Characteristics of students who enroll and succeed in psychology web-based classes. J. Educ. Psychol. **92**(1), 137 (2000)
28. Yoo, J., Kim, J.: Can online discussion participation predict group project performance? investigating the roles of linguistic features and participation patterns. Int. J. Artif. Intell. Educ. **24**(1), 8–32 (2014)

Using Cortical Learning Algorithm to Arrange Sporadic Online Conversation Groups According to Personality Traits

Roberto Agustín García-Vélez[1], Martín López-Nores[2(✉)],
Yolanda Blanco-Fernández[2], and José Juan Pazos-Arias[2]

[1] Área de Ciencias Exactas, Universidad Politécnica Salesiana,
Calle Vieja 12-30 y Elia Liut, Cuenca, Ecuador
rgarciav@ups.edu.ec
[2] Departamento de Ingeniería Telemática, AtlantTIC Research Center
for Information and Communication Technologies, EE Telecomunicación,
Universidade de Vigo, Campus Universitario s/n, 36310 Vigo, Spain
{mlnores,yolanda,jose}@det.uvigo.es

Abstract. Online conversation spaces are becoming an increasingly popular tool for language learning. Various portals on the Internet offer technological platform where groups of students can meet native teachers and arrange conversation sessions in convenient dates and times. The students' satisfaction is very important in this context because potential new users pay much attention to the comments and ratings provided by others in the past. Therefore, the portals implement simple mechanisms for the students to rate their experiences, and use the feedback so gathered to promote the teachers who get the best evaluations. Notwithstanding, the current online conversation portals do not implement any means to proactively supervise the formation of the sporadic groups of students, aiming to ensure that the conversations will be balanced, engaging and pleasant to everyone. In this paper we look at the question of whether social data mining and machine learning technologies can be used to maximise the chances that the people put into the same group will get on well together. Specifically, we present one approach based on mining personality traits and using *Cortical Learning Algorithm* to aid in the planning of the sessions.

Keywords: Online language learning · Sporadic social networks · Personality traits · Cortical Learning Algorithm

1 Introduction

The concept of *sporadic* (aka *spontaneous*) *social networks* refers to groups of people (acquaintances or strangers) who happen to share a common space (physical or virtual) and have similar interests in it for a certain period of time [1–3]. Online conversation spaces are one context in which such sporadic groups form, specifically for the purposes of language learning. Various portals on the Internet

P. Zaphiris and A. Ioannou (Eds.): LCT 2016, LNCS 9753, pp. 429–436, 2016.
DOI: 10.1007/978-3-319-39483-1_39

(e.g. Verbling and HowDoYouDo) offer a meeting point for groups of students to meet native teachers and arrange conversation sessions (henceforth, classes) in convenient dates and times. The teachers' personality and capabilities are key aspects to achieve positive group dynamics, and for that reason those portals ask the students to provide one rating for their labor after the classes have finished. The students often consider the aggregate value of those ratings when choosing the next classes in which they would like to participate.

Previous studies [4,7,10] have shown that the personality traits are one of the most important aspects to take into account in the formation of collaborative learning groups, because positive dynamics can potentiate the participation of all individuals. Likewise, other studies [8] have shown that the teacher ratings are an important feature for online learning portals, as they encourage the teachers to always do a good job and the students' satisfaction improves. However, despite the importance of ensuring positive dynamics and engaging topics in online conversation spaces, nowadays there are no solutions in place to proactively supervise the formation of the sporadic groups of students, and neither to assist the teachers in the preparation of appealing material.

In this paper we look at the question of whether social data mining and machine learning technologies can be used to maximise the chances that the people put into the same group will get on well together. The goal is challenging because the sporadic groups are most often independent of one another and many of the participants do not know each other beforehand. Therefore, unlike in [4,7,10] and similar works that focused on long-standing learning communities, it is not possible to make a first distribution of students into groups, and then refine progressively after successive rounds of observation and feedback. In order to face the more dynamic context on online learning spaces, we have developed and approach based on (i) mining personality traits of students and teacher from social networks, and (ii) using the advanced machine learning features of the *Cortical Learning Algorithm* (CLA) [9] to discover which combinations work well and which ones do not. This approach has been implemented in a real portal and some early results are now available.

The paper is organized as follows. Following this introduction, Sect. 2 describes the main modules and information flows of our approach. Then, Sect. 3 summarizes the findings obtained after the first few months of the approach running. Finally, Sect. 4 indicates the contributions we expect to make out of this project in relation to the research questions we are addressing, and also explains how we plan to continue with this work in the short and medium terms.

2   The Proposed Approach

We are developing the doctoral work in collaboration with an online conversation portal that specialises in English teaching for Spanish-speaking people. Rather than merely displaying the available classes and letting any students book their places in them, we want to advertise the new classes selectively and proactively, so that they are first known to the students who would most likely get

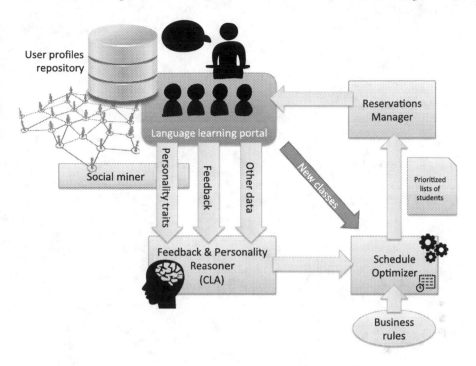

Fig. 1. Overall design of the proposed solution.

on well together. Of course, personality is assessed along with the data about the language level and the daily/hourly availability of teachers and students, bearing in mind a set of business rules about the number of classes each student is expected/allowed to attend during a period of time (depending on his/her type of subscription), the minimum average number of students in the classes to ensure that the portal makes profit, etc. The ultimate business goal is to achieve the greatest occupancy in the classes, so as to deliver service to more students with fewer classes.

The architectural scheme of our proposed solution is depicted in Fig. 1, comprising four main modules: the *"Social miner"*, the *"Feedback & personality reasoner"*, the *"Schedule optimizer"* and the *"Reservations manager"*. All the planning depends on a repository of student and teacher profiles, storing their personal data, learning needs and availability as usual, plus newly-added fields about personality traits. These are inferred from the users' activities in online social networks by the *"Social miner"* module. Currently, this module works with Facebook only, and gets data directly from the *Apply Magic Sauce Prediction API* (http://applymagicsauce.com/), which computes psycho-demographic profiles that include estimations of the classical *Big 5* personality traits [6] (one of the most popular frameworks used by psychologists to describe the human psyche along the dimensions of openness, conscientiousness, extraversion, agreeableness and neuroticism [6]) as well as estimations of intelligence, life satisfaction,

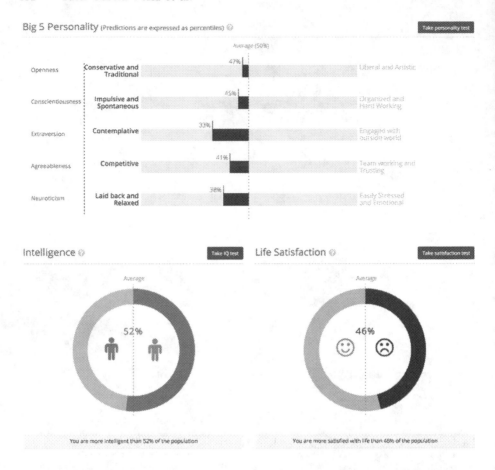

Fig. 2. Estimations of the *Big 5* personality traits, intelligence and life satisfaction.

sexual preference, political and religious orientations, education and relationship status. Figures 2 and 3 show graphical representations of the results obtained for one student.

The data obtained by the *"Social miner"* for all the profiles is fed into the *"Feedback & personality reasoner"* along with the feedback provided by students and teachers after the classes, as well as traces of the number and duration of everyone's interventions in the class, their ages, genders, locations and timezones. As regards the feedback, currently, we ask students to rate their satisfaction with the class, the teacher's labor and their interactions with the other students on a 5-point Likert scale (*"very negative"*, *"negative"*, *"neutral"*, *"positive"*, *"very positive"*). In turn, we ask the teacher to rate each student's attitude and performance with regard to the class objectives.

The *"Feedback & personality reasoner"* is expected to learn progressively which combinations of traits and other data ensure positive feedback and which ones do not, what are the proper balances, etc. The *Cortical Learning Algorithm*

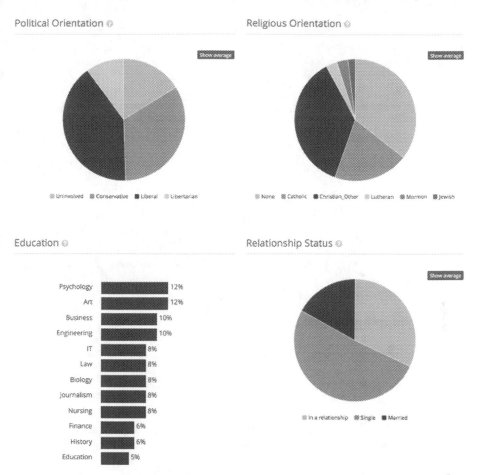

Fig. 3. Estimations of political and religious orientations, education, and relationship status.

models structural and algorithmic properties of the human brain's neocortex to discover patterns in more sophisticated ways than classical artifacts like Bayesian networks and neural networks do [9]. On the one hand, we use CLA in *learning mode* to assimilate new bundles of information coming after every class, which serves to continuously evolve a complex model of the aspects that may influence the satisfaction of students and teachers. On the other hand, we use it in *inference mode* to make predictions and aid in the arrangement of forthcoming classes, in a loop with the "*Schedule optimizer*".

The "*Schedule optimizer*" is based on the code of the open-source project OptaPlanner (http://www.optaplanner.org/), which provides a lightweight, embeddable constraint satisfaction engine that optimizes planning problems (typically, problems which are probably NP-complete or harder). Our module tries to harmonize the composition of the conversation groups with the availability and interests of every teacher and student, as well as with the business rules of the online conversation portal. At the output, we get a prioritized list of potential students for each new class, which is used by the *"Reservations manager"* selectively deliver warnings about the available classes, to filter the lists of classes offered on the web site to each student, and to inform teachers about opportunities to offer new classes. The list of potential students is revised as the places in the classes are booked, until they are full.

3   Preliminary Evaluation

Our approach is being tested and some early results are now available, following some training of the *"Feedback & personality reasoner"* module. The data gathered thus far suggests that the average satisfaction does improve with regard to statistics from previous months, when there was no artificial intelligence aiding in the planning of the classes. However, ANOVA tests [5] indicate that the amount of data is not yet sufficient to fully confirm this hypothesis. Besides, we have found that the reported levels of students' ratings of other participants improve as more of them come from the lists computed by the *"Schedule optimizer"*.

4   Conclusions and Future Work

The approach presented in this paper will serve to address the following research questions:

1. Is it possible to predict the levels of satisfaction of students and teachers in a class before it takes place, considering their personality traits and topics of interest?
2. Is it possible to get consistently more positive feedback by arranging the conversation groups according to personality traits, mined from the students' and teachers' activities in online social networks?
3. What is the quickest, least cumbersome way of gathering feedback after a class, aiming to get relevant information about each participant's impressions of everyone else?
4. Does an increase in levels of satisfaction correlate with better learning outcomes, or do the students accept a trade-off between learning and socializing?

In replying to these questions, we expect to come up with a working solution to improve the experience in the collaborating portal, thereby gaining valuable insight (from the socioeconomic point of view) into the interrelations and trade-offs among the many factors involved: learning needs and availability, personality traits, social networking activities, business rules, learning outcomes, etc. Hopefully, some of the findings will be relevant not only to online conversation portals, but also to other areas of application of the concept of sporadic social networks.

As for the continuation of this work, we are seeking to complete the preliminary analysis of results with further evidence, gathered during at least one year of our approach running. Besides, we want to evaluate alternative solutions for the social mining and machine learning tasks. First, we want to compare the learning capabilities of HTM against those of *Big Data* tools like Weka (http://www.cs.waikato.ac.nz/ml/weka/). Second, we are working to optimize the conversation groups not only on the grounds of personality traits, but also topics of interest mined from social networks and, thereby, make CLA reason about broad categories of topics (e.g. "Culture", "Sports", "Health", etc.). Finally, in the medium term, we want to implement solutions of our own to get additional information about personality, by monitoring the students' and teachers' participation in the classes, using sound processing and face recognition tools to appraise shyness and mood, to recognise smiles and laughs, etc. This would be a significant improvement of the technological platform of an online conversation portal.

Acknowledgment. This work is being supported by the European Regional Development Fund (ERDF) and the Galician Regional Government under agreement for funding the Atlantic Research Center for Information and Communication Technologies (AtlantTIC), and by the Ministerio de Educación y Ciencia (Gobierno de España) research project TIN2013-42774-R (partly financed with FEDER funds).

References

1. Ben Nejma, G., Roose, P., Dalmau, M., Gensel, J.: Service discovery for spontaneous communities in pervasive environments. In: Wang, J., et al. (eds.) WISE 2015. LNCS, vol. 9419, pp. 337–347. Springer, Heidelberg (2015). doi:10.1007/978-3-319-26187-4_32

2. Boutet, A., Frenot, S., Laforest, F., Launay, P., Le Sommer, N., Maheo, Y., Reimert, D.: C3PO: a network and application framework for spontaneous and ephemeral social networks. In: Wang, J., et al. (eds.) WISE 2015. LNCS, vol. 9419, pp. 348–358. Springer, Heidelberg (2015). doi:10.1007/978-3-319-26187-4_33

3. Bravo-Torres, J.F., López-Nores, M., Blanco-Fernández, Y., Pazos-Arias, J.J., Ordióñez-Morales, E.F.: Leveraging ad-hoc networking and mobile cloud computing to exploit short-lived relationships among users on the move. In: al Saidi, A., Fleischer, R., Maamar, Z., Rana, O.F. (eds.) ICC 2014. LNCS, vol. 8993, pp. 84–102. Springer, Heidelberg (2015)

4. Dascalu, M., Bodea, C.N., Lytras, M., Ordez de Pablos, P., Burlacu, A.: Improving e-learning communities through optimal composition of multidisciplinary learning groups. Comput. Hum. Behav. **30**, 362–371 (2014)

5. Gamst, G., Meyers, L., Guarino, A.: Analysis of Variance Designs: A Conceptual and Computational Approach with SPSS and SAS. Cambridge University Press, New York (2008)

6. McCrae, R., Costa, P.: The five-factor theory of personality. In: John, O.P., Robins, R.W., Pervin, L.A. (eds.) Handbook of Personality: Theory and Research, 3rd edn, pp. 159–181. Guilford Press, New York (2008)

7. Mudaliar, D., Modi, N.: Contemplating crossover operators of genetic algorithm for student group formation problem. Int. J. Emerg. Technol. Adv. Eng. **2**, 192–197 (2012)

8. Neubaum, G., Wichmann, A., Eimler, S., Kramer, N.: Investigating incentives for students to provide peer feedback in a semi-open online course: an experimental study. In: Proceedings of 10th International Symposium on Open Collaboration (OpenSym), Berlin, Germany, August 2014

9. Numenta, Inc.: HTM Cortical Learning Algorithms. White paper (2011). http://numenta.org/resources/HTM_CorticalLearningAlgorithms.pdf

10. Sinha, T.: Together we stand, together we fall, together we win: dynamic team formation in massive open online courses. In: Proceedings of 5th International Conference on Applications of Digital Information and Web Technologies (ICADIWT), Bangalore, India, February 2014

Process Mining of Interactions During Computer-Based Testing for Detecting and Modelling Guessing Behavior

Zacharoula Papamitsiou$^{(\boxtimes)}$ and Anastasios A. Economides

IPPS in Information Systems, University of Macedonia, Thessaloniki, Greece
papamits@uom.edu.gr, economid@uom.gr

Abstract. Detecting, recognizing and modelling patterns of observed examinee behaviors during assessment is a topic of great interest for the educational research community. In this paper we investigate the perspectives of *process-centric inference of guessing behavior patterns*. The underlying idea is to extract knowledge from real processes (i.e., not assumed nor truncated), logged automatically by the assessment environment. We applied a three-step process mining methodology on logged interaction traces from a case study with 259 undergraduate university students. The analysis revealed sequences of interactions in which low goal-orientation students answered quickly and correctly on difficult items, without reviewing them, while they submitted wrong answers on easier items. We assumed that this implies guessing behavior. From the conformance checking and performance analysis we found that the fitness of our process model is almost 85 %. Hence, initial results are encouraging towards modelling guessing behavior. Potential implications and future work plans are also discussed.

Keywords: Assessment analytics · Educational data mining · Guessing behavior · Pattern recognition · Process mining · Student interaction analysis

1 Introduction

The rise of educational data mining and learning analytics promises to deconstruct the deeper learning processes into more simple, distinct mechanisms, for understanding and supporting human learning accordingly [1]. This is envisaged to be achieved by tracking *every type of interactions* within any type of information system supporting learning or education (formal, informal, ubiquitous, mobile, virtual or real-world), converting them into explorable educational datasets, subjecting them into mining, and coding them into interpretable and useful schemas. *Interaction analysis* covers a number of methods for empirically exploring the space of humans' activities with each other and with objects in their environment via the use of artefacts and technology, for identification of practices and problems, and the origins for their solution [2]. In the educational context, technology-mediated learning supports learners' ability to interact with other learners, tutors, content interfaces, features and digital environments, and provides a great opportunity for recording, filtering and processing logged interaction trace data regarding systems' usage and *user activity indicators* [3].

© Springer International Publishing Switzerland 2016
P. Zaphiris and A. Ioannou (Eds.): LCT 2016, LNCS 9753, pp. 437–449, 2016.
DOI: 10.1007/978-3-319-39483-1_40

Recently, researchers attempt to extract indicators of students' behavior from multiple and diverse logged data sources. The exploration of the underlying relationships between these indicators and learning outcomes, its forthcoming analysis and the endeavor to identify patterns and model students' performance based on their actual interactions, has attracted increased attention (e.g. [4–6]). In these cases, advanced data mining and machine learning techniques have been utilized, beyond traditional statistical analysis methods, in order to investigate the abovementioned relationships.

1.1   Problem Statement - Motivation of the Research and Research Questions

As apparent, *recognizing patterns of students' behaviors during assessment* – which is closely related to measuring performance – is crucial for the research community. When it comes to computer-based testing procedures – which is a typical, popular and widespread method of online assessment – one of the *observed unwanted examinee behaviors* that needs to be detected and appropriately managed and that critically affects the assessment result (e.g., score) is *guessing* of the correct answer on testing items.

The prevalent methods for modelling guessing behavior include Item Response Theory (IRT)-based techniques and Bayesian Knowledge Tracing (BKT), both of which adopt a probabilistic approach for hypothesizing and investigating students' behavior either within testing environments [7, 8] or within Intelligent Tutoring Systems [9]. In these approaches, researchers defined thresholds for discriminating noneffortful guessing responses from solution behavior upon test speededness (i.e., amounts of times to answer the question) [10, 11], explored different combinations of IRT-parameters (e.g. difficulty-based guessing models based on test-taking motivation, the corresponding effort expenditure, the correctness of the answer and the estimated examinee ability) [12], contextualized the estimation of the probability that a student has guessed or slipped [13], and enhanced previous results with skill difficulty driven by the estimation of knowledge acquisition during each step of the problem solution procedure [14].

However, the abovementioned methodologies (a) follow an *outcome-centric probabilistic consideration*, in terms of employing the student's ability/performance estimation, and (b) *do not "dive" into the causation and origins* of the occurring interactions.

In order to overcome these shortcomings, the novelty of the present approach resides in the following facts: (a) we investigate the perspectives of *process-centric (rather than outcome-centric) inference* of guessing patterns, (b) we explore *full-fledged process models with concurrency patterns,* unlike most of the traditional educational data mining techniques which focus on data or simple sequential structures [15], and (c) we associate *student's goal-orientation* to exhibiting guessing behavior during assessment. Thus, the research question (*RQ*) is:

> *"Can we discover behavioral patterns (sequence/repetition/alternation/frequency/duration) within event logs that can be associated with guessing during testing?"*

The underlying idea in the proposed approach is to employ process mining in order to extract knowledge from event logs tracked automatically by the testing environment [16, 17]. In particular, we suggest a three-step process mining methodology on logged trace data: (a) an initial control flow perspective, (b) next, the identification of sequences of events, (c) and finally, the classification of these sequences of events based on *students' time-spent* on correctly and wrongly answered questions, *student's goal-orientation* and *questions' difficulty*, and their mapping to respective behavior schemas.

In this paper we present the results from a study that we conducted in order to explore the capabilities of the proposed methodology on recognizing meaningful patterns that imply guessing behavior. 259 undergraduate students from a Greek University participated in an assessment procedure designed for the study. We employed the LAERS assessment environment [6] to collect the data (i.e., track students' interactions logs) during testing. For the mining purposes we used the ProM process mining tool [18] –a generic open-source framework for implementing process mining tools in a standard environment. The analysis revealed patterns of interactions in which low goal-orientation students frequently answered quickly and correctly on difficult items, without reviewing or altering them, while they submitted wrong answers on easier items. We classified this as guessing behavior. In order to measure the model's ability to re-reproduce all execution sequences that are in the log, we performed conformance checking and performance analysis. The fitness of our process model was almost 85 %. In essence, we suggest that process mining of temporal traces, taking into consideration each student's goal-orientation can be used for modelling guessing behavior during testing.

The rest of the paper is organized as follows: in Sect. 2, we provide an overview of process mining applied in the educational domain. In Sect. 3, we present the experiment methodology, the data collection procedure and the analysis methods that we applied, while in Sect. 4, we analyze the results from the case study. Finally, in Sect. 5, we discuss on the major findings, possible implications and future work plans.

2 Process Mining: An Overview

Process mining is a relatively new technology which emerged from the business community, and at the same time, a field of research situated at the intersection of data mining and business process management. The main objective of this technology is to allow for process-related knowledge extraction from event logs, automatically recorded by Information Systems [16]. The target is "to discover, monitor and improve real processes" [19, p. 34]. In other words, the purpose of process mining is to identify, confirm or extend process models based on actual data.

The core component of all process mining tasks is an *event log*. An event log is a set of finite *event sequences*, whereas each event sequence corresponds to a particular *process instance* (i.e., a *case*) of an activity, and can have a timestamp and an actuator executing or initiating the activity [19]. The sequence of events executed for a case is called a *trace*. Thus, within an event log, multiple cases may have the same trace.

The most prominent process mining technique is process model discovery (i.e., structures that model behavior), which includes the complete process model production from event-based data, without using any a-priori information. The constructed process model reflects the behavior observed in the original log and is able to reproduce it.

In the educational domain, typical examples of event logs may include learner's activity logs in e-learning environments (e.g. learning management systems, intelligent tutoring systems, etc.), use of pedagogical/educational resources, examination traces, participation and engagement in collaborative activities, etc. Examples of cases where process mining has been the central methodology, include the discovery of processes followed by the learners in different contexts, such as in self-regulated learning [20], in collaborative learning [21, 22], in collaborative writing [23, 24], in multiple-choice questions tests [25], and the discovery of learning habits based on MOOC data [26].

More precisely, in [25], process model discovery and analysis techniques (such as Petri nets, Heuristic and Fuzzy miner) were used to analyze assessment data (e.g. correctness of the answer, certitude, grade, time-spent for answering the question, etc.) from online multiple choice tests and to investigate the students' behavior during online examinations. In the collaborative learning context, the authors explored regulatory processes [21], and analyzed collaborative writing processes and how these correlate to the quality of the produced documents [23, 24]. In addition, the analysis of behavioral learner data (i.e., related to modeling and prototyping activities during a group project and the respective scores) with process mining techniques – targeting a complex problem solving process – shed light on the cognitive aspects of problem-solving behavior of novices in the area of domain modeling, specifically regarding process-oriented feedback [27]. Yet, in [26] the objective was to provide insights regarding students and their learning behavior (watching videos in a recommended sequence) as it relates to their performance. Finally, in the context of enhancing self-regulated learning [20], the authors analyzed the temporal order of spontaneous individual regulation activities.

In these examples from the educational domain, the prevailing process model discovery techniques were control-flow mining algorithms, which allow the discovery of educational processes and learning paths based on the dependency relations that can be inferred from event logs. The results of mining educational datasets with process mining provided useful insight regarding the improvement of understanding of the underlying educational processes, allowing for early detection of anomalies [23, 24]. These results were used for generating recommendations and advice to students [26], to provide feedback [27] to either students, teachers or/and researchers, to help students with specific learning disabilities, to improve management of learning objects [20], etc.

In our approach, we applied a three-step process mining methodology during a testing procedure, and explored its capabilities on recognizing meaningful patterns of guessing behavior during examination. We elaborate on this methodology in Sect. 3.

3 Methodology

3.1 Research Participants and Data Collection

In this study, data were collected from a total of 259 undergraduate students (108 males [41.7 %] and 151 females [58.3 %], aged 20-27 years old (M = 22.6, SD = 1.933, N = 259) from the Department of Economics at University of Macedonia, Thessaloniki,

Greece. 12 groups of 20 to 25 students attended the midterm exams of the Computers II course (related to introduction to databases, information systems and e-commerce). For the purposes of the examination, we used 34 multiple choice quiz items. Each item had two to four possible answers, but only one was the correct. Finally, the participation to the midterm exams procedure was optional. As an external motivation to increase the students' effort, we set that their score would participate up to 30 % to their final grade.

In our study, we used the LAERS assessment environment [6], which is a Computer-Based Assessment system that we are developing. At the first phase of its implementation, we configured a testing unit and a tracker that logs the students' interaction data. The testing unit displays the multiple choice quiz items delivered to students separately and one-by-one. Within the duration of the test, the students can temporarily save their answers on the items, before submitting the quiz, can skip or re-view them and/or alter their initial choice by selecting the item to re-view from the list underneath. They submit the quiz answers only once, whenever they estimate that they are ready to do so.

The second component of the system records the students' interaction data during testing. In a log file we tracked students' time-spent on handling the testing items, distinguishing it between the time on correctly and wrongly answered items. In the same log file, we also logged the times the students reviewed each item and the times they changed their answers, and the respective time-spent during these interactions. In a separate file we also calculated the effort expenditure on each item and estimated the item's difficulty level [28]. Finally, we embedded into the system a pre-test questionnaire in order to measure each student's goal expectancy (GE) (a measure of student goal-orientation and perception of preparation [29]) in a separate log file. The final collected dataset includes the features illustrated in Table 1.

Table 1. Features from the raw log files

1. The student's ID	*9. The total time the student spends on viewing the tasks and submitting the correct answers*
2. The task the student works on (question Id)	*10. The total time the student spends on viewing the tasks and submitting the wrong answers*
3. The answer the student submits (answer Id)	*11. How many times the student views each task*
4. The correctness of the submitted answer	*12. How many times the student changes the submitted answer for each task*
5. The timestamp the student starts viewing a task	*13. The student's effort required*
6. The timestamp the student chooses to leave the task (saves an answer)	*14. The item's difficulty*
7. The idle time the student spends viewing each task	*15. The student's goal-expectancy (GE)*
8. The student's total time on task	*16. The student's actual performance (final score).*

In this study we applied a three-step process mining methodology on logged trace data and explored its capabilities on recognizing meaningful patterns of interactions that imply guessing behavior: (a) initially we adopted a control flow perspective (Petri-Nets [30]), (b) next, we identified sequences of events (*traces*), and finally, (c) we classified these sequences of events based on the *students' time-spent* on correctly and wrongly answered questions, the *student's goal-orientation* and the *question's difficulty*, and mapped them to respective behavior schemas.

3.2 Data Pre-processing and Construction of the Petri Net

Data pre-processing allows the transformation of original data into a suitable shape to be used by process mining algorithms. During this process, and within the dataset, we identified abstract behaviors of students regarding the testing items (i.e. students' actions), which we then coded into *tasks*. In our study we define as *task* T = {View(v), Answer Correctly(ac), Answer Wrongly(aw), Review(r), Change to Correct(chc), Change to Wrong(chw)}, the simplest learner's action. In addition, and since students' time-spent on each task is a continuous variable, that is difficult to subject into mining, we classified the students' temporal behavior in 4 clusters by applying the k-means algorithm (with k = 4). We experimented and executed the k-means algorithm for a number of iterations with different values of k (k = 3, k = 4, k = 5, k = 10). We computed the sum of squared error (SSE) for these values of k and plotted k against the SSE. According to the "Elbow" method [31], we finally selected k = 4. For simplicity reasons we call *Cluster* C = {medium-slow(ms), quick(q), medium-quick(mq), slow (s)}. Table 2 shows a sample of the consolidated event log with each row representing one event.

Table 2. Features after the data pre-processing

CaseId	Resource	timestamp	questid	answid	spenttime	Cor/ness	task	Cluster
170	16610	13:36:38	59	231	54.487	0	aw	ms
172	30314	13:51:07	60	235	24.759	0	aw	mq
174	30314	12:33:30	61	239	65.909	0	aw	ms
175	22514	13:36:44	56	219	10.498	1	chc	q
177	16610	13:37:12	60	232	31.133	1	ac	ms
179	22514	13:36:59	57	221	11.391	1	r	q
180	22514	13:37:26	58	225	27.091	1	r	mq
181	18805	13:37:41	58	undef	32.591	2	v	ms
182	25711	13:37:44	56	219	30.332	1	ac	ms
184	16610	13:37:40	61	239	26.254	0	aw	mq
185	22514	13:37:51	59	231	24.562	0	chw	mq
187	18805	13:39:55	59	undef	110.063	2	v	s
188	30314	12:34:03	61	239	5.167	0	r	q

Our analysis of the logged data explores the temporal behavior of students. Hence, the final clustered tasks considered in this study included 24 *events classes* E = {quick view(qv), quick review(qr), quick correct(qc), quick wrong(qw),..}.

Next, we performed a dotted chart analysis in order to gain some insight in the underlying processes and the respective performance. Figure 1 illustrates the results of this analysis. All the instances (one per student) are sorted by the duration of the computer-based assessment.

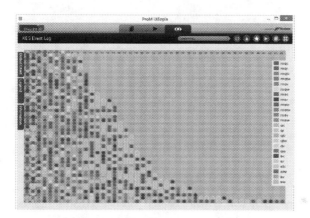

Fig. 1. Dotted Chart Analysis (Color figure online)

The basic idea of the dotted chart is to plot a dot for each event in the log according to the time. Thus, it enables visually examining the complete set of data in an event log and highlighting possible interesting patterns within the log. The dotted chart has *three orthogonal dimensions*: time and component types. The time is measured along the horizontal axis of the chart. The component types (e.g., originator, task, event type, etc.) are shown along the vertical axis. Note that the first component considered is shown along the vertical axis, in boxes, while the second component of the event is given by the color of the dot. Let us also note that in a dotted chart, common patterns among different cases are not clearly visible.

For detecting common patterns between the behavioral "traces" (response strategies) of the students during testing, in our case study, we mined the event log for Petri Nets using Integer Linear Programming (ILP). The ILP Miner is known for the fact that it always returns a Petri Net that perfectly fits a given event log [32]. Figure 2 illustrates the generated Petri Net which describes the generic pattern of answering questions, allowing for answer-reviews and changes. In this figure, the states (i.e., the events) and the transitions between them, including sequences, braches and loops between events are summarized for the whole sample, modeling the testing behavior of the participants. Every question can be answered correctly or wrongly and the student can spent a lot or less of time on answering the question. Further, a question can be viewed or reviewed and the student may change the submitted answer. The latter decision is modeled by an internal transition (painted in black) that goes to the final place of the net.

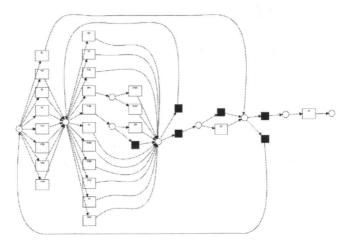

Fig. 2. The Petri Net that models the handling of testing items in our study

3.3   Identification of Traces - Conformance Checking and Performance Analysis

A process that specifies which event need to be executed and in what order is a workflow process model. In our study, we identified 47 sequences of events, i.e. *traces*. We define every unique sequence of events as *trace* $TR_i = \{TR_1 = \{qv,qw,qr,mqv, mqc, ...\}, TR_2 = \{sv,qw,msv,mqc,qr,msr,...\}, ...\}$. Figure 3 shows all the paths detected within the event log, corresponding to the solution strategies the students follow during testing. All the 47 traces are illustrated in this figure. The numbers on the arrows indicate how many cases follow the specific trace. Sequences of events, branches and loops are also illustrated in this figure.

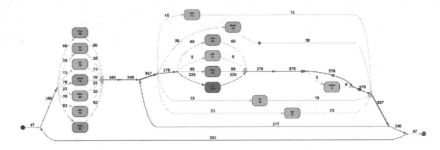

Fig. 3. Paths and traces detected in the event log of student's interactions with the testing-items

Before performing the conformance checking and performance analysis, we enhanced the process mining technique with trace alignment. In fact, trace alignment prepares the event logs in a way that can be explored easily and it complements existing process mining techniques focusing on discovery and conformance checking.

Trace alignment allows for similarity detection between traces, inducing interesting patterns of testing-item manipulation by the students during assessment. Given the great heterogeneity in traces, only few of the produced clusters delivered a good trace alignment.

Next, we performed conformance checking and performance analysis This analysis may be used to detect deviations, to locate and explain these deviations, and to measure their severity. We found that the fitness of our process model (i.e. whether the log traces comply with the description in the model) is almost 85 % (40 out of the 47 traces were re-produced correctly). This is particularly useful for finding out whether (or how often) the students exhibit guessing behavior. Then, we classified these sequences of events based on the students' time-spent on correctly and wrongly answered questions, their GE and the question's difficulty, and mapped them to respective behavior schemas.

4 Results

4.1 Recognition of "Guessing Behavior" Pattern

Figure 4(a) and (b) are samples of the traces followed by students who answered correctly and wrongly to the most of the questions respectively.

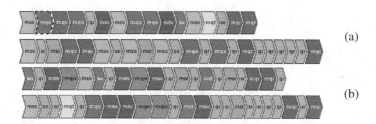

(a)

(b)

Fig. 4. Traces of (a) high achieving students, (b) low achieving students

As seen from Fig. 4(a), high achieving students answer correctly on the items, review the items and in those that they initially submitted a wrong answer, they revise it, think about it and submit a new, correct answer. Similarly, from Fig. 4(b) one can tell that low achieving students answer wrongly on the questions, they will not revise them and will not change their answers. Note that, high achieving students also denote high goal-expectancy (GE). In [6] it was found that there is a positive effect of GE on their time to answer correctly, while there is a negative effect of GE on time to answer wrongly, indicating that poorly prepared students will spend less time on questions.

However, the major category of the students are those who achieve an intermediate score. In this case, two major behaviors have been identified: those who will try their best, but not answer all items correctly and may have slipped some answers, and those who may have guessed some of the answers. The traces of these two categories are illustrated in Fig. 5.

(a)

(b)

(c)

Fig. 5. Traces of students exhibiting (a) solution, (b) guessing and (c) slipping behavior

As seen from Fig. 5 (a), the students view and review the items and try to "solve" the questions and submit the correct answers. They spent a considerable amount of time on dealing with the question and in some case, they might change their answers. On the contrary, Fig. 5 (b) corresponds to a trace that implies guessing behaviour. That is because in both traces, the students have answered fast and correctly on an item that has been found to be a difficult one, while they have submitted false answers on less difficult items. Furthermore, in both cases, the students do not revise the "suspicious" item. In an analogous way, in Fig. 5 (c), the students have slipped an easy item, by submitting fast a wrong answer, while answering correctly on the most difficult items.

5 Discussion and Conclusions

The issue of detecting and appropriately managing the observed examinee guessing behavior during testing is a central topic for the educational research community. In general, guessing behavior is expressed as rapidly occurring random responses, implying either that the students did not exhibit effort exertion or that they did not fully consider the testing item. Previous methods from related work, follow a probabilistic consideration on the identification of guessing behavior, that is outcome-centric and do not "dive" into the causation of the interactions that take place. In order to overcome these shortcomings, the novelty of the present approach resides in the following facts: (a) we investigate the perspectives of process-centric (rather than outcome-centric) inference of guessing patterns, (b) we explore full-fledged process models with concurrency patterns, and (c) we associate student's goal-expectancy to exhibiting guessing behavior during assessment. In essence, the core research question of this study concerned the discovery of behavioral patterns (sequence/repetition/alternation/frequency/duration) within event logs that can be associated with guessing during testing.

In the suggested approach, the underlying idea was to extract knowledge from event logs (i.e., real processes) tracked automatically by the testing environment. Hence, in order to address the research question, we applied a three-step process mining methodology on logged trace data. In our approach, we initially employed Petri Nets from a control flow perspective, next we identified sequences of tasks (traces), and finally, we classified these traces based on the students' time-spent on correctly and wrongly answered questions, their goal-expectancy and the question's difficulty, and mapped them to respective behavior schemas. We conducted a study with 259 undergraduate university students who participated in an assessment procedure appropriately designed. We employed the LAERS assessment environment to track examinees' interactions logs during testing, and the ProM process mining tool for mining the logs. We discovered 47 behavioral traces (patterns) in total. The analysis revealed patterns of interactions in which low goal-orientation students frequently answered quickly and correctly on difficult items, without reviewing or altering them, while they submitted wrong answers on easier items (Fig. 5). We classified this as guessing behavior. This is partially in agreement with previous research results [8, 10], according to which the response time of guesses is usually very short compared to the amount of time required for the items.

In order to measure the model's ability to re-reproduce all execution sequences that are in the log, we performed conformance checking and performance analysis. The fitness of our process model was almost 85 %, with 40 out of the 47 traces to conform to the description in the model, and be correctly re-produced. Initial results are encouraging, indicating that process mining of temporal traces, taking into consideration each student' s goal expectancy can provide reliable modelling of guessing behavior.

However, it is important to note that an event log contains only example behavior, i.e., we cannot assume that all possible traces have been observed. In fact, an event log often contains only a fraction of the possible behavior [16]. Moreover, and in agreement with [20], although the proposed methodology may be useful for gaining insight into the students' interactions with the learning and assessment items, however, one identified disadvantage of process mining and descriptive modelling is that they are not directly suitable for statistical testing (e.g., significance testing).

According to [33], guessed answers increase the variance error of test scores and lower the test reliability. The accurate modelling of guessing behavior could lead to using the frequency of this behavior as an indicator of students' disengagement with the test. Identification of guessing behavior patterns could also assist in assessing the quality of multiple-choice items, re-designing the testing items, and change those that have caused guessing behavior too frequently. Furthermore, and since process mining is a promising methodology for behavioral pattern recognition within educational logged data, one possible research direction would be to explore the optimum size of the test (number of items) as well as the position of the items within the test, and associate these with fatigue and lack of focus, that could hinder guessing behavior. In [25] the authors employed process mining on assessment data and found that 35 % percent of the students answered the first question right and had high confidence. It would be interesting to measure the correct answers on this item if it was delivered as the last item of the assessment process and considering the students' confidence [34].

In the educational context, the application of process mining to learner's interaction trace data can become valuable assets for discovering, monitoring and improving real processes by extracting knowledge from learning-oriented event logs. We believe that analysis of behavioral learner data with process mining can add value in addition to the currently available learning analytics tools and techniques.

References

1. Papamitsiou, Z., Economides, A.A.: Learning analytics and educational data mining in practice: a systematic literature review of empirical evidence. Educ. Technol. Soc. **17**(4), 49–64 (2014)
2. Jordan, B., Henderson, A.: Interaction analysis: foundations and practice. J. Learn. Sci. **4**(1), 39–103 (1995)
3. Donnelly, R.: Interaction analysis in a "Learning by Doing" problem-based professional development context. Comput. Educ. **55**, 1357–1366 (2010)
4. Huang, S., Fang, N.: Predicting student academic performance in an engineering dynamics course: a comparison of four types of predictive mathematical models. Comput. Educ. **61**, 133–145 (2013)
5. Macfadyen, L.P., Dawson, S.: Mining LMS data to develop an "early warning system" for educators: a proof of concept. Comput. Educ. **54**(2), 588–599 (2010)
6. Papamitsiou, Z., Terzis, V., Economides, A.A.: Temporal learning analytics during computer based testing. In: 4th International Conference on Learning Analytics and Knowledge, pp. 31–35. ACM, New York (2014)
7. Lee, Y.-H., Jia, Y.: Using response time to investigate students' test-taking behaviors in a NAEP computer-based study. Large-scale Assessments Educ. **2**(1), 1–24 (2014)
8. Kong, X.J., Wise, S.L., Bhola, D.S.: Setting the response time threshold parameter to differentiate solution behavior from rapid-guessing behaviour. Educ. Psychol. Meas. **67**(4), 606–619 (2007)
9. Baker, R.S., Corbett, A.T., Gowda, S.M., Wagner, A.Z., MacLaren, B.A., Kauffman, L.R., Mitchell, A.P., Giguere, S.: Contextual slip and prediction of student performance after use of an intelligent tutor. In: De Bra, P., Kobsa, A., Chin, D. (eds.) UMAP 2010. LNCS, vol. 6075, pp. 52–63. Springer, Heidelberg (2010)
10. Schnipke, D.L., Scrams, D.J.: Modeling item response times with a two-state mixture model: a new method of measuring speededness. J. Educ. Meas. **34**, 213–232 (1997)
11. Wise, S.L., Kong, X.: Response time effort: a new measure of examinee motivation in computer-based tests. Appl. Meas. Educ. **16**, 163–183 (2005)
12. Cao, J., Stokes, S.L.: Bayesian IRT guessing models for partial guessing behaviors. Psychometrika **73**(2), 209–230 (2008)
13. Baker, R.S.J.d., Corbett, A.T., Aleven, V.: Improving contextual models of guessing and slipping with a truncated training set. In: Baker, R.S.J.d., Barnes, T., Beck, J.E. (eds.) 1st International Conference on Educational Data Mining, pp. 67–76 (2008)
14. Gowda, S.M., Rowe, J.P., Baker, R.S.J.d., Chi, M., Koedinger, K.R.: Improving models of slipping, guessing and moment-by-moment learning with estimates of skill difficulty. In: Pechenizkiy, M., Calders, T., Conati, C., Ventura, S., Romero, C., and Stamper, J. (eds.) 4th International Conference on Educational Data Mining, pp. 199–208 (2011)
15. Trčka, N., Pechenizkiy, M., van der Aalst, W.P.M.: Process mining from educational data (Chapter 9). In: Romero, C., Ventura, S., Pechenizkiy, M., Baker, R.S.J.d. (eds.) Handbook of Educational Data Mining. pp. 123–142. CRC Press, London (2010)
16. van der Aalst, W.P.M.: Process Mining: Discovery, Conformance and Enhancement of Business Processes. Springer, Berlin (2011)
17. van der Aalst, W.P.M.: Process mining: making knowledge discovery process centric. SIGKDD Explor. Newsl. **13**(2), 45–49 (2012)
18. van Dongen, B.F., de Medeiros, A.K.A., Verbeek, H., Weijters, A., van der Aalst, W.M.: The ProM framework: a new era in process mining tool support. In: Ciardo, G., Darondeau, P. (eds.) ICATPN 2005. LNCS, vol. 3536, pp. 444–454. Springer, Heidelberg (2005)

19. van der Aalst, W.M.: Process mining in the large: a tutorial. In: Zimányi, E. (ed.) eBISS 2013. LNBIP, vol. 172, pp. 33–76. Springer, Heidelberg (2014)
20. Bannert, M., Reimann, P., Sonnenberg, C.: Process mining techniques for analysing patterns and strategies in students' self-regulated learning. Metacogn. Learn. 9(2), 161–185 (2014)
21. Schoor, C., Bannert, M.: Exploring regulatory processes during a CSCL task using process mining. Comput. Hum. Behav. 28(4), 1321–1331 (2012)
22. Bergenthum, R., Desel, J., Harrer, A., Mauser, S.: Modeling and mining of learnflows. In: Jensen, K., Donatelli, S., Kleijn, J. (eds.) ToPNoC V. LNCS, vol. 6900, pp. 22–50. Springer, Heidelberg (2012)
23. Southavilay, V., Yacef, K., Calvo, R.A.: Process mining to support students' collaborative writing. In: Baker, R.S.J.d., Merceron, A., Pavlik, P.I.Jr. (eds.) 3rd International Conference on Educatinal Data Mining, pp. 257−266 (2010)
24. Calvo, R.A., O'Rourke, S.T., Jones, J., Yacef, K., Reimann, P.: Collaborative writing support tools on the cloud. IEEE Trans. Learn. Technol. 4(1), 88–97 (2011)
25. Pechenizkiy, M., Trčka, N., Vasilyeva, E., van der Aalst, W.M.P., de Bra, P.: Process mining online assessment data. In: Barnes, T., Desmarais, M.C., Romero, C. and Ventura, S. (eds.) 2nd International Conference on Educational Data Mining, pp. 279–288 (2009)
26. Mukala, P., Buijs, J.C.A.M., Leemans, M., van der Aalst, W.M.P.: Learning analytics on Coursera event data: a process mining approach. In: Ceravolo, P., Rinderle-Ma, S. (eds.) 5th SIMPDA, pp. 18−32 (2015)
27. Sedrakyan, G., De Weerdt, J., Snoeck, M.: Process-mining enabled feedback: "tell me what I did wrong" vs. "tell me how to do it right". Comput. Hum. Behav. 57, 352–376 (2016)
28. Papamitsiou, Z., Economides, A.A.: A temporal estimation of students' on-task mental effort and its effect on students' performance during computer based testing. In: 18th International Conference on Interactive Collaborative Learning, pp. 1136–1144. IEEE (2015)
29. Terzis, V., Economides, A.A.: The acceptance and use of computer based assessment. Comput. Educ. 56(4), 1032–1044 (2011)
30. van der Aalst, W.M.P.: The application of petri nets to workflow management. J. Circuit. Syst. Comput. 8(1), 21–66 (1998)
31. Sugar, C.A., James, G.M.: Finding the number of clusters in a dataset: an information-theoretic approach. J. Am. Stat. Assoc. 98, 750–763 (2003)
32. van der Werf, J.M.E.M., Dongen, B.F., van Hurkens, C.A.J., Serebrenik, A.: Process discovery using integer linear programming. Fundam. Inform. 94(3–4), 387–412 (2009)
33. Bereby-Meyer, Y., Meyer, J., Flascher, O.M.: Prospect theory analysis of guessing in multiple choice tests. J. Behav. Decis. Making 15(4), 313–327 (2002)
34. Lamboudis, D., Economides, A.A.: Adaptive exploration of user knowledge in computer based testing. WSEAS Trans. Commun. 3(1), 322–327 (2004)

Learning Technologies

Coupled Persuasive Systems: A Case Study in Learning Japanese Characters

Dave Berque[1(✉)] and Hiroko Chiba[2]

[1] Computer Science Department, DePauw University,
Greencastle, USA
dberque@depauw.edu
[2] Modern Languages Department, DePauw University,
Greencastle, USA
hchiba@depauw.edu

Abstract. One of the challenges faced by Japanese language learners is becoming comfortable with three types of writing scripts: Hiragana, Katakana and Kanji (Chinese characters). The need to learn many characters often seems overwhelming to Japanese learners; however, instructors can play a pivotal role in assisting learners by helping them cognitively organize the information expressed in the scripts. This cognitive organization can help the learner develop better ways to memorize characters at an early stage and can also help accelerate the learning process later. This paper presents a case study in that shows how a human teacher can leverage a pen-based instructional technology system to provide Japanese learners with feedback and suggestions that persuade them to change the way they draw Japanese scripts.

Keywords: Persuasive technology · Japanese scripts · Kanji · Stroke order · Dyknow

1 Introduction

1.1 Persuasive Technology

Persuasive technology is a subfield of HCI that studies technology designed to persuade people to change attitudes or behaviors. In his book, Persuasive Technology: Using Computers to Change What we Think and Do, Fogg introduces this field and provides examples from varied domains including safety (persuading people not to drive after drinking) and education (persuading students to study regularly) [4].

Fogg categorizes persuasive technologies depending on how the technology persuades. For example, Fogg presents reduction technologies that work by making target behaviors easier, and suggestion technologies that give users feedback to help them understand how their behavior differs from a target behavior [4].

Fogg limits his work to technologies that work independently to facilitate a behavior change. We build on Fogg's work by showing why it can be important to consider what we call a "coupled persuasive system." Such systems consist of a human component and a technology component that work together to enable behavior change.

© Springer International Publishing Switzerland 2016
P. Zaphiris and A. Ioannou (Eds.): LCT 2016, LNCS 9753, pp. 453–462, 2016.
DOI: 10.1007/978-3-319-39483-1_41

While Fogg would argue that this is simply a form of computer mediated communication (communication between humans, mediated by a computer), we present a situation in which a human and computer work synergistically as a persuasive system. Specifically we present a case study that couples a human teacher with a pen-based instructional technology system to provide Japanese learners with feedback and suggestions that help change the way they draw Japanese scripts.

1.2   Challenges for Japanese Language Learners

One of the challenges faced by Japanese language learners is becoming comfortable with three types of writing scripts: Hiragana, Katakana and Kanji (Chinese characters). There are 46 basic letters in each of the Hiragana and Katakana scripts, and approximately 2000 Kanji characters that the learners eventually need to master (for simplicity, we will refer to letters and characters simply as "characters" in the remainder of this paper).

The need to learn many characters often seems overwhelming to Japanese learners; however, instructors can play a pivotal role in assisting learners by helping them cognitively organize the information expressed in the scripts. This cognitive organization can help the learner develop better ways to memorize characters at an early stage and can also help accelerate the learning process later.

Although each writing script is used for a different purpose in sentences, writing the characters requires similar organizational patterns across all three scripts. For example, learners must focus on their stroke order (the order in which individual strokes are drawn to form a single character) and on their ability to shape the characters correctly. Internalizing patterns in stroke order and character shape can help students cognitively organize their learning. Additionally, the visual attributes of the characters can work together with motor memory to lead to automaticity in writing characters. This, in turn, is one of the keys to successfully learning Japanese.

Teaching stroke order has been strongly encouraged in Japanese education, especially in elementary school. During the 6 years of elementary school, at least 1006 Kanji are introduced as mandated by Japan's Ministry of Education, Culture, Sports, Science, and Technology [6]. The widely accepted Kanji test, *Nihon Kanji Noryoku Kentei* (*Kanji Kentei* or *Kanken*), has six sections that deal with Kanji stroke orders [7]. The most advanced of these levels covers 1006 Kanji characters, which is aligned with the Kanji studied in the first six years of schooling [7]. According to Hiroshi Matsumoto, stroke order can serve as a means to "orderly construct" an aesthetically pleasing Kanji by continuously connecting dots and lines [5]. Knowing the stroke order also help learners identify the number of strokes in radicals (parts). This is crucial when looking up a new Kanji in a paper dictionary, as well as when looking up a Kanji in an on-line dictionary if we cannot copy and paste the Kanji into the dictionary, such as when looking up a Kanji that we see on a sign or in a book.

2   Classroom Solution

For several years we have explored the use of networked pen-based computers, a collaborative instructional technology software system called DyKnow [3], and a human instructor to support student learning in college level courses [1, 2]. In this paper we focus on the use of this system to help students master Japanese scripts in two courses taught by the second author.

In addition to regular meetings, the courses "Elementary Japanese I" and "Elementary Japanese II" meet once per week for a laboratory that takes place in a classroom that provides each student (as well as the instructor) with a pen-based computer. DyKnow software allows Japanese characters drawn by the instructor to be shared with students in real time. The instructor can also use the system to collect and view characters drawn by students and optionally to display this work for the entire class to see.

During class, the instructor demonstrates how to draw Japanese characters while the system transmits individual pen movements to the student's computers where the instructor's writing is displayed. The students can repeatedly replay the instructor's writing stroke-by-stoke to reinforce the stroke order and character shape. Figures 1, 2 and 3 show the Kanji character for mountain (pronounced *yama*), originally written by the instructor, at three stages of replay by a student. Figure 1 shows the character after the first stroke has been drawn, Fig. 2 shows the character after the second stroke has been drawn and Fig. 3 shows the completed character.

Fig. 1. Kanji after the first stroke was drawn

The student can use the software's controls to step through the sequence stroke by stroke. The software provides an option to display each stroke as a completed unit (the entire stroke is displayed at once) and also provides an option to replay each stroke dynamically to show the direction of the original drawing.

Fig. 2. Kanji after the second stroke was drawn

Fig. 3. Kanji after the third (final) stroke was drawn

After replaying the instructor's strokes, students practice drawing the character in the software using their own styluses. Sometimes, the students use the software to practice privately while the instructor moves throughout the room and provides feedback. At other times, the instructor uses the software to share some of the student writing with the entire class simultaneously, which allows the instructor to provide feedback to the entire class (see Fig. 4). In either case, the instructor can provide students with detailed feedback on their stroke order and shape by using the software to replay the student's writing stroke by stroke.

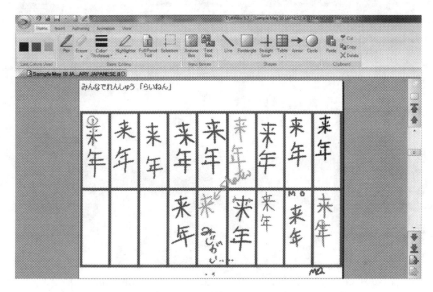

Fig. 4. In-class interactive exercise

Periodically, students take quizzes that require them to draw characters and submit them to the instructor through DyKnow. While grading quizzes, the instructor can review each student's writing process stroke by stroke. Once again, this allows the instructor to give the students precise feedback. Figure 5 shows an example of a student's response to a quiz question along with feedback from the instructor. The student's response, along with the instructor's feedback are then returned to the student using the software.

In each of the use cases described above, the DyKnow software is used to augment the instructor's ability to give the students feedback that persuades them to adjust their writing style. In addition, the instructor's choice to periodically share student work makes learning more interactive and social. This can make learning more enjoyable while also motivating students to do a better job while drawing Japanese characters.

3   Survey and Results

With approval from the DePauw University Institutional Review Board we invited 81 undergraduate students to complete an online anonymous survey regarding their experiences using DyKnow software in Japanese courses. We received 30 responses from students who had experience with the software.

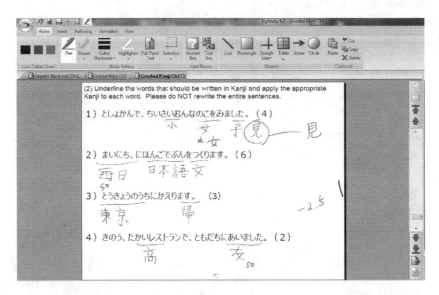

Fig. 5. Kanji quiz (SO stands for stroke order)

The survey included a set of objective questions that students responded to using a five point Likert scale as well as open ended questions. A summary of the responses to objective questions is provided in Figs. 6, 7, 8, 9 and 10. All percentages are rounded to the nearest integer.

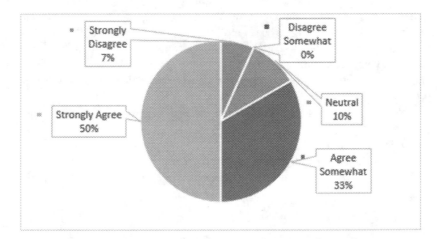

Fig. 6. Using DyKnow helped me learn to write the Japanese scripts (Color figure online)

Of the 30 survey respondents, 9 indicated that they had significant experience with writing Japanese scripts before enrolling in their Japanese language course. We believe these students were native Mandarin speakers who were studying abroad in the United

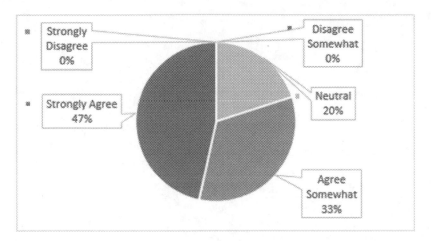

Fig. 7. I have become more aware of stroke orders because we used DyKnow (Color figure online)

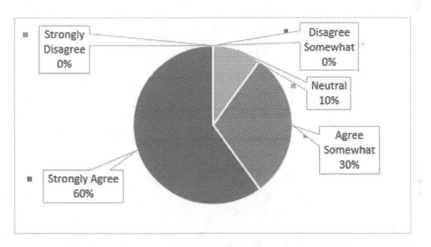

Fig. 8. Replaying how the letter/character is written facilitated learning stroke order (Color figure online)

States. Table 1 shows the percentage of students who agreed or strongly agreed with the survey statements broken down by prior familiarity with Japanese writing scripts.

The survey also invited students to provide additional feedback through several open-ended questions. For example, students were asked to describe the biggest advantages of using the DyKnow system. Out of 30 responses, 19 students specifically mentioned stroke order or the system's replay capabilities. Representative comments are presented below.

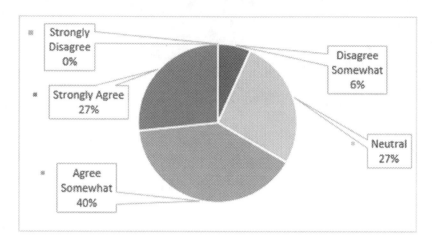

Fig. 9. Feedback through DyKnow (quizzes, in-class writing) helped me to correct stroke orders and shapes of Kana and Kanji (Color figure online)

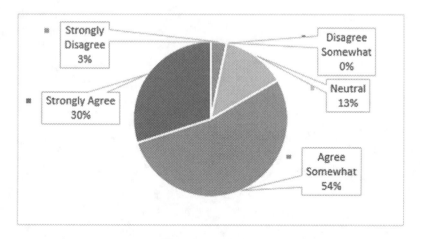

Fig. 10. Using DyKnow is enjoyable (Color figure online)

- "Getting the stroke order correct and replicating Japanese characters"
- "I think the biggest advantage was being able to see the stroke order and the ability to replay it"
- "Replaying the slides to see how kanji are written. It's very helpful when studying"
- "It helped a lot with stroke order"
- "Stroke order could be easily seen"
- "Seeing stroke order and movement"
- "Witnessing the strokes through a clear, large perspective"
- "Learning stroke order".

Table 1. Comparing presumed native Manderin speakers to other students

	Percent of students with prior experience with Japanese scripts	Percent of other students
Using DyKnow helped me learn to write using the Japanese scripts	33 % agree somewhat	33 % agree somewhat
	22 % strongly agree	62 % strongly agree
I have become more aware of stroke orders because we used DyKnow	11 % agree somewhat	43 % agree somewhat
	33 % strongly agree	52 % strongly agree
Replaying how the letter/character is written facilitated learning stroke orders	44 % agree somewhat	24 % agree somewhat
	33 % strongly agree	71 % strongly agree
Feedback through DyKnow helped me to correct stroke orders and shapes of Kana and Kanji	33 % agree somewhat	43 % agree somewhat
	11 % strongly agree	33 % strongly agree
Using DyKnow is enjoyable	33 % agree somewhat	62 % agree somewhat
	44 % strongly agree	24 % strongly agree

In response to this question, as well as on a question that invited students to provide any additional information they wanted to share, several students commented *explicitly* about the interaction between instructor, fellow students and the software as a means to facilitate learning. Representative comments are presented below.

- "Easy to follow teacher's instructions"
- "Direct comparison to other's writing"
- "Our whole class could learn at the same time"
- "The student teacher interaction"
- "It allowed me to playback the teacher's stroke order. This is especially useful when you are very new to Japanese"
- "The best part of DyKnow is everyone can write each word at the same time and teacher can also edit and correct them at the same time".

Many other students *implicitly* referenced the importance of both the teacher and the technology. For example, one student wrote "I think the biggest advantage was being able to see the stroke order and the ability to replay it". While this student did not mention the instructor by name, the student implies that the system enabled him to see the teacher's stroke order.

4 Discussion and Conclusion

The data suggest that students believe that using DyKnow helped them learn Japanese writing scripts. In fact, 83 % of the students agreed or strongly agreed with this statement. More specifically, 90 % of the students agreed or strongly agreed that replaying how a letter of character is written facilitated learning stroke orders, 67 % agreed or strongly agreed that receiving instructor feedback through DyKnow was helpful, and 84 % agreed or strongly agreed that using DyKnow was enjoyable.

While students perceived benefits of using DyKnow regardless of their previous knowledge of Japanese writing scripts, the data suggests that students who had no significant prior knowledge of Japanese scripts were more likely to perceive a benefit. We assume that most of these students were native Mandarin speakers who were studying abroad in the United States. While 55 % of these more experienced students agreed or strongly agreed that DyKnow helped them to learn the Japanese scripts, an overwhelming 95 % of the less experienced students agreed or strongly agreed with this statement. Similarly, while 77 % of the more experienced students agreed or strongly agreed that they benefited from replaying letters and characters, 95 % of the less experienced students agreed or strongly agreed with this statement. Finally, while 44 % of the more experienced students agreed or strongly agreed that the teacher's feedback (provided through DyKnow) was helpful in learning correct stroke orders, 86 % of the less experienced students agreed with this statement.

This case study demonstrates that coupling a human teacher with a pen-based instructional technology system provides Japanese learners with feedback and suggestions that help them learn to write Japanese scripts. However, our results are limited to young adults who are learning Japanese as a foreign language. Further investigation would be needed to determine if the results generalize to children who are learning the Japanese writing system as their native language.

References

1. Berque, D., Bonebright, T., Gough, M., Smith, C.: Leveraging the interplay between a grassroots pen-based computing pilot and an institutional laptop initiative. EDUCAUSE Q. Mag. **32**(4), (2009). http://er.educause.edu/articles/2009/12/leveraging-the-interplay-between-a-grassroots-penbased-computing-pilot-and-an-institutional-laptop-initiative
2. Berque, D.: An evaluation of a broad deployment of DyKnow software to support note taking and interaction using pen-based computers. In: Proceedings of CCSC: NE 2006 Annual Conference, Holy Cross College, 21–22 April 2006. Journal of Computing Sciences in Colleges
3. DyKnow Web Site. http://www.dyknow.com
4. Fogg, B.J.: Persuasive Technology, Using Computers to Change What We Think and Do. Morgan Kaufmann, San Francisco (2003)
5. Matsumoto, H.: Hitsujun no hanashi (Stories About Stroke Order). Chuōkōronshinsha, Tokyo (2012)
6. Ministry of Education, Culture, Sports, Science, and Technology Web Site. http://www.mext.go.jp/a_menu/shotou/new-cs/youryou/syo/koku/001.htm
7. Nihon Kanji Noryoku Kentei Web Site. http://www.kanken.or.jp/kanken/outline/degree.html

Game Design Recommendations Focusing
on Children with Developmental Dyscalculia

Matheus A. Cezarotto[(✉)] and André L. Battaiola

Department of Design, Federal University of Paraná, Curitiba, PR, Brazil
matheus.cezarotto@gmail.com,
ufpr.design.profe.albattaiola@gmail.com

Abstract. Children with Developmental Dyscalculia's difficulties include those which affect the normal acquisition of arithmetic abilities. In order to improve their mathematic skills, these children are moved by the use of based-game interventions during neuropsychological rehabilitations. These games seek arithmetic training but present several game design constraints, which limit the real possibilities of use specially regarding motivational aspects. This paper presents a combination of studies on neuropsychology and game design to enhance user's motivation. In order to achieve such purpose, it comprises four steps: literature review, case study, data triangulation, and experts' evaluation. As a result, we offer a set of game design recommendations focused on user's motivation. This paper is a result of the first author's dissertation for the postgraduate program in Design.

Keywords: Game design · Motivation in games · Interventions for developmental dyscalculia

1 Introduction

Electronic games are considered a significant entertainment media able to captivate the user's attention, acting as an expressive mechanism to provide fun for players [1, 2]. Nowadays, modern society needs make the use of games not just an entertainment, extending this tool for serious contexts and activities to provide motivation. This is process of Gamification [3].

Neuropsychology has been using computer games during neuropsychological rehabilitation in order to motivate children with developmental dyscalculia [4–6]. Developmental dyscalculia is a specific learning disability which affects arithmetic abilities, meaning that children with this disorder have a severe and persistent difficulty on developing these skills [7, 8].

Several authors have presented positive results in using game-based interventions for remediating dyscalculia [4–6, 9, 10]. Despite the relevance of these authors' contributions to the design of arithmetic training, some problems remain to be solved regarding how can we develop games for this specific application. The lack of game design studies in general leads to non-systematized development of these game-based interventions. Constraints in game design limit the real possibilities of use for these games, particularly affecting the player's experience. This paper attempts to fill this gap

© Springer International Publishing Switzerland 2016
P. Zaphiris and A. Ioannou (Eds.): LCT 2016, LNCS 9753, pp. 463–473, 2016.
DOI: 10.1007/978-3-319-39483-1_42

in the development of games for children with developmental dyscalculia by relating neuropsychology and game design studies, aiming to define a set of recommendations focused on user's motivation. Thus, our research problem is "how to increase children's motivation using game-based interventions for dyscalculia?"

As a methodology, the research approach is exploratory and qualitative, comprising four procedures: literature review, case study, data triangulation, and expert's evaluation. In this paper, we present these procedures hierarchically, sequenced leading to the research results.

2 Literature Review

Through a narrative literature review, this phase established a conceptual framework based on accomplished studies on the specific area of this research. Moreover, we present information regarding game settings to increase user's motivation and highlight some dyscalculia characteristics. Hereinafter, we discuss the main results of this review.

2.1 Motivational Elements in Games

Regarding the game definition, this study adopt game as system in which players engage in an artificial conflict, defined by rules, resulting in quantifiable outcome [11]. In this case, system is a group of parts or elements forming a complex whole [11].

A review in game design studies implicitly or explicitly demonstrates that games are formed by elements, which are responsible for contributing or defining the player's experience [12]. Taking into account the idea that a game has forming elements, we have considered for this study seven elements for games [13].

- **Components:** They are the game objects that the player is able to manipulate physically or virtually in the course of game. For example, characters, ships, cards among others.
- **Rules set:** This element is responsible for defining the goals and procedures in the course of game. For example, scoring more points than the opponent, being first to achieve the goal, saving the princess etc.
- **Environment:** Game environment is the physical or virtual constraints of the game system. For example, board, levels, virtual worlds, etc.
- **Game mechanics:** This element describes the actions, which players can take in order to complete the game goals. For example, moving characters, maneuvering cars, throwing objects etc.
- **Theme:** The game theme is the subject matter, a fictional context or a metaphor used for contextualizing the rules set and the game system.
- **Graphical interface and information:** This category unifies two elements from the game system [13], interface and information, due to the interface element used for this study, which considers not just physical characteristics but also interface graphical aspects. Interface is the element used to allow the player to interact with informational game elements. Thus, information is the status of game shown to the player by the system (through the interface). For example, scores, visual instructions, etc.

- **Player(s):** This category represents the human factor in the game, the players and their behavior interacting with game system.

The preceding studies bring up an important perspective regarding the game system, highlighting that the game experience happens with the player interacting either with other players or with game elements [13, 14]. Thus, in order to enhance motivational and fun aspects in games, the most relevant part is how to establish and present the game elements to the player.

Game design publications referring to player's experience focused in intrinsic motivation usually adopt The Flow Theory [15]. Such theory refers to the player's mental state and best performance called "optimal experience", likely to occur when there is a balance between challenges and user skills leading to a deep sense of enjoyment [15]. Some studies expanded the Flow Theory to attend a specific application in game design [16, 17]. In this regard, there are eight recommendations to serve as guides on development of animations and games, aiming to increase learner's motivations [17]. We have adapted these recommendations to the context of this study, which we describe hereinafter.

- **Challenges:** Using challenges to promote user's motivation requires that the player's skills and challenge difficulty matches. When achieving goals, the amount of challenge must not exceed the player skills or underestimate the player's capacity.
- **Clear goals:** The goals in activity must to be as clear as possible to the player, clearly informing which goals the player must accomplish.
- **Performance Feedback:** It is the component which provides performance information to the player. Feedbacks are essential in games, for they sustain motivation once they provide the necessary information to keep the player up with the goals.
- **Emotional appeal:** It is customized information provided by means of narrative and characters in order to intensify the user's interest and motivation for the activity.
- **Cognitive process:** Metaphors and visual analogies work as a component to facilitate mental processing of information, assisting the player in understanding new contents with knowledge already processed by memory.
- **Sensory curiosity:** It means visual expression used for communicating information. Thus, in order to attract the user's attention, using graphical language can promote an aesthetic standard.
- **Control:** Offering to the user control and choice during the tasks or activities facilitates interaction and extends motivation for learning.
- **Immersion:** Flowing optimal experience offers some characteristics which promote engagement, interest and attention for an object. Such characteristics are full concentration in the activity, distractions exclusion from consciousness, and the distortion of time perception. This flow results from the preceding recommendations.

The foregoing discussion creates a framework of game information focused on improving player's experience. As a second part of literature review of this study, we present in the following pages some information related to developmental dyscalculia, and game-based interventions.

2.2 Developmental Dyscalculia

Developmental Dyscalculia is a disorder of mathematical abilities, not determined by intellectual difficulties or inadequate educational instruction [7, 8]. Dyscalculia presumably is a result of a specific impairment of brain function [7]. The prevalence of this disorder is around 3 to 6 % of the school-aged population [8, 18]. Diagnosing dyscalculia is a complex activity and a task for psychologists. All in all, in the diagnosis, standardized arithmetic assesses arithmetic skills in children [19]. These test shows if there is a significant discrepancy in the child's arithmetic achievement in relation to age, chronologic grade, and intelligence [18, 19].

Treatment for developmental dyscalculia should focus on educational interventions to enhance the assimilation of arithmetic concepts in particular [18]. In this sense, neuropsychological rehabilitation aims to increase children's learning using cognitive and behavioral techniques [20].

We have searched for information concerning neuropsychological interventions by means of a technical visit to the Developmental Neuropsychology Laboratory (DNL) at Federal University of Minas Gerais (Brazil). In DNL, a psychologist provides neuropsychological rehabilitation for children individually, using specific material with activities structured in seven modules, considering hierarchic arrangement of mathematics. Such modules are number sense; counting; transcoding; addition; subtraction, math problem solving; and multiplication. The laboratory credits the success of this rehabilitation treatment to three elementary concepts. They are

- **Motivation:** This concept is present in all rehabilitation activities. The purpose is keeping the child in a playful environment. Moreover, activity goals are configured in intermediate levels, focusing on the child cognitive profile, avoiding challenges which are too difficult or too easy.
- **Self-perception:** This concept provides the user some performance information. Thereby, graphical representations show the child their performances, highlighting his/her progress during the intervention activities, promoting a successful experience.
- **Errorless learning:** In this approach, rehabilitation activities prioritize the avoidance of errors during learning [21]. For this, the presented tasks have adequate levels for child's performance, reducing errors and offering more successful experiences.

Additionally, taking into account the aspects presented by DNL (UFMG), we summarize some instructional principles in literature, as relevant for using in neuropsychological interventions in order to increase the mathematical learning effectiveness [22, 23]. We filtered these principles considering those relevant for the present study:

- Individualized interventions are more effective [22].
- In interventions, repetition is necessary for learning, enhancing the learning process [22].
- A segmentation of the learning content is effective [22].

- Computer interventions allow children to practice and automatize math facts, also providing direct feedback. Therefore, in general, traditional intervention (with a teacher or psychologist) is more effective [23].

In rehabilitation treatments, neuropsychology publications have been studying the use of game-based interventions [4–6]. Game-based interventions are a positive tool for the neuropsychological rehabilitation, once it provides intense training on mathematical abilities in an entertaining environment. Additionally, they capitalize the attraction that children naturally have for computer games [6]. Nowadays, interventions use adaptive games in a large scale [4]. The development of these games aims to adapt task difficulties to individual abilities. Thus, software games are designed with an algorithm, which constantly evaluates player's actions in order to increase or decrease difficulty, maintaining an adequate difficulty [6].

After describing what the literature defines to enhance user's motivation in games, we present from now on the next phase, i.e. a case study with children diagnostic with dyscalculia.

3   Case Study

In the case study phase, two children aged 10 and 12 years old diagnosed with dyscalculia participated in a rehabilitation program conducted to evaluate motivation in games focused in this kind of learning disability. This rehabilitation program took place in the Developmental Neuropsychology Laboratory (DNL), located at Federal University of Minas Gerais in Belo Horizonte, Brazil. The DNL is a collaborator of this study, offering a significant support as well as their experience with diagnosis, interventions, and neuropsychological rehabilitation for developmental dyscalculia.

The small sample recruited is justifiable for three reasons: complexity to diagnose children with dyscalculia; necessity of a professional (psychologist) for each child during the rehabilitation; and the qualitative approach of the study. However, the study profited from the rehabilitation program longitudinal aspect along six weeks. We have used a codename to protect the identity of the research participants. They are group 1 (child 1 and psychologist 1) and group 2 (child 2 and psychologist 2).

This case study accomplished 12 rehabilitation sessions. From these, 6 sessions consisted in half an hour using games for each child once a week, assisted by the psychologist. After each game session, the children answered to structured interviews, aiming to obtain information related of the motivation and game experience among the weeks. Additionally, those psychologists responsible for conducting the rehabilitation program provided information using questionnaires regarding the children's behavior during the game interaction.

De Castro et al. developed both games used in case study [10]. They are *Shark*, and *Dance Dance and Dance!* (Fig. 1). Each child played each game three times. The used games are part of study sample and we selected them for this case study orientated by researchers of DNL. We have used as case study procedures a structured interview for children and a questionnaire for psychologists.

Fig. 1. Games used in case study (Source: De Castro et al. [10])

3.1 Case Study Results

We have analyzed the case study data in a qualitative approach, using the user's perspective to describe what was motivational or not in the games used during rehabilitation program.

Results for each child were distinct: for child 1, the games were motivational; on the other hand, child 2 considered the games not motivational. We infer that this heterogeneity occurred due to distinct children's profile concerning previous experiences with entertainment games. In this sense, child 1 is not an entertainment game user, contrary to child 2, who frequently use this type of game. Thus, there is a direct relation between user's motivation and their level of experience with games. Therefore, higher experience turns the user more critical of the game settings.

During game interaction, the children highlighted some elements that called their attentions. They were character, scenery, and rewards. However, the flow element "challenge" was the most responsible to increase or decrease user's motivation. This was evident when observing child 2's data. In both games, child 2 was motivated when starting the interaction, but along other sessions with the game, this motivation did not persist, tending to boredom. This occurred on game 1 (*Shark*), due to the task goals being too difficult for that child's skills. In contrast, game 2 (*Dance Dance and Dance!*) presented tasks goals which were too easy for that child. Accordingly, the game elements can be well set (e.g., characters, rewards), however if the balance between challenges and user's skills is not appropriate, the game will not be motivational. Additionally, for child 2, the excessive repetition was another aspect responsible for decreasing motivation.

Regarding improvements in the games, in order to enhance fun experience, the children have indicated some points, which are

- **The possibilities to manipulate character:** Taking into account that both games allowed limited action for the avatar, the children suggested extending these actions. For instance, actions can be extended in levels throughout the game, providing the player new possibilities of interaction and avoiding repetition.
- **Solving mystery in the game consisting of several challenges:** For the children, it is important a fictional context for the game, wherein challenges (game goals) are

present in a playful environment comprising different types of activity. This idea provides the player a not so evident cognitive training (e.g., addition calculations), once it is part of a narrative.

4 Establishing Recommendations

In this phase of the study, we provide an answer for the research problem based on previous information discussed. We established a set of game design recommendations for developing games for children with dyscalculia focused on user's motivation. As a methodology, we used data triangulation to intersect all study results in order to establish these recommendations (literature review + case study).

Moreover, in order to schematize the recommendations, we segmented our research problem into two secondary questions, which consider both neuropsychology and game design perspectives. As answers to these questions, we elaborated a set of preliminary recommendations structured in categories (Table 1).

Table 1. Establishing recommendations

Research problem	Secondary questions	Recommendations categories
How to increase children's motivation using game-based interventions for dyscalculia?	What should be considered in the conception of games from **Neuropsychology perspective**?	· Trained mathematical ability · Content structure · Activities
	What should be considered in the conception of games from **Game Design perspective**?	· Components · Rules set · Environment · Game mechanics · Theme · Graphical interface

After establishing these preliminary recommendations, experts evaluated a trial version, aiming to evaluate the recommendations' applicability on developing game-based interventions for children with dyscalculia. The evaluation consisted in a value judgment based on the experience of small set of evaluators. The experts were structured in two group composed by two game designers and two psychologists. Finally, in the last phase of this study, we examined the adjustments proposed by the experts. As a result, we offered the final version of the recommendation set, which we present hereinafter.

5 Set of Recommendations

This section presents a set of game design recommendations. These recommendations do not cover technical aspects of the development of games, focusing on the **pre-production,** considering game production cycle [24]. **Preproduction** is the first phase in a game production cycle, when producers define elementary game information as concept, planning, main characteristics, limitations, and project requirements. Considering this, the following recommendations cover preproduction issues.

5.1   Neuropsychology

Trained Mathematical Ability

- **Use modules for training or teaching mathematical content based on a hierarchic arrangement.** Modules are number sense; counting; transcoding; addition; subtraction, math problem solving; and multiplication.

Content Structure

- **Structure the module's activities adaptively to child's (player's) cognitive profile.** An alternative is using an algorithm to analyze player's actions during the game, based on challenge intensity, adapting challenge intensity based on the performance of each individual player. Thus, there will be additional content when the player becoming proficient in the tasks.

Activities

- **Use repetitions in activities,** however too much repetition is unwelcome for user's motivation. Explore a fictional game context composed by levels, where repetition for learning is arranged as part of a narrative, not too evident to the player.
- **Single player games composed by individual tasks are more efficient.** However, it is possible to promote competitions using the player's own performances, stimulating him/her to seek even better results.
- **Use game-based interventions guided directly by a psychologist or teacher.** Use the game as part of a system, providing structured data about the user's performance in an interface for the rehabilitation administrator. This system can quantify the user's performance in several aspects, for example, activity, session, comparison with children the same age, among other relevant possibilities for neuropsychological rehabilitation.

5.2   Game Design

Components

- **Use character as a visual stimulus in order to attract the player's attention to the activity.** Allow the player to manipulate the character, additionally allowing a customization of their features. An alternative for this is providing new characters throughout the game with more possibilities of manipulation and customizations.

Rules Set

- **Provide the player instructions related to the game's goals, rules and possible actions.** An alternative is using animated tutorials, also offering an option "help" during the game for eventual doubts.

Environment

- **Use the scenery as part of a ludic game context, acting as a background for the game activities.** In this sense, by means of graphical expression, the scenery can promote an emotional appeal attracting user's attentions.

Game Mechanics

- **Promote automatizing arithmetic by game mechanics,** thus gradually stimulating the player to solve problems using the less time possible and with less errors. This automatizing must consider the individual child's ability.
- **Game mechanics must consider a balance between challenges and player's skills.** Provide challenges in an intermediate level for the player, not too difficult or too easy. This balance must consider player's performance, so the player may interpret those challenges as possible and motivational. An alternative is providing challenge tasks solution in levels or steps, gradually increasing difficulty.
- **Accomplish an initial placement test to locate players in different levels of game challenges based on individual player's skills.** This placement can occur in the own game system, using activities before starting to play.
- **Offer chances for the player "to survive" in the game activities.** This allows the player to recover from errors and not blocking their progress in the game.
- **Use errorless learning, avoiding negative feedback (punishment).** Change the negative feedback into an orientation (e.g. tips to be successful in the tasks), considering player's errors. The purpose is promoting the player's progress in the game activities instead of discouraging them with punishments.
- **Locate the game mechanics in a playful environment based on a narrative,** for example, solving a mystery (large challenge) in the game by means of several small challenges.

Theme

- **Use graphical elements based on a narrative, for example, character, scenery, mechanics, activities, rewards etc.** The narrative may use a metaphor or analogy as an alternative to improve the player's learning, and additionally form a graphical expression for the game.

Interface

- **Interface elements are part of the game's graphic expression**, which focused in player's motivation, being possible to use creativity in their design. In this sense, in order to design these elements, use consistency in typography, color, layout and arrangement. Moreover, avoid excesses, making visible only relevant information not to overload the player's mental processing.
- **Use graphical elements which allow player's navigation into the game system.** These elements allow the user to set elementary functions before playing.
- **Use graphical elements providing instructions to the player.** These elements present information about game components, set of rules, and game mechanics.

- **Use graphical elements providing immediate feedback and self-perception,** in order to show the players their performances during the intervention activities. For instance, scores, badges, leaderboard, missions, achievement, progress, levels etc.
- **Offer positive feedback to the player resulted from correct actions, in order to increase engagement.** Use different types of rewards, as intangible (digital on game system) and tangible (out of game system, such as small gifts). Systematically design these rewards to keep player in flow. In this sense, provide small or big rewards based on the difficulty of completed challenges.

6   Final Considerations

The set of game design recommendations established in this study is an alternative to enhance motivation for children with dyscalculia during the neuropsychological rehabilitation. This result contributes for orienting the design process of these games. Based on the study results, we highlight a need for systemizing the development of game-based interventions, contemplating the role of each game element for user's motivation. In this sense, we point out the necessity of considering user's perspective, knowing their needs and preferences for game settings.

Finally, we emphasize that our results are not final solutions. However, the recommendations provided in the current study are initial instructions, which may guide new studies, aiming to enhance the effectiveness of game-based interventions in neuropsychological practices. Moreover, the recommendations may increase the development of games focused in Brazilian children with dyscalculia, who nowadays lack games-based interventions.

Acknowledgements. CAPES provided founding for this research. Thanks also to the researchers from Developmental Neuropsychology Laboratory (UFMG) who contributed to this project.

References

1. Prensky, M.: Aprendizagem baseada em jogos digitais (in Portuguese). SENAC, São Paulo (2012)
2. Johnson, S.: Tudo que é ruim é bom para você: como os games e a TV nos tornam mais inteligentes (in Portuguese). Zahar, Rio de Janeiro (2012)
3. Werbach, K., Huner, D.: For the Win: How Game Thinking Can Revolutionize Your Business. Wharton Digital Press, Philadelphia (2012)
4. Kadosh, R.C., et al.: Interventions for improving numerical abilities: present and future. Trends Neurosci. Educ. **2**(2), 85–93 (2013)
5. Butterworth, B., Varma, S., Laurillard, D.: Dyscalculia: from brain to education. Science **332**(6033), 1049–1053 (2011)
6. Wilson, A.J., et al.: Principles underlying the design of "the number race", an adaptive computer game for remediaton of dyscalculia. Behav. Brain Funct. **2**(1), 19 (2006)

7. Wilson, A.J., Dehaene, S.: Number sense and developmental dyscalculia. Hum. Beh. Learn. Dev. Brain Atyp. Dev. **2**, 212–237 (2007)
8. Shalev, R.S., Gross-Tsur, V.: Developmental dyscalculia and medical assessment. J. Learn. Disabil. **26**(2), 134–137 (1993)
9. Käser, T., et al.: Design and evaluation of the computer-based training program Calcularis for enhancing numerical cognition. Front. Psychol. **4**, 489 (2013)
10. De Castro, M.V., et al.: Effect of a virtual environment on the development of mathematical skills in children with dyscalculia. Plos One **9**, e103354-16 (2014)
11. Salen, K., Zimmerman, E.: Rules of Play: Game Design Fundamentals. MIT Press, Cambridge (2004)
12. Almeida, M.S.O., Silva, F.S.C.: Towards a library of game components: a game design framework proposal. In: XII SBGames, Proceedings Art & Design Track, São Paulo, SP (2013)
13. Järvinen, A.: Games Without Frontiers: Theories and Methods for Game Studies and Design. Tampere University Press, Tampere (2008)
14. Mattar, J.: Games em educação: como os nativos digitais aprendem (in Portuguese). Person Prentice Hall, São Paulo (2010)
15. Csikszentmihalyi, M.: Flow: The Psychology of Optimal Experience. Harper Perennial Modern Classics, New York (1990)
16. Fu, F., Su, R., Yu, S.: EGameFlow: a scale to measure learners' enjoyment of e-learning games. Comput. Educ. **52**(1), 101–112 (2009)
17. Alves, M.M.; Battaiola, A.L.: Recomendações para ampliar motivação em jogos e animações educacionais (in Portuguese). In: X Simpósio Brasileiro de Games e Entretenimento Digital-SBGames 2011, Salvador, BA (2011)
18. Shalev, R.S.: Developmental dyscalculia. J. Child Neurol. **19**, 765–771 (2004)
19. Haase, V.G., et al.: Discalculia e dislexia: semelhança epidemiológica e diversidade de mecanismos neurocognitivos (in Portuguese). Dislexia: novos temas, novas perspectivas, pp. 257–282 (2011)
20. Haase, V.G., Pinheiro-Chagas, P., Andrade, P.M.O.: Reabilitação cognitiva e comportamental (in Portuguese). In: Teixeira, A.L., Kummer, A. (Orgs.) Neuropsiquiatria clinica, pp. 115–123. Rubio, Rio de Janeiro (2012)
21. Middleton, E.L., Schwartz, M.F.: Errorless learning in cognitive rehabilitation: a critical review. Neuropsychol. Rehabil. **22**(2), 138–168 (2012)
22. Swanson, H.L., Sachse-Lee, C.: A meta-analysis of single-subject-design intervention research for students with LD. J. Learn. Disabil. **33**(2), 114–136 (2000)
23. Kroesbergen, E.H., Van Luit, J.E.H.: Mathematics interventions for children with special educational needs a meta-analysis. Remedial Spec. Educ. **24**(2), 97–114 (2003)
24. Chandler, H.M.: The Game Production Handbook, 3rd edn. Jones & Bartlett Publishers, Burlington (2013)

A Live Virtual Simulator for Teaching Cybersecurity to Information Technology Students

Margus Ernits[1,2(✉)] and Kaido Kikkas[2,3]

[1] Tallinn University of Technology, Akadeemia tee 15a, Tallinn, Estonia
margus.ernits@gmail.com
[2] Estonian Information Technology College, Raja 4C, 12616 Tallinn, Estonia
[3] School of Digital Technologies, Tallinn University,
Narva Road 25, 10120 Tallinn, Estonia
kaido.kikkas@kakupesa.net

Abstract. This paper introduces an Intelligent Training Exercise Environment (i-tee), a fully automated, open source platform for cyber defense classes and competitions. The platform allows to simulate realistic cyberattack situation in virtual and sandboxed environment to give a hands-on experience of a critical situation.

The main outcome is an open source virtual cyber simulator that enables hands-on, practical learning. The platform can be integrated into existing curricula or used to create a new subject or a competition event. A student needs only a web browser and a remote desktop protocol client to start exploring the system.

Keywords: e-learning · Cyber security · Simulation

1 Introduction

On-line hands-on cybersecurity competitions and courses are an effective way to educate students in the field of ICT and to raise security awareness [3,19]. Today, cyber competencies and awareness are a must for all ICT students. Yet many ICT curricula contain perhaps only one theory-oriented course about security which is not sufficient today [11]. Developers need knowledge and skills to design secure information systems. System engineers need to know how to protect the system and how to act in an actual crisis. In order to study secure system design and programming we need a practical hands-on course. In order to train people to defend the system in a critical situation, a cybersecurity competition as part of the course can be a powerful educational tool [3].

We may ask why are practical hands-on cybersecurity courses and competitions not part of every ICT curriculum and why do most curricula contain only one course which is not of hands-on type? Even practical classes tend to be limited to designing and programming a secure system but do not cover live attacks and defense [19]. One possible reason for this is that creating a practical security

© Springer International Publishing Switzerland 2016
P. Zaphiris and A. Ioannou (Eds.): LCT 2016, LNCS 9753, pp. 474–486, 2016.
DOI: 10.1007/978-3-319-39483-1_43

course demands much more resources than a theoretical one, and it has to be updated every term due to rapid changes in the field. Moreover, if the course is designed by only a small group of people there may be not enough diverse competencies to build a practical course containing a live exercise. In addition, a practical and nontrivial cybersecurity course needs a realistic sandboxed information system with servers, services and workstations for each student or group. This makes such an approach more expensive compared to traditional courses.

Today we see data breaches every day, from banks to healthcare to popular websites to governmental institutions. Cyber security is a rapidly changing and growing field. We expect that every ICT specialist is security aware, being able to design secure systems and defend existing systems. The growing amount of malicious activities online causes increasing need for security experts - yet ICT specialists sometimes expect that their security department will find all problems in company's systems by penetration testing and security event monitoring. However, the security problems cannot be solved by one department because security should be designed along with the system rather than added later.

We believe that every ICT specialist should be aware of cyber threats and able to avoid known security mistakes when developing a new system. Today, we use IT systems that were developed years ago with little security in mind, which means that those systems are exploitable by cyber criminals using common attack methods. Thus a skill of defending IT systems is needed in addition to knowledge of how to design a secure system.

Security awareness for ICT specialists should be an integral oart of their education - every ICT student needs to know how to design a secure system and how to defend existing systems against cyber criminals.

Our solution is an open-source virtual sandboxed simulator for practical cybersecurity classes and competitions. The platform is called i-tee (in Estonian it can be interpreted as 'information way' or 'information path') the main features of which are (a) automated grading/scoring for competitions, (b) automated attacks to simulate cyber criminals and malicious activities, (c) immediate feedback using a virtual teaching assistant, and (d) virtual computer user simulator to make the simulation more realistic [4].

The i-tee platform, released under the MIT license, is available in Github[1]. At the time of writing, it is in use at four institutions. The platform has also been tested in cybersecurity competitions in Estonia (24 students) and Moldova (21 students).

The aim of this paper is to provide one possible starting point for academics who want to integrate hands-on cyber security elements into existing courses without having to develop their own tools.

2   Background

As the role of cyber security is increasing, every ICT curriculum should provide necessary coverage of cyber field [11]. Usually the studies consist of lectures,

---

[1] Source code of the i-tee platform – https://github.com/magavdraakon/i-tee.

practical classes and independent work. The distribution between practical classes and lectures varies but cyber security courses tend to be more theoretical and usually focus on the design and development of new system, this aspect also prevails in practical classes and homework. The traditional lecture-based approach is still dominant [19]. However, we feel that this approach is not suitable to teach the defense of IT systems which should rather focus on a simulation of an actual critical situation. It is possible to simulate cyber attacks using roleplay and groupwork (e.g. tabletop exercises) but defending complex IT systems is a skill that can be mastered only with hands-on, practical training. The hands-on approach has also proven an effective teaching method for science [17].

The approach used in the Cyber Defense Exercises (CDX) is an efficient way to study cyber security and increase information assurance awareness [3,14]. Students often get bored when learning mere theory but the realistic element of cyber attacks that occurs in CDX provides excitement and demands full commitment from the students. However, using CDX as learning tool does not replace lectures or other learning approaches such as tutorials, projects, mentoring etc. However, using the CDX yields best results when combining different approaches [19]. Also, preparing for the exercise motivates students to learn as they see a practical output for the knowledge [1]. The CDX'es are widely used as teaching tools at universities [6] and private companies, e.g. SANS NetWars [13].

Some examples of cyber security exercises are Defcon's Capture the Flag (CtF) [2], Cyber Defense Exercise (CDX) [14], International Capture the Flag Contest (iCTF) [18], Locked Shields [9] and Collegiate Cyber Defense Competition [16]. The number of exercises is constantly increasing - the European Union Agency for Network and Information Security has identified over 200 national and international cyber security exercises [10].

2.1   Types of Cyber Security Exercises

The exercises can feature different goals: develop capabilities; evaluate capabilities of individuals, organisations and systems; measure knowledge, ability, endurance and/or capacity; train the participants and provide an opportunity to gain knowledge, understanding and skills [10].

One possible taxonomy of exercises and distribution [10]:

- Simulation – 35 %
- Tabletop – 26 %
- Workshop – 20 %
- Red-team/Blue-team – 11 %
- Drill – 3 %
- Discussion based game – 2 %
- Seminar – 1 %
- Capture the flag – 1 %
- Other – 3 %

Cyber security exercises may be individual (develop skills) or team competitions (develop skills and teamwork). Based on size they can be divided into

– small-scale, suitable for students and universities, and
– large-scale, such as international live exercises with complex infrastructure

Based on objectives, exercises may be divided into defense-oriented, offense-oriented and mixed approaches.

To promote hands-on experience and situation awareness we focus on the live exercises such as Red-team/Blue-team and Capture the Flag.

Red-team/blue-team type of exercises contain attacking (red) and defending (blue) teams. Attackers may compete with each other or just provide attacks for all blue teams.

In the Capture the Flag type of exercises, an offending team should gain control over the attacked system, acquiring a critical piece of information (known as the flag) as a proof of success. For example, a flag can be a database record, a passwords or its hash, or some files or hashes from the targetted file system. This type of exercises usually focuses on offensive but may also contain defensive parts as well - e.g. at iCTF where each team defends their own vulnerable network and tries to compromise other team's networks. The vulnerabilities are same for all teams - thus, after discovering and mitigating security issues at their own systems, competitors can use the found vulnerabilities to attack other teams [18].

Various types of exercises have been used in academic setting: [7]

– Defensive cyberexercise – defending a vulnerable infrastructure against Red-team attacks. Some examples are: Cyber Defense Exercise (CDE) [15], Locked Shields [9].
– Small-scale, internal exercises – usually standalone rather than integrated into the curriculum.
– National Capture-the-Flag exercise – may feature additional teams besides red and blue, such as the green team are responsible for providing and maintain an infrastructure of the game, the white team handling aspects of gameplay, scoring and rules, or the yellow team dealing with situation awareness and providing background information.
– Semester-long class exercise – they are integrated into curricula and have learning objectives, but tend to be less competitive compared to the CTF type of exercises [7].

2.2   Typical Design of the Cyber Security Exercise

Designing cyber security exercise can be divided into seven steps: Objectives, Approach, Topology, Scenario, Rules, Metrics and Lessons Learned [6].

Objectives are defined according to the goal of the exercise: participants are able to implement security configurations and defend the systems; participants are able to find security vulnerabilities and improve penetration testing skills; students are able to perform reconnaissance and defense in depth approach; students are able to mitigate common web, network and system attacks etc. Design of objectives gives pedagogical value to the cyber exercise and allows reuse of existing work [5].

Approach can be either defense oriented; offense oriented or mixed [6]. In practice the mixed approach is preferred because knowing the attack methods gives advantage to defense. However, knowledge about attacks and tools do not provide skills and qualities to work under pressure in a stressful situation [9].

Topology is designed to support objectives of the exercise and consider technical capabilities of the platform used.

Scenario should support objectives, consider topology restrictions as well as provide a mission and an engaging story for the students.

Rules must address different aspects: who can participate - some exercises exclude students already working in the field of security; what methods are allowed for competitors; which parts are graded (e.g. functionality and uptime of services, successful attacks, recovery time etc.). Rules must be known to the participants.

Metrics and Lessons Learned include collection and processing of feedback, description of exercise system failures (in a complex environment some parts are likely to fail). A published post-activity report containing a Lessons Learned section can be a valuable source of information for designing next exercises. A good example of post-activity report is presented by the Locked Shields competition [9]. The metrics determine how to measure of effectiveness of the exercise and how are the objectives achieved [6].

2.3   Components of Competition Platform

We will look at common components of cyber security platforms and their usage in different exercises.

VM Provisioning. Cyber exercises are usually executed on dedicate virtualized platform to provide a sandbox for attacks and vulnerable systems. The tools used by students are common and used by cyber criminals as well. Therefore, a sandboxed isolated environment is a must for exercises. Some platforms use virtualization technologies, e.g. VMware vSphere used at Locked Shields [9], KVM was used at early stages of Locked Shields in early stages and VirtualBox was used at iCTF [18] and CyberOlympics [4].

Network Provisioning. In order to provide sandboxed network environments for each team the cyber exercise platform should able to configure several virtual networks for each team.

Attacking Systems. Red-team/Blue team exercises may use live attack traffic from a dedicated Red team, alternately all teams may perform offensive operations or attacks can be made by competition system itself.

Attacks must be provided for all teams/competitors in a coherent way to ensure equal chances, they must stay within the environment and not hit public hosts by accident.

Locked Shields uses a red team with more than 50 members to provide consistent traffic for all teams [9]. However, *live fire* from the red team can be expensive and for small grade exercises it can be replaced with automated attack engine [4].

Sometimes the attacking systems have a Command and Control module similar to the ones found in botnets [4].

Scoring. The exercise objectives should be graded by a scoring system. The iCTF used scoring mechanism called *scorebot* which periodically tests service functionality to ensure that mitigation methods used by teams did not break any services [18].

Network Traffic Generator. The system contains responsive, centrally managed network traffic generator to provide realistic operational experience during CDX's and trainings. Realistic network traffic and user emulation in system is a important part of every CDX platform. Without any 'background noise' it would be too easy for the participants to isolate the attacking traffic.

2.4   Platforms for Exercises

Internet-Scale Event and Attack Generation Environment (ISEAGE) is a testbed that focuses on hands-on laboratory exercises. The ISEAGE provides a sandboxed environment enabling controlled attacks against students' systems and networks [12]. The architecture of ISEAGE contains a background traffic generator, an attack module, an attack amplification module as well as a Command & Control module. It can be used in classroom and in cyber exercises, as some attack targets are publicly available[2]. However, as of 2015, the complete system is not freely available.

The *Information Warfare Analysis and Research Laboratory Range (IWAR Range)* is developed by US Military Academy and used in the IA curriculum at West Point. The Range uses a virtualized environment with base infrastructure of sample organization and several networks such as the attack network called a Gray Network, the research network called Black Network to support development of the Range and IA course, and the Gold Network for targets. The IWAR Range is isolated from outside networks. For virtualization a VMWare Workstation was used for the Gray Network [15].

The *Locked Shields Range* is developed by Estonian Defense Forces with NATO Cooperative Cyber Defence Centre of Excellence (NATO CCD COE) and used for the biggest annual international technical exercise called Locked Shields (over 400 participants from 16 Nations[3]. The competition is designed for professional defenders of national critical IT infrastructure but Locked Shields has also a test instance where Cyber Security Master students act as blue team

---

[2] ISEAGE github page – https://github.com/ISEAGE-ISU.
[3] https://ccdcoe.org/locked-shields-2015.html.

members; this is organized as an elective part of the curriculum at Tallinn University of Technology. For VM provisioning, the proprietary Virtual Lab Manager (VLM) is used to configure VMware VMs. Live red team is used to perform a wide range of attacks against 40 targets per team. The attackers are divided into network, client-side, web-applications, and SCADA teams [9]. No public repositories or competition designs are publicly available.

The Blunderdome platform is designed for teaching students using linear paths to break into a web application which simulates a grade management system, the goal for the students is to change their grade. The students need to break into a vulnerable Linux server. This system is designed to provide a symmetric and linear learning experience with one deterministic path for students [8]. The platform is not publicly available.

The SANS Net Wars is a proprietary platform with relevant content [13].

The survey from European Union Agency For Network And Information Security identified more then 200 different exercises [10]. Yet while the number of cyber exercise platforms can be in the same rank, to our knowledge no open source, publicly available platform with relevant cyber content exists.

3   Our Cyber Simulator Solution

In a student's perspective, using the cyber simulator starts with login page in a web browser. After successful login, the student can choose a mission (in case of ordinary studies) or join a competition if a cyber competition event is opened. The student will read the scenario of the exercise and then start his/her own sandbox with VM-s and virtual networks. The student can log in to each workstation or server using Remote Desktop Protocol (RDP) included in MS Windows. For Mac users several RDP clients exist, such as Cord or Microsoft RDP client. Linux users can easily use *rdesktop* or *xfreerdp*.

Sometimes, access to the environment needs setting up a Virtual Private Network (VPN) [9,14]. However, we decided that access to the environment should be as easy as possible and not require special software or settings at the students computer. Therefore, we believe that time needed to start with cyber mission for first time user should not exceed 15 min including viewing a video introduction.

When in exercise mode, the Scoreboard displays the current state of the services and historical count for states: service OK counter (green), service interruption counter (red), service vulnerable or in warning state (yellow) as seen on Fig. 1

The Leaderboard gives information about competition leaders - missions completed and score for the first 20 users as seen on Fig. 1. When the exercise starts, the objectives are opened according to the scenario and students can read detailed description of objectives and see the score in real time.

Each mission contains a network topology, virtual machines and objectives that are graded automatically or based on feedback from students. For example,

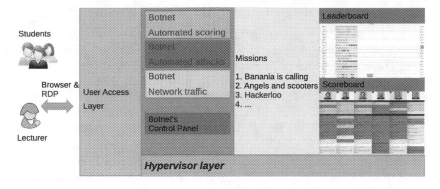

Fig. 1. The architecture of the system (Color figure online)

in the introductory mission called Angels and scooters the scoreboard automatically detects whether the objective Configure apache virtualhost is achieved, but in the mission of Hackerloo the system asks information that the student should obtain from a web application using a SQL injection vulnerability.

The web interface is built with Ruby on Rails. Users can be authenticated using LDAP, Active Directory or SAMBA4 services. For virtualization layer we use VirtualBox Headless due to its capability to provide console access using common RDP protocol. Low-level RDP access allows to design a scenarios where VM is broken and boots only from CD image; the student should fix the problem. For networking we use VirtualBox's internal networks created when the mission starts [4].

The scoring is done by a configurable botnet which performs checks for each objective opened. For competition missions the checks are switched on manually, using a control panel of botnets as seen on Fig. 2. When using non-competition mode missions, the scoring switched on automatically according to the mission scenario and the progress of the student.

For attacks a separate botnet is used because in most of the missions the students are allowed to block the attacker's IP address using a firewall - if scoring and attacks were done by the same botnet with same addresses, students would be unable to use common practices to block the attackers. The nature of the attack depends on the mission.

Both botnets are controlled using a GUI application seen on Fig. 2 which uses a Fabric framework[4] to control bots and execute scripted scoring and attacks.

Fig. 2. The control panel of botnets

---

[4] Fabric Framework – http://www.fabfile.org/.

Virtual Machines are provisioned using custom script and configured using declarative configuration management via Puppet[5] with serverless setup.

This platform provides a responsive application level traffic generator that simulates real users and covers the attacks. The network traffic is initiated from hosts from several network segments. It uses an IRC-based and encrypted communication channel between bots and CnC server to receive commands and send status messages. The network traffic generator is tested on Linux (Ubuntu, Debian), Windows (XP, Vista, 8, 8.1, Server 2008, Server 2012, 10) but is designed to work on every platform supported by Python with YAML libraries.

Traffic generators are controlled by the central control server (CnC) and the amount of traffic is tunable during the exercise. The platform allows for simultaneous run of different labs (missions or virtual learning spaces) [4].

4   Discussion

Various sources (and also our experience) suggest that students are better motivated to learn cyber security via live exercises. Therefore, cyber exercises are increasedly used by universities [10]. We can just ask why aren't they a part of every ICT curriculum - but as suggested above, designing a cyber exercise and virtual lab platform is expensive and time consuming task [3].

We tried to use different existing open source projects like OWASP Web-Coat[6], Damn Vulnerable Web App (DVWA)[7] and OWASP Hackademic[8] - even if we had some success, those projects are vulnerable targets and need a laboratory system to run them. We tried to find an open-source cyber exercise and competition platform that can be integrated into curriculum. However, such a system did not exist for the time being.

For raising security awareness and motivate students and lecturers we implemented a novel cyber security platform i-tee. The main contribution is the platform itself because it allows to implement cyber exercises into curriculum with relatively low effort compared to developing an exercise from ground up. We believe that the i-tee system can lower the cost and setup time to level that single instructor/lecturer/teaching assistant can install this platform and start using it as part of a semester-long class or one-time event.

To install and use the i-tee platform, a certain level of Linux knowledge is needed. We tested the installation guide on students and those who managed to complete basic Linux course were also able to install a new i-tee instance. For running a full cyber competition, the organizer will need additional knowledge about attacks and vulnerabilities implemented in the open source missions.

---

[5] Open Source Puppet – https://puppetlabs.com/puppet/puppet-open-source.
[6] OWASP WebCoat – https://github.com/WebGoat/WebGoat.
[7] Damn Vulnerable Web App – http://www.dvwa.co.uk/.
[8] OWASP Hackademic – https://github.com/Hackademic/hackademic/.

We developed several missions for i-tee and open sourced a sample mission implementation: "The Kingdom of Banania" is available from bitbucket[9] This mission is suitable for competitions, workshops and semester-long courses.

Mission: The Kingdom of Banania – According to the storyline, the participants are offered an internship in the Kingdom of Banania as a sysadmin of Bananian e-Government. They will discover that the websites are riddled with various well-known vulnerabilities which are already being actively exploited for different pranks and web defacement. The participants are then tasked to restore the websites and patch the vulnerabilities.

During the repairs the participants will discover that the website of the largest newspaper of Banania, bandemia.ban, displays ever more nonsensical news stories. The involved journalists ensure that they have never seen those (and some hint a possible political diversion by the neighbouring Empire of Pineapplia). Finally, King Bananius XII Magnus appoints all participants to clean up the situation. If successful, they are promised a lifetime supply of bananas from the Royal Banana Garden. Those who fail will instead face a lifetime of hard labour at the Banana Curvature Measurement Tool Calibration Office.

In addition, the scenario features a hacker group called Acronymous attacking all websites. The infrastructure of each student is seen on Fig. 3.

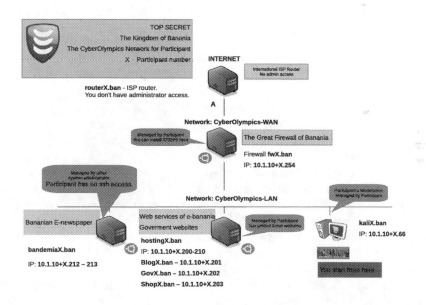

Fig. 3. Network topology of the mission

---

[9] Mission: The Kingdom of Banania – https://bitbucket.org/magavdraakon/ cyber0lympics.

The goals are restoration of disrupted systems and patching various security holes (every participant will have a small private network that will be constantly under attack during the competition; see Network topology for details).

The graded metrics are: availability and functionality of web applications; resistance for attacks; recovery time after successful attacks. This mission implements eleven learning objectives for example: student installs and configures proper web application firewall; student finds attacks from log files and implements security configurations for web servers; student are able to reconnaissance and enumerate all web applications and databases and backup them.

Vulnerabilities and attacks used include HeartBleed, SQL injection, XSS, ShellShock, DDOS, path traversal, weak security configuration.

5   Future Work

The main goal for the future is to build a community of academics who use i-tee platform and contribute missions and updates. We also plan to involve students in the content creating process and experiment with different learning methodologies. For community we plan to develop a web interface for content contribution and mission design.

6   Conclusions

Setting up a cyber exercise environment requires involvement of multiple people due to the time spent on tasks. Also, the needed skillset is rarely possessed by just one person.

We developed an open source live virtual simulator i-tee that can be integrated into existing curriculum. The time needed for downloading, installation and executing a cyber simulator i-tee is a fraction compared to the time it takes to design the whole system by themselves.

The i-tee can be used in online learning and for instructor lead classroom studies. The platform is suitable for different cyber exercise approaches (Red team/Blue team; Workshop and Capture the Flag). The platform was successfully tested on 10 events with more then 200 users and as of 2016, is used by three higher education institutes in Estonia. We raised security awareness amongst Estonian students and developed system allows other universities and countries do the same.

The platform allows to integrate practical hands-on learning approach to ICT curricula without developing a solution from scratch. We hope that the platform will get contributions from community, as it is open source and publicly available. In future we will experiment with different learning approaches and develop an automated virtual teaching assistant system for supporting students.

References

1. Adams, W.J., Gavas, E., Lacey, T., Leblanc, S.P.: Collective views of the NSA/CSS cyber defense exercise on curricula and learning objectives. In: Proceedings of the 2nd Conference on Cyber Security Experimentation and Test, CSET 2009, p. 2. USENIX Association, Berkeley (2009)
2. Cowan, C., Arnold, S., Beattie, S., Wright, C., Viega, J.: Defcon capture the flag: defending vulnerable code from intense attack. In: DARPA Information Survivability Conference and Exposition, vol. 1, p. 120 (2003)
3. Doupé, A., Egele, M., Caillat, B., Stringhini, G., Yakin, G., Zand, A., Cavedon, L., Vigna, G.: Hit 'em where it hurts: a live security exercise on cyber situational awareness. In: Proceedings of the 27th Annual Computer Security Applications Conference, ACSAC 2011, pp. 51–61. ACM, New York (2011)
4. Ernits, M., Tammekänd, J., Maennel, O.: I-tee: a fully automated cyber defense competition for students. In: Proceedings of the 2015 ACM Conference on Special Interest Group on Data Communication, SIGCOMM 2015, pp. 113–114. ACM, New York (2015)
5. Fulton, S., Schweitzer, D., Dressler, J.: What are we teaching in cyber competitions? In: Frontiers in Education Conference (FIE 2012), pp. 1–5 (2012)
6. Furtună, A., Patriciu, V.V., Bica, I.: A structured approach for implementing cyber security exercises. In: 2010 8th International Conference on Communications (COMM), pp. 415–418, June 2010
7. Hoffman, L.J., Rosenberg, T., Dodge, R., Ragsdale, D.: Exploring a national cybersecurity exercise for universities. IEEE Secur. Priv. **3**(5), 27–33 (2005)
8. Louthan, G., Roberts, W., Butler, M., Hale, J.: The blunderdome: an offensive exercise for building network, systems, and web security awareness. In: CSET (2010)
9. NATO Cooperative Cyber Defence Centre of Excellence: Cyber defence exercise locked shields 2013 after action report (2013). https://ccdcoe.org/locked-shields-2015.html
10. Ogee, A., Gavrila, R., Trimintzios, P., Stavropoulos, V., Zacharis, A.: The 2015 report on national and international cyber security exercises survey, analysis and recommendations (2015). https://www.enisa.europa.eu/activities/Resilience-and-CIIP/cyber-crisis-cooperation/cce/cyber-exercises/latest-report-on-national-and-international-cyber-security-exercises/at_download/fullReport
11. Rowe, D.C., Lunt, B.M., Ekstrom, J.J.: The role of cyber-security in information technology education. In: Proceedings of the 2011 Conference on Information Technology Education, SIGITE 2011, pp. 113–122. ACM, New York (2011)
12. Rursch, J., Jacobson, D.: When a testbed does more than testing: the Internet-Scale Event Attack and Generation Environment (ISEAGE) - providing learning and synthesizing experiences for cyber security students. In: 2013 IEEE Frontiers in Education Conference, pp. 1267–1272, October 2013
13. SANS Institute: Sans netwars (2016). https://www.sans.org/netwars
14. Schepens, W.J., James, J.R.: Architecture of a cyber defense competition. In: IEEE International Conference on Systems, Man and Cybernetics, vol. 5, pp. 4300–4305, October 2003
15. Schepens, W.J., Ragsdale, D.J., Surdu, J.R., Schafer, J., New Port, R.: The cyber defense exercise: an evaluation of the effectiveness of information assurance education. J. Inf. Secur. **1**(2) (2002)

16. Sroufe, P., Tate, S., Dantu, R., Cankaya, E.C.: Experiences during a collegiate cyber defense competition. J. Appl. Secur. Res. **5**(3), 382–396 (2010)
17. Stohr-Hunt, P.M.: An analysis of frequency of hands-on experience and science achievement. J. Res. Sci. Teach. **33**(1), 101–109 (1996)
18. Vigna, G., Borgolte, K., Corbetta, J., Doupé, A., Fratantonio, Y., Invernizzi, L., Kirat, D., Shoshitaishvili, Y.: Ten years of ICTF: the good, the bad, and the ugly. In: 1st USENIX Summit on Gaming, Games, and Gamification in Security Education (3GSE 2014) (2014)
19. Yurcik, W., Doss, D.: Different approaches in the teaching of information systems security. In: Proceedings of the Information Systems Education Conference, pp. 32–33 (2001)

MADE Ratio: Affective Multimodal Software for Mathematical Concepts

Reza GhasemAghaei[✉], Ali Arya, and Robert Biddle

Carleton University, Ottawa, ON K1S 5B6, Canada
Reza.GhasemAghaei@carleton.ca
http://hotsoft.carleton.ca/

Abstract. This paper addresses the use of multiple sensory modalities and affective strategies in learning mathematics. A case study is presented where these domains are used to design a mathematical ratio system. We adopted a multimodal approach used by other researchers, and applied our proposed design methods to create the MADE Ratio system. We then recruited participants to test the usability of the system. Our findings were that the design methods were effective, but we also gained insight about how they could be improved.

Keywords: Multimodality · Affect · Educational software

1 Introduction

In this paper we focus on interaction design and evaluation for a multimodal learning system called "*MADE Ratio*". The system is a case study of our *MADE* (*Multimodal Affect for Design and Evaluation*) framework. We are considering the sensory modalities, affective and cognitive strategies and trying to solve mathematical learning challenges. Using a multimodal affective learning system should increase the motivation in learning, and will help students develop better understanding of some tasks in mathematics. We first describe our framework, then the design process and the system, and last present the study and results.

2 MADE Framework

Human-computer interaction (HCI) and education can be improved with the help of affective and cognitive strategies in a multimodal user interface (UI) environment. This multimodal environment recognizes two or more combined user input modes (multiple sensory modalities) and recognition-based technologies such as audio or gesture in a coordinated manner with multimedia system output such as images, text or audio [8,9].

We wish to support affective aspects of learning. We reshaped the three domains of *Bloom's taxonomy* [1], a classification of the different kinds of objectives that educators distinguish, and created a framework called MADE. We are

© Springer International Publishing Switzerland 2016
P. Zaphiris and A. Ioannou (Eds.): LCT 2016, LNCS 9753, pp. 487–498, 2016.
DOI: 10.1007/978-3-319-39483-1_44

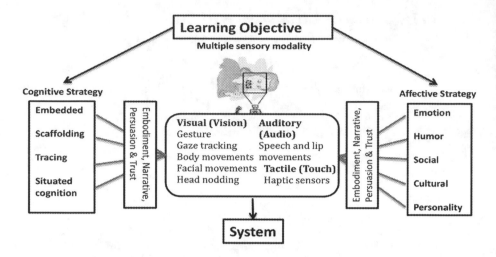

Fig. 1. The MADE framework

considering the *multiple sensory* and *quasi-sensory* modality domains to help the *affective* and *cognitive* domains (Fig. 1).

The MADE framework is based on principles for multimodal design considering emotional and cognitive aspects of learners while interacting with a multimodal educational system. While interacting with educational software, a student can employ the sensory modalities (e.g. 3D motion controller, face detection and tracking, vision or audio); they may also need to employ some quasi-sensory modalities (e.g. embodiment, persuasion or narrative) while interacting with a supportive technology [5]. We follow Kort et al.'s affective model [7]. This identifies four phases of learning and the affective character of each: encouraging exploration with positive affect, challenges and negative affect, supporting overcoming challenges and reducing the negative affect, and affirming learning so restoring positive affect.

3   Design Process

Our case study was to design a system to help learn the concept of a mathematical ratio. The modality involves embodied cognition to support pedagogy, and is based on the work of Howison et al. [6].

This design should increase the proprioceptive, kinesthetic and episodic memory experience, as the controller that we use requires physical motion of the arms and the hands. The proprioceptive memory involved will aid remembering how to perform intended physical actions in the future. The learning takes place by the students carrying out a physical activity by moving their hands and body movements to interact with the UI. By using affective strategies we can increase the episodic memory, which actually happens to learners; the learner will think about the time back when they did this with their hands. The system supports discovery learning and exploration using sensory modalities.

In our system, one of the tasks is that learners have to make a requested ratio. Feedback is provided by showing the screen in different colors and giving persuasive feedback i.e. praising messages, audio, icons or images. The learners move their left and right hands in regard to a specific ratio and distance between their hands.

We used two design methodologies, *Affective Personas* and *Affective Essential Use Cases*. Affective Personas identify key aspects of the emotional state of users, and Affective Essential Use Cases describe goals for emotional aspects of user experience to be supported by the system. We described these design processes in detail elsewhere [4].

4   System

Our system uses a Leap Motion 3D Controller (https://www.leapmotion.com/), an easy to use, low-cost hand-motion tracking controller to support the software by remote manipulation interaction (see Fig. 2). The physics-based manipulation is more than just hand waving. It can be an opportunity for the mind to reflect on what the body can already do. Embodied interaction suggests that UI becomes even more visible and available for a wider range of engagements and interactions [2]. It can drive both the understanding and solving cognitive conflicts between student's implicit assumption and her/his own observable enactment, providing experiences that are recast in terms of emerging mathematical concepts [6].

Fig. 2. The Leap Motion Controller

Figure 3 shows a snapshot of the main screen of our system when the ratio task has been completed. It shows how a student is interacting with a Leap Motion device using his hands and moving them to indicate a proportion of 1:3. For developing the software we used JavaScript and the Raphael graphics library (http://raphaeljs.com/) as well as PHP and MySQL.

The main elements are as follows:

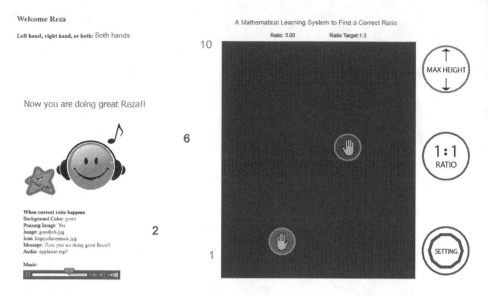

Fig. 3. A student sitting at a desk is moving the right hand higher from the desk searching for equivalent proportions 1 to 3 or 2 to 6; a ratio of 1:3 is reached, maintaining the goal proportion and resulting in affective feedback of audio, a message, icon, image and screen color change. (Color figure online)

- Main window: the main part of the screen shows two circles representing each hand. The circles move as the student moves her/his hands up and down. The background color is gray when the correct ratio is not achieved (here it is green as a ratio of 1:3 has been reached).
- Left section: provides the student with affective feedback (audio, messages, icons, images, music and color), when the task is successfully done.
- Right sidebar: the student and teacher can modify the affective settings, height, and ratio. The teacher can view and change the cognitive and affective strategies in the database.

5   Study

In this study we considered the usability of our system. Below we explain the study, talk about the expectations, our participants, the equipment, the procedure, and the analysis methods. The study was approved by our university research ethics board. We were not doing formal hypothesis testing, but simply doing usability testing and comparing the results with our expectations. Our expectations were as follows:

1. The Leap Motion Controller is easy and engaging
2. Fun results from the physical interaction
3. The affective design supports learning

Participants

Eleven undergraduate and graduate students (3 females and 8 males) from two universities in Canada volunteered to participate in this study. They ranged in age from 21 to 60, with a mean age of 33 (S.D. $= 12$). All participants were able to use their hands and arms freely and had ability to work in English. All participants reported using computers daily, and most participants (85 %) reported using them for 11–20 years. All participants stated they had used pencil and paper, or mouse and keyboard, when they learned about ratios while in school. Seven participants were right-handed, three were left-handed, and one was ambidextrous.

Equipment

A Leap Motion Controller, a Dell desktop computer with a 22-in. high-resolution LCD monitor, and two speakers were used. We used an audio recorder to capture the participant's voice comments.

Procedure

The study took thirty minutes for each participant. We taught the participants how to interact with the system using their hands before the study, for five minutes. We used a think aloud protocol, and did audio recording. The main part of the procedure had four steps:

1. Training phase: We had a five minute testing phase, providing a short training exercise for the user before starting with the ratio task, asking them to have their both hands to position 5, and then space left-hand and right-hand four units apart to get familiar with the system.
2. Testing phase: After the training phase we had a testing phase of fifteen minutes. First they had to do the default tasks and see the affective feedback we provided them, and we monitored their reactions. Next they would customize their settings, and we monitored their reactions and saw their preferences.
3. A Usability questionnaire that we explain in the "Quantitative Results" section, below.
4. An Open-ended questionnaire that we explain in the "Qualitative Results" section, below.

We collected both qualitative and quantitative data at the same stage of the study. We used thematic analysis for the qualitative aspects of the study. We collected the data from comments and answers to open ended questions, went through it all, and identified themes.

6   Quantitative Results

First we address our stated expectations:

1. The Leap Motion Controller is easy and engaging: Almost all participants (82 %) agreed that there is no fatigue involved while interacting with the UI.
2. Fun in the physical interaction: Regarding the pleasantness and how pleasant is to interact with the UI, 91 % of participants agreed that using Leap Motion Controller would be more engaging than using mouse and keyboard.
3. Affective design support of learning: Regarding the affective strategies 72 % of participants agreed that it would help in motivating students in learning ratio.

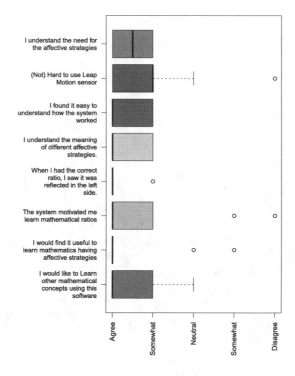

Fig. 4. Usability questionnaire about the MADE Ratio system (Color figure online)

Figure 4 shows the usability questionnaire results. On the left side there are eight statements. The participants were given a questionnaire to evaluate and rate their experience and subjective impressions of the system. For each question, subjects were given a Likert scale between agree and disagree. For analysis we used R (https://www.r-project.org/). The results of this analysis are shown in Fig. 4. The responses are shown as boxplots, where the inner quartiles are shown as colored boxes, the outer quartiles with whiskers, and outliers as circles.

The first statement is about understanding the need for affective strategies in this learning system; all the participants agreed. For the second statement (Not hard to use Leap Motion Controller) mostly everyone agreed. By providing a training phase at the beginning of the study, everyone understood how the system worked. The forth statement was understanding the meaning of different affective strategies, which everyone understood. The fifth statement was about task affirmation and reflection on the UI, and everyone but one agreed. The sixth statement explore whether the system motivated the participant in learning about mathematical ratios, but not all agreed. The seventh statement was whether it is useful to use affective strategies in learning mathematics; only two of the participants were neutral but the rest agreed. The last statement was if the participant would like to learn other mathematical concepts using this software; almost everyone agreed except one participant somewhat agreeing, and another was neutral.

Overall, the rating indicated approval of the system design; however, some differences were observed among participants.

7   Qualitative Results

At first we did a pilot study with one participant to capture firsthand behaviors and interactions that might have not been noticed. We found some problems with the system, and fixed them for the real study. One issue was that the Leap Motion Controller was far from the participant, which meant the participant was not feeling comfortable and had some fatigue with his hand. Having it closer made it easier to hold up his hands, giving a finer control over the height making it easier to use with no fatigue. Another concern was the participant said that the text wording could be improved in a lot of places, and we fixed all those instances. Another issue was brought up was the audio. He said: *"I'm not a fan of audio in general, but the applause seemed over the top, and the music was in the way because we were talking."* So we provided controls for the audio.

7.1   Multiple Sensory Modalities

Fun and Engaging: Almost all the participants agreed this system would be fun and engaging for children. They said the Leap Motion was easy to use and quite fun to try for the first time. One participant said: *"I personally have cousins who are currently learning ratios, and believe this would be an interesting way for them to learn, that they would enjoy"*. Another participant said: *"I think having Leap Motion is an effective and innovative approach for kids to be engaged in learning mathematics. The device is small, light and easy to use and having a friendly interface would be successful in my opinion for learning."* Another participant said this system is great for allowing students to respond in the modality that they have the most comfort with. He said the Leap Motion is good for visualization representations for how a ratio scales. He had a suggestion that there be option to interact in a horizontal way as well, suggesting that would more directly correspond to hand positions.

Easy to Use But Could Be Improved: One participant said the Leap Motion is mostly easy to use but it is a bit finicky. Some participants mentioned there should be a physical reference such as a ruler displayed vertically. Another said it would be nice to have a ruler (scale) guide on the side as reference points to help user more accurately move up and down.

Learnability and Memorability: One participant said that the Leap Motion would help with learnability and memory, because you've experienced it yourself. Another participant said it was very smooth and there was no lag-time when interacting with the Leap Motion.

Control of Audio: One participant said the audio output would be suitable as long as it is controllable. Another participant mentioned: *"While performing a task, if the music is playing, it might be distracting for some people, but the praise (e.g. clapping) when the job was complete can be a good thing."*

7.2   Affective Strategies

Effect on Learning: One participant said this multimodal system had benefits by providing multiple interaction modes including audio, visual and using an embodied interaction approach; the Leap Motion can make UI learnable and memorable. One participant said: *"I feel proud of myself when I hear applause."* He said that the happy face is encouraging, audio is motivating, but he did not like the specific music in the background, and he said it depends on type of music. Another participant said: *"The affective strategies are great for kids, and it's very encouraging."* Another participant said: *"The affective strategies like music are helpful in learning, since it challenges the students to try, and in the meantime it presents a mathematical problem like a computer game. This interactive approach is helpful since it draws students attention more than traditional learning techniques."* Most of the participants said this system could be very good for children, e.g. music, audio, color, text and using humor and funny things can be engaging for kids. One participant said: *"I like the idea of giving different types of feedback and customizing that feedback."* She said that affective strategies present in this system are appropriate for kids but not for adults.

Challenges: Some participants would have liked if the system provided the learner with a score. This possible addition could be a mechanism to make the learning seem more like a game that would keep the students' attention and challenge them. One participant suggested that there be continuity to the music during the task (e.g. each part of the task for 30 s, and eventually music finishes when the person completes the whole task and it is done. Another participant suggested that when a user wants to start using the system, it can ask the user their favorite color for the background choice. Some participants had concerns for the location of content on the screen. Some liked the affective feedback's location on the screen, but they said it should not go on top of the learning objective.

Some participants suggest the ratio can move closer to the hand circles on the main screen as maybe a better idea.

Virtual Characters: A participant mentioned adding virtual characters; an avatar of the learner. For example, there is an appeal to emotional investments of virtual characters like Pokemon, and we could provide for the student to choose an avatar that reacts to their performance, and lets them earn token currency as a reward for success – which could be spend to customize the avatar – and allow custom themes for success/fail sounds, a custom look and feel theme to the interface as personalization.

7.3   Facial Recognition

We suggested that our system might use analysis of facial expression to detect emotional state, and asked for their comments.

Useful for Teaching: The participants agreed with having a facial recognition with the system, and they said it might be a great way for adapting difficulty to success/failure e.g. frustrations vs. excitement. One participant said: *"I think that facial recognition should be used, as it would allow the teacher to be able to monitor individual performance of students, to know when to modify the difficulty or focus on a skill that doesn't seem to be understood."* This approach might be useful to help better understand the students' moods and feelings and how they feel about solving mathematical problems. Teachers might then adapt the exercise based on the learner's frustration with difficulty. If a student feels that they are behind, facial expressions would help teacher to adjust/modify level of difficulty. It might be interesting data to collect for a teacher to reflect back on and use in their assessment of teaching methods, and assessing their student's performance.

Privacy Issues: At least two participants said: "Showing the student's face in the screen would be distracting." One of these participants mentioned people may not like capturing their face (privacy) and added: *"Probably not? It would have to be done very well, so that it's not really telling you how you feel. [There is a] danger of being creepy monitoring. How would it improve my experience? and is it going to be worth the costs?"* Another participant said that she is not sure how useful it would be. Almost all the participants agreed that it would be very interesting for the teacher to user a facial recognition. Only one of the participants said: *"Would there not be some privacy concerns here? I personally would not like it. Some people do not like to express or have their emotions show/being monitored. E.g. with frustration/anger/sad. Learning environment should be more visual/interactive rather than computer monitoring; the human touch is needed here".* Therefore, they felt it could be useful for the teacher to see the video, but it would be more distracting if there was a real time video on the same page, and some people might not like having their image recorded.

7.4   General Advantages

As one participant mentioned, this system has a lot of potential for some people who have problems focusing on written material (e.g. ADHD). He added that this system provides a visual, auditory and physical interaction which is the environment they learn best in. He said: *"I find it very effective for my age and personality: I don't like voice; I'm more visual."* He would like the system to somehow show the movements of his hands on the screen. Other participants agreed on the following general advantages:

1. This system is fun and is more engaging compared to the traditional way of learning ratios.
2. Customization in this system is an advantage.
3. The system provides a hands-on physical interaction.
4. The system would raise the curiosity of children in learning.

7.5   General Disadvantages

"The User has to focus on each the left and right side of the screen. It took his attention and made he look at different directions while looking at numbers and make calculations." This was said by one participant, who suggested that more coherence on the main screen. Another participant said: *"If you could combine the points of attention; you have three-points of attention: our hands, hands shown on the screen and ratios on the left, which causes three focal points. Combine them into one."* This issue was perhaps the most prominent disadvantage; the entire list was:

1. Potential problem of different places to focus.
2. More visual cues about what is going on.
3. Need for challenges and game-like structure.
4. Potential problem with motor skills hand-eye coordination.

8   Discussion

We have described our rationale for, and implementation of, the MADE Ratio system, including our design-based research approach and reporting on qualitative and quantitative studies with eleven undergraduate and graduate students who engaged in problem-solving tasks with the MADE Ratio. Our study is consistent with the work of Howison et al. [6], while they have not emphasized the multimodality aspect and affective strategies. Out tasks were performed by the participants who had prior experience with ratios and proportions, but not in a multimodal environment. They had learned mathematical concepts with pencil and paper, or using mouse and keyboard.

The math topics we considered in this system were ratios and proportions. We tried to implement a multimodal system with a super-simple affective experience to increase engagement and attention of the students. This system is customizable, meaning the teacher can select different learning objective, affective and cognitive strategies in the database for different personas. The teacher monitors the students understanding of the material and provides different learning strategies to each student. These strategies employ sensory and quasi-sensory modalities, which we explained earlier.

Reflecting on our experience, we now suggest that the system might also have elements of *persuasive technology tools*, as described by B.J. Fogg [3]. Specifically, the system might be seen to be using *tailoring*, which is persuasion through customization (the teacher is able to customize the database according the each student's interest), as well as *reduction* approach to make the complex ratio task simpler (by using the Leap Motion Controller) to increase a student's motivation to engage in the task more frequently. Fogg has proposed that tailored information is more effective than generic information in changing attitudes and behaviors; the information provided by a system will be more persuasive if it is tailored to the individual's needs, interests, or other factors relevant to the individual. We also discussed affect and so we might be seen as employing Pathos, from Aristotle's modes of rhetoric. Pathos represents an appeal to the emotions of the students, and elicits feelings that already reside in them.

The reflections of our participants also leads us to consider *gamification in education* as a potential new approach we might explore in refining the system.

9   Conclusions

The ability to communicate emotionally and cognitively plays an essential role in HCI and education. This paper focused on UI design and implementation for a multimodal system in affective education, and conducted usability testing. We presented the rationale, design, implementation, and early results from our study of a novel educational technology. The goal of this study was to determine if this system can motivate and engage students in learning ratios and proportions. The affective strategies and the Leap Motion Controller were well suited for this environment.

We validated our three expectations: The Leap Motion Controller was easy and engaging, the system did support fun through the physical interaction, and the affective design support will increase the motivation in learning and the students did better understand some tasks in mathematics.

Our next steps will consider the following potential improvements. First, the interface should show a list of the tasks for the students to attempt, rather than relying on a teacher. Second, the system should show the student their learning progress. Third, and perhaps the most important, the system could allow the teacher to monitor and see current student status and how he/she is doing, showing the affective status, and allowing changes to be made to the task list and the affective feedback strategies. We also plan to upgrade the system adding facial recognition to it to support this. We plan to do another user study to monitor the task difficulties/easiness, and do more quantitative analysis on the data we collect. We will use an updated, modified version of the questionnaire and will consider all the feedback participants provided in this study.

In future, we will see what other relevant tasks can be specified and used with this system, and if the framework and the system could also be applicable to other domains. In the design of this system, we used two design methodologies, Affective Personas and Affective Essential Use Cases. It is hoped that these methodologies may support designers in the creation of multimodal affective software for teaching environments.

Acknowledgments. We thank the participants in this study, and lab colleagues for comments. We acknowledge a Discovery Grant through the Natural Sciences and Engineering Research Council of Canada (NSERC), and funding from the Industry Canada GRAND Network of Centres of Excellence.

References

1. Bloom, B.S.: Taxonomy of educational objectives: the classification of education goals. In: Handbook 1: Cognitive Domain. Longman (1956)
2. Dourish, P.: Where the action is: the foundations of embodied interaction. MIT press (2004)
3. Fogg, B.: Persuasive Technology: Using Computers to Change What We Think and Do. Morgan Kaufmann, Amsterdam (2002)
4. GhasemAghaei, R., Arya, A., Biddle, R.: Design practices for multimodal affective mathematical learning. In: 20th International Symposium of Computer Science and Software Engineering, IEEE CSSE (2015)
5. GhasemAghaei, R., Arya, A., Biddle, R.: The MADE framework: multimodal software for affective education. In: EdMedia: World Conference on Educational Media and Technology, vol. 2015, pp. 1864–1874 (2015)
6. Howison, M., Trninic, D., Reinholz, D., Abrahamson, D.: The mathematical imagery trainer: from embodied interaction to conceptual learning. In: Proceedings of the SIGCHI Conference on Human Factors in Computing Systems, pp. 1989–1998. ACM (2011)
7. Kort, B., Reilly, R., Picard, R.W.: An affective model of interplay between emotions and learning: reengineering educational pedagogy-building a learning companion. In: ICALT, p. 0043. IEEE (2001)
8. Oviatt, S.: Multimodal interfaces. In: Jacko, J.A., Sears, A. (eds.) The Human-computer Interaction Handbook, pp. 286–304. L. Erlbaum Associates Inc., Hillsdale, NJ, USA (2003). http://dl.acm.org/citation.cfm?id=772072.772093
9. Preece, J., Sharp, H., Rogers, Y.: Interaction Design: Beyond Human-Computer Interaction. Wiley, New York (2015)

Pedagogical Document Classification and Organization Using Domain Ontology

Ali Shariq Imran$^{(\boxtimes)}$ and Zenun Kastrati

Faculty of Computer Science and Media Technology,
Norwegian University of Science and Technology (NTNU), Gjøvik, Norway
{ali.imran,zenun.kastrati}@ntnu.no

Abstract. One of the challenges faced by today's web is the abundance of unstructured and unorganized information available on the Internet in form of educational documents, lecture notes, presentation slides, and multimedia recordings. Accessing and retrieving the massive amount of such resources are not an easy task, especially educational resources of pedagogical nature. Much of the pedagogical content available on Internet comes from blogs, wikis, posts with little or no metadata, that suffer from the same dilemma. The content is out there but way out of the reach of the intended audience. For content to be readily available, it has to be properly organized into different categories and structured into an appropriate format using metadata. This paper addresses this issue by proposing an automated approach using ontology-based document classification. The paper presents a case study and describes how our proposed ontology model can be used to classify educational documents into predefined categories.

Keywords: Domain ontology · Document classification · eLearning · SEMCON

1 Introduction

People have been educating themselves since the era of dawn, shaping their minds to adapt to the changing needs. Not only education has helped mankind acquaint themselves with better tools and skills, and to find solutions to everyday problems, it has also helped progress in the field of technology. Over time, it has resulted in a technologically advanced society we now live in today.

Massive amount of digital content from all walks of life is produced on a daily basis with the advancement of technology, and education is no different. Hundreds and thousands of educational videos, audio recordings, presentation slides and lecture notes are uploaded to the Internet, creating a massive wealth of information and digital libraries of educational content. Most of which is, however, unstructured and unorganized, thereby making it difficult to find them amongst the wealth of information available on the Internet.

According to IBM, a computer giant, roughly 2.5 quintillion bytes of data is produced every day. This data is coming from various sources in forms of emails,

© Springer International Publishing Switzerland 2016
P. Zaphiris and A. Ioannou (Eds.): LCT 2016, LNCS 9753, pp. 499–509, 2016.
DOI: 10.1007/978-3-319-39483-1_45

chats, blogs, posts, social media, eLearning platforms, among others. This huge amount of data is expected to grow even at a faster pace in coming years. More than 80 % of the information coming from various sources is unstructured and unorganized [1]. This results in a loss of data and the information fail to reach to the users. This holds true for educational material roaming around on the Internet as most of it never reach to the audience.

To ensure easy retrieval and access to massive amount of digital data, we need to organize and structure it accordingly. Having said that, organizing and structuring massive wealth of information is a momentous task for humans. It is labour intensive, prone to errors and is time-consuming. Automatic approaches and methodologies such as the use of ontologies can help play a vital role in this regard.

The rest of the paper is as follow. In Sect. 2 we present the related work on ontology and eLearning. Section 3 describes the importance and the role of ontologies in organizing pedagogical content. Section 4 presents a case study where we show how our proposed ontology model can play an effective role in organizing educational material while Sect. 5 concludes the paper.

2   Related Work

Ontologies are being used in web portals and eLearning systems for nearly two decades to generate knowledge and aid processes of collaborative learning. 1999 was the start of era when the role of ontologies for intelligent educational systems was first recognized in a workshop [2]. With the boom of web 2.0 in 2004, ontologies gained popularity. By then numerous workshops, conferences, and journals were dedicated to ontologies for educational systems [2–8], which resulted in a significant amount of researches. This lead to the development of semantic tools (Jena, Sesame, KAON, JRDF, Protege (Pugin for Protege for OWL) and ontology based languages (DAML + OIL, RDF, RDF-S, OWL and its sublanguages: OWL Lite, OWL DL, and OWL Full). Thus giving rise to a semantic web, semantic databases and semantic searches in last decade. Since then ontologies have become an essential part of many eLearning systems.

Ontologies are now being used in eLearning systems for domain knowledge, metadata, and entity representation. Use of ontologies in the context of eLearning can be categorized into [9]: (a) curriculum modeling and management, (b) describing learning domains, (c) describing learners data such as profile and personal data and, (d) describing eLearning services, all for the purpose of better content structuring and organization, and easy search and retrieval mechanisms. CURONTO is an ontology designed for entire curriculum management. Others include Gescur [10] and Crampon project [11] that aid curriculum designing. Learning ontologies consists of domain (subject) specific ontologies [12,13], and task-based ontologies involving pedagogy design [14,15], assessments [16,17], search and retrieval [18], and feedback [19,20]. Adaptive courseware Tutor [21], ONTODAPS [22], and work done by Panagiotopolos et al. [23] provides information about student's knowledge, progress, and personal information. They also provide information describing learners data such as IMS learner information package (LIP), IEEE public and private information (PAPI), and friend of a friend (FOAF). While [24] and [25] are service related ontologies for creating learning object repositories (LOR) and mapping learning objects (LO) to a single common ontology. These facilitate the existing metadata standards such as Dublin Core DCMI, IMS learning resource metadata, IEEE LOM and SCORM via ontologies.

3   Importance of Ontologies in eLearning

This section briefly discusses eLearning platforms' content organization, defines ontology and establishes how ontology can play a role in the content organization in eLearning platforms.

3.1   eLearning Platforms

Over the years, numerous eLearning platforms and management systems have emerged. These platforms and websites such as Coursera, edX, Khan Academy, offers many online courses from all walks of life. These courses are usually divided into modules. Each module is further divided into different lessons and each lesson consists of a topic. The topics may be further split into smaller chunks of educational resources called LO. On a daily basis, hundreds and thousands of LOs are created and uploaded on various educational platforms. The benefit of these resources is certainly undeniable, however to benefit from the wealth of information available on the Internet, these resources have to be structured and grouped together into categories for easy search and retrieval. A domain ontology can play a vital role in this regard by incorporating semantics into eLearning platforms.

3.2   Ontology

Ontology is a fundamental element in semantic web and artificial intelligence (AI) based systems and is often defined as a *'specification of conceptualization'* [27]. It is a description of the real world concepts as entities and the relationship between them. Ontologies can be used in context of knowledge sharing and reuse. Given a domain ontology, queries, questions, and assertions can be made via AI agents/programs for content organization, structuring, and classification. Thus, It can also be described as a set of vocabulary of a particular domain.

A domain ontology consists of concepts and the relationships between these concepts for a particular domain (course) rather than specifying only generic concepts, as found in the upper ontologies such as SUMO, DOLCE, Cyc, among others. In other words, a domain ontology represents the vocabulary of a particular domain in a formal way and therefore it should closely match the level of information found in a text document in that domain.

3.3   Ontology Role in eLearning

Many learning management systems (LMS) and online learning platforms use open educational resources (OER) delivering high-quality pedagogical content in a form of LO. These OER and LO are often manually structured and organized into different categories, which demands a lot of manual work and is a time-consuming process. The OER and LO consist of different topics from various fields which can be depicted as concepts.

For instance, for a given chemistry domain, a list of commonly used terms can be prepared. These terms can be used as concepts to build an ontology for chemistry domain. The ontology is usually a hierarchical representation of these terms and the relationships between them. Thus, the terms for a chemistry domain can be represented as a hierarchical structuring consisting of classes and subclasses. To give an example, the term 'atom' can be a subclass of the term 'substance'. As both of them are concepts belonging to a chemistry domain, therefore, these terms can be used as labels in a domain ontology. Once the ontology is populated with a list of all the important concepts from the chemistry domain, it can be used to classify and organize different OER and LO using it.

In today's era, ontology plays a vital role in structuring and organizing pedagogical content on eLearning platforms. The next section presents a case study describing how ontologies can be used to structure and organize educational resources into different categories.

4   Case Study

In this section, we are introducing an example of classifying unlabelled text documents in the appropriate category within a pedagogical platform using the domain ontology. Employing a domain ontology enables to move from a document classification based on keywords to a classification based on content meanings (concepts), thus moving from lexical to semantic interpretation. The example presented in this section is composed of 4 components.

4.1   Domain Ontology

Text document classification presented in this case study is in line with ontology-based classification approach, therefore, it takes as a starting point the existence of a domain ontology. A domain ontology represents concepts for describing a domain and interpreting a description of a problem in that domain. A 5-tuple based structure [28] shown in Eq. 1 is commonly used to describe the concepts and their relationships of a particular domain.

$$D = (C,\ I,\ H,\ type,\ rel) \tag{1}$$

where:

- C is a finite set of concepts

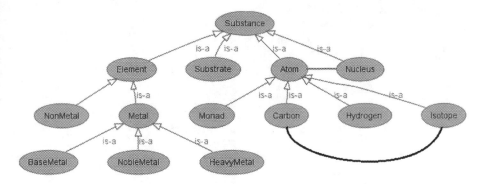

Fig. 1. A part of substance ontology from the domain of chemistry

- I is a finite set of lexical entries (Instances)
- H is a finite set of concept to concept relationships
- *type* is a finite set of instance to concept relationships
- *rel* is the finite set of instance to instance relationships.

Figure 1 shows a part of substance ontology built according to the Eq. 1. Additionally, it illustrates concepts (Element, Atom, Metal), instances of concepts (Carbon, Hydrogen) and the three types of relationships used to link these concepts. These relationships are (1) concept-to-concept (Metal is an element, Nucleus is part of an atom), (2) instance-to-concept (Monad is an atom with valence one), and (3) instance-to-instance relationship (Carbon has isotopes).

4.2 Predefined Categories and Semantics

The second component shows categories which have been predefined in a pedagogical platform. In this case study, the category shown in Fig. 2 is the subject of chemistry and the documents contained within this domain. The documents are organized into appropriate categories manually by an expert of that domain. At this point, these documents are represented as plain texts and there is no semantics associated with them.

The semantic information is added in using a domain ontology as defined in Subsect. 4.1. The semantic of documents, as shown in Fig. 3 (Doc_1, Doc_2,..., Doc_n), is incorporated by matching the terms t in a document Doc with the relevant concept c from the domain ontology. Adding semantics is possible thanks to (1) the presence of at least one of the concept labels within documents and/or (2) through identification of terms which are semantically close related to these concepts.

The former is a straightforward process. It simply employs the matching method [29] to find the concepts label within documents. A domain ontology consists of single label concepts such as Substance, Element, Atom and compound label concepts (BaseMetal, HeavyMetal) as well. For single label concepts, we use only those terms from the document for which an exact term exists in

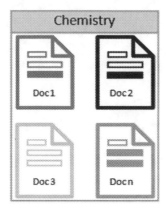

Fig. 2. Representation of a predefined category

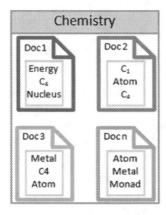

Fig. 3. Representation of documents after semantics have been incorporated

the domain ontology. For example, for concepts in the domain ontology such as Substance, Atom, and Element, there exists the same term extracted from the document. This process is known as exact term matching. For compound label concepts, we use those terms from the document which are present as part of a concept in the domain ontology. This type of concept matching is known as partial matching, and it represents cases when concept label contains terms extracted from the document in the corpus. The formal definition of exact and partial matches is given as follows.

If DO is the domain ontology, C the corpus composed of documents of this particular domain and $Doc \in C$ a document defined as a finite set of terms $Doc = \{t_1, t_2, ..., t_n\}$.

The mapping of term $t_i \in Doc$ into concept $c_j \in DO$ is defined as exact match $EM(t_i, c_j)$, where

$$EM(t_i, c_j) = \begin{cases} 1, & \text{if } label(c_j) = t_i \\ 0, & \text{if } label(c_j) \neq t_i \end{cases} \tag{2}$$

The mapping of term $t_i \in Doc$ into concept $c_j \in DO$ is defined as partial match $PM(t_i, c_j)$, where

$$PM(t_i, c_j) = \begin{cases} 1, & \text{if } label(c_j) \text{ contains } t_i \\ 0, & \text{if } label(c_j) \text{ not contain } t_i \end{cases} \tag{3}$$

If $EM(t_i, c_j) = 1$, term t_i and concept label c_j are identical and term t_i is then replaced with concept c_j.

If $PM(t_i, c_j) = 1$, term t_i is part of concept label c_j and term t_i is then replaced with concept c_j. For example, the *BaseMetal* compound ontology concept shown in Fig. 1 contains terms extracted from the document such as *Base* and/or *Metal*.

The latter is a more complex process. It searches for new terms within documents which are associated semantically with ontology concepts. To find these terms, we employ the SEMCON model [26] which uses an aggregated contextual and semantic information of the particular term. SEMCON exploits the statistical features such as frequency of occurrences of a term, term font type, and term font size to build the observation matrix. Contextual information is then defined by using the cosine measure where the dot product between two vectors of the observation matrix reflects the extent to which two terms have a similar occurrence pattern in the vector space. In addition to the context information, the SEMCON incorporates the semantic information to a term, by computing a semantic similarity score between two terms - a term that is extracted from a document and term that already exists in the domain ontology as a concept.

The next step is incorporating semantics of the categories. This is a process where the overall classification system tries to replicate the way an expert organizes/categorizes the documents into each category. The category semantics is built by aggregating the semantics of all documents which belong to the same category, as shown in Fig. 4.

Figure 5 shows all the steps taken through the process of incorporating the semantics of the chemistry category.

Each category is represented by a vector with two members: (1) concepts of a domain ontology, and (2) weight of these concepts. Category vector representation is given in Eq. 4.

$$Cat_j = \{(c_1, w_1), (c_2, w_2), (c_3, w_3), ..., (c_j, w_j)\} \tag{4}$$

Where, c_j is a concept appearing in the domain ontology and w_j is the weight of this particular concept.

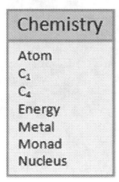

Fig. 4. Incorporating category semantics

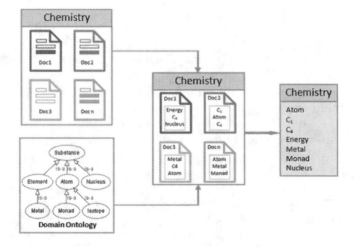

Fig. 5. The overall process of incorporating category semantics

Weight of concepts of the category vector is computed by aggregating the concept importance and concept relevance. The value of a concept weight given in Eq. 5 is in the range of [0,1].

$$w(c_j) = Imp(c_j) \times Rel(c_j) \tag{5}$$

Concept importance shows how important a concept is in the domain ontology and this is reflected in the number of relations this particular concept has to other concepts. The concept importance is computed automatically using the approach described in [30]. More concretely, the approach takes the ontology and map that into a graph and then implements one of the Markov-based algorithms (PageRank) to compute the concept importance.

Concept Relevance reflects the contribution of a particular concept to a category vector by the frequency of the occurrences of this concept in that category alone and it is computed using the Eq. 6.

$$Rel(c_j) = \sum_{i=1}^{m} Freq(c_j) \tag{6}$$

Where, $Freq(c_j)$ is the frequency of occurrences of a concept c_j in the corpus.

4.3 Representation of Unclassified Documents

The last component deals with the unlabelled documents which have to be classified into the appropriate category. The following preprocessing steps have to be undertaken to bring these new and unclassified documents into the appropriate form for further processing: text is cleaned by removing all punctuation and capitalization, and a tokenizer is used to separate the text into individual terms (words); all terms resulted by tokenization process are passed through the term stemmer to convert them into their base or root form to develop a list of potential terms which are a noun, a verb, an adverb or an adjective; the stop words are removed; and finally the weight of terms is computed using one of the techniques from the Information Retrieval such as Term frequency *tf* or Term Frequency Inverse Document Frequency *tf*idf*.

After the preprocessing step, the incoming unlabelled document is finally represented as a document vector composed by a finite set of weighted terms and it is described by the tuple given in Eq. 7.

$$Doc_i = \{(t_1, w_1), (t_2, w_2), (t_3, w_3), ..., (t_i, w_i)\} \tag{7}$$

Where, t_i is the ith term appearing in this particular document and w_i is the weight of this particular term.

The final task, after the unlabelled document is brought in the document vector form according to Eq. 7, is then to classify it into its appropriate category automatically. This ultimate goal is achieved using the similarity measure. It finds the similarity between category vector and document vector. The higher the similarity score, the closer the relationship between the document and the category. In other words, the higher the similarity score between a document and a category, the document more likely belongs to this category. The mathematical definition of similarity measure is given in Eq. 8.

$$Similarity(Doc_i, Cat_j) = \frac{\overrightarrow{Doc_i} \times \overrightarrow{Cat_j}}{\| \overrightarrow{Doc_i} \| \cdot \| \overrightarrow{Cat_j} \|} \tag{8}$$

Where, Doc_i and Cat_j represent the document vector and category vector, respectively.

5 Conclusion and Future Work

In this paper, we presented a case study depicting how the proposed ontology-based model can be used to classify educational documents into predefined categories in a pedagogical platform. The model classifies documents based on the content meanings thereby trying to replicate the way an expert organizes/categorizes the documents into each category. To achieve this, the model initially build the semantics of the documents using the domain ontology. Aggregating the semantics of all these documents belonging to a particular category builds the semantics of category. Finally, an unlabelled document is classified into a category which has the highest similarity score with this particular document.

The proposed approach can be an ideal choice for educational platforms such as massive open online courses (MOOC) and LMS where content organization and structuring is inevitable for easy search and retrieval. In the future we are planning to implement the proposed model to classify documents for a particular course within a pedagogical platform.

References

1. Raghavan, P.: Extracting and exploiting structure in text search. In: SIGMOD Conference, p. 635 (2003)
2. Workshop on "Ontologies for Intelligent Educational Systems", in conjunction with AI-ED 1999, Le Mans, France, 18–19 July 1999
3. Workshop on "Concepts and Ontologies in Web-based Educational Systems", in conjunction with ICCE 2002, Auckland, New Zealand, 3–6 December 2002
4. Workshop on "Semantic Web for Web-based Learning", in conjunction with CAISE 2003, Klagenfurt/Velden, Austria, June 2003
5. Workshop on "Applications of Semantic Web Technologies for Web-based ITS", in conjunction with ITS 2004, Macei-Alagoas, Brazil, 30 August–03 September 2004
6. Workshop on "Learning Design and Topic Maps", Oslo, Norway, 26–27 January 2005
7. Anderson, T., Whitelock, D.M.: The educational semantic web: visioning and practicing the future of education. J. Interact. Media Educ. **2004**(1), p.Art. 1 (2004). http://doi.org/10.5334/2004-1
8. Sampson, D.G., Lytras, M.D., Wagner, G., Diaz, P.: Special issue on Ontologies and the Semantic Web for E-learning. J. Educ. Technol. Soc. **7**(4) (2004)
9. Al-Yahya, M., George, M., Alfaries, A.: Ontologies in e-learning: review of the literature. Int. J. Softw. Eng. Appl. **9**(2), 67–84 (2015)
10. Dexter, H., Davies, I.: An ontology-based curriculum knowledge-base for managing complexity and change. In: 9th IEEE International Conference on Advanced Learning Technologies, pp. 136–140 (2009)
11. Fernandez-Breis, J.T., Castellanos-Nieves, D., Hernandez-Franco, J., Soler-Segovia, C., Robles-Redondo, M., Gonzalez-Martinez, R., Prendes-Espinosa, M.P.: A semantic platform for the management of the educative curriculum. Expert Syst. Appl. **39**(5), 6011–6019 (2012)
12. Lee, M.-C., Ye, D., Wang, T.: Java learning object ontology. In: 5th IEEE International Conferences on Advanced Learning Technologies, pp. 538–542 (2005)
13. Sameh, A.: Ontology-based feedback e-Learning system for mobile computing. In: Mastorakis, N., Mladenov, V., Kontargyri, V.T. (eds.) Proceedings of the European Computing Conference. LNEE, vol. 27, pp. 479–488. Springer, New York (2009)
14. Isotani, S., Mizoguchi, R., Capeli, O., Isotani, N., Jaques, P.: A semantic web-based authoring tool to facilitate the planning of collaborative learning scenarios compliant with learning theories. Comput. Educ. **63**, 267–284 (2013)

15. Cobos, C., Rodriguez, O., Rivera, J., Betancourt, J., Mendoza, M., Leon, E., Viedma, E.: A hybrid system of pedagogical pattern recommendations based on singular value decomposition and variable data attributes. Inf. Process. Manag. **49**(3), 607–625 (2013)

16. Castellanos-Nieves, D., Fernandez, J., Garcia, R., Martinez, R., Moreno, M.: Semantic web technologies for supporting learning assessment. Inf. Sci. **181**(9), 1517–1537 (2011)

17. Litherland, K., Carmichael, P., Garcia, A.: Ontology-based assessment for accounting: outcomes of a pilot study and future prospects. J. Account. Educ. **31**(2), 162–176 (2013)

18. Lee, M., Tsai, K., Wang, T.: A practical ontology query expansion algorithm for semantic aware learning objects retrieval. Comput. Educ. **50**(4), 1240–1257 (2008)

19. Del, M., Breis, J., Castellanos, D., Morales, F., Espinosa, M.: Semantic web technologies for generating feedback in online assessment environments. Knowl. Based Syst. **33**, 152–165 (2012)

20. Kazi, H., Haddawy, P., Suebnukarn, S.: Leveraging a domain ontology to increase the quality of feedback in an intelligent tutoring system. In: Aleven, V., Kay, J., Mostow, J. (eds.) ITS 2010, Part I. LNCS, vol. 6094, pp. 75–84. Springer, Heidelberg (2010)

21. Grubii, A., Stankov, S., Žitko, B.: Adaptive courseware model for intelligent e-learning systems. In: International Conference on Computing, e-Learning and Emerging Technologies, vol. 16, no. 1 (2014)

22. Nganji, J., Brayshaw, M., Tompsett, B.: Ontology driven disability-aware e-learning personalisation with ONTODAPS. Campus-Wide Inf. Syst. **30**(1), 17–34 (2012)

23. Panagiotopoulos, I., Kalou, A., Pierrakeas, C., Kameas, A.: An ontology-based model for student representation in intelligent tutoring systems for distance learning. In: Iliadis, L., Maglogiannis, I., Papadopoulos, H. (eds.) Artificial Intelligence Applications and Innovations. IFIP AICT, vol. 381, pp. 296–305. Springer, Heidelberg (2012)

24. Raju, P., Ahmed, V.: Enabling technologies for developing next generation learning object repositories for construction. Autom. Constr. **22**, 247–257 (2012)

25. Arch-Int, N., Arch-Int, S.: Semantic ontology mapping for interoperability of learning resource systems using a rule-based reasoning approach. Expert Syst. Appl. **40**(18), 7428–7443 (2013)

26. Kastrati, Z., Imran, A.S., Yayilgan, S.Y.: SEMCON: semantic and contextual objective metric. In: 9th IEEE International Conference on Semantic Computing, pp. 65–68 (2015)

27. Gruber, T.R.: A translation approach to portable ontologies. Knowl. Acquisition **5**(2), 199–220 (1993)

28. Maedche, A.: Ontology Learning for the Semantic Web. Kluwer Academic Publishers, Norwell (2002)

29. Deng, S., Peng, H.: Document classification based on support vector machine using a concept vector model. In: Proceedings of the IEEE/WIC/ACM International Conference on Web Intelligence, pp. 473–476 (2006)

30. Kastrati, Z., Imran, A.S., Yayilgan, S.Y.: An improved concept vector space model for ontology based classification. In: 11th International Conference on Signal Image Technology and Internet Based Systems, Bangkok, Thailand (2015)

A Study of Gender Similarity Between Animated Pedagogical Agents and Young Learners

Anne-Laure Kervellec[✉], Eric Jamet, Virginie Dardier,
Séverine Erhel, Gaïd Le Maner-Idrissi, and Estelle Michinov

Centre de Recherches en Psychologie, Cognition et Communication, Université
Rennes 2, Rue du Recteur Paul Henry, 35000 Rennes, France
{anne-laure.kervellec,eric.jamet,virginie.dardier,
severine.erhel,gaid.lemaner-idrissi,
estelle.michinov}@univ-rennes2.fr

Abstract. Gender is strongly involved in the organization of interactions. According to the similarity-attraction hypothesis, learners may be more attracted to animated pedagogical agents that are similar to them, especially with regard to gender. Research on gender matching has so far yielded mixed results. However, the frequent use of tasks related to science, technology, engineering or mathematics may have interfered with the similarity-attraction relationship in these studies, as gender stereotypes suggest that boys are more associated with these fields than women. The aim of our study was to examine the effect of gender similarity on young learners (N = 47) performing a neutral task. Gender similarity was found to have a positive impact on learners' perceptions of animated pedagogical agents, but in the opposite-gender condition, learners were more engaged in the task. We discuss our results in the light of theory and previous research on gender matching.

Keywords: Human–computer interface · Gender studies · Elementary education · Interactive learning environments

1 Introduction

The social cues conveyed by animated pedagogical agents (APAs) can have an impact on learners in multimedia learning environments (e.g., Baylor and Kim 2004). In most cultures, gender is the primary social categorization (DeFrancisco and Palczewski 2007), and is strongly involved in the organization of interactions (Ridgeway and Smith-Lovin 1999). Gender stereotypes appear at an early age (e.g., Arthur et al. 2008). It is well known that people regard computers and other media as though they were real people (i.e., media equation theory; Reeves and Nass 1996). Gender stereotypes may also exist in the virtual world. For example, when computers provide gender cues, users produce stereotypical responses based on gender (Nass et al. 1997). Gender stereotypes lead to expectations about men and women. Men are regarded as agentic (i.e., independent, masterful and competent), and women as communal (i.e., friendly, unselfish and concerned with others; Eagly and Wood 1991). According to Schunk (1987),

© Springer International Publishing Switzerland 2016
P. Zaphiris and A. Ioannou (Eds.): LCT 2016, LNCS 9753, pp. 510–517, 2016.
DOI: 10.1007/978-3-319-39483-1_46

a model's perceived competence can enhance observational learning. Interactions between learners and APAs can be affected by gender stereotypes. As a consequence, male APAs could benefit from gender stereotypes and therefore be more effective.

Some reports, for instance, indicate that male agents are more effective for learners than female ones, as they are judged more positively (Kim et al. 2007; Experiment 1 & 2), arouse greater interest in the task (Kim et al. 2007; Experiment 1) allow for better self-regulation (Baylor and Kim, 2004; Experiment 1) and give rise to enhanced self-efficacy (Baylor and Kim 2004; Experiment 1) or learning outcomes (Kim et al. 2007; Experiment 1; Moreno et al. 2002).

Others, by contrast, suggest that female agents are more beneficial to learners, contributing to their self-efficacy (Baylor and Kim 2004; Experiment 2). Shiban et al. (2015) found a positive effect on learners' interest in the subject (statistics) for the female, young and attractive agent, compared to the male, older and less attractive agent. Schroeder and Adesope (2015) didn't find any effect of agent gender.

It is, however, important to emphasize that most of these studies did not take the learners' sex into account, even though some research in social psychology on the similarity attraction hypothesis (SAH) suggests that it is important to consider gender similarity between learners and APAs.

According to the similarity-attraction hypothesis (SAH), people tend to be more attracted to others who are similar to themselves (Byrne 1971). Same-sex preferences are observed from an early age (e.g., Martin et al. 1999).

In a computer-based learning context, learners could therefore be more attracted to same-sex APAs. Gender similarity has a positive impact on judgments, with girls and boys considering their own gender more favorably (e.g., Yee and Brown 1994). Moreover, according to Bandura (1997) similar attributes, such as gender, between social model and learner can affect self-efficacy which, in turn, has an impact on persistence and achievement (Schunk 1995). In the light of this knowledge, we would therefore expect gender similarity between APAs and learners to give rise to better outcomes. However, studies have yielded heterogeneous results. For example, some studies have highlighted an effect of agent gender independently of the learner's sex. Baylor and Kim (2003) for instance, demonstrated a main effect of APA gender, with a male agent being judged more extrovert and agreeable in an instructional plan development task. Participants also expressed greater satisfaction with their performances and reported that the male agent facilitated self-regulation more than the female agent did. Furthermore, Arroyo et al. (2009; Experiment 2) observed that girls work better with the male agent. In another study, male and female agents exposed gender-fair beliefs, and provided a twenty-minute narrative about four female engineers, followed by five benefits of engineering careers (Ashby Plant et al. 2009). They observed a positive effect of a female versus male agent on the career interest dimension and mathematics performance.

Arroyo et al. (2009; Experiment 1) meanwhile, found that students tended to perform better in mathematics with a learning companion of the opposite gender, thus contradicting the SAH, although participants did not express a preference for this agent in the similarity condition. As for Behrend and Thompson (2011), they failed to demonstrate any effect of learner–APA gender similarity on either learning, engagement or perceptions of utility – be it of the agent or of the office software training program. That said, the SAH was corroborated in studies, in which Ozogul et al. (2013; Experiment 1) observed that 12-year-old girls rated a program on electrical circuits more positively after working with a gender-matched agent. In another study, Arroyo et al. (2013) found that female characters had a positive effect on girls. Male students had more negative outcomes when a learning companion was present; they obtained their worst outcomes with female characters. Research on the gender of agents and participants has therefore yielded mixed results so far, with no clear endorsement of the SAH. Students' judgments, motivation and even learning outcomes are not necessarily more positive when the APA's gender matches their own.

Furthermore, a task's gender orientation may influence interactions (Ridgeway and Smith-Lovin 1999). For example, children evaluate a computer-synthesized speech more positively and show better self-confidence when voice gender matches either content gender (i.e., female topics: skin care and makeup, princesses, dance; male topics: dinosaurs, football, knights) (Lee et al. 2007). Moreover Lee (2003) showed that participants exhibited a greater conformity with male character about typical male subject (i.e., sport) and with female character about typical female subject (i.e., fashion).

It should be noted that up to now, APA gender studies have usually featured tasks about science, technology, engineering or mathematics (STEM; e.g., Ozogul et al. 2013; Shiban et al. 2015; van der Meij et al. 2015) (often in order to develop girls' self efficacy in STEM). This may have interfered with the similarity-attraction relationship and could explain equivocal outcomes, as women are underrepresented in the STEM field (Beede et al. 2011), and people associate science and mathematics with men (e.g., Nosek et al. 2009).

The aim of our study was to examine the effect of gender similarity on learners performing a nonstereotypically gendered task. Based on SAH, we predicted that learners would judge the same-sex APA more positively (Hypothesis 1), exhibit greater engagement (Hypothesis 2), and perform better (Hypothesis 3) with a same-gender APA than with an opposite-gender one.

2   Method

2.1   Pretest

We conducted a pretest in order to select a neutral learning task. Participants included 62 children (32 girls, 30 boys) with a mean age of 9.52 years ($SD = .31$). Consistent with previous studies (Becky 2000; Miller and Budd 1999). We measured children's preferences for and perceived competence in different academic disciplines according to gender.

This pretest revealed that a foreign language task could be regarded as nonstereotypical, in contrast to mathematics or participants' native language.

2.2   Test

Participants and Design. The sample comprised 47 children (24 girls, 23 boys) attending schools in western France. Participants' mean age was 10.53 years ($SD =$ .27). All of them had French as their mother tongue. They were randomly assigned to a same-gender ($n = 25$) or opposite-gender APA ($n = 22$) (see Fig. 1). (Perception of gender of APAs has previously been pre-tested with students).

Material and Procedure. The children had to learn new items of English vocabulary presented by the APA on a 12.1" touchscreen tablet. After the learning phase, they could practice in an engagement phase, before undergoing a learning test. Children's perception of the APA was assessed by a post-task printed questionnaire. The session lasted 40 min.

Measures. We evaluated learning, engagement, and APAs' perception.

Learning: children had to recall some of the words learned in the lesson. They had to recall eight English words cued by the French ones (e.g., How do you say *journal* in English?). To receive a point, the child must remember the word and its pronunciation must be correct. Scores ranged from 0 to 8 points.

Engagement: we measured the number of exercises completed in a revision task (e.g., Behrend and Thompson, 2012). Between the learning phase and learning test, children could practice saying the new words. They could see and listen again twice to each of the 10 words featured in the lesson. Each time, the participant chose to listen the same word again, they received a point. They could end this phase whenever they liked. This allowed us to score their engagement out of 20.

APAs perception: We examined two dimensions of the APAs: their legitimacy and their attractiveness.

Legitimacy: the three items for the 5-point legitimacy scale were adapted from Bavishi et al. (2010); inspired by Choi and Mai-Dalton (1999). Cronbach's alpha reliability coefficient was .94 for this scale.

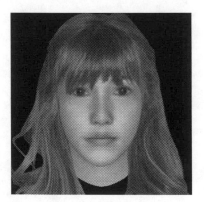

Fig. 1. Boy and girl APAs in the learning environment

Attractiveness: comprising four items, the 5-point scale for measuring attractiveness was adapted from two existing scales (i.e., Khan and De Angeli 2009; McCroskey and McCain 1972; Pratt, Hauser, Ugray and Patterson 2007). Alpha reliability was .94 for this scale.

3 Results

Regarding participants' perceptions of the APAs, we observed effects of gender similarity on both legitimacy, $F(1, 45) = 9.030$, $p = . 004$, $\eta^2 = .167$, and attractiveness, $F(1, 45) = 6.027$, $p = .018$, $\eta^2 = .118$. Participants who had been assigned to a same-gender APA rated the latter as more legitimate (same-gender APA: $M = 3.83$, $SD = 1.07$; opposite-gender APA: $M = 2.77$, $SD = 1.3$) and also more attractive (same-gender APA: $M = 3.86$, $SD = .70$; opposite-gender APA: $M = 3.32$, $SD = .82$). As Levene's homoscedasticity test showed that there was significant heterogeneity of variance ($p > .10$) for engagement, we ran a Mann–Whitney test. Engagement was greater among learners who had worked with an opposite-gender APA ($M = 6.73$, $SD = 6.2$) than with a same-gender APA ($M = 3$, $SD = 3.46$), ($U = 158$, $p = .012$).

We failed to find any difference in learning, $F(1, 45) = .130$, $p = .72$, between learners who had been assigned a same- versus opposite-gender APA.

4 Discussion

Consistent with SAH, and with our first hypothesis, learners judged the same-gender APA more positively than the opposite-gender APA.

Concerning engagement, results failed to confirm our second hypothesis, as learners were more engaged with the opposite-gender APA. There are two possible explanations for this result. First, our participants may not have sought to compete with the opposite-gender APA, and were thus more strongly engaged. Second, they may have felt more competent with the same-gender APA, and therefore saw less of a need to persevere in order to succeed. Regarding performance on the learning task, results also failed to confirm our third hypothesis.

Our study shows that results can differ and even be contradictory, depending on which measures are used. This might explain the mixed results of previous studies.

Further research with children of various ages is needed to explore these results.

Moreover, the gender orientation of a particular task may strongly influence the user–system relationship, making it necessary to compare several different types of task. It is therefore crucial to conduct further experiments to understand this effect.

Acknowledgement. Support for this work was provided by the French National Research Agency (ANR) under grant number ANR-11-TECS-0013.

References

Arroyo, I., Burleson, W., Tai, M., Muldner, K., Woolf, B.P.: Gender differences in the use and benefit of advanced learning technologies for mathematics. J. Educ. Psychol. **105**(4), 957 (2013)

Arroyo, I., Woolf, B.P., Royer, J.M., Tai, M.: Affective gendered learning companions. In: Proceedings of the 2009 Conference on Artificial Intelligence in Education: Building Learning Systems that Care: From Knowledge Representation to Affective Modelling, pp. 41–48, Amsterdam, The Netherlands. IOS Press, The Netherlands, Consulté à l'adresse (2009). http://dl.acm.org/citation.cfm?id=1659450.1659461

Arthur, A.E., Bigler, R.S., Liben, L.S., Gelman, S.A., Ruble, D.N.: Gender stereotyping and prejudice in young children. In: Levy, S.R., Killen, M. (eds.) Intergroup Attitudes and Relations in Childhood Through Adulthood, vol. 66, pp. 1072–1087. Oxford University Press, Oxford (2008)

Plant, E.A., Baylor, A.L., Doerr, C.E., Rosenberg-Kima, R.B.: Changing middle-school students' attitudes and performance regarding engineering with computer-based social models. Comput. Educ. **53**(2), 209–215 (2009). http://doi.org/10.1016/j.compedu.2009.01.013

Bandura, A.: Self-efficacy: The Exercise of Control, vol. ix. W H Freeman/Times Books/Henry Holt & Co, New York (1997)

Bavishi, A., Madera, J.M., Hebl, M.R.: The effect of professor ethnicity and gender on student evaluations: Judged before met. J. Divers. High. Educ. **3**(4), 245–256 (2010). http://doi.org/10.1037/a0020763

Baylor, A., Kim, Y., Baylor, A., Kim, Y.: The role of gender and ethnicity in pedagogical agent perception. In: Présenté à E-Learn: World Conference on E-Learning in Corporate, Government, Healthcare, and Higher Education, vol. 2003, pp. 1503–1506, Consulté à l'adresse/p/12158/ (2003)

Baylor, A.L., Kim, Y.: Pedagogical agent design: the impact of agent realism, gender, ethnicity, and instructional role. In: Lester, J.C., Vicari, R.M., Paraguaçu, F. (eds.) ITS 2004. LNCS, vol. 3220, pp. 592–603. Springer, Heidelberg (2004). Consulté à l'adresse http://www.springerlink.com/content/bfw9rj3y4fd8qn7g/

Becky, F.: The gendered subject: students' subject preferences and discussions of gender and subject ability. Oxford Rev. Educ. **26**(1), 35–48 (2000). http://doi.org/10.1080/030549800103845

Beede, D.N., Julian, T.A., Langdon, D., McKittrick, G., Khan, B., Doms, M.E.: Women in STEM: a gender gap to innovation (SSRN Scholarly Paper No. ID 1964782). Social Science Research Network, Rochester. Consulté à l'adresse (2011). http://papers.ssrn.com/abstract=1964782

Behrend, T.S., Thompson, L.F.: Similarity effects in online training: effects with computerized trainer agents. Comput. Hum. Behav. **27**(3), 1201–1206 (2011). http://doi.org/10.1016/j.chb.2010.12.016

Behrend, T.S., Thompson, L.F.: Using animated agents in learner-controlled training: the effects of design control (SSRN Scholarly Paper No. ID 2171592). Social Science Research Network, Rochester (2012). Consulté à l'adresse http://papers.ssrn.com/abstract=2171592

Byrne, D.E.: The Attraction Paradigm. Academic Press, New York (1971). Consulté à l'adresse http://catalog.hathitrust.org/api/volumes/oclc/204468.html

Choi, Y., Mai-Dalton, R.R.: The model of followers' responses to self-sacrificial leadership: an empirical test. Leadersh. Q. **10**(3), 397–421 (1999)

DeFrancisco, V.P., Palczewski, C.H.: Communicating Gender Diversity: A Critical Approach. SAGE Publications, Thousand Oaks (2007)

Eagly, A.H., Wood, W.: Explaining sex differences in social behavior: a meta-analytic perspective. Pers. Soc. Psychol. Bull. **17**(3), 306–315 (1991). http://doi.org/10.1177/0146167291173011

Khan, R., De Angeli, A.: The attractiveness stereotype in the evaluation of embodied conversational agents. In: Gross, T., Gulliksen, J., Kotzé, P., Oestreicher, L., Palanque, P., Prates, R.O., Winckler, M. (eds.) INTERACT 2009. LNCS, vol. 5726, pp. 85–97. Springer, Heidelberg (2009). Consulté à l'adresse http://link.springer.com/chapter/10.1007/978-3-642-03655-2_10

Kim, Y., Baylor, A., Shen, E.: Pedagogical agents as learning companions: the impact of agent emotion and gender. J. Comput. Assist. Learn. **23**(3), 220–234 (2007)

Lee, E.-J.: Effects of "gender" of the computer on informational social influence: the moderating role of task type. Int. J. Hum. Comput. Stud. **58**(4), 347–362 (2003)

Lee, K.M., Liao, K., Ryu, S.: Children's responses to computer-synthesized speech in educational media: gender consistency and gender similarity effects. Hum. Commun. Res. **33**(3), 310–329 (2007). http://doi.org/10.1111/j.1468-2958.2007.00301.x

Martin, C.L., Fabes, R.A., Evans, S.M., Wyman, H.: Social cognition on the playground: children's beliefs about playing with girls versus boys and their relations to sex segregated play. J. Soc. Pers. Relat. **16**(6), 751–771 (1999)

McCroskey, J.C., McCain, T.A.: The Measurement of Interpersonal Attraction (1972). Consulté à l'adresse http://eric.ed.gov/?id=ED071140

Miller, L., Budd, J.: The development of occupational sex-role stereotypes, occupational preferences and academic subject preferences in children at ages 8, 12 and 16. Educ. Psychol. **19**(1), 17–35 (1999). http://doi.org/10.1080/0144341990190102

Moreno, K., Person, N., Adcock, A., Van Eck, R., Jackson, T., Marineau, J.: Etiquette and efficacy in animated pedagogical agents: the role of stereotypes. In: Présenté à AAAI Symposium on Personalized Agents (2002)

Nass, C., Moon, Y., Green, N.: Are machines gender neutral? gender-stereotypic responses to computers with voices. J. Appl. Soc. Psychol. **27**(10), 864–876 (1997). http://doi.org/10.1111/j.1559-1816.1997.tb00275.x

Nosek, B.A., Smyth, F.L., Sriram, N., Lindner, N.M., Devos, T., Ayala, A., Greenwald, A.G.: National differences in gender–science stereotypes predict national sex differences in science and math achievement. Proc. Natl. Acad. Sci. **106**(26), 10593–10597 (2009). http://doi.org/10.1073/pnas.0809921106

Ozogul, G., Johnson, A.M., Atkinson, R.K., Reisslein, M.: Investigating the impact of pedagogical agent gender matching and learner choice on learning outcomes and perceptions. Comput. Educ. **67**, 36–50 (2013). http://doi.org/10.1016/j.compedu.2013.02.006

Pratt, J. A., Hauser, K., Ugray, Z., Patterson, O.: Looking at human–computer interface design: effects of ethnicity in computer agents. Interact. Comput. **19**(4), 512–523 (2007)

Reeves, B., Nass, C.I.: The Media Equation: How People Treat Computers, Television, and New Media Like Real People and Places. Center for the Study of Language and Information, Chicago (1996)

Ridgeway, C.L., Smith-Lovin, L.: The gender system and interaction. Ann. Rev. Sociol. **25**(1), 191–216 (1999). http://doi.org/10.1146/annurev.soc.25.1.191

Schroeder, N.L., Adesope, O.O.: Impacts of pedagogical agent gender in an accessible learning environment. J. Educ. Technol. Soc. **18**(4), 401–411 (2015)

Schunk, D.H.: Peer models and children's behavioral change. Rev. Educ. Res. **57**(2), 149–174 (1987). http://doi.org/10.3102/00346543057002149

Schunk, D.H.: self-efficacy and education and instruction. In: Maddux, J.E. (ed.) Self-Efficacy, Adaptation, and Adjustment, pp. 281–303. Springer, New York (1995). Consulté à l'adresse http://link.springer.com/chapter/10.1007/978-1-4419-6868-5_10

Shiban, Y., Schelhorn, I., Jobst, V., Hörnlein, A., Puppe, F., Pauli, P., Mühlberger, A.: The appearance effect: influences of virtual agent features on performance and motivation. Comput. Hum. Behav. **49**, 5–11 (2015). http://doi.org/10.1016/j.chb.2015.01.077

van der Meij, H., van der Meij, J., Harmsen, R.: Animated pedagogical agents effects on enhancing student motivation and learning in a science inquiry learning environment. Educ. Technol. Res. Dev. **63**(3), 381–403 (2015). http://doi.org/10.1007/s11423-015-9378-5

Yee, M., Brown, R.: The development of gender differentiation in young children. Br. J. Soc. Psychol. **33**(2), 183–196 (1994). http://doi.org/10.1111/j.2044-8309.1994.tb01017.x

Evaluating the Usability Using USE Questionnaire: Mindboard System Use Case

Tulio Vitor Machado Faria[✉], Matheus Pavanelli, and João Luiz Bernardes Jr.

PPgSI, University of Sao Paulo (USP),
St. Arlindo Bettio, 1000, Ermelino Matarazzo, Sao Paulo, SP, Brazil
tuliofaria@usp.br, tuliofaria@gmail.com

Abstract. Currently, children and young people have more access and contact with digital technologies and they are also more present in schools. The aim of this study is to validate a set of functionalities proposed and implemented in an educational system, evaluating its usability and how it can be improved. The web-based system, called Mindboard, aims to facilitate collaboration in class and beyond it. The experiment involved students during a brief summer course to evaluate its use regarding collaboration and usability. After the last class, students answered a USE questionnaire about the system's usability. This usability analysis showed that the system has, overall, good ease of use. Furthermore, the questions about positive points showed some advantages that we did not expect at first and lead us to interesting future works.

1 Introduction

Currently, children and young people have more access and contact with digital technologies. Government programs in many countries are also promoting the availability of mobile devices, computers and Internet access to students and teachers in public schools. Students are also bringing their own devices to classrooms more and more often, in a trend known as "Bring Your Own Device" (BYOD), notebooks, tablets and smartphones are more present and used in class, and are also used to study after class. These devices could enrich the learning experience no matter in which place or time it occurs and not being restricted to in-class periods [1]. According to the Horizon Report [2], worldwide education institutions are gaining increasing quality and availability of internet access in their dependencies. With all these facts, a large ecosystem to support the use of technologies during classes and after them is being formed.

In this scenario, the aim of this study is to validate a set of functionalities proposed in an collaborative educational system, designed and developed with the intention of facilitating collaboration in class and beyond it but this relies, of course, on teachers pedagogical use of the tool. We will focus, then, in evaluating the usability of the system and how these results could be used to improve future versions.

This web-based educational system, named Mindboard, had a prototype developed with the chosen set of features. These features include allowing teachers and students to collaborate with each other during classes and outside them.

P. Zaphiris and A. Ioannou (Eds.): LCT 2016, LNCS 9753, pp. 518–527, 2016.
DOI: 10.1007/978-3-319-39483-1_47

During classes, teachers can share slides and source-code (or other forms of textual content generated during the class) and answer student questions in real-time. On the other hand, students can receive all shared content, annotate it and choose whether to share their notes and with whom, ask questions, answer questions from other students or from the teacher and supply anonymous feedback to teachers about their understanding of the class at each moment. All this information is logged and accessible to students and teachers later. Figure 1 shows a screenshot of Mindboard during a class.

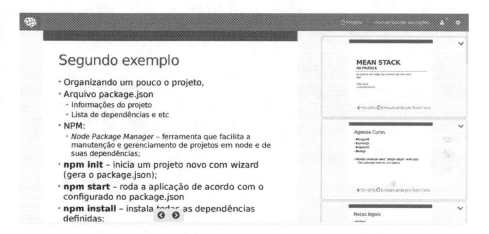

Fig. 1. Mindboard screen during class. Teachers can display a presentation (*left*) and the class history is shown (*right*) allowing to every user to jump to a specific point of the class.

Figure 2 shows another Mindboard feature: the display of textual content in real-time. In this example, the content was a Javascript source code.

Out of the class, users can watch classes again as video lessons, enriched with meta-data created during the class, such as the annotations, questions and answers, all synchronized with the content. During a programming online class, for instance, the video may show a piece of code and a note in the system is highlighted. Student can also ask questions and takes notes during online and asynchronous video lessons. The system can also be used in distance-only learning with these features.

After prototype development, Mindboard was used in an experiment with students in a summer course to evaluate its use regarding collaboration and usability.

In the next section we will talk about Computer-Supported Collaborative Learning and usability questionnaires. In Sect. 3 we discuss our experiment and in Sect. 4 we analyze its results. Later on, in Sect. 5 we leave our considerations and examine possible future work.

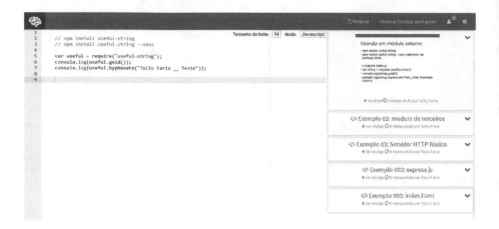

Fig. 2. Mindboard screen during class sharing textual contents in real-time. In this case, we are presenting a source code in Javascript.

2 Background: CSCL and Usability Questionnaires

This paper describes an experiment using a computer system called Mindboard. Since it is a collaborative system, we need to understand the context in which it is inserted. Later in this section we describe the usability questionnaires that we considered and the USE Questionnaire, which was selected for use during the experiment.

2.1 Computer Supported Collaborative Learning

Educational systems are computational tools that aid in one or more of the processes involved in teaching and learning activities [3]. Their uses could serve one or more activities, such learning management, simulation, tutoring, or as a mean of communication and information exchange. When an educational system is used collaboratively it can be named as Computer Supported Collaborative Learning (CSCL).

CSCL is a special case of Computer Supported Collaborative Work (CSCW). CSCW as a way to supply a possible demand of the work market as early as 1985. By that time, researchers already saw a new scenario emerging in which workers could do their jobs collaboratively and not necessarily in the same place [4].

Mindboard is considered a CSCL system since it allows users to identify their role, share information with each other and allowing the users to discuss with each other about the class subject.

2.2 Usability Questionnaires and the USE Questionnaire

Usability analysis can be performed in many different ways such as interviews, behavior analysis and through questionnaires. Because mostly of time considerations and ease of recordability and data extraction, we choose to use questionnaires to study Mindboard's usability. There are many already validated and well known questionnaires that could be used for this task. Some of those we considered for this work are described below.

The Questionnaire for User Interaction and Satisfaction (QUIS) is a tool created by a multidisciplinary team in human-computer interaction in lab of the Maryland University [5]. It is relatively long and attempts to break down usability in several specific aspects. In this work we opted for using a tool less focused in such details to get an overview of the question.

The questionnaire Computer System Usability Questionnaire (CSUQ) was designed by Jim Lewis and is licensed as public domain. It is reliable but it lacks for a standard [6].

The questionnaire Usefulness, Satisfaction and Ease of Use (USE), designed by Arnie Lund, has as its goal to analyze and summarize graphical interface usability using a model composed of three factors: usefulness, satisfaction and ease of use [7]. We believe these factors are the most important for our application, which should be used voluntarily, picked up quickly with as little training as possible or none whatsoever and be used transparently to avoid being an obstacle during classes or study time. It also gives an overview of these factors without going into very specific details in its questions, instead opting for providing ample opportunity for participants to make qualitative comments, which was our goal in this particular instance. It is also licensed as public domain and was the questionnaire we chose to use.

The USE questionnaire uses 27 questions with the Likert scale, with users answering questions split in 3 groups: Usefulness, Satisfaction and Ease of Use. For each question there is also a field where the user can enter some comment about it. At the end of the questionnaire, the user is prompted to name 3 positive and 3 negative points found in the system. In Sect. 3.1 we describe how we use and get the answers during the experiment and in Sect. 4 we discuss the results.

3   Experiment Description

The experiment was approved by USP's Ethics Committee with protocol number 39888114.0.0000.5390.

3.1   Setting up the Course

The experiment was conducted during a programming course in another institution named "MEAN Stack in Practice", in which students were introduced to web programming using NodeJS. The course was promoted online only, using local Facebook Groups about Information Technology and using the personal Facebook profile and contacts of one of the authors. After registration, we had 16 enrolled students, which were divided in two groups, one using the Mindboard system with 9 students and a control group not using it with 7 (the difference in the size of both groups happened mostly due to student schedules and other decisions outside our control).

The course took only four days and each group had classes in separate weeks. We conducted 3 classes in-locus and 1 online, using video-screen-casting. The course presented four main topics: MongoDB, ExpressJS, AngularJS and NodeJS. The main objective of the course was to introduce students to web programming using these technologies, allowing them to apply these subjects even during the classes. The two groups were exposed to the same content but in the Mindboard group we sent and presented all the material and source code using Mindboard, while the control group sometimes received class material via email. Students could access class content at any time after it was presented. Course registration was completely open to the public and only a small fee was charged to cover the costs of a coffee break during classes.

3.2   Data Collection

During the experiment a lot of usage and behavioral data was collected. Figure 3 shows the laboratory setup and how we captured the course in audio and video for posterior analysis. The web-cam used was a Logitech C920 and we captured the video in a resolution of 720p. These video records were used to count collaborations between students and with the teacher. We also used a survey to ask how the students collaborated with each other out of the classroom and without using Mindboard in both groups and to get a general idea how frequent this collaboration was. In the group that used Mindboard we also logged usage data using the system. After the last day of course, we presented participants in the Mindboard group with the USE questionnaire to inquire about the system's usability. Google Forms was used as the medium for all questionnaires and surveys.

Fig. 3. Laboratory capture setup. The left image shows the lab arrangement during classes and on the right shows the position of the camera used to capture the experiment for posterior analysis.

4   Results

The experiment occurred during the planned period as expected, but we had some problems with the collected usage data. The main problem that we encountered was the lack of a good amount of participants. We expected at first around 40 students split in two equal groups, but we had 16 (7 students in the first group and 9 in the second one). When we combine this fact with the short duration of the course, we ended up collecting a relatively small amount of usage data for Mindboard, compared to what we planned. Another fact that created a bias in our experiment was that, in this small universe of users, some groups of students already knew each other, what led to collaboration between them more naturally. Collaboration was an important metric in the analysis of Mindboard because it had been designed to aid mainly in this activity. Finally, collaborations were counted using the audio and video streams recorded during classes, but only during the analysis did we discover that the audio was unusable (the room was too large to be captured using only one microphone). Another problem we faced was related to the use of a single camera, which was occluded in certain moments. These factors led to our collaboration count having less quantitative importance than we expected at first and to a more careful analysis of the qualitative feedback supplied by students (and, of course, to the USE questionnaire to evaluate Mindboard's usability).

With those caveats in mind, the number of interactions per student recorded in both Mindboard's group and the control group was approximately the same. Qualitative analysis of these interactions, however, considering mostly student feedback and also, to a smaller degree, teacher feedback, suggests that in the control group, between 20 % and 30 % of interactions occurred because of difficulties in seeing the content being projected on a screen during classes, particularly when showing code, while in the Mindboard group there were no instances of this problem since students could and did follow content in their own devices. Thus the Mindboard group reported having more interactions of higher quality, collaborating and discussing about the content itself instead trying to decode it from what was projected. Another situation in which we detected a lot of interactions of little relevance in the control group was when the teacher alternated between source code files during class. In this kind of situation, one student or another always asked to go back to the last file, while others were already thinking about the new file, which caused unproductive interruptions during classes and appeared to have a negative impact on the stream of thought for both teacher and students. The feature that allows students to go back and forth in content and review it as they wish in their own device during classes helped many students in this sort of situation.

Students also reported that they suffered less with lack of attention using Mindboard to navigate within the content than in conventional classes. Finally, we had a couple students with moderate visual impairment who were quite thankful and excited about the system for facilitating their access to the content during classes (Mindboard has options to control parameters such as font size that help in this situation, but we confess we had not foreseen this advantage in accessibility before the experiment since it was not our primary focus).

Analyzing the USE Questionnaire data we discovered some interesting things. Regarding the system's usefulness, Mindboard averaged 5.6 out of 7. Table 1 shows each question with its average score.

Table 1. Usefulness questions

Usefulness questions:	Score:
It helps me be more effective	5,5
It helps me be more productive	5,4
It is useful	6,3
It gives me more control over the activities in my life	6,5
It makes the things I want to accomplish easier to get done	5,4
It meets my needs	5,3
It does everything I would expect it to do	4,8
Usefulness score:	5,6

The mean score of 5.6 suggests that students considered the system with a good level of utility. The lowest score in this set of questions is about whether the system does everything that students expect it to do. We believe this occurred because many students would like to see more specific features in the system, such as, some way to integrate the real time text sharing with an Integrated Development Environment (which was specifically mentioned in the comment section of this question).

The set of questions about Ease of Use aims to measure the experience of the user with the system. Mindboard scored well in this aspect too, with a mean of 5.76 of 7. Table 2 shows each question and its average score. The question with the highest score was about whether the user could easily learn how to use it without instructions, with a score of 6.2.

In the set of questions related to user satisfaction, Mindboard also scored well, with an average of 5.7 out of 7. Table 3 shows each question's score. The question with the highest score was about whether the user could easily remember how to use the system, with a score of 6.7. Considered along with the answers showing high learnability discussed above this shows that Mindboard is both easy to learn without instructions and easy to use without much effort once its learned. Because the system is designed for use in education, these aspect of high learnability and memorability are considered very important (even more than efficiency and more than they would be for production software) [8], both to encourage users to adopt the system and so that its use does not take attention away from the learning process.

Besides these scores and the comments for each question, the USE Questionnaire has one feature that was very useful for our analysis of Mindboard:

Table 2. Ease of use questions

Ease of use questions:	Score:
It is easy to use	5.8
It is simple to use	6.1
It is user friendly	5.8
It requires the fewest steps possible to accomplish what I want to do with it	5.8
It is flexible	5.4
I can use it without written instructions	6.2
I don't notice any inconsistencies as I use it	5.2
Both occasional and regular users would like it	6.0
I can recover from mistakes quickly and easily	5.3
I can use it successfully every time	6.0
Ease of use score:	5.76

Table 3. Satisfaction questions

Satisfaction questions:	Score:
I learned to use it quickly	6.3
I easily remember how to use it	6.7
It is easy to learn to use it	6.6
I quickly became skillful with it	6.2
I am satisfied with it	6.0
I would recommend it to a friend	6.3
It is fun to use	5.7
It works the way I want it to work	5.3
It is wonderful	5.1
I feel I need to have it	5.4
It is pleasant to use	5.3
Satisfaction score:	5.9

it asks participants about the positive and negatives points of the system. It may look like a simple question, but the results of it were quite important for us in gathering qualitative feedback, explaining some of the scores and to collect suggestions to improve the system or for future features.

The positive points that were mentioned most often were related to ease of use and learning and having a friendly, intuitive and functional user interface. Many other comments mentioned the real-time content sharing as an important positive point as well as the integration with between annotations and video.

Negative points included complaints about the long time it took to load the system (because we only found out too late, already during the experiment, that we would only have internet access with rather low bandwidth). Other negative points mentioned were related to integration with other systems, such as Integrated Development Environments (IDE) and the lack of a real-time chat. After this experiment, we do have plans to perhaps include IDE support in future versions, even if it is an improvement very specific to a particular area of teaching. Regarding chat, however, we designed Mindboard with the intent of being used along with other learning management systems already adopted by institutions, not to replace them, and many of these systems already have support to several features that we consider very interesting but do not plan to replicate, such as real-time chat, discussion forums etc. During the experiment, however, we opted to use Mindboard on its own, which explains this lack of certain features many users commented on.

Based on the above, we consider these 3 groups of questions and, particularly, the comments after each question and the positive and negative points at the end of the questionnaire provided us with a very good opportunity to analyze our system's usability and to help us find where we could improve it. Having the qualitative comments to rely upon meant that even though USE's questions were not as numerous and specific as, for instance, those in QUIS, we could still find very specific positive and negative aspects of the system, but it was made less complex by the fact that we only had a relatively small sample size. If we had to analyze hundreds of questionnaires, it would likely be easier to dispense with so many comments, which are more difficult to treat than the numeric answer data, and instead have more and more specific questions.

5   Conclusion

Except for some problems we had with the small amount of usage data collected, the experiment could show us some interesting things about Mindboard's utility and ease of use of Mindboard in and out of classes. The USE Questionnaire proved to be the right choice for our context as well, providing us with a lot of information about which aspects of the system we could improve and with the collections of positive and negative points so we can create a better version of Mindboard. The qualitative comments encouraged by USE were very important for us and our amount of participants, but we believe that they would be considerably more difficult to treat if we had a much larger sample, for instance in the hundreds.

As future work, we would like to conduct more experiments so we can capture more data. The main thing we would like to change is the size of the class. We plan on running the next experiment in two classes, each with 40 to 60 students, and for a longer period of time instead of only 4 classes (one of which was online only). We also plan to test the system with more teachers, not only more students. Finally, we will discard the idea of trying to record the sound of interactions and attempt to work with them only through a combination of video records and self-reporting. Regarding video, we intend to record it with multiple cameras (at least two) to reduce the problem of occlusion.

For the next versions of Mindboard we plan to add a new set of features, such as: integrate it with development environments (for programming classes) and allow users to annotate with drawings instead of only with text. We also plan to show examples of integration between Mindboard and other systems already used in education, such as Moodle [9].

Acknowledgments. Authors would like to thank CAPES - Brazilian Federal Agency for Support and Evaluation of Graduate Education within the Ministry of Education of Brazil for financing the scholarship that supported this work.

References

1. Johnson, L., Adams, S., Cummins, M.: The NMC Horizon Report, 2014 K-12 Edn. The New Media Consortium, Texas, Austin (2014)
2. Johnson, L., Adams, S., Cummins, M.: The NMC Horizon Report: 2012 Higher, Education edn. The New Media Consortium, Texas, Austin (2012)
3. Tchounikine, P.: Computer Science and Educational Software Design. Springer, Heidelberg (2011). http://link.springer.com/10.1007/978-3-642-20003-8
4. Greif, I.: Computer-Supported Cooperative Work: A Book of Readings. Morgan Kaufmann Publishers, San Mateo (1988)
5. Norman, K., Shneiderman, B., Harper, B.: QUIS.: The Questionnaire for User Interaction Satisfaction (1987). www.cs.umd.edu/hcil/quis/
6. Lewis, J.R.: IBM computer usability satisfaction questionnaires: psychometric evaluation and instructions for use. Int. J. Hum.-Comput. Interact. **7**(1), 57–78 (1995)
7. Lund, M.: Measuring Usability with the USE Questionnaire (2001). http://www.stcsig.org/usability/newsletter/0110_measuring_with_use.html
8. Shneiderman, B.: Designing the User Interface: Strategies for Effective Human-Computer Interaction. Addison-Wesley, Reading (1998)
9. Moodle. http://moodle.org

Tomorrow's On-Board Learning System (TOOLS)

Manuel Oliveira[1(✉)], Joao Costa[2], and Hans Torvatn[1]

[1] Sintef, Technology and Society, S.P. Andersensv. 5, 7465 Trondheim, Norway
{manuel.oliveira, hans.torvatn}@sintef.no
[2] HighSkillz, London, UK
joao.costa@highskillz.com

Abstract. Efficient maritime training is important to build a competent workforce of seafarers, able to operate safe, following rules and regulations. The most widely used methods of onboard training is the so called Computer Based Training (CBT), which simply is a set of electronic lectures and multiple choice tests afterwards. While widely used this method has been criticized for being individualistic, difficult to apply in a practical setting, boring and demotivating for learning. Alternative methods have not been developed, partly because of the dominance of the CBT method, but also because bandwidth and connectivity issues for ships have restricted both use of more interactive and internet based tools. The Tomorrow's onboard learning system (TOOLS) was a project to research and develop an innovative game-based learning platform for on-board training, along with a course on energy efficiency. The chosen topic was of keen interest to the ship owners that took part of the project, aiming to achieve fuel savings whilst reducing the impact on the environment. The paper describes the TOOLS platform, the course developed and the evaluation results from two vessels, one from each participating shipping company.

Keywords: Maritime training · Serious games · Onboard training

1 Introduction

A competent workforce implies more than knowing, but being capable of applying knowledge effectively and efficiently within the work context. Consequently, talent management, including training and education is a key element to success in any industry today, including the maritime industry. There is little disagreement on this, and there exists a plethora of training centres, of formal certificates as well as on-board training systems in the form of Computer Based Training (CBT). Further, ship-owners as well as vetting organizations, certificate providers, port authorities, and other agencies inspect and control actual work practice on-board. The seafarers are required to follow a long list of procedures and standards, in order to regulate work practice. It is acknowledged that the standard work practice is in general more than sufficient to ensure safe and agreed upon transportation of goods and people. However, in reality, what exists are erroneous and potentially dangerous work practice that can destroy the reputation of responsible ship owners, be costly to the shipping company due to fines

© Springer International Publishing Switzerland 2016
P. Zaphiris and A. Ioannou (Eds.): LCT 2016, LNCS 9753, pp. 528–538, 2016.
DOI: 10.1007/978-3-319-39483-1_48

and necessary improvement work, be environmentally un-friendly and dangerous. In short there is a need for improving the competence of the workforce even though the appropriate knowledge acquisition occurs.

Experience in the maritime industry and research pivoting around these topics, indicates that there is a gap between so-called intended and actual work practice among the officers on board (i.e. [3]). While officers seem to be familiar with the correct and preferred work routines given in steering documentation, training manuals, engine manuals and company policy, they sometimes use alternative work practices in their daily work on board. Unfortunately, since work operations at sea are quite risky, wrong or insufficient, work practice may lead to serious incidents. In addition, most department managers at sea such as the captains or other senior officers, do not have managerial training or education, with the result that on-board management style is left to each individual and varies substantially from vessel to vessel or from one sailing period to another [7].

This paper describes the Tomorrow's on-board learning system (TOOLS) platform, an attempt to improve the training methods by developing new game based methods intended as a substitution to one of the more popular on-board training methods. As part of the research work, a course for energy efficiency was developed that was composed of two episodes, with distinct intended learning outcomes. The rest of the paper is structured as follows: Sect. 2 describes current training practice, strengths and weaknesses, Sect. 3 and Sect. 4 describe the TOOLS platform and game respectively, both resulting from the co-design activities; Sect. 5 describes two formative evaluation studies carried out and finally conclusions are summarized in Sect. 6.

2   Current Onboard Training Practices

Several training methods are in wide spread use in the maritime sector today; training centers in-house or externally delivering training course, on-board computer based training (CBT), simulator training (usually delivered by external training centers specializing in this), video based training and of course drill and training on board. The methods fall into two big categories: On-board an on-shore. The off-shore methods are training centers and simulation centers, the on-board are drills and training, video based lectures and CBTs. The off-shore methods are more expensive and less flexible than the on-shore, because on-boards require travel and subsistence costs as well as a need for planning the training.

As a relatively cheap and flexible on-board training method CBTs have become quite popular. CBT can cover all topics, does not require the seafarer to go anywhere and the infrastructure required is simply a PC and the CBT course itself on a disk from the CBT provider. No connectivity to anything is required, which has been important because of low bandwidth and high prizes of satellite connectivity for ships. The seafarer is put in front of the computer and starts the CBT program, which is an old fashioned e-learning module. It is a lecture based teaching method, in the CBT the seafarer reads a text, or listens to a text spoken to him if it is a modern version and answers a multiple choice questionnaire based on this text. The course then assesses a total score and tells the seafarer if he/she has passed the text or not. The CBT provider logs the use and if certificates are needed provides this.[1] However, the CBT training programs have not fully handled the transition from training sessions to actual work practice and they have the following limitations:

- The learning environment on board does not support experiential learning;
- Operational mistakes are costly, but there is no safe environment for experimentation;
- CBTS are individual and ignores social learning and community building
- There is no support for reflection, thus internalization of knowledge does not take place;
- A necessary characteristic of learning is motivation and the current delivery mechanisms for on board training are boring, which leads to low engagement and consequently poor learning.

2.1   Looking for New Training Methods

In 2012 two medium sized Norwegian ship owners wanted to try to do something different than CBTs working jointly with the contract research agency SINTEF. In an earlier collaborative R&D project (ended 2009) on bureaucracy and reporting the gap between theory and practice had been clearly exposed. In a survey to the seafarers (deck officers) it was discovered that more than a third of the officers reported breaking company procedures regulating use of auxiliary engine (several instances) and other safety and environmentally issues to a lesser degree [3]. This was the acknowledged breach of procedures which was admitted in a survey, and the possibility of underreporting such breaches was of course quite large.

Additional use of engines are both costly and environmentally unfriendly[2]. The same goes for using wrong kind of fuel, another type of error often seen. Avoiding excessive use of engines, and thus fuel, will lower costs as well as avoid pollution and emissions. The Transpacific Stabilization agreement, a research and discussion forum of major ocean container shipping lines that serve the transpacific trade in both directions between Asia and the USA states that: "*Fuel accounts for 60 % or more of total voyage operating costs for a typical scheduled container service. Even small changes in fuel costs have dramatic impacts on service levels and/or carrier balance sheets.*"[3] Thus, the breach of procedures had impact.

Not satisfied with its current training regime nor its operational effectiveness the shipping companies wanted to work with SINTEF on the possibility of creating improved training procedures that was better suited to bridge the gap between theory and practice, and the TOOLS project was created.

---

[1] Exact testing and certification procedures vary. They can be relatively complex.

[2] While not using enough when necessary creates a safety hazard.

[3] http://www.tsacarriers.org/fs_bunker.html.

2.2   The Seafarers Use and Assessment of Training Methods

As part of the project a survey was carried out among the officers of two shipping companies participating in the TOOLS project. The surveys were distributed to each ship be email, printed out onboard, answered and sent back by post. This method was chosen because it was relatively easy to reach all seafarers on board and no email lists of respondents were needed neither did the seafarers need to be on-line to answer the questionnaire. The respondents were all officers in all ships in the two companies. A total of 374 answers were received from 750 possible respondents, a response rate of 50.

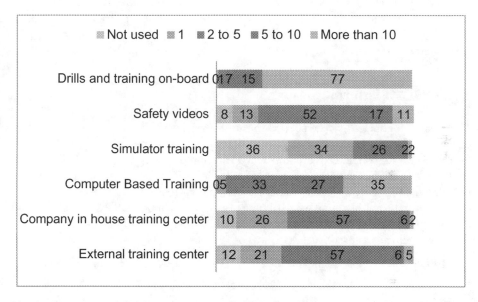

Fig. 1. Frequency of training methods in TOOLS participating companies, last 12 months, N = 374.

From Fig. 1 we can see that during a year the typical seafarer (officer) is subject to several training sessions. The method most frequently used is drills and trainings on-board, 77 % did that more than 10 times per year. CBT was the runner up in frequency, 34 % had more than 10 exposures to this, an additional 27 between 6 and 10 times. The least frequent method was simulator training, 36 % of the officers had not done this, and another 34 done it once.

Looking at the usefulness of the training as assessed by the seafarers we found that it was in general perceived as relevant and useful. Looking only at the on-board training we find that 68 % perceived on-board drills as very useful, 35 the same for safety videos and 30 % for CBTs. The most practical training was the most popular, but all training forms were viewed as useful. The problem is of course that questions like this does not measure learning outcome, only "happiness" with the training.

Since CBTs was of particular interest to the shipping companies some additional questions were asked on this. It was found that CBT training was done individually (79 % always did CBTs alone), and most of the seafarers (75 %) had to repeat the course before passing exam. Results from CBTs were sometimes discussed (61 %) but 32 % rarely or never discussed them. CBT is an individual training form.

One of the reasons for using CBTs has been concerns about connectivity and the need for additional devices for conducting training. We therefore surveyed the actual frequency of personal devices that could be employed for training and the use of internet for personal reasons. We found that 93 % had personal PCs (approximately half had either tabled and or smart phone) 86 % claimed to have local wireless connected to internet at all times, and Facebook was in daily usage by 76 % of the sailors. Overall we concluded that the infrastructure for doing a gamebased training platform with internet connectivity was in place.

3   TOOLS Platform

The survey conducted gave credence to the grievance of both the ship owner companies and seafarers that current on-board training solutions based on CBT failed miserably to support effective competence development. However, the survey also confirms that all stakeholders consider the relevance of on-board training, thus it is a need that is not being successfully addressed from current service providers. As documented in relevant literature e.g.: [6], namely in communities related to learning and technology enhanced learning, there are several limitations to both the process and delivery mechanisms used, such as:

1. **Motivation.** The key complaint for both the seafarers and the shipping companies is the failure of content to engage successfully, thus a pre-requisite for learning is not met [5];
2. **Delivery mode.** Learning content is based on the tell premise, using non-interactive content, which studies (e.g.: [6]) show such delivery modes yield the lowest form of retention;
3. **Shallow learning.** The didactical design is poor, with the focus on the meeting the minimal required to support the content certification. There is little consideration to the actual return on learning (ROL), thus what the seafarer acquires in terms of knowledge and their ability to apply the competence in the appropriate time and attitude.
4. **One size fits all.** Learning is not personalized to the particular needs of the seafarer, thus achieving flow [2] is difficult as one-size-fits-all does not accommodate the differences between each individual.

The above are an illustrative sample of the limitations of the existing on-board training solutions, which as put forth by Aldrich [1] resembles fast food where the nutritional value is low, in particular when compared to the well balanced diet of home-made food.

Building upon the recognized challenges of onboard training, the TOOLS project aimed to research and develop an innovative on-board training solution that is game-based learning, focused on the effective and efficient competence development of the seafarers. The overall process is depicted in Fig. 2, which starts with the login of the seafarer onto the TOOLS platform either with a dedicated account or with a social account, such as facebook or linkedin.

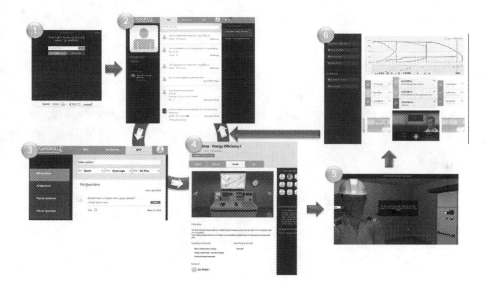

Fig. 2. TOOLS platform and learning process

Once successfully signed-in, the seafarer has three distinct options to consider:

- **Wall (step 2).** This section of the platform consists of a social activity line where the seafarer may publish their thoughts and share them with the students in the same classroom and their friends. The platform also publishes events concerning the activities of the seafarer.
- **Q&A (step 3).** This section of the platform consists of questions and answers shared within the community of seafarers across the fleet. The seafarers can pose questions, search and rate answers, with the one posing the question being responsible for overseeing the responses, deciding when the question was answered by deciding on best answer.
- **Courses (step 4).** This section of the platform contains all the courses that the seafarer has been engaged with and subscribed to. For each course, the seafarer has an atypical course description, including the break-down into lessons, the additional seafarers that have taken or are taking the course and recommended reading. In addition, the seafarer can access the detailed post-action review of their own past sessions and that of other seafarers, having the capability of searching best performances.

All the steps 2, 3 and 4, are interchangeable and not a linear process with precedence between the different steps. Step 5 corresponds to when a seafarer engages with a course, which provides them a believable immersive context where they need to make cognitive decisions (Sect. 4). After the session, the seafarer is presented with a detailed post-action review (step 6) where they are presented with 3 distinct layers:

- **Performance Curves.** The layer presents the performance curves depicting the competence (e.g.: trust building, decision making, etc.) of the seafarer at each sampling interval. These curves are determined by equations based on observable behavior indicators;
- **Events.** The layer indicates the events captured during the engagement with the session, which are correlated to the performance. Atypical events correspond to achieving particular objectives, learning outcomes, mistake committed, etc.
- **Context.** The layer presents snapshots taken at given intervals, which provide the seafarers with an important contextualization for both the performance measurements and events.

4   TOOLS Serious Game

The TOOLS platform is a game-based learning platform where the courses provide experiential learning through the engagement of believable contexts where the seafarers are required to make decisions.

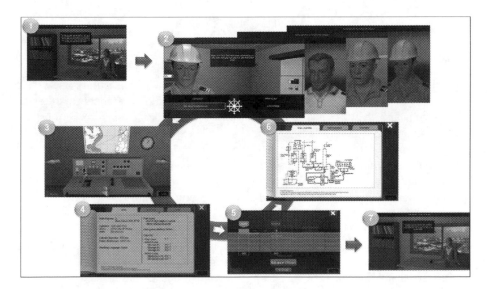

Fig. 3. TOOLS learning content

The diagram of Fig. 3 reflect the interaction cycle with the course on energy efficiency, consisting of two main lessons:

- **Emission Control Area (ECA).** The learning of the outcome of the lesson is to have the seafarer to determine the crucial point in time when to switch from high sulfur fuel to low sulfur fuel to reduce the impact of emissions when entering a ECA, aligned with what regulations permit. The decision needs to take into account the fuel in the engine and the rate of consumption, thus calculating how long it takes to switch effectively the fuel.
- **Fuel Efficiency.** The intended learning outcome is to achieve the optimal fuel efficiency whilst in port. A seafarer needs to determine how many auxiliary engines to have in operation taking into account the necessary power consumption depending on the activities taking place.

Both lessons were co-created with multiple stakeholders, involving in addition of the development team, seafarers, management, subject matter experts and experienced instructors. The development process was iterative with frequent releases for testing the concepts and instructional design of the course. As important to the intended learning outcomes, the lessons of the course have-inbuilt pitfalls indicative of poor work practice, thus the seafarer needs to apply critical thinking and follow procedure.

As illustrated in steps 2–6 of Fig. 3, the seafarer engages in dialogue (step 2) with multiple characters, from higher and lower ranking officers. The higher ranking officers provide orders, which essentially corresponds to guiding the seafarer in what goals to achieve in a step-wise manner. However, the use of lower ranking officers facilitated the abstraction to the particulars of a shipping vessel since evidence demonstrated a signification absence of layout and design standardization. Consequently, the seafarer would decide what to action to take and instruct their team mate to carry it out. The dialogue was carefully crafted to encourage particular behaviours, such as to always ask instead of making assumptions, to demonstrate principles of leadership by communicating well and building rapport with the remainder crew members, and ensure that lower ranking officers understand and commit to the given orders. Due to the prominence of Filipinos in the seafarer population, the dialogue was carefully created to eliminate potential cultural stereotypes.

In addition to the dialogue interaction, the seafarers is required to consult with the engine room log book (step 4), specifications of the vessel (step 6) and the company procedures. Both are actions that are seldom followed by seafarers, who usually follow whatever is the existing practice onboard even if wrong. This was another key learning outcome designed into the course's lessons as a result of the co-design activities.

Finally, in step 5, the seafarer is given the chance of controlling how time is governed thus allowing real-time for decision making whilst permitting to advance time to verify the outcomes of particular decisions.

Steps 1 and 7 correspond respectively to in-game briefing and debriefing of the course. Although the seafarer is given a detailed post-action review, it is important to include in-game debriefing where the human resource manager can provide relevant feedback to the seafarer.

5   Evaluation Study

For the formative evaluation of the TOOLS platform, two studies were carried out with population of seafarers from two different shipping vessels, belonging to two different shipping companies (Grieg Star and KGJS). However, both consisted of predominately Filipino population. To support the evaluation, both quantitative and qualitative measures using questionnaires, which were complemented by observational studies involving two facilitators, one involving a member of the development team and another being an occupational psychologist.

A total of 37 seafarers, 13 from Grieg Star and 24 from KGJS, took part of the two studies. The setup used was to have a server installed onboard with two laptops for seafarers to engage with the course on energy efficiency. For this reason, only two seafarers at a time would take part of the study as shown in the photograph of Fig. 4.

Fig. 4. Evaluation session involving officers onboard

One questionnaire was used to capture user satisfaction and it was designed with two distinct parts, the first part consisted of three questions with 7-point likert scale (Fig. 5), ranging from "not at all" to "strongly agree"; the second part consisted of an additional three open-ended questions (Fig. 6).

> Did you enjoy playing the training game?
> Would you play it again if you had the time?
> Do you think you know more about energy efficiency after playing the game?

Fig. 5. Questions based on 7 point likert scale

The second questionnaire was to measure usability, thus the standard System Usability Scale (SUS) was used without modification, entailing the 10 questions each with a 5-point response.

> What did you like?
> What would you change?
> Anything else you want to share with the development team?

Fig. 6. Qualitative open-ended questions

The seafarers would engage with the platform and asked to do the course on energy efficiency. Once they completed the course, they were asked to complete both the questionnaires on user satisfaction and usability. There was no assistance or clarification provided to the seafarers, which impacted negatively the SUS score due to seafarers not being English native speakers [4].

As a result of the user satisfaction questionnaire, 78 % enjoyed the course, 80 % would play again if they had the time and finally 81 % reported knowing more about energy efficiency. Although the usability questionnaire yielded an average SUS score of 60, which is below the recommended 68, there was a clear distinction between two groups of the seafarer population. A third of the population averaged a score of 71, whilst two thirds consistently scored 50 with a standard deviation of 3.5.

6   Conclusions

The paper presented the TOOLS game-based learning platform as an innovative solution to support the competence development of seafarers. Although the use of serious games for training and development of competences is not novel, their use in the maritime sector has been limited with the incumbent service providers remaining limited to traditional CBTs.

The solution was co-created with multiple stakeholders within two shipping companies concerned with addressing the evidenced gap between the traditional training and the demonstrable on-board work practices. The results from summative evaluation have yielded very promising results, with seafarers having a very high acceptance. Although the SUS questionnaire was used with less promising results, there was clear improvements from one study to another as improvements were made to the TOOLS platform based on the feedback collated. An important factor that had a negative impact on the SUS scores is based on the fact that the seafarer population was not native English speakers. In addition, the poor digital literacy of the seafarers created significant barriers to usability.

Acknowledgments. The authors would like to thank the funding of the TOOLS project from the national Norwegian research council.

References

1. Aldrich, C.: The Complete Guide to Simulations and Serious Games: How the Most Valuable Content Will be Created in the Age Beyond Gutenberg to Google. Jossey Bas, San Francisco (2009)
2. Csikszentmihalyi, M.: Flow: The psychology of Optimal Experience. Harper & Row, New York (1990)
3. Lamvik, G.M., Wahl, A.M., Buvik, M.P.: Professional culture, work practice and reliable operations in shipping. In: Briš, R., Martorell, S. (eds.) Reliability. Risk and Safety. Taylor & Frances Group, London (2010)
4. Lewis, J.R., Sauro, J.: The factor structure of the system usability scale. In: Kurosu, M. (ed.) HCD 2009. LNCS, vol. 5619, pp. 94–103. Springer, Heidelberg (2009)
5. Mahanta, D., Ahmed, M.: e-Learning objectives, methodologies, tools and its limitation. Int. J. Innov. Technol. Explor. Eng. (IJITEE) 2(1), 2278–3075 (2012)
6. Noesgaard, S., Ørngreen, R.: The effectiveness of e-Learning: an explorative and integrative review of the definitions, methodologies and factors that promote e-Learning effectiveness. Electron. J. e-Learn. 13(4), 278–290 (2015)
7. Oltedal, H.A., Tvedt, S.D.: Filipino cadets' attitudes and expectations to-wards safety in work at sea. In: Scandinavian Maritime Conference, 28–29 November 2012 (2012)

Adaptable and Adaptive Human-Computer Interface to Recommend Learning Objects from Repositories

Thomas Quiroz, Oscar M. Salazar, and Demetrio A. Ovalle(⊠)

Universidad Nacional de Colombia, Sede Medellín, Medellín, Colombia
{tquirozv,omsalazaro,dovalle}@unal.edu.co

Abstract. In the last decades, some useful contributions have occurred to human-computer interfaces and e-learning system developments such as adaptation, personalization, ontological modeling, as well as, learning object repositories. The aim of this paper is to present the advantages of integrating ontologies as knowledge representation scheme in order to support adaptable and adaptive functionalities that can be offered by a human-computer interface when recommending LOs from Repositories. A human-computer interface model is proposed which is composed of several modules that allow deploying adaptable and adaptive functionalities such as the following: (1) store and retrieving of LOs from repositories, (2) representation of events by learners within the GUI, (3) performing of inferences through ontological reasoned, (4) adaptation of the GUI for each of the users' profiles and (5) monitoring of all changes made by the user on the GUI and storing of them in the system database for further processing. In order to validate the model a prototype was built and tested through a case study. Results obtained demonstrate the effectiveness of the proposed human-computer interface model which combines adaptability along with adaptive characteristics.

Keywords: Human-computer interfaces · Personalization · Adaptable and adaptive systems · Ontologies · Learning objects (LO) · LO repositories

1 Introduction

Nowadays, the access to a large amount of information is easier through the Web that allows data and knowledge repositories to be connected among them. However, it becomes a great challenge for people wishing to learn in a virtual way to assimilate this knowledge since it does not always fit with their learning styles, preferences, or even considering inappropriate ways of deployment of these digital educational resources.

Personalized Adaptive interfaces currently play a very important role in virtual learning environments since they seek to adapt the presentation and display of educational content, such as learning objects (LO), through the preferences, needs and cognitive characteristics of the students. According to Lopez [1] it should be distinguished between adaptability and adaptivity in user interfaces. Within an adaptable interface the user is who explicitly adapts the interface so that it fits their preferences and features. For example, window managers can allow the user to change the settings

© Springer International Publishing Switzerland 2016
P. Zaphiris and A. Ioannou (Eds.): LCT 2016, LNCS 9753, pp. 539–549, 2016.
DOI: 10.1007/978-3-319-39483-1_49

on the appearance of the desktop with respect to colors, fonts, desktop background or behavior of some of its components. In contrast, on an adaptive interface the same system is the responsible actor for activating the actions necessary to perform the adaptation. Thus for instance when a word processor automatically detects a grammatical error, the same processor marks it or even edits it without human intervention. Personalized Adaptive interfaces can then be defined as those parameters of the interface that automatically adapt to the characteristics of the users [2], allowing the improvement of the satisfaction and the permanence of the user interacting with the application on its computer, personal device or on the web site. Current trends are toward the web information retrieval systems allowing adapting results using personalized adaptive interfaces that consider the properties and settings of the users [3, 4].

The aim of this paper is to present the advantages of integrating ontologies as knowledge representation scheme in order to support adaptable and adaptive functionalities that can be offered by a human-computer interface known as GUI (graphical user interface) when recommending Learning Objects (LO) from Repositories. We propose a GUI model and develop a prototype which is composed of several modules that allow deploying adaptable and adaptive functionalities.

The rest of the paper is organized as follows: Sect. 2 presents the conceptual framework of this research. Section 3 reviews some related works concerning adaptable and adaptive interfaces. Section 4 describes the proposed model. Section 5 offers the model implementation and validation of the proposed model. Finally, the main conclusions and future research directions are presented in Sect. 6.

2   Conceptual Framework

This section provides main definitions used in this research work such as adaptable vs adaptive interfaces, learning objects, repositories, ontologies, among others.

2.1   Adaptable vs. Adaptive Interfaces

Human-computer interfaces have evolved in last decades from predominantly textual interfaces to more complex interfaces using multimodal interaction (e.g. communication by natural modes such as speech, handwriting, etc.). In addition, it is important to distinguish between adaptability and adaptivity [5, 6] in graphical user interfaces (GUI). An adaptable GUI allows users to explicitly customize several aspects of the interface so that he/she can fit its preferences and needs [7]. On the other hand, when using an adaptive GUI the system activates itself the actions necessary to perform the adaptation [8].

2.2   Ontologies

Ontologies can be defined as a formal representation of a particular domain using a well-defined methodology that allows the representation of the domain entities and the relationships existing among them [9]. Based on this, it is important to generate a formal representation of the adaptive learning course structure, in order to make inferences and generate recommendations for improving the learning process. Similarly, designing formal representations of a specific domain allows having readable and reusable information for computers and intelligent systems [10].

2.3 Learning Objects, Repositories and Federations

According to the IEEE, a LO can be defined as a digital entity involving educational design characteristics. Each LO can be used, reused or referenced during computer-supported learning processes, aiming at generating knowledge and competences based on student's needs [11, 12]. LOs have functional requirements such as accessibility, reuse, and interoperability. The concept of LO requires understanding of how people learn, since this issue directly affects the LO design in each of its three dimensions: pedagogical, didactic, and technological. In addition, LOs have metadata that describe and identify the educational resources involved and facilitate their searching and retrieval. LORs, composed of thousands of LOs, can be defined as specialized digital libraries storing several types of resources heterogeneous, are currently being used in various e-learning environments and belong mainly to educational institutions [13].

Federation of LORs serve to provide educational applications of uniform administration in order to search, retrieve and access specific LO contents available in whatever of LOR groups [14].

3 Related Works

This section examines some related research works that focus on adaptable and adaptive interfaces seeking to contrast the advantages and disadvantages of each work.

Letsu-Dake and Ntuen [5] design an adaptive interface for controlling a complex system where the user has to monitor an industrial process that has multiple variables. The main function of the adaptive interface is to help the user to maintain proper operation of the system by providing some warnings and alerts, graphics, identification of damaged components, among others. To verify the impact of the adaptive interface and its components authors compare the performance (measured in terms of the times the system needs to reach the goal) of two groups of users, one using the system with the adaptive interface and the other group using the system without adaptive interface.

Park and Han [6] develop a research about the effects of a help provided by an adaptive interface and user control through adapting menus. They use a variety of interface prototypes to validate the impact of the adaptation provided by the system. Each interface is distinguished by the amount of control of the user or system in the adaptation of the interface. Authors measure performance and satisfaction of the user with each of the interfaces. Another measured variable is the time that the user takes to find a specific option; his/her perceived efficiency, and user preferences on interfaces regarding menus.

Shakshuki et al. [7] present a distributed system based on software agents for obtaining and monitoring health metrics in real time. These metrics consider pulse, blood oxygenation or any other metric that can be monitored through the use of sensors. In addition, the system incorporates learning techniques for the deployment of an adaptive interface that accommodates the features of system users (patients or healthcare professionals). Learning techniques allow the system to collect and store historical data of user interaction with the system interface (Human-Computer Interaction). This process is carried out through three sub-components: learning, evaluation, and adaptation.

The learning component categorizes the data collected by the agent's sensor component into two categories: action (choices and preferences) and behaviour (statistical interactions with the interface). The evaluation component compares the new information with historical data and sends the differences to the next component. Finally, the adapting component updates the user model depending on the information received and adapts the interface to user needs.

Jorritsma et al. [8] integrate some mechanisms of adaptive customization to support natural work environment: the Picture Archiving Communication System (PACS) in radiology. The adaptive support is offered in the form of personalized suggestions, generated based on user behavioral data that can be accepted or ignored by participants. The adaptive customization support is designed to help users to effectively personalize the PACS's custom region. It is based on users' function usage, which was logged by the PACS's built-in logging tool, and consist of a table that gives insight into a user's function usage and a set of suggestions about which functions the user should add or remove to his or her custom region. To validate the system 12 Radiologists interacted with it, one half of the Participants received support and the other half did not. Participants who received support used the PACS's customization facilities more effectively than participants who did not receive support.

Ravi et al. [15] develop a system that categorizes MOOCs (Massive Open Online Course) teachers with different computer proficiency using learning authoring environments to provide adapted interfaces. To achieve this, authors categorize teachers in four broad classes by collecting data about teacher's computer performance during authoring process. The four classes are the following: Class A (Expert Users), Class B (Users' with a sound of knowledge), Class C (Knowledgeable intermittent users) and D (Novice users). The system uses this information to specify the design features in order to adapt its interface to teacher's profile. In addition, the system uses ADDIE (Analysis, Design, Development, Implementation, and Evaluation) instructional design model for supporting teachers to complete their authoring effectively in a step by step manner. Experiments made by authors attempt to compare the existing MOOCs authoring environment with their system. Results obtained by analytics showed a better performance among teachers using the system proposed.

Shakshuki et al. [16] propose an architecture of a multi-agent system designed to provide healthcare information about specific patients through continuous monitoring. It is important to highlight that the resulting data produced by the system is accessible not only by the patient to whom it belongs but also by his or her healthcare professional. The proposed system uses an adaptive user interface to improve the overall experience for users with poor vision or motor skills. Authors focus on the implementation of several of the key components involved in the adaptive user interface: learning component and the user model. The system architecture is composed of two kinds of agents: user agent and resource agent. User agents are in charge of three following goals: (1) adapt the UI to improve user experience, (2) manage health data, and (3) respond to healthcare professional user agent requests for health data. On the other hand, the resource agent is responsible to authenticate information requests among user agents, and to archive patient health data for long-term storage. To validate the system proposed two scenarios are provided that demonstrates the feasibility of the adaptive user interface.

From the previously reviewed research works we can conclude that several enhancements can be performed that allow improving the GUI (graphical user interfaces) by adding adaptivity and adaptability features. However, some of these works still present shortcomings such as the following: (1) do not recommend new content; (2) do not allow adapting the panels that contain specific functionalities; (3) do not offer the possibility of finding new educational resources; (4) some of them just adapt menu features; (5) the interfaces are not flexible for adaptation processes, i.e., the system adapts the interface but does not allow that users operate on it. The aim of this paper is to face these shortcomings and to provide a comprehensive solution concerning the use of adaptive and adaptable HCI interfaces in virtual learning environments.

4 Model Proposed

Figure 1 shows the model proposed, which considers five processes that can offer adaptivity and adaptability functionalities within a virtual learning environment, those functionalities will be detailed later. Processes that compose the model are described as follows:

- LO Recovery Process: This process is responsible for the search and compilation of LOs, which takes place from the integration of the system with the LOs repository called ROAP [13]. In this instance both metadata and LO contents are recovered in order to store them in the system central database.
- Grabber Events Process: This process is responsible for monitoring and storing interaction records performed between user and interface, with the aim of collecting those events that user performed when using interface adaptability features. In fact, this information is useful for supporting the intelligent adaptation of the GUI.
- Ontology Generator Process: This process allows the deployment and generation of records within the ontology, from the information concerning user profiles, performed events performed by the user within the GUI, and the interface structure. Subsequently, the generated ontology is delivered to the ontological reasoner. The details associated with the development of the ontology are presented later.
- Ontological Reasoner: is responsible for generating the inferences that allow obtaining relevant information for the interface presentation. The inferred information is sent to the adaptation process.
- Adapter Process: This process is very relevant since it enables the intelligent adaptation of the interface, from the information provided by the ontological reasoner. Adaptations performed to the GUI are presented in the following section.

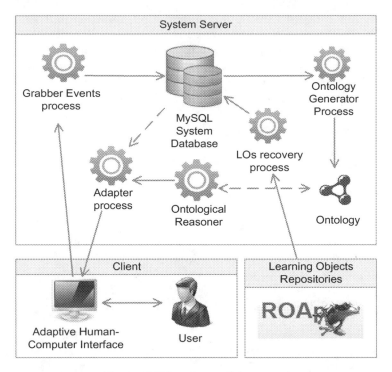

Fig. 1. HCI interface model proposed

Concerning the development of the ontological structure, the following two stages have been considered: the first one examines the characterization of user profiles and the second the structure of the GUI. The student profile is composed of personal information (name, identification, etc.), as well as features and preferences of specific learning process (learning style, font sizes, favorite formats, etc.). The structure of the interface in turn, is divided into five panels that offer the different system functionalities (detailed later). Figure 2 shows the ontology that describes characteristic informations of the GUI panels (height, width and position) and associates it with a specific student profile. The GUI performs this with the aim of storing the display preferences for every student.

The result of applying these two stages allows the generation of inferences from the ontology in order to perform real-time recommendations to users concerning the GUI adaptation. Likewise, the system can infer new kinds of adaptations by detecting new events (interactions) generated by students within the interface. This inferential knowledge abstraction is depicted by using SWRL (Semantic Web Rule Language) rules, some of which are presented in Table 1.

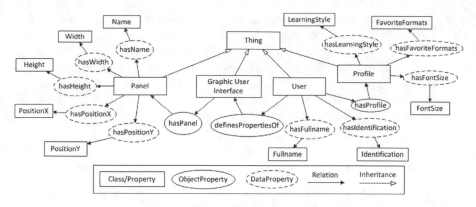

Fig. 2. GUI & User-profile ontological structure

5 Implementation and Validation

The model prototype along with its graphical user interfaces are developed using the Framework GWT-Google Web Toolkit [17]. This framework includes open source libraries that allow web developers to create and maintain complex front-end applications in JAVA.

Table 1. Ontological inference rules

Goal	SWRL Rule
Getting the height and width for a panel, defined by a particular user	PREFIX ont: <http://www.adaptivegui/#> SELECT ?subject ?panel ?height ?width ?name WHERE {?subject ont:hasIdentification 12345 . ?subject ont:definesPropertiesOf ?gui . ?gui ont:hasPanel ?panel . ?panel ont:hasName ?name. ?panel ont:hasHeight ?height . ?panel ont:hasWidth ?width . FILTER regex(?name, "search") }
Getting the position for a panel, defined by a particular user	PREFIX ont: <http://www.adaptivegui/#> SELECT ?subject ?panel ?positionx ?positiony ?name WHERE {?subject ont:hasIdentification 12345 . ?subject ont:definesPropertiesOf ?gui . ?gui ont:hasPanel ?panel . ?panel ont:hasName ?name. ?panel ont:hasPositionX ?positionx . ?panel ont:hasPositionY ?positiony . FILTER regex(?name, "LO Reposito- ries")}

Regarding installation and deployment of the central database we use MySQL database engine for all requirements about relational models that the system needs. For the ontological integration, we use JENA framework [18]. It is important to highlight that the ontology was mapped to OWL language by Protégé framework. As a result, SPARQL query language is used to perform inferences from the ontology. This language is supported by the W3C to perform queries on RDF and OWL graphs, thus enhancing the information search and selection on the semantic Web.

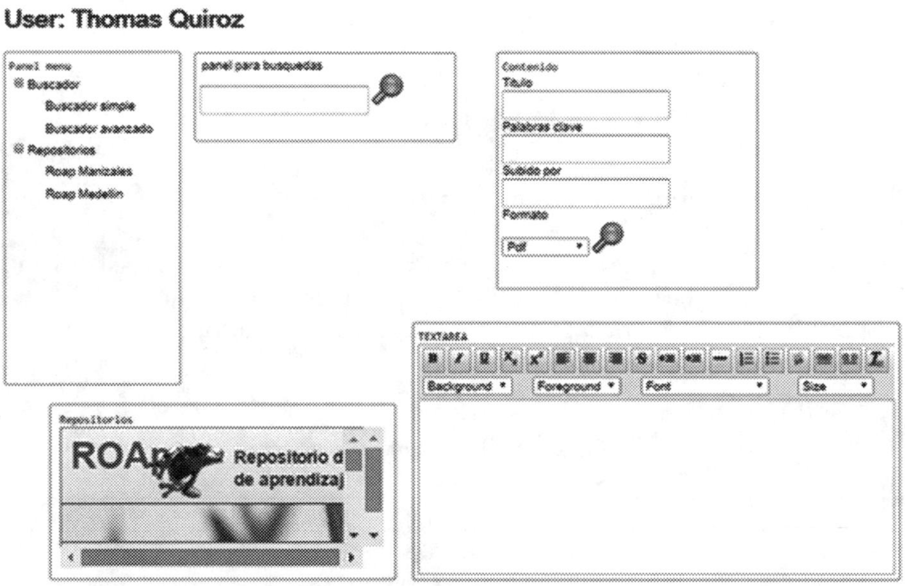

Fig. 3. GUI deployment

User profile is represented through a domain-specific ontology, which also involves the knowledge related to the GUI structure consisting of five panels, as follows:

1. LO Displaying Panel (on the upper right corner of the Fig. 3): This panel is responsible for showing the search engines (Simple and Advanced) and the list of found LO according to the search performed by the user on repositories. After an LO is selected by the system this panel is in charge of deploying it to the user.
2. All the searches performed by a specific user are stored by the system in order to feedback the LO recommendation mechanism. Furthermore, the system adds into the menu panel other objects that may be useful to the user according to his/her learning profile.
3. Menu Panel (on the upper left corner of the Fig. 3): This panel displays a specific user menu that involves a LO search engine (Simple or Advanced); a list of LO repositories, so the student can use them to find more objects that the ones shown by the system; finally, this panel contains a list of relevant LOs according to student learning style and preferences.

4. Search Panel (on the upper center of Fig. 3): It includes the functionalities of the LO simple search engine working like a shortcut mechanism avoiding the use of the menu panel.
5. Notes Panel (on the bottom right of Fig. 3): It enables students to build in real time their own writing notes without moving or change to another program. In addition, this functionality allows exporting these writing notes as plain text files that can be accessed later.
6. LO Repositories Panel (on the bottom left of Fig. 3): It allows a quick access to different LO repositories allowing students personalized searches. This functionality allows to find others LO that cannot be directly found by the system.

An important advantage exhibited by the GUI is the possibility of changing the position and size of each panel (adaptability characteristics). In addition, the GUI can be autonomously adapted to each of the users interacting with the GUI (adaptivity characteristics).

To validate the model prototype, several student profiles are considered and several LO searches are performed using the Colombian LO federation well known as FROAc (http://froac.manizales.unal.edu.co/dnia/main.php). We started with a single user, who applied a test in order to define his/her learning style and thus a user profile is created in the system. The system learn how the user organize size and position of all the panels (depending on the LO type that was displayed). Later, when similar users (i.e. having the same learning style) access the model prototype, it adapts the GUI based on information gathered from previous users that shared similar profiles.

Another case study to validate the proposed model is interacting with an experienced user who already has a lot of time interacting with the GUI and has defined his/her distribution for all panels with different types of LO. To this user the prototype presents a distribution based on all the knowledge it has about the user and all other users with the similar profile and learning style. Then the system assesses whether the user likes the distribution; also whether the user considers well the panel size according to the deployed LO.

6   Conclusion and Future Work

Using the advantages of user profiling in virtual learning environments our proposed model, which combines adaptive with adaptable issues, learns from a specific user-interface interactions in order to propose a similar distribution of the panels that compose the GUI to other users with similar profiles. In addition, the proposed model has the ability to adapt the GUI according to the deployed LO types. This fact facilitates the process of adaptation performed by the user.

However, some recommendations given by some users that used the prototype address following issues that will be considered as future work:

– Simple Search Panels should be removed in order to be added as part of functionalities offered by the content panel wherein the LO are displayed; making in this way the area of the GUI to be expanded.

- The area wherein different panels can move should not be restricted for users. However, since there is a restriction on the graphical libraries used by the system this issue would not be possible to change.
- The model proposed should incorporate user contextual characteristics in order to improve the GUI adaptation mechanism.

Results obtained from case studies demonstrate the effectiveness of the proposed human-computer interface model which combines adaptability along with adaptive characteristics.

Acknowledgments. This research was developed with the aid of the master grants offered to Oscar M. Salazar and Thomas Quiroz by COLCIENCIAS through "Convocatoria 645 de 2014. Capítulo 1 Semilleros-Jóvenes Investigadores". This research was also partially funded by the COLCIENCIAS project entitled: "RAIM: Implementación de un framework apoyado en tecnologías móviles y de realidad aumentada para entornos educativos ubicuos, adaptativos, accesibles e interactivos para todos" from the Universidad Nacional de Colombia, with code 1119-569-34172.

References

1. Lopez, J., Victor, M.: Interfaces de usuario adaptativas basadas en modelos y agentes software. Tesis de Doctorado, Departamento de Sistemas Informáticos, Universidad de Castilla-La Mancha, p. 324 (2005)
2. Gavrilova, T., Voinov, A.: An approach to mapping of user model to corresponding interface parameters. In: Proceedings of the Workshop Embedding User Models in Intelligent Applications, pp. 24–29 (1997)
3. Smyth, B., McGinty, L., Reilly, J., McCarthy, K.: Compound critiques for conversational recommender systems. In: IEEE/WIC/ACM International Conference on Web Intelligence (WI 2004), pp. 145–151. IEEE (2004). doi:10.1109/WI.2004.10098
4. Steichen, B., Ashman, H., Wade, V.: A comparative survey of personalized information retrieval and adaptive hypermedia techniques. Inf. Process. Manage. **48**(4), 698–724 (2012). doi:10.1016/j.ipm.2011.12.004
5. Letsu-Dake, E., Ntuen, C.A.: A case study of experimental evaluation of adaptive interfaces. Int. J. Ind. Ergon. **40**(1), 34–40 (2009)
6. Park, J., Han, S.H.: Complementary menus: combining adaptable and adaptive approaches for menu interface. Int. J. Ind. Ergon. **41**(3), 305–316 (2011)
7. Shakshuki, E.M., Reid, M., Sheltami, T.R.: An adaptive user interface in healthcare. Procedia Comput. Sci. **56**, 49–58 (2015)
8. Jorritsma, W., Cnossen, F., van Ooijen, P.M.A.: Adaptive support for user interface customization: a study in radiology. Int. J. Hum.-Comput. Stud. **77**(4), 1–9 (2015)
9. Tramullas, J., Sánchez-Casabón, A.-I., Garrido-Picazo, P.: An evaluation based on the digital library user: an experience with greenstone software. Procedia Soc. Behav. Sci. **73**, 167–174 (2013). doi:10.1016/j.sbspro.2013.02.037
10. Gaeta, M., Orciuoli, F., Paolozzi, S., Salerno, S.: Ontology extraction for knowledge reuse: the e-Learning perspective. IEEE Trans. Syst. Man Cybern. Part A Syst. Hum. **41**(4), 798–809 (2011)

11. Rodriguez, P., Salazar, O., Ovalle, D., Duque, N., Moreno, J.: Using ontological modeling for multi-agent recommendation of learning objects. In: Workshop MASLE – Multiagent System Based Learning Environments, Intelligent Tutoring Systems (ITS) Conference, Hawaii (2014)
12. Learning Technology Standards Committee: IEEE Standard for Learning Object Metadata. Institute of Electrical and Electronics Engineering, New York (2002)
13. Rodríguez, P.A., Moreno, J., Duque, N.D., Ovalle, D., Silveira, R.: A model for the semi-automatic composition of educational content from open repositories of learning objects. Rev. Electrónica Invest. Educ. (REDIE) **16**, 123–136 (2014)
14. Van de Sompel, H., Chute, R., Hochstenbach, P.: The aDORe federation architecture: digital repositories at scale. Int. J. Digit. Libr. **9**, 83–100 (2008)
15. Ravi, R., Kumar, A., Bijlani, K., Sharika, T.R.: Self-adaptive interface for comprehensive authoring. Procedia Comput. Sci. **58**, 158–164 (2015)
16. Shakshuki, E., Reida, M., Sheltami, T.: Dynamic healthcare interface for patients. Procedia Comput. Sci. **63**, 356–365 (2015)
17. GWT Documentation (2016). http://www.gwtproject.org/. Accessed 10 Feb 2016
18. Ameen, A., Khan, K.U.R., Rani, B.P.: Extracting knowledge from ontology using Jena for semantic web. In: International Conference for Convergence for Technology 2014, pp. 1–5 (2014)

Usable, Aesthetic, Sociable and Motivating Interface for Students' Online Knowledge Sharing

Prasanna Ramakrisnan[1,2,3]($\boxtimes$) and Azizah Jaafar[3]

[1] i-Learn Centre (i-LeC) University Technology MARA,
40450 Shah Alam, Malaysia
prasanna@fskm.uitm.edu.my
[2] Faculty Computer and Mathematical Sciences (FSKM),
Universiti Teknologi MARA (Melaka), Melaka, Malaysia
[3] Institute of Visual Informatics (IVI),
National University of Malaysia, Bangi, Malaysia
azizahj@ukm.edu.my

Abstract. Online knowledge sharing is an important factor in ensuring students continues learning outside the classroom. The advancement of technology now allows the students' sharing of knowledge to take place regardless of time and place in an online learning environment using an online discussion interface. Efforts have been taken by many higher education institutions to encourage students to share their knowledge in online discussion interface, but however it fails to sustain the knowledge sharing activities. This poses the question of how to promote the knowledge sharing activities among students. While previous research adopted the usability and sociability as antecedents for the online knowledge sharing activities, this study further explores visual aesthetics and intrinsic motivation design as additional two antecedents. We propose a set of contextual gamification and social media strategies which apply self-determination theory to self-motivate students for online knowledge sharing. It was found the game and social media elements can motivate the user in the online interface. The implementation of game elements in online interface can engage users while encouraging their activities for learning. Thus intrinsic motivation was designed using a set of gamification and social media specifications to enhance students' self-motivation for knowledge sharing activities. The research model with 53 items was tested for content validity to identify the initial measures for online knowledge sharing. Based on the content validity analysis, 20 items that does not fit into the criteria was discarded from the instrument. Our finding reveals that 33 items from usability, visual aesthetics, sociality and intrinsic motivation design can be used for initial development of online knowledge sharing model.

Keywords: Online knowledge sharing · Gamification · Motivating interface

© Springer International Publishing Switzerland 2016
P. Zaphiris and A. Ioannou (Eds.): LCT 2016, LNCS 9753, pp. 550–561, 2016.
DOI: 10.1007/978-3-319-39483-1_50

1 Introduction

Screen interface is a key aspect for enabling online knowledge sharing activities. The designers should think how design an interface to support the online knowledge sharing activities. Students need to support knowledge sharing activities should be emphasized rather than designing the interface based on the interest of the designer or software developer. It will make it easier for students to engage in online knowledge sharing activities. Thus the interface designer should combine their technical knowledge and skills with the best aesthetics that will attract the students to share knowledge.

In recent years, most of the online learning system provides a communication tool (discussion forum) for sharing of knowledge among students and teachers in addition to the development and distribution of learning content. This has resulted in the universities to use a blended learning approach, consisting of face-to-face instruction and the use of e-learning tools to support online learning. The e-learning tool which is proposed as an addition to the face-to-face traditional classroom discussions is the discussion interface [1]. Based on previous study, few shortcomings in the discussion interface design were identified [2]. Thus, the discussion interface should be designed to facilitate online knowledge sharing activities.

2 Conceptual Model for Online Knowledge Sharing

Interface for knowledge sharing is concerned with the ability of the students to use interface for knowledge sharing discussions. The challenge is to determine the criteria of online discussion interface that enables the sharing of knowledge among students'. Various criteria has be taken into account to assess the online discussion interface. Among the evaluation criteria that often been discussed are usability, visual aesthetics and intrinsic motivation design.

The interface design plays an important role in providing an online space for interaction among students. Thus the interface design should be made interesting and to make students feel interested in using it for knowledge sharing. This study shows that the interface design should be given attention to support for knowledge sharing. Issues such as usability, visual aesthetics, sociability and intrinsic motivation design are the most important factors to be assessed. Earlier studies looked at usability and visual aesthetics as one single factor, but they are actually two different factors and it is important to investigate both the factors separately to understand users' behavior [3]. Usability traditionally was defined as "people who use the product can do so quickly and easily to accomplish their task" [4]. But the traditional usability evaluation is insufficient for e-learning [5]. Thus the user, task and context that taken into account in traditional usability is extended to learning in formal and informal environments [6]. Learning occurs in online discussion interface through the students' interaction in an informal environment. In this context, usability is concerned with how intuitive and easy it is for students to learn to use and interact with the online discussion interface. The online discussion interface should be designed in a way in which students can interact easily for knowledge sharing activities.

Apart from usability factor, the visual aesthetics factor plays an important role in the evaluation of interface and relatively limited research in other contexts such as online discussion interface [7]. In addition, it also was found that the visual aesthetics of the interface can define user satisfaction and pleasure by using measurement constructs [8]. Therefore, this study makes extension to measure empirically the visual aesthetics of the online discussion interface for knowledge sharing. So looking at the usability and visual aesthetics of the interface alone is not enough. Researchers must also pay attention to the technology that enables social interaction in online discussion interface [9]. Hence, sociability concept was introduced to examine support of social interaction in the online interface. Sociability is concerned with developing the software, policies and practices to support social interaction online. Though practical sociability and usability are closely related, both of these factors have significant differences. Usability is very dependent on how users interact with technology while sociability is related with how users interact with the support of technology. Therefore the online discussion interface need to be evaluated to see how the interface support students' interaction online.

As the interface combines intrinsic motivation design factor in online discussion interface, intrinsic motivation design factor need to be considered for inclusion in the online discussion interface evaluation. It was found the game elements can motivate the user in the online interface [10]. But the use of game elements in the context of non-game is known as gamification [11]. This gamification was used in intrinsic motivation to predict students' attitudes toward the use of game elements and the intention to continue using it [12]. The implementation of game elements in online interface can engage users while encouraging their activities for learning [13]. Besides that social media elements also can increase students learning [14]. Thus intrinsic motivation design factor will be assessed using a set of gamification and social media specifications to enhance students' motivation for engaging them in knowledge sharing activities.

From the result of literature review, a conceptual model was developed. This conceptual model is designed to investigate students' knowledge sharing ability in online discussion interface using four important factors; usability, sociability, visual aesthetics and intrinsic motivation design.

3   Intrinsic Motivation Design for Online Knowledge Sharing

The motivation theory that mainly behind this study is Self Determination Theory (SDT). SDT is a general theory of human motivation and personality [15], which concerns people's inherent growth tendencies and innate psychological needs. In this study, three psychological needs that enhances intrinsic motivation: autonomy (self-determination in resolving what to do and how to do it), efficiency (to develop and implement skills for manipulation and control of the environment), and relatedness (in relation to others through pro-social relationships).

Autonomy. Autonomy refers to the degree of selection that students have to perform academic tasks; and about when and how to perform the task [16]. Ryan and Deci

(2000) said that the autonomy occurs when individuals take action on their desire or for personal reasons and not due to be controlled by others [17].

Number of activities under the concept of autonomy as proposed in the discussion interface to improve students' motivation to meet their autonomy needs:

A1: Allow the students to choose appropriate avatar to represent them in the online knowledge sharing activities.
A2: Allow the students to choose the way to receive feedback immediately about their online knowledge sharing activities
A3: Allow the students to choose the types of media that wants to be shared in online knowledge sharing activities.

Competence. Competence is the ability of students to complete a task assigned to the successful and efficient in continuous interaction with the social environment. For the students to build their own competence, it is suggested to support the perceived extend of learners' own behaviors [18]. The feeling of competence is enhanced by (1) unexpected, direct and positive feedback, (2) an optimal challenge and (3) freedom of demeaning evaluations [15]. For example, early studies shows that positive feedback can improve the performance of intrinsic motivation, whereas negative performance fccdback rcducing intrinsic motivation [19]. In addition, fcclings of compctcncc also can be enhanced by displaying the progress of students in the interface [20]. When displaying the progress of students to other students, it can also stimulate the relatedness needs [21].

So knowledge sharing activities should be designed interestingly to enable online knowledge sharing activities. Below are some of the suggested activities to help increase student motivation with fulfilling the basic psychological needs for competence.

C1: Provide the student unexpected response when they achieve required performance in online knowledge sharing activities.
C2: Provide the student direct response about their position in online knowledge sharing activities.
C3: Provide the student positive feedback for their effort in online knowledge sharing activities
C4: Provide the student view of their progression in online knowledge haring activities.

Relatedness. Relatedness is the last requirement for intrinsic motivation. It refers to the need to belong to or dependent on a particular group. Therefore, the feeling of relatedness is connected, belonging and interaction with others in the discussion interface. Feeling a sense of connection not only to share knowledge but also to compete in the leaderboard [20]. Relatedness support social interaction with other students with various elements such as tagging, ratings, commenting and visualization of social status and reputation [18]. Number of activities to enhance the feeling of relatedness among students for online knowledge sharing is proposed:

R1:   Allow students with similar interest to be connected.
R2:   Allow the students to visualize their social status, reputation and contribution in online knowledge sharing activities.

Allow the students to show appreciation to other students' contribution.

4   Gamification Strategies in Intrinsic Motivation Design

This section presents the gamification features introduced into the discussion interface based on the proposed activities in intrinsic motivation design.

Avatar Selection. The discussion interface allow the students to choose appropriate avatar to represent them in online knowledge sharing activities (see Fig. 1). This feature was designed based on the suggestion A1 from the activities.

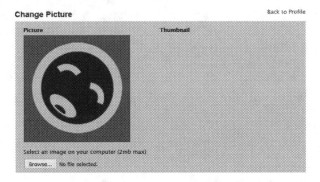

Fig. 1. Avatar selection

Immediate Feedback. The discussion interface allow the students to choose the way the feedback about the online knowledge sharing activities given immediately. For instance, the student can choose the option to send the feedback straight to their email. So that they can read immediately the feedback about their discussion directly using their smart phone without login to discussion interface. This feature was designed based on the suggestion A2.

Media Selection. Customization of type of media used for the online knowledge sharing activities can be determine by the students themselves. By this students feel more autonomous. This feature was design based on the suggestion A3.

Unexpected Response. The discussion interface provides unexpected responses when the student fulfill some requirement needed in the online knowledge sharing activities. For instance, award in the form of badge will be given if the total count of comments a user has ever made meets or exceeds the target criteria. Badges are visual representations of students' achievements in online knowledge sharing activities, which can be collected within the discussion environment [22]. When the badges are awarded unexpectedly, it will keep up students' interest levels [23]. The badges are **advertised**

on students profile so other students' can see the online knowledge sharing level. These features were designed based on suggestion C1 and R2.

Direct Response. The discussion interface will rank the students success in online knowledge sharing activities. For instance, students' can view their position in knowledge sharing activities directly in the discussion interface (see Fig. 2). This **view can be shared** with all the students in the discussion interface. For students at the top ranking, feelings of competence can arise. Besides that, the students' ranking can create competition among the students to be at the top ranking. These features were designed based on the suggestion C2 and R2.

Positive Feedback. The discussion interface allows the student provides positive feedback to other students' contribution in online knowledge sharing activities. This

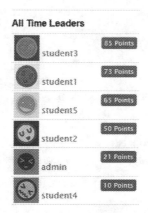

Fig. 2. Direct response on students' online knowledge sharing activities

allows the student to **show appreciation** to other students' contribution. For instance, students' can use the discussion interface to show "kudos" and encourages the students' to involve more in online knowledge sharing activities. These features were designed based on suggestion C3 and R3.

View Student Progression. The discussion able to show student progression in online knowledge sharing activities. Students' progression represent their ability and level of engagement in online knowledge sharing activities. The more student engage in online knowledge sharing, the higher students' progression will be. The students' **progression level can be seen by other students** in their profile (see Fig. 3). These features were designed based on suggestion C4 and R3.

5 Social Media Strategies in Intrinsic Motivation Design

This section presents the social media features introduced into the discussion inter-face based on the proposed activities in intrinsic motivation design.

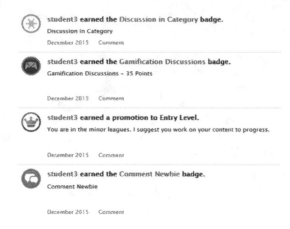

Fig. 3. Student progression level

Connected with Their Peers. Students feel more connected with peers when they participate in social media [24]. The hashtag is an important element of social media strategies. Thus to keep students' connected in similar interest topics, tagging is used. The tagging allow students to group key words and discussions so they are easily searchable (see Fig. 4). The purpose of using tagging in the discussion interface is to allow the students to easily connect on discussion topics, sharing their thoughts and opinions. This feature was designed based on suggestion R1.

6   Method

6.1   Participants

Fig. 4. Tagging the key words

The participants for this study are panel of experts. The selection panel of experts depends on the required amount of expert, desired level of experts, experience of experts, qualifications of the experts and experts' diversity of knowledge [1, 2]. The panel of expert panel may consist of content or lay experts. Content experts are professional with research and working experience in the study area while lay experts are potential research subjects [3]. The aim using the subject from the target group as one of the panel of expert is to ensure that the population which the instrument developed is represented. Additionally lay experts can also give opinions on items that are less clear and item that are important in the study. The purpose sample from actual population is used as lay expert because they know the research construct through direct personal experience [2].

The recommended amount of experts is between three to ten experts for each group (content expert and lay expert) in the content validity test [3, 4]. Although using larger number of experts provide more information about the measures but the possibility to reach agreement on the items used in instruments would decrease [5]. After determining the panel of experts for content validity test, the views of a panel of experts on the items in quantitative and qualitative manner researchers was collected and analyzed. For this study four panels of experts were selected (3 senior lecturer with Doctorate and 1 Phd student).

6.2 Instrument

A response form with the developed items were created as instrument for this study. Five criteria's were used to evaluate the items in the response form: (1) relevance, (2) clarity and (3) necessity. Each item were rated on a scale of 1–4 for relevance and clarity; and scale of 1–3 for necessity. In literature it is recommended for dichotomizing the ordinal scale during the process of content analysis. Finally an empty space is given bottom of each items for the experts to add any comments. The suggested format of response form was adapted from [3]. Addition to it, a brief demographic questions can be included at the top of response form to gather some information about the experts. Thus the response form can be divided in three section: (1) brief demographic questions, (2) instructions to the experts, (3) construct theoretical definition, scales and list of factors or sub factors for the measures with its definition and lastly (4) items that need to be accessed.

6.3 Procedure

Once the panel of expert have been identified, email or call should be given to the selected experts requesting their interest in the content validity test. Duration about one week was be given to the experts to respond to the request. As soon as the experts accepted the invitation to involve in content validity test, a cover letter and response form sent to the panel of experts. Cover letter included the purpose of study and description of the response form. Duration one week was given to the panels of experts to provide constructive feedback on the study items.

7 Data Analysis

There are three types of analysis that can be performed on data collected for the content validity test: (1) content validity ratio (CVR), (2) content validity index (CVI) and (3) reliability or inter-rater agreement (IRA) [3, 6]. The elimination of item is done by using two commonly used method for content analysis; the content validity ratio (CVR) [6] and content validity index (CVI) [4]. While the reliability of the expert's rating was seen from the value of IRA.

8 Finding

Once all the panel of judges completed the response form, data was analyzed for CVI, CVR and IRA. The detail analysis of content validity is extended to another research paper. Out of the 53 items assessed, 20 were considered to have insufficient content validity. The final items included the initial online knowledge sharing model were displayed in Table 1.

Table 1. Online knowledge sharing model

Factor	Item	References
Usability	I can read, navigate, seek and contribute knowledge in this discussion interface	Self-developed based on [25, 26]
	I can quickly learn how to share knowledge in this discussion interface	
	I can easily share knowledge in this discussion interface	
	I will get confirmation message if I want to remove my discussion from this discussion interface	
	I can easily read the information in this discussion interface	
	I can quickly find the information in this discussion interface	
	The information in this discussion interface is well organized	
	I can navigate into this discussion interface easily	
	I can easily go back to my discussions in this discussion interface	

(*Continued*)

Table 1. (*Continued*)

Factor	Item	References
	I can move quickly between the discussion topics in this discussion interface	
Visual aesthetics	The layout of this discussion interface is clear	Adapted from [27]
	The layout of this discussion interface is easy to understand	
	The layout of this discussion interface is well-structured	
	This discussion interface design appears inspired	
	This discussion interface design is interesting	
	Attractive color composition used in this discussion interface design	
	Proper choice of colors in designing this discussion interface	
	This discussion interface appears to be designed to support the online knowledge sharing activities	
Sociability	This discussion interface enables me to easily connect with other students online	Adapted from [28]
	This discussion interface allows informal conversations	
	I feel comfortable to share knowledge in this discussion interface	
	This discussion interface allows for non-task-related conversations	
	This discussion interface enables me to make close friendships with other students involved in the discussion	
Intrinsic motivation design	I can select an appropriate avatar to represent me in this discussion interface	Self-developed based on [15]
	I can make a choice in receiving discussion feedback in this interface	
	I can select suitable type of media for the purpose of sharing knowledge online	
	I will receive unpredicted responses for my achievements in this discussion interface	
	I can track my performance in knowledge sharing activities directly in this discussion interface	
	I received positive feedback for my knowledge sharing efforts in this discussion interface	
	I can see my progression in knowledge sharing activities	

(*Continued*)

Table 1. (*Continued*)

Factor	Item	References
	I can easily follow discussion with a specific theme or content which interests me in this discussion interface	
	I can view the status of my knowledge sharing activities, reputation and contribution visually in this discussion interface	
	I can show appreciation (like) to the contribution made by other students in this discussion interface	

9 Conclusion

This study demonstrates quantitative feedback was received from the experts for identification of initial online knowledge sharing measurement. Four factors were identified to measure the online knowledge sharing. They are usability, visual aesthetics, sociability and intrinsic motivation design. Panels of experts were requested to give constructive feedback on the identified measures from literature. Then content analysis were conducted and items were judged for explaining the construct of study (online knowledge sharing). Then items were removed and modified based on the feedback obtained from the panel of experts. Once the content validity study completed, further pilot study can be conducted to identify any problems with the instrument before final testing is done. For future work, we will validate the items using a statistical procedure. To conclude, gamification and social media strategies can be used to design intrinsic motivation in an interface. To keep student to share knowledge online we proposed usability, visual aesthetics, and sociability and intrinsic motivation rooted in self-determination theory using gamification and social media strategies.

References

1. Sulisworo, D.: Designing the online collaborative learning using the Wikispaces. Int. J. Emerg. Technol. Learn. **7**, 58–61 (2012)
2. Preece, J., Maloney-Krichmar, D.: Online communities focusing on sociability and usability. In: Jacko, J., Sears, A. (eds.) Handbook of Human-Computer Interaction, pp. 596–620. Lawrence Erlbaum, Mahwah (2003)
3. Mahlke, S.: Understanding users' experience of interaction. In: Proceedings of the 2005 Annual Conference on European Association of Cognitive Ergonomics, pp. 251–254. University of Athens (2005)
4. Dumas, J.S., Redish, J.: A Practical Guide to Usability Testing. Intellect Books, Exeter (1999)
5. Zaharias, P., Poylymenakou, A.: Developing a usability evaluation method for e-learning applications: beyond functional usability. Intl. J. Hum.-Comput. Interact. **25**, 75–98 (2009)

6. Mehlenbacher, B., Bennett, L., Bird, T., Ivey, M., Lucas, J., Morton, J., Whitman, L.: Usable e-learning: a conceptual model for evaluation and design. In: Proceedings of the 11th International Conference on HCI International (2005)

7. Tractinsky, N.: Toward the study of aesthetics in information technology. In: ICIS, pp. 771–780 (2004)

8. Lavie, T., Tractinsky, N.: Assessing dimensions of perceived visual aesthetics of web sites. Int. J. Hum. Comput. Stud. **60**, 269–298 (2004)

9. Preece, J.: Sociability and usability in online communities: determining and measuring success. Behav. Inf. Technol. **20**, 347–356 (2001)

10. Hamari, J., Koivisto, J., Sarsa, H.: Does gamification work?–a literature review of empirical studies on gamification. In: 2014 47th Hawaii International Conference on System Sciences (HICSS), pp. 3025–3034. IEEE (2014)

11. Deterding, S.: Situated motivational affordances of game elements: a conceptual model. In: Gamification: Using Game Design Elements in Non-Gaming Contexts, a Workshop at CHI (2011)

12. Hamari, J., Koivisto, J.: Social motivations to use gamification: an empirical study of gamifying exercise (2013)

13. Raymer, R., Design, E.-L.: Gamification: using game mechanics to enhance eLearning. Elearn. Mag. **2011**, 3 (2011)

14. Tarantino, K., McDonough, J., Hua, M.: Effects of student engagement with social media on student learning: a review of literature. J. Technol. Stud. Aff. **1**, 1–8 (2013)

15. Deci, E.L., Ryan, R.M.: Handbook of Self-determination Research. University Rochester Press, Rochester (2002)

16. Deci, E.L., Eghrari, H., Patrick, B.C., Leone, D.R.: Facilitating internalization: the self-determination theory perspective. J. Pers. **62**, 119–142 (1994)

17. Ryan, R.M., Deci, E.L.: Self-determination theory and the facilitation of intrinsic motivation, social development, and well-being. Am. Psychol. **55**, 68 (2000)

18. Shi, L., Cristea, A.I., Hadzidedic, S., Dervishalidovic, N.: Contextual gamification of social interaction – towards increasing motivation in social E-learning. In: Popescu, E., Lau, R.W., Pata, K., Leung, H., Laanpere, M. (eds.) ICWL 2014. LNCS, vol. 8613, pp. 116–122. Springer, Heidelberg (2014)

19. Deci, E.L., Ryan, R.M.: Intrinsic Motivation. Wiley Online Library (1975)

20. Barata, G., Gama, S., Jorge, J., Gonçalves, D.: Engaging engeneering students with gamification. In: 2013 5th International Conference on Games and Virtual Worlds for Serious Applications (VS-GAMES), pp. 1–8. IEEE (2013)

21. Stott, A., Neustaedter, C.: Analysis of gamification in education, Surrey, BC, Canada (2013)

22. Sailer, M., Hense, J., Mandl, H., Klevers, M.: Psychological perspectives on motivation through gamification. IxD&A. **19**, 28–37 (2013)

23. Exton, G., Murray, L.: Motivation: a proposed taxonomy using gamification (2014)

24. Jackson, C.: Your students love social media… and so can you. Teach. Toler. **39**, 38–41 (2011)

25. Preece, J.: Online Communities: Designing Usability and Supporting Socialbilty. Wiley, Chichester (2000)

26. Preece, J., Shneiderman, B.: The reader-to-leader framework: motivating technology-mediated social participation. AIS Trans. Hum.-Comput. Interact. **1**, 13–32 (2009)

27. Moshagen, M., Thielsch, M.T.: Facets of visual aesthetics. Int. J. Hum. Comput. Stud. **68**, 689–709 (2010)

28. Kreijns, K., Kirschner, P.A., Jochems, W., Van Buuren, H.: Measuring perceived sociability of computer-supported collaborative learning environments. Comput. Educ. **49**, 176–192 (2005)

Engaging Chinese Children with Autism to Interact with Portable Hand- and Finger-Gesture Based Applications: Experiment and Reflections

Tiffany Y. Tang[1], Mary Falzarano[2], and Patricia A. Morreale[3(✉)]

[1] Media Laboratory, Department of Computer Science, Kean University,
Wenzhou, Zhejiang, China
yatang@kean.edu
[2] Department of Occupational Therapy, Kean University, Union, NJ, USA
mfalzara@kean.edu
[3] Department of Computer Science, Kean University, Union, NJ, USA
pmorreal@kean.edu

Abstract. Recent work by researchers in China has demonstrated the potential for collaborative play as an educational tool for children on the Autism Spectrum Disorder (ASD). In this paper, researchers in the United States and China investigate the potential for accessible interface design and learning by students with ASD. Through the use of known tools and interventions, an educational protocol has been designed to evaluate two applications. The pilot studies, including experimental design and outcomes, are presented here, and provide a solid foundation for comparative assessment of mid-air finger-gesture interaction as well as hand-gesture interaction. Early results in China are promising, based on experiences in the United States.

Keywords: Autism · Hand-and-finger gesture · Accessible interface design · Collaborative play

1 Introduction

Our understanding of the effectiveness of using games enabled by a portable marker less finger and hand position capture device (e.g. the Leap Motion Controller) to train children with Autism Spectrum Disorder (ASD) fine motor and motor gesture skills is very limited due to few empirical studies. The study described in this paper is believed to be one of the first to shed light on the suitability and degree of effectiveness of such a training approach to improve children's motor impairments.

ASD is a neurodevelopmental disorder affecting 1 in 68 children in the US [1]; it is characterized by such core impairments as repetitive and constrained behaviors and lack of social communication knowledge and skills [1]. Of note, many children with autism demonstrate severe impairment with reciprocal interaction significantly impacting their joint attention [2] and collaborative interaction and play [3] which in turn decreases their ability to participate in meaningful learning, social and play interactions [4].

© Springer International Publishing Switzerland 2016
P. Zaphiris and A. Ioannou (Eds.): LCT 2016, LNCS 9753, pp. 562–572, 2016.
DOI: 10.1007/978-3-319-39483-1_51

In this paper, we report on two pilot studies conducted in the classroom of a large Children's Educational Development Center in a southern Chinese city for children with ASD. To the best of our knowledge, it is one of the first attempts to study the acceptability, usability and possible benefits of finger- and hand-gesture enabled interactions for special education.

2 Related Work

Few previous empirical studies have provided us with sufficient understanding of both the acceptability and usability of the finger- and hand-gesture based motionless games/applications for individuals with ASD. However, two indirect lines of prior research are relevant to our current study.

Recent studies revealed that the under-explored motor abnormalities are also prevalent in ASD [5] and are believed to interfere with the development of adaptive skills [6, 7]. The motor abnormalities, known as associated symptoms [8] may include problems with gross and fine motor skills [9, 34], skilled motor gestures [6, 10] and motor learning patterns [11]. However, children with autism often demonstrate strong visual perceptual abilities for objects as they have been found to be drawn to consistency of visual stimuli (both static and dynamic), matching and discriminating salient features [12–15, 33], while conversely there have been impairments noted in the visual perception abilities for facial features [14–16].

Although a wide variety of games and applications have been developed to improve individuals' social communication, eye-hand coordination and cognitive skills etc., fewer games and applications target the individual's motor impairments.

2.1 Benefits of Motion-Based Games and Applications

Several recent studies on the possible advantages motion-based touchless games provide for children with ASD [17–20] have been found. In particular, these studies revealed that the whole-body interaction enabled by Kinect games can enhance children's motor skills and social behaviors [19, 20, 35], reduce their distress and increase emotion-releasing abilities [17]. Custom-made Kinect games can further be used for attention and cognitive skills training [18]. The field studies conducted in [17] indicate that motion-based gaming can promote cognitive learning and attentional skills, supporting both selective and sustained attention.

2.2 Use of Gesture Games and Applications for Fine Motor Skills Training

In addition to Kinect, Leap Motion, an increasingly popular touchless hand and finger motion tracking device, has been examined to demonstrate its accuracy in measuring hand movement in pointing task among healthy adults [21]. Due to its extreme portability, Leap Motion offers a greater advantage than Kinect for training on fine motor skills, such as that needed by individuals with ASD. A full understanding of the benefits of motion-based games (including both whole-body and hand-finger gesture-based interactions) requires examining that of the latter. However, little previous empirical evidence directly addresses the issue, especially in China where technology-based application use is rarely used in both the school and at home [22].

Following this path of research, we have seen so far one attempt which includes a series of Leap Motion-based games to train children's fine motor skills empirically studied in a special education center in Beijing [23]. Results showed that the 'innovative' interaction poses bigger challenges—children have difficulty adjusting their hand gestures in a 3D space.

3   Experimental Design and Assessment

3.1   Study One: Drawing Game

The Game. A simple drawing game was implemented using C#. Players can use both hand or finger gestures to draw on the canvas (Fig. 1). In order to assess children's attention and engagement level and their emotional state, we made the game rules very simple by supporting only two simple actions—drawing through hand-finger air gesture (depicted by the boy in Fig. 2) and cleaning via a circle gesture.

Participant. Five pairs of boys and their family members were recruited by the Center to participate in this game. (In the Center, close to 90 % of the children are boys). The boys participating in this study have comparable (similar) intelligence and abilities (M = 4.8, SD = 1.8), referred to as C1 (the oldest, 8 years old), C2, C3, C4 and C5 respectively.

Experimental Conditions. One purpose of this experiment was to examine whether finger-gesture based manipulation would bring more fun and usability (in terms of ease

Fig. 1. The game entry user interface of the drawing game

Fig. 2. During testing, a grandma helped her grandson with ASD drawing in the canvas

of use) to the children. Therefore, we tested the game in the school with which children feel familiar and comfortable. The game was projected onto a wall via a projector; and to avoid children's curiosity towards the tiny Leap Motion controller, we 'hid' the controller into a box leaving the interaction area open (as depicted in Fig. 2). Each family member/child pair was given a maximum 15 min of play in order not to fatigue the children [17, 18] due to their young age.

Measures. Qualitative data, such as the level of enjoyment and engagement, and the degree of attention on screen objects were collected through observations, commonly seen in the literature [17, 24, 25]. These variables were among the behavioral and emotional signals examined in previous research [17].

Experiment Procedures. Before the experiment, the head teacher was given the Chinese translation of the game including a short description of how to play it. Parents were informed of the purpose of the experiment, experimental procedures and their rights. Each child entered the testing room with their parents (except for one with his grandmother, C3). The developer first introduced the Leap Motion device, and demonstrated how to draw with two finger-gestures. Then, the parent/grandmother-child pair interact with the game together. After the testing was over, structured interviews based on the one developed in [26] for a Chinese family were conducted at the end of the play session. The aim was to obtain information on the child's behaviors and prefer-ences, and phone- and computer-game uses at home.

Results and Discussions. In contrast to previous findings that children were mostly reluctant to touch a singing plant [22], both children and their family members showed high engagement in the drawing game; their attention level was very high during the entire game-playing session. All children showed high levels of sustained attention, and most of the time when they were playing the game with the help of the parents, their eyes remained focused towards the visual stimulus in the game. Both children and parent/grandma's emotional states were enthusiastic. Structured interview with all family members indicate the high satisfaction of the family with the game, especially regarding the Leap Motion device since it was their initial encounter with such a 'magic' controller. Overall, for all of the parents, it was the very first time they were aware of the existence of such a device and they all expressed amazement at such an innovative way of user interaction. While all children had been given opportunities to play with mobile phones at home, their family members claimed that none of the games and applications are specifically designed for their children; in fact, according to the teachers at the Center, this was the first-ever such educational application. An earlier game, the Yuudee (Little Rain Drop), launched in May 2015 [27], lacks the personalization mechanism where teachers can adaptively change the contents based on children's responses and conditions, therefore, it has not gained popularity among special education schools in China. With this said, the teachers at this Center were very open to our drawing game. However, it was observed that the children had difficulty manipulating and using their fingers; we designed a second more portable web application which utilizes hand-gesture.

3.2   Study Two: Zoo and House Game Study

The Application. The improved version was implemented using JavaScript and can be accessed at: http://www.tmywk.com/ as a web-enabled application (a Leap Motion gesture controller is required). Currently, there are two available scenes: a zoo and a house. When the child interacts with one screen object (an image), its Chinese name (a word) will be shown accompanied by a sound file to spell out its name (see Fig. 3). This learning process is commonly used in the famous Lovass model of Applied Behavior Analysis (ABA) in which individuals with ASD are required to pair a word with a corresponding image (through the use of familiar materials and intermittent rewards with an aim to enhance children's vocal language understandings). Since it is well known that children with ASD frequently experience sensory overload and may be averse to excessively loud and high pitched sound [28], the auditory sound was presented at a moderate volume, and the tones fall into the frequency range of human speech. None of the children in our experiment demonstrated any observable startle response; instead, the children's attention to the screen objects was continuously dedicated. Teachers also voiced no complaints about the sound and the tones.

Participants. Five boys with the same intelligence and abilities participated in this study (M = 6.3, SD = 2.4), referred to as C1, C2, C3, C4 and C5 respectively; four boys were reported to have interest in playing computer games (C1, C2, C3, and C5). Their head teacher recommended the children because they were informed of the nature of the game beforehand (as required by the Autism Center).

Fig. 3. The zoo interface in the zoo and home game

Experimental Conditions. One of the purposes of this second experiment was to examine whether hand-gesture based manipulation would bring more fun and usability (in terms of ease of use) to the child, therefore, we tested the game in the school again with which children feel familiar and comfortable.

Measures. Qualitative data included the level of enjoyment and engagement, the degree of attention on screen objects, and additionally, the degree of independent manipulation by children were collected through observations (commonly seen in the literature [12, 17, 24, 25]). These variables were among the behavioral and emotional signals examined in previous research [17]. Although the conclusions derived from these data cannot provide a convincing picture of the design patterns for such a game, they are sufficient to inform the designers of whether the new design managed to serve its intended goals.

Experiment Procedures. Each child entered the testing room with either the home-room teacher or the head-teacher. The teachers had been informed earlier about the nature of the experiments (with a Chinese translation of our game). The game designer provided brief instructions to the children on how to play the game through a short demonstration (lasting less than one minute). After the instruction, the children were given the time to play the game. Prior to this experiment, and unlike some other testing in which a given time is allocated, Chinese children had seldom been exposed to such gesture-based game and technology-enabled games before [22]. This is only the second time such a gesture-based application has ever tested in the ten-year period that the Center has been educating children. Therefore, free-play was administered in order to assess the usability of the application. After each play round, teachers were interviewed to provide their perspectives on the children's noticeable behaviors and the overall benefits of the game.

Fig. 4. During testing, a boy was observed interacting with the application at ease

Results and Discussions. All the children showed high enthusiasm while playing the game, and with very minimum training needed (see Fig. 4 on one testing moment). Among the five boys participating in the game, three older boys C3, C4 and C5, were extremely attentive to the game, played it with ease, and showed high sustained attention [17]. Among the qualitative data collected through the analysis of the videos and observations during the testing, the level of enjoyment and engagement, the degree of attention on screen objects and the degree of independent manipulation were all very high. Compared to the similar observations in Study One, the children needed less assistance to activate the device and play the game. Since the game was also projected into the wall, two younger boys C1 and C2, demonstrated high interest during game-play as they were observed to stare at the wall display instead of the computer screen. Of note, child C4 stopped working in the application when it was time for him to attend a class; however he later went back on his own to the game during the class break. According to the homeroom teacher this was the first time he had independently initiated participation in an activity.

In summary, all the children were able to show sustained attention to the on-screen stimuli. They demonstrated high skills in mimicking the developer's demonstration. The results lead us to believe that the usability of such a hand-motion based touchless application is very satisfactory. To our surprise, the teachers' feedback and reactions in Study Two were much more positive when compared to those from Study One: they revealed that although it is the first time they had ever seen such a type of game tested in their center, it was beyond their expectations to observe the children's reactions to the application as well as their quick and deep immersion in it.

Unlike previous studies [17, 18] examining the learning benefits of such motion-based touchless games relative to children's attentional skills, our work attempts to understand the acceptability of such games (Study One and Two) and the learnability and usability of it (Study Two). It is unclear what design rules would best be formulated in both gesture-based and multi-modal interactive applications since some cultural issues unique to this population have contributed to the overall acceptance of these applications. In addition, children seldom receive strengthened in-home intensive training in parallel to their school-based ABA training programs. Chinese parents largely rely on the Autism Center to undertake all the interventions. However, our two experiments have drawn attention from both the teachers and parents who have encouraged us on in further development of such games.

4   Lessons Learned

Our current understanding of the possible benefits of motion-based application/games for individuals with ASD are extremely limited, partly due to the small number of empirical studies, particularly in China. Hence, overall, the two studies conducted and reported here offer a valuable first glimpse into the acceptability and usability of motion-based touchless games for Chinese children with ASD.

Results of our two pilot studies reveal practices and perspectives on the use of finger- and hand-gesture enabled interactions that add depth to our previous understanding of such use. In particular, while mid-air finger-gesture interaction is challenging for younger children with ASD, hand-gesture interaction offers more fun and playability in the learning process. However, we expect some resistance from parents and special education teachers who may remain suspicious of the use of such games/applications.

5   Conclusion

The research presented here provided an opportunity to learn about how cause and effect contributes to motor skill acquisition and learning. In particular, the researchers observed that when the child is engaged in a motivating task he will practice the required movements, and through this practice develop motor control accompanied by true learning to build a foundation and provide carryover into more complex movement patterns. Additionally, and perhaps more importantly, when the parent/caregiver observes the child's ability to activate and sustain engagement in a task, the parent is more likely to carry over the practice at home further solidifying the child's skill development. This training protocol is beneficial for both the teachers and the parent/caregiver, as they recognize the ease of use when provided with the initial instructions, reinforced with observation of the child's focused and sustained engagement in the activating the game and attending to the visual stimulus that results from the child's motor movement (either the full hand gesture or the more refined 1 or 2 finger gesture).

Teachers can build on the visual motor abilities the children gain through the use of the games provided here to integrate learning concepts (examples include matching colors/shapes; categorization of images and finally matching words to pictures to promote reading and language acquisition). Finally, children can develop social skills through turn taking and collaborative play with the computer games. Developmentally the child is given the opportunity to simultaneously link the kinesthetic and visual systems together. For example, the child will move his hand or fingers and watch the visual stimulus that results from the movement. This is foundational for numerous necessary eye hand coordination tasks for daily living skills (buttoning a jacket, opening containers/book bags, folding clothes) and school/learning skills (using scissors, arts and crafts, drawing, letter formation and handwriting). In the United States, occupational therapists who work with children with ASD, use play and school based activities to promote the children's bilateral hand coordination and eye hand coordination (visual motor integration). For example, for handwriting, children must hold the paper with one hand and write with the other. Foundational eye hand coordination activities, such as the finger- and hand-gesture enabled interactions with fun and engaging computer games and programs, provides children the opportunity to develop these abilities. Additionally, multiple studies have reported the positive impact of the use of a multi-sensory approach to teach children with ASD and to promote social interactions and engagement [29–31]. Through the use of motion based visual interactive computer games and programs, the child with ASD benefits from a multisensory approach to learning (the motor act of activating the device and the viewing the visual stimulus).

For a nation where even the prevalence study has only started two years ago [32] and government-funded special education is both expensive and limited, in terms of both quality and quantity, affordable and portable technological solutions such as those outlined here could offer great helps to families living with ASD. We hope our study sheds light on the degree of benefits of such hand and figure motion control games for Chinese children with ASD, and also provides preliminary data to call for more HCI community engagement in such research in China.

Acknowledgements. We acknowledge Kean University's financial support to Tiffany Tang under Wenzhou Kean University's Student Partnering with Faculty (SPF) Research Program. The authors are grateful to children and their families at Wenzhou XingLe Children's Educational Development Center for participating in the experiments; thanks also go to Tina Xiaoting Fu, and Esther Mingyue Tang for developing the two games and their efforts during both the experiment and interviews as well as Leila Zeqiang Huang and Relic Yongfu Wang for their helps during the experiment.

References

1. American Psychiatric Association. DSM-V: Diagnostic and statistical manual of mental disorders, 5th Edition. American Psychiatric Publishing, Section 299.00 (2013)
2. Kasari, C., Freeman, S., Paparella, T.: Joint attention and symbolic play in young children with autism: A randomized controlled intervention study. J. Child Psychol. Psychiatry 47(6), 611–620 (2006)
3. Machalicek, W., Shogren, K., Lang, R., Rispoli, M., O'Reilly, M.F., Franco, J.H., Sigafoos, J.: Increasing play and decreasing the challenging behavior of children with autism during recess with activity schedules and task correspondence training. Res. Autism Spectrum Disord. 3(2), 547–555 (2009)
4. Case-Smith, J., Arbesman, M.: Evidence-based review of interventions for autism used in or of relevance to occupational therapy. Am. J. Occup. Ther. 62, 416–429 (2008)
5. Sacrey, L.-A.R., Germani, T., Bryson, S.E., Zwaigenbaum, L.: Reaching and grasping in autism spectrum disorder: a review of recent literature. Front. Neurol. 5(6), 1–12 (2014)
6. Mostofsky, S.H., Dubey, P., Jerath, V.K., Jansiewicz, E.M., Goldberg, M.C., Denckla, M.B.: Developmental dyspraxia is not limited to imitation in children with autism spectrum disorders. J. Int. Neuropsychol. Soc. 12, 314–326 (2006)

7. Leary, M.R., Hill, D.A.: Moving on: autism and movement disturbance. Ment. Retard. **34**, 39–53 (1996)
8. Ming, X., Brimacombe, M., Wagner, G.C.: Prevalence of motor impairments in autism spectrum disorders. Brain Dev. **29**, 565–570 (2007)
9. Fournier, K.A., Hass, C.J., Naik, S.K., Lodha, N., Cauraugh, J.H.: Motor coordination in autism spectrum disorders: a synthesis and meta-analysis. J. Autism Dev. Disord. **10**, 1227–1240 (2010)
10. Jones, V., Prior, M.: Motor imitation abilities and neurological signs in autistic children. J. Autism Dev. Disord. **15**, 37–46 (1985)
11. Haswell, C.C., Izawa, J., Dowell, L.R., Mostofsky, S.H., Shadmehr, R.: Representations of internal models of action in the autistic brain. Nat. Neurosci. **12**, 970–972 (2009)
12. Battocchi, A., Pianesi, F., Tomasini, D., Zancanaro, M., Esposito, G., Venuti, P., Sasson, A.B., Gal, E., Weiss, P.L.: Collaborative puzzle game: a tabletop interactive game for fostering collaboration in children with Autism Spectrum Disorders (ASD). In: Proceedings of the ACM International Conference on Interactive Tabletops and Surfaces (ITS 2009), pp. 197–204. ACM Press (2009)
13. Grandin, T.: My experiences with visual thinking sensory problems and communication difficulties. Center for the Study of Autism (1996)
14. Grandin, T.: Visual abilities and sensory differences in a person with autism. Biol. Psychiatry **65**(1), 15–16 (2009)
15. Simmons, D.R., Robertson, A.E., McKay, L.S., Toal, E., McAleer, P., Pollick, F.E.: Vision in autism spectrum disorders. Vision. Res. **49**(22), 2705–2739 (2009)
16. Behrmann, M., Thomas, C., Humphreys, K.: Seeing it differently: visual processing in autism. Trends Cogn. Sci. **10**(6), 258–264 (2006)
17. Bartoli, L., Corradi, C., Garzotto, F., Valoriani, M.: Exploring motion-based touchless games for autistic children's learning. In: Proceedings of the ACM International Conference on Interaction Design and Children (IDC 2013), pp. 102–111. ACM Press (2013)
18. Bartoli, L., Garzotto, F., Gelsomini, M., Oliveto, L., Valoriani, M.: Designing and evaluating touchless playful interaction for ASD children. In: Proceedings of the ACM International Conference on Interaction Design and Children (IDC 2014), pp. 17–26. ACM Press (2014)
19. Garzotto, F., Gelsomini, M., Oliveto, L., Valoriani, M: Motion-based touchless interaction for ASD children: a case study. In: Proceedings of AVI, pp. 117–120. ACM Press (2014)
20. Ringland, K.E., Zalapa, R. Neal, M, Escobedo, L. Tentori, M. Hayes, G.: SensoryPaint: a natural user interface supporting sensory integration in children with neurodevelopmental disorders. İn: CHI 2014 Extended Abstracts, pp. 1681–1686. ACM Press (2014)
21. Tung, J.Y., Lulic, T., Gonzalez, D.A., Tran, J., Dickerson, C.R., Roy, E.A.: Evaluation of a portable marker less finger position capture device: accuracy of the leap motion controller in healthy adults. Physiol. Meas. **36**(5), 1025–1035 (2015)
22. Tang, T., Winoto, P., Wang, R.: Having fun over a distance: supporting multiplayer online ball passing using multiple sets of kinect. In: CHI 2015 Extended Abstracts, pp. 1187–1192. ACM Press, New York (2015)
23. Zhu, G., Cai, S., Ma, Y., Liu, E.: A series of leap motion-based matching games for enhancing the fine motor skills of children with autism. In: 15th International IEEE Conference on Advanced Learning Technologies (ICALT 2015), pp. 430–431. IEEE (2105)
24. Greis, F., Silva, M., Raposo, A., Suplino, M.: Exploring collaboration patterns in a multitouch game to encourage social interaction and collaboration among users with autism spectrum disorder. Comput. Support. Coop. Work **24**(2-3), 149–175 (2015)

25. Goh, W., Shou, W., Tan, J., Lum, G.T.J.: Interaction design patterns for multi-touch tabletop collaborative games. In: CHI 2012 Extended Abstracts on Human Factors in Computing Systems (CHI EA 2012), pp. 141–150, New York, NY, USA (2012)
26. La Valle, C.: Chinese cultural factors impacting the educational schooling of children with autism in China. DePaul Discoveries, Vol. 2, Issue 1, Article 10 (2013). http://via.library.depaul.edu/depaul-disc/vol2/iss1/10
27. Wang, S.: In China, the making of an app for autism. The Wall Street Journal, 19 May 2015. http://blogs.wsj.com/chinarealtime/2015/05/19/in-china-the-making-of-an-app-for-autism/
28. Marco, E., Barett, L., Hinkley, N., Hill, S., Nagarajan, S.S.: Sensory processing in autism: a review of neurophysiologic findings. Pediatr. Res. **69**(5 Pt 2), 48R–54R (2011)
29. Goldsmith, T.R., LeBlanc, L.A.: Use of technology in interventions for children with autism. J. Early Intensive Behav. Interv. **1**(2), 166 (2004)
30. Hayes, G.R., Hirano, S., Marcu, G., Monibi, M., Nguyen, D.H., Yeganyan, M.: Interactive visual supports for children with autism. Pers. Ubiquit. Comput. **14**(7), 663–680 (2010)
31. Silver, M., Oakes, P.: Evaluation of a new computer intervention to teach people with autism or Asperger syndrome to recognize and predict emotions in others. Autism **5**(3), 299–316 (2001)
32. Clampton, N.: China moves to tackle autism with first study of prevalence. South China Morning Post (2013)
33. Grandin, T.: Thinking in Pictures, Expanded Edition: My Life with Autism. Vintage, New York (2008)
34. Frith, C., Law, J.: Cognitive and physiological processes underlying drawing skills. Leonardo **28**(3), 203–205 (1995)
35. Harper, R., Mentis, H.: The mocking gaze: the social organization of kinect use. In: Proceedings of ACM CSCW 2013, pp. 167–180. ACM Press, New York. (2013)

Proactive Functions of a Pedagogical Agent – Steps for Implementing a Social Catalyst Function

Madlen Wuttke[1]([✉]), Michael Heidt[2], Paul Rosenthal[3], Peter Ohler[4], and Nicholas H. Müller[4]

[1] Media-Psychology, Faculty of Humanities, Chemnitz University
of Technology, Reichenhainer Straße 39, 09126 Chemnitz, Germany
madlen.wuttke@phil.tu-chemnitz.de
[2] Visual Computing Laboratory, Faculty of Informatics, Chemnitz University
of Technology, Reichenhainer Str. 39, 09126 Chemnitz, Germany
michael.heidt@informatik.tu-chemnitz.de
[3] Visual Computing Laboratory, Faculty of Informatics, Chemnitz University
of Technology, Straße der Nationen 62, 09111 Chemnitz, Germany
paul.rosenthal@informatik.tu-chemnitz.de
[4] Media-Psychology, Faculty of Humanities, Chemnitz University
of Technology, Thueringer Weg 11, 09126 Chemnitz, Germany
{peter.ohler,nicholas.mueller}@phil.tu-chemnitz.de

Abstract. The development of pedagogical agents has been focused on the empirical relevance of outward appearance and the voiced conveyance of information. Rather than following these steps of analysing agents' looks, the following paper is focused on having pedagogical agents function proactively in regard to the environment the learner is situated in. This means agents are able to listen and react to noise disturbances or obvious attention diversion by the learner. Furthermore, the agent is enhanced by a social catalyst routine, enabling the system to facilitate cooperative learning through the use of narrative techniques for the retention of information.

Keywords: Pedagogical · Agent · Proactive · Narrative · Learning · Social catalyst

1 Introduction

As it has been previously mentioned [45], the underlying technical aspects of pedagogical agent designs have been analyzed in various detail regarding their outward appearances. Examples being their depiction regarding the displayed gender and its influence on learners [2, 15, 16], the inclusion of facial action movement capabilities in order to convey non-verbal cues [1, 14], ethnicity [13] or whether or not the inclusion of animations is hindering or beneficial within the learning context [4, 18, 22].

Compared to these varying degrees of investing resources to have a pedagogical agent appear more lifelike, we propose a shift in effort to reengineer the mechanisms of an agent and to enhance its capabilities to not only convey information but to include

© Springer International Publishing Switzerland 2016
P. Zaphiris and A. Ioannou (Eds.): LCT 2016, LNCS 9753, pp. 573–580, 2016.
DOI: 10.1007/978-3-319-39483-1_52

the environment, other learners than the one in front of the screen and other elements into the learning experience. Therefore, building on the described exhibition context described earlier [18, 46] we present the interactions of different technological aspects, working towards a social catalyst function due to proactive elements. Thereby we integrate works about passive aspects of pedagogical agent design like the politeness and the social conversational style, as in the wording choices of information conveyance, the amicability of the agent and whether or not it would be useful to include discussions about topics not related to the information material at hand [28, 30], the creation of a beneficial learning environment regarding communication beyond the learning material [29] as well as the possibilities of including gestures and facial mimics [9] or non-verbal input [3]. For a broader view on the topic, refer to [12].

Therefore, a systematic consideration of individual learning requirements is not yet the focus of empirical research. So, while there is ample research about the various facets of the depiction of a pedagogical agent inside an information transfer situation, there is very little about the human-computer-interface-features which an agent might be able to provide to the user. But to integrate a pedagogical agent into a learning environment and in order to have it be able to integrate active listening, visual observations and additional information just-in-time, the system has to perform pro-actively and include these aspects into the predetermined learning context.

2 Proactive Enhancements of the Agent System

Reeves and Nass [23] have already proposed that there is a deep social link between users and computer systems. They postulate that there is a human tendency to act social in a conversational situation, even if this communication is aimed at a machine. However, Lester et al. [17] formulated a persona effect which includes the observed behavior by Reeves and Nass and expand it by focusing on the anthropomorphic depiction of an agent. But if a user is acting socially towards a machine, then it appears only logical to assume that a user will in turn expect to receive socially adequate responses from an agent system. Nevertheless, human to human conversational strategies are not limited to the rather limited input devices of modern day computer systems. Instead, they are heavily dependent on the decoding capabilities of non-verbal communication attempts like for example intonation, facial expressions and the gaze of the conversation partner. Therefore a way of including the sensor-array of currently available hardware into the communication with a pedagogical agent was developed. A commonly used webcam is consequently utilized to detect a user's gaze upon the display. Should it divert away from the presented information material, the presentation is stopped. Furthermore a microphone is used to check for ambient noise levels and checks, whether or not the verbal output of the agent can be understood by the learner in front of the screen. Hence, the pedagogical agent is upgraded to the real world capabilities of any other teacher tasked with conveying learning materials: if the student is not attentive or if it is too noisy, the agent will suspend the presentation and continue, once the environment or non-verbal cues by the learner allow it.

As previous experience has shown, incorporation of narrative elements can be an effective tool towards strengthening visitor engagement [21]. Therefore we are going to enhance the previously outlined museum installation [46] by aspects of technical and narrative learner engagement. For example, due to the added microphone to listen in on the environment, the agent system would be able to check for background noises which might hinder the experience of a specific museum exhibit (e.g. of musical instruments or the presentation inside a cinema). Furthermore, the agent might be listening for keywords uttered by nearby visitors, which could indicate a common interest for an exhibit and therefore initialize the social catalyst routine, as described in [46]. The webcam on the other hand would be capable to check for signs of confusion or other unwanted emotions which would indicate a hindered experience of the exhibitions. Using libraries of the Facial Action Coding System [14] the 'brow lowerer' could indicate that something has not been understood or that the visitor does not recognize the elements as described by the agent system. Therefore, the system might explain the last part in a different way or with a different visualization, until the 'brow lowerer' is either not recognized anymore or might even be replaced by an 'outer brow raiser', which might indicate, that a user has found something that was missing before. Our constructive efforts are informed by a methodology for interdisciplinary development [20] based on analyses of interdisciplinary practice [7, 18, 19].

Obviously, other forms of physiological interaction with the agent system are within the bounds of possibility for current technology. Smartwear, like the Android-wear or fitness-trackers, offer a wide range of available biophysiological information about the user. The Microsoft-Band [2] for example offers skin-conductance measurements next to continuous heart-rate monitoring and movements. These kinds of measurements were limited to expensive and specialized research hardware a few years ago, but offer new perspectives for user-centered agent designs. Changes in biophysiological feedback can signal the system not to pursue an available connection between two visitors [46] and changes in the usual physiological measurement when looking at an exhibition can be used to determine interest within a topical domain or not. Additionally, gaze tracking via webcams is already widely researched as being capable of facilitating new forms of interaction with a device [5, 7] while real eye-tracking devices tend to become more readily available [27], allowing for the implementation of interaction strategies for handicapped or incapacitated persons [19, 24].

Furthermore, narrative techniques are used to enhance the learning context, to facilitate an interaction process between the strangers visiting the exhibition, enabling the agent system to provide the previously described social catalyst capabilities while reporting the current status of software development and hardware integration.

Due to narratives being a form of information conveyance, its origins can be found in a time when writing was not available to the population [8, 25, 33]. As Gerrig [16] points out, the information processing is the same, whether the received information is fictional or real. Regarding the proactive pedagogical agent, it has to be deemed trustworthy in order to facilitate a believability, but possesses the power to convey complex information in a more accessible way [20]. Within this context, Bruner [6] states that experiences and memories are stored as stories. This in turn should lead to a better retention of conveyed information when it is already presented while taking narrative structures into account.

So by being mindful of narrative structures, like temporal cohesion, progression of storyline and the individual complex developments of the characters [48], the learning material is anchored [26]. But this means a greater complexity for the agent system itself, since it has to obey the basic narrative structures and has to include the acquired environmental information. In order to achieve this goal, the learning material has to be pre-structured according to narrative rules.

- Narrations are recognizable patterns of characters, events and have to regard cultural storytelling techniques [35].
- Stories itself are not considered to be interesting. Only by the inclusion of one or more relatable characters, a narration is able to function [36].
- Since characters are pivotal, the current living situation has to be 'threatened' [6, 37, 38, 40, 44] but the crisis can be resolved by implementing newly experienced events.
- Stereotypical applications of characters can be used to reduce the complexity of the narrated scenario [42].

In order to keep the development of the learning material at a lower level of complexity, the narrative technique of five acts should be implemented [43].

1. Characters and the basic setting is described, upcoming challenges are insinuated but kept vague.
2. Events are depicted in greater detail and the introduced characters are confronted with the challenges ahead.
3. Depicted occurrences culminate into a cataclysmic event which the characters are not able to solve with the acquired knowledge up to this point.
4. The characters are given time to reevaluate their attempts, their knowledge and to complement their learned lessons.
5. A reintroduction of the events in step three, accompanied by ways of implementing the learned and trained knowledge to succeed in the storyline.

By implementing these features, the learner is able to gather relevant information in a concrete and tangible way while maintaining an easy to memorize structure of the learning material.

3   The Agent as a Social Catalyst

Due to the necessity of relatable characters and based on the narrative structure, the agent system is then capable of integrating other visitors of the exhibition into the learning scenario. By implementing the already described steps [46] to facilitate a communication between former strangers, the proactive pedagogical agent is able to structure learning material according to the storyline. Therefore the aforementioned model [46] is augmented by the narrative elements.

1. Based on information about the users beforehand, the system makes an initial analysis about user interest compatibility
2. The initial connection to another user is facilitated by the two respective agents onscreen, depending on the proximity of the users to each other and an exhibit which is used as an anchor for the initiation

3. Once the agents acknowledge each other, the storyline is adapted to the specific interests and used to engage the users into a conversation by pre-structuring the knowledge elements
4. Users have the option to decline this event in a courteous way without offending the other person – the agents then disengage and continue to function as a traditional information system while increasing the distance to the failed interaction
5. If the interaction is confirmed by both parties, the agents join each other visibly on the shared screen adjacent to the exhibition and initiate the information conveyance by building on the narrative structure

4 Proactively Enhanced Museum Exhibition

In accordance with the published scenario, the two level system of a handheld mobile device and a wall mounted installation is retained [46]. The tablet is used to display information about the exhibit in conjunction with environmental information like location, chain of visited exhibits and predetermined interests of the user. Wall mounted displays transmit information via RFID or simple QR Code like information encoding and trigger adequate reactions inside the electronic educational instance (EEI) [45, 47] (Fig. 1).

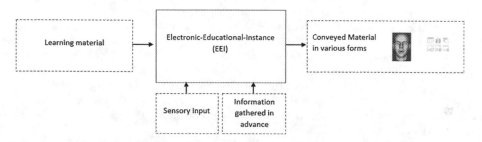

Fig. 1. Enhanced model of the Electronic Educational Instance (EEI) [45, 47]

Within this enhanced EEI, the additional environmental information of the sensory input is obtained, analysed and a corresponding variation of the learning material is prepared. Thereby, the proactive pedagogical agent is capable of detecting potentially hindering elements and is able to form a situational context within the exhibition. Accordingly, in conjunction with the previously entered person specific information, the learning material can be adapted to information about the users and is capable to proactively prepare the learning material for people with impairments.

The newly integrated sensory input devices is capable of gathering information about the environment and to adapt to the individual preferences and outside information. Due to the expanded social catalyst function, the visitors of the exhibition are, with the help of their information devices as well as their personal agents, enabled to learn on their own or in cooperation with other, like-minded visitors.

5 Conclusion

The presented paper discussed the pre-requirements for the development of pedagogical agents as well as the current steps being undertaken to enable the proactive functions of the agent system in the form of the aforementioned model regarding the enhanced electronic educational instance. This EEI model is currently used to integrate already established learning material and to integrate sensory input on stationary and mobile devices.

References

1. Agada, R., Yan, J.: Research to improve communication by animated pedagogical agents. J. Nextp Gener. Inf. Technol. **3**(1), 58–69 (2012)
2. Baylor, A.L., Rosenberg-Kima, R.B., Plant, E.A.: Interface agents as social models: the impact of appearance on females' attitude toward engineering. In: Conference on Human Factors in Computing Systems (CHI 2006), Montreal (2006)
3. Baylor, A.L., Kim, S.: Designing nonverbal communication for pedagogical agents: when less is more. Comput. Hum. Behav. **25**, 450–457 (2009)
4. Baylor, A.L., Ryu, J.: The effects of image and animation in enhancing pedagogical agent persona. J. Educ. Comput. Res. **28**(4), 373–395 (2003)
5. Becker, L.: Apple erhält Patent auf Eye-Tracking-Technik. (2015). http://www.heise.de/newsticker/meldung/Apple-erhaelt-Patent-auf-Eye-Tracking-Technik-2523025.html
6. Benjamin, W.: Erzählen - Schriften zur Theorie der Narration und zur literarischen Prosa. Suhrkamp Verlag, Sinzheim (2007)
7. Bischof, A., Obländer, V., Heidt, M., Kanellopoulos, K., Küszter, V., Liebold, B., Martin, K.-U., Pietschmann, D., Storz, M., Tallig, A., Teichmann, M., Wuttke, M.: Interdisziplinäre Impulse für den Begriff "Interaktion". In: Hobohm, H.-C. (ed.) Informationswissenschaft Zwischen Virtueller Infrastruktur Und Materiellen Lebenswelten. Tagungsband Des 13. Internationalen Symposiums Für Informationswissenschaft (ISI 2013), pp. 448–453. Hülsbusch, Glücksstadt (2013)
8. Bruner, J.: Actual Minds, Possible Worlds. Harvard University Press, Cambridge (1986)
9. Campbell, J.: The Hero with a Thousand Faces, 2nd edn. Princeton University Press, New York (1968). (Third Printing 1973 Ausg.)
10. Cheng, J.: Samsung Takes Eye-Scrolling Technology to Disabled Community (2014). http://blogs.wsj.com/digits/2014/11/25/samsung-takes-eye-scrolling-technology-to-disabled-community/?mod=WSJBlog&utm_source=twitterfeed&utm_medium=twitter
11. Cobley, P.: Narrative. Routledge, New York (2014)
12. Craig, S.D., Gholson, B., Driscoll, D.M.: Animated pedagogical agents in multimedia educational environments: effects of agent properties, picture features, and redundancy. J. Educ. Psychol. **94**(2), 428–434 (2002)
13. Crittenden, C.: Fictional characters and logical completeness. Poetics **11**, 331–344 (1982)
14. Ekman, P., Friesen, W.V., Hager, J.C.: Facial Action Coding System - The Manual. Research Nexus division of Network Information Research Corporation, Salt Lake City (2002)
15. Freytag, G.: Die Technik des Dramas. Verlag von S. Hirzel, Leipzig (1863)
16. Gerrig, R.J.: Experiencing Narrative Worlds. On the Psychological Activities of Reading. Westview Press, London (1993)

17. Heidig, S., Clarebout, G.: Do pedagogical agents make a difference to student motivation and learning? Educ. Res. Rev. **6**, 27–54 (2011)
18. Heidt, Michael: Examining interdisciplinary prototyping in the context of cultural communication. In: Marcus, Aaron (ed.) DUXU 2013, Part II. LNCS, vol. 8013, pp. 54–61. Springer, Heidelberg (2013)
19. Heidt, M.: Reconstructing coding practice - towards a methodology for source-code. In: Boll, S., Maaß, S., Malaka, R. (eds.) Mensch & Computer 2013 - Workshopband, pp. 271–275. Oldenbourg Verlag, München (2013)
20. Heidt, M., Kanellopoulos, K., Pfeiffer, L., Rosenthal, P.: Diverse ecologies – interdisciplinary development for cultural education. In: Kotzé, P., Marsden, G., Lindgaard, G., Wesson, J., Winckler, M. (eds.) INTERACT 2013, Part IV. LNCS, vol. 8120, pp. 539–546. Springer, Heidelberg (2013)
21. Heidt, M., Pfeiffer, L., Berger, A., Rosenthal, P.: PRMD. In: Mensch & Computer 2014 - Workshopband. De Gruyter Oldenbourg, pp. 45–48 (2014)
22. Hendricks, W.O.: The structural study of narration. Poetics **1**(3), 100–123 (1972)
23. Huang, H.-H., Cerekovic, A., Pandzic, I.S., Nakano, Y., Nishida, T.: Toward a multi-culture adaptive virtual tour guide agent with a modular approach. Artif. Intell. Soc. **24**, 225–235 (2009)
24. Kapoor, A., Qi, Y., Picard, R. W.: Fully automatic upper facial action recognition. In: IEEE International Workshop Analysis and Modeling of Faces and Gestures AMFG 2003, pp. 195–202 (2003)
25. Kim, Y., Baylor, A.L., Shen, E.: Pedagogical agents as learning companions: the impact of agent emotion and gender. J. Comput. Assist. Learn. **23**, 220–234 (2007)
26. Kim, Y., Wei, Q.: The impact of learner attributes and learner choice in an agent-based environment. Comput. Educ. **56**, 505–514 (2011)
27. Lebowitz, M.: Creating characters in a story-telling universe. Poetics **13**, 171–194 (1984)
28. Lester, J.C., Converse, S.A., Kahler, S.E., Barlow, S.T., Stone, B.A., Bhogal, R.S.: The persona effect: affective impact of animated pedagogical agents. In: Pemberton, S. (ed.) Human Factors in Computing Systems: CHI 1997 Conference Proceedings, pp. 359–366. ACM Press, New York (1997)
29. Lusk, M.M., Atkinson, R.K.: Animated pedagogical agents: does their degree of embodiment impact learning from static or animated worked examples? Appl. Cogn. Psychol. **21**, 747–764 (2007)
30. Majaranta, P.: Communication and text entry by Gaze. In: Majaranta, P., Aoki, H., Donegan, M., Hansen, D.W., Hansen, J.P., Hyrskykary, A., Räihä, K.-J. (eds.) Gaze Interaction and Applications of Eye Tracking. IGI Global, New York (2012)
31. Mar, R.A.: The neuropsychology of narrative: story comprehension, story production and their interrelation. Neuropsychologia **42**, 1414–1434 (2004)
32. Mattila, Anna S.: The role of narratives in the advertising of experiential services. J. Serv. Res. **3**(1), 35–45 (2000)
33. Mielke, C.: Zyklisch-serielle Narration: erzähltes Erzählen von 1001 Nacht bis zur TV-Serie. Walter de Gruyter GmbH & Co KG, Berlin (2006)
34. Moreno, R., Flowerday, T.: Student's choice of animated pedagogical agents in science learning: a test of the similarity-attraction hypothesis on gender and ethnicity. Contemp. Educ. Psychol. **31**, 186–207 (2006)
35. Parker, P.: Die Kreative Matrix. UVK Verlagsgesellschaft, Konstanz (2005)
36. Reeves, B., Nass, C.: The Media Equation: How People Treat Computers, Televisions, and New Media like Real People and Places. Cambridge University Press, New York (1996)

37. Scovsgaard, H., Räihä, K.-J., Tall, M.: Computer Control by Gaze. In: Majaranta, P., Aoki, H., Donegan, M., Hansen, D.W., Hansen, J.P., Hyrskykary, A., Räihä, K.-J. (eds.) Gaze Interaction and Applications of Eye Tracking. IGI Global, New York (2012)
38. Sugiyama, M.S.: On the origins of narrative. Hum. Nat. **7**(4), 403–425 (1996)
39. Vanderbilt, T.C.A.T.G.: Anchored instruction and its relationship to situated cognition. Educ. Researcher **19**(6), 2–10 (1990)
40. TheEyeTribe: The World's first $99 eye tracker with full SDK (2015). https://www.theeyetribe.com/
41. Veletsianos, G.: The impact and implications of virtual character expressiveness on learning and agent–learner interactions. J. Comput. Assist. Learn. **25**, 345–357 (2009)
42. Veletsianos, G.: How do learners respond to pedagogical agents that deliver social-oriented non-task messages? impact on student learning, perceptions, and experiences. Comput. Hum. Behav. **28**, 275–283 (2012)
43. Wang, N., Johnson, W.L., Mayer, R.E., Risso, P., Shaw, E., Collins, H.: The politeness effect: pedagogical agents and learning outcomes. Int. J. Hum. Comput. Stud. **66**, 98–112 (2008)
44. Wood, S.: Writer's Digest - Write Better Get Published. Abgerufen am 18. März 2010 von 9 Tricks to Writing Suspense Fiction (2008). http://www.writersdigest.com/article/nine-tricks-to-writing-suspense-fiction
45. Wuttke, M.: Pro-active pedagogical agents. In: Fakultät für Informatik (ed.). Proceedings of International Summer Workshop Computer Science, pp. 59–62 (2013)
46. Wuttke, M., Heidt, M.: Beyond presentation - employing proactive intelligent agents as social catalysts. In: Kurosu, M. (ed.) HCI 2014, Part II. LNCS, vol. 8511, pp. 182–190. Springer, Heidelberg (2014). doi:10.1007/978-3-319-07230-2
47. Wuttke, M., Martin, K.-U.: Natural forms of communication and adaptive behaviour in human-computer-interaction. In: Kurosu, M. (ed.) HCI 2014, Part II. LNCS, vol. 8511, pp. 641–647. Springer, Heidelberg (2014). doi:10.1007/978-3-319-07230-2
48. Wuttke, M., Belentschikow, V., Müller, N.H.: Storytelling as a means to transfer knowledge via narration–a scenario for a narrating pedagogical agent. i-com **14**(2), 155–160 (2015). doi:10.1515/icom-2015-0034

Collaboration Technologies

On the Effectiveness of a Collaborative Virtual Pair-Programming Environment

Ahmad Al-Jarrah$^{(\boxtimes)}$ and Enrico Pontelli

Department of Computer Science, New Mexico State University,
Las Cruces, NM, USA
{jarrah,epontell}@nmsu.edu

Abstract. In this paper, we assess the effectiveness of an extension of Alice, named *AliCe-ViLlagE,* which allows two students to work on the same project, with synchronous communication mechanisms and shared view of the same virtual working environment. The virtual environment supports multi-modal interactions among students (e.g., video, instant messaging). *AliCe-ViLlagE* collects statistics about each team members contributions, allowing for evaluation of the effectiveness of the collaborative environment, and supporting teacher's assessment of the team work. The paper describes the first formal evaluation of the *AliCe-ViLlagE* platform with a group of undergraduate students. The results show impressive results in terms of number of interactions between the students, enabled by the *AliCe-ViLlagE* framework, levels of satisfaction of the students, and completion time.

1 Introduction

AliCe-ViLlagE [1] is a novel extension of the Alice introductory programming environment [15], that enables interaction and collaboration among students in the development of programs. In this paper, we assess the *Collaborative Virtual Pair Programming (CVPP)* model and *AliCe-ViLlagE* . In this evaluation, we aim to investigate the benefits of using a collaborative virtual environment for learning programming. The evaluation tests two hypotheses: **(1)** Building a collaborative virtual learning environment for learning programming through extending the standard pair-programming model to CVPP makes the group interaction more effective and usable in the programming group. **(2)** Extending Alice into a collaborative virtual learning environment that implements the CVPP model makes learning programming within a group more effective and creates more interaction between the group members. In this paper, we present the evaluation of *AliCe-ViLlagE* in the context of learning programming with entering undergraduate computer science students.

Motivations. The Computer Science community is facing a complex question [8]—how to engage more students in gaining competency in computing (and possibly pursue academic degrees in the field of computing), in order to meet the pressing demand for trained computing workforce. Unfortunately, while more

© Springer International Publishing Switzerland 2016
P. Zaphiris and A. Ioannou (Eds.): LCT 2016, LNCS 9753, pp. 583–595, 2016.
DOI: 10.1007/978-3-319-39483-1_53

and more jobs demand sophisticated computing skills, the number of students considering careers in this field remains abysmally low [7,12,14]. According to the United States Bureau of Labor Statistics, the number of professional positions in computer science is increasing at a rapid pace. The projections indicate growths in number of positions of more than 20 % by 2022 in all core areas of computing, making computing the fastest growing cluster among all occupations. Moreover, according to statistics from the *Computing Research Association (CRA)*, women represent 51 % of the US population while only 12.9 % of undergraduate degrees in computer science are granted to women [22].

The somber numbers of students pursuing computing can be attributed to a variety of factors—e.g., negative image [3,20], fear of offshoring. But a critical factor lies in the CS gaps in the K-12 system. While other countries have enhanced their educational efforts in computing (e.g., China has integrated CS throughout the high school math curricula [16]), the CS Teachers Association (CSTA) reports a neglect of CS at the high school level in the U.S. From 2005 to 2009, the percentage of schools offering CS courses dropped from 40 % to 27 %, due to lack of interest and lack of teachers; CS courses often count only as general electives, not as college-preparatory electives [19]; many of them are more about use of applications than actual CT. Students are often faced with scarce access to introductory computing courses, and they are often isolated in their learning experiences, especially when the learning experience takes place in afterschool programs and in rural communities.

AliCe-ViLlagE. In this paper, we describe an evaluation of a collaborative virtual pair programming model (CVPP) and its implementation in a novel collaborative environment for *Alice programmers,* called *AliCe-ViLlagE* . The CVPP model is an extension of a standard pair programming (PP) model. Two programmers collaborate to solve a shared programming task. The design of CVPP allows programmers to work together over distance—e.g., each programmer sits in a different room, building, city. CVPP supports the original pair programming model (i.e., a driver and a navigator) as well as allowing variations of this model. The ability to provide dynamic modifications of roles allows CVPP to support more flexible pair programming models, where the two team members can play the two roles (driver role and navigator role) at the same time. There is a significant value in allowing this type of extension:

- It allows both team members to act as concurrent navigators—which is important for brainstorming and debugging;
- It allows both team members to act as concurrent drivers—enabling modular development of an Alice project.

The implementation of CVPP in the context of Alice requires the addition of new features and functionalities to facilitate concurrent programming of 3D worlds by a *group of programmers*. We refer to the new environment as AliCe-ViLlagE [1]. The environment combines the benefits of using Alice in teaching programming and the benefits of using a collaborative PP model in programming and learning, e.g., increased technical experiences and skills exchange, sharing of information, better program quality with fewer bugs, and enhanced student confidence.

The first version of *AliCe-ViLlagE* focuses on two-people teams. The *AliCe-ViLlagE* framework is designed to meet the following requirements:

- The assignment of roles to team members should be dynamically changeable;
- The system should allow roles to be *assigned* (e.g., a teacher requiring the two students to maintain fixed roles) as well as roles that can be modified on-demand by the team-members;
- Each team member should be allowed to view the code on his/her own display, and the two team members should be allowed to collaborate even if not physically at the same location;
- *AliCe-ViLlagE* should provide a *synchronous* behavior: each change to the code made by one team member should be immediately reflected on the view provided to the second team member.

The environment provides a number of functionalities aimed at maintaining a record of the contributions of each team member to a given project (e.g., for review by an instructor). *AliCe-ViLlagE* records the contribution of each member in a log file; these contributions can be reviewed in summary form (e.g., in a table or a bar chart). *AliCe-ViLlagE* allows the instructor not just to monitor the progress for each team, but it provide him/her with all required information to evaluate the individual contributions of each member. Thanks to these features, *AliCe-ViLlagE* is more than a programming environment: it is a collaborative virtual learning environment, promoting collaboration, simultaneous code development, and interaction regardless of physical location. *AliCe-ViLlagE* programmers work on the development of a 3D world by programming in a virtual environment. Furthermore, consistency controls are present to prevent conflicting modifications of the same entity. The contribution of this paper is the first evaluation of *AliCe-ViLlagE* with students in an actual learning setting.

2   Brief Literature Review

While the practices of programming have always acknowledged the importance of teamwork and collaboration, it was only in the 1980s that software engineering research started highlighting the benefits of software development activities conducted by teams of two people at the same workstation. Larry Constantine was perhaps one of the first researchers to investigate the benefits of working in pairs in programming tasks, like producing code faster with fewer errors; he referred to this practice as *Dynamic Duos* [6]. Working in pairs is not new, but studying pair programming as methodology started by the end of 1990s. The authors of [13] reported that pair programming started gaining traction and popularity around 1995.

Software engineering research has, since then, widely explored pair programming (e.g., [2,4,9,11,17,21]). Pair programming is one of the practices of Extreme Programming (XP) and is one of the Agile Methods [9] in software development. In pair programming, two programmers work collaboratively at one computer on the same design, algorithm; researchers emphasized the importance to control such interaction—e.g., the authors of [5] require a single keyboard, monitor, and mouse to be shared between the pair. One of the team members in a pair is assigned the role of the *driver,* where s/he has the control of the keyboard and the mouse; the second member plays the role of the *navigator* (also known as *observer* or *pointer*) [2,4]. The navigator has a more strategic role, such as looking for errors, thinking about the overall structure of the code, finding necessary information and brainstorming with the driver [9].

Several case studies reported a positive effect of pair programming. The authors of [4] indicate that a good pair programming team is fast, efficient, and effective. According to [4], pair programming leads to fewer bugs, a better understanding of the code structure, higher quality of code, better design and improved morale. The authors of [11] conclude that students who work in pairs, produce better programs and pair programming can be used effectively in an introductory programming class. The authors of [21] strongly support such conclusions; students in pair programming tend to develop a positive attitude towards collaborative programming, while developing stronger individual programming skills—thus, working in pairs does not affect the ability to work individually in the future. Also, the conclusion of [18] include that pair programming affects people's habits, helping them to focus more on productive activities.

3   Methodology

In this investigation, we design two programming assignments which ask students to build a 3D world. Students in the team are located at different sites, and they need to use Alice or *AliCe-ViLlagE* to build a solution to the two assignments. In the case of Alice, students are required to use "traditional" communication mechanisms (e.g., email) to communicate and transfer ideas and information among them. In *AliCe-ViLlagE* , students are asked to use the built-in communication channels (e.g., text chat, audio, video conference).

Participants to the study are randomly assigned to teams, each consisting of two students. Each team has to work on both programming assignments. To make the comparison fair, half of the teams start by solving the selected assignment using Alice and then switch to *AliCe-ViLlagE* for the second assignment, while the other teams start by using *AliCe-ViLlagE* and then switch to Alice. The two members of each team are placed in two different rooms, and they are unable to see each others or directly interact. After completing each assignment, the students are asked to complete a survey.

3.1   Background of the Participants

The experiment is targeted to entering computer science undergraduate students. Participation to the experiment has been solicited through email announcements sent to the mailing lists in the Computer Science Department at New Mexico

State University. We recruited 10 students, organized in 5 teams. Throughout the study, the identities of the participants have been kept anonymous and no personal information was revealed or required—except for information regarding the students' academic background. At the beginning of the session for each team, students have been asked to complete a pre-survey, in order to assess their academic background and programming skills (Table 1).

In the pre-survey, students are asked to describe their experience levels in the different related topics (as shown in Table 1). the overall programming experience of participants is low. Figure 1(left) summarizes the overall level of confidence of the participants in all the areas related to programming, Alice, and collaborative environments. Figure 1(right) summarizes the level of experience for the different areas.

Table 1. The Pre-survey

Part 1: You need to answer the following question at the beginning of the study.				
1.	Rank your knowledge/experience with the Alice language			
	Very Low			Very High
	1	2	3	4	5
2.	Rank your experience working with partner programming teams			
	Very Low			Very High
	1	2	3	4	5
3.	Rank your experience working with collaborative tools (e.g. shareflow, Dooster, Asana, etc.)			
	Very Low			Very High
	1	2	3	4	5
4.	I usually work physically close to my teammate(s).			
	Strongly Disagree			Strongly Agree
	1	2	3	4	5
5.	Rank your programming experience level.			
	Very Low			Very High
	1	2	3	4	5
6.	Rank your experience level with using IDE (e.g. Eclipse, NetBeans, Visual studio, et.)			
	Very Low			Very High
	1	2	3	4	5
7.	Rank your experience with Block-Based programming (e.g. Scratch, App Inventor, ToolBox, etc.)			
	Very Low			Very High
	1	2	3	4	5

3.2 Assignments

The assignments are group assignments. Therefore, the team members have to work together to finish the assignment's requirements. In each assignment, the team has to build a 3D Alice world. In the first assignment, the story talks about city life, while the second talks about kids that are playing in a farm. In both assignments, students need to add all components of the scene, such as incrementally building the city in the first assignment (e.g., by adding buildings, roads, traffic sign, cars, people, etc.) and the farm components in the second assignment (e.g. farm house, animals, trees, kids, etc.). In each assignment, the students have to add the program components (e.g., objects, methods, function, statements, etc.), and they need to discuss within the team what other components are required to complete the assignment. As part of the assignment, we are requesting students to communicate among themselves the issues encountered during the resolution of each assignment and to coordinate within the team on the completion of the work (e.g., by agreeing on who does what). In Alice, the team has to select a "standard" communication channel, while *AliCe-ViLlagE* provides dedicated communication channels that are built in the environment.

3.3 Questionnaire Design and Measures

After completing each assignment, the students have been asked to fill out a survey about the environment adopted in the work. Table 2(a) and (b) show the

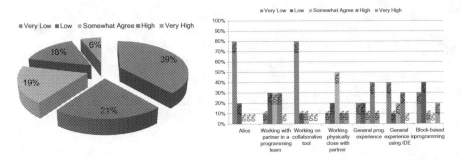

Fig. 1. The overall experience in all fields (left) and experience by area (right) (Color figure online)

questions that students have to answer after completing their work using Alice and *AliCe-ViLlagE* , respectively. Each question in the survey is used to rate one aspect of the programming and collaboration experience, rated on a Likert scale from *"Strongly Agree"* = 5 to *"Strongly Disagree"* = 1.

Table 2. The Post-survey

(a) Alice

(b) *AliCe-ViLlagE*

4   Discussion and Findings (Descriptive Analysis)

In this section, we discuss and analyze the students' behavior during the team-based resolution of the assignment, and analyze their answers for each question in both surveys. At the beginning, we study the students behavior and interaction while they work on each assignment. Parameters that we observe include the number of transactions—a transaction is any event that the student perform in the development of the program, such as adding an object, adding a method, adding a function, editing a method, changing a value, etc.—the amount of time to complete each task, and the percentage of time spent on other activities (e.g., communication).

4.1   Analysis of the Time-Line During Software Development

AliCe-ViLlagE records the students' events and transactions in a log file, and provides statistical representation of the activities in charts and tables. Unfortunately, Alice does not offer comparable analytical capabilities. Therefore, we use a free application to record the student screen in Alice environment. Figure 2 shows the total of transaction that each group completed using Alice and *AliCe-ViLlagE* . The figure shows that the percentage of transactions successfully completed by each team using *AliCe-ViLlagE* is significantly larger than the corresponding percentage of transactions completed using Alice. Each group used each environment for thirty minutes, and the amount of works finished by each group in *AliCe-ViLlagE* are larger than the amount of works finished in Alice. In other word, respect to the required time to complete the assignment, we found that the time required to complete the whole assignment using Alice will be around the double time that required to complete the same assignment using *AliCe-ViLlagE* .

The reason of the big gab between the number of finished transactions is related to the total of time that each student in the group spends working on the program. In Alice, one of the group member should work while the other member wait until his/her partner finishes and sends the 3D world using any communication channel (e.g., email). Figure 3 shows the time line for each team. The figure shows that, in the case of Alice, it is

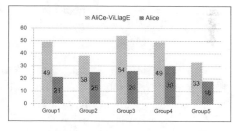

Fig. 2. Percentage of completed transactions for each team under different environments(Color figure online)

common for one student to work at a specific time while the other member is often idle, waiting for the partner to share the partially completed project. The idle student cannot easily brainstorm, looking for errors or share immediate ideas with his partner because, s/he does not have access to the latest version of the program and does not know exactly what aspect of the project the other team member is specifically working on. This type of situation instead does not

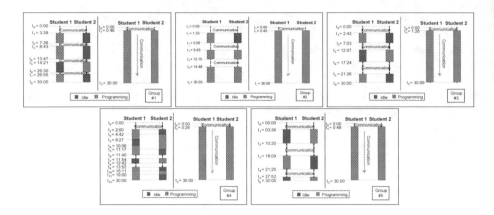

Fig. 3. The time line of each team solving the same assignments—Alice on the and *AliCe-ViLlagE* on the right

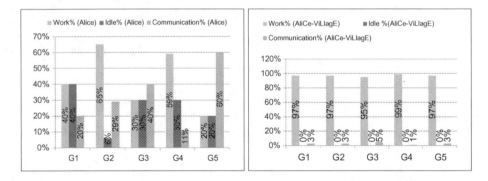

Fig. 4. Percentage of time dedicated to programming, idle, communication in Alice (left) and *AliCe-ViLlagE* (right)(Color figure online)

occur in *AliCe-ViLlagE* . *AliCe-ViLlagE* allows both students to work at the same time, sharing the same synchronized view of the 3D world, immediately reflecting any modifications made.

Figure 4 shows the percentage time for each team that has been dedicated to coding, communication, and idle time during the team activities. Comparing the percentage of coding time for each team in Alice against *AliCe-ViLlagE* (Fig. 4), we observe that students in *AliCe-ViLlagE* spend the majority of their time coding (from 95 % to 99 % of the time). In Alice, students spend a high percentage of time idle. We can also observe that in all the experiments, the idle time in *AliCe-ViLlagE* is actually 0.

In Fig. 3, teams 1, 3, and 5 work smoothly using Alice, while teams 2 and 4 face difficulties. Figure 4(left) shows that the coding time for the two groups is high, especially in team 2, and idle time is very low. This percentages for these two teams are derived from a very undesirable pattern: each student in the team works on a local copy of the 3D world and does not wait for his/her partner to send him/her the file. This results in miscommunication and conflicting solutions in the project. Team 2 discovers this problem at the end, when one of the students send a message to his/her partner about it; *"It is like passing a file from one person to another"*. They found that the file that each one have contains a different contents from the file on his/her partner side, and the result that they got is presented by a message when a member send to his/her partner said: *"We cannot integrate our work"*.

4.2   Post-survey Part2

Each team has to build a story in Alice by following one of the two assignments. After finishing the assignment within a given time limit (30 min per assignment), each student completes a survey about working in Alice with a partner over distance. The questions assess the effectiveness of using Alice in collaborative group to solve an introductory programming assignment.

The first two question asks the student to assess the communication channels used in the project. Figure 5(a) shows that all teams use emails as a main communication channel, to exchange information, questions and to transfer files between team members. The results also show that no team opted to use (audio) phones for communication, while 20 % of participants use text messages in addition to emails. The students' satisfaction of the communications channels used is summarized in Fig. 5(b) (the percentages in the graph are related to the number of participants that use the communication channel).

Participants face difficulties in solving the assignments using Alice, as can be seen in Fig. 5(c). We can observe that more than 50 % of students rank the difficulty of the problem solving process as high. The group face an issues in working together because of; **(1)** the miscommunication between team members (as in teams 2 and 4, as shown in Fig. 3), **(2)** the amount of time that each member spends working compared with the time that the member spends idle (waiting his/her partner to send him/her the file and switch the work between them). According to these difficulties, the overall level of satisfaction of the students in the team is quite low—as can be seen in Fig. 5(d).

From the students' responses summarized in Fig. 5(d), we can observe that the level of satisfaction of the students is distributed over four levels. On the other hand, the students identify the possibility of errors to occur to be as high—only 20 % of the students indicate a level of confidence to ensure a low probability for errors.

Finally, the survey asked the students to suggest a modification of Alice to enhance the team-work and support the collaboration between team members operating at a distance. Some students suggest the integration of dedicated features to support team-work; interestingly enough, some of the students who experience Alice for the first time indicate as needed specifically the features present in *AliCe-ViLlagE* , while students that experience Alice after using *AliCe-ViLlagE* recommend the collaboration features of *AliCe-ViLlagE* as the recommended extensions for Alice (e.g., S3, S4).

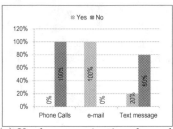

(a) Used communication channels

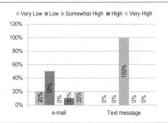

(b) Participant satisfaction about the used communication channels

(c) The assignment difficulty

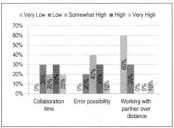

(d) Solving the assignment Problems

Fig. 5. Responses to the survey part 2(Color figure online)

4.3 Post-survey Part3

AliCe-ViLlagE is developed with the goal of providing students with collaboration features to facilitate team communication and collaborative code development in the context of a shared assignment. After each team finishes the resolution of the assignment using *AliCe-ViLlagE* , we collect answers to the corresponding survey (Table 2(b)).

The first question inquires about the overall level of satisfaction of the students in using *AliCe-ViLlagE* to solve the assignment. We can observe from the responses that 50 % of the students rank their overall experience as very satisfactory; furthermore, no student ranks his/her experience as low or very low. These results confirm that *AliCe-ViLlagE* is a simple and enjoyable environment to use collaboratively. The bar chart in Fig. 6(a) shows that the students did not face any particular difficulty in solving the assignments; these results are fairly different than what we observed in the case of Alice. Moreover, the students found that the communication components are easy to use (Fig. 6(a)) and they provide an effective communication media between team members (Fig. 6(c)).

The students' responses in rating the quality of collaboration and the quality of interacting with a partner at a distance are also significantly different than Alice. Figure 6(b) shows that 70 % of the students demonstrate a very high level of satisfaction in the use of *AliCe-ViLlagE* to collaborate with a partner at a distance (the corresponding question for Alice shows 60 % of participants rating the solution as very low satisfaction). On the other hand, the students rank the

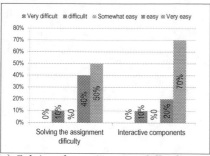

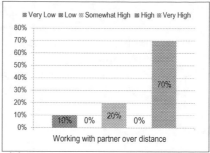

(a) Solving the assignment difficulty and using the interaction components

(b) Solving the assignment Problems

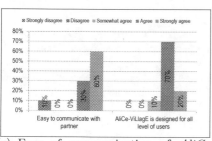

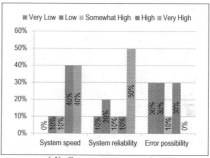

(c) Ease of communication of *AliCe-ViLlagE*

(d) System properties

Fig. 6. Responses to the survey part 3(Color figure online)

features of *AliCe-ViLlagE* (system speed and reliability) as high—this relates to the ability of *AliCe-ViLlagE* to automatically maintain synchronized copies of the code/3D world on the monitors of the two students. Finally, most of students rank the possibility of errors to occur as low or very low.

5   Conclusion and Future Work

The first part of this project is to build a collaborative virtual pair programming model. The model is designed and implemented as an extension of Alice—leading to a first effective prototype, named *AliCe-ViLlagE* . The resulting experience in the use of *AliCe-ViLlagE* by students, compared to the use of Alice, provides evidence of high levels of satisfaction and effectiveness. The features included in *AliCe-ViLlagE* to enable synchronized code development and communication simplifies distributed code development, enhancing team work and effective collaboration. Furthermore, *AliCe-ViLlagE* provides an instructor with capabilities to oversee the activities of each team, track contributions, identify difficulties, and determine team performance. The feedback from the students shows that the resolution of assignments using *AliCe-ViLlagE* is faster, easier, and more reliable than working with Alice at a distance.

A second prototype of *AliCe-ViLlagE* has been recently completed and it is now ready for evaluation. In this new prototype, we allow a group of students (more than two) to collaborate to solve shared programming assignments. The role of students are extended to include more than just a navigator and driver role (e.g., leader, time keeper, analyzer, designer, etc.). The second version is an extension of the Affinity Research Group (ARG) model [10].

References

1. Al-Jarrah, A., Pontelli, E.: AliCe-ViLlagE: alice as a collaborative virtual learning environment. In: Frontiers in Education Conference, pp. 1–9. IEEE (2014)
2. Arisholm, E., Gallis, H., Dyba, T., Sjoberg, D.I.K.: Evaluating pairprogramming with respect to system complexity and programmer expertise. IEEE Trans. Softw. Eng. **33**(2), 65–86 (2007). doi:10.1109/TSE.2007.17
3. Baker, L., Snow, E., Garvin-Poxas, K., Weston, T.: Recruiting Middle School Girls into IT: Data on Girls' Perceptions and Experiences from a Mixed Demographic Group. MIT Press, Cambridge (2006)
4. Begel, A., Nagappan, N.: Pair programming: what's in it for me?. In: Proceedings of the ACM-IEEE International Symposium on Empirical Software Engineering and Measurement, pp. 120–128. ACM (2008)
5. Comman, I., Sillitti, A., Succi, G.: Investigating the usefulness of pair-programming in a mature agile team. In: ¡CHECK¿Abrahamsson, p, Baskerville, R., Conboy, K., Fitzgerald, B., Morgan, L., Wang, X. (ed.) Agile Processes in Software Engineering and Extreme Programming. LNBIP, pp. 127–136. Springer, Heidelberg (2008)
6. Constantine, L.L.: Constantine on Peopleware. Yourdon Press, Englewood Cliffs (1995)
7. Cuny, J.: CS 10K Project: Transforming High School Computing for the 21st Century. Presentation, CE21 Community Meeting (2012)
8. Cuny, J., Wilson, C., Johnson, M., Margolis, J.: A Week to Focus on Computer-Science Education. National Science Foundation, Predds Release **09–234**, (2009)
9. Fronza, I., Sillitti, A., Succi, G.: An interpretation of the results of pair programming during novices integration in a team. In: International Symposium on Empirical Software Engineering and Measurement, pp. 225–235. IEEE CS (2009)
10. Gates, A.Q., Roach, S., Villa, E.Y., Kephart, K., Della-Piana, C., Della-Piana, G.: The Affinity Research Group Model Creating and Maintaining Effictive Research Teams, IEEE Computer society (2008)
11. McDowell, C., Werner, L., Bullock, H., Fernald, J.: The effects of pair-programming on performance in an introductory programming course. In: 33rd SIGCSE Technical Symposium on Computer Science Education, pp. 38–42. ACM (2002)
12. National Center for Women and Information Technology: Computing Education and Future Jobs: National. State and Congressional District Data. Technical report, NCWIT (2012)
13. Nawrocki, J., Wojciechowski, A.: Experimental evaluation of pair programming. European Software Control and Metrics (Escom), pp. 99–101 (2001)
14. NCWIT: Women and Information Technology: By the Numbers (2011). http://www.ncwit.org/pdf/BytheNumbers09.pdf
15. Pausch, R., et al.: Alice: rapid prototyping system for virtual reality. IEEE Comput. Graph. Appl. **15**(3), 8–11 (1995)
16. Powell, B.: Five Things the U.S. Can Learn from China. Time Magazine (12) (2009)

17. Salleh, N., Mendes, E., Grundy, J., Burch, G.S.J.: The effects of neuroticism on pair programming: an empirical study in the higher education context. In: International Symposium on Empirical Software Engineering and Measurement, pp. 22: 1–22: 10. ACM (2010)
18. Sillitti, A., Succi, G., Vlasenko, J.: Understanding the impact of pair programming on developers attention: a case study on a large industrial experimentation. In: International Conference on Software Engineering, pp. 1094–1101. IEEE (2012)
19. Simard, C., Stephenson, C., Kosaraju, D.: Addressing Core Equity Issues in K-12 Computer Science Education: Identifying Barriers and Sharing Strategies. Technical report, Anita Borg Institute for Women and Technology (2010)
20. Thom, M., Pickering, M., Thompson, R.: Understanding the barriers to recruiting women in engineering and technology programs. In: 32nd ASEE/IEEE Frontiers in Education Conference (2002)
21. Williams, L., McDowell, C., Nagappan, N., Fernald, J., Werner, L.: Building pair programming knowledge through a family of experiments. In: International Symposium on Empirical Software Engineering. IEEE Computer Society (2003)
22. Zweben, S.: 2009–2010 Taulbee Survey. Technical report, Computing Research Association (2011)

Using Image Processing Technique
for Supporting Healthcare Workers
in Collaborative Works

Salin Boonbrahm, Lanjkorn Sewata, and Poonpong Boonbrahm(✉)

School of Informatics, Walailak University,
Tha Sala, Nakorn Si Thammarat 80160, Thailand
salil.boonbrahm@gmail.com, lsewata@gmail.com,
poonpong@gmail.com

Abstract. Collaborative work is an activity done by more than one person to get a job done. For healthcare workers, several jobs are considered as collaborative work such as consulting or diagnosis. In this study, medical images were used as the objects manipulated by physicians at different locations. They could manipulate and provide comments or opinions to each other during collaborative sessions which included time proximity: at the same time or at different time. The system composed of application program for managing collaboration and image processing functions. Two case studies have been done on analysis of tumor and diabetic retinopathy. The first case dealt with real-time collaboration at different locations while the second case dealt with different time collaboration.

Keywords: Collaborative work · Medical image · Processing · Healthcare worker

1 Introduction

Collaboration is an act of someone working with other people on a joint project. In real life, there are two kinds of job achievement i.e. by doing it alone or having other people to help or participate with. Actually, using software to get a job done by more than one person may require an enhancement of tool or software that one person uses to do their job to a tool that support more than one person to do the job together. Decision making, for example, starts with having a decision support system (DSS) for one decision maker and later when there are situations that the decisions have to come from a group of people, the board or committee for example, a group decision support system (GDSS) is then introduced [1, 2].

In order to be able to collaborate for decision making, the number of people involved are not the only matter, the tool for supporting collaboration is also important as well. To set up a tool, there is also the proximity for time and space involved. For the time, it can be at the same time or different time while space can be in the same place or different place [2]. The combination of time and space that will be benefit from using software for collaboration are two cases. For the first case, users are in different location

© Springer International Publishing Switzerland 2016
P. Zaphiris and A. Ioannou (Eds.): LCT 2016, LNCS 9753, pp. 596–606, 2016.
DOI: 10.1007/978-3-319-39483-1_54

and they use the system at the same time. This means that they have to set the schedule to use the system. The second case is the situation that users are in different locations and they use the system at different time. If this tool is used in healthcare unit such as hospital, the staff at different hospitals can have a floor for the diagnosis without any needs to travel.

When we focus on the use of computer applications in healthcare organization such as hospital, there are several examples including the information system that are based on healthcare information, decision support and quality assurance [3]. For healthcare, decision making is more complicated than others, so information and tools to support the decision must be accurate and easy to work with.

Nowadays, medical Imaging plays the key role in helping physicians diagnose and make decision to treat the patients. We can have the digital images of the patients from X-rays machine, Computed Tomography (CT) Scanner and MRI (Magnetic Resonance Imaging) machine. Interpreting those images may need some experts or someone with more experience to consult with, especially in an unusual case. With the advance in telecommunication network, transferring images from one location to others for discussion or consultation may not be a problem. It would be more useful if the image can be manipulated by healthcare workers at different sites in consulting session.

Since there are many types of images that are related to health information and the use of those images should be analyzed and discussed by more than one expert in the field for accurate result, there should be a tool to support real time collaborative work for problem solving, decision making or consulting in healthcare.

In this research we are interested in setting up a software program to help healthcare worker in one location to collaborate in real time with experts from other locations for decision making using information gathered from medical image processing. Users can use the program to analyze medical images acquired from CT scanner, MRI machine or any devices that provide digital image for specific purposes which would benefit in decision making and all the visual images can be shared amongst experts in real time.

2 Related Works

There are several papers on the use of computer for collaborative works in many areas such as in education [4–6], government services [7] and healthcare [3, 8, 9]. In education, collaborative learning is implemented in different ways [4, 6]. By using the internet, the community of learners could be constructed and applications were implemented to support distance learning especially web-based applications like chat rooms, blogs, wikis. For government service such as transportation, the use of computer in the collaborative works have been implemented as a training tool for transportation teams to practice on how they should response in emergency events [7]. The computer-based system provided the team with the drills for different situations with details like daily traffic situations and unusual situations. In healthcare, when computers were used in hospital units such as patient wards, laboratories, and departments, computerized data were every where. Now, global computer network makes it possible to connect with external units such as patient residents and other hospitals [3, 9].

With the advance in technology, especially computer graphics, all the new scanning machine for healthcare have a digital output, making them easy to process. Right now there are many software tools which can speed up and enhance the operation of the analysis of medical image. Fifteen of these software programs were compared in several aspects such as function, system language, platform and etc. [10]. Some researchers emphasized on finding new algorithm that could be used in image processing such as image reconstruction, image enhancement, image smoothing and etc. [11] While other used parallel algorithm for tumor edge detection which could detect cancer tumor at early stage [12]. Methods and algorithm for detecting different categories of cancer such as breast, liver and brain tumor were also investigated [13]. The methods used were, a restively loaded bowtie antenna with genetic algorithm approach, FPGA (Field programmable Gate Array) - 3-D Ultrasound computer tomography with adapted matched filtering algorithm, in pentetreotide SPECT-A Collimator based on Monte Carlo simulation, and Cellular automata (CA) based segmentation method – MR (Magnetic Resonance) Images.

3   Use of Medical Image Processing in Collaborative Works

Medical images are usually used for radiographic technique in diagnosis, clinical studies and treatment planning, so it is quite important to life and death situation. Today with the advance in the field of computerized image processing and digital equipment, all the medical imaging system such as X-Ray, Computer Tomography (CT), Magnetic Resonance Imaging (MRI) and etc. provide the output in a digital form, making them easy for transferring and interpreting. When interpreting the data, sometimes the physicians rely more on their experiences than the output from the machine. The decision may come from one physician or from a group of physicians which means that they might prefer to get some help or opinions from others. For example, two dimensional images from the imaging devices may look unclear or may have some suspicious points to be considered, if there are some collaboration process before progressing into the next step of processing, the decision may be more reliable. Figure 1 shows the flow chart of the process.

3.1   Experimental Setup

In order to test the concept that collaboration in healthcare for real time decision making using medical image processing can be done for users who are in different places, we have developed the software applications to support the work flow shown in Fig. 1. This software was installed in a server which acted like a host for the system where users could join in and behaved like clients.

In real life situation, MRI digital images from local hospital can be diagnosed by the physicians at the hospital or with the help of experts or other physicians at that

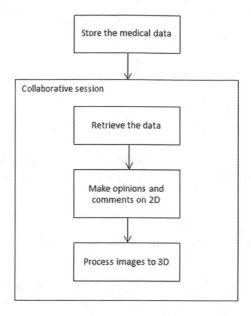

Fig. 1. Flow chart of the collaborative session

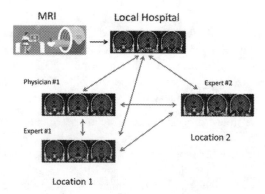

Fig. 2. Flow of medical image to and from experts

hospital or experts somewhere else. If the decision did not need real time analysis, then each person can get the image by mail or by other means. If the decision must be in real time, video conferences may help. In the case that images need to be manipulated by someone or everyone before making any decisions, then we have to create a new application to support these activities. Figure 2 shows how each person interacts with the image.

The hardware requirements for this setup were one standard server attached to local

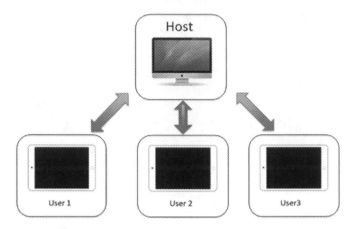

Fig. 3. System setup for collaboration

area network and few clients which could be tablets or laptop computers. The only condition was that all of them must be in the same network. The system flowchart is shown in Fig. 3.

3.2   Software Development

For healthcare collaboration in which real time decision making on medical image is required, the software should support the users to work on the same image at the same time. For example, all three users would like to discuss about the tumor on the same image, they can mark on the tumor, paint them with different color and etc. Few properties of the software are as following:

- Basic functions for image processing such as image enhancement, edge detection, segmentation an etc.
- 2D image from medical imaging devices can be stored and retrieved to display on each users screen.
- Manipulation on each screen can be done and image on each screen can be saved as individual or can be accumulated to new image under assigned condition.
- Information related to the same image that has been evaluated can be analyzed and can be used to formed 3D image.
- 3D image that has been created can be transformed i.e. rotate, translate, enlarge and etc.
- Manipulated Image by different techniques or different users can be compared.

The user interfaced and menu for the program are shown in Fig. 4.

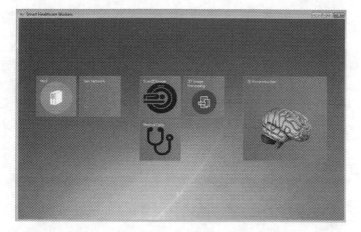

Fig. 4. User interface and menu for the collaborative software.

4 Case Study 1: Collaborative in Brain Cancer Diagnostics Using Image from CT Scan

Usually, visualization of human tumor can be done by analyzing the cross sectional image of the human body from CT scanner in the suspicious area. CT is the abbreviation for computed tomography or computerized tomography that will provide the cross-sectional images of human body. Analyzing the tumor for its shape or whether it is cancer tumor or not sometimes need more than one physician opinion. Figure 5 shows the conceptual framework of collaborate physicians analyzing the CT image of a brain cancer patient.

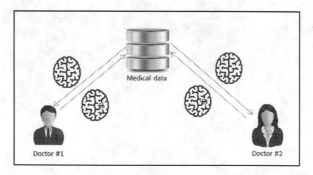

Fig. 5. Conceptual framework for physicians collaboration

In order to prove whether collaboration can be applied to the image processing analysis, we have set up the experiment using modified image from CT scanner and then stored in our program. We proposed that two users (physicians or experts) helping each other to estimate the size and shape of the tumor. With the help of the software

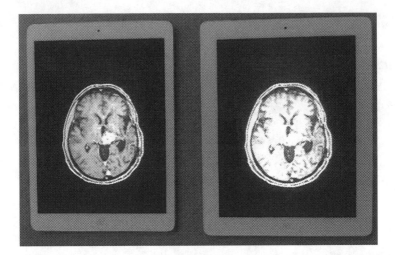

Fig. 6. Image from CT scanner showing the suspicious part to be identified

functions, the image has been enhanced and the shape of 2D tumor cells could be seen easily on each user's iPads in Fig. 6.

In real life, the machine can only differentiate the objects under conditions that we have created, so there is a room for skill physician to make different opinions. In this case, these two experts may identify the boundary of the tumor differently and the shape may be different from the machine proposed. Figure 7 shows how the two physicians identified the boundary of the tumor differently.

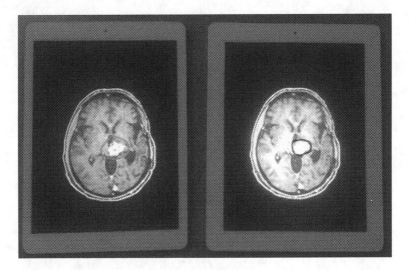

Fig. 7. Two physicians identify the boundary of the tumor differently

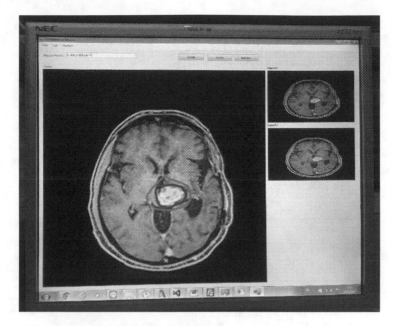

Fig. 8. Accumulation of two images from two experts

By accumulating all the new boundaries of the tumor from 2D CT layers images (Fig. 8), the program could put them together and construct them into a 3D image as shown in Fig. 9.

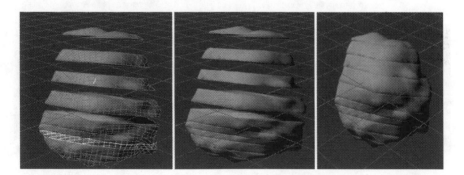

Fig. 9. Using 3D construction function, 3D tumor cell can be constructed

5   Case Study 2: Detection of Diabetic Retinopathy

Diabetic retinopathy is the leading cause of new blindness in diabetic patients. The exact mechanism by which diabetes causes retinopathy remains unclear, but if it is detected in early stage, treatment can be provided to save the vision. In the initial stages of diabetic retinopathy, red dots caused by the breakdown of blood vessels appears in the superficial retinal layers of the patients. If these dots or hemorrhages can be detected and identified using image processing and collaborative technique, then treatment can be provided. Figure 10 shows the initial sign of the symptom compares to the normal one.

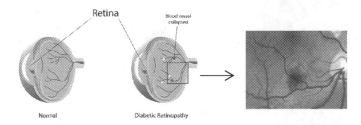

Fig. 10. Diabetic retinopathy compare to the normal one (Color figure online)

Since the dot is very small at the early stage, identifying them is very difficult. Using the software to process the image and then by consulting with experts using collaborative function, the diagnostic result should be more accurate than by one judgment.

Figure 11 shows the retina images before and after processing in which we could see the dots and blobs clearly and experts can identify them whether the patients has Diabetic Retinopathy or not.

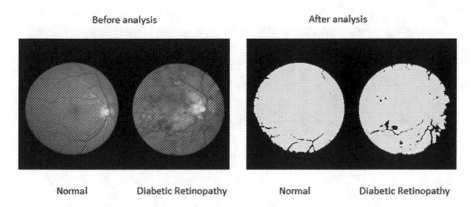

Fig. 11. The retina images before and after processing

6   Result and Discussion

In the first case study, by implementing our system to help identifying the location and shape of the tumor, each user (medical doctor or expert) could identify the parts that they considered as tumor. The system would collect all the information that each user provided such as the boundaries of the tumor, the remarks and etc. and then put them together to form the results, which in this case was the shape of the tumor. This kind of collaboration will help the workers in identifying uncertain areas and providing more accurate result. In the second case study, users could manipulate retinal images and processed them so that all the red dots caused by the breakdown of blood vessels could be identified. Depending on the image processing method each user used, the results from each user may be different. Since the system also had functions for comparing the results, so the final correction could be made after all users read the results from others and an agreement was made.

The differences between these two cases was that, the first one made real time collaboration from users who were at different locations while the second one, the collaboration was done in different locations and at different times.

7   Conclusion

Even though, there are some software for collaborative decision-making available in the market, but they are mostly designed for business purposes. With the software tools that support both collaborations through network and having functions for image processing, healthcare work could be processed in real time with results more accurate than from the judgment of only one expert. In this paper, we have tried to show that real time collaboration in group support systems for medical purposes by using data analyzed using image processing is possible. More detail works should be done which to people in healthcare businesses to work more effectively.

References

1. Power, D.J.: A Brief History of Decision Support Systems (2007). http://DSSResources.COM/history/dsshistory.html
2. DeSanctis, G., Gallupe, B.: Group decision support system: a new frontier. ACM SIGMIS Database 16(2), 3–10 (1984)
3. Fitzmaurice, J.M., Adams, K., Eisenburg, J.M.: Three decades of research on computer applications in health care. J. Am. Med. Inform. Assoc. 9(2), 144–160 (2002)
4. Stahl, G., Koschmann, T., Suthers, D.: Computer-supported collaborative learning: an historical perspective. In: Sawyer, R.K. (ed.) Cambridge Handbook of the Learning Sciences, pp. 409–426. Cambridge University Press, Cambridge (2006)
5. Sung, H.Y., Hwang, G.J.: A collaborative game-based learning approach to improving students' learning performance in science courses. Comput. Educ. 63, 43–51 (2013)
6. Beldarrain, Y.: Distance education trends: integrating new technologies to foster student interaction and collaboration. Distance Educ. 27(2), 139–153 (2006). doi:10.1080/01587910600789498
7. Velasquez, J.D., Yoon, S.W., Nof, S.Y.: Computer-based collaborative training for transportation security and emergency response. Comput. Ind. 61, 380–389 (2010)
8. Sandars, J., Langlois, M., Waterman, H.: Online collaborative learning for healthcare continuing professional development: a cross-case analysis of three case studies. Med. Teach. 29(1), e9–e17 (2007)

 9. Fitzpatrick, G., Ellingsen, G.: A review of 25 years of CSCW research in healthcare: contributions, challenges and future agendas. Comput. Support. Coop. Work **22**, 609–665 (2013). doi:10.1007/s10606-012-9168-0. Springer
10. Lee, L.K., Liew, S.C.: A survey of medical image processing tools. In: 4th International Conference on Software Engineering and Computer Systems, pp. 171–179 (2105)
11. Wang, Y., Zheng, J., Zhou, H., Shen, L.: Medical image processing by denoising and contour extraction. In: IEEE International Conference on Information and Automation, pp. 618–623 (2008)
12. Sulaiman, H., Said, N.M., Ibrahim, A., Alias, N.: High performance visualization of human tumor detection using WTMM on parallel computing system. In: IEEE 9th International Colloquium on Signal Processing and Its Applications, pp. 205–208 (2013)
13. Velusamy, P.D., Karandharaj, P.: Medical image processing schemes for cancer detection: a survey. In: International Conference on Green Computing Communication and Electrical Engineering. IEEE Xplore (2014). doi:10.1109/ICGCCEE.2014.6922267

Theory and Tools in Learning Methods for Medical Doctors

Karim Elia Fraoua[1]([⊠]), Christian Bourret[1], Claude Amar[2],
and Stéphane Mouly[3]

[1] Université Paris Est Marne-La-Vallée, Equipe Dispositifs d'Information et de
Communication à l'Ere Numérique (DICEN IDF), Conservatoire national des
arts et métiers, Paris-Est Paris-Ouest, EA 7339, Paris, France
{Fraoua,Bourret}@u-pem.fr
[2] C&A Audit & Conseil, 92100 Boulogne Billancourt, France
AmarCLAUDE@caauditconseil.com
[3] Université Sorbonne Paris Cité-Diderot, Unité Fonctionnelle de Médecine
Interne 1 - Département de Médecine Interne, Pôle Médecine - Aval des
Urgences APHP - Groupe Hospitalier Lariboisière-Fernand Vidal, 75010
Paris, France
stephane.mouly@aphp.fr

Abstract. In this work we try de demonstrate that implementing new tools for
medical doctors must be discussed using some aspects of the game theory and
from a sociological point of view. Taking into account this interaction, we could
help to better fit the needs of medical doctors and help them to succeed in
private area. We will discuss the process under Hayek and Boudon approaches,
in order to explain the non-normative behavior of these specific users, and to
push them in the best way, using learning structure, introducing the important
role of mediator and the measurement of feedback using lexicomotric tools.

Keywords: Information · Learning processes · Hayek · Medical doctors ·
Boudon · Allais paradox

1 Introduction

In France the Private Health System is considered in crisis for many constraints. An
important one is how to motivate medical doctors to choose private sector and not to
remain in hospital despite the fact that sometimes they are under a precarious situation
[1]. They have in fact a fixed-term contract and are not considered as a permanent staff
of the hospital.

This paradoxical situation, push the official organizations in France (ARS,
HAS, …) or the town halls, and the regions to invite a foreign doctors to settle in
France, which does not necessarily meet all the needs, and mainly does not address the
situation of the management of medical graduates in France [2].

This situation causes a major problem of the management of the French health and
implies major problems in some areas named "medical deserts" because of the problem
of the replacement of retired doctors or lack of attractiveness of some areas [3].

© Springer International Publishing Switzerland 2016
P. Zaphiris and A. Ioannou (Eds.): LCT 2016, LNCS 9753, pp. 607–615, 2016.
DOI: 10.1007/978-3-319-39483-1_55

These isolated and depopulated rural areas but also deprived suburbs of large cities, suffer greatly from this problem and can't face to offer an efficient care to their citizens. These areas need to improve the attractiveness for the installation of new practitioners, especially doctors, who themselves are reluctant to go or sometimes consider that there are a lack in their cursus program during their graduation in the field of management. Avoiding this tension, is a vital need for people and the best performances of distribution of practitioners, especially young doctors, it is one of the major challenges that is facing our health system. It is therefore become essential to understand why medical doctors are not interested by this project and focus on motivating young graduates doctors based on innovative training practices in managing of medical office.

The Admedico project is addressed to medical doctors, in order to help and push them to understand the main mechanism of managing a medical office [4]. Indeed, we aim to optimize the organization of getting medical doctors into private practice for the first time and link them the various operators, economic or administrative. In this work, we have chosen to evoke the notion of game theory because of the issue of uncertainty that can arise during learning process. We will try to justify the use of such an approach and do not get into a playful dimension only and purely innovative effect.

In this work, we will inevitably raise the important issue of understanding of both the nature of doctors in terms of risk-taking and decision-making in a field to which they are not necessarily prepared but doomed to perform, and also what would be the best learning tools for a subject like management approaches while they are in a very behaviorist learning process, but also very specifically about their job considered as purely technical.

For this purpose, we will expose briefly the approach of Boudon in learning process [5] and we will consider the work of Allais [6] and Hayek [7] to better situate stakeholders including learners, their learning strategies and the role of the trainer, since we have implemented remote learning strategy through a variety of tools such as video, educational games, etc.

2   The Profile of Concerned Doctors

Hayek is the first to oppose the so-called "constructivist" school or construction of a social reality by the agents [8]. This approach in which human are all equal in their social construction, is confronted to the true social reality. Hayek will seek to demonstrate that the reality is more complex and we need to adapt the tools to this reality. This idea is in the same approach of the work of Moscovici [9] and Abric [10] which attempts to show that the concept of group, is more complex and that our values may overlap the values of others. This work is contiguous to the work of Mead of the concept of social interactionism to model a social being [11]. We can of course build more easily on a group of doctors agents since they often come from the same social spheres and that this identity or social affiliation is relatively high.

Hayek's work shows the concept of the absence of collective standards and that individuals are different [12], which goes against Durkheim's approach on rules of a collective standard [13]. Indeed on the basis of Hayek, Nonaka develops the idea that more the person acquires knowledge and more its relationships and strategies with others change or evolve [14]. This multiplicity of facets of the individual justifies the multiplicity of tools. The aim is obviously to develop sufficient tools but also the interaction between the learners to achieve the goal of common knowledge.

The configuration must be a cooperative game in which agents are engaged through a guaranteed contract by the learning structure [15]. It is essential to develop this organizational architecture, this will create the prior idea of mutual trust and the organization of the learning structure and actor's interaction. This entirely fulfill in the preceding description of our work in a socio-constructivist approach [16]. This last is actually opposite to the utilitarian approach, that established rules are based on igno-rance of the actors. In our case, all players know and the contract is completely symmetrical. The objective of learners is pursued by trainers and tools implemented consolidate that.

3   Reasons that Penalize Doctors to Try the Private Sector

This forces each player to an accepted or tolerated ignorance of the circumstances of the future and raises the question of forecasting, including my future, if I have to leave this situation where I work so sometimes "precarious" in the hospital, so I program training that encourages me to settle my own behalf and that is necessary for the success of my plans. It must then establish objective information. These rules play in the role of behavior standards and facilitate the learning process of agents, on which Hayek questions from Economy and Knowledge [7].

According to Hayek, the agents are moderately rational, meaning they decide to share a little with assumptions developed. They are only partially informed, to the extent that they base their behavior on limited sequences of observations from the past behavior of other agents that shape their social environment. They can abandon their project on the basis of this information partition.

In conclusion, we understand that agents must in a hypothesis of the presence of an artifact, which should lead to the more rational patterns of learning, through examples of video testimony, correct the informational bias. Through the work of Boudon, we will show that the establishment of a multi-tool system meets current needs of agents that appear to be socially or culturally identical but may ultimately be different and should therefore require a different approach [17].

Thus taking into account Bourdon work, which shows the clear role and importance of the system of interactions to account for social phenomena and draws attention to the effects of aggregation or goal congruence. It indicates that sociology cannot be done without the interest to the agent,, it must refer to a subject with intentions and a some autonomy. The tool that we develop must consider this essential aspect to ensure success. It is in the spirit of Hayek when non standardized layout of the individual especially in a complex task of learning [18]. Indeed, the sociological parameters for Boudon cannot explain everything about human behavior. The individual is always with a certain autonomy [19], which can lead to a paradoxical situation or perhaps explain some irrational choices.

The role of the mediator artifact is here reinforced by its influential role on the learner group (according to Boudon). Beyond this influence, the adherence to training cannot occur without the mediator. It is certain that in order to an agent to adopt this innovation, it is necessary that the agent must be informed by its existence, its benefits, its situation and its representations to led him to expose to the influence of others. Besides this, Boudon shows that on another aspect namely the development of new therapeutic treatments with private doctors where the network is less dense than in hospitals, the role of the medical representative is primordial which shows here the role of mediator and his importance.

To consolidate the above and take account from the idea of Boudon [19], that the individual may react to other aspects that sociological elements, we will discuss decision-making mechanisms and that could help us understand why doctors do not want to integrate the liberal sector, and also explain how the choice of tools could affect their decision making. The physician's interaction with the tool could become an incentive tool.

In conclusion, and according to Boudon terminology [5], there are two ways to see the agent, as an individual player, we speak in the case of functional systems which explain here the development of different which could explain also the vision of Hayek on the non-normativity of agents and as a social agent in the interdependent systems. This justifie the presence of learning modalities and measurement feedback with the necessity of artifact presence or mediator.

Finally we get into to the essence of game theory in order to better explain the situation experienced by learners. We will use the Allais paradox on the commitment of the agents in a risky or a uncertain situation [20]. Von Neumann and Morgenstern [21] and John Nash [22] obviously, develop this theory that will show that individuals contribute to maximize their welfare or the utility function, utility that can manifest itself in many ways and can vary according to circumstances. In fact the agents take decision considering whether or not the decisions taken by others, and it measures the interactional and strategic decisions between actors. They will establish access probability to this outcome depending on the strategy that other agents will set up, avoiding risky situations, hence the obvious connection with the learner profile will have a fear of uncertainty and therefore can accept a lower gain if the strategy is risky to achieve a higher gain.

In our work, we'll look at the consolidation of the aforementioned profiles, showing that individuals avoid risky situations but also that every individual is unique and that the notion of individual is not a normed standard. There are certainly social groups previously explained, but in the context of learning, certain specific features may appear including even within supposedly homogeneous groups.

Maurice Allais provides an essential element to the issue of management of uncertainty by agents [20]. This will involve doctors who leave a precarious situation to a risky situation even uncertain. In fact, the precarious situation in which there is a contractual physician at the Hospital is considered almost certain due to information available to the agent components; In fact, the hospital itself suffers from a lack of practitioners, therefore, the physician under contract knows that his contract will be renewed continuously from authorizing it to believe that it will eventually become part of the permanent staff of the hospital.

Indeed, we can evaluate this almost paradoxical situation as defined by the evaluation of the decision following the work of Maurice Allais [20]. Following the work of Bernoulli commented that the first through the paradox of St. Petersburg in 1738 which states that players have a risk aversion [23], which is formulated by replacing the gain or wealth of the player by his utility function. It is in this spirit that Maurice Allais, on the basis of the work of Savage on the theory of expected utility [24], will build a lottery in which players will be confronted to different situations, in this example we expose only the principle of risk aversion:

A situation, where is the gain of € 5 million with a 10 % chance, 1 M € with 89 % chance, and finally zero gain with 1 % risk.

B situation with a gain of € 1 million with a 100 % chance and therefore no risk of loss.

The result that interests us here is that the money will choose the least risky or the one with the least uncertainty about the B. This option is less interesting in terms of pay but less risky option because the risk of loss is zero. Indeed the overall allocation in the A version is more important than in version B.

This can fit a priori to our case of the learner profiles and will introduce the question of the learner towards risk, and the main question, of ability to understand the mechanism of management and to be well accompanied in the installation process. For the first point, it is essential to take account of this mathematical approach that will reduce the risk sentiment due to the multiplicity of tools to implement, to their complementarities and a to their partial recovery, some concepts, to be so to speak, can exist in other tools.

4 The Organization of Learning and Its Context

The current field of education and training is subject to the pressures of the economic context. International competition is driving companies or the state to invest in new educational and several ideas emerge in the field of educational innovation [25]. Employees are also required to develop new skills and versatility, being always more qualified, with new technical skills including those in information and communication [26].

With regard to the first element, namely learning, the first question is the motivation to learn, and how learning can add value to the learner as the fulfillment of a professional project that will include both aspects, the skills and the financial well-being. Berbaum shows that adults in the public training, have poor intellectual work habits that can be an obstacle to the acquisition of new skills [27].

Concerning adult education, many often believed incorrectly that they are only sensitive to the learning of know-how or skills. We forget that it is part of a comprehensive approach that includes, learning to know, and about learning techniques including the issue of accumulation of knowledge [28]. The acquisition of the knowledge, skills and attitudes are not the subject of a transmission based on a classical approach but a comprehensive transformation involving all actors. We must now be aware of the added value of learning structure in terms of methods and tools, notwithstanding the resources that it can offer [29]. The place of the learner must be motivated by learning outcomes that will acquire and personal investment by learning how to learn helped by the mediator or artifact. The latter will be the one who will accompany the learner by putting it in a learning situation by providing the necessary assistance, by challenging the learner.

5   Presentation of ADMEDICO Project

5.1   Description

The Education Project of a "usual practice", is the creation of a learning platform and scalable digital learning housed on the Web, the theme of which is to popularize the essential knowledge of practices to the installation for liberal health professionals. ADMEDICO is an innovative online learning solution that responds to digital educational and interactive questions that will arise to any medical professional and/or paramedic during his first installation in liberal way. This transversal project covers the information technology, teaching methods, learner interactivity, validation of skills and the understanding of the ongoing optimization of the format and content, all of which find their justification in the different Recent work on the development of teaching techniques and understanding of psycho-socio-cognitive phenomena involved in the transmission and use of knowledge and which will be detailed below.

5.2   Methodology

AdMedico The platform is a participatory educational approach through continuous exchanges with learners, and will include:

(1) A dynamic approach:

A tutorial teaching as a film composed of six to ten video sequences (episodes) of six to ten minutes maximum each, having the same structure (introductory video of the problem followed by a video of using as a creative and educational tutorial adapted with final synthesis and return to the forums and/or appropriate interlocutors), interactive with learners (through quizzes and/or exercises to achieve online and corrected between each session) to cover all the issues raised by a great theme (instances, the installation process, social security, taxation, accounting, partnerships).

(2) An online support, whose forces are based on:

- Attractive presentation that uses audiovisual professionals to render captivating
- Content designed by men (and women) experience who share a deep understanding of their complementary visions
- A validation of knowledge through QCM/QUIZ which induces a participative logic for learners
- A "human" help available for each step in real life (in the form of a "hotline" or "hotline").

The educational content will be developed by a doctor in charge of the project within a drafting committee. The technical aspects of this digital optimization and innovative educational format will be optimized and the footage will be broadcast on a dedicated web platform, open to learners, live or with the intervention of the mediator.

(3) AdMedico will be updated permanently

The student is co-producer of content and not only consumer, in our conception and point of view during the implementation of Admedico, regarding to the theory described before. ADMEDICO will also optimize the collection learners feed-back for the purpose of continuous improvement and real-time interface and learning tools (questionnaires, interviews, exchanges) through the learners' suggestions.

5.3   Audience

Every year in France, 40 000 new doctors, dentists, nurses, physiotherapists, midwives are facing the problem of the successive steps of the liberal system. Professionals are facing difficulties such as the declaration of liberal activity, administrative and usual constraints, often some fees unanticipated of and therefore anxiety, administrative burdens and malfunctions without having practical knowledge. The platform AdMedico would initially be built for the Liberal installation of the medical profession, then in a second time evolve into content specific to the needs of each health profession.

6   Measuring Feedback Using Lexicometry Tool

This technique allows text analysis in "natural language", keeping the speech as it is written or said [30]. In this way, in the open questions in surveys, we analyze the responses to lead to a critical judgment in improving the process of evaluation and feedback. Several points emerge in the use of lexicometry, mainly the creation of knowledge in an unknown area through the corpus construction which does not appear in the tool that was introduced and consequently on the construction of new approaches to learning where the terminology of knowledge engineering [31].The second relevant factor would be the critical analysis of the content or pedagogy of the new educational approach for an audience that does not know this new educational approach.

The interaction, justified both by the uses of the tools, will be measured by a number of tools such as quizzes, direct interaction but also by corpus analysis of questionnaires sent to learners but also those visible on the forums in place. In a society dominated by the use of Web 2.0, it is certain, as we turn to a professional group, that the mechanisms underlying the functions of the social network will appear. The role of lexicometric tools is to gather the main idea widespread in this tools to reconstruct the reality of the speeches [32].

7   Expected Results for the Project and ADMEDICO and Criteria/Indicators to Evaluate These Results

We want to optimize the first installation of medical doctors, it's the main goal of this project, shorten the startup time of liberal activity avoiding the dead time, and through precise targeting and personalized support (specific activity, discipline, geographical), to connect the various economic and administrative actors with the future liberal doctor according to their needs. Outcome indicators should first assess the capacity of this innovative teaching method to transmit knowledge but also in measuring the impact of this tools on the real number of medical doctor installed after this learning process.

This type of education developed by doctors, scientists, teachers and experts from the Liberal professional world allows the pooling of complementary areas of expertise (pedagogy, ICT) and could be a bridge between the world of education and practical reality. It is these mediators that fully enable the success of the educational platform.

8 Conclusion

In this paper, after analyzing the situation of liberal medicine and current gaps to fill a glaring structural deficit despite the strong financial incentives, we observe that the situation do not evolve in the right way over time but quite the contrary. We show through factual analysis, taking into account the situation of doctors towards learning methods and that new practices of better training to deal with the administrative and fiscal procedures can succeed. Our tool Admedico can fully participate in finding a solution, to help medical doctors to settle in private area.

A look worn by Hayek's vision but also by Boudon, according to these specific actors from both as an individual and as social agent, shows the non-normativity of actors faced to learning methods which justifies the multiplicity of tools but that this learning process will reduce both the risk and the uncertainty as defined by Allais. This will help us appropriately, according to the completeness of the methods and approaches, facilitate the installation of physicians in private area.

References

1. http://www.sccahp.org/ArticleDossier.php?CleDossier=95
2. Schweyer, F.X.: Démographie de la médecine générale. Métiers Santé Social, 41–54 (2015)
3. Bourret, C.: E-health and societal and territorial intelligence in France collective knowledge production issues and new networked interface organizations (Chap. 12). In: David, A. (ed.) Competitive Intelligence and Decision Problems, pp. 247–268. ISTE – John Wiley Ed., London (2011)
4. Fraoua, K.E., Bourret, C., Mouly, S., Amar, C.: New training approaches to support the installation of medical doctors in neglected areas in France. In: 8th International Conference of Education, Research and Innovation Seville, Spain, 18–20 November 2015
5. Boudon, R.: Le juste et le vrai: études sur l'objectivité des valeurs et de la connaissance. Fayard (1995)
6. Allais, M., Hagen, G.M. (eds.): Expected Utility Hypotheses and the Allais Paradox: Contemporary Discussions of the Decisions Under Uncertainty with Allais' Rejoinder, vol. 21. Springer Science & Business Media, Dordretch (2013)
7. Von Hayek, F.A.: Economics and knowledge. Economica 4(13), 33–54 (1937)
8. Sicard, F.: La justification du libéralisme selon F. von Hayek. Revue française de science politique, pp. 178–199 (1989)
9. Moscovici, S.: Notes towards a description of social representations. Eur. J. Soc. Psychol. 18 (3), 211–250 (1988)

10. Abric, J.C.: 8 L'étude expérimentale des représentations sociales. Sociologie d'aujourd'hui **7**, 203–223 (2003)
11. Stryker, S.: From Mead to a structural symbolic interactionism and beyond. Annu. Rev. Sociol. **34**, 15–31 (2008)
12. Hayek, F.A.: Individualism and Economic Order. University of Chicago Press, Chicago (1948)
13. Durkheim, E.: Emile Durkheim on Morality and Society. University of Chicago Press, Chicago (1973)
14. Nonaka, I.: A dynamic theory of organizational knowledge creation. Organ. Sci. **5**(1), 14–37 (1994)
15. Johnson, D.W.: Cooperative learning: increasing college faculty instructional productivity. ASHE-ERIC Higher Education Report No. 4. ASHE-ERIC Higher Education Reports, George Washington University, One Dupont Circle, Suite 630, Washington, DC 20036-1183 (1991)
16. Vygotsky, L.S.: Mind in Society: The Development of Higher Psychological Processes. Harvard University Press, Cambridge (1980)
17. Boudon, R.: La Logique du social-Introduction à l'analyse sociologique. Hachette, Paris (1979)
18. Lanneau, G.: R. Boudon et l'individualisme methodologique. Dynamiques Sociales et Changements Personnels, ISBN: 2-222. Centre National de la Recherche Scientifique, Paris (1989)
19. Boudon, R.: La logique du social (1979)
20. Allais, M.: Le comportement de l'homme rationnel devant le risque: critique des postulats et axiomes de l'école américaine. Econometrica: J. Econometric Soc. **21**(4), 503–546 (1953)
21. Von Neumann, J., Morgenstern, O.: Theory of Games and Economic Behavior. Princeton University Press, Princeton (2007)
22. Nash, J.F.: Equilibrium points in n-person games. Proc. Nat. Acad. Sci. USA **36**(1), 48–49 (1950)
23. Bernoulli, D.: Exposition of a new theory on the measurement of risk. Econometrica: J. Econometric Soc. 22(1), 23–36 (1954)
24. Friedman, M., Savage, L.J.: The utility analysis of choices involving risk. J. Polit. Econ. **56**, 279–304 (1948)
25. IDEA: Projet d'accompagnement de formation innovant. http://idea.univ-paris-est.fr/fr
26. Depover, C., Marchand, L.: E-learning et formation des adultes en contexte professionnel. De Boeck Supérieur (2002)
27. Berbaum, J.: Apprendre à… apprendre – *Sciences humaines*, hors série n°12, février–mars 1996
28. Fillol, C.: Apprentissage et systémique. Revue française de gestion **2**, 33–49 (2004)
29. Pelletier, G., Solar, C.: L'organisation apprenante: émergence d'un nouveau modèle de gestion de l'apprentissage. Apprendre autrement aujourd'hui, Cité des sciences et de l'industrie (1999)
30. Leblanc, J.-M.: Approches textométriques du web: corpus et outils. (Fiala, P., Barats, C., Leblanc, J.-M.) Dans Manuel d'analyse du Web (Barats, C. (dir.)). Armand Colin (2013)
31. Bernardini, S.: Corpora in the classroom. In: Sinclair, J.M. (ed.) How to Use Corpora in Language Teaching, pp. 15–36. John Benjamins, Amsterdam (2004)
32. Lebart, L., Salem, A., Berry, L.: Exploring Textual Data, vol. 4. Springer Science & Business Media, Dordrecht (1997)

Using Actor Network to Enhance Maritime System Design

Yushan Pan[1,2(✉)] and Hans Petter Hildre[1]

[1] AMO, Norwegian University of Science and Technology, Aalesund, Norway
{yushan.pan,hans.p.hildre}@ntnu.no
[2] Department of Informatics, University of Oslo, Oslo, Norway

Abstract. Designing a cooperative system in Computer-Supported Cooperative Work (CSCW) is a description-oriented approach. Maritime engineer emphasizes that such an approach is inadequate to convey 'how to solve problems' although it can describe 'what the problems are'. An approach called the Knowledge Transfer Technique (KTT) has recently been developed with the purpose of bridging the distance between the 'how' and the 'what' for the maritime engineering community. This article applies KTT to a maritime example in which a CSCW researcher and a maritime engineer cooperate to produce a system framework involving humans and their activities in machinery processes for designing cooperative systems. It highlights the CSCW designer to communicate better with the engineer. In turn, KTT has the potential to aid engineers in understanding how they can effectively implement engineering design in creating products to be used in cooperative material environments.

Keywords: Knowledge transfer technique · CSCW · Systems engineering · Maritime technology

1 Introduction

Maritime Technology, as defined by WEGMT (Western European Graduate Education in Maritime Technology), focuses on the "safe use, exploitation, protection of, and intervention in, the maritime environment" [1]. It is anticipated that engineering knowledge will be used to manage safety in offshore operations with the support of computer systems [2]. Despite recent advances in technology, the humans in cooperative operations still have a significant impact on the computer systems used [3], and this is particularly true of maritime technology.

In the maritime domain, the design of machinery with its integrated computer systems involves engineers rather than designers from the fields of informatics and the other design disciplines [4]. Although engineers can offer brilliant machine systems with the necessary functionalities, the understanding of how a system should look [5] is seldom able to satisfy the user's expectations of machine use as it relates to safety operations. It therefore remains a challenge to include the perceptions of humans into the development of maritime products. Investigations in other research fields have illustrated that a purely engineering understanding of a system in use is generally unsatisfactory due to its inadequate awareness of cooperative systems [6, 7].

© Springer International Publishing Switzerland 2016
P. Zaphiris and A. Ioannou (Eds.): LCT 2016, LNCS 9753, pp. 616–627, 2016.
DOI: 10.1007/978-3-319-39483-1_56

Designing cooperative systems is not new. However, using a theoretical analysis to inform design is not enough because it is hard (for example, for maritime engineers) to deploy this without a professional informatics background [8]. Cooperative work, with its supported systems, is very different from the engineering field where tasks can be accomplished by solo machines. Maritime technology is a complex and interactive environment where humans' activities are combined with machinery to create a social technical system [9]. It may erroneous to understand maritime technology as being solely about control and automatic systems [10]. Humans and their activities affect the computer systems in use. Thus, cooperative systems must acknowledge the interactive relations among and between humans and their support by the computer systems, and the combination of these factors in the material environment [11]. This is crucial and fundamental to the design of cooperative systems aimed at safety operations in maritime technology. In this article, we present how the knowledge transfer technique could help to combine the 'what' and 'how' questions to promote a picture for designing cooperative systems.

2   Knowledge Transfer Technique

KTT is based on a theoretical analysis of cooperative systems—known as awareness in actor-network theory [10]. It is central to note that in this article awareness refers to the human's awareness of activities and work procedures rather than the mental process of acquiring information and humans' awareness of their world [10]. This is fundamentally different from Endsley's concept of situation awareness and user supported design in engineering [12]. From the CSCW point of view, awareness in cooperative settings is used to describe how the individual monitors and perceives information that is available from their colleagues and from the surrounding material environment in which they are functioning [13]. It involves the processing of pre-known knowledge to reflect any issues related to design in the material environment [10]. Awareness is not subject to design; however, we can use computer systems to support it. KTT is based on this philosophy and customizes actor network theory (ANT) [14] to explore a critical approach to thinking for designers against an engineering field.

Awareness in KTT is defined under three categorizes [15]: self-awareness, we-awareness, and group-awareness. Self-awareness is explained as occurring when an operator is the focus of his own attention, or when he becomes aware of himself acting on his work. For example, an operator may wonder whether his work influences other operators [15] and could be monitored and understood by his colleagues. Self-awareness happens when an operator tries to reduce the discrepancy between his standard activity and his outcome expectations. We-awareness refers to the extent to which collaborative activity in the material environments depends on the participants' ability to remain sensitive to each other's conduct whilst engaged in their own distinct activity [16]. Group-awareness is a specific task procedure in which a group of operators work cooperatively on subtasks. During the group-awareness procedure, self and we awareness are allied in subtasks, and may occur in relationship to one another, while the group may be involved in different operations simultaneously.

Awareness alone could not adequately represent the interactive relationships occurring when humans are involved in maritime technology in actual use. In order to understand the interactive relations in a material environment, we have to understand how humans, computer systems, and the physical environment are connected and how they interact. ANT is a useful tool for analyzing social-technical environments, and deals with objects as part of an interactive network [14]. Researchers state that in order to make a social technical system readable and visible, it is essential to visualize the actor network [10, 17, 18]. Figure 1 shows the procedure by which information is processed (see Fig. 1). This is an iterative process that integrates cooperative work and social interactions together with technological systems to create a social-technical system.

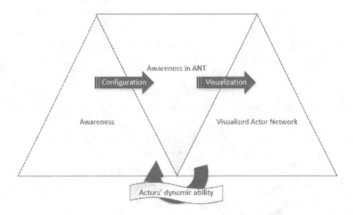

Fig. 1. Framework for designing a cooperative system

Maritime technology is complex. Hence, a maritime operation may involve more than one task and many subtasks [19, 20]. People sometimes misunderstand fieldwork [21] and that has resulted in a failure to categorize the types of awareness. In addition, the configuration of awareness in ANT is a process that deploys different types of awareness. Interactive relationships can establish a network where different actors are connected toward the accomplishment of a specific task. Hence, the connected actors in a network can be portrayed as a visualized actor network. Schoffelen et al. [17] argue that visualized actors can be read as things to be included in design. In addition, humans may practice cooperative systems with different objectives. This opens up the dynamic capabilities of actors in an actor-network to function in cooperative systems. Hence, the IT designer has to iteratively categorize awareness until humans and their interactive relations can be interpreted into an operating technical system via the visualized actor network [17].

3   An Empirical Case

An offshore supply vessel has to execute four offshore tasks simultaneously with two systems (Integrated Automatic Systems (IAS) and Dynamic Positioning System (DP)): providing and retrieving water, providing mud, uploading and reclaiming cargoes, and exercising its dynamic positioning operations. Two officers work on these offshore services. The chief officer first checks which crane is available for use, and then turns from the dynamic positioning operation checklist to the workload checklist. From this checklist, the chief officer can see which cargo needs to be uploaded to the platform and which cargo should be taken back from the platform (see Fig. 2).

Fig. 2.   Crane information on oil platform and cargo plan. (Color figure online)

In Fig. 2, different colors on the cargo plan mean that the vessel has different tasks at different platforms. At the same time, the first officer uses a communication channel to contact the platform and request it to put down pipes for providing and retrieving water and mud. Deck crews help to connect the pipes to the vessel. After these activities, the first officer starts his operations involving the water and mud tasks. The chief officer starts to monitor the cargo operations and records the cargo information on the paper. In addition, the chief officer shares this information verbally with the first officer. Simultaneously, the deck crews and the crew on the oil platform also assist the first officer via the communication channels. While interacting with the IAS, the first officer is concerned with safety issues, so all operation information is important to him.

IAS involves the integration of four individual systems: the liquid mud system, the stripping system, the tank cleaning system, and the bulk handling system. These four systems each have just two displays to show all their information. Hence, the first officer has to shift between screens based on his needs. Every time a cargo is uploaded to the platform or reclaimed from the platform, the chief officer records this information on the checklist and tells the first officer the weight of the cargo based on the number marked on it. The first officer also obtains information about the cargo's position on the deck as reported by the deck crew via the communication device.

The IAS can show only limited information about the speed at which water is piped, and about the amount of water and mud; furthermore, the first officer does not know which container has the water or mud because the onshore crew usually does not share this information immediately. When the first officer is doing his job, he therefore has limited information about which side of the vessel has the water and which the mud. Due to this, there is a risk that the vessel may roll over due to an imbalance, exacerbated by the sea waves and wind. In addition, the tons of cargo being loaded up and down from the oil platform make this risk more unpredictable. Furthermore, there is no alarm system for such an imbalance issue. The alarm system is used only for identifying if the vessel is too close to something, such as the platform or the coastline. Inside the vessel, there is another alarm system for tank cleaning, which is used to indicate if the container is too full of water or mud. It is also important to know that first officer has to maintain the dynamic positioning system. This becomes necessary when sea waves change the vessel's position making it unsuitable for delivery of the offshore services.

4   KTT-Based Systems Engineering

Self-, we, and group-awareness are grounded and intertwined in this offshore service. The actors have to make sure that their activities are visible to one another and are communicated to the other actors — the first and chief officers, the deck crew and platform—via communication channels. They need to ensure that their activities can be "heard" and observed [16]. For example, the first and chief officers transmit their communications to other actors (whether humans or machines) in different locations on the vessel or on the platform. Simultaneously, the computer systems are involved in these transmission processes through the actions of their operators who interact with the computer systems to communicate important information. This back and forth communication in the offshore service involves interactive relationships where different actors participate through practicing their role in the operation and thereby create an actor network facilitating a successful operation. In the offshore services, the actors in such an operation network are the platform, the first officer, the chief officer, the deck crew, and the supported computer systems.

Awareness happens during the activities when officers are working on their own tasks and task procedures. For instance: (1) The first and chief officers are aware of the position of the vessel and whether it is correctly positioned. The checklist and form preparation work have to be completed in a self-aware manner. The platform needs to know information when cooperating with the bridge. This is very important for the offshore services. (2) The deck crew also has to be involved in the offshore services. They manually help to check the valves. The officers have to exchange information with the deck to ensure that the cargo operation is adequate. This is important for balancing the vessel during its offshore services. (3) The first and chief officers need to exchange information about the cargoes because this information is necessary to enable the first officer to calculate how much mud and fresh water he can provide to the platform, and from which side of the vessel—the left or the right? In addition, the deck crew, officers, and platform are all aware of the offshore services that ensure cargo, piping, and positioning services go smoothly. The offshore services are conducted on the basis of the calculations made, yet even so, breakdowns in operations do happen because the systems' functions are outside the domain of the maritime technology.

4.1   Self-Awareness

Both officers also need to be aware of their actions when interacting with the digital systems and with other people. For example, the first officer needs to know information regarding the crane position before positioning the vessel in the correct position. To do this, he needs help from the deck, the platform, and also from his colleague, the chief officer. Information about the IAS system also needs to be confirmed by the first officer, such as the status of the containers for liquids, stripping, tank, or bulk systems. All of these factors build up the actor network from the first officer's position. The chief officer needs to check the cargo information and monitor the cargo operations as well as report information to the first officer. Hence, an understanding of the system's architecture will provide a focus indicating how to design the systems so that they can support the operator's self-awareness in the material environment.

Figure 3 shows the first officer's practice of self-awareness with other actors in the network (in the box) as well as manipulated computer systems and supported tools (forms and checklists). Current maritime technology can support his awareness by checking information from the IAS system. However, it is impossible for him to process information which must be provided by the other actors, such as the chief officer, the platform crew, and the deck crew, all of whom have to communicate with the first officer during the dynamic positioning operation. The first officer has to make his self-awareness visible and public by means of the communication tools. Maritime technology, to some extent, must support such self-awareness, although this is outside the functionalities of the dynamic positioning system. However, without these self-awareness oriented activities, the dynamic positioning operation is pointless regarding safety operations in some extent. KTT integrates social interactions into machinery via connecting actors (human and nonhuman) in the network by weakening the system borders between social world and machine world (see Fig. 3).

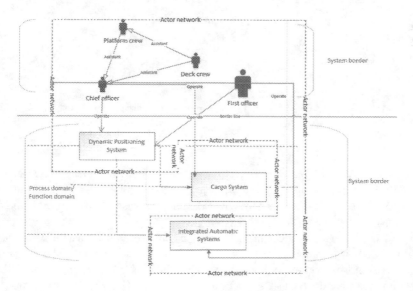

Fig. 3. First officer's self-awareness

4.2   We-Awareness

Interactive relationships lead both actors toward task accomplishment in a safe manner through their joint effort. The chief officer needs information from both the platform and the deck crew when doing the cargo service. The platform needs to let the chief officer know what cargo needs to be conveyed up and down from the platform. In the meantime, this information about the cargo needs to be forwarded to the deck crew by the chief officer because the deck crew needs to double check the cargo information and coordinate with the platform to position the cargo in a suitable place. In addition, the chief officer needs to tell the deck crew where to position the cargo on the deck. Hence, the chief officer, the deck crew, and platform have to be aware of each other's tasks and understand the activities that are done by the other actors (see Fig. 4) with respect to purposes of safety in the actor network they built jointly.

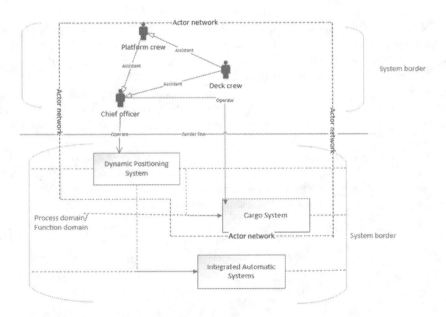

Fig. 4. We-awareness in chief officer, platform and deck crew's interaction

4.3   Group-Awareness

An offshore service is complex. The offshore service demands a high level of cooperation between the DP operation and the cargo operation because work conditions at sea are unstable. The first officer needs to make sure the vessel is in the correct position and has a good balance to counter the sea waves. When servicing the platform with water and mud, the first officer must be assisted by the chief officer in knowing the cargo information in order to decide which container under the deck should be used. Such a decision is important for his DP operation since the IAS system is impossible to notify him regarding the balance status of the vessel [22]. The cargo information cannot be processed directly by the chief officer as he needs to confirm it with both the platform and deck crew. Therefore, in this process, when the DP, cargo operation, and offshore service come together, the maritime operation becomes a single operation, its parts organized to function together to accomplish a specific maritime task. It grounds the interactive relationships between the actors consisting of both self- and we-awareness through dynamically changing work procedures that are connected and re-connected from task to task.

The intricate relationships arising from awareness result in system functions that are unlike the process order of most engineering processes. In order to ensure better safety precautions through the design of maritime technology, our critical thinking needs to address the human activities. In addition, how these activities affect the maritime technology when in use. This is crucial for designing maritime simulation. There is a need to use this new understanding to reframe maritime technology. In relation to system operations, tools and artefacts must support the human activities. This requires CSCW researchers to design supplementary systems from a higher level than the basic technical process [23]. In addition, it is necessary for the process sequence of a system function to fit with the human activities that involve the different tasks conducted under cooperative work conditions.

4.4   Supportive from KTT to Maritime System Design

Maritime system in engineering discourse sees cooperative work as a process of connecting individual operators and interacting machines [8] through frameworks, functions, and models [24]. It is a logical process in which elements of machines are assembled, and integrated in an automatic machine as engineers believe that dividing a system's problems into small pieces can solve the overall problem of designing a product [19]. For example, system modes are connected together as system function-alities to realize offshore operations. Operators might interact with one individual mode in servicing offshore with water and mud. However, if we assume that the mode used for providing water to platforms can cause the vessel to become imbalanced, due to the sea waves and the cargo's weight, then other system modes cannot simply be con-nected to the offshore service mode, since this mode's only function is to run piped water and mud from the containers. It is not possible for the two officers to convert this offshore operation into an automatic process as the engineers expected as shown in Figs. 3 and 4 where machinery has a flowchart-based process, i.e., cargo and IAS systems must be done after DP is finished. Officers have to engage with the DP and the cargo operation to process necessary information to assist with their own work with the offshore services. Such engagement in other work naturally has a significant impact on the human activities in the maritime technology. Humans must coordinate in order to realize the maritime technology's functions in the material environment via digital systems, devices and other possible tools on the vessel. This reflects the current shortage of engineering design using cooperative systems in maritime technology [7] may need supportive tools, services to help offshore operations toward to safety consideration.

With KTT to support engineering design, we are able to highlight awareness in maritime operations with the purpose of visualizing the actors involved in each section of the maritime technology, the machine functions in particular. By extending each mode of function, we believe it has the potential to enhance current maritime operations toward a safer situation by zooming in a specific problem area in different actor network (see Fig. 5) to figure out possible supportive solutions and tools. This is because extending each part of engineering design for maritime technology allows each mode involving human activities and their influences to be respected and engaged in the maritime operations at the engineering process level. This additional function will be used to control the engineering process by giving humans and their awareness activities supported tools that coordinate the workflow in maritime operations, whether parallel or non-parallel.

Researchers have suggested that CSCW knowledge does not inevitably show how to bring design knowledge into practical design [25]. CSCW researchers collect people and material artefacts in order to deploy a different approach, informing design about cooperative systems [26], for example through workshops [25]. However, the extent to which systems engineers can benefit from engaging with CSCW researchers and users in workshops remains an unanswered question [8]. It is a dilemma for both the CSCW researcher and the engineer. Researchers have also suggested that design should use the visualized actor network [27]. All these suggestions are important and to be respected. Designers are not engineers, they are outsiders to the professional mechanical area who raise critical questions and promote design requirements according to their ability to ensure the success of the final product, so that it will be safe to use. CSCW researchers are free of the institutional and political [25] influences of the engineering world and are free to respect human values in technology and to encourage engineering design to acknowledge human activities. Engineers could benefit from the critical questions which are asked by CSCW researchers regarding human influences on technology use in order to create a more comprehensive account of the cooperative situation [25]. Hence, we believe that by applying awareness in actor networks during offshore operations, system architecture could be designed as a process that involves humans and their supported tools in order to coordinate maritime technology in use.

Analyzing awareness in ANT allows engineers to become aware of the interactive relations among humans and with machines. In addition, it suggests how an interactive relationship can be built around machine activity. This process would allow the designer to scrutinize the design for cooperative situations on which to focus attention [25] and thereby design between-ness [18] in order to make interactive relationships, or in other words the actor network, more readable and designable [17]. Simultaneously, it would inform engineers that engineering systems need to allow room for human values and supported tools in coordinating the human activities with the running of the machine. Hence, the assembly of a single machine to represent cooperative work becomes a challenge, but human values and human activities, with their supported tools, can successfully contribute to meeting this deficiency. It may be incorrect to change the whole structure of the engineering process involved in maritime control functions. However, we can transfer design knowledge to notify engineers where designers can contribute to enable human activities to be appreciated in the application of maritime technology. KTT stands for this point of view.

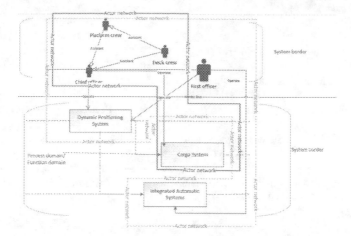

Fig. 5. Adding humans and their activities into the engineering process

5   Conclusions

We applied KTT to a maritime example to show how KTT could support engineering design through categorizing awareness in the design of cooperative systems and through visualizing the actor network. KTT does not aim to redefine the whole design process in the engineering field; rather, it offers a supportive suggestion based on knowledge of CSCW design to enhance maritime system to provide a better framework for taking human values into consideration in designing cooperative systems and systems structure. Awareness cannot be designed; however, researchers can design tools that support awareness of the group functions in cooperative systems to support humans' activities in machinery world. Grouping functions involves an understanding of how humans function in operations and what materials they use. Designing cooperative systems thus becomes a way to design supportive tools for actors and their relationships with other actors. We conclude that KTT is a not standalone tool. It is a process that integrates design knowledge from interdisciplinary fields. Maritime technology is no exception. This field needs a fresh approach to motive and promote the engineering society. This can be achieved by embracing CSCW as a means to understand humans and their values in the design of engineering products.

Acknowledgements. This research is found by the Research Council of Norway. Special thank you go to the reviewers for their constructive comments on our early manuscript. The first author would like to thank Sichao Song at Japan National Institute of Informatics for his suggestions and discussions on engineering design.

References

1. WEGEMT. Maritime Technology (2015) [cited 2015 03.01]. http://www.wegemt.org.uk
2. Storey, N.R.: Safety Critical Computer Systems, p. 453. Addison-Wesley Longman Publishing Co., Inc., Boston (1996)
3. Bjørneseth, F.B., Dunlop, M.D., Hornecker, E.: Assessing the effectiveness of direct gesture interaction for a safety critical maritime application. Int. Hum. Comput. Stud. **70**(10), 729–745 (2012)
4. Eder, W.E.: Engineering design vs. artistic design - a discussion. In: Canadian Engineering Education Association Conference (2012)
5. Pan, Y., Vederhus, L., Hildre, H.P.: Procedure verification using customized training facilities in offshore simulator environments: experiences from a specific subsea case. In: Åsgard project internal report 2015, pp. 1 – 10. Norwegian Univ. of Science and Technology (2015)
6. Rogers, Y., Yuill, N. Marshall, P.: Contrasting lab-based and in-the-wild studies for evaluating multi-user technologies. In: SAGE Handbook of Technology Research, pp. 359 – 373. SAGE (2013)
7. Pan, Y., Hildre, H.P.: Reflections on systems engineering in maritime design education. WMU j. Marit. aff. (2016, Under review)
8. Baxter, G., Sommerville, I.: Socio-technical systems: from design methods to systems engineering. Interact. Comput. **23**(1), 4–17 (2011)
9. Qureshi, Z.H.: A review of accident modelling approaches for complex socio-technical systems. In: 12th Australian Workshop on Safety Related Programmable Systems, Adelaide (2007)
10. Pan, Y. Finken, S.: Visualising actor network for cooperative systems in maritime technology. In: 12th IFIP TC9 Human Choice and Computers Conference, Manchester (2016)
11. Pan, Y.: Designing the interactive relations of complex systems: offshore operations asresearch resources. In: 18th International Conference on Dilemmas for Human Services. Linnæus University, Växjö (2015 in press)
12. Endsley, M.R.: Designing for Situation Awareness: An Approach to User-Centered Design. CRC, Boca Raton (2011)
13. Gutwin, C., Greenberg, S.: A descriptive framework of workspace awareness for real-time groupware. Comput. Support. Coop. Work (CSCW) **11**(3–4), 411–446 (2002)
14. Latour, B.: Reassembling the Social: An Introduction to Actor-Network-Theory. Oxford University Press, New York (2007)
15. Pan, Y., Finken, S.: Systems Architecture for Cooperative Systems: Utilising Awareness to Characterise Interactive Relationships (2015, Manuscript)
16. Schmidt, K.: The problem with 'awareness': introductory remarks on 'awareness in CSCW'. Comp. Supported Coop. Work **11**(3–4), 285–298 (2002)
17. Schoffelen, J., et al.: Visualising things. perspectives on how to make things public through visualisation. CoDesign **11**(3–4), 179–192 (2015)
18. Akama, Y.: Being awake to Ma: designing in between-ness as a way of becoming with. CoDesign **11**(3–4), 262–274 (2015)
19. Pahl, G., et al.: Engineering Design A Systematic Approach. Springer, London (2007)
20. Hallam, E., Ingold, T.: Making and Growing: Anthropological Studies of Organisms and Artefacts. Anthropological studies of creativity and perception, Ashgate (2014)
21. Ingold, T.: That's enough about ethnography. J. Ethnographic Theory **4**(1), 383–395 (2014)

22. Pan, Y.: Design of digital environments for operations on vessels. In: 12th International Conference on the Design of Cooperative Systems, Trento (2016)
23. Eder, W.E.: Theory of technical systems and engineering design science - legacy of Vladimir Hubka. In: International design conference, pp. 19 – 29 (2008)
24. Liu, C., et al.: Conceptual design of multi-modal products. Res. Eng. Des. **26**(3), 219–234 (2015)
25. Bjørn, P., Boulus-Rødje, N.: The multiple intersecting sites of design in CSCW research. Comput. Supported Coop. Work **24**(4), 319–351 (2015)
26. Williams, A., et al.: Multisited design: an analytical lens for transnational HCI. Hum.-Comput. Inter. **29**(1), 78–108 (2014)
27. Storni, C.: Notes on ANT for designers: ontological, methodological and epistemological turn in collaborative design. CoDesign **11**(3–4), 166–178 (2015)

Natural-Language Neutrality in Programming Languages: Bridging the Knowledge Divide in Software Engineering

Ivan Ruby[1] and Salomão David[2(✉)]

[1] Osmania University, Hyderabad, India
ivanrubyds@gmail.com
[2] Universitá Della Svizzera Italiana (USI), Lugano, Switzerland
salomao.david@gmail.com

Abstract. This paper introduces an approach to allow English Language Learners (ELLs) to collaborate in the Software Engineering field using their individual native languages. Natural-Language Neutrality (NLN) aims to bridge the Knowledge Divide in Software Engineering by providing tools and methodologies to allow speakers of different Natural Languages to learn, practice and collaborate in an environment that is Natural-Language agnostic.

A Knowledge Divide in Software Engineering is constituted by the differences in the knowledge assimilation capability, between native English-speakers and ELLs, due to the English-language barrier.

NLN intends to provide standardized methods to enable already-existing and new Programming Languages to be accessible to learners in their Natural-language context. The tools created to achieve this purpose, Glotter, Glotation and the Collaborative Model, are described.

Keywords: Human Computer Interaction · Computer Science Education · Learning & Collaboration Technologies · Programming Languages

1 Introduction

A Programming Language (PL) is a formal constructed language used to create a program, a list of instructions, to perform a task.

Although a PL specifies a notation (Aaby 1996) to write programs, these are often written with a combination of mathematical and everyday language characters, words and phrases.

According to World Language Statistics (SIL International 2015), English is the 3rd most spoken language in the world, with 5.43 % of speakers, behind Chinese[1] and Spanish with 14.4 % and 6.15 %, respectively. Nonetheless, a survey of the most used PLs' (TIOBE Software BV 2015) Syntax, Semantics, Standard Library and Runtime System indicates that the most popular are all English-based.

---

[1] A group of related varieties of languages spoken in China described as dialects of a single Chinese language.

© Springer International Publishing Switzerland 2016
P. Zaphiris and A. Ioannou (Eds.): LCT 2016, LNCS 9753, pp. 628–638, 2016.
DOI: 10.1007/978-3-319-39483-1_57

Although Non-English-based PLs exist (Wikipedia 2015), currently the most used have syntax, learning resources, Runtime, and Development Environments that are developed with an English-speaking audience in mind.

Hypothetically, in a universe of more than 7 Billion people, to make usage of the speed and computational capacity of machines to solve problems, approximately 94 % of the people would have to be able to express their instructions to the computer in English, even though not speaking it as a native language.

Software Engineering is a fast changing and evolving field. Thus, it is a challenge to translate and distribute the learning material in languages other than English, keeping pace with the technology development. This fact often categorizes a non-native English speaker student of Software Engineering as an English Language Learner (ELL) since the learning process makes usage of material and tools that are in English, regardless of whether the medium of instruction is English or not.

The discrepancy between the English Language not being the most spoken Natural-Language but being the most widely used in the most popular PLs, inability of ELLs to use their native languages and the constraint of being taught in one language while practicing the concepts (programming) in a different language altogether create a Knowledge barrier, or Knowledge Divide, to ELLs in Software Engineering.

To keep pace with innovations and generate ideas, people need to be able to produce and manage knowledge. However, the increase in the 21st century of access to information has resulted in an uneven overall ability to assimilate it.

Knowledge Divide is a term that denotes the differences between those who have access to knowledge and can assimilate it, participating in knowledge-sharing and using it as a tool for development, and others who are impaired in this process (Bindé and Matsuura 2005).

A Knowledge Divide in Software Engineering is constituted by the differences in Software Engineering-related knowledge assimilation capabilities between native English-speakers and ELLs, due to the English-language barrier.

ELLs need to develop English language and literacy skills in the context of the subjects being taught to keep up with English-speaking students (Lee 2005). However, the linguistic knowledge that students already possess is often not taken into consideration (Janzen 2008).

By allowing students to employ their existing language skills, the Knowledge Divide can be decreased.

Thus, this paper proposes a methodology to bridge the aforementioned Knowledge Divide.

2   Data Collection

During the month of April of 2015, a Survey was conducted to 78 students of the University College of Engineering, Osmania University. The students were from different streams of Engineering but had common introductory Programming courses in C and C++.

The sample was split into two groups, of 34 and 44 students to have a representative sample, and the questions presented to the students intended to study the following factors:

- Perceived importance of comments in source code
- Perceived importance and difficulty in understanding source code written in a native language.

3   Results

Students found a program without comments easier to understand but when presented a choice the version with comments was more favorable. When asked about the importance attributed to comments the majority (54 %) of the students was neutral. This inconsistency might suggest that comments are under-used, although of considerable importance in reading and understanding the source code (Fig. 1).

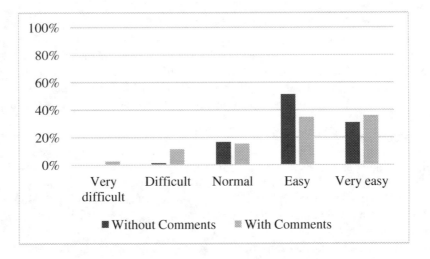

Fig. 1. Perceived difficulty in understanding a program's source code

Regarding the difficulty and importance of the usage of Native languages in source codes, a similar scenario could be verified.

58 % of the students found understanding a program written in their mother tongue difficult. Although a small portion would prefer reading a program written in their native language, when asked about its importance 45 % were neutral (Fig. 2).

It is this considerably undecided portion of the sample that led to the following questions being raised regarding students' perceptions:

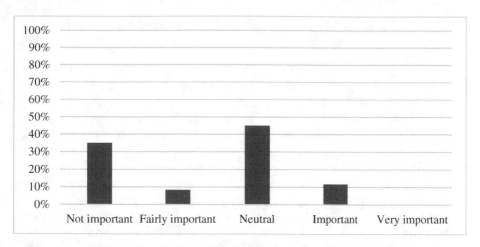

Fig. 2. Perceived importance of a native-language in understanding source code

- Are students aware of the resources available to them?
- Are the resources being presented and contextualized to suit the students' learning process?
- What determines the outcome of the learning process in Software Development: students' usage of their existing resources or their ability to adapt to the already established required resources?

Having this questions in mind, we decided to venture in the construction of a learning and practice model that would highlight the importance of using students' existing resources.

4   Multilingual vs. NLN Programming Languages

In one hand, Multilingual PLs, also called International PLs, allow the usage of more than one Natural Language for writing programs. Such are the cases of ALGOL 68 (van Wijngaarden et al. 1969) and BabylScript (Iu 2011).

ALGOL 68 is the 1968 version of the Algorithmic Language. It is an imperative PL, which succeeds ALGOL 60, and provides translations of its Standard in Russian, German, French, Bulgarian, Japanese and Chinese. The translations allow the internationalization of the PL.

BabylScript is an open-source, multilingual scripting language that compiles to JavaScript. It is implemented using the Java PL, by modifying the open-source Mozilla Rhino JavaScript engine. BabylScript has different language modes in which keywords, objects, and functions names are translated into non-English languages. With this feature, it allows programmers to write programs in languages other than English. BabylScript also allows a mixed language model, on which the same source code can contain code written in more than one language.

At the time of writing, BabylScript has 17 language translations including Chinese, Hindi, Swahili, Spanish and Russian.

Although Multilingual PLs reduce the initial language barrier, they pose a threat to their development and adoption for being Natural-language isolated. A larger audience can be engaged, but ultimately only speakers of the same language can collaborate.

So far, the approaches used for the creation of Multilingual PLs have not been standardized and a single approach to enable the feature to different PLs, existing as well as newly created, has not been identified.

On the other hand, NLN is an approach that intends to provide tools and methodologies to allow speakers of different Natural-Languages to learn, practice and collaborate in an environment that is Natural-Language-agnostic.

By allowing learners with different Native languages to interact in a unified platform, the Single Natural Language (English) knowledge requirement can be reduced.

The English-language is still required in Software Engineering. However, re-establishing a balance between its usage as a Lingua franca and native languages is desirable, recognizing the existing linguistic diversity (Bindé and Matsuura 2005).

NLN can be integrated into an already existing or newly created PL, taking advantage of the most used English-based ones (Fig. 3).

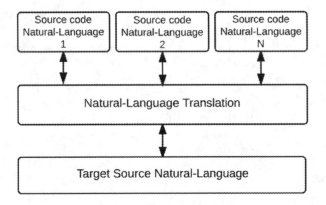

Fig. 3. Natural-Language Neutrality model

At the core of the NLN approach is a Natural-Language Translation mechanism. The required translation is only of the PL's keywords, not of the complete source code. Hence, we came up with a Translation mechanism that can be further exploited.

5 Tools

The proposed tools contemplate the source code keywords, comments and Collaboration between programmers.

Although each tool is designed to iterate over the elements of Bloom's Taxonomy Cognitive Dimension (Bloom et al. 1956), they mainly intend to stimulate the Affective Dimension elements in students, through the inclusion of their existing linguistic knowledge in the problem-solving process.

5.1   Glotter: A Compiler-Level Natural-Language Neutrality Enabler

A Glotter is a Lexical Analysis tool that converts the source code Lexical Units (tokens) from a Source to a Target Natural-Language.

A *Source Natural Language* can be any existing Natural Language while the *Target Natural-Language* is a predefined Bridge Natural Language, a Lingua Franca, which will enable all other Source Natural Languages to be translated to and from it.

The name is derived from the Latin word *glot*, which means Language, and the English word enabler. Therefore, a Glotter is a *Language Enabler.*

The Glotter receives a list of tokens, a list of Language Dictionaries and a selected Natural-Language, which serves as the context for the translation.

Its integration to a compiler enables the possibility of different (translated) versions of the same keywords being compiled into a single version. This process ultimately serves the purpose of enabling a single PL to be used with various Natural Languages, while maintaining all the syntactic and semantic structure and rules.

Upon processing, if the keyword is present at the selected Language Dictionary its value is substituted by the matching value. Otherwise, it is left intact. Although it is possible to implement an error reporting functionality upon detection of a non-existent keyword version in the selected Language, this feature might exceed the responsibilities of a Lexical Analyzer. Furthermore, this error can be reported by the Syntax Analyzer.

Implementation Methods

Embedded. By integrating the Glotter to the compiler, each token can be translated at a time. This approach is more flexible and does not add a performance impact on the normal working of the compiler. An Embedded Glotter requires modification to the compiler source code for an existing PL, what poses a disadvantage in case a seamless integration is expected (Fig. 4).

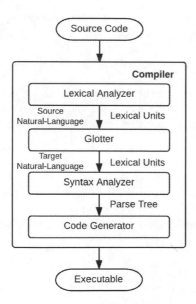

Fig. 4. Embedded Glotter Implementation

Standalone. In this alternative method, the Glotter is separated from the Compiler. The complete source code (input) is parsed by the Glotter, in a process that involves a Lexical Analysis (Tokenization) of the given code. Therefore, the source code is Tokenized twice. This process requires no modification of an existing compiler's source code, a fact that constitutes an advantage to enabling NLN in already existing PLs (Fig. 5).

Algorithm

```
Algorithm Glotter
   Input: A List of Lexical Units L, A List of Language
          Dictionaries LD, a selected Language S
   Output: A List of Lexical Units L

   if S = null, then
     S:="default"

   for each token in L, do
     translatedToken := null
     if token(type) = "Keyword", then
       translatedToken:= isPresentInLanguageDictionary(LD,
       S, token(value))
       if translatedToken != null, then
         token := translatedToken

 return L

 Algorithm isPresentInLanguageDictionary
   Input: A List of Language Dictionaries LD, A selected
          Language S, a Lexical Unit token
   Output: A String representing the a token or null

   for each selectedDictionaryToken in LD(S), do
     if selectedDictionaryToken(token) != null, then
       return selectedDictionaryToken(token)

 return null
```

Note:
It is assumed that the List of Lexical Units comprises of a list of objects with at least **type** *and* **value** *properties and upon not finding an entry or entry-value in a dictionary null is returned.*

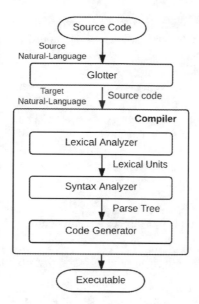

Fig. 5. Standalone Glotter implementation

5.2   Glotation: Natural-Language Annotated Comments

A Glotation is a special kind of comment that includes a source Natural Language attribute and the comment message.

The name is derived from the Latin word *Glot*, which means Language, and the English word *Annotation*, metadata attached to text (in this case, attached to source code).

The source language attribute can later be used to translate the comment message to a different Natural Language.

Syntax.

@xx message
Where:
@ is a Symbol that denotes a Glotation, **xx** is a two-letter lowercase ISO 639-1 Language code[2] and **message** is the Comment message or text.

Example:

@en This is a Glotation
@pt Esta é uma Glotação
@fr Ceci est un Glotation

The example above creates Glotations in English, Portuguese and French with the equivalents of *"This is a Glotation"*. Each time a user will access the source code, an option to translate the Glotations, *Glotate*, can allow the translations to occur, provided

---

[2] http://www.infoterm.info/standardization/ISO_639.php.

the user specifies to Environment (target) Language. Therefore, although the comments can be written in different languages, a user can choose to visualize all comments in his/hers context-Natural-Language.

The @ symbol is desirable since its usage is not common among the most used PLs. Therefore, it is possible to avoid confusion between a general comment and a Glotation.

A Glotation translation can be achieved using a Third Party translation service, which might require an internet connection.

To implement Glotations, the rules of the Syntax Analyzer (Parser) should be modified. The rules should detect a Glotation by the symbol @ and build an Abstract Syntax[3] node with the following properties:

- *type:* "Glotation"
- *language:* two-letter country code (content immediately following the @ symbol)
- *value:* the message text (separated from the country code by a whitespace).

Therefore, the rules for a well-formed Glotation can be deduced as:

1. Starts with the @ symbol
2. Has no space between the symbol and the following text
3. The text immediately following the @ symbol consists of a two-character string
4. Immediately following the two character string, there is a whitespace
5. After the whitespace follows the comment message with alphanumeric and special characters, including whitespace.

A message should only be translated if the Glotation language is different from the Language currently being used in the Development Environment by the user. Therefore, there should be a mechanism to obtain the Development Environment language.

Algorithm

```
Algorithm Glotation
   Input: List of Comment nodes LC, Environment Language L
   Output: List of Comments LC

   for each comment in LC, do
     if comment(type) = "Glotation", then
       if comment(lang) != L, then
         comment(value) := Translate(comment(value),
                                     comment(lang), L)
   return LC
```

---

[3] Tree representation of the Abstract syntactic structure of source code written in a programming language.

5.3   Natural-Language Neutrality Collaborative Model for Programming Languages

Making usage of the Glotter and Glotations, a collaborative model can be implemented to allow dissimilar Natural-Languages to be used in a programming environment. Such model should employ a mechanism to allow a user to write a program with keywords and comments in his/hers Natural-Language granted that this same program can be understood by a user with a different Natural-Language.

Translation of keywords and comments can be achieved by the Glotter and Glotations, respectively, but the key factor lies in the data format being used when storing and exchanging the program among the users (Fig. 6).

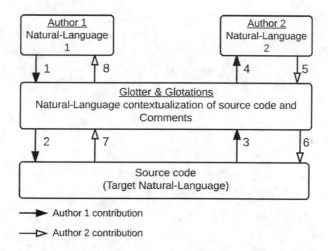

Fig. 6. NLN collaborative environment workflow

Upon creation, the source code to be exchanged should desirably possess only Glotations, instead of only comments or a mix. Such process can be automated on the Source code editor by automatically replacing general comments with Glotations, granted that the user has already permitted the functionality and chosen the environment Natural-Language. Similarly, the source code should always be stored with the keywords in the target Natural-language.

Such source code file, with Glotations and keywords in the target Natural-Language, will serve as the intermediate file format, the essence of the collaborative model.

When a different user receives this same source code, the process of contextualization can be performed by applying the Glotter and Glotation functionalities, joint or separately.

Therefore, the inverse process can take place by the second author editing the source code file, storing it in the intermediate file format and sending it back to the first author.

6 Conclusion

Language plays a critical role in a student's effective education. This process also depends on the teaching institutions taking into consideration the sociocultural aspects of the learners, such as their identity and experiences (Janzen 2008; Lee 2005).

Making the current trends and developments in the Software Engineering field available should be accompanied by processes, tools, and resources that will enable or, at least, ease the ability to assimilate this knowledge to the underprivileged. This increase in literacy would benefit not only the disadvantaged but the society as a whole since more people would be brought to an acceptable level of literacy and employability, becoming active contributors in combating poverty.

Although Multilingual PLs exist, a standardized and methodological approach is required to explore the context of Bridging the Knowledge Divide in Software Engineering thoroughly. Such can be accomplished through the proposed NLN approach.

Further research should be undertaken to understand its underlying factors, provide quantitative as well as qualitative indicators of its effectiveness and to incorporate new tools and methodologies to support it.

References

Aaby, A.: Introduction to programming languages. Computer Science Department, Walla Walla College. http://www.worldcolleges.info/sites/default/files/aaby.pdf

Bindé, J., Matsuura, K.: Towards knowledge societies. UNESCO world report, vol. 1 (2005)

Bloom, B.S., Engelhart, M.D., Furst, E.J., Hill, W.H., Krathwohl, D.: Taxonomy of Educational Objectives: Handbook 1 Cognitive Domain. Longmans, Green and Co. Ltd., London (1956)

Iu, M.-Y.C.: Babylscript: multilingual JavaScript. In: OOPSLA 2011: Proceedings of the ACM International Conference Companion on Object Oriented Programming Systems Languages and Applications Companion, pp. 197–198 (2011). http://doi.org/10.1145/2048147.2048204

Janzen, J.: Teaching english language learners in the content areas. Rev. Educ. Res. 78(4), 1010–1038 (2008). http://doi.org/10.3102/0034654308325580

Lee, O.: Science education with english language learners: synthesis and research agenda. Rev. Educ. Res. 75(4), 491–530 (2005). http://doi.org/10.3102/00346543075004491

SIL International: Summary by language size | Ethnologue Languages of the World (2015). https://www.ethnologue.com/statistics/size. Accessed 13 May 2015

TIOBE Software BV: TIOBE Index for June 2015 (2015). http://www.tiobe.com/index.php/content/paperinfo/tpci/index.html. Accessed 23 April 2015

van Wijngaarden, A., Mailloux, B.J., Peck, J.E.L., Koster, C.H.A.: Report on the Algorithmic Language ALGOL 68. Mathematisch Centrum, Amsterdam (1969)

Wikipedia: Non-English-based programming languages (2015). http://en.wikipedia.org/wiki/Non-English-based_programming_languages. Accessed 8 May 2015

Predictions on Service Adoption and Utilization Meet Reality

First Results from the Sciebo (Science Box) Project

Raimund Vogl[1]([⊠]), Holger Angenent[1], Dominik Rudolph[1],
Andreas Wilmer[1], Anne Thoring[1], Stefan Stieglitz[2],
and Christian Meske[2]

[1] University of Münster, Münster, Germany
{r.vogl, h.angenent, d.rudolph, a.wilmer, a.thoring}
@uni-muenster.de
[2] University of Duisburg-Essen, Essen, Germany
{stefan.stieglitz, christian.meske}@uni-due.de

Abstract. A large academic cloud storage service was launched in the beginning of 2015 by the majority of the public research and applied science universities in the German state of North Rhine-Westphalia (NRW) under the brand name "sciebo". One year after the start, we will examine if the predictions made on service adoption in the preparatory project phase based on the well-known diffusion model by Rogers apply to reality. This is the first study about the adoption of a specific cloud service at several universities. We identify two factors affecting the speed of diffusion: share of technophiles and the use of marketing measures. Organization size does not seem to influence the speed of diffusion .

Keywords: Diffusion of innovations · Adoption · Cloud-storage · Project report

1 Introduction

Cloud storage services like Dropbox or Google Drive became quite popular in the course of the last half decade, not least in the academic context among students and researchers, making it possible to easily share documents with others and to synchronize data across multiple devices. Those commercial services are very comfortable in use, but security concerns about their data utilization arise, especially after the Snowden disclosures. In 2013, as a consequence, the majority of the public research and applied science universities in the German state of North Rhine-Westphalia (NRW) formed a consortium to start a jointly operated private cloud service for the academic community. This sync and share storage platform should be free of charge, easy to use and, most importantly, it should be hosted on premise at several university data centers to be fully compliant with German data protection regulations [1]. With respect to the software functionality and the required hardware setup for potentially 500.000 users, the system design was grounded on empirical user studies.

© Springer International Publishing Switzerland 2016
P. Zaphiris and A. Ioannou (Eds.): LCT 2016, LNCS 9753, pp. 639–649, 2016.
DOI: 10.1007/978-3-319-39483-1_58

A first exploratory survey on the demand for a university operated alternative to Dropbox etc. was conducted among potential users at Münster University in 2012 and extended to a multi-site survey with more than 10.000 participants from three major universities in late 2013 [2]. Both surveys focused on the participants' intention to use such a university operated cloud service, their demand for storage space and client platforms, the type of content (file types) they intended to store, and the communities they wanted to collaborate with using the service's file sharing functionalities. The procurement of the software solution as well as the sizing of the hardware platform were based on the adoption and usage estimates derived from these surveys.

In February 2015, after extensive preparatory work done for the funding proposal, the procurement process, and the system setup and commissioning, the sync and share cloud storage service was launched under the brand name "sciebo – theCampuscloud" (sciebo being short for science box) with three university data centers (Bonn, Duisburg-Essen and Münster) hosting the system platforms on premise. Almost exactly one year after the start, it is now the right time to review how the initial expectations on service adoption and usage correspond with reality. After a year of operation (as of Feb 02 2016), exactly 40.000 users from 24 universities (out of 33 in NRW) and one public research center have signed up for sciebo through the self-enrollment web portal.

The case of sciebo is unique because it allows us to observe the diffusion of a technical innovation from the beginning in a well-controlled setting. There is plenty of literature about the adoption of cloud systems in organizations like SMEs [3–5] or special industries [6–13], but only little is known about the adoption behavior of end-users who can decide freely if they want to use a new cloud service or not [14]. Universities are a special case: On the one hand, they are organizations with a quite uniform population and a manageable size. On the other hand, because of the principle of freedom of research and teaching held high in Germany, there is no possibility to command the use of a system, so users have to be convinced.

1.1 Predictions

According to Rogers [15], innovativeness, i.e. the readiness and the degree to which a person or an organization adopts an innovation (i.e. a new product) compared with the other members of his population, follows the Gaussian distribution. He identifies five adopter categories (innovators, early adopters, early majority, late majority, laggards; see Fig. 1) who have different characteristics referring to their innovativeness. If you accumulate the adoption decisions of all those adopters over time, you will get an S-shaped curve, the diffusion curve. The faster the innovation is adopted the more steeply this curve will rise. The speed of diffusion depends on the characteristics of the innovation, in particular its relative advantage compared to other existing products, compatibility with existing values and practices, simplicity and ease of use, trial ability and observable results.

As our data from a large user survey conducted in 2013 [2] show, Dropbox is the most used storage service among members of the universities with about 80 percent of market share. This value recurs in another survey conducted in 2015 at the same universities (unpublished work), so we conclude that Dropbox obviously has reached

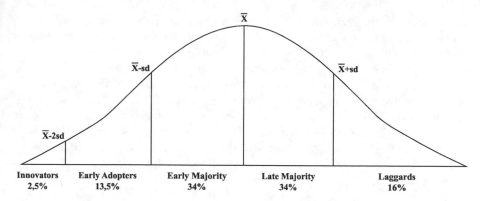

Fig. 1. Adopter Categories according to Rogers [15]

the saturation of demand five years after its inception in 2007 and two years after the release of the first stable version 1.0 in 2010. Examining Dropbox's worldwide diffusion (see Fig. 2), a flat growth is visible in the first two years and a take-off in the third year.

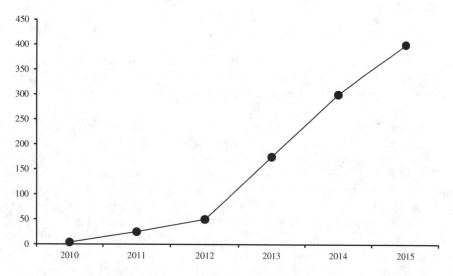

Fig. 2. Diffusion of Dropbox (in mio. users) [16]

For sciebo, we predicted an even faster diffusion because the technology is already known from Dropbox. Moreover, sciebo's high security standards and bigger free storage space seem to be significant relative advantages as stated by the participants of a survey in 2013 [2]. According to Diffusion Theory, market potential is not the total of all potential users (i.e. all members of the participating universities), but the total of all those persons who will realistically use a new service. In the survey, 92.5 percent of the participants stated that they wanted to use sciebo. Being informed that their usage authorization would be revoked when leaving university, the count dropped to 65 percent. Thus, 65 percent of all members of the participating universities – that is about 252.000 individuals – constitute the estimated market potential of sciebo.

Based on the distribution of per user storage demands from the survey, we could refine the initial assumption that each user would utilize the planned 30 GB quota to the max and were able to predict an average storage volume of 8 GB (pessimistic scenario) to 16 GB (optimistic scenario) per user and could ascertain that a maximum storage space of 30 GB should fit most users. Assuming that users would switch their academic data from another platform to sciebo in the first days after the registration, we expected a quite linear growth with a 30 percent basis synchronization at the beginning and just small gain of 3 percent a month.

Considering the predictions on service adoption and storage demand, different scenarios were derived to estimate the size of storage systems to be procured and the internet bandwidth required. The total storage volume required for the operation of sciebo in the long term was estimated at 1.7 PB (pessimistic) to 5 PB (optimistic), and the internet connection bandwidth requirement for service operation was estimated at 3 Gbps in the optimistic scenario.

2   Findings

2.1   User Diffusion

Nearly one year after the official launch, sciebo hit another milestone with now 40.000 users – this means an actual market share of 17.3 percent. In terms of the Diffusion Theory, this implies that sciebo's diffusion has already reached the early majority phase.

However, diffusion speed varies significantly at the different universities. Figure 3 shows the state of diffusion at the 14 universities that started sciebo in Feb 2015. The spectrum ranges from 6.7 percent at the University of Paderborn to 33.9 percent at RWTH Aachen. University size might serve as one explanation, as information should flow very fast at a small campus with a manageable number of departments. As stated by Rogers [15], diffusion can be seen as a communication process: In smaller and spatially closer populations, communication between the members is much more likely and easier than in a complex university with lots of different departments distributed over the whole city.

Though in theory size suggests itself as a reason for the different diffusion speeds, it does not seem to be a good explanation in our case: Comparing same-sized universities – e.g. the Universities of Münster, Duisburg-Essen and RWTH Aachen with about 44,000 to 49,000 members each (see Fig. 4) – the differences in market share are still evident. Results show a remarkable variance of 24.5 percent between RWTH Aachen (33.9 %) and the University of Duisburg-Essen (9.2 %), with the University of Münster (23.0 %) ranking mid.

Taking all universities into account, RWTH Aachen appears to be an outlier with its high market share. Both, the University of Münster (23.0 %) and the University of Duisburg-Essen (9.2 %), rank much closer to the overall average. One possible

Percent of Adoption

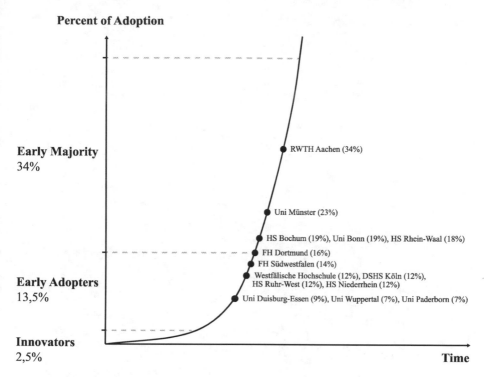

Fig. 3. Diffusion of sciebo after one year (only universities starting in Feb 2015)

explanation for RWTH's high performance is that, unlike the Universities of Münster and Duisburg-Essen, RWTH is a technical university with many technophiles. They resemble the innovators described by Rogers and are the first to adopt new technologies. Logically, a technical innovation like sciebo diffuses faster in a technophilic environment than in other populations.

The low performance of the University of Duisburg-Essen, compared with the same-sized universities and the overall average diffusion, is similarly interesting. A closer look reveals that the universities' commitment in terms of marketing activities might be another decisive factor. While RWTH Aachen and the University of Münster, in particular, performed a variety of marketing activities (i.e. direct mailings to all members), the University of Duisburg-Essen did not to that extent. Therefore it is likely that only innovators and early adopters who are interested in innovations and actively search for information on their own account for their share of sciebo users. Further monitoring will show if an early majority can be reached with no marketing and just word of mouth, or if the number of users will be stagnating. According to some authors there is a gap between the early adopters and the early majority which has to be bridged by marketing activities [17, 18], while Rogers [15] considers both groups as a continuum.

Examining the diffusion curves of the different universities (see Fig. 4), deviations from the ideal S-curve of the diffusion model are clearly visible. Usually, they are

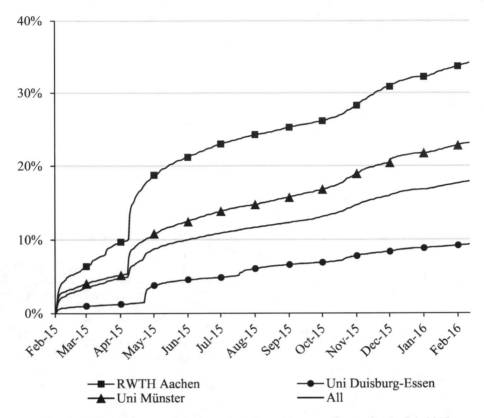

Fig. 4. Diffusion curves of chosen universities with same size starting in Feb 2015

caused by special events. The first boost in February 2015 is the official launch of the service. In the run-up we realized a large Facebook campaign with posts in over 400 user groups related to the participating universities. Also, test users were now added to the statistics. The second and largest user increase in April, at the start of the summer term in Germany, is triggered by direct mailing, that most participating universities did send to their members. The diffusion curves of those universities passing up this opportunity show no such steep rise. In October most universities welcome their largest share of new students for the winter term, explaining the next boost. In December, some universities used direct mailing to promote an online survey related to sciebo, again gaining attention and an additional boost for new users for sciebo.

As regards storage space, we initially expected 9 GB (30 % of the intended per user quota limit of 30 GB) right after registration and a monthly growth of 3 percent (until the quota limit is reached). Currently, the average volume needed by an active user (i.e. a user who uploaded some data) is 3.3 GB, amounting to a total of 99.8 TB storage space used in sciebo. Those universities which grant access to sciebo only to their staff have a substantially higher storage demand per active user (e.g. Düsseldorf University with 7.4 GB) than most other universities where usually three out of four active users are students (e.g. Münster University with 4.7 GB).

2.2   Data Storage

In Fig. 5 we analyzed the storage load on an individual user basis. In particular, we looked at the dependency between the consumed storage space of a single account and its age. Shown is the mean used disk storage for user accounts in dependency of the account lifetime (solid black line), the 0.05-quantile (lower grey line) and the 0.95-quantile (upper grey line) in a logarithmic plot. The broken black line represent the expected and the dotted black line the observed linear model of the user behavior.

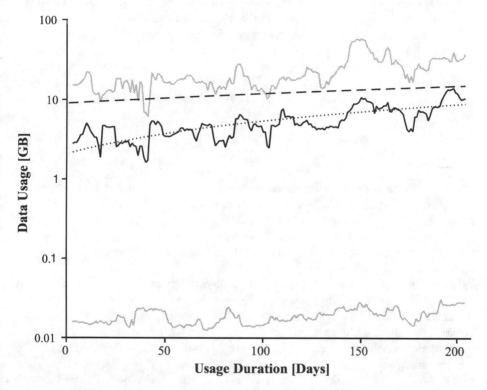

Fig. 5. Storage load on individual user basis per time vs. model (broken line)

Altogether 6,581 user accounts were analyzed on a day-wise basis. The statistical values were computed across an ensemble of user accounts for a specific account age. In addition, two data-sets from different time points are independent from each other because accounts were not tracked over time. The analysis was restricted to active accounts with a used storage capacity of more than 10 MB. Thus, inactive accounts from seasonal side effects, such as beginning of a new semester, are excluded from analysis. In addition, a moving average with a window size of 7 days was used to accumulate the number of user accounts for statistical analysis, i.e. in average $N = 225 \pm 92$ accounts were analyzed for each day.

We observed two main findings: First, we predicted that on average an account initially requires 30 percent of its full 30 GB quota and grows in a linear fashion with 3 percent of its quota per month. One can rewrite this assumption to a linear equation of the form f(x) = A + Bx with the function f describing the disk usage in dependency of the time x and the coefficient A as the initial off-set, B as the slope of the function, i.e. we expected Aexp = 9000 [MB] and Bexp = 29.6 [MB/Day]. However, we observed an offset aobs = 2077.1 ± 239.3 [MB] and a slope bobs = 33.5 ± 2.0 [MB/Day] with a linear Least-Squares Fit (p < .001 and adjusted R-Squared 0.578). The observed results show that on average a user synchronizes less data directly after the subscription than initially expected, but fairly consistent with 30 % of the average storage space per user of 8 GB in the pessimistic scenario deduced from the survey findings. However, the growth of the data synchronized is higher than expected.

Second, sciebo has to handle a variety of usage scenarios. In Fig. 5 the close distance of the average to the 0.95-quantile indicates a positively skewed underlying distribution, which is caused by an extensive disk usage of some few accounts. This indicates on the one hand that usage scenarios will differ in strong fashion between users and, on the other hand, that sciebo is capable to deal with a wide variety of use cases.

2.3   Bandwidth

The initial estimates of bandwidth requirements were essential to make sure that the internet connection bandwidth of the three university data centers hosting the sciebo platform was not entirely consumed by the new sciebo service. Based on simply models of service utilization (up- and downloads) an overall limit of 3 Gbps sustained for the whole sciebo system, thus approx. 1 Gbps for each of the datacenter sites, was predicted as being sufficient.

One year after the start of operation, this sustained data rate has not been reached by far, but temporary bandwidth peaks at each of the three sites are in the 800 Mbps range (see Fig. 6). With continuous growth of the sciebo user base and storage volume, bandwidth demands will necessarily grow, but negative effects on the internet connectivity of the hosting universities (each currently has a 10 Gbps internet link) are, as initially predicted, not to be expected, especially since traffic policies limiting the bandwidth allocated to individual connection could still be imposed. The mutual data backups between the three sites are schedules in the 12am to 6am timeframe where service utilization is low and thus do not negatively impact the bandwidth budget.

2.4   Additional Findings

Apart from those findings related to our predictions, some additional outcomes are worth mentioning. The first finding broaches the issue of user activity: 38 percent of the registered users are inactive, i.e. they have not uploaded any data to sciebo yet. Based on Rogers' Diffusion Theory [15], this inactivity of a substantial user fraction could be interpreted as either a prolonged phase of decision making or as discontinuance (without having used the service apart from signing up) [19, 20]. This finding needs further research.

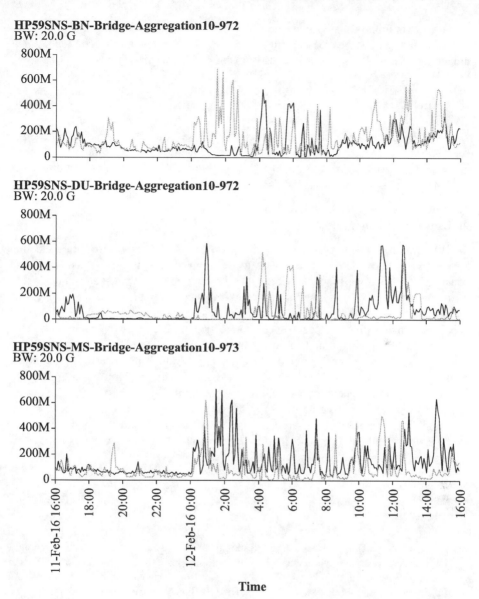

HP59SNS-BN-Bridge-Aggregation10-972
BW: 20.0 G

HP59SNS-DU-Bridge-Aggregation10-972
BW: 20.0 G

HP59SNS-MS-Bridge-Aggregation10-973
BW: 20.0 G

Time

Fig. 6. Internet bandwidth (in = black, out = grey) consumed by the 3 sciebo sites at Bonn (BN), Duisburg-Essen (DU) and Münster (MS) on a typical day after one year of operation. Corre-lated in/out peaks between two sites in the 12am – 6am timeframe are due to mutual backup copy operation.

The second finding focuses on the key collaboration feature of sciebo – sharing data with other sciebo users or externals (share via hyperlink). With an overall average of 2.4 shares per active user, this feature is not used very strongly yet. Folders (66.5 %) are shared more often than files (33.5 %). Approximately 50 percent of all shares are performed via link (primarily intended for external exchange), contrary to expectations from the survey [2], where 65 percent of the participants intended to share within their university and only 21 percent intended to share with externals.

3   Conclusion

These first results shows that the predictions phrased in the aftermath of the 2013 survey [2] are – up to now – in line with the service's adoption, and, moreover, Rogers' diffusion theory has proved to be an adequate model. We could identify two factors influencing the speed of diffusion of the sciebo cloud-service:

1. Share of technophiles in the organization
2. Use of marketing measures

Both findings are supported by the diffusion model. As known from the diffusion literature, an innovation is more likely to be adopted if it is not too complex and consistent with known products. Consequently, technophiles who understand a technical innovation much better and usually find it less complex than other people, will be more likely to adopt an innovation quickly. As noted by some authors, there might be a gap – in terms of missing peer-to-peer connections – between innovators and early adopters on the one hand and the early majority on the other hand, because of the significant differences between those groups [17]. Marketing measures like direct mailings, Facebook posts, YouTube videos etc. can bridge this gap by informing the early majority about a new service, and thus speed up the diffusion process. According to our data, organization size does not influence the diffusion speed.

Finally, the universities' heterogeneous rate of adoption and the high fraction of inactive users leave a wide field for further research. In the upcoming months, analyzing the reasons for discontinuance of use will be a key focus.

References

1. Vogl, R., Angenent, H., Bockholt, R., Rudolph, D., Stieglitz, S., Meske, C.: Designing a large scale cooperative sync&share cloud storage platform for the academic community in northrhine-westfalia. In: Sukovski, U. (ed.) ICT Role for Next Generation Universities - 19th European University Information Systems. Riga Technical University, Riga (2013)
2. Stieglitz, S., Meske, C., Vogl, R., Rudolph, D.: Demand for cloud services as an infrastructure in higher education. In: Proceedings of International Conference on Information Systems, ICIS 2014 (2014)
3. Trigueros-Preciado, S., Pérez-González, D., Solana-González, P.: Cloud computing in industrial SMEs: identification of the barriers to its adoption and effects of its application. Electron. Mark. **23**, 105–114 (2013)
4. Tehrani, Shima Ramezani, Shirazi, Farid: Factors influencing the adoption of cloud computing by small and medium size enterprises (SMEs). In: Yamamoto, Sakae (ed.) HCI 2014, Part II. LNCS, vol. 8522, pp. 631–642. Springer, Heidelberg (2014)

5. Alshamaila, Y., Papagiannidis, S., Li, F.: Cloud computing adoption by SMEs in the north east of england: a multi-perspective framework. J. Enterp. Inf. Manage. **26**, 250–275 (2013)
6. Oliveira, T., Thomas, M., Espadanal, M.: Assessing the determinants of cloud computing adoption: an analysis of the manufacturing and services sectors. Inf. Manage. **51**, 497–510 (2014)
7. Moryson, H., Moeser, G.: Consumer adoption of cloud computing services in germany: investigation of moderating effects by applying an UTAUT model. Int. J. Mark. Stud. **8**, 14 (2016)
8. Low, C., Chen, Y., Wu, M.: Understanding the determinants of cloud computing adoption. Ind. Manage. Data Syst. **111**, 1006–1023 (2011)
9. Lian, J.-W., Yen, D.C., Wang, Y.-T.: An exploratory study to understand the critical factors affecting the decision to adopt cloud computing in taiwan hospital. Int. J. Inf. Manage. **34**, 28–36 (2014)
10. Khanagha, S., Volberda, H., Sidhu, J., Oshri, I.: Management innovation and adoption of emerging technologies: the case of cloud computing. Eur. Manage. Rev. **10**, 51–67 (2013)
11. Ivanova, M., Ivanov, G.: Cloud computing for authoring process automation. Procedia-Social Behav. Sci. **2**, 3646–3651 (2010)
12. Gupta, P., Seetharaman, A., Raj, J.R.: The usage and adoption of cloud computing by small and medium businesses. Int. J. Inf. Manage. **33**, 861–874 (2013)
13. Cegielski, C.G.: Allison Jones-Farmer, L., Wu, Y., Hazen, B.T.: Adoption of cloud computing technologies in supply chains: An organizational information processing theory approach. Int. J. Logistics Manage. **23**, 184–211 (2012)
14. Shin, J., Jo, M., Lee, J., Lee, D.: Strategic management of cloud computing services: focusing on consumer adoption behavior. IEEE Trans. Eng. Manage. **61**, 419–427 (2014)
15. Rogers, E.M.: Diffusion of Innovations. Free Press, New York (2003)
16. Dropbox, https://www.dropbox.com/
17. Moore, G.A.: Crossing the Chasm. Marketing and Selling Disruptive Products to Mainstream Customers. Harper Business, New York (2014)
18. Christensen, C.M.: The Innovator's Dilemma. The Revolutionary Book that Will Change the Way You do Business. Harper Business, New York (2011)
19. Parthasarathy, M., Bhattacherjee, A.: Understanding post-adoption behavior in the context of online services. Inf. Syst. Res. **9**, 362–379 (1998)
20. Black, W.: Discontinuance and Diffusion: Examination of the Post Adoption Decision Process. Adv. Consum. Res. **10**(1), 356 (1983)

Organizational Self-Determination and New Digital Self-Study Applications as Means for Developing Nuclear Power Plant Operation Training

Mikael Wahlström[✉] and Timo Kuula

VTT Technical Research Centre of Finland Ltd, Espoo, Finland
{mikael.wahlstrom, timo.kuula}@vtt.fi

Abstract. New learning is required from nuclear power plant operators: subtle changes to work emerge as new changes to safety improvements are introduced. This study reports challenges, trade-offs and potential solutions related to career long learning in NPP operation. A NPP operating organization was studied with two focus groups sessions (N = 9). The focus group session outline was generated based on individual (N = 2) and group interviews (N = 6) along with existing published studies and concepts of learning theory. The identified challenges reflect limited resources and limited self-determination of a specific functional group as part of bigger organization.

Keywords: New learning · Nuclear power plant operation · Training development

1 Introduction

New learning and rehearsing the learnt is crucially important for nuclear power plant (NPP) operators: improvements to nuclear safety involve constant development of safety procedures and these, in turn, have to be learnt by the operators. Additionally, the operators should maintain and enhance their capability to handle challenging emergency situations, although these situations might never actualize during their career. Despite these needs, it is not at all certain that new learning is organized in the best possible fashion at power plants. Operating organizations in the NPP domain are typically large and fairly old, given the big resources needed and that the nuclear technology has been in widespread civilian use for more than half a decade already. These, along with extremely stringent safety requirements, could imply hierarchical and slowly developing organizations with limited flexibility and capability to adopt new learning trends and methods efficiently. Therefore it could beneficial to consider the current learning practices with an evaluation and perspective by an outsider, such as, a researcher, consultant, or, say, new leader. This study provides an example on how to consider and develop operator training at a NPP operating organizations. Additionally, our study findings – involving both solutions and challenges in training – may provide useful insights to other domains as well.

© Springer International Publishing Switzerland 2016
P. Zaphiris and A. Ioannou (Eds.): LCT 2016, LNCS 9753, pp. 650–660, 2016.
DOI: 10.1007/978-3-319-39483-1_59

The theoretical and methodological background of this study draw from the resilience engineering thinking and from the change laboratory method. Resilience engineering [1] emphasizes the positive impact of human activity as a part of a larger system in maintaining safety. This is to say that safety does not only involve the reduction of human errors (in the design of the system or during the operation), but also the problem solving capability of an active operator in special situation; no system can be considered totally safe, and eventually capable human is needed in solving or, even better, foreseeing and preventing an abnormal situation.

Our study draws inspiration from the change laboratory method [2] where development of training can be seen as a process, which firstly involves identifying the challenges the current training practices, along with the explicative background reasons to these, as well as solutions; these draw from the discussions with the workers within the organizations. In other words, change laboratory is a collaborative method: new concept for training can be identified and generated together with the operators. The change laboratory would also involve testing and establishing the new learning practices, while our study is not yet in this stage of the method.

Firstly, background understanding on training was acquired through interviewing two training developers and through two freeform interviews of operator teams; two simulator training sessions were observed as well. Based on these and background studies in NPP operation and in learning, focus group session outline was developed. Nine individuals participated in two focus group sessions.

Our study identifies a handful of practical challenges in the current learning practices and two basic sources explicating these. Firstly, it seems that the operators simply does not have sufficient time resources for optimal learning in the current work context: they would need more time to apply and more freely "play" with the simulator; this would allow better capability for handling abnormal situations. They would also need opportunities to witness and exchange the practices of operators in other shifts; this would allow the proliferation of good practices between the teams. Another basic "problem source" is being part of a hierarchical organization. This involves several aspects, such as, lack of influence on the content of learning and therefore perceived suboptimal content during learning days. Also, reflecting hierarchy and that the safety critical nature of the nuclear domain, learning the system holistically and by criticizing and inventing new practices with simulator training, can be seen as challenging due to the fact that the current safety procedures dictate operator activity very specifically. In addition to these challenges, we will also discuss preliminary solutions, that is, new training practices.

2   The Study Context: NPP Operation

Our study concerns a European NPP site; the site applies pressurized water reactors – this is typical reactor type at plants. At the studied NPP site, the operator shifts entail three types of work tasks: (1) shift supervisor (who is responsible of the overall operating activity), (2) reactor master (i.e., the primary circuit controller), and (3) turbine technician (i.e., the secondary-circuit controller). The work is in essence shift work and takes place day and night. The operators' main tasks are to monitor the NPP process and operate the plant safely and economically in all possible situations. In order to achieve this, the operators need to maintain clear understanding on state of the process. They have to be capable to act and to perform the procedures in any given time and to work in collaboration with the other staff.

Prior entering to training at the operating organization all operators have an engineering degree. The training at the plant consists of class room training, co-working and observation with the existing operators (i.e., an apprentice training), written exams, visits to the varying parts of the plant (during yearly maintenance when usually restricted areas are accessible). Fifteen work-weeks will be spent at the simulator.

After the training for new operators, the career-long new learning consists of simulator training, classroom lessons, and self-study. Any safety enhancement or other change at the plant translates into content that has to be learnt by the operators; new procedures, for example, are reviewed by the operators, as needed. The continuation training for the operators is mandatory as well, as the authorities dictate a minimum of days in simulator training.

The applied simulator is an almost exact mock-up of the operating room and, in a functional sense, it replicates the plant dynamics meticulously. The operating room and simulator consist of three walls filled with analogue controls. The control layout "replicates" power plant system itself, that is, the control devices on the walls follow the dynamics and causal links at the plant (including connections between steam lines, generators, pumps, and such). There are some newer digital devices as well, that is, computers, which are mainly used for monitoring the plant parameters; there is also one relatively newly fitted digital control device, but this too is linked to the analogue relays controlling the plant. The shift supervisor monitors the plant at the centre of the large room. One the left side operates the reactor master who controls the heat and pressure transfer, as produced by fission, at the shielded core of the plant; the turbine technician on the right, in turn, monitors and controls the heat and pressure transfer rotating a turbine connected to a generator that ultimately produces electricity.

In emergencies the plant operation relies heavily on alarms and procedures. The aim is that a procedure would be available for any given critical situation; as an alarm sets of the shift supervisor selects the corresponding procedure, that is, a specific and numbered flow-chart-filled paper leaflet. Each of the three operator types has their own dedicated procedures. During emergencies (and emergency training), a supplementary safety engineer will be asked to join the team; s/he monitors the plant state, based mainly on measures, and has her/his own set of procedures. There is, however, variation in this activity as the shifts seem to differ in the way in which they use the procedures. Some shifts have been found to express parameter-based anticipation, critical consideration of multiple sources of information, discussion and double-checking activity more than others [3]; assumedly, with dialogical interpretation of the situation, the work shifts entail better problem solving capabilities and more profound shared view of the plant state is generated [4].

Overall, NPP operation is complex and responsible work requiring career-lasting new learning. Abnormal situations are, in principle, dictated by the procedures. However, one may consider the resilience engineering thinking [1] according to which no system is complete safe and that therefore human understanding and problem solving capabilities would eventually be needed.

3   Methods

3.1   Background Studies

For background understanding, NPP's training experts and two operator teams were interviewed. Two simulator training sessions were observed as well.

The first of the training expert interviewees works as a trainer for trainers and developer at the NPP site. S/he has a long background career as a shift supervisor. The other expert informant works as a training developer and has academic training as well as vocational background in teaching and adult education. At the observer simulator training certain emergency procedures were rehearsed. After observing the training, the two shifts were interviewed in a freeform manner, in two separate sessions.

Based on these observations and interviews, as well as on literature [3, 4], basic understanding on the training and the features of the work were developed. Additionally, the first ideas of the possible challenges in training were created. This understanding was used to form the outline for two focus group sessions, which validate the findings of the background studies and provide the main data source for this study.

3.2   The Focus Group Sessions

The two focus groups consisted of the two training expert interviewees mentioned above, operator trainers, and regular NPP operators (total N = 9). Most of the participants were regular operators (N = 5).

Firstly, to provoke thinking and initiate discussion among the focus group, general challenges related to NPP training, as interpreted by the researchers, were introduced to the focus groups; these challenges were identified during the background studies (as explicated above). Firstly, a general issue found in the preliminary study was that "remembering the taught details is challenging." The issue was voiced in the after-training interviews and it reflects the complexity of procedures and the NPP system itself. Secondly, a related finding was introduced, this being the issue that "plant dynamics are not learnt as before with the simulator:" formerly the emergency procedures were much less specific, with targets rather than precise tasks. As explicated by our informants, with these more unspecific procedures, the operator had to consider the system functioning in order to actualize the procedure – this, assumedly, provided better basis for learning the system dynamics. Thirdly, it was noted that "motivation towards self-study varies strongly between the operators" – some interviewed operators expressed enthusiasm while others where less interested. Fourthly, a general observation on the curriculum was that "challenging and abnormal situations were rehearsed only seldom by the operators." Fifth, based on the literature [3] and overall observation of the work, it was concluded that NPP operation entails a general challenge of "the complexity of work and need for holistic understanding on the system."

After discussing these five potential challenges, four themes were discussed with session participants. The themes were mainly theoretically justified, but also partly derived from training expert interviews. First theme was "learning together;"

collaborative learning is a common theme in learning literature – dialogue between peers enhances exchange of good practices and new ideas, for instance [5, 6]. Second theme was called "learning goals." Prioritization between aims and the issue of who will be setting the goals was discussed here. This theme thus links to the theoretical ideas (such as constructivism) on learners being active and critical subjects (able to learning goal setting, among other things) rather than mere objects [5]. "Development of problem-solving ability" was the third theme. This connects to the resilience engineering line of research according to which safety is not merely the "negative" lack of mistakes, but also "positive" capability to solve and anticipate problems [1]. The final fourth theme was "inventing new." This is in line with the "expansive learning" [7] concept, according to which learning involves creative generation of new ideas rather than mere "input" of existing thinking.

The themes were first introduced by the researcher (the authors of this paper) and discussed with the whole focus group. Then the focus group was split into half and the participants discussed each theme without researcher participation (the operators were allowed to discuss without the trainers). The participants were guided to consider challenges and practical development ideas in view of different modes and aspects training, these being (1) simulator, (2) class room lectures, (3) self-study, and (4) evaluation: As an example, the group considered simulator-related challenges and ideas from the viewpoint of "learning together". Finally, the participants' ideas were discussed with the whole focus group and the researchers. Overall, the focus group session consisted of three types of conceptual "stimuli" for initiating discussion among the operators and their trainers: initial findings and assumptions on challenges, theoretically justified themes, and the four ways and aspects of training.

3.3   Qualitative Content Analysis

The analysis of data followed roughly the principles of basic qualitative content analysis [8], that is, the participants remarks were bundled together into fewer categories. The categories were not predefined per se, but the overall aim was to pinpoint practical training-related challenges and possible solutions. This process took place intuitively, based on perceived similarity between the participants' suggestions. The categories were generated on different levels of abstraction for the purpose of generalization of the study results: viewing the study findings more generally might help to consider whether the challenges and solutions could apply to several work contexts.

4   Results

The practical development ideas, resulting from the focus groups, reflect the challenges and problems of the current training. The ideas in Table 1 were listed after the group work sessions and they represent the possibilities and wishes that the participants considered as realistic to implement in the current training, given the current training resources and means. Of these ideas, simulator training without the dictating procedures seemed popular as this was consider to better improve understanding on the plant dynamics. Additionally, to further develop self-study was seen interesting and inspiring. The contradiction between current theory training (class room lectures) and the operators' needs for more targeted and practical learning content could be identified.

Table 1. Operators' ideas by focus group learning themes and modes of training

Focus group learning themes:	*Modes of training:*		
	Simulator	Class room lectures	Self-study
Learning together	More collaboration between shifts.	More (collaborative) hands-on exercises. Group work that enhances discussion.	Preparing for exams through collaboration in shifts. Other self-study through collaboration (e.g. transferring tacit knowledge from experts to novice).
Learning goals	More ideas from the operators included in training.		Use of digital applications (such as digital exams).
Development of problem-solving ability	"Blind" plant dynamic training without procedures. Diffusion of best practices between shifts.	More examples from real-life situations.	Development of background material for procedures.
Inventing new	More collecting needs for procedure improvements.		More self-studying new procedures and major changes in NPP before the simulator training.

Table 2 also presents results of the study, these involving now both problems and solutions, and being further categorized by the researchers. The table presents "specific sources of challenges" (second column), which entails issues that were presented at the discussion by the focus group participants or were presented by the researchers agreed upon by the participants (this taking place in one result cell "procedures now more specific than before"). The third column entails "implied practical challenges," that is, potential problems related to the abovementioned sources of challenges as assumed either by the participants or the researchers; all of these were voiced at the focus group. "Specific solutions" column (fourth column) refers to solutions discussed at focus group sessions, the solutions being voiced either by the researchers or the participants. Finally, "generic sources of challenges" and "generic solution category" (on the extreme left and right columns, respectively) are abstractions as interpreted by the researchers.

Table 2. Challenges and development solutions regarding career-long operator training at a NPP site

Generic sources of challenges	Specific sources of challenges	Implied practical challenges	Specific solutions	Generic solution category
limited resources	limited possibilities for applying simulator	limited "routine capability" in emergency situations	laptop-based simulator; another simulator	resources, new digital training applications
	limited training days	limited time for study needed issues	some less-crucial issues to self-study	resources, organizational development
	no possibilities for seeing colleagues in one's own task	lack of exchange in good work practices; lack of comparative understanding on one's own performance	new means for representing simulator performance and post-simulator self-study; simulator performance observations	resources, new digital training applications
limited self-determination of a specific functional group as part of bigger organization	the class-room training content of learning days is largely dictated top-down	lack of appropriate prioritization in content (as perceived by the operators)	some less-crucial issues to self-study (would require a special status within the whole organization)	organizational development
	limited background knowledge about procedures (at times)	limited learning by understanding and criticizing; limited bottom-up development	more resources for distributing information	resources
	procedures now more specific than before	plant dynamics not learned as before in simulator	more freeform simulator use; post-simulator self-study; laptop-based simulator	new digital training applications
	bureaucratic obstacles	reductions in the amount of training development	reconsidering some bureaucratic obstacles	organizational development

Firstly, a bundle of challenges seem to relate to the notion that there are only limited time resources available for training. The discussion recurrently reflected the issue the operators had only limited possibilities for applying simulator and limited days for training the content they felt pertinent for NPP operation. It was complained by an operator that limited simulator days do not provide sufficient experience for handling the emergency situation in "routinized manner." Simple solution would be to add more training days and, since the current simulator now seems to be well utilized, another simulator. Some additional solutions, which would not require much less dedicated training hours as provided by the energy company, emerged as well. Firstly, the idea of laptop-based "minisimulator" was discussed: apparently this had been in the making for several years now. This would allow training with the simulated plant dynamics more freely and often in self-study.

A specific problem, related to lack of training days, was that the operators lacked the possibility to witness colleagues actualizing the same task as oneself. There is rotation between teams, that is, a reactor master, for example, would not spend the whole career with the same shift leader. However, a reactor master would practically never see another reactor master in action during the career – this would only take place in the apprentice training phase. Lack of possibility to compare oneself to others implies insufficiency in both diffusion of good practices and in professional self-knowledge. There is no specific reason inhibiting this, but the training is organized in a manner such that there are in practice never opportunities for this.

Better prioritization in selecting content for training was also discussed as the means for overcoming the problems of limited time allocated for training. However, there were only limited possibilities for this, reflecting the second general problem source identified by us: limited self-determination of operators as part of the overall power company organization. Much of the content of class-room training days is dictated top-down, with issues mandatory for the whole organization. The operators generally complained that some of these mandatory-for-all issues could be transferred to self-study (as being not in the top priority, in their view) while other issues, more crucial for operation of the plant, could be studied during the learning days. For example, if the content of lectures on, say, information security, could be studied at home or during easy phases at plant – it was suggested that instead of following these lectures time could be spent, say, in visiting some parts of the plant for more profound understanding on the plant dynamics.

The subordinate nature of the operators within the hierarchical power point organization can be seen as explicative of some other issues as well. It was explained by the operators that at times they felt that sufficient background knowledge about procedures was not provided. This implies difficulties in learning by understanding and criticizing as the procedures are simply given without explication of the logics beneath the provided rules. There is also no bottom-up operator-driven development of the procedures in this approach. This varied, however, since, at times, the operators were well integrated into procedure development.

The hierarchy also relates to an issue identified in the background study and agreed upon in the focus group: emergency procedures were now much more specific than before. With the previous type of procedures, the operators could assumedly achieve more profound understanding of the plant dynamics during exceptional situations at simulator training as they had to figure out the exact operating actions by themselves. It was considered that more freeform use of simulator could be beneficial due to this. This could take place with the abovementioned laptop-based simulator. It was also discussed that developing training is generally challenging due to plant bureaucracy. We did not go much to specifics, but information security, for instance, is vigorous within the plant site and apparently a common reason for precluding developing ideas. Overall, the emerged solution options involve increasing or re-allocating time resources for training, new digital training applications and organizational development.

5   Discussion

The background studies and the focus-group sessions provided a rich set of suggestions on potential challenges and solutions (see Table 1 and Table 2). Based on these findings, we may consider potential general tensions between training and operating within an ultra-safe industry. In addition, we will also further consider solution options; self-study will be discussed in particular.

5.1   Some Learning-Related Contradictions in Ultra-Safe Industries

Bainbridge (1983) has discussed general safety-related challenges related to automation. A contradiction lies there that as the reliability of the system increases, less common will it be to experience abnormalities and problems at work – this, in turn, implies limited on-the-work learning needed for solving these situation, which could eventually lead to under-achievement in emergency situations. In other words, creating an 'ultra-safe' and highly reliably system could, in principle, create counterproductive safety results.

Similarly, creating exact foolproof procedures seems to entail an element of paradox: if the procedures can be actualized by simple rule-following, training with these procedures does not necessarily create understanding of the overall system. Simulator training would thus need to entail situations to which procedures do not exist. Actualizing simulation training of this kind might not be as simple as one might imagine: if the aim is that the system would be safe in all imagined realistic situation, creating abnormal situation to which procedures do not exist would imply a fail in the system design. Indeed, the focus group participants remarked that this kind of training takes place too seldom.

The contradictions above – that is, (1) between comprehensively dictating procedures and learning as well as (2) between the aim of absolute system safety and creation of simulator training with surprising system failures – imply challenges in cultivating problem solving capabilities. Yet, as assumed by the researchers within the resilience engineering community [1], no system can be completely safe and ultimately there may be a need for human problem solving capabilities.

5.2   Developing Self-Study

The role of self-study and self-directed learning has apparently been a recent topic of interest at the studied NPP. It could be developed by supporting collaborative learning within and between shifts, and supporting the personal and group learning goal setting. Transferring more resources for self-studying requires new organization of training and new kind of learning materials. More profoundly, it could require a mindset that supports shifting the training away from predetermined learning goals and methods. This might be a challenge in an ultra-safe context, and the development efforts should be made in close collaboration between NPP personnel and suitable stakeholders, such as learning experts and researchers.

There are many ways in which new digital possibilities could contribute to self-study as the digital laptop-based "minisimulator" could be applied by the operators as they wish. In addition to solving emergency situations and actualizing procedures, more freeform use could in principle be possible with this application, that is, the operators could more freely make their own try-outs with the programmed plant dynamics. Additionally, "gamification" is a trend in training [10], which could be of inspiration here; game elements could be introduced to the simulator use – the operators could compare "results" or they could even design tasks and emergencies one for another. This would, however, require additional programming and design.

New digital possibilities could also contribute to post-simulator self-study: automatically created representation of the performance can be imagined, this including video clips synced with time-line of simulator events; audio could be represented visually for indicating collaboration. With this kind of media representation of the simulator performance, the operators could be able to better reflect and compare activity in discussion after simulator sessions.

5.3   Limitations and Future Study Plans

A limitation of this study is certain one-sidedness: we have had the operators' opinion on training and our study entails an element of critique towards the energy company organization – some identified challenges seem to reflect inhibiting hierarchy and bureaucracy. However, a fuller understanding and alternative points of views could be achieved by discussing with representatives at higher-levels of the organizational hierarchy. We are planning to do this in the future. Additionally, reflecting the discussion above, we will also develop and test new self-study methods for further developing NPP training.

Acknowledgements. The study was supported by the SAFIR2018 programme, the Finnish State Nuclear Waste Management Fund (VYR), VTT Technical Research Centre of Finland Ltd, and Finnish Institute of Occupational Health FIOH. We would like to thank Marika Schaupp (FIOH) for planning and participating in background data collection and analysis, and Heli Heikkilä (FIOH) for commenting the focus group outline draft. Warm thanks also for the personnel at the studied NPP site.

References

1. Hollnagel, E., Woods, D., Leveson, N.: Resilience engineering: Concepts and precepts. Ashgate Publishing Ltd, Vermont (2007)
2. Virkkunen, J.: The Change Laboratory: A tool for collaborative development of work and education. Springer, New York (2013)
3. Savioja, P., Norros, L., Salo, L., Aaltonen, I.: Identifying resilience in proceduralised accident management activity of NPP operating crews. Saf. Sci. **68**, 258–274 (2014)
4. Norros, L., Savioja, P., Koskinen, H.: Core-Task Design: A Practice-Theory Approach to Human Factors. Synthesis Lectures on Human-Centered Informatics (2015)
5. Jonassen, D.: Designing constructivist learning environments. nstructional-design theories and models: A new paradigm of instructional theory, vol. II, pp. 215–239 (1999)
6. Wenger, E.: Communities of practice: Learning, meaning, and identity. Cambridge University Press, Cambridge (1999)
7. Engeström, Y.: Expansive learning at work: toward an activity theoretical reconceptualization. J. Educ. Work **14**(1), 133–156 (2001)
8. Hsieh, H., Shannon, S.: Three approaches to qualitative content analysis. Qual. Health Res. **15**(9), 1277–1288 (2005)
9. Bainbridge, L.: Ironies of automation. Automatica **19**, 775–779 (1983)
10. Kapp, K.: The gamification of learning and instruction: game-based methods and strategies for training and education. Wiley, New York (2012)

Cultural and Social Aspects of Learning and Collaboration Technologies

Gender Differences in Usage Motivation for Social Networks at Work

Juliana Brell, André Calero Valdez[✉], Anne Kathrin Schaar,
and Martina Ziefle

Human-Computer Interaction Center, RWTH Aachen University,
Campus-Boulevard 57, Aachen, Germany
{brell,calero-valdez,schaar,ziefle}@comm.rwth-aachen.de

Abstract. In times of demographic change, skill shortage, and disruptive innovations, organizational knowledge and innovative capacity are the key to a company's success. But how can knowledge be retained with fast staff-turnover, global project-based work and parental leaves? Using social networking sites to improve knowledge dissemination at work seems promising, when looking at the success of private social networking sites. In this article we investigate how user diversity influences the motivation to use such a site at work. We conducted a survey in a company that successfully implements social networking for knowledge dissemination (n = 50) and analyzed differences in usage motivation using multiple linear regression analysis. Among other effects, we found that women use such a system because of a stronger need for social interaction and information. From our findings we derive practical implications for designing a social networking site for work.

Keywords: Social networking sites · User diversity · Motivation · Knowledge management · Web 2.0 technologies

1   Introduction

Globalization processes, rising international competition, and a constantly aging population [1] cause knowledge to be a key resource with indispensable value in any innovation process [2]. As the maintenance, management, and expansion of a companies employees accumulated knowledge is no easy task, a functioning knowledge management becomes important. A well prepared and cared knowledge management tool can not only compensate for staff leaving the company for e.g. parental leave or retirement [3], but provide the essential support for the company's success in the era of digital technology.

The usage of social networking sites (SNS) for business purposes seems to be a promising approach for enhanced connectivity and communication among employees independent from space, time and position [4–6]. Since social media services like Facebook, Twitter and other SNS are part of our daily private lives [7], their implementation as a business support tool spread with amazing

P. Zaphiris and A. Ioannou (Eds.): LCT 2016, LNCS 9753, pp. 663–674, 2016.
DOI: 10.1007/978-3-319-39483-1_60

rapidity [8]. Day-to-day tasks, which previously used to be solved by unsystematic mailing lists and shared servers, are now shifted into social media related technologies. This is particularly important in cases of short-term and project related employment, or for steadily growing companies, which continuously have to integrate new, sometimes inexperienced staff. But even if a company manages to implement a business community, it sometimes generates low user rates and fails to succeed.

But studies concerning usage motives for SNS have been conducted on a merely hypothetical level, which should also be supported by studies in real applications. The approaches do not include local, hands-on investigations, so that answers about prospective usage still remain unclear. Therefore, we need to investigate employee motivation in success stories of already existing companies with a functioning SNS, so that everyone's personal needs and motivation are met.

2   Related Work

In order to identify where to start we must determine which factors to investigate first. Research from the field of knowledge management has investigated success of knowledge management systems but implementing these as a social networking site brings new challenges. Here individual motivation seems to play a major role in usage, as the network benefits when all users participate. Therefore one must reach the largest number of users possible. In order to customize a system that it meets all user emotive and motivational requirements, diversity of employees must be regarded.

2.1   Social Networks for Knowledge Management

Leonardi et al. [9] were among the first to systematically investigate the advantages of social network systems for knowledge management. They describe SNS as the "leaky pipe", "echo chamber", and "social lubricant". Enterprise social networks allow information to passively leak to a broad set of employees and provide a space to strengthen existing communities of interest. At the same time they provide insights into what others are doing. On the other hand these properties come with problems, such as information leak to outsiders, groupthink of isolated groups, and the illusion of social connection. Still both these advantages and disadvantages are based on the assumption of actual implementation and acceptance.

A study conducted in 2008 reveals that there are differences between use and user motivations in enterprise versus private SNS usage [5]. Even though the usage of social networks in business is becoming standardized, ubiquitous, mobile and less costly [10], the challenge of meeting individual needs remains. Otherwise users might reject yet another platform [11]. From the plethora of possible criterias that influence acceptance and rejection, one must first determine the criteria by which a work-based portal should be evaluated [12,13].

2.2 User Diversity and Usage Motivation

Over time many studies about success and motivational factors concerning SNS were conducted. Research has indicated that users would use such a system, if it addresses their need for information, self-portrayal, feedback and social interaction [14].

Findings by Lin and Lu [15] reveal the importance of enjoyment as the most influential factor for continued usage. Right after the fun during usage comes the number of peers, followed by usefulness. In addition, the authors found notable differences concerning motivational factors due to gender. Others state that general diversity factors like gender and age are not of great or even any importance when regarding motives for business community usage [6,14].

Schaar et al. [14] found out that there are correlations of usage motives with technology related diversity factors like social media usage frequency. They claim the need for information and autonomy as the most important motives. But diversity not only influences why a system is used, they also influence how it is used. There are crucial differences in what different users are willing to share on social networking site, depending also on its usage context [16]. Still, the findings from existing literature are not unanimous but rather depend on the specific user group, so that the specifics of user diversity should be investigated further.

2.3 Research Question

Often research has investigated usage of social networking sites at work as a proposal for future implementation. But users projections of their own desires and future behavior may differ from reality. Often real-life implementation leads to different conclusions about why users actually use a system and why they reject such a system.

For this reason we wanted to investigate what really drives users to use a social networking site, in contrast to a prospective study [6]. We wanted to conduct a study at a relatively young company that uses a SNS at work to streamline all communication and knowledge management.

Our investigation took place in international, online-operating clothing retailer in Germany founded in 2008. The company with about 110 employees is constantly growing and they implemented *yammer*[1], a social network solution offered by Microsoft, as a central institution for any internal communication and exchange purposes.

Here, we investigate the usage motives reported by users and determine which user factors influence motivation in this real-life scenario. For this purpose we use factors established in earlier research and examine how they interact with four usage motives (see Fig. 1).

---

[1] https://products.office.com/de-de/yammer/yammer-features.

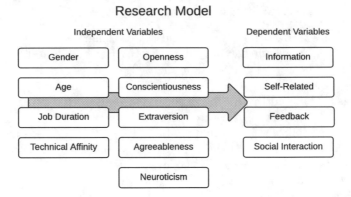

Fig. 1. Our case study investigating explanations for differences in usage motivation.

3   Method

In order to understand how user diversity and personality influence usage motivation, we conducted a study at a company that uses a social networking site
at work. The questionnaire was conducted online, using survey monkey and was
sent to all, approx. 110 employees by email. For all participants we assessed their
age, gender and how long they have been working at this company (job duration). We measured the usage motivation and technical affinity with 21 items
from previous research. As personality measures, we use the BFI-10 inventory
to measure big five personality attributes [17]. We used six-point Likert scales
and normalized to this scale range for all other cases. We also measured which
features of social networks were used how often depending on the usage context
(work or private). This usage frequency was measured on a logarithmic scale
(i.e. daily, 2–3× per week, every week, 2–3× per month, every month, rarer).

3.1   Statistical Procedure

The survey contained items developed from previous research, namely usage
motives (see Table 1) and technical affinity (see Table 2). For these we also provide a short summary on their factorial structure and internal reliability (i.e.
Cronbach's α, see Table 3) from our data-set. We used principal component-
analysis with vari-max rotation to identify the factorial structure, but report
only factorial load of individual items.

We use $\alpha = .05$ as the level of significance and $\alpha = .01$ as the threshold for
highly significant findings. We do not assess power for our statistical tests, so we
can not conclude from non-significant findings that no differences exist. Since we
assume that our measurements are normally distributed, we used student's t-
tests to assess differences of means between groups. In cases were this assumption
might have been violated, non-parametric tests were conducted. Since parametric

Table 1. Dependent variables: Item texts and scales. Loading refers to the factor-loading of the principal component analysis after varimax rotation with Kaiser-Normalization.

I use the software because,...	Scale	Loading
I can access information more easily	Information	.825
I can access information that is relevant for me	Information	.817
I will get informed about activities in my department	Information	.775
I can present my ideas	Information	.697
I can show my successes	Self-Related	.610
I can show what my skills and competencies are	Self-Related	.726
I can work more autonomously	Self-Related	.721
I can work independent of place and time	Self-Related	.691
I can plan my work on my own	Self-Related	.675
I get feedback from my colleagues on my work	Feedback	.900
I get feedback on my work	Feedback	.881
I get feedback on the results of my work	Feedback	.864
...my work is valued in the system	Social Interaction	.726
I can exchange with my colleagues regularly	Social Interaction	.714
...my colleagues are reachable immediately	Social Interaction	.710
I can stay in touch with colleagues I don't see often	Social Interaction	.654

tests are quite robust against the violation of the assumptions, non of these tests revealed differing results. Thus we only report results from parametric tests. As effect size we report Cohen's d.

We use multiple linear regression analysis to identify the strength of multiple factors on outcome variables. The step-wise method was applied to identify all possible predictors for all our models. Gender is dummy-coded (female $= 1$) to allow it as a predictor in our models. For all predictors, variance inflation factors are not reported, as they never exceed a level of 1.5. We report the full regression table, including standardized slopes (β) to identify the size of effect for each predictor.

Table 2. Independent variables: Item texts and scales. Loading refers to the factor-loading of the principal component analysis after varimax rotation with Kaiser-Normalization.

I agree with the following statement:	Scale	Loading
I can understand technical processes easily	Technical Affinity	.931
I have no troubles in using technical devices	Technical Affinity	.922
I understand physical and technical cause-effect relationships	Technical Affinity	.839
I can get excited about technology	Technical Affinity	.823

4   Results

In the following section we present the results from our online study. We first describe our sample to provide an overview of the employees in our company. We then look into variables that influence the usage motivation and try to determine the strength of influence by using multiple linear regression analysis. This allows us to compare the relative influence of each predictor on our outcome variables.

4.1   Description of the Sample

A total of 50 participants completed the online questionnaire, 36 of which were women and 14 men. This matches the relation of men and women employed at this company. The age of participants ranges from 19 to 61 years with a mean age of 28.5 years ($SD = 8.06$). The employees have been working on average for 1.5 years at the company ($SD = 1.13$, range 0–6 years).

Our sample shows a relatively high *technical affinity* (see Table 3), which is expected for an Internet company. Yet, there is a difference in *technical affinity* between both genders ($t(36) = 2.638$, $p = .012$, $d = 1.04$). Men show a higher score ($M = 5.0$, $SD = 0.79$) than women ($M = 4.04$, $SD = 1.06$).

The participants are moderately *extraverted* ($M = 4.04$, $SD = 0.77$) and show a high level of *conscientiousness* ($M = 4.72$, $SD = 0.81$). The latter could be slightly biased towards the top-end of the scale, as employees might over-report their level of dedication for work in this measure. *Openness* also scores moderately high ($M = 4.46$, $SD = 1.05$), similar as *agreeableness* ($M = 3.97$, $SD = 0.73$). The employees are open to new experiences and team-capable. *Neuroticism* scores slightly below the scale mean (i.e. 3.5) with a mean of $M = 3.23$ ($SD = 0.87$). We find that women ($M = 3.44$, $SD = 0.88$) show a higher score on this scale ($t(36) = -2.463$, $p = .019$, $d = 1.51$) than men ($M = 2.73$, $SD = 0.60$) as found in multiple other studies. Sadly, not all participants completed the personality questionnaire (n = 37).

4.2   Usage Motivation

All usage motives scored moderately high, with the exception of the need for information, which scored very high (see Table 3). Interestingly we found differences in usage motivation, when looking at gender. Overall, women reported high scores on all four scales (see Fig. 2). But, these differences are not significant in all cases.

The need for information is reported more strongly by women ($t(39) = -2.36$, $p = .023$, $d = 2.36$) than by men, indicating that women use the yammer system in order to find *information*. Needs that are *related to oneself*, such as organizing work autonomously and presenting ones successes show no difference between genders ($t(39) = -1.59$, $p = .120$, n.s.). A similar finding can be found for the need for *feedback* ($t(39) = -1.418$, $p = .164$, n.s.). Both genders have a similar need for *feedback* as a motivation to use a SNS. Still, there is another gender difference in the need for *social interaction* ($t(39) = -2.49$, $p = .017$, $d = 2.5$). Women also use the SNS out of a higher need for *social interaction* within the company.

Table 3. Description of the sample with internal scale validity and sample means with standard deviation.

Scale	Cronbach's α	M	SD
Information	.870	5.07	0.84
Self-Related	.891	4.02	1.05
Feedback	.969	3.92	1.12
Social Interaction	.827	3.91	0.95
Technical Affinity	.920	4.32	1.07

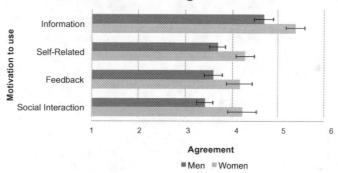

Fig. 2. Usage motivations show differences between genders. Error-bars denote the standard error.

4.3   Linear Regression Analysis

In order to determine whether these differences are actual gender differences and not effects of other confounding factors we conducted a linear regression analysis with all our independent variables. First, we look at the need for *information*. The multiple linear regression outputs a model with three predictors ($F(1, 33) = 4.201$, $adj.r^2 = .321$, $p = .048$). This model can explain 32 % more variance than using the scale-mean alone. The strongest predictor is still gender ($\beta = .383$), but agreeableness ($\beta = .348$) and age ($\beta = .289$) show similarly strong influences on the motive *information* (see Table 4). This means that women show a strong need for information that increases with age and with a team-focused personality. Younger men report to use the SNS less out of the need for information.

Self-Related motivation to use can be predicted with a model that has two predictors ($F(1, 34) = 4.881$, $adj.r^2 = .187$, $p = .034$). This model explains 18.7 %

Table 4. Linear regression tables for three models used to predict usage motivation.

Model	Predictor	B	SE B	β	p
Information	(const)	1.080	0.895	-	.236
	Agreeableness	0.421	0.169	.348	.018
	Gender	0.745	0.273	.383	.010
	Age	0.035	0.017	.289	.048
Self-Related	(const)	5.991	0.741	-	.000
	Job Duration	−0.354	0.139	−.385	.016
	Technical Affinity	−0.341	0.155	−.334	.034
Social Interaction	(const)	2.380	0.607	-	.000
	Gender	0.870	0.340	.397	.015

more than the scale mean. Job duration and technical affinity have similar negative influence on the *self-related* motivation (see Table 4). This means that employees that have been longer with the company and/or show a higher affinity use the SNS less in order to portray themselves or to become more autonomous at work.

A true gender effect can be seen at the motive *social interaction*. Here a model with only one predictor was significant ($F(1, 35) = 6.548$, $adj.r^2 = .134$, $p = .015$). Indicating that the gender difference found by the t-test before has no confounding variables hidden underneath it (to our knowledge and measurement). Women do report that they use the SNS at work to socialize with coworkers more then men.

Interestingly, no model could be found for *feedback* that had significantly improved the explained variance in the ANOVA of the linear regression procedure. Thus women and men use the SNS to get *feedback* with the same intensity. The need for feedback is not strong but universal in our sample.

4.4   Results on Usage Features

Beyond understanding which user diversity factors influence *why* users access a SNS, we want to understand *how* users use the system and how their usage differs from using a private social networking site like facebook. For this purpose we asked users how often they used certain features of a social networking site in two contexts (privately and at work). Features that are more typical for work related scenarios are functions such as *sharing documents* as well as *creating and using polls*. On the other hand *posting music* or *posting photos* are features that are more suitable for a private context.

When we focus on the usage frequency of different features in our sample, we see that *following news, chatting, sending messages* and *liking content* are the most frequently used features in both private and work settings (see Table 3). Most people in our sample do not post music or photos often, neither at work nor privately. These two typical private features get even less attention than the typical work-related feature *sharing documents* (see Table 3). This indicates that sharing information at work is actually used more than sharing photos in a private setting. The SNS site is actively used for knowledge management and organizational learning (Fig. 3).

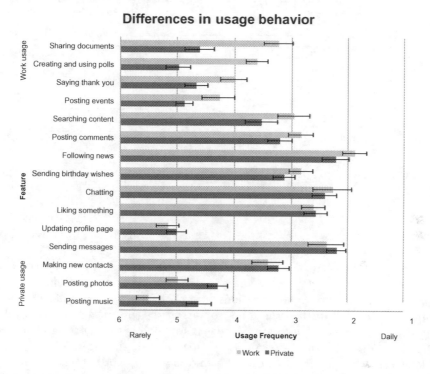

Fig. 3. Usage frequency ordered by the strength of difference between contexts. The diagram starts with typical work-related features and ends with typical private features. Features in the middle are used in both contexts and also get the highest usage. Error-bars denote the standard error. Usage Frequency is a logarithmic scale.

5   Discussion

In this article we investigated the effect of user diversity on the motivation to use a social networking site at work. The study was conducted at a company that successfully manages all knowledge exchange based on a Yammer system and included fifty participants. These participants were asked to report on why they use the system and which features they use.

We found that gender, age, agreeableness, and technical affinity influence specific motives to use the system (see Fig. 4). Women use the system because of a greater need for *social interaction* and *information*. The need for information will also become an increasing reason to use the system, when an employee becomes

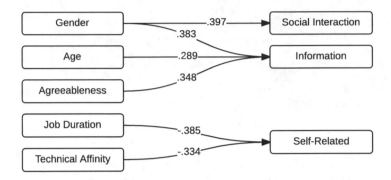

Fig. 4. Outcome of the multiple linear regression analyses. Numbers denote standard-ized slopes (β).

older and is more agreeable. Employees that are team-focused (or agreeable) might want to know how well the team is doing and how far they have progressed. Older users might need more information from the network, as they could be less experienced in using social media. Another explanation could be that older employees are often in higher positions and thus require more information to complete their job. On the other hand being on the job for a longer period of time or having a high *affinity to technology* is related with reporting to use the system out of reasons that are less *self-related* (e.g. self-portrayal). People who are longer on the job might already be known at company or just perceive a lower need to portray themselves. Employees with high technical affinity could experience some of the *self-related* items differently. That is, they already feel independent through use of technology. It is interesting to point out, that all users report to use the system for feedback similarly. Either feedback is a universal need satisfied equally across diversity factors in our sample or any explanatory variable has not been assessed.

5.1 Implications for Businesses

Depending on the structure of diversity factors in a company, one must make careful decisions when planning a social networking site for work. The features and structure of the system must address the needs of the users otherwise it will get rejected. From our results we see that features for social interaction, even if not-directly business related form a major component in usage motivation; even more so for women. A social networking site should therefore allow communication and self-portrayal as well as provide information needed by employees.

5.2   Limitations and Caveats

We must be careful when extending the results from this study. All participants come from a single company, which happens to be a very young company. Start-ups often have a vibe that stems from selecting personnel often highly alike. This sample is highly social-media affine and atypical. Diversity in this company is present but might drastically underestimate the diversity found in older companies. Specific and customized analyses must be performed when trying to implement a similar solution to ensure acceptance of such systems.

References

1. Buck, H., Kistler, E., Mendius, H.G.: Demographic change in the world of work: opportunities for an innovative approach to work - a German point of view. Fraunhofer-Gesellschaft zur Förderung der angewandten Forschung eV (2002)
2. Gourova, E., Toteva, K.: Enhancing knowledge creation and innovation in SMEs. In: 2012 Mediterranean Conference on Embedded Computing (MECO), pp. 292–297. IEEE (2012)
3. DeLong, D.W.: Lost Knowledge: Confronting the Threat of an Aging Workforce. Oxford University Press, Oxford (2004)
4. Schuh, G., Stich, V., Behrendt, S., Bender, J., Calero Valdez, A.: Zukunft gestalten: Soziale Technologien in Organisationen in Zeiten des demografischen Wandels: Wissen - Innovation - Demografie (2015)
5. DiMicco, J., Millen, D.R., Geyer, W., Dugan, C., Brownholtz, B., Muller, M.: Motivations for social networking at work. In: Proceedings of the 2008 ACM Conference on Computer Supported Cooperative Work, pp. 711–720. ACM (2008)
6. Schaar, A.K., Calero Valdez, A., Ziefle, M., Eraßme, D., Löcker, A.-K., Jakobs, E.-M.: Reasons for using social networks professionally. In: Meiselwitz, G. (ed.) SCSM 2014. LNCS, vol. 8531, pp. 385–396. Springer, Heidelberg (2014)
7. Stocker, A., Müller, J.: Exploring factual and perceived use and benefits of a web 2.0-based knowledge management application: the Siemens case references+. In: Proceedings of the 13th International Conference on Knowledge Management and Knowledge Technologies, p. 18. ACM (2013)
8. Koch, M., Richter, A.: Enterprise 2.0: Planung, Einführung und erfolgreicher Einsatz von Social Software in Unternehmen. Oldenbourg Verlag (2009)
9. Leonardi, P.M., Huysman, M., Steinfield, C.: Enterprise social media: definition, history, and prospects for the study of social technologies in organizations. J. Comput. Mediated Commun. 19(1), 1–19 (2013)
10. Von Krogh, G.: How does social software change knowledge management? Toward a strategic research agenda. J. Strateg. Inf. Syst. 21(2), 154–164 (2012)
11. Löcker, A.K., Eraßme, D., Jakobs, E.M., Schaar, A.K., Calero Valdez, A., Ziefle, M.: Yet another platform? Motivational factors for using online communities in business contexts. In: Advances in the Ergonomics in Manufacturing: Managing the Enterprise of the Future, vol. 13, p. 152 (2014)
12. Calero Valdez, A., Schaar, A.K., Ziefle, M.: State of the (net)work address developing criteria for applying social networking to the work environment. Work 41(Supplement 1), 3459–3467 (2012)

13. Calero Valdez, A., Schaar, A.K., Bender, J., Aghassi, S., Schuh, G., Ziefle, M.: Social media applications for knowledge exchange in organizations. In: Razmerita, L., Phillips-Wren, G., Jain, L.C. (eds.) Innovations in Knowledge Management, pp. 147–176. Springer, Heidelberg (2016)
14. Schaar, A.K., Calero Valdez, A., Ziefle, M.: User-centered design of business communities. The influence of diversity factors on motives to use communities in professional settings. Procedia Manufact. **3**, 645–652 (2015)
15. Lin, K.Y., Lu, H.P.: Why people use social networking sites: an empirical study integrating network externalities and motivation theory. Comput. Hum. Behav. **27**(3), 1152–1161 (2011)
16. Schaar, A.K., Calero Valdez, A., Ziefle, M.: The impact of user diversity on the willingness to disclose personal information in social network services. In: Holzinger, A., Ziefle, M., Hitz, M., Debevc, M. (eds.) SouthCHI 2013. LNCS, vol. 7946, pp. 174–193. Springer, Heidelberg (2013)
17. Rammstedt, B., John, O.P.: Measuring personality in one minute or less: a 10-item short version of the big five inventory in English and German. J. Res. Pers. **41**(1), 203–212 (2007)

Enhanced Affective Factors Management for HEI Students Dropout Prevention

Emmanuelle Gutiérrez y Restrepo[1,2], Fernando Ferreira[3],
Jesús G. Boticario[1], Elsa Marcelino-Jesus[3], Joao Sarraipa[3(✉)],
and Ricardo Jardim-Goncalves[3]

[1] aDeNu Research Group, Artificial Intelligence Department,
Computer Science School, UNED, C/Juan del Rosal, 16, 28040 Madrid, Spain
{egutierrez, jgb}@dia.uned.es, emmanuelle@sidar.org
[2] SIDAR Foundation, Madrid, Spain
[3] CTS, UNINOVA, DEE, Faculdade de Ciências e Tecnologia,
Universidade NOVA de Lisboa, 2829-516 Caparica, Portugal
{flf, ej, jfss, rg}@uninova.pt,
http://www.sidar.org

Abstract. Among the problems affecting Higher Education Institutions (HEI) in Latin America and the Caribbean there is the dropout, which relates to a more general issue consisting in dealing with the diversity of students. Here provided solutions are to detect and deal with student's particular capacities and needs. To cope with this situation the ACACIA project has defined a framework that develops both CADEP centers and technological infrastructure. The former consists of an organizational unit focus on Empowering, Innovating, Educating, Supporting, Monitoring and leveraging institutions in dealing with such diversity. The latter is based on building the required infrastructure to tackle those issues and covering both face-to-face and eLearning educational settings. This comprises non-intrusive affect detection methods along with ambient intelligent solutions, which provide context-aware affective feedback to each student. Preliminary experimentation results open interesting avenues to be further progressed thus taking advantage of current developments on affect computing technologies.

Keywords: Emerging technologies for collaboration and learning · Recommender systems for technology-enhanced learning

1 Introduction

UNESCO in its Post-2015 Education Agenda presents evidence of problems affecting Higher Education Institutions (HEI) in Latin America and the Caribbean. This has been useful to identify critical situations. Among those situations there is the dropout, which is caused mainly by affective and academic factors, as well as cultural, economic or social exclusion or disability.

Nicaragua, Colombia, Brazil, Peru and Chile share key priorities in their development programs for education, which to be achieved would require to open regional mobility for the students in higher education institutions based on the optimization of

© Springer International Publishing Switzerland 2016
P. Zaphiris and A. Ioannou (Eds.): LCT 2016, LNCS 9753, pp. 675–684, 2016.
DOI: 10.1007/978-3-319-39483-1_61

resources and international cooperation processes. These aspects can be found in European Union priorities for the region (European Commission 2014).

In order to tackle the student retention problem, the importance of evaluating students' motivation and attention to the class is of major importance. This entails dealing with class evaluation and further planning. Aiming at performing such evaluation, it is possible to obtain information by distributing surveys or by performing measurements, which may involve psycho-physiological information sources. The first case allows subjective assessment and depends on the will of participants to contribute. When the approach is to use measurements, this requires the proper consent of participants and their parents (when dealing with underage students). Here, although the approach should be as minimally invasive as possible, even non-invasive at all, there is the problem of collecting and dealing with sensitive data such as psychological and physiological information. This information is expected to provide more reliable means of getting assessments. Although the prospect of invasive measurements can be seen reluctantly by students, or any other people, who tend to resist such approach. Here there is the problem of invading each one's privacy as with such measurements it is possible to surpass a person's will by measuring their physiological information and not depending on his/her voluntary deployment of information.

This paper addresses how the ACACIA project is dealing with the student retention problem in terms of setting up an organizational unit, so-called CADEP centers, which deals with the educational and managerial issues involved, and developing the required technological infrastructure, which needs to be established in order to detect and manage the affective issues involved in such problem. To present such view, this paper is organized as follows. First the problem of the student's retention and the required infrastructure for detecting affective related issues are described in terms of related literature. Then the ACACIA approach to deal with those issues is presented covering both, the ACACIA-CADEP strategy and the technological infrastructure that has been developed to detect and manage the affect state of students, which affects their retention. The paper concludes with a summary of main conclusions and future work.

2   Student Retention and Affective Related Issues

The problem of student retention is well known and widely studied, as can be seen in (Summerskill 1962), (Astin 1977, 1993), (Bean 1980, 1983), (Bean and Metzner 1985) and (Spady 1970) among others. Studies by the Centre for the Study of College Student Retention indicate that despite the efforts of universities retention policies have not succeeded in increasing retention rates (Seidman 2015).

There is evidence for problems affecting higher education in Latin America and the Caribbean (LAC) which relates to how these countries are dealing with the concept of education for all (UNESCO 2014), were following critical situations arise:

- Dropout derived from emotional factors, academic, economic or social cultural marginalization, or disability;
- Lack of educational resources among faculty staff to meet the requirements affecting vulnerable students;

- Gaps in communication and cooperation among teachers, researchers, administrators and managers, which hampers collective action that is needed to address cross-section issues related to access and successful stay in college.

Studies by the Center for Student Retention -CSCSR- indicate that despite the efforts of universities in retention policies there has not been any significant increase in retention rates. The main strategies proposed by the CSCSR have to do with the setting up of the so-called Retention Committee in institutions, which is focused on identifying both students at risk of dropping out and problems within the classroom such as a little attention, getting poor grades and little class participation, among others. Nearly one in two students drops out of high school before graduating (Busso et al. 2013) and besides the quality of the educational system this can also be affected by low self-esteem, self-motivation, study habits, persistence and frustration tolerance, expectations and student's own personal values, which makes it even more difficult for institutions to adapt their system to address these issues.

Teachers, as any other human being, are able to sense and detect affect states from their students, which relate to their attention and restlessness states, their "boredness" or their motivation towards the class. The problem arises when students are learning remotely, as in eLearning, or even in live classes while students are interacting with computational devices. In this sense, the identification of students' affect features is required. To this with this issue it is well-known that humans display their emotions through different channels, including facial expressions, body movements and physiological reactions, which have been considered as elements of the non-verbal communication forms (Pantic and Rothkrantz 2000). Thereof the idea is to collect these human features and investigate to what extent they confirm a particular affective state. To deal with this issue affective computing is currently an active research field with significant efforts and advances linked to the emergent devices and gadgets.

There have been well-known studies in affective computing and the affective relation of humans with computers, which can provide insights on possible solutions for the aforementioned problems (Picard 1997). The affective assessment, which has to deal with both eLearning and face-to-face student, could be based on using different computational equipment and approaches. Since most laptops have cameras, can be used locally or remotely to give emotional information to professors and trainers using text assessment (Shivhare and Khethawat 2012) or reading facial expressions (Adolphs 2002). The analysis of such emotional clues, generated by real-time physiological signal readings from aforementioned devices, can provide information (e.g. analytics) on students' attention and motivation. The teacher will then be able to adapt the teaching process and later report the successful methods to the community.

There is vast research including reviews on the state of the art in emotions detection beyond the aforementioned examples. For instance, a review of available works on emotions detection with facial gestures was published in (Saneiro et al. 2014). As for using more intrusive psycho-physiological sensors, in (Villarejo et al. 2013) authors introduced a commercial pulsimeter and alternatively skin conductance to detect stress, where the skin conductance presented wider differences in the relaxed and stressed stages. Here it is noticeable that most successful approaches have applied several information sources. In particular most of them comprise verbal, non-verbal and physiological measures. Heart rate is used in (Van den Broek 2013), which is combined with speech along with the Self-Assessment Manikin scale - SAM (i.e., a non-verbal pictorial assessment technique that directly measures several emotional dimensions) (Bradley and Lang 1994). There is work that has used Blood Volume Pulse, Galvanic Skin Response, Pupil Diameter and Skin Temperature to detect stress (Zhai and Barreto 2006).

There are as well many examples on the progress of affect computing in educational settings. For instance, a framework has been proposed to recognize learner's emotions using electroencephalography, skin conductance and blood volume pressure (Jraidi et al. 2014). In (Handri et al. 2010) authors made use of the e-learning material provided to learners in relation to their galvanic skin response. Electrodermal activity was used to detect the 12 proposed emotions in (D'Mello 2014). There are also instances on using non-verbal communication, such as body movements and facial expressions, which were used for evaluating learners' states (Afzal and Robinson 2007).

Some of this paper authors are also conducting a study related to the attention evaluation of students attending e-learning courses, where such analysis is conducted using physiological measurements as ECG. This work intends to increase the efficiency of students' attention in attending courses in this case related to the aquaculture business processes of the project AquaSmart. The AQUASMART project mission is driven by the business need of the European aquaculture companies, when companies have business objectives that cannot be achieved due to lack of instruments that would enable them to manage and access global knowledge and big data, in a multi-lingual, multi-sector and cross-border setting. Therefore, although this is a completely different domain still the main objective of the study reported in this paper is focused on supporting students' motivation while achieving their learning objectives, which in this case comes from an effective knowledge transfer from a specific industry research project.

3   The ACACIA Approach

The ACACIA project defines a system to address the above-mentioned issues, thus covering organizational and technological requirements involved in dealing with the student retention. The latter is addressed by building the required technological infrastructure.

3.1   The Acacia-CADEP Strategy

From the organizational viewpoint, the approach consists in supporting centers for education and professional development, which are called CADEP. It integrates modules named as: Empower ("Empodera"), Innovate ("Innova"), Educate ("Cultiva"), Support ("Apoya") and Convenes ("Convoca"), that all together create the appropriate framework for (1) monitoring students at risk; (2) providing training and supporting equally both the academic staff and technical and administrative staff of the institution;

and (3) exploring, via its laboratory system, new strategies for university teaching and innovative use of ICT in teaching practices, encouraging entrepreneurship among students and teachers. This system articulates the educational community to deal with each student's capacities and needs.

The model of CADEP is the result of analyzing multiple theoretical approaches that address the problems of student retention. Thus, it is proposed the creation of a committee in institutions for the identification and analysis of students at risk of dropping out. These committees intends to contribute for the demanding target of keeping and encouraging student's interests in an active participation in class, and empowering teachers with the skills and tools that will allow the adoption of new teaching models. This should cope in the best way with their students' differences and needs.

Innovation is an essential part of each module within the Acacia CADEP, thereof:

- Innovation in dealing with social affection issues at the university, through information systems capable of generating educational recommendations that meet the student's emotional states, which are to be detected and tracked in order to improve students' academic level and prevent dropout (Apoya).
- Technological innovation in university teaching, by using knowledge management systems and personalized solutions based on students' interaction tracking and machine learning analysis of collected data, which are to be provided with tool that detects emotions, using among others the paradigm of the Internet of Things (IoT) and the creation and reuse of applications and devices, encouraging university entrepreneurship (Innova and Apoya)
- Innovation in teaching in university environments through: the development of applications to support teaching and learning differentiated according to cognitive, affective and cultural conditions of students who achieve lower levels. Innovation in every respect to deal with individual needs and preferences, thus considering the use of 3D printers, which serve as educational support material for blind students. Ultimately the approach consists in adding new references to the current university curricula to make them more flexible and suitable to care for students with a wide variety of personal and social needs, which also implies to provide accessible learning environments for populations with differences in access to knowledge (Cultiva and Empodera).
- Innovation in the university academic management through a knowledge management system for partnership, which detects and transfers innovations related to affective, technological and didactic issues throughout the CADEP network system (Convoca).

The specific objectives of each of the modules are as follows:

Empodera: Providing training in areas of eLearning standards, accessibility and usability; Maintaining the Kit & Thesaurus ALTER-NATIVA knowledge base; as well as dealing with the creation of adaptations that cannot be performed directly by teachers, e.g. sign language interpretation.

Innova: Innovating in terms of new infrastructure, applications and programs which are developed and used to meet special educational needs and diversity, e.g. using ambient-intelligence solutions and 3D printers.

Cultiva: Training faculty through innovative programs with the support of the ALTER-NATIVA's curricular elements and VLO, which are to promote educational development of vulnerable populations from the perspective of a Community of Welfare.

Apoya: Detecting, tracking and supporting emotions of students with disabilities and critical family situations through both regular and advanced techniques (e.g. automatic emotion detection systems) to improve academic performance and avoid abandonment. And, train administrative and teaching staff, techniques and strategies for dealing with students at risk.

Convoca: Organizing and controlling the activities in the establishment of the different centers (e.g. space, physical resources and institutional rules). Addressing the development and continuous evaluation of capacity building issues though the various CADEP.

3.2   Technological Infrastructure Developed for Managing Affect

From the technological infrastructure standpoint, aforementioned developments on affect computing are expected to leverage the possibilities of taking care of students' retention. Here, the aDeNu Research Group at UNED has designed, implemented and evaluated the Ambient Intelligence Context-aware Affective Recommender Platform (AICARP) infrastructure to explore the potential of context-aware affective feedback beyond computer-based recommendation approaches taking advantage of the possibilities of ambient intelligence (Santos et al. 2015). The corresponding personalized support is provided without interrupting the learning activity by delivering the recommended action to the learner at the same time she is carrying out the learning activity (e.g. while the learner is talking, the system can tell her to slow down by switching on a light or playing a sound). This requires enriching the system with capabilities to detect changes in the learners' affective state (e.g. from physiological sensors), as well as to interact with the user through the preferred sensorial channel (e.g. sight, hearing, touch, smell). Different experiences are taking place within two related research projects, MAMIPEC and BIG-AFF, from where it is expected to progress on the results to date and thus provide valuable feedback to ACACIA (Fig. 1).

It is expected that monitoring students affective states, especially in what regards to their attention in classroom will become a reality in pilots for the South and Central American countries participating in ACACIA. That is an on-going process partially verified by the physiological trials performed in lab or in classrooms (Salmeron-Majadas et al. 2015), which also takes advantage of other developments such as evaluation frameworks (Marcelino-Jesus et al. 2015) or those ontologies that were successfully implemented in the project ALTERNATIVA.

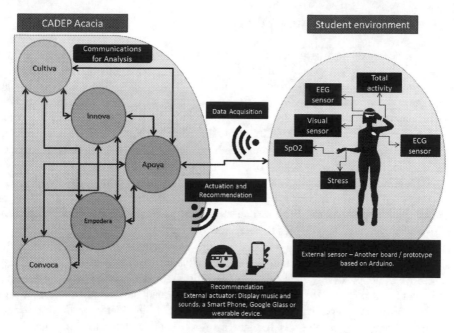

Fig. 1. AICARP platform

The approach proposed here covers both small-scaled (i.e., intra-subject) and detailed lab experiments limited in time to be carried out from the scientific viewpoint, which are expected to clarify the main issues involved, and on a larger-scale (i.e. inter-subject), try to use non-invasive measurements. As for the latter, the eye-tracker becomes one of the best options because it does not depend on wearing additional detector devices. It is also planned to use heart-rate variations and even galvanic skin response measurements, both of interest for the evaluation of emotional states and attention, which are minimally invasive, as they become part of the equipment of smart-watches and other consumer products. This work ultimately aims at providing lessons learned from the evaluation, which is expected to determine which type of detectors, contents, media and multimedia should be used in a particular class and context.

Another expected outcome of performing such studies is an increase of teachers' awareness of the actual involvement of students in class and consequently supporting their responsibility in actively assessing, adapting and developing class activities towards student's success. This way it is expected a better identification of students at risk. Thus problematic individuals can be spotted early and intervention can be readily prepared in order to improve the success rate of such rehabilitation actions.

In general, it is expected that such approach lead to a successful upgrade in the classroom towards students' commitment and success. The proposed methodology aims at making a difference to traditional classroom behavior where problems used to be identified in a too late stage or not identified at all until the student abandons school.

4   Conclusions and Future Work

The work described in this paper is a continuum from previous work developed by members of the consortium and from relevant scientific publications in the field. Thus it is consistently aiming at supporting students in their learning process and addressing specifically the problems associated with demotivation and withdrawal from studies. The proposed approach here is focused on managing affect related issues that impact students at risk of abandonment and aims at the empowerment of an attentive school community, continuously updating their methods and instruments towards its success. The objective is that the on-going work will prove its usefulness during the course of ACACIA project so that results can be made available for the community. Future work will be based on the achieved results and it is foreseen that the conjunction of self-assessment with physiological measurements will generate results that will improve the overall process. From those results, future work will aim at the selection of the best methods and eventually include new physiological measures that increase the quality and readiness of the evaluation process so that the proper measures can properly be deployed and positively help students towards success in studies and in personal fulfillment. Additionally, the work conducted will be also integrated in different projects and contexts. In particular, e-learning programs as in AquaSmart, which main objective is to develop solutions for increasing the student attention in courses and better integration of different types of materials available online. Within MAMIPEC and BIG-AFF the affect detection infrastructure will be evaluated in different scenarios ranging from laboratory to real world settings.

Acknowledgements. The authors acknowledge the European Commission for its support and partial funding and the partners of the research projects from ERASMUS+: Higher Education – International Capacity Building - ACACIA – Project reference number – 561754-EPP-1-2015-1-CO-EPKA2-CBHE-JP, (http://acacia.digital); and Horizon2020 - AquaSmart – Aquaculture Smart and Open Data Analytics as a Service, project number - 644715, (http://www.aquasmartdata.eu/). This work has also been partly supported by the Spanish Ministry of Economy and Competitiveness through projects MAMIPEC (TIN2011-29221-C03-01) and BIG-AFF (TIN2014-59641-C2-2-P.

References

Adolphs, R.: Recognizing emotion from facial expressions: psychological and neurological mechanisms. Behav. Cogn. Neurosc. Rev. **1**(1), 21–62 (2002)

Afzal, S., Robinson, P.: A study of affect in intelligent turoring. In: Supplementary Proceedings of the 13th International Conference of Artificial Intelligence in Education (AIED 2007), Marina Del Rey, CA, USA, 9 July 2007 (2007)

Astin, A.: What Matters Most in College: Four Critical Years. Jossey-Bass, San Francisco (1977)

Astin, A.: What Matters Most in College: Four Critical Years Revisited. Jossey-Bass, San Francisco (1993)

Bean, J.: Dropouts and turnover: the synthesis and test of a causal model off student attrition. Res. High. Educ. **12**, 155–187 (1980)

Bean, J.: The application of a model of turnover in work organizations to the student attrition process. Rev. High. Educ. **6**, 129–148 (1983)

Bean, J., Metzner, B.: Conceptual model of nontraditional undergraduate student attrition. Rev. Educ. Res. **55**, 485–540 (1985)

Bradley, M.M., Lang, P.J.: Measuring emotion: the self-assessment manikin and the semantic differential. J. Behav. Ther. Exp. Psychiatry **25**, 49–59 (1994)

Busso, M., Bassi, M., Muñoz, J.S.: Is the Glass Half Empty or Half Full? School Enrollment, Graduation, and Dropout Rates in Latin America, October 2013. IDB Working Paper No. IDB-WP-462. SSRN: http://ssrn.com/abstract=2367706, http://dx.doi.org/10.2139/ssrn.2367706

D'Mello, S.K.: Emotional rollercoasters: day differences in affect incidence during learning. In: The Twenty-Seventh International Flairs Conference (2014)

European Commission: Latin America - Regional Cooperation - funding - European Commission. European Commission (2014). https://ec.europa.eu/europeaid/regions/latin-america/latin-america-regional-programmes-eu-funding_en. Accessed Nov 2015

Handri, S., Yajima, K., Nomura, S., Ogawa, N., Kurosawa, Y., Fukumura, Y.: Evaluation of student's physiological response towards e-Learning courses material by using GSR sensor. In: 2010 IEEE/ACIS 9th International Conference on Computer and Information Science (ICIS), pp. 805–810 (2010)

Jraidi, I., Chaouachi, M., Frasson, C.: A hierarchical probabilistic framework for recognizing learners' interaction experience trends and emotions. Adv. Hum. Comput. Interact. **2014**, 16 (2014). Article ID 632630

Marcelino-Jesus, E.; Sarraipa, J.; Ferro-Beca, M.; Jardim-Goncalves, R.: A framework for technological research results assessment. IJCIM – INT. J. COMPUT. INTEG. M. 24 February 2016. doi:10.1080/0951192X.2016.1145806

Pantic, M., Rothkrantz, L.J.M.: Expert system for automatic analysis of facial expressions. Image Vis. Comput. **18**, 881–905 (2000)

Picard, R.: Affective Computing. The MIT Press, Cambridge (1997)

Saneiro, M., Santos, O.C., Salmeron-Majadas, S., Boticario, J.G.: Towards emotion detection in educational scenarios from facial expressions and body movements through multimodal approaches. Sci. World J. **2014**, e484873 (2014)

Salmeron-Majadas, S., Arevalillo-Herráez, M., Santos, O.C., Saneiro, M., Cabestrero, R., Quirós, P., Arnau, D., Boticario, J.G.: Filtering of spontaneous and low intensity emotions in educational contexts. In: Conati, C., Heffernan, N., Mitrovic, A., Verdejo, M. (eds.) AIED 2015. LNCS, vol. 9112, pp. 429–438. Springer, Heidelberg (2015)

Santos, O., Saneiro, M., Boticario, J., Rodríguez-Sánchez, M.: Toward interactive context-aware affective educational recommendations in computer-assisted language learning. New Rev. Hypermedia and Multimedia, 22(1–2), 27–57 (2016). 07 August 2015. doi:10.1080/13614568.2015.1058428

Seidman: Center for the Study of College Student Retention. http://www.cscsr.org/. Accessed Oct 2015.

Luís-Ferreira, F., Sarraipa, J., Jardim-Goncalves, R.: Framework for adaptive knowledge transmissionsupported by HCI and interoperability concepts. In: Stephanidis, C., Antona, M. (eds.) UAHCI 2014, vol. 8514, pp 370–377. Springer, Heidelberg (2014). doi: 10.1007/978-3-319-07440-5_34. ISBN: 978-3-319-07440-5

Spady, W.: Dropouts from higher education: an interdisciplinary review and synthesis. Interchange **1**(1), 64–85 (1970)

Summerskill, J.: Dropouts from College. In: En, N.S. (ed.) The American College, pp. 627–655. Wiley, New York (1962)

UNESCO: EFA Global Monitoring Report 201. The Education for All Global Monitoring Report - Teaching And Learning: Achieving quality for all, facilitated and supported by UNESCO (ED - 2014/GMR/GS/1). http://unesdoc.unesco.org/images/0022/002266/226662e.pdf. Accessed Jan 2016

Van den Broek, E.L.: Ubiquitous emotion-aware computing. Pers. Ubiquit. Comput. **17**, 53–67 (2013)

Villarejo, M., Zapirain, B., Zorrilla, A.: Algorithms based on CWT and classifiers to control cardiac alterations and stress using an ECG and a SCR. Sensors **13**, 6141–6170 (2013)

Zhai, J., Barreto, A.: Stress recognition using non-invasive technology. In: FLAIRS Conference, pp. 395–401 (2006)

Towards a Digital Teaching Platform in Brazil: Findings from UX Experiments

Andrew Koster[1], Renata Zilse[1(✉)], Tiago Primo[1], Állysson Oliveira[1],
Marcos Souza[2], Daniela Azevedo[2], Francimar Maciel[2], and Fernando Koch[1]

[1] SAMSUNG Research Institute Brazil, Campinas, Brazil
{andrew.k,renata.borges,tiago.t,allysson.o,fernando.koch}@samsung.com
[2] SAMSUNG SIDIA, Manaus, Brazil
{marcos.muniz,daniela.as,francimar.m}@samsung.com

Abstract. This work discusses the usability experiments conducted around a proof-of-concept implementation of a novel tablet-based Digital Teaching Platform (DTP). The platform is intended to address specific issues with tablet usage in a classroom setting, and address problems with technology adoption in education, particularly in Brazil. We evaluated the DTP in two separate studies, a Usability experiment in a laboratory setting, and an in-situ experiment in Brazilian classrooms, with the aim of identifying specific problems with the current solution, and identifying usage patterns that better engage students in the classroom. We found that our DTP leads, overall, to a very satisfactory experience. However, any such platform aimed at classroom usage should take special care to address note-taking, and tasks related to collaboration, sharing, and general social aspects of the classroom experience.

1 Introduction

Student engagement has long been recognized as integral to both performance and retention of learning [4]. Nevertheless, it is still an ongoing research and policy topic to understand the aspects that could lead to improve students engagement [2]. Digital Teaching Platforms (DTPs) in the classroom have been identified as a tool for engaging students, however only if suitable pedagogical methods and Learning Objects are adopted to meet the teachers pedagogical plan and classroom needs [7].

In this paper we evaluate the proof-of-concept implementation of a novel tablet-based DTP, designed from the ground up to support teachers in Brazilian classrooms. After in-loco interviews with specialists and students, classroom observations and review of the literature, we found two significant research opportunities: (1) the existent solutions rely on a stable broadband internet connection, which in Brazil is not always available; and (2) teachers indicated that they did not know how to use the existent platforms due to an over-abundance of features and lack of support. The principal requirements were thus an easy-to-use out-of-the-box platform that enables teachers to incorporate the use of tablets into their regular lesson plan and stimulates student engagement.

P. Zaphiris and A. Ioannou (Eds.): LCT 2016, LNCS 9753, pp. 685–694, 2016.
DOI: 10.1007/978-3-319-39483-1_62

We developed a proof-of-concept implementation of the DTP consisted of four principal components: (i) a light-weight content server, running on a Raspberry Pi, (ii) a wifi router, (iii) one tablet per person (students and teacher), and (iv) a SmartTV or interactive whiteboard and tested in two different ways: in a usability lab where we identify hurdles in how students navigate through the content, and in field trials where we evaluate the response from both students and teachers when using the system.

The DTP we developed can be categorized in the scope of Mobile Learning, as described by Pereira et al. [8]. They found that through the evolution of Learning Models, traditional learning techniques could be enhanced by Electronic Learning and Mobile Learning. Our principal difference from current works in this area regards the user-centric research in order to build our software solution.

The work of Samuel et al. [10] presents IGLOO, a mobile learning technology that intends to support educators and students in learning environments. IGLOO consists of an administrative interface and a mobile application to run of the educator's device. The administrative interface is used by the educators in order to create quizzes. The educators interface will receive those quizzes by SMS or Bluetooth. Their evaluation is based on achieved tasks rather than the student performance. The difference from our work is that we are proposing a solution that encompasses different aspects regarding educational activities; for example, the association of the educational contents with the program of the discipline.

Potts et al. [9] propose an m-learning application for administering quizzes that offers a multi touch interface compatible with Android and iOS devices. After the students answers tests, the results are sent to the educator by email. The presented work, developed a prototype that is flexible to provide such feedback during a class. In our point of view, this approach provides more dynamic classes and improves the communication between teachers and students.

We believe that this is the first work that collects best-practices and usability results for a digital teaching platform in the classroom. In the next section we describe the study in the usability lab, and in Sect. 3 describe further research in classrooms. We then conclude the article highlighting the principal findings from both experiments.

2 Usability Tests

2.1 Methodology

The usability lab study evaluated the DTP with 14 students (1 female and 13 male) with ages between 18 and 35 years old and enrolled in vocational education programs. The study was conducted with one student at a time, and each test took approximately 45 min to 1 h. The task analysis was based on the 5 quality attributes of usability proposed by Nielsen [5]: learnability, efficiency, memorability, errors and satisfaction. The test was designed to verify issues regarding the natural process, and teaching methodology, by emulating a classroom environment: each test was conducted with two mediators, one of whom acted as a teacher to enhance the immersion of the subject. The test

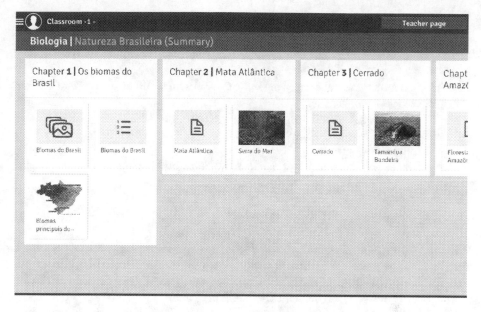

Fig. 1. The educational content in the DTP Player. Note that the UI is in English to enhance understanding, but we used a localized Portuguese version for the actual tests.

simulated a lesson on Brazilian biomes (see Fig. 1), a topic that has nothing to do with the students' studies, but was indicated as an interesting general topic. The other mediator acted as interviewer and thus played a more traditional role in usability studies.

Five activities were scripted, that are related to different types of content available in the platform (e.g. watching a video, studying a slideshow, and answering exercises). As this is performed in a usability lab, all movements, speeches, questions and errors in the experience of the student-subjects were recorded. Eye tracking was used to identify attention hotspots in heat maps and gaze plots. After completing all the tasks, each subject was invited to reflect on their general experience, and what went well or not. Each user answered questions regarding their experience in each activity on a Likert scale from 1 to 7.

The study was divided into three phases: introduction (self-exploration), completing the set of tasks, and an interview and debriefing.

Phase 1: The experimental process started with a short warm-up. We received the participants and asked them questions about their technology preferences and hobbies, trying to relax them and make them as comfortable as possible. They were invited to explore the system by themselves.

Phase 2: Two researchers conducted the experiment, one acting as a teacher and the other monitoring the eye tracker results. The users were invited to sit and be positioned adequately in front of the X2-30 eye tracker [11]. It was quickly explained what would be requested, and what the students would do through the Digital Teaching Platform. The evaluation was conducted following the sequence of tasks divided by the activities described below:

- video tasks: tasks related to interacting with the video player
- reading texts: tasks related to textual content
- slide navigation: tasks related to paging through a gallery of educational slides
- navigation: tasks related to navigation, in which the students had to find the teacher's page
- exercises: tasks related to answering exercise questions

Phase 3: After completing the tasks all the users were invited to watch their session, which was recorded. The goal was to enhance the results and comprehend why specific areas were the focus of attention. The study was concluded with an interview and questionnaire.

2.2   Results

Watch Video. Most users like to see the title and the description of the video and had no problem watching the video. An example of the focus from eye tracking can be seen in Fig. 2. However, the users did suggest a reorganization of the page: they expect the features "Like", "Share" and "Notes" below the video, as opposed to next to it; we noticed that YouTube[1] is the main reference for the arrangement of elements on the screen. Furthermore, some users expect functionality that is not currently offered, such as easy access to content that they "liked" for future access. Moreover, they would like to be able to take notes while watching the video (the video pauses when the users pull up a keyboard). Another feature that users would like is more cohesion between the different contents, such as direct hyperlinks from the video to texts, or slides, that give more details.

Reading Texts. All users consider texts to be very important for the application, despite large texts on the screen being unattractive. The digital text — together with the price and a lighter backpack — are mentioned as the most positive and practical points for tablet usage in a classroom, and they leave the users satisfied. The users like to have a zoom feature for reading. According to the users the figures in the text draw more attention while reading. Most users would like to have more options for note taking and highlighting, and mention a tool bar with options to make it possible to select, copy, paste, highlight and bold parts of the text. The users would like to have an option to consult a dictionary for the meaning the words they do not know. Most users would like to send the text to their personal email, or otherwise access the texts outside of the application.

Slide Navigation. Swiping between slides did not cause problems, but users indicated they would like further navigation options, such as a bar with thumbnails and previous/next buttons. Moreover, as with viewing videos, most users

---

[1] www.youtube.com.

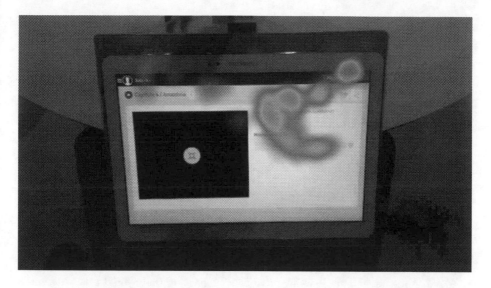

Fig. 2. Heatmap generated by the X2-30 eye tracker during a video task.

want it to be easier to take notes. There was also some confusion of the UI elements, where we noted that the icon for viewing the slides in a timed slide show draws more attention than the icon for viewing the slides in full screen.

Exercises. The users felt there was feedback missing when answering exercises: they were confused that there was no confirmation that their answer had been accepted, or that the quiz did not proceed automatically to the next question. They also missed buttons to navigate forward and backward through the questionnaire, in addition to the current option of clicking on any question to open it. Finally, the users would like the ability to take notes while doing the exercises (for instance, to write down the intermediate solutions in a math question). The users very much liked receiving feedback of their performance — an optional screen for the teacher displays the correct answers and a percentage of the students who gave each answer.

Navigation. The button to navigate straight to the teacher's page was identified by all, but not associated with that action: most students thought it accessed a special page for the teacher and ignored it. They navigated to the teacher's page by navigating back to the class overview page and finding the content the teacher had opened. They all identified it as an important functionality once told about its use.

Relevance Map. A relevance map of application was created according to the users expectations. We asked the users how relevant to a classroom content application they judged all activities they had seen, answered on a 7-point likert scale, with 1 being irrelevant, and 7 extremely relevant. The main areas and the "teacher's page" feature were considered for the analysis. In general, the content and functionality was seen as very relevant by the users. To validate the social features (Like, Share and Notes) a ranking of preferences was created. The users were asked about "what they do after accessing an interesting content". The ranking was created according to the users decisions and choices. These rankings can be seen in Fig. 3.

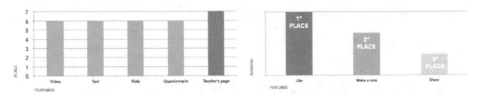

Fig. 3. The relevance of all the functionality tested to the educational process, according to the students; and the ranking of what social action they would take with interesting content.

3   Field Trials

In the field trials, we tested the platform with teachers and students of middle-school mathematics in three different school environments: two public schools in Manaus, AM, and an institute providing extracurricular school activities for students in Campinas, SP. The students were between 13 and 16 years old. In addition to observing the classes and capturing automatic interactions, we conducted on-the-spot satisfaction surveys asking the participants to fill out a questionnaire after the classes, using the User Engagement Scale [6], and conducted interviews with some of the students and the participating teachers.

The field trial focused on mathematics classes on the topic "functions", and the content was created by the respective teachers, using a slideshow, video, questionnaire and interactive content. The content was divided into two classes: introductory knowledge and enrichment on the topic. Using this content, the two class hours were used to evaluate two aspects of the DTP:

- to measure the satisfaction with the DTP on the first contact (first impression);
- and to evaluate specific usage issues that appeared in a classroom setting.

3.1   Methodology

We used an adaptation of the Experience Sampling Method (ESM) [3], a method originally developed to perceive people's emotional response to events, and since adapted to measure users' satisfaction, particularly in situated mobile scenarios [1]. While there are different ways of applying the method, we adopt a straightforward application for situations where both the evaluator and the subject are in the same physical location: the evaluator asks the subject to point out his or her current emotional state (with regards to satisfaction) on a printed card (Fig. 4), which gives a choice of five states ranging from very dissatisfied to very satisfied at the time of the app use.

Fig. 4. The five emotional states the users could indicate on a card for applying the ESM method.

In addition to asking students about their emotional state during the class, we asked all participants (including the teacher) to participate in a short self-reporting survey based on the User Engagement Scale (UES). The UES is a self-report measure that builds upon earlier work in the area of educational multimedia. Many applications of the method were found and analyzed by O'Brien and Cairns, who suggested that "the UES is a "good" measure that can assist researchers in capturing the users' perception of information interactions, and be used in mixed methods studies to help make sense of, for example, behavioral data" — O'Brien and Cairns [6]. The original survey they proposed has 31 questions, which is too long for the quick application of a survey after the class. We adapted the survey to focus on the dimensions that O'Brien and Cairns indicated were most stable, and reduced the survey further by not asking the questions in their negative form, resulting in six questions on the dimensions *aesthetics*, *usability* and *focused attention*, and we added a final question that conflates some of the other dimensions into what we call *perceived experience*, as a way to measure the user's engagement with the app. The questions can be found in Table 1. The questions were answered on a Likert scale from 1–5, with a similar emotional aid as in the ESM method.

Finally, we augmented the self-report methods with observation and interviews with some of the students and the teachers. A summary of the times and methods applied is provided in Fig. 5.

3.2   Results

The principal findings are that both the students and the teachers were very satisfied with the usage of the DTP in the classroom, and showed a high level of engagement, in particular in the dimensions of aesthetic appeal and perceived experience, as showed in Fig. 6.

Table 1. Questions used in the user engagement survey during the field trials, categorized by dimension.

Aesthetic Appeal	I think the app is beautiful
	I think the graphics and images used in this app are beautiful
Focused Attention	I was so involved in the task that I lost track of time
	I realized that the class went faster
Perceived Usability	The application responds the way I expected
	I think the application is easy to use
Perceived Experience	I felt excited while using the app

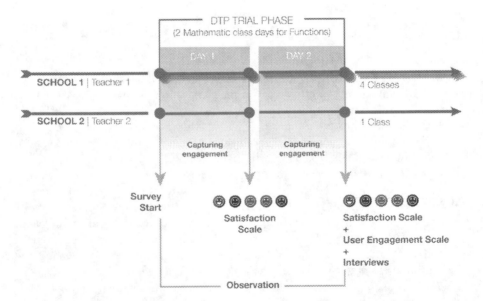

Fig. 5. Overview of the field trials and the evaluation methods applied throughout this experiment

The DTP app is an easy, focused, interactive and richer way to learn, according to the students we asked. One finding was that they reported that in a traditional setting without tablets they had to copy the teacher's notes manually, whereas on the tablet with the DTP this is unnecessary, and does not "waste their time": they can concentrate on the content itself and use the time to comment, take their own notes and answer the teacher's questions. Students think that is also improves the teacher's performance: "He explains better and students be more engaged". Finally, the students report that they were required to participate in the exercises: "in the DTP app we must do the exercise. In the textbook we can pretend".

Fig. 6. Satisfaction at the moment of use (left) and the outcome of the survey for each dimension (right)

Specific usability issues also arose, most importantly: (i) the login and material download process is too slow, and cost the teacher minutes that could have been spent teaching. (ii) it is essential that students notes (whether made with a stylus or a keyboard) are prominently displayed together with the content.

A more general observation is that the students (and teachers) expect a more collaborative behavior: they want students to contribute to the class content and activities; proposing exercises, topics, videos and also suggesting approaches to the teachers. All of this appears to be more evident and easy in a digital setting. In their opinion, during the experiment with the DTP, the students interact more with each other because of the tablets. We observed this in particular when the exercises were corrected, and the students' integration became effusive and very participatory. Creating more tools for sharing ideas and content among students and teachers is a direction we intend to explore in a future version.

4   Conclusion

Our research is preliminary, nevertheless we conclude that despite usability issues of the proof-of-concept, the DTP appears to motivate teachers performance and engage the students in a classroom setting. User feedback indicates that our DTP offers advantages in class time optimization and interactivity. The findings show that tablet usage is an important tool to motivate students in the classroom setting. We must however place a caveat; while the students had all used tablets in the classroom before, it was not common practice, and the novelty may play a part in the positive evaluation: long-term evaluations are scheduled to better evaluate this and to identify additional features to incorporate in the DTP.

References

1. Desmet, P., Overbeeke, K., Tax, S.: Designing products with added emotional value: development and application of an approach for research through design. Des. J. **4**(1), 32–47 (2001)

2. Harding, K., Parsons, J.: Improving teacher education programs. Aust. J. Teacher Educ. **36**(11), 4 (2011)
3. Meschtscherjakov, A., Weiss, A., Scherndl, T.: Utilizing emoticons on mobile devices within ESM studies to measure emotions in the field. In: Proceedings of MME in Conjunction with MobileHCI, Bonn, Germany, 1–4. ACM (2009)
4. Newmann, F.M.: Student Engagement and Achievement in American Secondary Schools. Teachers College Press, New York (1992)
5. Nielsen, J.: Usability 101: introduction to usability (2003). https://www.nngroup.com/articles/usability-101-introduction-to-usability/. Accessed 10 Feb 2016
6. O'Brien, H., Cairns, P.: An empirical evaluation of the User Engagement Scale (UES) in online news environments. Inf. Process. Manage. **51**(4), 413–427 (2015)
7. OECD: Students, Computers and Learning. Making the Connection. PISA, OECD Publishing (2015). http://dx.doi.org/10.1787/9789264239555-en
8. Pereira, O.R.E., Rodrigues, J.: Survey and analysis of current mobile learning applications and technologies. ACM Comput. Surv. **46**(2), 27: 1–27: 35 (2013)
9. Potts, J., Moore, N., Sukittanon, S.: Developing mobile learning applications for electrical engineering courses. In: Proceedings of IEEE Southeastcon 2011, 293–296. IEEE (2011)
10. Samuel, O.O., Botha, A., Ford, M., Tolmay, J., Krause, C.: IGLOO: mobile learning system to facilitate and support learners and educators. In: 2nd International Conference on Adaptive Science Technology (ICAST2009), 355–360. IEEE (2009)
11. Company, T.: Manual of eye tracking solution for mobile device testing (2016). http://www.tobiipro.com/siteassets/tobii-pro/brochures/tobii-pro-mobile-device-standbrochure.pdf. Accessed 4 Feb 2016

Bridging Digital Divide in Schools in Developing Countries: Perceptions of Teachers of Free Software Opportunities

Edmund Laugasson(⊠), James Sunney Quaicoe, Eka Jeladze,
and Triinu Jesmin

School of Digital Technologies, Tallinn University,
Narva Road 25, 10120 Tallinn, Estonia
{edmund.laugasson,james_sunney.quaicoe,eka.jeladze,
triinu.jesmin}@tlu.ee

Abstract. 21st century information society requires more and more use of ICT (information and communication technology) in everyday life. Nowadays there is much talk about the digital divide, which means economical and social disparities in digital technology use and availability in society of a particular country and among different countries. In this paper we sought to explore teachers knowledge and use of ICT resources in the context of free/*libre* and open-source software (FLOSS). When relying permanently on free tools there are several benefits which in turn will grow sustainable information society and will fortify economy in larger scale. For the mentioned purpose we use Technology Acceptance Model (TAM) first version. We found that TAM model is not ideal to accomplish mentioned tasks, especially in educational institutions. If teachers will be aware of FLOSS then they can increase ICT resources use in schools in a meaningful way. This in turn will reduce also disparity in schools and we may call it as a digital turn.

Keywords: Technology Acceptance Model · Adoption · Digital divide · Free/*libre* and open-source software

1 Introduction

Contemporary information society is sequenced by the emergence of different 21th Century Technologies, ICT (information and communication technology) particularly. Educational institutions are preparing students for tomorrows life [4,14]. This phenomenon have had immense influence in the educational systems in both developing [13] and developed [6] countries. The scenario of digital divide cannot be overlooked in educational institutions; giving rise to inequity and various shades of digital disparities in those schools. Disparities could be seen in several ways among educational institutions: these include a lack of hardware and software resources, however, what is most important, is the know-how to use them in a pedagogically efficient and meaningful way. We do not argue the

© Springer International Publishing Switzerland 2016
P. Zaphiris and A. Ioannou (Eds.): LCT 2016, LNCS 9753, pp. 695–706, 2016.
DOI: 10.1007/978-3-319-39483-1_63

ICT importance in education, but we contend that the suitable knowledge how and what to use in terms of ICT. Also its availability and use in educational institutions in the first place. This all will provide sustainable and equal access to information society resources to ensure tomorrows workers but also teachers' competitive achievement ability. We assume that through the use of free/*libre* and open-source software (hereinafter: FLOSS) it would be possible to reduce the digital divide in schools to the nearest minimum. This will happen due to released funding resources to establish the minimal level of ICT equipments in educational institutions. The opened funding can be then used to achieve other goals that will facilitate teachers and students engagements in accessibility to ICT resources and raising knowledge awareness and how to use technologies in reasonable ways.

In this paper we sought to explore teachers' knowledge and use of ICT resources in the context of FLOSS. When relying permanently on free tools there are several benefits which in turn will grow sustainable information society and will fortify economy in larger scale.

We used the Technology Acceptance Model v1 (hereinafter: TAM1) [3] were adopted it as the research framework to explore constructs associated with FLOSS and digital divide in Estonian, Ghanaian and Georgian schools. Teachers voluntarily participated in the survey Fig. 1.

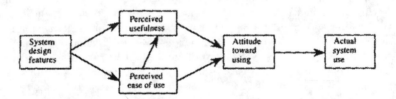

Fig. 1. Technology acceptance model [3]

Not less important is the social mechanism around the FLOSS. This means that the community of users holds together and shares the knowledge and teaches each other in addition to sharing tools the software itself. This makes equal opportunities for participating in information society regardless of students' or teachers' wealth.

Having access to ICT resources implies ability to participate in nowadays information society. FLOSS plays crucial role here with not only saving money but also freeing educational institutions from vicious circle of paying money continuously in a ascending direction and as often as software companies ask. This in turn gives the opportunity to ensure given education competitiveness at labour market and economy in general of whole country.

2   Background

In our study we have three countries: Ghana, Georgia, Estonia and we are giving a short overiview of these countries about ICT use, especially in education.

2.1   Ghana

The use of digital technologies of ICTs on a day-to-day basis in digitally divided communities has become widespread in spite of the digital limitation [15]. Ghana, a Sub Saharan African country has been identified as among the ten ICT proactive nations in Africa, though located in the block of developing nations; and characterised globally as digitally disadvantaged. Nonetheless, there is a window of digital opening for such countries. In the opinion of James [11] developing countries could generate substantive savings and also to a large extent bridge the global digital divide if they migrated to the use of FLOSS applications. He further observed that to meet the demands of the proprietary software, computer users in developing countries resort to piracy and illegal procurement of applications. Unfortunately, the use of FLOSS applications has not caught up with most developing nations. According to the article [12], developing nations are making more conscious efforts towards the advancement of FLOSS initiatives. He observed that from 2006 to 2010 FLOSS advancing FLOSS initiatives in Africa arose from four (4) to eight (8). However, not so dramatic increase, it is a token of the progressive awareness of FLOSS in digital divided communities.

Not oblivious to the global digital trends and developments, ICT integration into teaching and learning at the pre-university level of Ghanas education system was rolled out 2007; marking a New Education Reform (NER). Relying on the merits of FLOSS, government commenced the supply of laptops to a target over 60,000 schools. The first set of laptops came with FLOSS operating system but later agitations resulted in the change of the operating system to proprietary (MS Windows 7) [8,9,19]. A study [18] indicated that some digital disparities exist across basic schools in Ghana. This Digital Divide (DD) was found across the schools ICT culture components; which included teacher ICT competence, activities in the classroom, confidence in use and availability for digital equipment resources [17]. It could be speculated that digital divide resulting for teacher digital literacy in schools, less use of digital resources might be the results of contention between the use of proprietary software and FLOSS. Through observation and literature, it has been established that in the ICT terrain in Ghana, people are more inclined to the use of proprietary software, mainly Microsoft Windows (hereinafter: MS Windows) operating system than FLOSS and it holds true for teachers as well. In related article [22] found out that 84,7 % of organisations run their systems on MS Windows operating system, 11,9 % on GNU/Linux (hereinafter: Linux) while 3,4 % on UNIX. It further noted that generally FLOSS operating systems are used on servers; while the proprietary operating system is predominantly used on desktop computers and laptops. This clearly adds to the fact to controversy of teacher use of FLOSS in lieu what is known to be the status quo in the context of their ICT use. In the light of the forgiving, it makes sense that teacher position on the use of FLOSS will be a challenging if they are well versed and prone to the use of MS Windows operating systems. In this context the case of divide across the schools digital culture could persist; in the form of disconnection between human and material (digital) resources [18]); unless there occurs holistic digital paradigm shift on the part educators and trainers. Literature acknowledges why possible challenges will exist when it came to the mainstream ICT practices in Ghana. In his view, [22] noted that some of the challenges accounting for less use of FLOSS is the fact that Ghana has no FLOSS policy to generate actions and interest is this of aspect of ICT activities. Accordingly, in the reviewed ICT in Education policy has factored in the need of bringing FLOSS into the digital practices in schools [9]. He further realised that many proprietary software users live with the perception that it is difficult to migrate to the use of FLOSS owing to its complex systems and applications and navigations; as new skills and knowledge are needed to be acquired. Nevertheless, bringing FLOSS applications into education and training systems will go a long way to eliminate the obstacles propriety software pose in the integration of ICTs in schools. Thus, teachers, well trained on FLOSS could possibly have access to a lot more of educational applications for daily use than his/her colleague who will be required to pay for the use of applications. In this paper the situation of teachers knowledge and engagement in digital activities using FLOSS based application are compared with other two nations: Georgia and Estonia.

2.2   Georgia

The first successful attempt of ICT integration in the general education of Georgia began in 2005 by replicating Estonian Tiger Leap program into Georgian Deer Leap. The goal of the Deer Leap program was to support development of ICT infrastructure and utilization of modern information technologies into the general education (Decree of the President of Georgia) [5]. The program built on equipping all the schools of Georgia with computers and Internet connection, ensuring fast adoption of ICT by teachers and pupils across various disciplines and age levels in primary and secondary schools, developing e-learning environment with corresponding e-resources. Technology inheritance of the program was in relatively bad condition in the country: outdated and insufficient amount of computers without Internet connectivity; despite informatics being a compulsory subject in all secondary schools, the content was often taught without computers. At the end of the first phase of Deer Leap program, by 2008, 26 520 new computers were provided to schools (with a 20:1 student-computer ratio) equipped with Linux operating system and a collection of open-source software applications; Web-based collaboration environment was developed and integrated into LeMill.net in order to support eLearning with sharing opportunities; 60 % of all primary and secondary pupils had access to Internet at school; Basic computer literacy training were carried out for 21 540 teachers out of 70 000 on the Linux operating system basis. 8158 laptops were provided for excellent pupils within Presidential program - My First Computer. By the end of the first phase of Deer Leap program the master plan was developed for Deer Leap Plus (2009–2012) programme with the goals to establish digitally enriched learning environment by integrating ICT into curriculum as a cross-curricular theme via innovative e-learning methods. With the change of ministry officials the realization of the goals defined by Deer Leap plus program took different turn. The program components came apart to different agencies under the Ministry of Education and Science of Georgia, instead of cumulating them within one program. The responsible MoES agencies according to a new structure were: Education and Science Infrastructure Development Agency, Education Management Information System, Teacher Professional Development Center, national curriculum department of MoES. Major shift occurring besides the restructuring of Deer Leap program was switching of computer parks from Linux to Microsoft proprietary software. The memorandum between Microsoft and Ministry of Education and Science of Georgia was signed in 2008 [21]. As a result all the schools of Georgia was equipped with MS Windows operating system and MS Office software under the Microsoft academic licensing terms. Accordingly Teacher ICT training programs were converted to the use of Microsoft software. As a transitional period a dual boot Microsoft and Linux operational systems were installed on school machines to let teachers and students select suitable working environment. At the moment the only operating system working in school computers is Microsoft software. We might conclude that the Ministry decision was partially based on the FITS (Focus on ICT in Schools) [21] survey that was held in 2008 on the use of ICT in the schools of Georgia. The objectives of FITS was to analyze the scope and ways of integrating ICT into learning/teaching processes and the problems related with educational use of ICT; According to the survey the majority of teachers (75 %) used mainly MS Office software. However, 43 % of the teachers were satisfied with the availability of software in schools and $\frac{1}{3}$ of teachers estimated that the situation is good. About $\frac{1}{4}$ of teachers estimated the situation with software as very good. Only 5 % of teachers were not satisfied with the availability of software. There was disparity between the popularity of MS Office among teachers and the satisfaction level of the availability of software if considering that absolute majority of computers in schools were Linux-based. This contradiction was explained by a hypothesis that teachers used MS Office mainly at home [21]. Another ambitious initiative - Netbooks for Primary Schools - took start in 2010 in Georgia [3]. The program aims to provide quality education to the students and develop their ICT skills in order to support their integration in international educational space. All the pupils as well as their mentors get netbooks for personal educational use on their first day at school. Up to now all the classes 1 to 4 are equipped with computers to use in the learning process. Teachers go through intense training course of how to use ICT-enhanced pedagogy in teaching and learning process (91 contact hours). The netbooks are equipped with Microsoft software and Intel-powered Mythware classroom management system. Mythware platform enables teachers to digitally manage classroom, supervise individual students as well as groups activities by sharing resources through intranet connection.

2.3   Estonia

Tiger Leap (1997–2000) was the first national-level strategy on computerization of Estonian schools, aiming at equipping all schools with computers and

Internet connection, providing the basic ICT skills for all teachers and educational software for all subject areas. The follow-up strategy (called Tiger Leap Plus, 2001–2005) focused primarily on the implementation of this technology by integrating it into everyday teaching an learning in all age levels and all subject areas across the secondary education. During this period, majority of the teachers passed Intels 40hrs course Teach to the Future, Virtual Learning Environments were taken into use by shcools. The third strategy Learning Tiger (2006–2009) focused on integrated e-learning. The new educational e-services have been developed and/or implemented within local and international projects: collaborative Learning Object authoring portal LeMill.net, Learning Object Repository (called Waramu) which is connected to all-European repository network LRE, virtual learning environments (Moodle, Krihvel) and online testing tools (TATS, PETS). A new teacher training programme DigiTiger has been developed and implemented by a group of enthusiastic teachers, this programme focuses on the use of Web 2.0 tools in teaching and learning. The implementation of all three strategies has been led by the Tiger Leap Foundation, a non-profit organisation that was founded by the Ministry of Education and is financed mostly from the state budget and European projects [16].

One of the main issues related with Tiger Leap project was renunciation of platform neutrality quite in the beginning. Mainly proprietary Microsoft software platform was chosen. This has been influencing Estonian society, especially educational institutions, until today.

During December 2014 to April 2015 there was FLOSS pilot project in Tallinn educational institutions (3 schools and 2 kindergartens) [7]. Even though the project had obstacles, the overall result was positive and the mentioned educational institutions remained to use the FLOSS. Today there is even some schools additionally joining the project. The use of FLOSS still lasts and there has been developed a massive deployment tool [1].

3   Methodology

There are different methodologies used to investigate digital divide and its possible solutions. Mainly we are concidering here disparities in society which also affects information society. The most famous approaches are different acceptance models. Technology Acceptance Model was used to carry out current research. We used the research instrument created in University of Michigan, Business School [3]. The instrument contains of 20 questions: ten for Perceived Usefulness (PU) and ten for Perceived Easy of use (PEU).

Procedure. Data was collected in January 2016 from three countries: Estonia, Ghana and Georgia. We used the convenience sample and collected 209 responses: 168 from Georgia, 34 from Estonia and 7 from Ghana. We have to admit that these samples are not representative but this is the data we could collect. We created a web questionnaire in three languages: English, Georgian, Estonian in order to collect the data during 2 weeks in all coutries. After data was collected, all Georgian and Estonian text was translated into English. The situation of each country was relatively different. As the questionnaire was online, accessibility to the internet was required in order to answer. This was relatively challenging issue in Ghana, where access to the internet is quite limited. This fact is also reflected in the results. In Estonia we had also relatively small, but reasonable sample. In Estonia there are proportionally large amount of different research regularly carried out and it would be also quite challenging to collect data among others. In Georgia we had best opportunities as one of the authors was in place and visiting schools so this also reflects in the results.

We used 7-point Likert-scale where 1 was strongly agree and 7 strongly disagree. Additionally we asked some questions about teaching and ICT experience and terms. The questionnaire was selective: participants were asked whether they use free and open-source or proprietary software. Both cases teachers answered same questions but with previously selected focus.

We formulated the following research questions:

1. What is the opinion of teachers about the meaning of FLOSS and PRS?
2. What perceptions do teachers hold about the usefulness and ease in using either FLOSS or PRS?
3. What principal constructs are influencing differences in perceptions about FLOSS and PRS in different countries?

... where: *FLOSS* means *free/libre and open-source software*
PRS means *proprietary software*

4 Results

The study drew participants from Ghana, Estonia, and Georgia. In all 209 teachers participated, whom 89.5% were females and 10.5% males. The age distribution of participants stood as follows; 30 or less years (10%), 31–40 (37.3%), 41–50 years (39.7%) and 51 and more years (12.9%). We collected data from three different countries and as the samples were quite different, also results are as follows (Table 1). For statistical analysis we used IBM® SPSS® Statistics v23 and GNU PSPP v0.8.5.

Table 1. Samples from participated countries

	Sample	Percentage	Teacher		School type			
			ICT	Non-ICT	P[a]	E[b]	E+G[c]	G[d]
Ghana	7	3,3%	100,0%	-	100,0%	-	-	-
Estonia	34	16,3%	-	100,0%	5,8%	73,5%	17,7%	3,0%
Georgia	168	80,4%	24,2%	75,6%	6,6%	92,3%	-	1,1%

legend: [a] primary school | [b] elementary school
[c] elementary + gymnasium (or highschool)
[d] gymnasium (or highschool)

The sample age reflects also age of teachers in each of country. When in Ghana there were mainly younger teachers, then in Estonia and Georgia we can see more older ones. This reflects also teaching experience, which is relatively higher in Estonia and Georgia.

Research Questions. *RQ1: What is the opinion of teachers about the meaning of FLOSS and PRS?*
This question sought to establish the knowledge what participants have about FLOSS and PRS. We have to admit that awareness of terms is still relatively low (Table 2)

Table 2. Awareness of terms and choices

	Terms correct, %		Use, %	
	FLOSS	PRS	FLOSS	PRS
Ghana	28,6	71,4	14,3	85,7
Estonia	26,5	68,6	23,5	76,5
Georgia	34,5	47,6	22,6	77,4

RQ2: What perceptions teachers hold about the usefulness and ease in using either FLOSS or PRS?
This question explored the variations existing in the perceptions participants have on the perceived usefulness and ease of use (Table 3). The lower the mean, the higher the agreement. A independent t-test was conducted to evaluate participants perceived usefulness and ease of use of free/libre and open-source software (FLOSS) and that of proprietary software (PRS). There is statistically significant higher mean on the usefulness of PRS (M=3,07; SD=1,44) over FLOSS (M=2,59; SD=0,80), t(-4,0163)=208; p<0,001; with eta squared value=0,07) indicating a large effect for the benefit of FLOSS as we used Likert scale where the value 1 were strongly agree and the value 7 was strongly disagree. While, in the case of perceived ease of use for FLOSS and PRS; a statistically significant higher mean was recorded for PRS (M=3,95, SD=0,70) over FLOSS (M=3,73; SD=0,36); t(208)=-4,015; p<0,001; with eta squared value=0,07); indicating a large effect for the benefit of FLOSS.

RQ3: What are the variations of different countries in perceptions about FLOSS and PRS? This question explored country perceptions about FLOSS and PRS. Table 4 shows the descriptive statistical analysis of the participants responses. We also analyzed Perceived Usefulness (PU) and Perceived Easy of Use (PEU) all together to get overall picture of Technology Acceptance Model (TAM) capabilities. First we compiled independent t-test to compare PU and PEU over all participated countries. Variable "greater control over the work" (2nd question in PU part) was rated higher by free software users (M=2,57; SD=1,612)

Table 3. Means of PRS an FLOSS

		Mean	N	Std. deviation
Pair 1	FLOSS PU	2,59	47	1,69
	PRS PU	3,07	162	1,64
Pair 2	FLOSS PEU	3,73	47	0,76
	PRS PEU	3,95	162	0,80

than proprietary software users (M=3,22; SD=1,847) (p=0,032). "Software easier to use" was rated higher by free software users (M=2,23; SD=1,386) than the proprietary software users (M=2,78; SD=1,759) (p=0,029). As there was relatively small sample from Ghana, we repeated separate t-test between Estonia and Georgia to see possible influences there. In Estonia the free software users (M=2,13; SD=1,126) rated the use more easier than proprietary software users (M=3,54; SD=1,679) (p=0,034) about the 10th question in PEU part. Georgia there were several significant results. All questions in Perceived Usefulness were significant and overall PU module t-test showed that free software (M=2,29; SD=1,48) users appreciated perceived usefulness higher than proprietary software (M=3,13; SD=1,71) (p=0,007). ANOVA test was compiled but it did not show any statistical significance among participated countries according to chosen significance level of 5 %. When we compared mens and womens among countries then there was no difference of statistical significance in t-test. ANOVA test among different types of schools has been compiled with Tukey honest significance test comparison at Post Hoc option and did not show any statistical significance. T-test between Estonia and Georgia compared PU (Perceived Usefulness) and PEU (Perceived Easy of Use) did not show any statistical significance. But in Estonia we see that PEU has important significance free software users (M=3,77; SD=0,33) assess their software easier to use than proprietary software users (M=4,15; SD=0,44) (p=0,035). The overall Cronbach's Alpha in case of PU (Perceived Usefulness) was 0.974 (N=209) and in case of PEU (Perceived Easy of Use) it was 0,498. As we see the PEU reliability is lower than expected (0,7). When to look per country then we see that Estonia has most influences here: Ghana ($\alpha_{PU} = 0,987$; $\alpha_{PEU} = 0,542$), Estonia ($\alpha_{PU} = 0,961$; $\alpha_{PEU} = 0,359$), Georgia ($\alpha_{PU} = 0,975$; $\alpha_{PEU} = 0,543$). One influence in Estonia is recent FLOSS project [7] which has influenced the PEU component has brought some confusion among users due to some misunderstandings among organizers.

Discussion. Initial objective of the study was to evaluate FLOSS (free/libre and open-source software) in the context of TAM1 model. We intended to use the outcome to explore country variations in the use of FLOSS and PRS (proprietary software). In the process we establish that in the context of varying ICT policies and implementations structure in the three countries using TAM 1 turned out to be challenging; as participants did not respond proportionally the required

Table 4. Country variations regarding FLOSS and PRS

Country	TAM component	Mean	Std. deviation
Ghana	FLOSS PU	3,22	1,665
	FLOSS PEU	3,92	0,519
	PRS PU	1,78	0,777
	PRS PEU	3,44	0,673
Estonia	FLOSS PU	2,80	0,888
	FLOSS PEU	3,74	0,155
	PRS PU	3,09	1.083
	PRS PEU	4,10	0,391
Georgia	FLOSS PU	2,53	0,707
	FLOSS PEU	3,72	0,378
	PRS PU	3,12	1.506
	PRS PEU	3,94	0,742
Total	FLOSS PU	2,59	0,794
	FLOSS PEU	3,73	0,358
	PRS PU	3,07	1,443
	PRS PEU	3.95	0,701

constructs for measuring of the model. In lieu of exploring the model, a comparative analysis was carried out across the variables Perceived Usefulness (PU) and Perceived Ease of Use (PEU). Even we see that countries are mostly using proprietary software (PRS): Ghana 85 %, Estonia 76,5 % and Georgia 77,4 % - users perceive FLOSS easier and more useful. Also noticeable would be understanding the terms and there is better understanding of PRS than FLOSS terms which reflects also in usage. All school levels perceive software usage similarly and there is no significant difference. Estonia has been the driving force with the experience of Tiger Leap project and this has been reflected and used to develop similar processes in Georgia and would be as one example for future developments in Ghana. Despite great projects in Estonia and Georgia the digital divide is still there, especially in Ghana but could be mitigated by deploying FLOSS [2]. There are many good projects running to reduce the digital divide [10] and it does not only affect developing countries but even developed ones [20].

5   Conclusion

TAM depends on user attitude and will but at school context the choice of technology (software particularly) does not depend only on that. There are also situations where there have been software usage decided by decisionmakers: local authority, usually the school owner or sometimes by school management board. In such situation there is quite often not much discussed the technology choice with teachers and the choice does not very much depend on teachers' preferences. This in turn may cause frustration among teachers as were also mentioned in current research comments. There are also different groups of teachers: in current research we had 25 % of ICT and 75 % of non-ICT teachers. It is obvious that ICT-teachers have been more influenced by technology, certain software particularly, and therefore more biased than non-ICT teachers. One moment would be also challenging according TAM to maintain or preserve FLOSS + PRS ecosystem at educational institutions. Based on the previous discussion we may say that TAM did not measure all aspects that affect technology choices, especially at educational institution context.

References

1. Butterknife provisioning suite (2016). http://butterknife.rocks/
2. Caudill, J.: Helping to bridge the digital divide with free software and services. Int. J. Open Source Soft. Process. **2**(4), 13–27 (2010)
3. Davis, F.D.: User acceptance of information technology: system characteristics, user perceptions and behavioral impacts. Int. J. Man Mach. stud. **38**(3), 475–487 (1993)
4. Dede, C.: Emerging influences of information technology on school curriculum. J. Curriculum Stud. **32**(2), 281–303 (2000)
5. Deer Leap Foundation creation (2005). https://matsne.gov.ge/ka/document/view/95170
6. Ein-Dor, P., Myers, M.D., Raman, K.: Information technology in three small developed countries. J. Manage. Inf. Syst. **13**(4), 61–89 (1997)
7. Free software project in educational institutions (2016). http://www.tallinn.ee/est/haridusasutused/Vabavara-projekt-haridusasutustes
8. ICT in Education Policy. Ministry of Edcuation/Government of Ghana (2008). http://www.moe.gov.gh/assets/media/docs/ICTinEducationpolicy_NOV2008.pdf
9. ICT in Education Policy. Accra: Ministry of Edcuation/Government of Ghana (2015). http://www.moe.gov.gh/assets/media/docs/ICT_in_Education_Policy_August_2015_new.pdf
10. Internet World Stats: The Digital Divide, ICT, and Broadband Internet (2016). http://www.internetworldstats.com/links10.htm
11. James, J.: Free software and the digital divide: opportunities and constraints for developing countries. J. Inf. Sci. **29**(1), 25–33 (2003)
12. Karume, S.M., Mbugua, S.: Trends in adoption of open source software in Africa. J. Emerg. Trends Comput. Inf. Sci. **3**(11), 1509–1515 (2012)
13. Lee, J.W.: Education for technology readiness: prospects for developing countries. J. Hum. Dev. **2**(1), 115–151 (2001)
14. Lever-Duffy, J., McDonald, J., Mizell, A.: The 21st-Century Classroom: Teaching and Learning with Technology. Addison-Wesley Longman Publishing Co. Inc., Boston (2002)
15. Measuring the Information Society Report. Geneva, International Telecommunication Union (2014). https://www.itu.int/en/ITU-D/Statistics/Documents/publications/mis2014/MIS2014_without_Annex_4.pdf
16. Poslawski, G., Sipelgas, K.: Estonia's tiger leap into the world of design. Des. Manage. Rev. **21**(4), 44–51 (2010)

17. Quaicoe, J.S., Pata, K.: Factors determining digital divide in Ghana's basic schools. In: IST-Africa Conference 2015, pp. 1–8. IEEE (2015)
18. Quaicoe, J.S., Pata, K.: The teachers digital literacy: determining digital divide in public basic schools in Ghana. In: Kurbanoğlu, S., Boustany, J., Špiranec, S., Grassian, E., Mizrachi, D., Roy, L. (eds.) Information Literacy: Moving Toward Sustainability, pp. 154–162. Springer, Switzerland (2015)
19. Sector News: 4,853 Teachers in Western Region to Receive Laptops (2014). http://www.moe.gov.gh/site/media/nws_0037.php
20. Stanford University: The Digital Divide (2016). http://cs.stanford.edu/people/eroberts/cs201/projects/digital-divide/start.html
21. The memorandum between Microsoft and Ministry of Education andScience of Georgia (2008). http://www.mes.gov.ge/old/index.php?module=multi&page=detals&multi_id=1&id=1232
22. Worlali, S.: Free and Open Source Software in Ghana Information Technology Essay (2010). http://ict4d.at/2010/09/18/free-and-open-source-verses-proprietary-softwares-the-case-of-ghana/

A Model to Evaluate Digital Safety Concerns in School Environment

Birgy Lorenz[1,2]([⊠]), Kaido Kikkas[1,2], Mart Laanpere[1,2], and Edmund Laugasson[1,2]

[1] School of Digital Technologies, Tallinn University,
Narva Road 25, 10120 Tallinn, Estonia
{Birgy.Lorenz,Kaido.Kikkas,Mart.Laanpere,
Edmund.Laugasson}@tlu.ee
[2] Estonian Information Technology College,
Raja St 4C, 12616 Tallinn, Estonia

Abstract. In cyber security of a modern information society, digital safety is becoming more and more important regarding governance and schools as well as well-being of common people, especially children. There are models to evaluate cyber-attacks and technical risks in institutions and ICT services, but there are no good models yet to help understanding the concerns and issues of everyday e-life of commoners, including students and teachers - especially the ones that can be encountered at schools (from primary to upper secondary). This makes digital safety an essential part of innovation and cooperation at schools as well as in teacher training. The aim of this paper is to propose a model that helps to build up internet security training and other activities that will improve children's and teachers' safety skills and resistance to security threats.

Keywords: Digital safety contextual model · Internet safety · Security risks at schools · Security training · Innovation and cooperation in teacher professional development

1 Introduction

Our society allows having online connections with nearly anyone or any device. This has developed new types of crimes - cybercrime, cyber-bullying, online social manipulation etc. Despite the rules and regulations to enhance safe online behavior it has not been sufficient. For example, according to the Eurostat 7.02.2011 newsletter 21/2011, Estonia belongs to top 3 countries using secure software in EU; the EU Kids Online II [15] study stated that it is one of the top countries where children are facing online threats whereas most parents don't have a clue about the online life of their child. The situation has not changed since. The wider use of cloud services, social and automated software solutions (Internet of Things) at schools also brings larger risks and misuse of technology. In addition to their intended targets, attacks and abuse can also influence third parties (institutions, but sometimes even the whole country).

In this article, we define digital safety as a branch of cyber security that deals with people and the levels of online comfort, privacy and reputation, especially in the educational context. Earlier Estonian studies used the term "internet safety", but we feel

© Springer International Publishing Switzerland 2016
P. Zaphiris and A. Ioannou (Eds.): LCT 2016, LNCS 9753, pp. 707–721, 2016.
DOI: 10.1007/978-3-319-39483-1_64

it being too narrow - as we are also talking about the use of mobile technology and other parts of wider digital context. The cyber security approach has been mostly focusing on technological and institutional aspects, the laws and regulations prioritizing critical infrastructure of the government and businesses. At the same time, commoners including children and teachers lack necessary support, as this task has been relegated to voluntary workers or NGO-s. Luckily, political support and interest to develop this field has been growing. It has recently been stressed that commoners are an important part of information warfare [17] - e.g. as reflected by Estonian strategic documents Cyber Security Strategy 2008–2013 [7] and follow-up documents like the same strategy in EU 2013.

1.1 Cyber Security Related Strategy and Policy Documents in Estonia

We have looked at the strategy and educational policy documents in Estonia to propose a cyber-security model for schools. There are not many documents related to digital safety and cyber security (only the Cyber Security Strategy and Defense Strategy), but there are documents that mention digital literacy skills of commoners.

The new Cyber Security Strategy 2014–2017 [8] highlights understanding and discovery of cyber threats and finding ways to ground them. This document emphasizes the rise of digital threats and cybercrime targeting modern technologies, at the same time it is pointed out that the weakest link can be also be human itself. This means that training and digital security related life skills should be taught not only to specialists but also every citizen (including children) that can be targeted in cyber war through social manipulation. The Information Society Development Plan 2020 [11] forecasts the rise of different technologies, suggesting that the added value from using ICT and mobile technologies can only be achieved by enhancing digital literacy skills, including safety skills in this area. The Local Authority Information Society Development Plan 2015 [16] and the Internal Security Development Plan 2015–2020 [13] suggest that the awareness about needed skills for a digital society is a big issue. At the same time they state that as important as the skills are, the values and attitudes that affect our security behavior in this technology rich and global world would be even more important. And finally the National Defense Strategy [22] mentions again the need for better psychological defense: prevention of panic, influencing and containing hostile mindset spread, as well as ensuring trust to the state and defense activities from the commoners' view. It will be also important to ensure that traditional media channels would work in a case of attack; informing population in an emergency situation would be of prime importance. Finally, an important strategy is to eliminate economic incentives for cybercrime.

In Estonia there are many different institutions and companies that deal with digital security in every day basis. As up to 2014 the main issues and campaigns were related to the project "Be smart online!" [1] that had its limitations in focusing on internet only. From 2014 on, the ICT companies have started their own campaign "Connected with mobile safety" [5]. These projects help to promote the discussion in the society - e.g. parents are increasingly demanding that schools should take action, as parents themselves lack necessary knowledge to support their child.

Based on the strategies, we conclude that the most important is to train citizens who cannot be manipulated, can detect when someone attempts it, and can deal with digital crime or difficulties. At the same time they should preserve good attitudes towards technology, be enthusiastic about present and future developments and keep up the trust in authorities. These goals are expected to be delivered by the teachers and education system.

1.2   Education Strategy and Guidelines

The problem with digital safety in education is that it is not considered important enough. Proper educational use of technology is still lagging behind its social use, there is also opposition from older teachers who think that "school and teaching should be free from digital intervention". Such attitudes may stem from diverse reasons, such as lack of skills, learning aids or devices, or even slow connection speed. At the same time the younger generation and lot of innovative schools are up to the task regarding needs of the modern society. The problem with security is that while digital skill standards have not been implemented yet (they are optional), there is less consensus about whether digital safety should be a responsibility of school or parents - while parents provide the students with devices, the students usually learn most of the skills and develop attitudes "by themselves" or "through social media and real life experience".

We find that our educational strategies that strive to include everyone from the kindergarten to university actually support only the digital skills needed by the labor market. Guidelines that influences schools doings are national curricula (evaluated in the Digiturvis study as explained below) and International Society for Technology in Education (ISTE. NETS) [14] standards that are also optional. As Teachers Professional Standard V [26] also points to ISTE, it is the most important document to understand which problems should be solved through education in digital safety. ISTE standards were introduced to Estonia 2013–2014 when the governmental NGO called the Information Technology Foundation for Education (HITSA) started to implement in in its trainings to teachers and programs for students. The main 5 focus areas are: overall ICT competences in every level of educational; specific competences in vocational and higher education; ICT specialist training; teaching and learning in a digital age; information system in education. Digital safety areas are scattered between every section, e.g. understanding internet safety trends; choosing secure devices to surf online; recognize potential insecure behavior or threat; know how to act when something bad happens or seek help when needed; understand your own and others online behavior; knowledge about account maintenance; help students to learn how to act nice and consider others online. A parallel can be drawn with cars - a good car in the hands of an inexperienced and/or ignorant driver can pose a major danger.

We also looked at the national curricula (from kindergarten to university level), but could find only a fraction of what is really needed. For example, to effectively prevent cyber-crime, students should keep up with the changing technology in education, communities in personal and institutional life. The whole Digiturvis [9] study results can be found here in Estonian: http://1drv.ms/1N7KmtZ.

In conclusion, digital safety topics and areas are mentioned in different strategies. Usually the development is focused on positive aspects – developing services, accessibility, raising awareness and develop skills and competences. Drawbacks are less mentioned, but we see a lot of hints that suggest that future documents will deal with the issue more thoroughly. However, at the moment the documents contain no clear goals to be reached. This means that digital safety area has not been fully understood and this makes it really hard for teachers and schools to understand what is or is not their responsibilities.

1.3   Related Studies in Estonia

As mentioned, the digital safety research done in Estonia so far has mostly been focusing on the positive – overall evaluation of the situation where the youth nowadays live in (social media, online communication). Specifically, no one yet has fully focused on digital safety as it is often hard to separate from its context. The most important study that dealt with the issue on European level was the 2009 EU Kids Online II [15] that gives some insight to young people's online behavior (online habits, exposure to threats, parental supervision). Internet safety issues for the EU countries have been also focused through European Union project InSafe (In Estonia Safer Internet SIC) [12] and European SchoolNet gives out award E-Safety Label [10], that sadly focuses only in the management level and collecting some cases (e.g. cyberbullying and privacy-related issues).

In Estonia we can also refer to international studies like PISA [24] and PIAAC [23] or TALIS [25] that ask some interesting questions about technology. Estonian adults tend to have good basic e-skills, but as the workplace does not value these skills directly, they will deteriorate. At the same time, Estonian schools lag behind the rest of society. The digital literacy level of students almost uniformly exceeds that of teachers - but unfortunately, this does not apply to digital safety skills.

The CreativeClass [6] and "Conceptual framework for increasing society's commitment in ICT" [6] studies point out the autonomy of the schools to interpret the curricula and also reveal different priorities. The digital literacy is one of the main goals/challenges for the Ministry of Education, but it is not always so for the schools. This means that not every school has computer labs, technology lessons, or e-learning. The results show that schools have a lot of autonomy at primary and secondary school level – every school did something differently, but some of them supported it through optional or mandatory courses or extracurricular lessons.

An interesting study in terms of digital safety was the Mobile/Smart Security study carried out by the ICT industry representative Look@World Foundation in 2014 [21] that gives overview of mobile technology use among Estonian adults and children (usage, attitudes and security knowledge). The results show good access to mobile technology which will increasingly be the focus of personal technology use. Unfortunately, the safety awareness is again rudimentary and practical defense skills are low - usually, people are aware of dangers in general, but do not know specific threats. For example, only 2 out of 5 people locked their phones. And importantly, parents are unable to support their children, as they are helpless themselves.

The issue is also that in digital safety, people rely on "friends" more than they rely on official help [19]. Principals really think that technical limitations will help [20]. Depending on the school's traditions, these regulations will be developed by principal, teachers or involving students, parents or outside experts. Importantly, the effectiveness of these regulations depends heavily on the level of cooperation - authoritarian rulesets will be much more likely ignored by students.

In conclusion, in the "Education Guidelines to Schools" there are some mention of digital safety and digital literacy skills, but it is still unclear who is responsible and how it is being implemented. Schools' freedom in organizing education and applying curricula makes this really difficult task, as there is no clear understanding what the cases that education should concur. For example, considering things like phishing, seeing/sharing inappropriate content, trust to government, reputation, illegal content, technology over usage, cyber bullying, harassment, public data, identity theft – are they issues that should be dealt with as they appear, or after turning 18 when the youth enter workforce? Would the questionable attitudes (internet is a no-man's land; do but don't get caught) that can foster in the heads of youngsters easier to counter when they are already grown up and have their own opinions how the digital society really works?

Thus, there seems to be a need for a model that education sector could use to understand and teach digital safety issues on the commoners' level rather than in cyber security level that already involves criminal acts. The low-level pranks and disturbances can be dealt with by the educational sector, to raise more responsible and aware people that can really stand up to social manipulation and solve low level situations by themselves, not always seeking help immediately when e.g. somebody sends a spam e-mail. The model should help to detect, explain, solve and choose an awareness training for different low level cases that happen in the schools and usually go unnoticed. This should be a basis in the teacher professional development training regarding digital safety issues.

2 The Model and Its Evaluation

2.1 The Model

We have developed a model based on the research done about students' and teachers online behavior. The digital safety contextual model is based on the school as a smaller-scale model of society dealing with digital world risks on institutional and personal level.

The model is divided into zones, types, challenges and levels, and solutions.

2.1.1 Zones

The model involves different stages. The first is Zones that "people are concerned or not or how much" are divided into two: public and private. For common people (including students) the public zone is something that is not part of the person's immediate interest; school, online friends, acquaintances and society. The private zone includes family, friends, but sometimes even really close online friends (see Fig. 1).

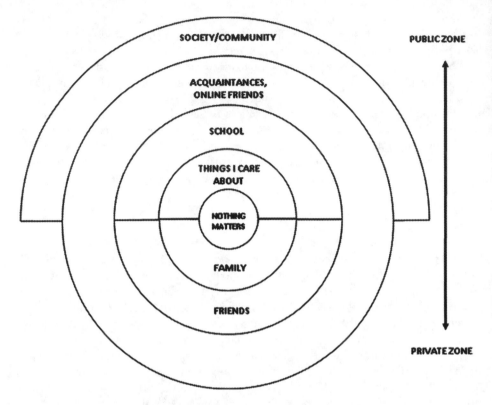

Fig. 1. Personal zones of concerns in digital safety

For a teacher as a representative of an institution (school), the public zone includes his/her classroom, school board and expectations from society. The private zone includes colleagues, students and their parents. In the center there is a zone of ignorance called "nothing matters" (see Fig. 2).

2.1.2 Types

Cyber security and digital safety cases can be divided into two areas based on their nature: a. technical concerns, where the solution involves technical approach (e.g. technical restrictions or monitoring) and b. behavioral concerns, where solutions usually are related to internal procedures, habits, guidelines etc.

At the same time, cases can also divided into institutional and personal (based on "who will solve it"). Yet in digital safety, both categories must be addressed - for example, a person can function well on institutional level (he/she follows secure practices at work) whereas being at serious risk on personal level (disregards security guidelines e.g. on Facebook), especially as the latter can have wider consequences (see Fig. 3).

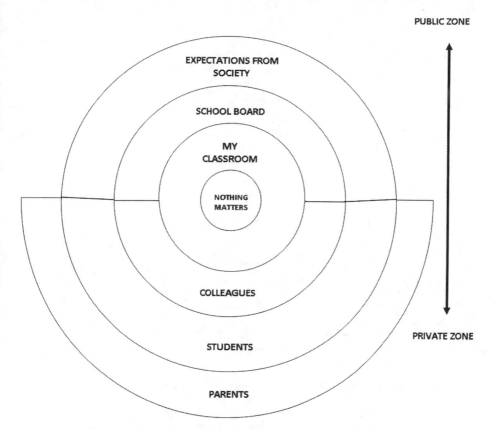

Fig. 2. Institutional zones of concerns in digital safety

2.1.3   Challenges/Concerns

Challenges or concerns of digital safety and security can be divided into 5 categories (reputation, data, fraud, health, freedom) that in turn will be divided into 9 areas of challenges with 7 layers of each. This is the basic conceptual model or taxonomy we are proposing that is inspired from the Concerns-Based Adoption Model (CBAM) (2006).

1. **Reputation**
   a. **Self-inflicted damage** (others think I am incompetent) – as I have no skills to deal with the issue, others see me as stupid. This situation can occur when the person is forced to use technology and there is no or little help available. At school the common occurrence is when people start to use BYOD solutions. In the end there can be issues with technology overuse, misuse and other risks. Without regulations there can be chaos. People can become incompetent when using websites, answering emails, translating digital content or even when the technology is not working properly;

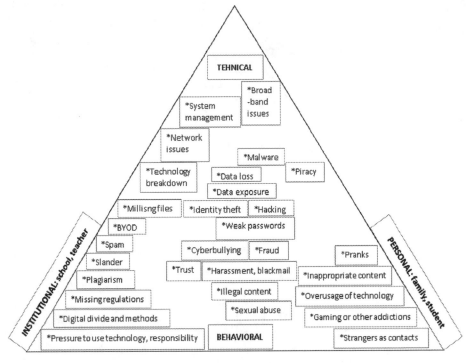

Fig. 3. A model for understanding digital safety incident types (Lorenz 2012b)

   b. **Outside damage** – it can result from spreading false information, bullying and harassment. Countermeasures are technical (know how to remove data from the internet) and psychological (raise self-esteem), there might be a need for legal or judicial assistance.
2. **Data**
   a. **Data loss** – the situation can occur on attacks on technology or when we don't have the skills to keep our data secure. A typical example can be sharing one account with more than one person;
   b. **Data exposure** – this is a concern about privacy. Examples include data leak through email, website, losing password, using spyware, hacking, too much contacts online that one does not personally know. There is a need to raise awareness how to make, store and share data in a secure manner.
3. **Fraud**
   a. **Dishonesty** – identity theft, but also spreading false information, prank calls, slandering, plagiarism or other cheating. This will often result in people becoming disillusioned as they lose trust to the society and people's honesty;
   b. **Money loss** – fraud involving material (including monetary) loss. Examples include fake bills or paid but undelivered services. These acts can often result in legal actions.

4. **Health**
   a. **Physical risk factors** – this involves technology misuse or overuse or even addiction (gaming, communicating etc.);
   b. **Mental risk factors** – includes exposure to inappropriate data (sexual abuse, child pornography, torture of animals etc.).
5. **Freedom** – various diverse issues: obstructive malware, connection and usage monitoring by others, manipulation how one is acting online, restricting freedom of speech.

2.1.4 Layers and Levels

To understand concerns or challenges we can divide them into 7 layers (see Table 1). Personal layers are quite similar to organizational levels (school as an institution). In different layers there are different solutions that can help to evolve into the next higher level of understanding. This means that when person or institution is in a lower level then it is not wise to offer them a high level solutions, or you can just predict that probably they will be stuck in "this kind of situation" that "can be solved with a help of this and this".

More examples can be found at https://goo.gl/HwExq3.

2.1.5 Solutions

Solutions in security field example in aviation safety are tied with the Bowtie model (2009), where the problem is in the middle with its causes and solutions on both sides. On the right there prevention tactics that include identifying the case, reasons and effectiveness for the tactics to solve the case before it will occur; on the left there are collected tasks that are related to damage detection, minimization of the effect and finding helpers/responsible persons to solve the bad situation (see Fig. 4).

This model gives us tools to find ways to solve one or another concern and at the same time raise awareness level and develop skills (see Fig. 5).

Example of different levels understanding we can use this simple case where teacher asked primary students to send her their email passwords to make another environment users (see Table 2).

In the students' view, there were no problem as the case was not recognized. They were happy that teacher offered this kind of solution where they could use the same password in several places. At the same time it was manipulating them to think this is a good practice. Problems in this case could be lack of privacy or hacking, as now teacher had a list of students' passwords which can be considered a serious offense. A solution for this will be awareness training to students. In the parents' view - as the parent was competent in digital safety, he insisted that this incident would be treated as cyber security expected it to be treated. Even if it was a semi-criminal case, it was not treated in that way, as in education there should be a way to people learn from the mistakes (the school board opinion). In the teacher's' view it was an easy solution as the students forget their passwords all the time, so it had affected the e-learning quality as most of the class time was spent changing passwords or fixing accounts. The solution would be to have a discussion with the school board as the institution needs

Table 1. Personal layers and Institutional levels

Layer/Level	Personal	Institutional
1 Nothing matters	"It does not involve me, I don't care". It can be solved through awareness training – to let people know these things are out there in the world	This concerns me a little or not at all
2 Need for more information	"I should know about this more". In this stage we can offer guidelines like "when you see something like this, you might want to act like that"	It's someone else's concern (parents, ICT manager, students themselves)
3 Attitude	"It is important to me as well". The support will be related to explain cases, discussions in a small group, but also public presentations and mass media influence	This can be dealt with technological restrictions – where there is a regulation that you cannot pass, then the behavior will be more secure (e.g. obligation to use 15 character password)
4 Skills	"How can I do that". There is a need for training, practice	Issues occur, we must start to deal with them with a help of experts (class teacher, psychologist, ICT manager)
5 Trial and error	"I will test it myself". In this stage people are searching for sharing experiences to another, coaching, supervision or other	At school it can be dealt with regulating the field – when it is publicly not visible, there is no problem. Schools involve also external experts like child welfare. Everyone must obey the rules and regulations even when testing the limits
6 Implementation of routines	"I don't think in that matter anymore, it's a kind of elementary, hygiene level to me". In this layer there can be only a shocking cases that can shake the person's mind or he/she has developed a need to give something back to the community, to be asked to be involved making others life easier	This is our concern. We need to discuss and solve it together. If needed there should be an active board to solve cases. Cases are also measured and logged
7 Expert	Future developments, creation of the law, development plans, finding out new threats and reporting it to the community, helping others and taking responsibility of it	We include everyone to the process of agreements and we believe in it. All concerns will be dealt with. There is an action plan. And everyone that is needed are involved in the solution finding process

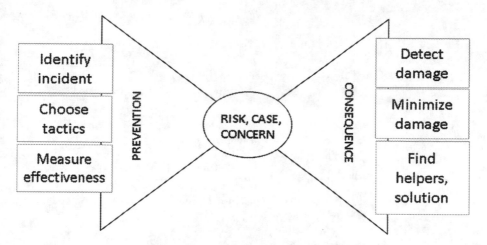

Fig. 4. A simplified bow-tie model for dealing with digital safety risks

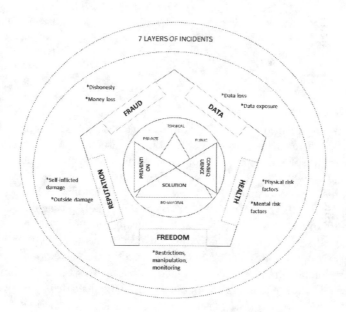

Fig. 5. The complete model to evaluate digital safety concerns of commoners

more clear regulations and understanding responsibilities of different parties, as well as to inform the teacher that this kind of action would not be a good practice.

The validation process shows that the schools still lack understanding about different internet safety issues and their solutions. We also understood that the level of action is related to school culture and the level they are on. Most schools are lagging behind in the level 2–4 depending of the situation as in every school there are teachers that "don't use the internet and so don't see it as his/her problem" and most of the schools have had first entry level training in internet security but see the solution to be

Table 2. Sample cases

Connected persons	Students	Parents	Teacher
Personal/Public	Personal	Personal	Personal
Technical/Behavioral	Technical	Behavioral	Technical/Behavioral
Concern	Freedom	Dishonesty	Self-inflicted damage
Layers/Levels	1	7	2
Prevention	Can't use services that are offered	Understanding the nature of the issue (why it can happen, is it a malicious act or not)	Knowledge about personal data security issues was low
Consequences	Cannot participate in school's activities	Trust in the institution will decrease	Data exposure, hacking
Who will I get help from/What is needed to be done	ICT personnel will help	Web Police, School board, talking to the teacher	Need for rules and regulations in the institution regarding personal data protection and passwords

part of ICT managers, the psychologist's or class teacher's job. Only one school had an idea for a plan where teachers and students would get training once in every three year or had a board to solve the cases. No one had significant written regulations, logging the events and knowing where to turn when they needed external help, except e-police services as this kind of campaign has been going on in Estonia for 4 years by now.

We propose that this model can be used to develop a tool that can collect cases from a everyday life of a student - both personal and institutional. First it helps to reflect to the student itself what she/he can do in this situation, if she/he really is thinking of the solution. Also, as these cases can be collected and refused to give good examples how different ways in different levels people can solve issues. This can be a learning tool, at the same time it can be a tool to also not only understand the cases, but solve them and improve awareness training both in teacher's professional development studies and students.

3   Conclusions

A big problem is that digital safety issues seem either to be of equal importance to the overworked school administration or are dismissed completely as "parental challenge", not an educational one. The biggest security risk in the future is predicted to be "located between the keyboard and the chair", defense always lagging behind attackers and challenges. Training security mindset is not only a workplace and adults challenge, it should be dealt already on a basic school level, where the school can give students appropriate digital skills and security understanding that can help them throughout their lives.

For different levels of awareness, different solutions are needed. Our model helps to detect low level incidents and disturbances that influence commoners' attitudes. Some students are in the level that they don't know and they don't care, others in the same citations might see lot of things that can go wrong and prepare for it, that the threat will not realize. Model helps also teacher and school leader to understand in what areas they are in a low level position and where they might be already an expert. Model also helps to choose solutions – will we need regulations, awareness trainings, specialist help, technical regulations or other.

Based on the model above, most digital safety issues found at school are related to data, reputation, free will and fraud (people are not honest). When students or teachers act then there is a fine line between ethics and real life regulations as policy and law. Usually at school, even the cases that has a hint of criminal behavior (sharing personal data without permission, weak passwords and password sharing etc.) will not be prosecuted with full intent. Eventually these cases are solved by removing the offending data from the internet and hoping for the best or changing the password and account regulations. Most of the time the issues are not dealt with as the threat is not being recognized or is taken as not so serious that the case might need. Sometimes the case is being noticed but no one knows how to act on it. At the same time most cases can escalate rather quickly to more serious issues that needs police or court attention, depending of the country, school and people. When solving these cases, the solutions fell into the field of awareness training; arguing and discussing with each other and community; implementations of new rules and regulations both technical and behavioral.

So we also propose to develop a tool using our model to let digital safety incidents be simulated - the tool should reflect in which direction should think before acting or when something has already happened, the tool can point you in the right direction to solve the case. So we could call the tool also as "prevention" not only "solution" but definitely both cases are presented. The perspective would be students anonymously tell stories, through which also feedback as solution is given by the model. In this way the model will be enriched with new cases and solutions. This model is for younger people to analyze cases independently or together with teacher and find the solution. For time to time experts will look at the given solutions and correct the model if needed. Also web police and teachers are engaged to develop understanding of cases and its solutions.

The tool based on our model would help to raise awareness and through this also solve problems ("It helped me without having to reveal my ignorance or involve the police!").

Acknowledgements. This study was supported by the Tiger University Program of the Information Technology Foundation for Education.

References

1. Be Smart Online: NPO Estonian Union for Child Welfare (2012). http://www.targaltinternetis.ee/en/projektist/
2. Bowtie model: Introduction to Bowtie model, Civil Aviation Authority (2009). http://www.caa.co.uk/default.aspx?catid=2786&pagetype=90
3. Conceptual framework for increasing society's commitment in ICT: approaches in general and higher education for motivating ICT-related career choices and improving competences for applying and developing ICT, Tartu University (2015). https://sisu.ut.ee/ikt/
4. Concerns-Based Adoption Model: American Institutes for Research (SEDL) (2006). http://www.sedl.org/cbam/
5. Connected with mobile safety: Look@World Foundation (2013). http://www.nutikaitse.ee/nutikaitse-2017-projektist/
6. CreativeClass: BalticComputerSystems Eesti (2014). http://www.bcskoolitus.ee/creativeclass/
7. Cyber security strategy 2008–2013 in Estonia: Republic of Estonia Ministry of Defence (2008). https://valitsus.ee/sites/default/files/content-editors/arengukavad/kuberjulgeoleku_strateegia_2008-2013.pdf
8. Cyber security strategy 2014–2017 in Estonia: Republic of Estonia Ministry of Economic Affairs and Communications (2014). https://www.mkm.ee/sites/default/files/kuberjulgeoleku_strateegia_2014-2017.pdf
9. Digiturvis: Tallinn University, Republic of Estonia Ministry of Economic Affairs and Communications (2015). http://1drv.ms/1N7KmtZ
10. E-Safety Label: European SchoolNet (2012). http://www.esafetylabel.eu/web/guest/about
11. Information Society Development plan 2020 in Estonia: Republic of Estonia Ministry of Economic Affairs and Communications (2013). http://www.riso.ee/sites/default/files/elfinder/article_files/infoyhiskonna_arengukava_2020_f.pdf
12. InSafe: European SchoolNet (2014). http://www.saferinternet.org/about
13. Internal Security Development Plan 2015–2020: Republic of Estonia Ministry of Interior (2015). https://valitsus.ee/sites/default/files/content-editors/arengukavad/siseturvalisuse_arengukava_2015-2020_kodulehele.pdf
14. ISTE standards - International Society for Technology in Education: Information Technology Foundation for Education (HITSA) (2012). http://www.innovatsioonikeskus.ee/sites/default/files/ISTE/ISTE_NETS_S%20%28Estonian%29.pdf
15. Livingstone, S., Haddon, L.: EU kids online. Z. Für Psychol./J. Psychol. **217**(4), 236 (2009)
16. Local Authority Information Society Development Plan 2015: Republic of Estonia Ministry of Interior (2011). http://kov.riik.ee/wp-content/uploads/2013/04/KOVIYAK_2012-EGA-l%C3%B5ppversioon.pdf
17. Lorenz, B., Kikkas, K.: Socially engineered commoners as cyber warriors-Estonian future or present? In: 2012 4th International Conference on Cyber Conflict (CYCON). IEEE (2012)
18. Lorenz, B., Kikkas, K., Laanpere, M.: Comparing children's e-Safety strategies with guidelines offered by adults. Electron. J. e-Learn. **10**(3), 326–338 (2012)
19. Lorenz, B., Kikkas, K., Laanpere, M.: Bottom-up development of e-Safety policy for estonian schools. In: Estevez, E., Janssen, M. (eds.) 5th International Conference on Theory and Practice of Electronic Governance (ICEGOV 2011), 26–28 September 2011, pp. 309–312. ACM International Conference Proceedings Series. ACM (2011)
20. Lorenz, B., Kikkas, K., Laanpere, M.: Exploring the impact of school culture on school's internet safety policy development. In: Stephanidis, C. (ed.) HCII 2013, Part II. CCIS, vol. 374, pp. 57–60. Springer, Heidelberg (2013)

21. Mobile/Smart Security study: Look@World Foundation (2014). http://www.vaatamaailma.ee/nutiturvalisuse-uuring-seitse-last-kumnest-saab-nutitelefoni-kasutada-piiramatult
22. National Defense Strategy: Republic of Estonia Ministry of Defence (2010). https://valitsus.ee/sites/default/files/content-editors/arengukavad/riigikaitse_strateegia.pdf
23. PIAAC Estonia: Republic of Estonia Ministry of Education and Research (2014). https://www.hm.ee/et/tegevused/uuringud-ja-statistika/piaac
24. PISA Estonia: Republic of Estonia Ministry of Education and Research (2012). https://www.hm.ee/et/tegevused/uuringud-ja-statistika/pisa
25. TALIS Estonia: Republic of Estonia Ministry of Education and Research (2008). https://www.hm.ee/et/tegevused/uuringud-ja-statistika/talis
26. Teachers Professional Standard V: Educational Qualification Board (2013). http://www.hm.ee/index.php?popup=download&id=4321

Digital Turn in the Schools of Estonia: Obstacles and Solutions

Birgy Lorenz[1,2(✉)], Kaido Kikkas[1,2], and Mart Laanpere[1,2]

[1] School of Digital Technologies, Tallinn University,
Narva Road 25, 10120 Tallinn, Estonia
{Birgy.Lorenz,Kaido.Kikkas,Mart.Laanpere}@tlu.ee
[2] Estonian Information Technology College, Raja St 4C, 12616 Tallinn, Estonia

Abstract. Schools from all over the world are moving into the direction of using more e-learning, digital gadgets and BYOD (*Bring Your Own Device*). In the Estonian Strategy for Lifelong Learning 2020, the switch to 1:1 computing in classroom is called "Digital Turn". The strategy relies on expectations that smarter use of personal digital devices will improve not only digital literacy of pupils, but also their academic achievements in various subjects. The Estonian government plans to allocate 47 million Euros of national and EU structural funds until year 2020 for this purpose. There is also interest in improving digital skills of school-leavers on the side of the industry, as the Estonian ICT sector expects to double the turnover within the next 4–5 years. The sectoral analysis estimated the need for 8000 new employees in ICT companies. To achieve this, the industry has supported various educational programs like the Look@World Foundation's Smart Lab project, Samsung Digital Turn project for schools, using Raspberry Pi-s at school supported by TransferWise, Microsoft's Partners in Learning projects and so on.

Challenges for the digital turn are related to people's involvement (teachers, school leaders, students, parents, officers); resources (gadgets, time, salary, maintenance); promises (this is beneficial for improving the students' skills and competences and also is the only way); lack of analysis (act more, measure less). In this article we will study the Samsung's Digital Turn project applications for the schools 2014 and 2015 in order to understand what are the goals for the schools when they think of digital turn; we also have asked school ICT administrators, educational technologists and school leaders to list seven issues that come into their mind that should be death with in the process, and surveyed teachers of one school over a 4-year period, tracking the changes in using technology as well as learning and teaching.

We will analyze the data to understand the trends and difficulties schools will face during this journey. This information is needed to train all other 450 schools that have not started their digital turn change yet, but are forced to act soon. The trends in digital turn projects will tell us the maturing process and goals that the schools have as opportunities and strengths while the list of difficulties shows the project's weaknesses and threats. Looking at one school over 4 years will help us to understand the change, especially the areas that have changed in teachers' practices.

© Springer International Publishing Switzerland 2016
P. Zaphiris and A. Ioannou (Eds.): LCT 2016, LNCS 9753, pp. 722–731, 2016.
DOI: 10.1007/978-3-319-39483-1_65

In the conclusion we propose a list of actions that can be used to meet the challenges that can ruin the digital turn for most schools. We also propose an area of measures where the digital turn is the most visible.

Keywords: Digital turn · Digital skills · Innovation at schools

1 Introduction

Digital media, digitalization and e-learning changes our behavior, transforms the way we do and experience things, work life and also education [28]. New literacy practices are arising that will benefit from current solutions in many fields [20]. Trends of the internet shows us that computer-oriented solutions are designed 'one size fits all' (like television) rather than more interactive ones (see also Gilster [7]).

Digital divide is not only a challenge of old vs new generation, it also lurks between students - over the years, there are many interesting studies pointing out that tech-savvy students rely more on internet to finish homework or experience social interactions [14]. Whether today's students learn differently or not is heavily debated - while common understanding is that "world and learning has changed", some researchers point out that it is not so [26]. At the same time there are socio-economic issues stemming from background and culture one comes from [10]. The PISA study also looks at connections between background and academic results and they show that this key difference is present in some countries, while in others (like Estonia) it is not that problematic [24].

In Estonia, some interesting discussions have been taking place over changed learning and teaching in the context of development of national curricula. Challenges that have been pointed out are related to student's focus, skills of planning, communication and presentation skills, problem solving, and motivation [14]. The Estonian Lifelong Learning Strategy provides guidelines for schools to emphasize students' special needs, cooperation with the industry and digital skills [5]. In 2015 there was coexistence of different learning theories at schools - some teachers lean towards older, more traditional approach, others being more liberal. The need to train teachers in both technological and theoretical aspects of learning has been stressed [1].

1.1 Situation in Estonia

1.1.1 Strategies

In Estonia, the sights have been set to the period of 2020–2050, attempting to predict what will happen in the world and what kind of students/workers will be needed by that time. At the same time, strategic plans and scenarios are often developed thinking of only near future, or even according to political election results. The Estonian Lifelong Learning Strategy mentioned above is one of the key documents that all of the stakeholders have agreed with. It includes ideas of changed learning, relearning and unlearning; motivating school leaders and teachers; benefits or effects of lifelong learning on workforce, digital turn and equality. Another strategy that focuses more on knowledge-based Estonia states that it is important to have good-quality, diverse and internationally competitive research sector to support economy and society [25].

The digital turn focuses mostly on schools improvements - there are many work-groups that discuss digital literacy skills of the students and teachers as well as ways of measuring them. For example, the EU Commission has published guidelines that all states can use to compare digital skills [6]. The Estonian Ministry of Education and Research website contains the Digital Turn Programme 2015–2018 that points out three directions: digital culture integration with teaching and learning; development and accessibility of digital teaching materials, and equipping the schools (network and technology) [4]. The Information Technology Foundation for Education (HITSA) has assured that they have means and goals to improve digital skills on every level (kindergarten to university), are able to support special digital education needs at voca-tional and university level and maintain the information system and structure needed [9].

1.1.2   Research

Research involving Estonian teachers, students and digital skills gives us a controversy - student's state that teachers do not use technology in class and teachers disagree. The common issue is that teachers in fact do use a lot of technology to prepare lessons and use presentation tools, but students in the classroom are considered active participants allowed to use technology. Also from TALIS research [29] we learned that school leaders are not that worried about lack of possibilities concerning computers and software. It is confirmed further when we look at the PISA 2009 [17] and PISA 2012 [11] results suggesting that school leaders do not see digital improvement as a priority task for their schools.

Overall the national curricula from 2012 supports digital technology use at schools and points out that every subject has its own commitment. For example, study of languages (Estonian, English, Russian, German or other) is meant to introduce digital communication tools, translation, using forums, email, social networks and blogs, and textual analysis; mathematics is to also promote cooperation, using different statistical programs, simulations and models, visualization and research; national sciences (Estonian language, history and culture) should include maps, videos and use of learning environments; social sciences should support individual or group activities, international cooperation, diagrams and data analysis; art and music are also obliged to teach about online museums, archives and databases, Creative Commons, sharing data, creativity as 3D, video and animation; and finally, informatics (which is voluntary) should focus on virtual identity, web meetings, wikis, podcasts, internet safety and security etc. [18].

The Digital Turn workgroup at the Ministry of Education and Research has also asked Norstat to survey teachers, students, parents, school leaders and local authorities to understand attitudes towards increased use of digital devices at school. The results are not published yet, but overall sentiment is that the respondents were positive about schools starting to use more technologies (mobile devices, laptops, develop WiFi and digital materials). There are some challenges regarding health, concentration and class management issues, manual skills development, support and training, or cost of tools. Also, teachers expect that the chosen solution rather leans towards using school devices than BYOD, and government should provide free learning and teaching materials for everyone. At the same time, students and parents are more or less interested of using their own devices.

Due to prominence of the ICT sector in Estonia, there are many different studies regarding ICT students and their profession. The Tartu University study shows that 20–25 % of all applicants are women - this ratio stays the same throughout the university and later work life, even if the probability to get accepted is 12 % higher than for men. The decision to go to the IT sector is often related to an earlier experience solving problems or doing something practical like creating a website or a game; other factors include IT lessons or personally knowing someone from the field [13]. The Praxis study predicts IT sector developments and workers need towards year 2020 [12]. According to that, there is a need for more support, database and system administrators and developers, a slightly smaller need is for leadership and design professions. Of people currently active in the sector only 57 % have some kind of academic degree, and 16 % have vocational education. According to the study, the IT Sector currently needs 2500+ new employees (the number for other sectors combined is estimated to be 4000), of which 2/3 should be specialists with higher education. In order to raise interest in the ICT field, many companies have started to run or support different educational programs.

1.1.3   Supporting Innovations and Projects

'Digital jumps' are characteristic to Estonia. Projects backed by the Tiger Leap Foundation have been present in our education starting from 1997. At first, the main goals were to change the way of thinking and harness the digital world - to get schools connected, teachers to develop their own materials and create their own training courses, also providing teachers with laptops. Since then, the Tiger Leap has moved into many other sectors in Estonia where innovation and change is needed. Today the project is managed by HITSA and they offer several training to teachers and school leaders regarding the digital turn. For example, the "Leadership in teaching and learning process" is a school team challenge where 4–6 people (principal, main teacher, ICT manager and teachers) set their school's goals and solve the problems with the help of external experts. The program lasts 6 months [8]. For teachers they offer various trainings starting from basic computer lessons to programming and from 3D printing to webinars. HITSA also provides support for coding, robotics and other technology use in classroom via the Progetiiger program and runs the Digital Innovative Classroom "Smart Lab".

From the university aside there are two-three major players - the Centre for Innovation in Education at Tallinn University (provides teacher training, project days and training for working teachers), the Pedagogicum at the University of Tartu pro-vides their own training and solutions via the Network of Innovation schools, and the Mektory Innovation Centre at Tallinn University of Technology provides schools with training for students and teachers about science. There is also the "Noored kooli" (Youth to Schools) initiative that is similar to "Teach for America" in the US.

The local authority has to maintain the schools' technical equipment and network connections as well as provide tools and services that help to improve education. Some authorities have stepped up to do even more. Usually they make a competition and let schools compete for the prize money. For example, some Pärnu area schools started their own Digital turn project [16]. Also the council of Tartu has started to test out "open learning area" and digital school implementations with assistance from EU funds

[21]. In Tallinn, the Department of Education initiated the "Digi-idea" project giving out three prizes for innovative projects [22].

Likewise, IT industry has pushed schools to reach higher quality standards and activeness level of changing the education and implementation of technologies. For, example, starting from 2009 Microsoft has run several projects under the aegis of their Partners in Learning program [19]. BCS Training has a Creative Classroom project that has been funded by Erasmus+ [3]. Samsung Baltics started several Digital Turn projects in Estonia and Latvia starting from 2014, with the common idea to train 6 members of the school (including school leaders) who will proceed to innovate the rest of the school and community. At the end of every year, there will be a prize of 10 000 euros for one of the schools [23]. Also, the SmartLab project that is funded by Estonian Association of Information Technology and Telecommunications runs small-scale projects focusing on robotics, coding and engineering education as extracurricular activity [27].

In conclusion, there is a drive from the industry as well as from the government to make education more digital and innovative. Yet, schools are worried about possible setbacks. We have followed the Samsung Digital Turn schools project over 2 years in order to find out which steps have the schools taken to implement various technological and theoretical aspects, what are the challenges, how to measure success, and what are suggestions to others.

2 Methods

During the last four years, we have seen different ways for schools to handle the digital turn. In this study we have collected data from experts to learn about current challenges, also looking at project proposals addressing the digital turn prepared by schools over the last two years and the published results and changes from a number of schools over several years.

Our aim is to find out:

- what are the first steps when they start to implement changes, what do they envision to be the catalyst for actual change?
- what are the changes that can happen in one school over 4 years?
- what are the common mistakes and problems that experts point out in the digital turn projects and how to avoid or solve them?

The first answer could be found through qualitative data analysis the Samsung Digital turn projects from 2014 and 2015. In this project, 109 schools applied (43 first year, 66 more schools joined later). The application consisted of information of their activity level in digital turn preparations, their dream project for 9 months. Every year 8–12 schools are chosen for the full training program and competition where the first prize is 10 000 euros. The program content and training is provided by Tallinn University experts - professors, lecturers and researchers. We also we studied the published data from three schools that have documented their digital turn over several years. These are large (over 700 students) schools from all over Estonia, known for their innovation and digital drive. The data was collected from their websites.

The second question was answered using input from ICT technologists, ICT managers, school leaders and active teachers that participated in open discussion about "what are the 7 mistakes that school can do regarding digital turn". Their ideas were collected in 7 days using a social media discussion board. Everyone was able to say something, comment others' sayings and ask questions. 26 people shared their thoughts, 12 of them provided a full list of difficulties. The respondents were identified (rather than anonymous) and they were experts in the area. We annotated given sentences using Open Coding method 2–3 people and analyzed the results using grounded theory to discover categories [2].

3 Results and Discussion

The results show that the schools that joined the project during its first year were already active or very active in the field, while 19 % of the late joiners were newcomers (no previous significant digital turn project experience). It should be noted that there was no visible correlation between the schools overall activity level in digital turn and technological steps like implementing online shared folders, mobile technology usage, public WiFi, also the size of the school did not matter.

Thus, while all the applicants had good idea what should be done to implement 1:1 computing, using and developing digital materials or creating more student-centered learning processes, there was difference regarding BYOD - most active schools were more willing to test out new gadgets brought in by students and implement them into everyday schoolwork.

The more active the school was in digital turn, the more higher and complex goals they were aiming at. Less active schools wanted to solve extracurricular and informal learning related challenges (setting up a robotics lab, improving WiFi quality in library etc.), while the active ones focused on more general categories like international relations, value-based learning, immersive language learning, qualitative feedback, developing their own materials and learning systems etc.

We also found that the manageable amount of students participating was in the range of 50–350. Thus small schools were able to engage in whole school projects, larger ones had to focus on a specific age or area group.

Most popular topics in 2014 were development of e-learning materials and using mobile technology, but also creating videos, cross-curricular activities and systematization of technology usage and improvement of digital skills of the students. In 2015 the focus shifted to teacher training and most important keyword was digital skills of teachers and students, but also learning stories, community involvement, nature trails etc. Thus we notice an evolution - at first they started with narrow, specific requirements, moving ahead to the community level later on. A follow-up of the three schools from a year after the Digital Turn project can be found at https://goo.gl/jkp7uv.

The second part of the study looked at the mistakes preventing the digital turn was the topic of a discussion involving school experts (mainly educational technologists and ICT managers, but also school leaders and active teachers), the main outcomes are listed below:

- **Lack of resources** - while the problem seems to be endemic in education, it is possible to find funding for digital turn activities if supporters can see the actual impact. While there is a need for mobile devices, new PCs, software and networking to start the digital turn project, schools make the abovementioned mistake of 'thinking too small', stating the specific need but failing to show its greater impact. Many schools obtain technology sporadically ("we have the sum X and have to spend it by the end of the year"), the fact that most local authorities are unaware of the actual needs of schools in their area does not help either.

- **Technology malfunctions resulting from misuse** - most smart gadgets of today are meant to be personal by definition, yet many schools designate e.g. tablets to common use (citing their small numbers). There are several maintenance issues that makes the school-owned tablets a security risk. This kind of "digital communism" results in devices being unmaintained ("if it belongs to everyone, who should care for it?"), there is also a serious lack of guidelines and lists of which applications should be used and which ones avoided. In addition, school WiFi networks are often designed with small loads in mind (as small is cheap) and do not handle the spiking workloads from BYOD well (e.g. a network designed for 120 users is actually used by 400).

- **Missing support** - this includes several aspects from general school management to tech support to training. This is exacerbated further by serious overload of teachers - as they are supposed to use their leisure time to familiarize themselves with the new technology, lack of support will result in 'dropping the ball', disillusionment and letting go.

- **Teachers are not on board** - due to the reasons mentioned above, many teachers are afraid of 'rocking the boat' - both fearing the unknown and an ever-increasing overload play a role here. Many teachers do not own the devices, using a shared one at school has but a limited training effect. Due to this, many teachers are actively against any increase of digital technology at school.

- **Lack of community involvement** - as digital skills and knowledge of students often exceed the teacher's, they will sometimes 'test' the teacher during classes or switch to other activities as the teacher is unable to manage the situation. One solution to instill the proper 'digital etiquette' could be at home, but parents often display the same symptoms as teachers (no time, ignorance and negativism, fear of costs etc.).

- **Immeasurable benefits** - this is possibly the most important factor in understanding the obstacles of implementing digital turn at school. Currently the impact measurement has mostly been limited to quantitative aspects (number of devices, speed of networks etc.) while it should become much more qualitative (impact on learning, changes of attitudes etc.).

- **Other issues** - this was the area with many different variables, e.g. school culture and its effect to the change; understanding of national curricula goals; digitalization of the sake of digitalization; going digital for a campaign not because there is a real need. Also some schools said that they are not motivated by being average in the field as then they will not benefit as much (as most projects and funding go to the 'stars'). And there is also lack of constructive criticism - while nobody dares to say that is a "bad thing", the discussion moves to the level of "is it for me" (in short, the question is whether the digital world is 'just for geeks' or everyone). In comparison, looking at the government programs and strategies, all of them assume that the matter is long settled.

We see that Estonian schools are quite independent in the things they do - they look for guidance from outside partners, national curricula and strategies, but decide their actions by themselves. The challenge is that also the teachers are so independent that sometimes even the school leaders and school goals can be overruled. This means that attempts to do the rapid digital turn by forcing it with strategies, programs and events (and even money) has a short-lived effect. So the key is to find a common ground with the schools, let them choose their own path and set the overall goals. If the schools get more people on board the chance to succeed is much greater than if starting alone and doing the digital turn with just a small group of people.

We have formulated the following suggestions:

- **Governmental stakeholders and ministries** should analyze strategies and the curriculum, refraining from politicizing action plans. For all important decisions, clear communication should be provided about where the funding comes from, what are the metrics and what are the expected roles for all sides. Partners on all levels should be included in this.
- **Local authorities** should accumulate knowledge about governmental level strategies and possibilities and share that information to school leaders in their area. Again, these activities should be inclusive, involving not only the top schools but also less successful ones.
- **Industry** should provide insights about future developments, employment and expectations to future employees. School need help in determining the goals and developing curricula, especially from practical perspectives.
- **Universities and research facilities** should provide academic insights of the development in schools and analysis of both positive and negative trends. They are essential in supporting schools in becoming able to develop the 'big picture' and setting the goals larger than just 'improve the WiFi in cafeteria'.
- **Schools** should focus on plans that are not only directed to acquiring technologies, but to change and develop learning communities and culture. They should strive to train teachers, students and parents about future learning perspectives and benefits on the school level.
- **Teachers** should become more welcoming towards new learning methods, seeing beneficial tools and methods that can be used to activate students. They also should provide an example by being lifelong learners themselves.
- **Students and parents** should strive to be part of learning culture rather than bystanders or opponents. Inclusion from both sides is the key.

4   Conclusion

In carrying out the digital turn, the most successful schools are dealing with the human resources. They discuss issues and developments with the wider community – their goal is to include everyone and aim high. Lack of technical resources can be dealt with the help of industry, local authority or various projects. A more difficult problem is the learning community and ideas about the curricula where new and old way of doing things clash. In order to solve them, a balanced approach is needed where all involved sides will be able to contribute. We set goals to explain obstacles and solutions to the digital turn program in Estonia and we have accomplished that by including real digital turn best exemplary schools stories and ICT technologists, ICT managers, school leaders and active teacher's ideas about what is wrong and how we can fix it inside out.

Acknowledgements. This study was supported by the Tiger University Program of the Information Technology Foundation for Education.

References

1. Altuna, J., Lareki, A.: Analysis of the use of digital technologies in schools that implement different learning theories. J. Educ. Comput. Res. (2015). doi:10.1177/0735633115597869
2. Borgatti, S.: Introducstion to Grounded Theory. Analytictech. http://www.analytictech.com/mb870/introtogt.htm. Accessed 21 Oct 2015
3. Creative Class: About the project (2014). http://www.bcskoolitus.ee/creativeclass/?page_id=79. Accessed 21 Dec 2015
4. Digipööre: Republic of Estonia Ministry of Education and Research web (2014). https://www.hm.ee/et/tegevused/digipoore. Accessed 21 Dec 2015
5. Estonian Lifelong Strategy 2020. Haridus- ja Teadusministeerium. https://www.hm.ee/et/elukestva-oppe-strateegia-2020
6. Ferrari, A.: DIGCOMP: a framework for developing and understanding digital competence in Europe. European Commission, Joint Research Centre, Institute for Prospective Technological Studies (Report EUR 26035 EN) (2013)
7. Gilster, P., Glister, P.: Digital Literacy. Wiley Computer Pub., New York (1997)
8. Haridusjuhtide koolitused. Hitsa (2014). https://www.innovatsioonikeskus.ee/et/events-tags/haridusjuhtide-koolitused
9. HITSA strateegia ja visioon: HITSA veeb (2014). http://www.hitsa.ee/sihtasutusest/visioon. Accessed 21 Dec 2015)
10. Hohlfeld, T.N., Ritzhaupt, A.D., Barron, A.E., Kemker, K.: Examining the digital divide in K-12 public schools: four-year trends for supporting ICT literacy in Florida. Computer. Educ. **51**(4), 1648–1663 (2008)
11. Jukk, H., Puksand, H., Kitsing, M., Lindemann, K., Henno, I., Tire, G., Lorenz, B.: PISA 2012-Eesti tulemused (2013)
12. Jürgenson, A., Mägi, E., Pihor, K., Batueva, V., Rozeik, H., Arukaevu, R.: Eesti IKT kompetentsidega tööjõu hetkeseisu ja vajaduse kaardistamine. Praxis (2013)
13. Kori, K., Pedaste, M., Niitsoo, M., Kuusik, R., Altin, H., Tõnisson, E., Murtazin, K.: Why do students choose to study information and communications technology? Eur. Procedia Soc. Behav. Sci. **191**, 2867–2872 (2014)
14. Levin, D., Arafeh, S.: The digital disconnect: the widening gap between Internet-savvy students and their schools (2002)
15. Liblik, P.: Ootused huvitavale koolile, Huvitav Kool, blogi (2014). http://huvitavkool.blogspot.com.ee/p/avalikkuse-ootused-huvitavale-koolile.html. Accessed 21 Dec 2016
16. Link, E-G.: Algas konkurss "Pärnu linna digipööre" Pärnu Postimees (2015). http://www.parnupostimees.ee/3211137/algas-konkurss-parnu-linna-digipoore. Accessed 21 Dec 2015

17. Lorenz, B.: Eesti õpilaste PISA 2009 IKT-alased küsimuste vastused vihjavad kasutamata ressurssidele koolides (2013)
18. Maadvere, I.: IKT uues põhikooli riiklikus õppekavas, Tallinna Haridusamet (2010). http://www.tallinn.ee/est/haridusasutused/g7677s51441
19. Microsoft Eesti: Võrgustiku partner Microsoft aitab arendada koolist innovaatilise kooli, Unistused ellu! (2013). http://www.unistusedellu.ee/content/v%C3%B5rgustiku-partner-microsoft-aitab-arendada-koolist-innovaatilise-kooli. Accessed 21 Dec 2015
20. Mills, K.A.: A review of the "digital turn" in the new literacy studies. Revi. Educ. Res. **80** (2), 246–271 (2010)
21. Pintson, M-L.: Avatud õpiruum aitab teisiti õppida, Tartu Postimees (2015). http://tartu.postimees.ee/3337229/avatud-opiruum-aitab-teisiti-oppida. Accessed 21 Dec 2015
22. Rannala, R.: Uuenduskonkursi „Digimõte" võitis "Põhja-Tallinna nutitsirkus" (2015) http://www.tallinn.ee/est/haridus/Uudis-IKT-konverentsil-autasustati-uuenduskonkursi-Digimote-voitjaid. Accessed 21 Dec 2015
23. Samsungi Digipööre: Projektist (2014). http://www.samsungdigipoore.ee/projektist/. Accessed 21 Dec 2015
24. Zoido, P.: How do some students overcome their socioeconomic background. PISA IN FOCUS, 5 (2011)
25. TA - Teadmuspõhine Eesti, Eesti teadus- ja arendustegevuse ning innovatsiooni strateegia 2014–2020. https://www.riigiteataja.ee/aktilisa/3290/1201/4002/strateegia.pdf
26. Thompson, P.: The digital natives as learners: Technology use patterns and approaches to learning. Comput. Educ. **65**, 12–33 (2013)
27. Vaata maailma: Nuti Labor - IKT huviringid noortele (2012). http://www.vaatamaailma.ee/projektid/ikt-huviringid-noortele. Accessed 21 Dec 2015
28. Westera, W.: The Digital Turn: How the Internet Transforms Our Existence. AuthorHouse (2012)
29. Übius, Ü., Kall, K., Loogma, K., Ümarik, M.: Rahvusvaheline vaade õpetamisele ja õppimisele. OECD rahvusvahelise õpetamise ja õppimise uuringu TALIS 2013 tulemused (2014)

Creating Digital Learning Environment for Design in India – Experiences in Institutional Collaboration for Content Generation

Ravi Mokashi Punekar[1]([⊠]), Ravi Pooviah[2], and Bibhudutta Baral[3]

[1] Indian Institute of Technology Guwahati, Guwahati, India
mokashi@iitg.ernet.in
[2] Indian Institute of Technology Bombay, Mumbai, India
ravi@iitb.ac.in
[3] National Institute of Design, Bangalore, Bangalore, India
bibhudutta@nid.edu

Abstract. The paper presents institutional experiences between three higher educational institutions of national excellence in India who were collaborating in the creation of a digital learning environment for Design in India undertaken under as a project under the Government of India funded project 'National Mission in Education - through Information Communication Technology' (NME-ICT).

Keywords: National Mission Project in Education · Design education · e-Learning · Higher educational institutions in India

1 Introduction

To face the challenges of the emergent knowledge economy, the Ministry of Human Resource Development (MHRD), Government of India, brought focus on the education sector into a national mission mode in early 2009. It formed an expert committee to formulate the broad framework for reforms necessary for the education sector and announced the 'National Mission Project in Education through Information Communication Technology' (NME-ICT). The objectives of this project were to be met by developing suitable pedagogical methods of various classes, intellectual calibers and research in e-learning and outline curriculum for the different knowledge in a systematic and unambiguous manner following well established pedagogical principles.

The committee laid out guidelines and invited leading Higher Education Institutions (HEI) to participate in development of courseware by proposing the following terms of reference:

1. It outlined the composition of the course design and development team and methodology to be followed.
2. Course content was to be delivered through a dedicated web portal specifically developed for this purpose.

© Springer International Publishing Switzerland 2016
P. Zaphiris and A. Ioannou (Eds.): LCT 2016, LNCS 9753, pp. 732–739, 2016.
DOI: 10.1007/978-3-319-39483-1_66

3. The inclusion of faculty members from partner institutions was strongly recommended.
4. Deliverables expected of the course team was articulated under the heads related to:

  – Curriculum Design activities.
  – Curriculum Development activities.

The learning out-comes was based on specifications and guidelines outlined in the Washington International Accord on Education.

This paper presents the outcome of one such project undertaken under the NME-ICT project. It focused on the domain of Design Education in India, the contents of which are available on an e-learning platform called D'source (http://www.dsource.in). Its relevance must be considered in the context of the current status of Design education in India and the importance of the need for such an online platform in design learning for prospective learners. It envisaged that it would add value to design education and contribute to the growing demands of the creative industry in India.

2 The Case for Creating Digital Learning Environment for Design Training in India

2.1 Design and the Creative Industry in India – Some Facts

The India Design Report 2011 published by the Confederation of Indian Industry (1), highlights an overview of the evolving nature of opportunities amongst various sectors of Indian Industry. The services extended by creative industries in India include visual communication design, product/industrial design, digital and multimedia design and needs of the vast social sector.

Leading Indian industrial houses meet their needs by sourcing in-house design talent, of design firms from abroad or from amongst these freelance design firms located in metro cities. There is increasing acceptance amongst Indian industry that investment in good design means good business. However the vast MSME sector in India still offers a vast potential for design intervention and needs design services to make them competitive.

The acceptance of Design as a contributor for industrial growth is reflected in the setting up of the India Design Council (IDC). The Government of India (GoI) has now put in place a National Design Policy document and a plan towards its implementation. Design Education forms an important focus in the National Design Policy. IDC has instituted the India Design Mark as a symbol of Good Design. Over the last few years there is seen an increasing trend in Indian manufacturers seeking recognitions for the India Design mark for their products.

2.2 Design Education and Professional Designers

Till early Nineties the National Institute of Design in Ahmedabad and the Industrial Design Centre, IIT Bombay in Mumbai were the only two leading Design schools in

India. In the three decades since then, there are nearly 30 Design Schools and over 100 commercial art colleges in India that offer different domains of specialization. The number of professional designers, around 8,000 in number, is still very small. This number is expected to grow exponentially in the next few years. It is probable that India will have over 200 design colleges by 2025 and over 1000 by 2030. Clearly making a case for supplementing training inputs through alternate channels such as ICT enabled synchronous and asynchronous modes of e-education.

To bridge the wide gap in knowledge dissemination in the design education domain, three of the leading institutions viz. National Institute of Design (NID) through its Bengaluru Centre; the Industrial Design Centre, IIT Bombay at Mumbai and the Department of Design, IIT Guwahati located at Guwahati in Assam came together to form a collaborative alliance and share its wide learning experience in Design Education. Geographically these institutions are located in South, West and North East region of the country. It was agreed that each Centre would act as the coordinating lead institute at each of these geographical locations and invite associate institutes to share their courseware in its efforts to generate content planned for the diversity of this ambitious pan-Indian coverage.

3   Planning the Design Content for the e-Learning Platform

The term 'Design', has over the past years, gathered many dimensions and definitions within the folds of its discourse. Considering that the nature of the profession has evolved to be multi-disciplinary and inclusive of a number of new fields of expertise, the plan for generation of content for on-line learning has necessarily to be broad based and divergent in terms of content. The need for an approach to introduce the concepts and approaches in 'Design Thinking' is articulated in the recently published Design Manifesto (2), which suggests that with inter-discipline convergence as the new paradigm, there is an urgent need for an introduction to the design thinking across various educational streams.

'...An interrogation and re-imagining of academic processes and structures, curriculum and pedagogy for enriching the existing design departments as well as the engineering, sciences, architecture, humanities and management streams within Centrally Funded Technical Institutions (CFTIs)'.

The aim and objectives of on-line education platform in design should therefore attempt to complement and enhance learning that these centers of learning offer and should at the same time meet the national objectives.

Drawing from the Design Manifesto, it was decided that the design content required highly porous boundaries between established disciplines and design, and the content should aim to position design thinking as a cognitive process central to all disciplines.

3.1   Statement of Objectives

The overall objective outlined amongst the collaborating partners was the creation and development of new learning environments related to Design that would provide greater access and enhancement to acquisition of critical knowledge, skills, and abilities for economic and social development in our country.

These initiatives will be based on the use of information and communications technology in the development of digital online content for learning Design with distance e-Learning programs on Design.

The main activities under this heading would be to:

a. Create online content for design learning through documentation of lectures, design exercises, design explorations, problem solving activities, and design process and design projects.
b. Create systems for online learning through distance education using suitable medium of instruction and ensure that the distance learning and dissemination of knowledge could be thorough the Internet with access to many media formats – video, documents, etc.

The dissemination could also be through synchronous live transmission of lectures, case studies and briefings through satellite TV transmission mode.

The content creation would be a joint initiative taken by co-ordination amongst the three partner institutes who would draw out a plan of action for carrying out the project activities.

3.2   Social Networking for Higher Learning with Collaborative Learning Space for Design for Synchronous and Asynchronous Interaction

The benefits of collaborative learning that can be expected from the use of group work are widely known but rarely practiced. These are academic, social, and psychological in nature and include factors such as building self-esteem, reducing anxiety, encouraging understanding of diversity, fostering relationships, and stimulating critical thinking.

The Internet seems to provide an ideal environment for exploring new forms of collaborative learning. The project aimed to research, experiment and build an online collaborative environment for learning applications on the net applicable for design learning.

The main activities under this heading were to:

a. Create a social networking platform for design learning that should have the potentials to get students interested in creating and building an environment for exchange of information with respect to design learning.
b. Create a collaborative space for both Synchronous and well as Asynchronous design learning that could be used to create problem-solving topics with both the teacher to students, students to students and teachers to other teachers being able to interact collaboratively.

3.3   Digital Design Resource Database Including the Craft Sector

The main activities under this heading were to:

a. Create systems for the documentation of existing knowledge of design and crafts both in the formal as well as in the informal sector. The documentation was planned to be through video, photos, documentaries, interviews, case studies, sketches, digital mappings, etc.
b. Create access to digital design resource database that will make information available to more numbers of people located in different places as well as enabling the access of this information at different times. Termed as a "virtual" or "digital" design resource database, this will have the capacity to allow the user access to information in multiple formats and media, independent of their physical location or ownership. In an efficient way it could help in the transformation, the generation, the storage, the dissemination and the management of knowledge.

4   Methodology

Prof. Ravi Pooviah as the Principal Project Head outlined and submitted the project proposal to the NME-ICT. Prof. Ravi Mokashi Punekar as center coordinator from the Department of Design, IIT Guwahati and Prof. Bibudatta Baral as the center coordinator from the National Institute of Design, Bangalore center joined as participating members of the partner institutions. Budget outlay proposed included salaries for project and administrative staff to be engaged on the project; space requirements; Equipment including video, photography and computers required for setting up the e-kalpa labs for each center. In addition the running costs and institute overheads were also factored in.

It was agreed that the administrative center for managing the web portal and integrating the contents submitted by the three centers would be the responsibility of the Industrial Design Centre. A common template for submission of content including visual documentation was agreed upon. Creative freedom was built into the approach to the study, based on the nature of the course content and diversity of the subject to be covered. It was agreed that the content should have a pan-Indian coverage. This would help to cover subjects that typify the rich diversity that is India.

Each center was free to build its own team and engage resource people and subject experts to cover the diverse domain of design including product design/industrial design; basic design; visual communication and new media; human factors; design methods; design management etc. Studies in craft documentation would be field study based with emphasis of documentation of the community of craftsmen, their making process, study of design elements etc.

Each center coordinator will build a network with other professional institutions, designers/subject experts from the region and be responsible in planning, execution and delivery of content. All contents will be sent to the e-kalpa lab at the Industrial Design Centre where it will be suitably adapted for uploading on the website to be created and administered. The web site was named www.dsource.in.

5 Results

The collaboration between the three partnering institutes has resulted in a unique collection of pan-Indian Design learning content being made available on an open platform at the web portal www.dsource.in. Presented below are specimen screen shots of the portal (Fig. 1).

Fig. 1. Screen shots from the site www.dsource.in

Nearly 15 subject experts, 25 faculty members, 30 project staff, 50 Design graduate students, 85 ongoing students from the undergraduate and graduate program and nearly 150 craftsmen have contributed content available on this website.

The content generated with an 'India Centric' focus is reflected in all its rich diversity of content categorized under the heads:

Courses: 85 courses have been developed in the form of modules from the domains of Design fundamentals (12 Courses), Graphic/Communication design (15 Courses), Animation design (28) courses), Product design (13 courses), Interaction Design, (7 courses), Design related other subjects (10 courses).

Resources: 235 field based documentation of the living traditions of handicraft and handloom practices of India have been documented making it one of the rich online visual inventories available on the subject.

Case Study: 85 design projects and experiments in creative learning undertaken by design students and faculty have been documented highlighting the design methodology followed in creative problem identification and solution seeking. The viewer gets an idea of the engagements and pre-occupations of design interventions that occupy the cross section of Indian designers and its relevance to the Indian society at large.

Showcase: 15 field based documentation of professional practice and entrepreneurship of Indian Designers work and their professional experiences in the field showcase the challenges and success of professional work offered to the creative industry in India.

Gallery: 600 different subjects, each containing 12 photographic images each with supporting descriptions has been generated through crowd sourcing. It captures the rich visual diversity of the land and the visual sensibilities of its people in every day life surroundings.

Videos: 45 video presentations capture impressions and inputs of various people and personalities, methods and process, tools and design assignments as live demonstrations are presented in this section.

The web portal was launched nearly 30 months ago. Nearly 45.0 gigabytes of content has been uploaded on this site. Analytics indicate that the site receives nearly 12000 page views per day, 300000 page views per month. It has 30 % return viewers. The website is visited by both national (68 %) and international (32 %) end users.

6   Institutional Collaborations for Content Generation – Some Insights and Conclusions

The success of the project is reflected in the increased awareness to Design reflected amongst prospective students who apply for admissions to the various design schools. Most of them have visited the site. A national level admission test is being administered amongst the design schools called (UCEED) for undergraduate admissions and (CEED) for graduate studies admissions. The number of applicants to these programs has significantly increased reflecting increased awareness amongst the applicants to the opportunities in pursuing Design profession as a career choice.

There is a steady flow of e-mail enquiries requesting for contact of the craft clusters for prospective business. These include exporters and inland retailers. This points to opportunities amongst crafts community for better returns to their craft.

Nearly 50 faculty members amongst the different design schools refer to the content on this site for teaching. The content is used for short training/awareness programs for industry professionals/executives. It is being showcased during national and international conferences and exhibitions.

The project outcome has received a very positive response from the MHRD who have now approved that this project should be further scaled up and the work continued during the second phase up to year ending 2017.

There is also need for critical review at this stage for identification of some course correction in the approach undertaken so far and future directions to be pursued. The medium of communication is all in the English language. This is both strength and a weakness. Firstly the reach is global and large international and national audiences who speak English have access to the content and benefit from it. But India is a land with nearly 23 official languages. Imagine if the medium of communication can be made available in all the Indian languages, the impact and reach it can ascertain. It will be phenomenal and this needs to be done. Following conventions of a standard educational model the courses can now be regrouped and formed into domain specializations. Assignment sand a model of assessment needs to be aimed for. This will enable possibilities of offering recognition to new educational program through on-line courses. In the next phase there will be a need to aim for a balance between the subject content for each domain of specialization.

The broad contours of the present contents and their coverage is perhaps one of its kinds in the world that has been initiated and offered through a national mission intervention of a nation state.

Acknowledgments. The authors would like to acknowledge the contributions of all faculty colleagues, resource persons, project associates who have contributed generously with their expertise and time in the generation of content put up on this website. A large numbers of professional designers were forthcoming in giving permission for using their case examples and giving interviews of their professional experiences in showcasing their works for the benefit of the larger audience. Learning of craft practices from the field has enriched the project experience in all its diversity and the generous contributions of all the crafts community who have contributed in the presentation of the rich diversity of crafts in India are acknowledged.

References

1. Piramal, R.A. (ed.): The India Design Report. Confederation of Indian Industry (CII), New Delhi (2011)
2. Government of India: Ministry of Human Resource Development Report 'Design Manifesto', Industrial Design Centre, IIT Bombay (2014)

Author Index

Printed in the United States
by Baker & Taylor Publisher Services